NATION, STATE AND THE ECONOMY IN HISTORY

At a time of persistent national strife on a world-wide scale, this book addresses the rarely explored subject of the reciprocal relationships between nationalism, nation and state building, and economic change.

Exploration of the economic element in the building of nations and states cannot be confined to Europe, and therefore these diverse yet interlinked case-studies cover all continents. Authors come to contrasting conclusions, some regarding the economic factor as central, while others show that nation-states came into being before the constitution of a national market. Above all, Central and Eastern Europe provides fertile ground for analysing divergent and convergent aspects of the relationship between the nature of political regimes and their economic performance. For Latin America, colonialism is the common point of departure, while for the USA and Australia the foundation of the state provided a striking basis for major economic development since the nineteenth century.

These deeply researched essays leave no doubt that the nation-state is a historical phenomenon and as such is liable to 'expiry' both through the process of globalisation and through the development of a 'cyber-society' which evades state control. Moreover the continuing integration of the EU heralds the further undermining of the traditional concept of sovereignty. Such developments fuel debates about the future of the nation-state against a background of reduced status and the increasing dominance of corporate power world-wide. By contrast, recent developments in South-Eastern Europe, the former USSR, and parts of Africa and the Far East show that building the nation-state has not run its course.

ALICE TEICHOVA is Emeritus Professor of Economic History, University of East Anglia and Honorary Fellow of Girton College, Cambridge.

HERBERT MATIS is Professor of Economic History at the Vienna University of Economics and Business Administration and Member of the Austrian Academy of Sciences.

NATION, STATE AND THE ECONOMY IN HISTORY

EDITED BY

ALICE TEICHOVA
HERBERT MATIS

CAMBRIDGE
UNIVERSITY PRESS

CAMBRIDGE UNIVERSITY PRESS
Cambridge, New York, Melbourne, Madrid, Cape Town,
Singapore, São Paulo, Delhi, Tokyo, Mexico City

Cambridge University Press
The Edinburgh Building, Cambridge CB2 8RU, UK

Published in the United States of America by Cambridge University Press, New York

www.cambridge.org
Information on this title: www.cambridge.org/9780521283137

First published 2003
Reprinted 2006
First paperback edition 2011

A catalogue record for this publication is available from the British Library

ISBN 978-0-521-79278-3 Hardback
ISBN 978-0-521-28313-7 Paperback

Contents

Figures

Tables

Contributors

BORIS ANAN'ICH is Academician at the Russian Academy of Sciences in Moscow. He is an authority on the economic, financial and political history of Russia in the nineteenth and twentieth centuries. His publications in English include 'Russia Falls Back, Russia Catches Up: Three Generations of Russian Reformers' (co-authored with V.G. Chernukh) in T. Tarnovski (ed.), *Reform in Modern Russian History: Progress or Cycle?* (Cambridge, 1995) and 'The Role of International Factors in the Formation of the Russian Banking System' in Rondo Cameron and V.I. Bovykin (eds.), *International Banking 1870–1914* (Cambridge, 1991).

ERNST BRUCKMÜLLER is Professor at the Institute of Social and Economic History of the University of Vienna. He is author of numerous publications, among them *Sozialgeschichte Österreichs* (Vienna, 1985) and *Nation Österreich. Kulturelles Bewußtsein und gesellschaftliche Prozesse*, 2nd edn (Vienna, 1996).

CATHERINE COQUERY-VIDROVITCH is Emeritus Professor at the University of Paris-7–Denis-Diderot and Adjunct Professor at Binghamton University. Among her numerous books the following were published in English: *Africa South of the Sahara: Endurance and Change* (Berkeley, Calif., 1987), *African Women: a Modern History* (Boulder, Col., 1998), and *African Urbanization from the Beginning to Colonialism* (Princeton, 2002).

FRANÇOIS CROUZET is Emeritus Professor of Modern History at the University of Paris-Sorbonne. His recent publications include *Britain and France in International Trade from Louis XIV to Victoria* (Aldershot, 1996). *Histoire de l'économie européenne, 1000–2000* (Paris, 2000) and *A History of the European Economy, 1000–2000* (Charlotteville, 2001).

KENT G. DENG is Reader at the London School of Economics and Political Science. His recent publications include *The Premodern Chinese Economy* (London and New York, 1999) and *Maritime Sector, Institutions, and Sea Power of Premodern China* (London and Westport, 1999).

PETER GATRELL is Professor at the Department of History of the University of Manchester. Among his recent publications are *Government, Industry and Rearmament in Russia 1900–1914: the Last Argument of Tsarism* (Cambridge, 1994) and *A Whole Empire Walking: Refugees in Russia during World War* I (Bloomington, Ind., 1999).

DOMINGOS A. GIROLETTI is Professor at the Universidade Federal de Minas Gerais. Recently he has published 'The Growth of Brazilian Textile Industry and the Transfer of Technology', *Textile History*, 16, 2 (1995), 'D. Brasil 500 Anos: a Formaçäo do Estado e a Luta pelo Desenvolvimento', *Universidade de Sociedade*, Brasilia 9, 19 (1999) and 'Balanço Critico sobre o Estado da Arte dos Estudos Organizacionais' (Florianópolis, 24° Encontro da ANPAD, 2000).

DAVID F. GOOD is Professor of History and Director of the Center for Austrian Studies at the University of Minnesota. Among his many recent publications are *Globalization and the Challenge of Institution Building: Lessons from Small European States* (edited with Randall Kindley) (Boulder, Col., 1997) and (as editor) *Economic Transformation in East and Central Europe: Legacies from the Past and Policies for the Future* (London, 1994).

GERD HARDACH is Professor of Social and Economic History at the University of Marburg. He has recently published *Der Marshall Plan. Auslandshilfe und Wiederaufbau in Westdeutschland 1948–1952* (Munich, 1994) and (with Sandra Hartig), 'Der Goldstandard als Argument in der internationalen Währungsdiskussion', *Jahrbuch für Wirtschaftsgeschichte*, 1 (1998).

CHRISTOPHER LLOYD is Professor of Economic History at the School of Economic Studies of the University of New England in Australia. Among his publications are the following studies: 'Capitalist Beginnings in Australia', *Arena*, 81 (1987) and 'Australian and American Settler Capitalism: the Importance of a Comparison and its Curious Neglect', *Australian Economic History Review*, 38 (1998).

CARLOS MARICHAL is Professor at the Centro de Estudios Historicos, El Colegio de Mexico. His most recent publication is *La Bancarrota del*

Virreinato: la Nueva Esapaña y los finanzos del imperii español, 1780–1810 (Mexico City, 2000).

HERBERT MATIS is Professor of Economic History at the Vienna University of Economics and Business Administration and Member of the Austrian Academy of Sciences. He is author of numerous publications of which the most recent are *Die Wundermaschine – Die Unendliche Geschichte der Datenverarbeitung* (Frankfurt and Vienna, 2002) and 'Vom Nachkriegselend zum Wirtschaftswunder – Der Schilling im "goldenen Zeitalter"' in Karl Bachinger, Felix Butschek, Herbert Matis and Dieter Stiepel (authors and eds.), *Abschied vom Schilling: Eine österreichische Wirtschaftsgeschichte* (Graz, Vienna and Cologne, 2001).

JACOB METZER is Professor of Economics at the Hebrew University of Jerusalem. His recent publications are *The Divided Economy of Mandatory Palestine* (Cambridge and New York, 1998) and 'Economic Growth and External Trade in Palestine: a Special Mediterranean Case' in Jeffrey G. Williamson and Sevket Pamuk (eds.), *The Mediterranean Response to Globalization before 1950* (London, 2000).

HIDEMASA MORIKAWA is Emeritus Professor at Toyohashi University in Japan. Among his publications are *Zaibatsu: the Rise and Fall of Family Enterprise Groups in Japan* (Tokyo, 1992) and *A History of Top Management in Japan Managerial Enterprises and Family Enterprises* (Oxford, 2001).

GÖRAN B. NILSSON is Emeritus Professor of Linköping University. His publications include *André Oscar Wallenberg (1816–1886),* vols. I–III (1984–94).

CLARA EUGENIA NÚÑEZ is Professor of Economic History at the Universidad Nacional de Educación a Distancia in Madrid. Among her recent publications are 'El Ministerio de Educación y la economía española 100 años después' in Pedro Álavarez Lázaro (ed.), *Cien años de educación en España. En torno a la creación del Ministerio de Instrucción Pública y Bellas Artes* (Madrid, 2001) and 'Educación y desarrollo económico', *Revista des Edicación*, 318 (1999).

PATRICK K. O'BRIEN is Centennial Professor of Economic History at the London School of Economics and Political Science. He is author and editor of many books. Among his recent publications are *The Industrial Revolution and British Society* (edited with R. Quinault) (Cambridge,

1993) and *The Rise of the Fiscal State in Europe 1200–1815* (edited with P. Hunt) (Oxford, 1999).

MICHAEL PALAIRET is Reader at the Department of Economic and Social History at the University of Edinburgh. Among his recent publications are *The Balkan Economies c. 1800–1914* (Cambridge, 1997) and *The Four Ends of the Greek Hyperinflation of 1941–1946* (Copenhagen, 2000).

VÁCLAV PRŮCHA is Professor at the Institute of Economic History at the Economics University Prague. He has published widely on the economic history of Czechoslovakia. Among his recent publications is the study 'Česká ekonomika. Cesty stoletím [1900–2000]' [The Czech Economy's Path through the Century 1900–2000], in *Ročenka Hospodářských novin* (2000).

ROMAN SANDGRUBER is Professor of Economic History at the Institute of Social and Economic History at the Johannes-Kepler-University Linz. His numerous publications include *Ökonomie und Politik Österreichische Wirtschaftsgeschichte vom Mittelalter bis zur Gegenwart* (Vienna, 1995).

FRANCIS SEJERSTED is Professor of Economic History at the Senter for teknologi og menneskelige verdier (TMV) of the University of Oslo. He is author of many books and articles. His recent publications include *Demokratisk kapitalisme* (Universitetsforlaget, 1993) and *Capitalism and Democracy. A Comparison between Norway and Sweden* in Haldor Byrkjeflot, Sissel Myklebast, Christine Myrvang and Francis Sejersteol (eds.), *The Democratic Challenge to Capitalism*: *Management and Democracy in the Nordic Countries* (Bergen, 2001).

ALICE TEICHOVA is Emeritus Professor of the University of East Anglia in Norwich and Honorary Fellow of Girton College, Cambridge University. Her publications are concerned with the economic and social history of Central Europe. Recently she published 'The Protectorate of Bohemia and Moravia (1939–1945)' in Mikuláš Teich (ed.), *Bohemia in History* (Cambridge, 1998) and she edited with Herbert Matis and Jaroslav Pátek, *Economic Change and the National Question in Twentieth-Century Europe* (Cambridge, 2000).

IBRAHIMA THIOUB is Associate Professor at the History Department of the Cheikh Anta Diop University at Dakar-Fann, Senegal. Recently he published 'Unification ou fragmentation des marches en Sénégambie. Des unités monétaires et instruments de mesure en usage dans le commerce (VIIIe–XIXe) siècles)' in C. Dubois, M. Michel and P. Soumille (eds.), *Frontiéres plurelles, frontiers conflictuelles en Afrique subsahari-enne* (Paris, 2000) and 'L'espace dans les travaux des historiens de "l'Ecole de Dakar": entre heritage colonial et construction nationale' in J.-Cl. Waquet, O. Georg and R. Rogers (eds.), *Les espaces de l'historien* (Strasburg, 2000).

B.R. TOMLINSON is Professor of Economic History at the University of Strathclyde. His recent publications include 'Economics and Empire: the Periphery and the Imperial Economy' in A.D. Porter (ed.), *The Oxford History of the British Empire: Vol. III, 1790–1914* (Oxford, 1999) and 'Technical Education in Colonial India, 1880–1914: Searching for a "Suitable Boy"' in Sabyasachi Bhattacharya (ed.), *The Contested Terrain: Perspectives on Education in India* (New Delhi, 1998).

STEVEN TOPIK is Professor of History at the University of California, Irvine. Recently he published *Trade and Gunboats: the United States and Brazil in the Age of Empire* (Stanford, 1996) and with Kenneth Pomeranz he edited *The World That Trade Created* (1999).

GABRIEL TORTELLA is Professor of Economic History at the Universidad de Alcala in Madrid. Among his recent publications is *The Development of Modern Spain: an Economic History of the Nineteenth and Twentieth Centuries* (trans. Valerie Herr) (Cambridge, Mass., 2000).

GAVIN WRIGHT is William Robertson Coe Professor of American Eco-nomic History at Stanford University. His recent publications include 'Can a Nation Learn? American Technology as a Network Phenomenon' in Naomi Lamoreaux, Daniel Raff and Peter Temin (eds.), *Learning by Doing in Markets, Firms and Countries* (Chicago, 1999) and 'The Civil Rights Revolution as Economic History', *Journal of Economic History*, 59 (1999).

Acknowledgements

This volume arose out of preparations for the Session of the International Economic History Association at the Nineteenth International Congress of Historical Sciences at Oslo, 6–13 August 2000. The papers were presented and discussed at the Pre-Congress Conference which met at the Vienna University of Economics and Business Administration in June 1999 and at a full day's session on 'Economic Change and the Building of the Nation-State in History' at Oslo. We should like to thank the authors of papers, rapporteurs and discussants for contributing to the success of both events. We greatly appreciated the helpful commentaries of the rapporteurs, which were taken into consideration by authors and editors for the final version of the volume: Håkan Lindgren (Stockholm) commented on chapters in Part I on Western Europe, Christoph Boyer (Berlin) and Alice Teichova (Cambridge) on chapters in Part II on Central and Eastern Europe, Patrick O'Brien (London) on chapters in Part III on Africa and the Middle East, Herwig Palme (Vienna) on chapters in Part IV on Asia, and Margarita Dritsas (Athens) on chapters in Part V on the Americas. The preparatory period gave authors time to revise their chapters and editors a chance to be in close contact with the contributors and rapporteurs.

We have incurred various debts to institutions which supported us financially: the Austrian Federal Ministry of Science and Education, the Ludwig Boltzmann Institut für wirtschaftshistorische Prozessanalyse and The Royal Historical Society. For their assistance we are truly grateful. We appreciated the help of Dr Charlotte Natmeßnig in the organisation of the Vienna Conference and we wish to thank Professor Even Lange, the President of the Nineteenth International Congress of Historical Sciences, for his assistance in making the meetings in Oslo a successful academic and a pleasurable social event. We wish to thank Mikuláš Teich who unsparingly advised and assisted us in preparing the conferences and the publication of the results. Special thanks are due to William Davies of Cambridge University Press for his interest and help in the completion of this volume.

Introduction

Alice Teichova and Herbert Matis

I

This book goes to press at a time of persistent national strife on a world-wide scale. The events in New York on 11 September 2001 have only underlined the relevance of gaining deeper insight into the subject of nation-states in historical context. At that time, the manuscript of this volume was ready to be edited for publication.

During the four years of preparation of its content the editors and authors could draw on the experience gained from the fruitful collaboration with colleagues on the collection of essays contained in *Economic Change and the National Question in Twentieth-Century Europe*.[1] The opportunity to expand the scale and scope of this theme occurred to the editors in connection with organising the Session of the International Economic History Association for the Nineteenth International Congress of Historical Sciences in Oslo (6–13 August 2000) on 'Economic Change and the Building of the Nation-State in History'. We had indeed been aware that the exploration of the economic element in the building of nation-states should not be confined to Europe and, therefore, cases cover all continents.

The notion of the 'nation-state' – as a distinctive framework of modern polity – has its roots in the late Enlightenment and early Romanticism. It connects with the materialisation of novel 'public sphere' in Europe against the background of the disintegration of the feudal system, including the repudiation of (Western) Christendom's claim to universality, and the rise of civil (*bürgerlich*) society.

In this process a major agency was the absolutist state. Thus the English and French absolutist courts, as discussed by Patrick O'Brien and François Crouzet, acted as a centralising force and the unification of administration promoted a sense of political unity among the royal subjects. At the same time, local and regional identities began to dissolve. What was originally an ethnically and linguistically heterogeneous population in a territory created through numerous contingencies (marriage, conquest, inheritance, etc.) gradually grew into a 'nation' by acquiring a common set of values, symbols, myths, rites, heroes, and legacies of memories. The standardisation of mental norms, as it were, aided by the standardisation of language out of vernacular forms, helped to engender a consciousness of belonging to a 'nation'. Furthermore, as pointed out by Gerd Hardach, by centralising and unifying administrative processes, introducing compulsory mass education and military service, and forging a common economic area, absolutism was able to assert the idea of state sovereignty over particularistic forces arising out of regionalism and the persistence of traditional social orders. But, as Clara Eugenia Núñez and Gabriel Tortella show, the Spanish state – with the Catalans and Basques battling to retain their identity – has had difficulties in amalgamating the political and economic realms throughout its history.

Looking into the case of Germany, Hardach begins where Crouzet ends, i.e. with the Napoleonic Wars of the early 1800s. Significantly, these authors come to different conclusions regarding the relative importance of economic factors in the building of the national state. Whereas Hardach (as well as Göran Nilsson examining the case of Norway between 1815 and 1880 and Francis Sejersted that of Sweden in the nineteenth and twentieth centuries) regards the economic factor, i.e. the formation of a 'national market', as central, Crouzet is guarded. The French nation-state came into being before the constitution of a national market.

II

Central and Eastern Europe is a highly fertile turf for probing divergent and convergent aspects of the theme of the volume. This is addressed in five contributions. In the first David Good offers an overview of the state of affairs in Central Europe by commenting on the multinational pre-1918 Habsburg monarchy and the post-1918 successor states on its former territory. Contrary to widely held views, Good propounds that state building did not precede the modernisation of the economic and social spheres in Central and Eastern Europe. Perhaps an even more challenging feature of his conclusion is that 'over the past century, there seems to be no systematic relationship between the nature of political regimes in the region and their economic performance'. Austria – the highly industrialised successor state – is the subject of the second joint-contribution by Ernst Bruckmüller and Roman Sandgruber. Specifically they consider the interaction between integrative and disintegrative forces in the Habsburg monarchy, the former spurred by economic interests and the latter actuated by national antagonisms. When it comes to post-First World War and Second World War developments, what emerges from the chapter is that a truly Austrian nation-state came into being when 'the economic development of the Second Republic went along with the confirmation and stabilisation of a distinct Austrian national consciousness'.

The contribution by Václav Průcha concerns Czechoslovakia, rivalling Austria as the most industrialised successor state. Průcha stresses that preconceived conclusions about the relationships between economics and politics and the state are unhelpful without meticulous historical research. He analyses the interplay of state, national conflict and the economy. His argument is based on differing economic levels which influenced the social structure in general, and that of nationalities in particular. In Czechoslovakia's case the fateful experiences from 1918 to 1992 are a virtual historical laboratory for variations in these relationships. Indeed, at the point in 1992 when the complete division of Czechoslovakia into the Slovak state and the Czech state occurred, the Czechoslovak economy had never before been so fully integrated. This Průcha shows in a telling table of the equalisation the economy had reached between the Czech Lands and Slovakia in the 1990s.

Michael Palairet's contribution guides the reader through the highly sensitive, complex and continuously changing scene of Yugoslavia. By discussing Serbia he presents provocative ideas and interpretations. Basically, Palairet defines Serbia as a nation-state by comparing nineteenth-century Serbia to post-1991 Serbia. In his analysis he concentrates on agriculture. By a nation-state – within the South-East European context – Palairet understands a state 'built upon the assent of a numerically predominant people sharing a common language and religion where interests of minorities are subordinated to those of the dominant nation'. From this definition he deduces that economic measures in multinational states (the Habsburg and Ottoman empires and Yugoslavia) are used to buy cohesion, and economic measures in national states are used to enhance state power. Thus economic development is subordinated to political stability. Ending the inquiry, Palairet peers into the future apprehensively: 'However, it remains to be seen if the corrupt and unstable structures of the European Union will be better able to integrate the nations of south-eastern Europe than were the corrupt and unstable multinational states of their recent past.'

The last contribution in this section, by Peter Gatrell and Boris Anan'ich, is also concerned with a long-term comparison. That is, they analyse the state–nation relationship extending over two centuries of economic development in multinational imperial Russia and the Soviet Union respectively.

The authors conclude: 'Under tsarism, economic change contributed to the creation of national sentiment and allegiance. In the Soviet case, the state sought to mobilise the population towards the goal of socialism, but ultimately many citizens became convinced that nationalism, rather than the pursuit of Soviet-style socialism, offered them better prospects of economic improvement.'

III

We turn to contributions that focus on the theme of the book outside Europe. In effect, aside from in Japan (Hidemasa Morikawa), it cannot be meaningfully explored without taking account of the ubiquitous impact and legacy of colonialism. The latter's objectives were primarily economic. 'Ever since colonial times, and even before that,' writes Catherine Coquery-Vidrovitch in her overview of Africa south of the Sahara, 'the economy had been oriented outward, ruled by an international market, located out of reach of African control.' In this respect, she finds, the situation was not essentially transformed when post-colonial formally independent states came into existence after the Second World War. Effectively, the dependence on foreign capital was not questioned. This contributed to failures in reaching the envisaged economic prosperity and nation building under the influence of the supremely nebulous concept of 'African Socialism'. On this, as well as other issues (corruption) emanating from the foundation of the colonial economy (groundnuts), Ibrahima Thioub has much to say in detail about Senegal, which became an independent state in 1960.

Amalgamation of economic and political matters constitutes the dominating feature of Jacob Metzer's guide to Jewish nation and state building (Metzer employs also the term: Jewish-Israeli nation). Its cornerstone has remained the principle of national landownership to which the Zionists as well as the government of Israel adhered throughout the Mandatory, pre- and post-1967 periods. As Metzer concludes: 'In executing... policies of colonising penetration into the occupied territories in an attempt to establish a Jewish-Israeli national existence there, and thereby a claim for future sovereignty, Israel has turned, essentially, full circle back to the "old" Zionist pre-state means of nation building.'

Can it be an accident that the English word 'loot' derives from the Hindi *lūt*? It reflects the manner in which ill-gotten material gains reached the shores of Britain after the East India Company established its rule over Bengal in 1757. India became the most important British colony – the jewel in the crown of the British empire. How the British government tried to retain it, after the First World War and during the Second World War, until the subcontinent's partition in 1947 into two separate states, India and Pakistan, is the subject of B.R. Tomlinson's scrutiny. Generally, he finds the current research still very diffuse and deprecates the neglect of the economic context in which decolonisation, partition and state formation came about. His starting point is the 1919 Government Act of India. Its object, Tomlinson points out, was threefold: to secure a market for British goods in India, to make use of an Indian army as an imperial strike-force and to have access to Indian revenues in the form of various charges. 'As the threat to imperial control of India's resources increased during the first half of the twentieth century', writes Tomlinson, 'so British efforts to maintain their rule by dividing their subjects intensified.' India's social, religious, linguistic and national variegation offered most favourable ground to operate the tried and tested *divide et impera* principle. Though in the end of no avail, it profoundly affected decolonisation and partition of India. A forceful reminder of its consequences is two wars and the threat of nuclear war between India and Pakistan over Kashmir.

The ancience of the Indian and Chinese civilisations has been well recognised and a subject of comparison. They differ in the fact that China remarkably has continued to exist as a political entity through centuries, despite weaknesses at the centre, internal political and social strife, and external military and commercial conflicts, such as the Anglo-Chinese war of 1840–2. This has gone down in history as the Opium War because it was precipitated by the Chinese government's opposition to importation of opium grown in India – a most profitable commercial operation for the British. In the face of bombardment of the south-east China coast by British warships the Chinese were forced to sign what is known as the Nanking Treaty (1842), by which Hong Kong was ceded to Britain and other areas, such as Canton and Shanghai, were opened to trade. In addition, China had to pay reparations. The view that, as a result, China was turned into a semi-colony Deng holds to be misconceived. He finds support for this contention in the notable value of state revenue derived from customs duties, mostly paid by foreign traders. This evidence awaits further evaluation. It is Deng's thesis that China, between 1840 and 1910, embarked on a series of reforms from the top which, alas, failed because 'the "social costs" for the majority exceeded the "social benefits" '.

Aptly, colonialism is the point of departure for the authors of the remaining four contributions dealing with Latin America, the USA and Australia. Not unlike Central and Eastern Europe, Latin America offers apposite comparative openings for the study of the theme of the volume. This is precisely what Carlos Marichal and Steven Topik undertake in their examination of the role of the state in economic activities in Brazil and Mexico in the period

1870–1910. In both countries, they find, the role was increasing externally as well as internally which, on the face of it, ran counter to the widely accepted principles of economic liberalism. Not so, conclude the authors:

Links to the international economy paradoxically forced some interventionist policies such as participation in commodity markets, tariff protection and nationalization of the railroads. Officials were not driven simply by ideology, and their actions changed over time. National sovereignty and political peace were as compelling as the balance of payments and per capita GNP. Markets did not run on their own; they required states' guidance.

This opinion finds an echo in Domingos Giroletti's chapter which approaches the history of the Brazilian state from a longer historical perspective from below.

When it comes to Gavin Wright's chapter on the USA, there is no doubt what its message is. The Declaration of Independence, adopted by the Continental Congress on 4 July 1776, was a political act signalling that American nationhood was coming into its own. It found reflection in measures, enacted during the 1780s and rounded off after the turn of the century, which Wright affirms laid the foundations for the striking US economic developments in the nineteenth and twentieth centuries. They included, crucially, the freeing of the land and labour to become capitalist market commodities. The latter applied to the northern but not to the southern territories. In the south the slave-based economy, Wright concludes, 'did not generate the same symbiosis between profit seeking and nation building that formed the core of the American experience for the rest of the country'.

Like some previous contributors, but even more so, Christopher Lloyd approaches the matter at hand comparatively. Also from this perspective, it is fitting that the chapter on Australia is the last in the volume. The comparative approach leads Lloyd to provide dialectically, as it were, a wide-ranging discussion of particular aspects of the economy–politics interplay in Australia from 1788 to the present. Lloyd's starting point is that 'Australia was born as a *modern* component or offshoot of the British state and developed in such a way that no pre-capitalist or anti-modern forces were permitted to influence significantly the infant society.' He continues by addressing topics such as colonial settler capitalism, including violent dispossession and partial eradication of the Aborigines; state–capital–labour compromise; and protectionism as an enduring framework of national (white Australian) policy from the end of the nineteenth century to the mid-1980s. Since then, Lloyd argues, the structure of Australia's political economy has changed enormously. From being a protected, mixed economy with a high degree of state ownership and regulation, toleration of monopolies and oligopolies, with an egalitarian income distribution by world standards, the economy and society have been opened to global competition and resulting inequality. Multiculturalism displaced 'White Australia', Aboriginal land rights and reconciliation moved to centre stage as national issues. Indeed, the beginnings of a new cultural formation, focusing on the special characteristics and influence of the natural environment, fusing Aboriginal, European and Asian cultural elements with environmentalism, can be discerned.

In effect, Lloyd raises the question of the forging of a new Australian national identity under the impact of globalisation.

IV

Although the authors' treatments of the subject vary in approaches, emphases, definitions, and geographical and chronological reach, certain comparative insights and perceptions emerge.

The existence of the nation-state is not questioned. By and large, it is accepted that its advent may be ascribed to interaction of economic, political and ideological forces in which national issues played a salient role. Here Václav Průcha's caveat that there is no simple answer regarding their relative importance is valuable. The nation-state is a historical phenomenon, and as such liable to 'expiry' fostered by the globalisation process, by the emanation of 'cyber-society' escaping the control of the state. The continuous integration of the European Union (on matters of law, border control, etc.), deepened through the introduction of the euro, heralds the undermining of the traditional concept of sovereignty. Developments such as these fuel debates about the future of the nation-state against the background of its reduced status and increasing dominance of corporate power world-wide. But recent developments in South-eastern Europe, the former USSR, parts of Africa and the Far East also demonstrate that nation-state building has not run its course. Rooted in chronic ethnic discords, these developments owe much to exclusionary strategies imbued with the dichotomy of the 'Self' and the 'Other'.

NOTE

1. Alice Teichova, Herbert Matis and Jaroslav Pátek (eds.), *Economic Change and the National Question in Twentieth-Century Europe* (Cambridge, 2000).

PART I

Political structures and grand strategies for the growth of the British economy, 1688–1815

Patrick K. O'Brien

The interest of the King of England is to keep France from being too great on the continent and the French interest is to keep us from being masters of the sea.

Sir William Coventry, 1673

STATE AND ECONOMY, 1688–1815

After the Glorious Revolution of 1688, a stable political regime gradually emerged. Within the 'kingdoms' of England, Wales, Scotland and Ireland, as well as the empire, over which the state exercised jurisdiction, *private* investors remained responsible for capital formation. Private businessmen (not civil servants) organized production, distribution and exchange. Businessmen and investors looked to central government for the provision of security. They expected to be protected from risks emanating from warfare on British soil or in home waters around the isles. From the time of the Interregnum onwards, an influential minority of traders, shippers, brokers, bankers, insurers, planters and investors engaged with the international economy expected the state to become proactive in defence of their ships, merchandise and wealth located beyond the borders of the kingdom. After William III took the throne they pressured their rulers to use diplomacy and armed force to extend opportunities for British enterprise overseas.

Somehow a succession of aristocratic governments (uninvolved in any direct way with trade and industry) managed to sustain political and legal conditions that turned out *on balance* to be conducive to the rise of the most efficient industrial market economy in Europe. Yet their foreign and domestic policies usually had other objectives in view and cannot be interpreted as a 'strategy' for the long-term development of the British economy. Ministers and Parliament allocated an overwhelming share of the taxes raised from 1688 to 1815 for military purposes, but that does not imply that Britain's foreign and imperial policies can be represented as a 'mercantilist vision' for empire and for the domination of world commerce.

This chapter will bypass the motivations and perceptions of the kingdom's political elite and focus upon *the long run*. I elaborate on how the *outcome* of major policies initiated and implemented by the state may have affected the actions of those engaged in the management and development of British industry, agriculture and commerce. No doubt kings, their ministers and Parliaments unwittingly promoted the Industrial Revolution. They may even be depicted as the closest approximation to a 'businessman's government' among the *anciens régimes* of Europe. But how exactly did the state assist in carrying the British economy forward to its status as the first industrial nation? How did industrialisation promote and configure the formation of the British state? One obvious way to start is to look at the allocation of taxes and loans at the disposal of ministers. Budgetary data do not encapsulate the economic role of the state precisely. Some important functions were performed at very little cost but tabulations of public income and expenditure do quantify changes in the scale and scope of its 'fiscal impact' on the macro-economy.

Deflated by indices of wholesale prices, the statistics do 'track' the ever-increasing role played by central government. In real terms its 'normal' or peacetime expenditures on goods and services climbed by a multiplier of 3.7 per cent from around £1.9 million in the 1680s to £7.1 million a century later. Wartime expenditures jumped even more – from around £5.7 million per annum in the 1690s to £22.5 million in the 1790s and by a factor of six if we compare average annual expenditures in King William's war against Louis XIV (1689–97) with those in the war against Napoleon (1803–15). Estimated as a share of gross national income the activities of the state accounted for a tiny proportion of gross national expenditure in 1688 and that proportion rose to reach nearly a quarter in the closing years of the Napoleonic War.

Thus this period cannot be presented as one of transition to the domination of private enterprise. On the contrary, the government's revenues and expenditures assumed a place of increasing importance for the growth and fluctuations of the British economy. Even in interludes of peace the share of the nation's resources absorbed overwhelmingly for military purposes by the state exceeded the share devoted to gross investment, while wartime allocations for the army and navy amounted to multiples of national expenditures on private capital formation. Over the entire period from 1688 to 1815 the British taxpayers and investors allocated more resources to military and naval objectives than they allocated to the formation and maintenance of the domestic economy's stock of productive assets – roads, canals, docks, buildings and machines as well as housing and other items of national wealth. Budgetary records expose the Hanoverian state's central preoccupation with national security and imperial expansion. Regardless of the rhetoric or pretensions of politicians to intervene in other areas of economic or social life, the state lacked the fiscal resources needed to regulate a national economy.

Eighteenth-century Parliaments, ministers and civil servants could spend something (but not too much) to make markets operate more efficiently; to promote the construction of social overhead capital; to safeguard internal law and order; to raise the quality of the nation's workforce; to foster technical progress or to engage just a little more effectively with almost any policy of a developmental nature. Parliament did push an increasing volume of economic and social legislation through to the statute book. It repealed laws perceived to constrict private enterprise. From time to time, ministers in London dispatched orders to Justices in the countryside. But neither the executive machinery nor the fiscal resources required to promote the development of the economy were available, either in Britain or, for that matter, in any other part of Europe. Only the integrated package of strategic, diplomatic, imperial, commercial and fiscal policies could be formulated systematically and implemented more or less effectively. As far as domestic policies (social as well as economic) were concerned *laissez-faire* not only proved to be ideologically attractive, but emerged as the only practical strategy for the regime to pursue.

Naval and military imperatives commanded shares of the public revenue that simply 'crowded out' possibilities for the execution (even the contemplation) of a more interventionist economic stance. In contrast to other countries that industrialised later, British businessmen and investors had to shoulder the costs and manage the plans required to build up the realm's networks of roads, navigable rivers and canals, ports and other forms of social and overhead capital. Their governments devoted almost no public money to the training of the workforce, to research and development or even to the dissemination of scientific and technical knowledge. In 1814 Patrick Colquhoun estimated that only 0.5 per cent of total public revenues collected during the long reign of George III had been devoted to purposes that might be defined as developmental. Monarchs and ministers preferred to leave the promotion of science and technology to the patronage of aristocratic, commercial and professional associations, with an amateur interest in 'natural philosophy'. They persisted however with Tudor and earlier traditions of encouraging foreigners to bring novel products and technologies into the realm while actively prohibiting the emigration of skilled artisans and the export of machinery. They continued to rely on that other 'cheap' but rather ineffective method of encouraging technological progress – the Elizabethan patent system – as codified in the Statute of Monopolies of 1624.

HIERARCHY AND GOOD ORDER

Although this inescapable fiscal constraint provided 'space' for private enterprise, the state left the framework for law and order within which factor and commodity markets operated within the realm in a less than satisfactory condition. Yet the new political order, which developed after the Revolution of 1688, maintained free trade within England and Wales although the Hanoverian regime took several decades to integrate Scotland into a single market and more than a century to incorporate Ireland into a unified kingdom and economy.

Parliament deposed James II peacefully enough, but William III's *coup d'état* provoked civil war and considerable destruction of life and property in Scotland as well as in Ireland. Despite the political union of 1707 the 'pacification' of Scotland was not secured until more than a decade after Cumberland's troops had savagely repressed a second and more serious Jacobite rebellion in 1745. William's victories at Boyne and Limerick created conditions for a partial but sullen acceptance of established property rights and Protestant authority in Ireland. Nevertheless, the threat of sedition and isolated outbreaks of disorder remained strong enough for governments in London to station a permanent garrison of troops in that troublesome Celtic province. Problems of internal security as well as Parliament's refusal to liberalise trade between the two nations precluded their integration into a common market.

Although the Hanoverian state held the realm together and eventually (after union with Ireland in 1801) effectively dismantled barriers to trade and factor flows, a truly unified domestic market did not emerge for a very long time. Meanwhile inside their 'partially unified' kingdom those well-protected aristocrats of Hanoverian England left economic affairs to be conducted against a discernible rise in the tide of crime against property. Furthermore, social historians have now uncovered too many episodes of collective protest, resistance, intimidation and violence for historians to assume that the landowners, farmers, millers, bakers, transporters, industrialists, merchants and retailers of Hanoverian Britain used their assets and managed their enterprises in the climate of security, approval and autonomy enjoyed by their counterparts during the heyday of Victorian capitalism. Unfortunately (as with criminal activity) no way exists of measuring the scale or severity of these potentially real social constraints on managerial authority and the rights of property owners to allocate their resources to uses that they perceived to be profitable. Over the eighteenth century disorder and challenges to property and authority certainly constituted economic as well as political problems.

Nevertheless, the capacity of 'paternal' governments of the day to deal viciously with the lower orders is also clear. Hanoverian authority came down persistently and effectively in favour of property and against customary rights, in support of masters and against the traditional expectations of workers and consumers who appealed to the traditions of an older 'moral economy'. Liberal historiography, which portrays eighteenth-century England as a 'free' market system, neglects to analyse the experience of large sections of the labour force (young people, women, semi- and unskilled labourers of all kinds) who lived out their working lives within an 'authoritarian' framework of law which severely curtailed their freedoms, including their rights to work or not to work, to select occupations, to withdraw their labour, to search for alternative employment or to engage with impunity in 'insubordinate' behaviour towards their bosses. Englishmen may have been free born but statutes of the realm dealing with masters and their servants, apprenticeship, poor relief for the able-bodied, vagrancy and delinquency gave employers political and judicial authority over their workers, which left the eighteenth-century labour market suspended somewhere between feudal servitude and the idealised free contractual system of political economy. Parliament maintained the traditional legal and political framework for labour relations in a condition that preserved hierarchy, authority and the extraction of optimal workloads. To counterbalance the paternalism and flexibility occasionally displayed by Justices at local level, from Westminster there came streams of injunctions designed to tighten up on the allocation of poor relief and the execution of vagrancy laws in order to force 'idle' workers, dependent juveniles and women to take up virtuous toil at low wages. Parliament also legislated to transpose traditional 'perquisites' attached to particular jobs into criminal acts of embezzlement. Recognising that the common law had not proved to be a deterrent to the formation of combinations of skilled workmen, the House of Commons also enacted no fewer than forty statutes prohibiting the formation of unions in particular crafts and locations, even before it passed the Combination Act of 1800 which outlawed all forms of collective bargaining.

Although the rights of property and the autonomy of masters could not depend on anything that could be recognised as effective protection from local police forces, serious and persistent challenges that could not be settled by established local authorities were on the whole put down by the military forces of the crown. It can no longer be claimed that Britain's constitutional regime lacked that will required to deal with a so-called 'ungovernable people'. Local militias and yeomanry could be embodied fairly quickly at the request of the magistrates. The War Office displayed little reluctance to dispatch troops to meet demands for armed force from any part of the kingdom, particularly after the rebellion in America, and with even more alacrity after the outbreak of revolution in France. With British troops mobilised to war for such a large part of the century Parliament's antipathy to a standing army looks irrelevant – at least when it came to coping with conceivable economic losses from problems of internal disorder.

Somehow the Hanoverian state presided successfully, and in fiscal terms at minimal cost, over a society on its way through an industrial revolution. It dealt with crime on the cheap by enacting a savage code of punishments for the unfortunate minority who happened to be convicted; it suppressed disorder and supported authority without difficulty in the countryside and surprisingly easily in the growing towns of the realm.

Perhaps its 'success' in maintaining the good order required for the spread of markets rested in large part on the polite and peaceable behaviour of the population at large. Loyal to the Protestant succession, patriots of a nation acquiring an empire and almost perpetually at or on the edge of war, open to persuasion from the established church, deferential towards birth, respectful to wealth and power, even those who actively resisted the encroachments of capitalism upon customary rights rarely confronted their superiors with anything more challenging than claims to paternal protection. Protesters could often be placated by minor concessions offered to uphold a dying moral economy or the common law.

Concessions for the sake of good order were, moreover, offered by England's hereditary ruling class – enforcing traditional and widely accepted codes of conduct. That aristocratic elite's reward for running offices of state, church, law and and local government had long been secured as rents levied upon agricultural production. Its authority could be extended at low fiscal cost to include new tasks involved in maintaining law, order and hierarchical systems of authority over the long period of transition to an industrial society. Britain's 'ancien régime' proved to be secure and flexible enough to accommodate gradual but, by 1815, rather profound structural changes to the economy. The 'good behaviour' of the majority of the populace coupled with the status and acceptance of aristocratic government ensured that a potentially unfavourable coincidence of rapid population growth and urbanisation, on the one hand, and serious challenges to established authority, on the other, did not occur. Unlike in France, the Netherlands or Spain, political disruption did not emerge to frustrate the course of economic change until it became irreversible. As Shelburne so aptly put it, 'providence has so arranged the world that very little governance is necessary'.

LAW AND THE OPERATION OF COMMODITY AND FACTOR

Nevertheless, Shelburne's 'Whiggish' comment should not conflate civil order with the legal conditions required for the operation of competitive markets. Most liberal historians applaud the stance taken by the Hanoverian state in allowing industries to escape from the fetters of guild controls, by relocating beyond the boundaries of corporate towns, but the economic costs of permitting guilds to survive in a very large number of towns right down to 1835 have not been assessed. They have also commended Hanoverian Parliaments and ministers for recognising the futility of attempts to regulate prices and wages and for resisting pressures for the rigorous enforcement of rules for apprenticeship embodied in an Elizabethan statute of 1563. That was generally but not invariably the case and Parliament did not repeal that statute until 1814; additionally the powers conferred on Justices of the Peace to assess wages and regulate food prices continued to be used from time to time. Parliament's failure to sweep away a penumbra of more or less obsolete statutes and to push the courts towards an assertion of free market principles created uncertainty among businessmen and traders and gave a semblance of legality to the actions of disorderly crowds and combinations of workmen seeking to use collective forms of organisation, intimidation and violence, to change prices and wages in their favour. Benign neglect can be represented as preferable to implementation of the state's extant powers to interfere with factor and commodity markets but its *laissez-faire* or inactivity in several respects looks less than masterly.

For example, as markets widened and specialisation increased the costs of transacting business across time and space went up. Well-defined and enforceable rules were required to promote the patterns of competition, co-operation and good behaviour required to make impersonal exchanges work efficiently. In England private property rights to land, minerals, houses, transport facilities, agricultural, industrial and commercial assets and to human skills and labour power had become legally enforceable under common or statute law long before 1688. Rules governing trade, exchanges and conditions of employment had also evolved over the centuries into modes of conduct widely accepted by businessmen and the workforce at large. During the industrial revolution commodity markets continued to operate within a heritage of law and codes of conduct. From 1688 onwards Parliaments engaged in a process of rescinding and amending a traditional body of law and adding new rules for the conduct of economic relations, but at the margin. Furthermore, laws might be interpreted more or less as Parliament intended by less than compliant courts and put into effect within wide margins of flexibility by the incompetent administrative machinery available for their execution. Historians are no longer seduced by *printed* statutes of the realm, but interpretations of the law by the courts (particularly of the common law) and the haphazard nature of law enforcement make it difficult to analyse connections between law and the spread of markets from 1688 to 1815. Whenever their transactions with each other broke down businessmen could appeal to the common law and turn to the established courts to safeguard and to indemnify them against risks from fraud, bankruptcy and breaches of contract between firms. But in all these matters the English legal system did not offer speedy, cheap and economically efficient ways of minimising risk and settling breaches of contract between firms. In dealing with disputes between businessmen and their customers, or in making arrangements for economically efficient settlements between creditors and debtors, reforms occurred, but the jurisdiction on offer to businessmen in Hanoverian England continued to be unpredictable, expensive to procure and suffused with considerations of equity, of custom and other anachronistic obstacles to the diffusion of competitive markets. Fortunately (and perhaps for an overwhelming share of their transactions?) businessmen abided by their own codes of practice, backed by sanctions which rested upon mutual interdependence and upon the preservation of 'reputation'. When necessary, they resorted to their own systems of arbitration, conducted by trade associations, guilds, chambers of commerce and other peer groups who applied commercial rules to disputes and to breakdowns in normal business relations.

From time to time Parliament stepped in and legislated, for example, to compel the courts to recognise promissory notes as assignable instruments of credit and in 1776 and 1779 passed bills designed to protect small debtors from imprisonment. Governmental interventions did not always operate with benign effect. Parliaments of landowners (antipathetic to forms of ownership that were not proprietorial or family-based and hostile to commercial dealing in 'paper' assets) passed the Bubble Act in 1720 and outlawed the 'infamous practice' of jobbing in stocks and shares thirteen years later. With these two acts the state placed barriers in the way of an ongoing evolution towards corporate forms of business enterprise which operated to depress the rate of investment and to maintain the capitalisation of industrial and commercial firms (particularly banks) at a scale which contributed to cyclical instability. Ultimately more baneful, the law sustained a tradition of family-based business organisations in Victorian Britain that proved itself to be ill-adapted to meet competitive challenges from American and German corporations during the second industrial revolution of the late nineteenth and twentieth centuries.

In 1688 Parliament took over responsibility for the management of the money supply from the crown, but it failed to meet demands from the growing economy for increasing supplies of coins or to legislate for the regulation of bank money and paper credit. Its *laissez-faire* stance towards the money supply left businessmen exposed to unnecessary deflationary pressures associated with shortages of coin and to instability associated with uncontrolled extensions of credit at one and the same time. All in all eighteenth-century governments exercised responsibility for the nation's coinage with manifest incompetence. They maintained fixed mint prices and parities which encouraged the export of gold and silver bullion and melted-down coins. This left the domestic economy chronically short of coin, especially silver coins of small denomination. Fortunately a network of financial intermediaries (merchants, bill brokers, London and country bankers) developed to fill the gap and to provide convenient and elastic forms of paper substitutes (banknotes, bills of exchange, book credit, cheques) for metallic money. Virtually unregulated, private commercial enterprise assumed responsibility for the expansion required in the nation's supply of money and the development of a financial system that carried the British economy through nine wars and an industrial revolution without widespread breakdowns, serious episodes of inflation or loss of confidence in paper credit. Nevertheless, cycles of economic instability, which occurred long before the famous crises of the years after 1819, can be associated with unregulated and imprudent extensions of bank credit. Throughout the period (indeed until well into the nineteenth century), neither the central government nor the governors of its chartered Bank of England wished to assume responsibility for the management of the money supply. Most classical economists remained unwilling to hand over that 'awesome' power to the state or the governors of the Bank of England, although they also expressed persistent and grave doubts about an unregulated, uncontrollable system of free and 'wildcat' country banking.

FOREIGN AND STRATEGIC POLICY

In an unstable international environment, Britain's monarchs and ministers had to cope with the omnipresent ambitions of France, the decline of Spain, the vulnerability of the Austrian Habsburgs, the expansion of Russia and Prussia, seditious Celts, a far-flung empire and, above all, with the unpredictable nature of dynastic crises of succession which afflicted all the royal houses of *ancien régime* Europe.

Taking the international order and the enmity of France (and its Bourbon ally Spain) as the givens of power politics, economic historians cannot ignore those vast and ever-increasing sums of public money allocated in order to preserve the security of the realm, to seize and defend Atlantic and Indian empires, and to safeguard the kingdom's increasing commitment to foreign trade, while also being used from time to time in the state's shameless efforts to weaken the competitive power of rival economies. They must at least inquire as to whether all that money was well spent. How far did the strategic policies pursued by successive Hanoverian governments contribute to the industrialisation of the economy? Perhaps a great deal of public revenue was (as radicals insisted) wasted in pursuit of dynastic aims with no obvious spin-offs for economic growth and the welfare of the people?

Such questions look more manageable than the idle pursuit of counter-factuals in the form of 'isolationist' scenarios for foreign policy and prompt economic historians to rejoin mercantilist discussions concerned with the political economy of diplomacy and military strategy. They lead to a re-engagement with the problem of analysing the potential benefits of public expenditures and to an escape from the entirely unbalanced preoccupation of liberal thought since the time of Adam Smith with the costs of taxes and loans.

Mercantilists and eighteenth-century statesmen argued a great deal about 'power and profit'. In going over debates of the day, modern military historians have distinguished two persistent and antagonistic refrains among the cacophony of contemporary views that can be read about the economic implications of Britain's military and diplomatic relations with the rest of Europe. Their separation between 'blue water' and 'continental commitment' approaches to grand strategy is instructive to contemplate.

Between 1688 and 1815 the Hanoverian state lacked the authority to conscript manpower on a large scale, as well as the fiscal base (and the political will) to maintain ground forces on the Continent for any length of time. Just as British governments carefully nurtured the nation's comparative advantages in seapower, its enemies France and Spain sustained their martial traditions on land. To mobilise the 'foreign' armed force required to counter the ambitions of two formidable Bourbon enemies within Europe turned out to be the most expensive and certainly the most controversial aspect of Hanoverian foreign policy. It gave rise to clamour for the more 'cost-effective' blue water option. Indeed a great deal of public revenue was allocated to maintain military alliances with European powers prepared for their own national interests to confront France and her allies on the mainland. In fiscal terms, that aspect of British 'grand strategy' involved three politically vulnerable courses of action: the hire of less than dedicated regiments of Hessian, Hanoverian, Swiss and other mercenaries; the alloca-tion of direct subsidies often transferred in the form of hard currency into the coffers of so-called friendly emperors, kings and princes; and finally the serious commitment (in 1689–97, 1702–13 and 1808–15) of British infantry and artillery to long campaigns on the Continent. Requests to send troops to European theatres of war were often made by Britain's Dutch, Austrian, Russian, Prussian and other European allies, but only rarely agreed to by governments in London. They sensibly sought to keep three options open: first, to retain soldiers at home in case the enemy managed to land on the kingdom's shores; second, to turn off flows of subsidies (including exports of military hardware) as and when it suited Britain's strategic interests to do so; and third, to wind up a war by serving notice on regiments of mercenar-ies, thereby avoiding the serious problems of crime and disorder associated with the demobilisation of masses of British troops in home ports. Further-more, the three occasions when William of Orange, Anne and George III did commit ground forces to campaign in Europe are all associated with drastic rises in levels of military expenditures, balance of payments crises, currency depreciation and an emergence of 'war weariness' among public opinion at home.

On the Continent 'Perfidious Albion's' devious diplomacy and the use of its wealth and fiscal advantages to 'buy' foreign armies to do its dirty work inspired distrust and resentment. As Europeans correctly observed, while their own manpower, capital assets, agricultures, towns and trade bore the brunt of armed attacks from France and her allies, Britain preserved her island security and exploited her naval superiority to expand territorial possessions and commercial opportunities overseas. No wonder all Europe gloated when George III lost his thirteen colonies in the Americas.

Then and now Englishmen hankered for the simple and ostensibly prof-itable blue water strategy. Did not European allies distrust their intentions, take their money and all too often fail to deliver effective and promised amounts of force to the fields of battle? Yet continental commitments surely represented an integral and necessary component of Britain's grand strategy. Of course, from time to time (examples are too numerous to list), British revenues, equipment and lives were wasted in ill-conceived or badly executed campaigns by armies on the mainland. Nevertheless, the 'aristocratic' view that rather high levels of expenditure on the ground forces of Britain and her allies were essential for the protection of the realm, the support of the navy and the containment of France turned out to be correct in the long run. But to the chagrin of merchants and mercantilists that policy did involve the acceptance of peace treaties and the granting of economic concessions to European powers that did not allow them to 'cash in' on the spoils of victory.

Meanwhile, the altogether more massive and consistent investment by the Hanoverian state in naval power paid off. Through nine wars (with three, perhaps four, conspicuous lapses when the incompetence of French and Spanish admirals saved the day), the Royal Navy remained in command of the English Channel and the North Sea. Its blockades and occasional first-strike actions prevented the combination of hostile fleets with sufficient fire power to outgun the Admiralty's men-of-war stationed in home waters.

European perceptions that the British economy gained more relatively from mercantilist warfare are surely correct. Between 1688 and 1815, foreign troops never ravaged the nation's towns, destroyed its capital equipment or ransacked its inventories of grain, animals, industrial raw materials and transport equipment. In wartime the share of the English workforce (particularly artisans) drafted into the army remained at manageable proportions because the War Office recruited from the unskilled and potentially under-employed (often Celtic) fringes of the workforce, because governments hired large numbers of foreign mercenaries, and because monarchs and ministers concentrated the bulk of military investment in waging more capital-intensive – that is to say naval and offshore – forms of military strategy.

In several significant respects this 'British way of warfare' complemented and sustained the long-term progress of the economy. In retrospect, that is why it seems sensible to represent expenditures on the navy and army as the Hanoverian state's implicit commitment to an integrated package of strategic, imperial and commercial policies for the long-term development of the kingdom. Even its most famous critic, Adam Smith, argues for 'defence before opulence', which is not perceptive enough. Defence formed an integral part of opulence. Expenditures upon armed forces (and the strategic concentration on the navy) provided 'preconditions' for a significant part of the economic growth achieved between 1688 and 1815. Links between power and profit connect the navy through the defence of the realm and foreign trade to the ongoing industrialisation of the economy. Naval power forestalled, repelled and protected the British Isles from invasion and provided its capitalists with the security required to invest in the long-term future of their economy and empire. True, a larger, more professional army stationed in barracks within the kingdom might have provided a cheaper and comparable measure of security, but that unpopular option could never allay the anxieties of businessmen and investors about the potential stability and predatory intentions of the crown, acting as the commander-in-chief of a larger standing army. At the end of the wars demobilised merchant seamen went back to sea.

Several overlaps (between public investment in the construction of warships, royal dockyards and naval organisation on the one hand and the mercantile marine, shipbuilding and foreign trade on the other) suggest that the allocation of skilled merchant seamen and other scarce resources to the Royal Navy carried in its train benefits for the civilian economy. Examples of such 'externalists', including improvements to the design of ships, to nautical instruments, maps, metallurgy, food preservation, to training in seamanship and even to medical care, have been detected as by-products of naval expenditures. The navy surely generated more spin-offs than can be found to have accrued from public money allocated to feed, clothe and arm soldiers.

Finally, the primary connection between expenditures on the navy and the growth of the nation's commerce with foreign and above all the imperial markets cannot be underestimated. Exports, imports, capital flows, shipping, services, marine insurance, international banking and commodity exchanges, and the growth of London, Liverpool, Glasgow, Bristol and other ports are all connected in so many ways to the Hanoverian navy. In a mercantilist age, the scale of economic development linked directly and indirectly to an ever-widening and deepening commitment to foreign trade and to the servicing of the international economy is inconceivable without persistent support from British seapower. As Pitt's Secretary for War, Henry Dundas, observed in 1801, 'it is obvious that the present strength and pre-eminence of this country is owing to the extent of its resources arising from its commerce and its naval power which are *inseparable*'.

Only the preoccupation of nineteenth-century liberals with the 'costs' of taxes and loans required to pay for it all makes it necessary to remind ourselves that ships-of-the-line, cruisers and frigates kept open trade with Europe, especially during those difficult years of Napoleonic blockade. The navy frustrated enemy attacks on British ships in the Channel and the North

Sea. The navy captured and maintained a fortified network of bases in the Mediterranean and along the perimeters of the Atlantic, Pacific and Indian oceans to protect British ships and their cargoes in blue waters far from home.

Naval organisation (convoys) eventually contained the long-running *guerre de course* waged with skill by French, Spanish, Dutch and American privateers against British trade. In most wars and thanks to superior naval organisation, the balance sheet of prizes (ships and their cargoes taken) exceeded domestic losses to enemy privateers by a considerable margin. That represents a victory for British public enterprise over the individualism of French and other privateers. Despite all the obstacles, interruptions and risks associated with the conduct of international trade in that dangerous international economic order, British exports continued to expand. Thanks to the Royal Navy, the nation's commerce was never crippled or even for long contained. The outward orientation of a rather small economy on the edge of Europe persisted as an endurable and effective strategy for its long-term transition to the status of a hegemonic power and workshop of the world.

Yet there are well-elaborated objections to representing foreign trade, linked with the Royal Navy, as *the* engine of Britain's economic growth from 1688 to 1815. Trade (it has been argued) was but 'the handmaiden of growth'. The increased volume of sales overseas emanated from the growing efficiency of the economy rooted in technical progress and entrepreneurial vigour. In theory there were always alternative growth paths to follow. In a fully employed economy, the gains from trade (exporting in order to consume imports at lower cost) are likely to have been small. Counterfactual 'Stuart' strategies for the long-run growth of the British economy (based on its partially integrated home market) are surely instructive to contemplate. Contemporaries would, however, have found it difficult to envisage how industrialisation and urbanisation (as well as the penumbras of favourable spin-offs that flowed from closer involvement with the world economy) might have emerged if British monarchs had radically constrained that involvement from the reign of William III onwards. Between 1688 and 1815, as the economy became more committed to international commerce (and its wealth increasingly vulnerable to hostile forces outside the kingdom), Hanoverian governments became more willing and the taxpaying public more compliant towards the expenditure of ever-increasing amounts of revenue in order to expand and defend Britain's interests in the Atlantic economy, the Mediterranean and the Indian Ocean. Only Jacobites fumed in the wilderness against this strategy. Aristocratic politicians (who disdained men of trade) entertained few doubts about promoting and protecting the nation's commerce. Merchants and industrialists lobbied for the use of force and diplomacy to open markets, to acquire territory overseas and to compel their colonial cousins to buy British. Mercantilists wrote pamphlet after pamphlet to extol the pursuit of power and profit. Was all this expenditure of political effort, bourgeois money and intellectual energy merely an unnecessary and economically flawed way to defend the realm, develop the economy and strengthen the state? Surely the Hanoverian regime's 'grand strategy' for the protection of the home market and for safeguarding the nation's commerce with the rest of the world created the necessary political conditions for the industrialisation of a relatively small market economy trading at the core of the largest occidental empire since Rome?

Along the way some misallocation of resources certainly occurred. There are numerous examples of inept diplomacy, military disasters, profligate expenditure and, by Gladstonian standards, the corrupt misappropriation of taxpayers' money raised to fund the army and navy. Spending by military departments of state, commanders of ships and gentrified but greedy colonels of regiments proved to be extremely difficult to control everywhere in Europe in the eighteenth century. Historians of public finance could follow up radical critiques of Britain's aristocratic governments and guesstimate the proportion of public money that they 'wasted' from all those millions of pounds raised and spent to carry the state and the economy through to that more peaceable international order which succeeded the decline of French power after 1815. Meanwhile economic historians can only assume that expenditures on military force by the Hanoverian state were basically unavoidable, and over the long run 'cost effective'.

TAXATION

To fund their interrelated military and commercial strategies Hanoverian governments raised taxes and borrowed sums of money way beyond the administrative capacity or the political comprehension of Tudor and Stuart regimes. Taxes rose in real terms by a factor of fifteen between the reigns of James II and George IV. Stable inflows of revenue into the Exchequer formed the indispensable basis for the accumulation of a perpetual national debt, which proved to be such a potent weapon for the rapid and sustained mobilisation of financial resources in wartime. To some extent the fiscal prowess of Orange and Hanoverian regimes might be regarded as fortuitous. A Dutch king took over an 'under-taxed' economy from an unpopular Stuart monarch, secured a political settlement with Parliament and embarked upon war to defend the Protestant succession. This enabled his ministers to increase revenues to previously 'unthinkable' levels. Taxes never again fell back to anywhere near the modest exactions 'extorted' by Charles II and his brother James II. Fortunately, the economy and the tax base continued to grow. Did that occur despite or because of the 'depredations' of the state? Industrial development, the spread of internal markets and growth of trade certainly assisted successive governments to innovate taxes and levy ever higher rates of duty. But clear jumps in the shares of national income appropriated as taxation (even in peacetime) confirm the discontinuity in politics and fiscal administration. That unmistakable outcome of the Glorious Revolution also points to the 'compliance' of England's taxpaying public with the aims of the new regime, as well as to a shrewd recognition by those who managed its fiscal policy that indirect taxes levied upon imports and, in growing proportion, upon domestically produced goods and services, would provoke less resistance than attempts to assess potentially more progressive, but ultimately unacceptable, direct taxes on income and wealth. Until Pitt the Younger introduced the first income tax in 1799, the fiscal system shifted steadily in favour of taxes on commodities and services. Furthermore, all chancellors recognised it would be expedient to tolerate rather high levels of fraud and evasion, particularly in Scotland and other potentially seditious provinces and virtually untaxable parts of the realm. Apart from the large and costly exception of the American rebellion, no tax revolts marked the upward rise in military expenditure.

Meanwhile industrialisation progressed in an economy 'afflicted' by an ever increasing 'burden' of taxation. For the times, the British enjoyed the distinction of being the most highly taxed nation in Europe, even if their government's military–fiscal matrix was transparent and widely admired. Taxes went up in wartime to fund interest bills on loans floated to cover suddenly enhanced levels of military spending. Taxes remained at higher levels over subsequent interludes of peace in order to service an irredeemable public debt – accumulating over time as a direct consequence of engagements in warfare. Economic historians cannot hope to conclude much about the economic effects of taxation. There were literally hundreds of taxes of every kind and their incidence is extremely difficult to determine empirically. To say anything at all, tax burdens must be related to social groups, economic activities and types of expenditure liable for taxation.

For example, the land and other directly assessed taxes, levied upon the wealthy, were increased radically and collected far more effectively during the wars against Louis XIV from 1689 to 1713. Thereafter, and especially when land values began their long upward climb from mid-century onwards, the nation's propertied elite transferred a diminishing share of their incomes to the state in the form of direct taxation. For political reasons such taxes levied directly on the rich could not be imposed at anything like progressive rates. All in all the Hanoverian state did not use the fiscal system to check growing inequality in the distribution of wealth and income: apart from the very poor, all groups in British society found themselves paying ever-increasing absolute amounts in direct taxes, but the non-progressive incidence of this form of taxation seems almost designed to contain any deleterious effects upon incentives to save and invest.

To make even tentative statements about the social and economic incidence of that more important and extraordinary range of customs, excise and stamp duties imposed by successive chancellors over the period is extremely difficult. In favouring indirect taxes, and spreading their burden across all ranks of society, the Hanoverian state maintained a fiscal strategy that became more and more regressive. But we must be clear what we mean by that loaded epithet. Necessities of the poor (their basic foodstuffs, clothing and shelter) remained exempt. Unlike today, chancellors of that time selected commodities and calibrated rates of taxation in order to take more money away from those with higher incomes. (For example, brandy and silk carried higher rates of duty than did beer and linens.)

Assuming, along with politicians of the period, that indirect taxes were in general passed on in the form of higher prices, enables us to suggest that between 1755 and 1815, the *share* of consumers' expenditure appropriated as customs, excise and stamp duties may have risen three to four times. An earlier jump from 1670 to 1720 may have been even more pronounced.

Most of the revenues passing through the hands of tax collectors circulated back into the domestic economy as expenditures for the food, clothing, equipment, ships and weapons supplied by British firms to keep navies at sea and armies in the field. Unfortunately a not insignificant proportion 'leaked out' of the realm into expenditures on imports and in wartime to fund mercenaries and British forces serving overseas. It is this 'share' that represents the macro-squeeze on consumption that operated, particularly in wartime, to depress the home market for British industry and agriculture.

The entire budgetary process of taxing and spending by the state altered patterns of demand and supply for goods and services. There was no value added tax and demands for more 'heavily' taxed commodities (such as beer, spirits, tobacco, salt and tropical groceries) were penalised. Other goods and services (textiles, processed foodstuffs, paper, metallurgical and engineering goods, household utensils and furniture, and internal transportation) escaped with lighter taxation. Rapidly growing and innovative industries were not, however, seriously burdened by taxes on their final outputs or raw materials. From the 1690s onwards, nearly all sectors of industry also enjoyed higher levels of protection in home and imperial markets. Despite a never-ending search for new taxes chancellors avoided whole areas of manufacturing activity. Their 'depredations' and 'distortions' tended to fall on established and taxable agro-industries – beer and its ingredients, spirits, vinegar, cider, salt, refined sugar, tobacco, soap, starch and candles. They also hit rapaciously at bourgeois families with aspirations to reside in more comfortable, spacious and civilised homes, to dress with style and to emulate the consumption patterns of those above them in the social scale. England's so-called 'consumer revolution' occurred in the teeth of the taxmen. Furthermore, British businessmen could avoid taxes by exporting their wares to foreign and imperial markets. Export duties almost disappeared in the late seventeenth century. If the mounting burden of indirect taxes narrowed the home market, drawbacks, bounties, imperial preferences and attacks on enemy (and even on neutral) commerce secured and safeguarded markets overseas.

Britain's fiscal policy (which complemented strategic commercial and imperial policies) promoted exports and encouraged the development of the mercantile, shipping and financial services required to integrate the populations of the kingdoms, the empire and (after 1846) peoples everywhere into a common and effectively policed international market.

BORROWING AND NATIONAL DEBT

Many an eighteenth-century commentator can be cited to support recent exercises in cliometric history which show how the massive rise in borrowing by the state (in order to provide immediately for the cash required to wage war) 'crowded out' the formation and maintenance of the stock of capital upon which the progress of the economy depended. 'Crowding out' almost certainly accompanied every Hanoverian war, waged largely on borrowed money. Dampening effects on private investment usually appeared in construction or similar lines of capital formation connected to urbanisation that were particularly responsive to variations in interest rates, and where investors competed directly with the state for loanable funds on the London capital market.

The Treasury experienced no difficulty in that competition because if necessary it could offer rates of interest above the legally allowable maximum of 5 per cent and because investors could reasonably anticipate capital gains at the end of hostilities. Securities or bonds sold by the state developed into a relatively riskless and highly attractive asset for nationals and for-eigners alike, not simply because the Hanoverian regime (unlike its Stuart predecessor) repaid debts and met its interest bills, but also because the English state devoted loans to winning wars and strengthening the fiscal base upon which the servicing of the government's debt depended. Despite the accumulation of a national debt which rose from a nominal capital of less than £2 million in 1688 to £834 million in 1816 (from less than 5 per cent of GNP to over twice its level), the cost of borrowing (on comparable public securities) declined from about 8–9 per cent in the wars against Louis XIV in 1689–1713 to below 5 per cent in the war against the French emperor, Napoleon, in 1802–15.

Between the Glorious Revolution and Waterloo, competition for loan-able funds between the government and the civilian economy diminished as savings rates rose to accommodate the voracious demands from the forces of the crown to fund their activities in wartime. In the short run and in a counterfactual sense, some potential capital formation failed to occur – particularly during the wars against France from 1793 to 1815 when inflows of foreign capital may have met a smaller proportion of the government's demand for loans than had been the case in previous conflicts. Modern economics suggests that military expenditures tend, over the long term and particularly in wartime, to depress consumption rather than investment ex-penditures. That almost certainly occurred during most of the wars Britain engaged in between 1689 and 1815.

Trends in the cost of borrowing indicate that the British economy (perhaps with rather strong assistance from inflows of foreign and refugee capital from Europe) found it progressively less difficult to fund the ac-cumulation of civil and military investment upon which its development was based. The accumulation and careful management of the national debt crowded 'in' as well as 'out'. It is not difficult to identify positive as well as negative economic consequences that flowed from public borrowing. For example, public debt diffused the habit of impersonal investment and encouraged saving, particularly in wartime when appeals to the propertied elite to buy bonds could elicit 'patriotic and prudential' as well as econom-ically rational responses to help their armed forces defeat foreign enemies who ultimately threatened their own wealth and status. Sales of bonds, of Exchequer and military bills provided British capitalists with portfolios of low risk and liquid paper assets – on the basis of which they could afford to venture more savings into commerce, industry and agriculture. Dealings in sound governmental paper also helped to integrate segmented capital markets within the kingdom. And metropolitan financial intermediaries developed the expertise required to attract Dutch, French, Swiss, German and even American capital into that reliable and militarily safe haven for money – the City of London. Is it plausible to regard the national debt as the engine of a conjoined eighteenth-century revolution in public and private finance? For example, the rise of the City first to become the hub of a national capital market and in short compass to surpass Amsterdam and all other European cities as the centre of the international monetary system occurred after a century of profitable and educational interactions between the Bank of England, London banks and the Stock Exchange on the one hand, and Hanoverian public finances on the other. Spin-offs for industry, agriculture and trade from the steady growth in London of institutions that eventually matured into the most efficient capital market in Europe must, in some degree, have compensated for crowding out effects in wartime.

Furthermore (as radicals noticed), the burden of debt servicing charges went up and up and laid claim to an ever-increasing proportion of taxes collected in peacetime. That significant fiscal constraint on central government's room for manoeuvre rose from a negligible amount in the reign of James II, to around a quarter of tax receipts at the turn of the eighteenth century and up to reach 55 per cent of total receipts in the aftermath of the Revolutionary and Napoleonic Wars. As commentators remarked at the time, the social effects of transferring income through a budgetary process, which collected revenue from taxpayers distributed across income bands in general and transferred it to holders of the national debt (concentrated in higher income brackets), could only be 'regressive' – and that effect intensified whenever price levels declined at the end of the hostilities. Politically the regime survived persistent attacks made on its debt by radicals, Tories and other believers in 'real' as distinct from 'fictitious' property. Economically the regressive transfer process associated with the rise of the national debt operated to raise rates of saving, investment and economic growth over the longer run.

CONCLUSION

A liberal and competitive world economy of the kind that prevailed from 1846 to 1914 forms a far superior environment for economic development than the 'mercantilist order' which British governments, merchants and industrialists operated from 1688 to 1815. Given the unavoidable fiscal constraints upon any pretensions it may have entertained to actively promote economic development at home, the Hanoverian state seems to have been remarkably successful in implementing policies that inflicted minimal damage upon the domestic economy. On balance, but not by any grand design, it promoted structural change and the long-term growth of per capita income.

For example, at home the new regime continued to operate a less than efficient system of common law and sustained authoritarian codes of labour control. Slowly the state became immune to Jacobite sedition and to lower-class threats to good order. At minimal fiscal cost, as a hereditary ruling elite, Hanoverian monarchs, ministers, Members of Parliament and Justices of the Peace successfully exploited feudal powers, status, deference and the Anglican religion to maintain political and managerial authority over a population growing rapidly in size, younger in age and more urban by the year.

Most mercantilists, as well as Malthus, believed the Hanoverian economy operated for long stretches of this period below full employment levels, particularly in peacetime. In their view, enhanced levels of military expenditure pushed the economy closer to full capacity utilisation and thus in some degree the wars of the age paid for themselves. Even so, by any standards the expenditures on the armed forces required to underpin the kingdom's foreign and strategic policies look massive and possibly profligate. On the credit side, between 1688 and 1815 no invasions of the homeland wasted the domestic economy. Before 1805 no great power emerged on the mainland of Europe capable of obstructing the kingdom's trade with the Continent. Foreign aggression against British commerce and territories overseas diminished. After the recognition of its independence in 1783, the United States was soon 'reincorporated' into the Atlantic economy which had Britain at its hub. Meanwhile diplomacy, backed by military force, had compelled the rival empires of Portugal, Spain and Holland in South America and Asia and the Moghuls in India to concede entrées to British trade ships. British privateering, together with blockades and assaults upon the mercantile marines of Holland, France and Spain by the Royal Navy (coupled with the vulnerability of Amsterdam and Frankfurt to invading French armies on the Continent), formed 'military preconditions' for the City of London's rise to a dominant position in international services.

Apart from that unmeasured windfall associated with the loot from India, which flooded in after Plessey, gains for the national economy took nine wars and decades of diplomatic activity to achieve – and even longer to mature into secure markets for exports and imports and into flows of private profits, rents and wages and jobs for the surplus population from the Celtic and other under-employed regions of the economy. During the eighteenth century, mercantilist intellectuals and aristocratic politicians claimed the gains from commerce represented real and sustainable returns for the ever-increasing burdens of funding defensive and offensive expenditures borne by British taxpayers. Ignored for too long by the proclivity of liberal political economy to concentrate on the costs of armed force, they form the 'credit' side of an unconstructable balance sheet to offset against the costs of crowding out, rising and regressive taxation and the instabilities in economic activity associated with those unavoidable cycles of war and peace that accompanied the British industrial revolution.

During that long, but by historical standards, rapid transition, Hanoverian statesmen entertained no illusions about the international order their businessmen had to operate within. For more than a century when the British economy was on its way to maturity as the workshop of the world, its governments were not particularly liberal or wedded to *laissez-faire*. Like the proverbial hedgehog of Aesop, the Hanoverians knew one big thing – that security, trade, empire and armed aggression really mattered. In fruitful (if uneasy) partnerships with bourgeois businessmen, they poured millions into strategic objectives which we can now see (with hindsight) formed preconditions for the market economy and night watchman state of Victorian England, as well as the liberal world order, which flourished under British hegemony from 1846 to 1914. By that time men of the pen, especially the pens of political economy, had forgotten and did not wish to be reminded of what the first industrial nation owed to men of the sword.

BIBLIOGRAPHY

In response to a request from the editors, the author is pleased to submit a chapter on Britain to substitute for that commissioned from Dr Anna Gambles, 'Regions, Nations and the United Kingdom. Conceptualizing the Economics of Union, 1783–1922'. Unfortunately Dr Gambles' health required her to withdraw from the project. This chapter does not have notes and draws heavily upon research, data and secondary reading on the state of the British economy included and fully referenced in the previously published papers and essays detailed below.

P.K. O'Brien, 'The Political Economy of British Taxation', *Economic History Review*, 41 (1988), 1–32.

'The Impact of the Revolutionary and Napoleonic Wars, 1793–1815 on the Long Run Growth of the British Economy', *Review Fernand Braudel Center*, 12 (1989), 335–83.

'Political Preconditions for the Industrial Revolution' in P.K. O'Brien and R. Quinault (eds.), *The Industrial Revolution and British Society* (Cambridge, 1993), pp. 124–55.

'Central Government and the Economy 1688–1815' in R. Floud and D. McCloskey (eds.), *The Economic History of Britain since 1700, Volume I: 1700–1860*, 2nd edn (Cambridge, 1994), pp. 205–41.

P.K. O'Brien and P. Hunt, 'England 1485–1815' in R. Bonney (ed.), *The Rise of the Fiscal State in Europe c. 1200–1815* (Oxford, 1999), pp. 53–101.

'Excises and the Rise of a Fiscal State in England 1586–1688' in M. Ormrod, R. Bonney and M. Bonney (eds.), *Crises Revolutions and Self-Sustained Growth: Essays in European Fiscal History* (Stamford, 1999).

CHAPTER 2

Economic factors and the building of the French nation-state

François Crouzet

There is a plentiful literature about the state's role in the history of the French economy and this literature is growing, as this problem is a matter of active controversy, not only among economists and economic historians, but also between politicians, in the 'chattering classes' and in the media. Free-marketeers consider the state to be responsible for most past or present ills and shortcomings in the French economy; socialists are convinced that intervention by the state has been and is both necessary and positive in its effects. The name of Colbert is bandied around, and abroad France is seen as a hopelessly Colbertist country.

On the other hand, the problem which is the theme of this volume – the impact of economic change upon the building of the nation-state (it is *de facto* the reverse of the one which has just been mentioned) – has been neglected, as in other countries, and this chapter will only put forward a number of rather desultory and elementary remarks. Moreover, it will mainly deal with the French state in the late medieval and early modern period, with the building of the *ancien régime* state. Indeed, I do not share the view that the 'modern' nation-state only developed in the era of industrial capitalism, i.e. the nineteenth century. The state, as we understand it, had emerged much earlier in Western Europe.[1]

COMPONENTS OF STATE BUILDING

In the case of France, the building of the nation-state was a typically *longue durée* affair, which developed over several centuries (from the twelfth to the nineteenth) and actually included several – let us say four – different processes.

The early Capetian kings (from 987 onwards) had real power only over a very small part of the kingdom of *Francia occidentalis*, created by the treaty of Verdun (843), which divided the Carolingian empire between Charlemagne's three grandsons. In a kingdom which was delimited eastward by the 'four rivers' – the Schelde, Meuse, Saône and Rhône – their fiat was only effective around Paris and Orleans and in the small area between these two towns.

Gradually, the royal *domaine* expanded, thanks to successful wars, to useful marriages, to the dying out of great feudal lords' dynasties.[2] There were, of course, temporary setbacks, because of military defeats, and also because of the creation of *apanages* in favour of kings' younger sons. One of those *apanages* led to the rise of the 'Burgundian state', which included both Burgundy and most of the Low Countries, and, in the fifteenth century, was powerful and quasi-independent. It disintegrated after the death of Charles the Bold (1477), but French kings recovered only the Duchy of Burgundy. Still, by the early sixteenth century, the royal *domaine* had so much expanded that it roughly coincided with the territory within the kingdom's frontiers (about 400,000 km²).

Well before this process had come to its end, French expansion had started beyond the limits of 843 and had taken over territories in the former Lotharingia, which were legally part of the Holy Roman Empire: Dauphiné (1349), Provence (1431) and later, in the sixteenth and seventeenth centuries, the three bishoprics of Metz, Toul and Verdun, Bresse and Bugey, Franche-Comté, Alsace, etc. By 1700 France had practically reached its present frontiers.

The rather slow and irregular advance of royal power and sovereignty made the French kingdom a mosaic of provinces with economic, social, legal and institutional specificities; some of them had negotiated their integration into the kingdom in return for privileges, such as the survival of provincial estates (which meant lower taxation). This was a major reason for the lack of uniformity within the French state, behind a façade of centralisation; it had important economic and fiscal consequences.

The effective governance of a kingdom which became increasingly larger (and was indeed immense, relative to the slowness and high cost of communications and transport) demanded the creation of a state apparatus, of a judicial, financial, military, administrative machinery – a creation which is at the heart of the process of state building. This edifice became increasingly complex as, from time to time, new strata were added while it was rare to abolish old institutions or offices. On the other hand, despite a sharp increase in the number of people who served the king from the early sixteenth to the late seventeenth century, the personnel of the state machinery was not very large in numbers.

Around 1515, France had about 5,000 *officiers* (office-holders), plus 7–8,000 clerks and other minor officials. By 1665, the number of royal office-holders had risen to 46,000 (including 8,648 judges and magistrates, and about the same number of financial *officiers*); tax-farming employed about 20,000 men. One must also take into account the standing army of 20,000 men in peacetime in the early sixteenth century, 30,000 at its end, 50,000 in the mid-seventeenth, 100,000 in the eighteenth century. Even if families are included, such numbers were only a small percentage of the country's population.

The words *office* (a public post which had become private property, and could therefore be bought, sold and inherited) and *officier* deserve some comment. The venality of *offices* existed in most of Europe, but the growth of *offices* and of an office-holding class went much further in France than elsewhere. By the early seventeenth century, office-holders had acquired a quasi-monopoly of the king's service (later, the tide ebbed). This system was typical of the early modern French state, but it was not particularly 'modern'. It was pervaded by patronage and cronyism; indeed ties of patronage were the vital force through which the wheels of the French government machinery worked. This is why concepts such as bureaucracy, centralisation, absolutism are somewhat anachronistic to describe *ancien régime* France. The absolute monarchy is a myth, except in so far as it could – and did – act, not unfrequently, with arbitrariness.[3]

The fourth – and last – element in the building of the nation-state is, of course, the rise of national consciousness, the feeling of belonging to a large community – the French nation. This is a difficult and controversial problem, on which I shall just touch here. According to nineteenth-century historians (who, in various ways, were almost to a man nationalists) French national consciousness awoke during the Hundred Years War (especially during its last stages, at the time of Joan of Arc) as a reaction against the devastations, massacres and other 'crimes against humanity' (as we would say today!) that English armies had committed for decades.

There has been a reaction against such views. It has been stressed, for instance, that most inhabitants of the French kingdom, up to the nineteenth century, did not speak French, but dialects, some of which were quite different from 'proper' French (e.g. *occitan*), while others were not even Romanic languages (Breton, Alsatian, Basque, etc.). It was also stressed that, as far as loyalty was concerned, many intermediaries – especially family lineages and patronage connections – stood between the king and most of his subjects. In a book that attracted much attention, Eugen Weber maintained that one cannot speak of a French nation before the late nineteenth century, under the Third Republic. Recently, in a book on the seventeenth-century

French army, J.A. Lynn concluded that the idea of 'France' made no sense to the ordinary infantryman.[4]

This reaction went too far. Recently, medievalists have maintained that, in France, nation preceded state, that a sense of French community emerged in the late Middle Ages.[5] For his part the late Denis Richet observed that we have evidence of hatred against English soldiers among the common people at the time of Joan of Arc, but that this is connected with a specific and temporary situation. Later on, and for a long time, we can have no idea of feelings among the lower orders. On the other hand, in the sixteenth century (and even earlier), educated men – lawyers, *officiers* (they often were the same persons) – frequently used the words 'French nation' in its modern meaning; they were critical of foreigners, whom they considered as guilty of turpitudes and vices, but they extolled the virtues of the French ... A national consciousness was obvious among such people, but they were a small minority.[6] Do we have to wait until the French Revolution – when the most popular motto was '*Vive la Nation!*' and when there was undoubtedly an explosion of 'nationalism' – to discover evidence of widespread national consciousness? I do not think so: this storm had been brewing for some time at least. Edmond Dziembowski has described a previous explosion of patriotism, among large segments of society, at the beginning of the Seven Years War, in anger against the seizure of French ships by the Royal Navy before war had been declared – not because many merchant vessels had been lost, but because king's ships had been taken – thus for reasons of honour, and not for commercial interest.[7]

ECONOMIC FACTORS OF STATE BUILDING

This brings me to the main theme of this chapter: what role did economic factors play in the processes I have sketched?

At first sight, they are not obvious. It was not for laying their hands upon riches that the Capetian and Valois kings extended their *domaine*. Admittedly, Normandy and Gascony, which were held as fiefs from the kings of France by the English kings, were rich provinces; the former was conquered in 1204, the latter in 1453, but the major objective in the case of Normandy was to expel the English from a region quite close to Paris, and in the case of Gascony to put an end to a conflict over that province which had lasted over two centuries and had been one of the causes of the Hundred Years War.

Conversely, the Valois kings, at the treaties of Arras (1482) and Madrid (1526), gave up to the Habsburgs sovereignty over the counties of Flanders and Artois, which were part of the kingdom of 843 and, since the eleventh century, had been one of the richest regions on the Continent. Admittedly, later on, France tried to reconquer those lost provinces, and partly succeeded, recovering Artois and a slice of Flanders (plus Hainaut), but this was for strategic reasons, in order to push northward a frontier which was dangerously close to Paris. Moreover Louis XIV did not intend to push further than the line he had reached by 1678, along which an 'iron belt' of fortresses was built (medals with the legend *Gallia clausa* were struck). In the eighteenth century, the idea that France was big enough was popular in government circles; during the War of Austrian Succession, Louis XV conquered the southern Netherlands (which, from being Spanish, had become Austrian), but he handed them back at the peace in 1748 (admittedly, their economic importance had much declined).

One could think that the 'wars of Italy', i.e. French attempts to conquer the Kingdom of Naples and the Duchy of Milan, which raged (with interruptions) from 1494 to 1559, had economic motivations because of Italy's wealth. Actually, they belong to a patrimonial view of politics: Charles VIII, Louis XII and Francis I wanted to recover territories of which they were, by inheritance, the legitimate owners and sovereigns. One can only observe that those wars also had a predatory aspect: thanks to transalpine conquests, gifts of fiefs, land and governorships of cities could be made to noblemen, a good deal of patronage became available, and the image of the king as a bountiful, generous prince was strengthened. Conversely, when the territories that had been occupied in Italy were given up by Henry II at the peace of Cateau-Cambrésis, in 1559, a dangerous crisis of the state was set in motion.

On the other hand, French colonial expansion in the seventeenth and eighteenth centuries had evident economic motivations: to secure for France its own supply of colonial produce, and to avoid imports from foreign countries which were detrimental to its balance of trade. But colonial expansion is no part of state building. Moreover, France started to establish colonies much later than the other powers, because there was no powerful group in French society to ask for and to support a policy of overseas expansion. Some mariners and merchants of port towns such as Dieppe and La Rochelle were pioneers, but they lacked capital and were not supported by the state, which was absorbed by civil or continental wars.

However, the economy, though not an active factor of territorial expansion, was at least a permissive condition. The power base of French kings was first the small region around Paris (the Ile-de-France), later the bigger Parisian basin, i.e. plains which are among the most fertile in Western

Europe. In those areas, the innovations which transformed medieval agriculture – the wheeled plough, the shoulder collar for horses, the three years'
rotation – were introduced quite early; large-scale clearings of forests and
waste took place from the eleventh to the thirteenth century, while serfs received or bought their freedom. The population increased fast and densities
of 40–50 inhabitants per km² were reached by the mid-thirteenth century.
As royal finances under the early Capetians were based upon resources that
were seigneurial in nature and depended heavily on the agrarian economy,
the latter's growth during the twelfth and thirteenth centuries (within an
expanding *domaine*, in addition) brought to the monarchy increasing receipts and supported its expansionist policies.[8] Moreover, in the territory
between the Somme and Loire, manors broke up early (from the eleventh
century onwards) into small units, over which the king could rather easily establish his authority and which he could use as his agents. The (not
quite) 'central' position of Paris and its region within the kingdom, rather
easy communications with most of its provinces and the navigable river
systems of the Seine and Loire must also be mentioned. Altogether, such
conditions may be more geographical than economic, *stricto sensu*, but the
control over a densely populated and 'rich' region gave to kings the financial
and military resources which they needed to extend their *domaine* over the
whole kingdom and beyond the limits of 843. Pierre Chaunu has rightly
seen a connection between the *monde plein* (a world at the full, with high
population densities) which the demographic expansion of the eleventh to
thirteenth centuries had created and the birth of the modern state.[9]

Moreover, France was the European state with the biggest population –
12 million inhabitants at least *c.* 1300 and 1500, 20 million in the seventeenth
century (within the borders of the time) and 28 million in 1789. This mass
of people – and of taxpayers – was a major factor in the succession of wars
which France fought against the Habsburgs, and which resulted eventually
in territorial aggrandisement, especially by the treaties of 1648 and 1659,
at Westphalia and the Pyrenees. It has been estimated that the financial
resources available to French kings were roughly equivalent in the mid-
sixteenth century, and in the first half of the seventeenth, to those of Spain,
despite the massive imports of silver which the latter received from America.

One may, in addition, wonder whether economic developments within
the French kingdom – in the twelfth to thirteenth century, then in the
sixteenth (and part of the seventeenth) century – did not have positive
consequences for state building.

Indeed, in the nineteenth century many liberal historians viewed French
history from the eleventh to the seventeenth century as a struggle between

the monarchy and a 'feudal', backward-looking and turbulent nobility. In this struggle to impose law, order and modernisation, the monarchy was supported by – and even relied upon – the bourgeoisie, as the nobility was their common enemy. In this view, economic development, especially the rise of towns, the progress of trade, handicrafts, manufactures, made a significant contribution to state building, as it made the bourgeoisie stronger.

Actually, despite a succession of revolts and conspiracies by grandees, despite a kind of secession by the gentry of southern France during the Wars of Religion, there was no persistent and general opposition to the central government by the nobility which, moreover, did not offer any alternative system of governance. On the other hand, most *officiers* (and some famous ministers of the crown, especially Colbert) had an urban and bourgeois background and had their roots in 'trade'. But they separated from the business bourgeoisie to form an 'estate' of their own, many members of which were ennobled. Although the *noblesse de robe* did not enjoy as much prestige as the *noblesse d'épée*, as its tasks were in courts of law or tax offices and not on battlefields, it had noble rank and enjoyed noble privileges.

The Old Regime was based much more upon co-operation by the crown with the elites than upon struggles against them (except in the eighteenth century, and this led to the regime's collapse). It was also based upon power-sharing: noblemen were dominant in the army, bourgeois in the financial sector of government, while both elements were present in the judiciary. Even in financial affairs, a good deal of the capital raised for the king on the Paris money market actually came from noblemen, courtiers, even from the royal family, but through the mediation of bourgeois financiers, who acted as strawmen and covers.[10]

There is no doubt, none the less, that the 'rise of the bourgeoisie' contributed to state building. First the state needed, as office-holders, not only men who were literate (who could read, write and reckon), but also – and increasingly, as administrative tasks became relatively sophisticated – men who had a training in law (and accountancy). Few members of the *noblesse d'épée* had such a training, while sons of well-to-do bourgeois or of office-holders had, not unfrequently, received a university education in law.[11] This was one reason why, from the early seventeenth century, the *noblesse de robe* superseded the *noblesse d'épée* in the king's councils. The venality of offices was the major channel of upward social mobility in *ancien régime* France. It has often been deplored that so much capital was diverted from productive investment towards offices; one major cause was the contempt for trade, for *la marchandise*, which was widespread and powerful within French society.

However, a shortage of investment opportunities in trade and industry may also have played a part.

The enrichment of the bourgeoisie (or the progress of capitalism, in other words) was also instrumental, especially in the matter of farming indirect taxes, as it allowed for a gradual concentration of such operations. In the fourteenth century, tax-farming was done piecemeal, at the village or small town level, and entrusted to well-to-do peasants or other ordinary men; in the fifteenth century it took place at the level of groups of villages. The late sixteenth and the seventeenth century did see the rise of wealthy financiers, who were able to undertake the collection of taxes (and to make large advances to the Treasury) for whole provinces or groups of provinces. In 1598, under Henry IV, his chief minister, Sully, united within one single farm contract the levy of the salt tax (*gabelle*) in the whole kingdom. In 1596, the 'Five Great Farms' (*Cinq Grosses Fermes*) had been created for collecting customs duties (*traites*) in a large group of provinces around Paris. Eventually, in 1726, the General Tax Farm was established, i.e. a private company that was in charge of collecting all leased taxes in France. It was a very large institution (with up to 30,000 employees) and an efficient one (which did not make it popular!). The Farmers General were wealthy men, who played a crucial role in eighteenth-century France. One can add that, in the fifteenth and sixteenth centuries, the government borrowed a great deal from town councils, and also that the latter guaranteed the king's debts, i.e. the regular payment of interest.

French campaigns in Italy during the sixteenth century were largely financed by loans from syndicates of Italian merchant bankers (mainly from Tuscany) who had settled in Lyons, where they had been attracted by the large fairs which took place there, and which were – for a time – a dominant centre of international settlements. The French state thus benefited from the rise of international banking at the time of the Renaissance. However, Italian bankers of Lyons suffered from the French state's 'bankruptcy' (rescheduling of debts) in the 1550s and from the economic decline of Italy; moreover, Tuscan bankers were superseded by Genoese bankers, who put their skills and capital in the service of Spain and not of France; they also transferred the hub of their transactions from Lyons to Besançon (in Spanish Franche-Comté) and then to Piacenza, in Lombardy. As far as France was concerned, the main capital market moved from Lyons to Paris in the late sixteenth century and henceforth the financiers who served the French state were mainly French.

Still, this was not the end of dependence upon international banking. The persecution of Protestants in France under Louis XIV led to an exodus and many Huguenot merchants and financiers emigrated to Protestant countries – especially Switzerland, Holland and England. These *émigrés* and their descendants remained in close touch with relatives and friends who had stayed at home (often after ostensible conversion to Catholicism). Those strong, family-based networks have been called 'the Huguenot International' by H. Lüthy, who showed that they had greatly assisted the French Treasury during the two difficult and expensive wars which raged from 1689 to 1713, and during which they drained enormous sums from all over Europe for their persecutor, Louis XIV. Later on, during the War of American Independence and in the 1780s, much French government stock (especially life annuities) was sold in Geneva, Switzerland and Holland, often through bankers who belonged to the 'Huguenot International'.[12]

RISE OF THE FISCAL-MILITARY STATE

We have thus been led to financial problems which, indeed, need more attention, as they played a crucial role in the building of the state apparatus.

As most others, the French state was at first – up to the late thirteenth century – a judicial state (*état de justice*); the major function of the king was to be the 'supreme judge', and his agents were first of all magistrates. Then a finance or financial state (*état de finances*) gradually developed, and this was the first stage of the 'modern' state; its major finality was to levy taxes, it originated in taxes. The judicial state had also been a 'domain state', in which the king was expected to *vivre du sien*, i.e. from the income supplied by the manors he owned, by payments from his vassals on various occasions, by tolls on trade, etc. Such rather limited resources decreased sharply because of the disasters which struck the seigneurial economy after the Black Death and during most of the Hundred Years War, just as the latter was causing a major rise in expenditures. So they had to be supplemented by entirely new revenues, i.e. taxes. Indeed, there is a very close connection between the traditional military function of the king as a warrior and the rise of the financial state: taxes were basically intended to maintain the army, to finance wars, and to repay and service the debts which had been incurred in wartime. The expression 'fiscal-military state' is perfectly appropriate, and the levy of taxes (especially direct taxes) was the main factor in the growth of state machinery.[13]

In a large country taxes can only be levied in money – though there are some examples of taxes in kind, but in special circumstances at late periods: in 1709–10, in time of war and during a subsistence crisis, special levies in kind (including transportation of goods) were exacted in the frontier provinces of Alsace and Franche-Comté, in order to supply troops operating nearby.[14] There was also, in the eighteenth century, the *corvée royale*, i.e. forced labour for work on the roads. Therefore, the finance state could only develop when marketisation and monetarisation of the economy had advanced enough – a stage which was reached in France in the thirteenth century. On the other hand, a succession of wars, especially the Hundred Years War, created urgent needs of ready money.

Still, the building of the financial state extended over four centuries and included four major stages, which are all connected with military crises. It will be useful to recall them briefly and to consider whether they have any connection with economic developments.

The first stage was in the fourteenth century, particularly from 1355 to 1380, when an enormous ransom of 3 million gold *écus* (14 tons of gold) had to be paid after King John had been taken prisoner at the battle of Poitiers, and when an embryo standing army of mercenaries was established to fight off the English.[15] Some taxes, formerly levied sporadically, were henceforth collected roughly every year. This included a hearth tax, which became known as the *taille*, from the verb 'to cut up or divide' – a very appropriate name when applied to the income of taxpayers! There were also indirect taxes: the *maltote* or *aide*, on various consumer goods (specially wine), and the *gabelle* or salt tax; in 1366, the king established his monopoly of salt sales in northern France. Simultaneously a corps of financial *officiers* was created.

This new fiscal system was thus established in a period of deep demographic and economic depression and stirred up much popular protest. However, the whole state structure largely disintegrated after new English victories over the French (Agincourt, 1415) and the English occupation of large parts of the kingdom, including Paris, which made Charles VII *le roi de Bourges* (in central France).

A second phase in the building of the financial state came in the mid-fifteenth century, after 1435, when the tide definitively turned in favour of the French in the Hundred Years War (which came to an end in 1453); actually there was a close connection between financial and military developments: the creation of a standing army (*Compagnies d'ordonnance*, 1445) contributed to victory on battlefields, but it was financed by taxation, on the same principles as earlier on. From 1439 onwards, the *taille* was levied every year in all regions which had no provincial estates; actually, in real terms and per capita, the *taille* was never as high as under Louis XI.

After a lull, a third stage came about in the sixteenth century, because of the demands of campaigns in Italy and the struggle with Spain, demands which peaked under Henry II (1547–59), because armies in the field had doubled in size and enemy resources had increased, thanks to American silver (within twelve years, the state net revenue increased 80 per cent in real terms). The financial-fiscal machinery was overhauled, and somewhat centralised – e.g. by the creation of a central treasury (*trésor de l'épargne*). New financial *offices* were created. The public sale of annuities, secured against the City of Paris's revenues, was started in 1522 (and, as mentioned above, much borrowing from Italian merchant bankers at Lyons took place).

After 1559, the state suffered a new crisis, mainly because of civil war – the 'troubles of religion'. It was succeeded in 1600–10 by a period during which order was restored in the country at large and also in finances. Then, starting in the 1620s, when the political and military power of the Huguenot party was broken by armed force, and accelerating in the 1630s, when France intervened in the Thirty Years War – at first under cover and then openly (1635) – there was a terrific and unequalled rise in government expenditures: 20 million *livres* per year in 1600–4, rising to 55 million in the 1620s, and escalating to 118 million in 1635–9. A good deal of this increase was paid by borrowing and by sales of *offices*; none the less taxes rose sharply (by over 100 per cent for direct taxes, from 1625 to 1634), and popular protest turned into large-scale and country-wide rioting. All taxation requires the threat of coercion, but this time coercion by the army had to be used in many provinces. Moreover, the central government, i.e. Cardinal Richelieu, Louis XIII's prime minister, realised that its control over the state apparatus, through large numbers of office-holders, was inadequate and created a new instrument of government, based on royal commissioners (*intendants*), who were sent to the *généralités* (roughly, provinces). Unlike *officiers*, they did not own their posts and received temporary commissions, which could be cancelled at any moment (but generally they belonged to offices-holders' families). There is a striking contrast between the effectiveness in the levy of direct taxes before and after fiscal powers were granted to the *intendants* in 1642.[16] As is well known, the *intendants* became a permanent institution and the lynchpin of the *ancien régime* system of government, which prevailed over the *officiers* (still Louis XIV did have only 300 full-time commissioners, of whom 30–35 were *intendants*, against 45,000 *officiers*).

This kind of 'revolution', of the years 1630–45, of which Richelieu was the contriver, was, roughly, the last stage in the building of the *ancien régime* state, as it also included the introduction of the ministerial system, in which government was conducted no longer by great officers of the crown (some of their posts were abolished) and by councils, but by ministers and secretaries of state; this was more bureaucratic and 'modern'. After disturbances during the minority of Louis XIV (*La Fronde*), his reign was mostly a period of consolidation under Colbert (1660–83),[17] who achieved many improvements in the financial and fiscal system (e.g. he reduced the cost of tax collecting and introduced more precise accounting), but no large-scale change – and no increase in the tax burden, which was not heavier by 1683 than under Richelieu or Mazarin. Admittedly, his successors, though they continued his reforms, had to face the hard task of financing two excessively expensive wars. But despite the creation of new taxes (*capitation* and *dixième*, which were rough kinds of income tax) and expedients, such as the issue of paper money (*billets de monnaie*), the fundamental traits of the financial state did not change.

ECONOMIC FLUCTUATIONS AND STATE BUILDING

We must now consider whether there was any relationship between the four stages in the building of the financial state and the major long-term fluctuations of the French economy, the two 'logistics' (in R. Cameron's words) of European economies between 1000 and 1800. Actually, it is remarkable that two of the four stages, when the financial state expanded and the fiscal burden increased, occurred during periods of demographic and economic depression or stagnation.

This is obvious, of course, for the first stage, in the fourteenth century shortly after the Black Death (which, moreover, was followed by renewed outbursts of plague in the late fourteenth and early fifteenth centuries), when the population had fallen by a third at least, and when, consequently, prices had dropped and production and trade had been greatly reduced. Moreover, France suffered more than its neighbours (e.g. Italy), because devastations by English (and French!) armies were added to the ravages which epidemics had caused.[18]

As for the fourth stage, in the seventeenth century, it took place during the downswing of the second logistic. Actually, France did not suffer as much in the seventeenth century as countries like Spain, Germany or Poland (but she did not prosper like the United Provinces or England), and recently historians have given up the idea of a 'tragic' seventeenth century; despite severe subsistence crises and epidemics, the population of the French kingdom was roughly the same (about 20 million) in 1700 as in 1600. Still, the 1620s and the 1630s, when the increase in the tax burden was at its maximum, were marked by two serious outbreaks of plague (which may have killed 2 million persons), by an economic slowdown, and by falling prices.[19]

On the other hand, stages two and three – in the mid-fifteenth and the mid-sixteenth century – occurred during a demographic and economic upswing. However, the earlier one came about when recovery and reconstruction were just starting, when the Hundred Years War had not yet ended, when the devastations it had caused had not yet been made good, and when the population – especially in several provinces (e.g. around Paris) which had been laid waste – was far below its pre-plague level.[20] Things were of course quite different in the mid-sixteenth century, but some writers observe that by the 1530s or 1540s, the most prosperous period of the sixteenth century was over, Malthusian pressures were felt, after a fast growth in population, and the latter stagnated from 1545 to 1560.

P. Chaunu has concluded that the state developed as an autonomous structure, relatively independent from the economic *konjunktur*, according to its own dynamics. The correlation between state building and economic development is to him clearly negative.[21] This conclusion seems to be valid. After all, as we have seen, the decisive factor in the building of the financial state was the requirements, the demands of war, and it would be difficult to find a causal connection between economic depression and *ancien régime* wars! It was bad luck for French taxpayers that expensive wars were fought when the economy was not in good shape; if it had been more buoyant, an increased tax burden would have been less painful. And, of course, the negative consequences of heavy taxation for the economy were aggravated by the gloomy *konjunktur* in which most increases in taxes took place.

Another problem to consider is whether the specific characters of the French economy had any significant impact upon the country's financial system. In this respect one must stress that, in the late medieval and early modern period and overlooking serious disparities between its different provinces, France was a 'moderately developed' country: less advanced and progressive than northern Italy, the Low Countries and England (from the seventeenth century onwards for the latter), less backward than Spain, most of Germany and, of course, Eastern Europe. P. Bairoch has calculated that, in the eighteenth century, French income per capita was close to the European average.[22]

Fernand Braudel and other writers have stressed that, during the long period we are considering, the centres of technological progress and of intense commercial activity, the birthplaces of capitalism, were outside the French kingdom – in the Low Countries and in northern Italy, plus an arc of merchant cities which united the two poles, at a distance from French borders. The only exception was during the relatively short period, in the twelfth and thirteenth centuries, when the Fairs of Champagne were the hub of trade in Western Europe. But the great cities which were in succession centres of 'world economies' – Venice, Antwerp, Genoa, Amsterdam, London – were not located in France, and the main routes which connected them avoided French territory. Indeed, it has been observed that the centres of commercial capitalism and those of modern states were geographically distinct. Lyons, economic capital of France in the sixteenth century, might be considered as an exception, but it was an 'Italian' city, dominated by Italian merchant-bankers, and thus evidence of the weakness of French capitalism. One could, of course, maintain that the existence in France of a large *état territorial* (Braudel's words), which was strong, authoritarian and fiscally demanding, prevented capitalism from developing; an objection, however, would be that the two economically advanced poles of Flanders and Italy existed before the rise of the French state.[23]

Anyhow, France was a country where agriculture was both overwhelmingly dominant and not particularly progressive and productive (it was even very backward in several – if not many – regions). It was a normal consequence that a large share of the state's revenue came from direct taxes – *la taille* or more exactly *les tailles* – upon the income of the peasantry. Moreover, agricultural production varied markedly, from year to year, according to weather conditions; bad harvests and subsistence crises occurred repeatedly and caused falls in government revenues, which were dangerous when they took place in the midst of a major war, as in 1693–4 and 1709–10.

On the other hand, France had no resource comparable to England's wool, from the export of which large taxes could be obtained. Except in the case of salt and wine, on which taxes were established in the fourteenth century, there were few opportunities for productive indirect taxes, as long as foreign trade had not developed on a large scale. Still, Sully and then Colbert reduced direct taxes and increased indirect ones, and in the eighteenth century, the fast rise of colonial trade, the growing consumption of new produce and the efficiency of tax-farming boosted indirect taxes. Revenue from the tobacco monopoly rose from 4 million *livres* in 1717 to 31 million in 1788. By 1788, 41 per cent of total revenue came from indirect taxes, 37 per cent from direct taxes. None the less, as P. Mathias and P. O'Brien have shown, in a classic article, indirect taxes supplied a smaller share of total revenue than in eighteenth-century England. In addition, they were more visible, more difficult to collect than in England, and highly unpopular.[24]

French governments were always short of hard and ready cash (admittedly this may not be specific to them!).[25] The absence of a bank of issue (such as the Bank of England) is often seen as responsible for the state's impecuniosity, while the high rates of interest on government borrowing have been considered a consequence of the French economy's backwardness. However, in both respects the behaviour of the royal government was more important than the condition of the economy. French kings were not reluctant to default on their debts, to reschedule them – specially in 1559, 1598, 1648 and 1661; later on, the 'System of Law' ended in 1720 with an actual bankruptcy and the cancellation of most debts which had been incurred under Louis XIV. It also discredited for a long time any idea of a bank of issue – up to the foundation of the *Caisse d'Escompte* in 1776. After the 'System', governments were more honest; the main bankruptcy – and a partial one – took place in 1771. Those periodical defaults were a major cause of the high interest rates which the king had to pay when he borrowed and which embodied an insurance premium against debt repudiation. Private persons, merchants, even non-state institutions were able to borrow at lower interest rates. This is why, in the eighteenth century, governments were prone to borrow *indirectly* as much as possible – from the General Farm, from provincial estates, from town councils, from the clergy, which all had much better credit ratings than the king. They borrowed sometimes at half the rate that was available to government and lent to the latter the money more cheaply than if it had borrowed directly. So everybody was happy, but the national debt and its servicing increased relentlessly.

Altogether, the financial state of the *ancien régime* had many serious shortcomings[26] – which eventually caused its collapse, as everybody knows. They included of course the webs of privileges, thanks to which many people, including the wealthiest, were exempt from *some* taxes, specially from the *tailles*. But the roots of such deficiencies are to be found in the structure of society and of institutions, rather than in the economy. Anyhow, in the eighteenth century, the British fiscal-military state was to become stronger and more efficient than its French counterpart, where absolutism was not much more than a façade for privilege, patronage, corruption and muddle.[27]

THE RISE OF MERCANTILIST INSTITUTIONS

Hitherto, we have only considered the state's three traditional functions – judicial, military and financial. For centuries, they were the only ones which the monarchy exercised. However, in the seventeenth and eighteenth centuries, the state assumed some new tasks, partly under the pressure of economic conditions.

In the early seventeenth century, the French economy was slowly recovering from the baneful effects of civil war, which had raged for almost four decades. But trade and manufactures suffered from competition by the rising and more advanced economies of north-western Europe – mostly the Dutch, but also the English. The penetration of Dutch and English ships in the Mediterranean and the diversion of the Levant trade to their benefit, which ensued, were harmful to the port of Marseilles. On the Atlantic coast, Dutch ships, thanks to their low freight rates, engrossed the export of French salt, wine and brandy towards northern Europe.[28] Many Dutch merchants settled in ports such as Nantes and Bordeaux, and their agents toured the hinterland to buy wines and brandies for export; they benefited from their knowledge of foreign markets, their networks of correspondents, the ready money they had available for making advances, and again low freights on their ships. They acquired a hold over the sea-borne trade of France and integrated some French provinces into a wide north-western European market. Unsurprisingly, French merchants felt marginalised, reduced to small-scale and even retail trade, and they loudly complained.

As a consequence, a strong current of economic nationalism developed in France from the late sixteenth century onwards. It had antecedents: on several occasions, steps had been taken to restrict imports of foreign goods, especially luxuries. What was new was the exasperation against foreign competitors, which turned into xenophobia, especially against the Dutch. The prohibition of imports of foreign goods and exports of French raw materials was demanded in many petitions from trading towns, at the assemblies of *notables* under Henry IV and Louis XIII, and at the Estates General of 1614 (the last ones before 1789). Moreover, several writers, especially Barthélemy Laffemas (in books of 1596 and 1598) and Antoine de Montchréstien (1615), put forward a kind of systematic doctrine which was capable of inspiring a coherent economic policy. They also explained the stagnation of the French economy and the fall in prices by the unfavourable balance of trade in France which had caused a drain of precious metals.

French mercantilism was therefore alive *before* Colbert and the latter's policies were anticipated during the decades which preceded 1660, especially by Sully and Richelieu: customs duties were raised, a 'Navigation Act' was passed in 1653,[29] the creation of new manufactures was encouraged by grants of monopolies, tax exemptions, subsidies and loans, several trading companies were started and some colonial ventures were launched. However, concrete results, though not entirely insignificant, were far below expectations.

It thus devolved upon Colbert to take up mercantilist policies again, on a grander scale and in a more systematic way than his predecessors. After having been excessively praised, he has recently been sharply disparaged (e.g. by P. Goubert). This is not the place to pronounce judgement upon him, nor to describe his policies. I shall just say that a median position seems to me sensible and that Colbert was no 'Colbertist', i.e. he was more pragmatic than is often said. From the point of view of state building, one must stress that Colbert created an 'economic administration', a machinery to supervise, encourage and direct the economy. In this field also there were antecedents: in 1601, a Committee of Commerce had been created; in 1602, Laffemas had been appointed Controller General of Commerce; but both committee and office were short-lived. In 1626, Richelieu had appointed himself Great Master and Superintendent of Navigation and Trade. In 1664, Colbert created, within the framework of the king's State Council, a special section, the Royal Council of Commerce, which was presided over by the king and where delegates from trading towns had seats. But this council was not very active and it was suppressed in 1676. Actually, all economic affairs came under the authority of the Controller General of Finances (a post created for Colbert in 1665) and in the provinces the *intendants*, who reported to him, were responsible for implementing his policies. Then, in 1669, Colbert established in each textile-manufacturing town an office for examining and stamping pieces of cloth (this was part of his policy to improve the quality of French goods, in order to promote exports), and he created fifteen posts of 'inspectors of manufactures' (by 1708, their number had risen to thirty-eight); these inspectors were to play an important role until their abolition in 1791, as Philippe Minard has shown.[30] One must also take into account the *enquêtes*, which Colbert ordered to gather economic information, the legislation which he passed (e.g. on trade law, forests, etc.), the foundation of dockyards for the navy (with their own administration), and a number of state-owned manufactures and armaments factories that he established. In addition, in 1700, one of his successors, Pontchartrain, established the *Bureau du Commerce* (which lasted until the French Revolution); under the authority of the Controller General, it was managed by a 'director', who was a quasi-minister for trade and industry, helped by four to six *intendants du commerce*.

From the 1660s onwards, and up to the fall of the *ancien régime* (despite the progress of *laissez-faire, laissez-passer* ideas in official circles during the eighteenth century), the state was, to some degree, responsible for the French economy (or at least for manufactures and foreign trade) and it had some instruments to act upon it. However, some qualifications must be made. We have presented the rise of French mercantilism as the product of difficulties which the French seventeenth-century economy suffered. But mercantilism is an economic ideology with objectives which are basically political, and even military. The policies which it inspired aimed at increasing the country's stock of precious metals and, therefore, the king's revenue, in order to support his *grande politique*: building up his army and navy, financing wars, paying subsidies to allies, etc. A second point is that 'Colbertism' was not well received by the French business community. They were glad to be protected against foreign competitors, but not to be prevented from using Dutch ships for exporting bulky commodities; they were ready to accept privileges, but not to be under strict control; they disliked Colbert's large and monopolist trading companies, which they considered as expedients to raise money for government, and they did not subscribe their shares (indeed, most of their capital came from financiers, tax-farmers and office-holders, who could not resist the minister's demand). I hesitate, therefore, to see economic factors as decisive in the rise of French mercantilism and of its institutions.

The take-over by the state of economic functions during the seventeenth and eighteenth centuries included public works, the infrastructure of transports, which had previously been completely neglected, but for the building of a few bridges (Pont Neuf in Paris, 1578); the government had felt responsible only for security on roads. The first move was the appointment in 1599 of Sully as *Grand Voyer* (let us say, Chief Inspector of Roads); he spent relatively large sums of money (6.5 per cent of total expenditures in 1609) in improving French roads; he also started the *canal de Briare*, which linked the Seine and the Loire – the two main arteries of traffic. It was a rather short canal, but it had a remarkable 'flight' (or staircase) of seven locks. Work was started by soldiers in 1607, but was only completed in 1642. Then nothing was done until the time of Colbert, who spent some money on roads, but whose main achievement was to sponsor and fund the *canal du Midi*, 242 km long, which joined the Garonne (and thus the Atlantic) to the Mediterranean; it was completed in 1681 and was the greatest public works project of the monarchy.

However, the great period of road-building was in the eighteenth century. An administration for bridges and roads (*Ponts et Chaussées*) was established, with a corps of professional engineers, who were trained in a special college. In 1738, a 'general plan' of main royal roads was drawn up; it was carried out in the fifty years which followed, under the supervision of *intendants*, who resorted to forced labour by the peasantry (*corvée royale*). By the 1780s, France had 40,000 km of well-built and well-maintained roads, which foreign visitors greatly admired – though Arthur Young observed that traffic was not intense. Undoubtedly, the state's intervention to improve transport had economic motivations (and had been demanded by the business community), but strategic considerations also played their role: better roads meant faster movements of troops – to the frontiers or to places where disturbances broke out. The star-shaped road system that radiated from Paris was not entirely in agreement with the needs of trade.

J.B. Collins has also seen a relation between the economic growth that took place during the eighteenth century and the expansion of the state's intervention (often at the request of local elites) in new matters: police (in the modern meaning, and mainly in Paris), poor relief (the incarceration of poor people in hospitals or workhouses – this was Michel Foucault's 'great confinement'), even education. I shall just mention these problems, as their origins are more 'social' than economic. But Collins' conclusion is worth recalling: this expansion of functions created a change in the nature of the state itself, which became fundamentally different from what it had been in the seventeenth century, much more 'modern'. He also observes – rightly – that, in the eighteenth century, the French government managed simultaneously to get stronger and to collapse. It could accomplish much more of what it set out to do, it was much better informed about conditions in the kingdom than earlier on, it was more centralised, its apparatus had expanded and become more like a real bureaucracy. On the other hand, it suffered an ideological bankruptcy; a growing gap, a dissociation developed, at the level of ideas and beliefs, between state and society. As D. Richet observed, the royal state and its authoritarian praxis, however enlightened, was not acceptable to public opinion any more.[31]

The *ancien régime* state was therefore destroyed by the French Revolution, which followed *tabula rasa* policies, and then undertook to build up a new system, though most of this task was actually achieved by Napoleon. While the state, which the monarchy had constructed, had remained – as Tocqueville pointed out long ago – an uncompleted, complicated, even ramshackle edifice, the Revolution and Napoleon finished the work of centralising and uniformising. The new French state was a truly modern and rational one, based upon the abolition of all kinds of privilege (both corporate and provincial) and upon uniformity of institutions.[32] In the economic field, France became a single unit (even though an effective national market was not achieved before the railway age), and free markets, free enterprise and *laissez-faire* succeeded corporatism and regulation. It has often been maintained that this new 'liberal' state conformed to the economic interests of the 'rising' bourgeoisie and was therefore the product of economic factors. Actually, this is a simplistic view: the French Revolution was 'made' by lawyers and not by businessmen; the motivations of its leaders and militants were first of all ideological, and economic factors were by no means dominant – just as they had played a role, but not a decisive one, in the building of the state which collapsed in 1789.[33]

NOTES

1. Recently a large-scale research project on the 'Origins of the Modern State in Europe, thirteenth to eighteenth Centuries' has been carried out under the auspices of the European Science Foundation; six volumes have been published (1995–8) as well as two complementary ones, edited by R. Bonney (see notes 2 and 14).

2. *Stricto sensu*, the term *domaine* refers less to a geographical entity than to a collection of rights, revenues and jurisdictions, but its extension also meant that kings re-established their lordships and control over the feudal lords within the realm and outstripped them in resources and military might; cf. J.B. Henneman, 'France in the Middle Ages' in Richard Bonney (ed.), *The Rise of the Fiscal State in Europe, c. 1200–1815* (Oxford, 1999; quoted further as Bonney, *Rise*), pp. 101–2. References have been reduced as much as possible.

3. Indeed, the venality of *offices* created a large administrative apparatus, which was largely independent from the crown; on the other hand, the capital invested in *offices* was the equivalent of a consolidated debt; Bonney, *Rise*, pp. 134, 152; also his *The European Dynastic States 1494–1660* (Oxford, 1991; quoted further as Bonney, *Dynastic*), p. 330.

4. E. Weber, *Peasants into Frenchmen: the Modernization of Rural France, 1870–1914* (Stanford, 1976); J.A. Lynn, *Giant of the Grand Siècle: the French Army 1610–1715* (Cambridge, 1997).

5. Cf. Colette Beaune, *Naissance de la nation France* (Paris, 1985).

6. D. Richet, *De la Réforme à la Révolution. Etudes sur la France moderne* (Paris, 1991), pp. 351 ff.

7. E. Dziembowski, *Un nouveau patriotisme français, 1750–1770. La France face à la puissance anglaise à l'époque de la guerre de Sept Ans* (Oxford, 1998).

8. Bonney, *Rise*, p. 103.

9. P. Chaunu, 'Une pesée globale', in F. Braudel and E. Labrousse (eds.), *Histoire économique et sociale de la France, Volume I: 1450–1660* (Paris, 1977), p. 27.

10. J.B. Collins, *The State in Early Modern France* (Cambridge, 1995); Bonney, *Dynastic*, p. 457.

11. Bonney, *Dynastic*, p. 341.

12. H. Lüthy, *La Banque Protestante en France* (2 vols., Paris, 1959 and 1961).

13. Bonney, *Rise*, pp. 161–2: 'The motor of fiscal change in France, as for all the main European monarchies, was expenditure on war', and the fiscal system was 'expenditure driven'.

14. R. Bonney (ed.), *Economic Systems and State Finance* (Oxford, 1995; quoted further as Bonney, *Systems*), p. 466.

15. Earlier on, under Philip IV (1285–1314), there had been a crisis in royal finances and early steps to build up a financial state. However, Henneman sees the capture (1356) and ransom of Jean Le Bon as the most decisive event in the

history of medieval French taxation, as a genuine revolution. During the 1370s, the new taxes supplied two and half times the large and exceptional subsidy which had been paid in 1304. Cf. Bonney, *Rise*, pp. 105, 116.

16. Bonney, *Systems*, p. 437.

17. A finance ministry emerged during the seventeenth century, but the official title of Colbert and his successors was *Contrôleur général des finances*.

18. One can add that the early steps in building the financial state, under Philip IV, had been taken near the end of the long upswing which had started in the tenth century, when Malthusian pressures were felt and an economic malaise prevailed.

19. In the short term, falling prices were not necessarily a negative factor: in the 1600s, they gave an opportunity to Sully to increase indirect taxes (and to reduce the *taille* at the same time), as this increase was hidden from the consumers. Chaunu, 'Une pesée globale', p. 179.

20. According to Henneman, 'France in the Middle Ages' (in Bonney, *Rise*, p. 119), the economic depression after 1410 – and for fifty years – was even worse than after the Black Death.

21. Chaunu, 'Une pesée globale', pp. 35, 47.

22. P. Bairoch, 'L'économie française dans le contexte européen à la fin du XVIIIᵉ siècle', *Revue Economique*, 40, 6 (November 1989), 939–64, esp. 961–3.

23. F. Braudel, *Civilisation Matérielle, Économie et capitalisme, XVᵉ–XVIIIᵉ siècle, Volume III: Le temps du monde* (Paris, 1979), pp. 269–99.

24. P. Mathias and P. O'Brien, 'Taxation in Britain and France, 1715–1810. A Comparison of the Social and Economic Incidence of Taxes Collected for the Central Government', *Journal of European Economic History* 5, 3 (Winter 1976), 601–50.

25. This was one reason why they could not give up any existing resources, even when they did not bring much revenue, while their economic consequences were obviously harmful. This was the case with tolls on rivers and road traffic, and with internal customs duties, the result being that France did not have a unified, single home market.

26. Including the corporate system of public debt, which has just been mentioned and which was less efficient than the British; also the fact that the 'finance ministry' had no unified control over expenditures; Bonney, *Rise*, pp. 128, 153.

27. Bonney, *Rise*, pp. 13–14. According to the Bonney–Ormrod model, France had passed from the 'domain' to the 'tax state', but only Britain had reached the higher stage of 'fiscal state' before 1815.

28. In 1651, 74 per cent of the tonnage of ships entering the port of Bordeaux or clearing from it (from or to non-French ports) were foreign. The Dutch also engrossed most of the trade with France's few colonies.

29. Foreign ships which exported French goods had to pay a duty of 50 *sous* per ton burden.

30. P. Minard, *La fortune du colbertisme. Etat et industrie dans la France des Lumières* (Paris, 1998).

31. Collins, *The State in Early Modern France*, pp. 184–5, 242; Richet, *De la Réforme*, p. 468; Michel Foucault, *Histoire de la folie à l'âge classique* (Paris, 1976).
32. A major change was the abolition of the venality of *offices*; *officiers* were replaced by elected officials or government-appointed *fonctionnaires*.
33. The views expressed in this last paragraph deserve to be set out at greater length, but space is short . . .

CHAPTER 3

Nation building in Germany: the economic dimension

Gerd Hardach

A BELATED NATION-STATE

Writing in 1832 on the division and unity of Germany, Leopold von Ranke remarked that in spite of the present tensions there had been for centuries a 'sentiment of essential unity of Germany'.[1] Ranke's words reflect the pride of the German national movement that Germany was one of the old established nations of Europe, and its frustration that the nation had failed to establish a modern state.[2] The sentiment of unity contrasted with a reality of political fragmentation. Ranke saw Germany 'between unity and dissociation', more unified than Italy, but less unified than France. His vision was a unified nation, bent towards the future, furthering its public weal.[3]

Ranke thought of nations as meaningful historical actors. Nations had their own identity, beyond the interests, designs and actions of their individual members.[4] In his *Geschichten der romanischen und germanischen Völker*, published in 1824, Ranke interpreted European history since the Middle Ages essentially as the interaction of six nations – the three 'Latin nations', France, Italy and Spain, and the three 'Germanic nations', Germany, England and Scandinavia. Two further actors in the shaping of European history were Turkey, an Asian nation, and Russia, a conglomerate of European and Asian provinces.[5] The definition of a nation was vague. A nation could be a comparatively homogeneous nation-state in the modern understanding, as France, England or Spain, where political power and cultural identity merged. It could be a cultural space fragmented into several political territories, as Germany, Scandinavia and Italy. It might also be a multicultural empire, as Russia or Turkey, with a dominant core culture and dependent regional cultures.

In a slightly different perspective, Ranke interpreted the history of Europe not as a system of nations, but as a system of powers. In his article on 'The Great Powers', published in 1833, Ranke argued that five states

56

as 'great powers' dominated European politics from the end of the seven-teenth century to the French Revolution of 1789: Austria, England, France, Prussia and Russia.[6] As the nation, a power had an identity of its own and was more than the sum of its members. But the power was defined more pragmatically than the nation as a political actor, and did not necessarily have the aura of cultural tradition, longevity and prestige. A power might be a nation, as England, France or Russia, or a part of a nation, as Austria and Prussia. Like persons, Ranke's nations and powers had their individual characteristics as represented by different constitutions, institutions and ideas.[7]

The role of politics and culture in the process of nation building was a recurrent theme in German historiography in the nineteenth and early twentieth centuries. As Ranke, many intellectuals took comfort from the assumption that the German cultural nation represented a long historical continuity in spite of the fragmentation and the fading political power of the old empire. It was only after the foundation of the German empire in 1871 that Friedrich Meinecke, a scholar of comparable stature to Ranke in German historiography, resolutely solved the dilemma. In his famous *Weltbürgertum und Nationalstaat*, published in 1907, he argued that the empire was the fulfilment of the national movement. Built on Prussian foundations, it had transformed the German cultural nation into a German political nation.[8] The convergence of national politics and national culture in the empire of 1871 continued to play a key role in the historiography of the German nation-state from the nineteenth century to the historical discourse of the late twentieth century.[9] With the imperial nation-state in the centre, the history of the nation-state falls into two periods: the straight road from the fragmented old empire to national unification in 1871, and the twisted path from the imperial nation-state to the republican nation, the racist nation, the two rival German states, and finally reunification in 1990.[10]

In this chapter, the emphasis is on the economic dimension of the nation-state. It is argued that economic performance was an important factor in the 'making, unmaking and remaking' of the German nation-state.[11] The eco-nomic dimension is rarely mentioned in historical syntheses of the German nation-state. Yet it seems obvious that economic growth contributed to the Prussian lead in the national unification movement of the nineteenth cen-tury, or the stability of the West German republican nation-state in the second half of the twentieth century, while economic crises played a central role in the failure of the republican nation-state in 1933, or the fall of the socialist nation-state in 1990.

The old German empire was politically fragmented, culturally hetero-geneous and economically decentralised. The origin of the old empire is usually traced back to the Treaty of Verdun in 843, when the empire of Charlemagne was divided. It took several generations, however, before the eastern part acquired an identity of its own. The medieval German empire claimed a direct succession from the Roman empire. In the late fifteenth century the Roman identity faded, and the empire acquired the title of 'Holy Roman Empire of the German Nation'. The first mention of this title seems to have been in 1474.[12] Unlike some of its western neighbours, the early modern German nation never became a territorial state. The attempt of the Habsburg rulers to establish a strong central government failed against the resistance of the numerous states and cities within the empire. In the late eighteenth century, the German empire was an ag-glomeration of 157 secular territories, 80 ecclesiastical territories and 51 free cities. While the political power of the empire faded, there remained a constitutional continuity. The political continuity of the empire created and supported a German identity, a popular proto-nationalism.[13] How-ever, the German identity competed with the allegiance to any of the many territories.[14]

The early modern territorial state claimed a monopoly of power, an iden-tifiable state territory, and a population living under its government. It relied on external controls, implemented by the twin institutions of the bureau-cracy and the military. People were expected to be loyal to the ruler, obey the laws of the land and pay taxes.[15] In Germany, the larger territories, and not the imperial government, built modern political institutions, provided administrative services, maintained military forces, enacted legal reforms, and implemented new fiscal and monetary policies. As other nation-states consolidated their power, Germany's political fragmentation was increas-ingly criticised as an anachronism.[16]

ECONOMIC UNIFICATION

The French Revolution of 1789 marked the transition from the early modern territorial state to the nation-state. The nation-state assumed a convergence of political institutions, cultural traditions and a national market. The supe-riority of the modern nation-state was demonstrated by the revolutionary wars, French hegemony over continental Europe from 1792 to 1815, and the fall of the old German empire in 1806. The challenge of the French revolutionary nation had a strong impact on the German movement for national unification.[17]

In the new bourgeois society, governance shifted from external to internal controls. The state requested from its citizens not only obedience but acceptance. General conscription, first introduced in revolutionary France, called young men from all social classes to fight for the state. Thus the role of the nation as an 'imagined community' was greatly enhanced.[18] The nation was not an autonomous historical force in the tradition of Ranke and German romanticism. It was an ideological construct, defined by the ruling elites to enhance the stability of power. The modern concept of the nation was a socially homogenising paradigm. It was based on the assumption that the 'imagined community' that was legitimised by tradition and culture was more important than the differences of class and gender. This contradicted the everyday experience that class and gender were far more visible in the individual life course than the remote imagined community of the nation. The early socialists argued that the working class had no stake in the nation-state.[19] Modern feminist historians discuss women's relationship to the national project.[20] Yet the historical longevity of the nation-state demonstrates that successive German governments did succeed in creating a national identity. Social cohesion in the modern nation-state was achieved in a permanent process of inclusion and exclusion. Traditions, real or invented, stable institutions and economic performance were the main instruments, in varying combinations, to create and maintain national identity and cohesion.

At the Congress of Vienna in 1815 the balance of power in Europe was restored. Germany became the German Federation of 1815–1866, a union of thirty-nine member states, ranging in size from Austria and Prussia to tiny principalities and free cities. The Habsburg monarchy was the presidential power of the German Federation, but it had no control over the other members. The boundaries of the German Federation corresponded approximately to the old Reich. The eastern and southern parts of the Habsburg empire and the eastern provinces of Prussia remained outside the frontiers of the German Federation. The old German empire may have had approximately 26 million inhabitants in 1800, including the territories west of the Rhine which were at that time occupied by France.[21] The population of the German Federation has been estimated at 30 million in 1816 and increased to 45 million in 1864. Austria was the largest German territory. In 1816 it had, without Hungary, a population of 14 million, of whom 9 million lived within the German Federation. Prussia had at that time 10 million inhabitants, of whom 8 million lived within the German Federation.[22] Culturally, the German Federation included Czechs, Italians, Slovenians and other minorities, but excluded Germans in Schleswig and in the eastern provinces of Prussia. Of the two leading powers of the German Federation, the Habsburg monarchy was a multicultural empire. Prussia was more similar to the West European nation-state, though 10 per cent of its population belonged to the Polish minority.[23]

In the early decades of the nineteenth century a capitalist market economy replaced the old feudal structure, and the industrial revolution changed German society. During the first half of the nineteenth century, economic growth was slow. Calculated for the territory of the future Reich of 1871, real net national product may have increased by 1.0 per cent from 1800 to 1850, and real net national product per capita by 0.1 per cent.[24] In the crisis of 1846, an agrarian crisis of the old type was linked to a new cyclical crisis. After 1850 economic growth accelerated. The crisis of 1857, the German–Danish war of 1864 and the civil war of 1866 interrupted the growth trend only briefly. From 1850 to 1869, calculated again for the territory of 1871, the average growth rate of real net national product has been estimated at 2.1 per cent per year, and the average growth rate of real net national product per capita at 1.4 per cent.[25]

During the industrial revolution, Germany's political fragmentation was criticised as a barrier to economic progress. As the rivalry between Austria and Prussia blocked the establishment of a nation-state, economic unification became a substitute for political unification. It may seem paradoxical that the national movement gained momentum in Germany at a time when the liberal doctrine reduced the role of the state. Far from the German idolatry of the state, British philosophers and economists took a pragmatic attitude towards government. They expected that the state provided institutions, justice and defence. But they regarded the attachment to a particular nation-state as circumstance and habit, rather than rational choice. Ricardo mentioned 'the natural disinclination which every man has to quit the country of his birth and connexions, and intrust himself with all his habits fixed, to a strange government and new laws'.[26] In modern economic jargon, Ricardo's remark suggests that the nation-state provided some psychic income. But as the rising international migration proved, the psychic income of belonging to a particular nation-state could be compensated by other considerations. Political economists demonstrated the advantages of free trade.[27] When Britain returned to gold in 1816, it created the foundation of an international monetary system with convertibility and fixed exchange rates. Most other countries adhered to a bimetallic currency or a silver standard at that time, but the parity between gold and silver was fairly stable in the short run. It was widely assumed that national currencies did not constitute 'optimum currency areas', to use a term coined by Mundell.[28] John Stuart Mill argued in 1848 that 'in the progress of political improvement', all countries would one day have the same currency. National currencies were a sign of economic and political backwardness: 'So much of barbarism, however, still remains in the transactions of the most civilized nations, that almost all independent countries choose to assert their nationality by having, to their own inconvenience and that of their neighbours, a peculiar currency of their own.'[29] Yet the internationalisation of production and consumption rested on a system of national economies and national economic policies. It was no contradiction, therefore, that the national movement was supported by economic interests.

Prussia and several south German states were the driving forces in the process of economic unification. Prussia established in 1818 a single customs line with a moderate tariff. During the following years, smaller territories were linked to the Prussian economic area. In 1833 Prussia, Bavaria, Württemberg, Saxony and several smaller territories of the German Federation founded a customs union, the Zollverein. The new economic area adopted the moderate Prussian tariff and thus held a middle position between the strongly protectionist Habsburg empire in the south, and the free-trading territories of Hanover, Oldenburg and the Hanse cities in north-western Germany. The Zollverein was gradually expanded until it included most of the territories of the German Federation. Austria remained outside as it did not want to give up its protectionism. It was linked to the customs union by a commercial treaty in 1853.[30]

The customs union was followed by a monetary reform. The German territories had different currencies, based on silver or gold. In Prussia and most other north German territories the Thaler was the standard unit of account, in south Germany and in Austria the Gulden. Various types of paper money were issued with fixed parities to silver. Austria had failed to consolidate its government finances after 1815, and therefore the Austrian Gulden was from 1811 to 1892 in fact a managed currency, with a flexible exchange rate to silver. In 1838 several territories of the German Federation formed a monetary union. The agreement defined a common mint parity of 1 Thaler to 1.75 Gulden. The currencies of member states were generally accepted as a means of payment, though they were not legal tender outside the issuing territory. The reform did not include the supply of paper money, and did not attempt a co-ordination of economic or fiscal policies. In 1857 a new monetary union was agreed, which included Austria. As the war of 1859 led to new government deficits, however, Austria found it impossible to implement the reform and remained on a paper standard. Thus the monetary reforms of 1838 and 1857 furthered the development of a national market dominated by Prussia, and separated from Austria.[31]

The revolution of 1848–9 gave a new impetus to political unification. The constitution that was accepted by the National Assembly in 1849 defined Germany as the territory of the German Federation, augmented by Schleswig and the eastern provinces of Prussia. Thus the revolutionary nation stretched from Aachen to Königsberg, and from Kiel to Trieste as a door to the Mediterranean. The definition of the revolutionary German nation was not uncontested. Some minorities, notably the Czechs and the Italians, had their own national ambitions. In Germany, some critics would have preferred a more homogeneous nation-state, led by Prussia and separated from the Habsburg monarchy. The Austrian government demanded a large federation, which would include the entire Habsburg empire. When the reactionary forces had defeated the revolution the decentralised structure of the German Federation was restored in 1850.[32]

Prussian historiography of the later nineteenth century celebrated the Zollverein as a far-sighted patriotic programme which prepared the nation-state of 1871. According to Heinrich von Treitschke, the customs union was a 'new link, solid and plain, in the long chain of historical events that led the margravate of the Hohenzollern to the imperial crown. The eagle's eye of the great king looked from the clouds, and in a far distance the clamour of the battle of Königgrätz could already be heard.'[33] This was, as historical research has shown, an exaggeration. The Prussian motives in 1833 were economic and financial: the Zollverein was regarded as an instrument for a larger market and more revenue. After the revolution of 1848–9, the Prussian government tried to use the Zollverein as a political instrument in its rivalry with Austria. In the short run, the strategy to use economic performance as a political weapon failed. In the civil war of 1866 which Prussia started to break up the German Federation and to separate Austria from national unification, seventeen members of the German Federation followed Prussia, while twelve states sided with Austria, though most of them were members of the Zollverein.[34]

In a wider sense, however, Treitschke's assertion that the Zollverein was a prelude to integration remains valid. As Prussia assumed leadership in the economic integration of Germany, it made a credible commitment to national unification. All those who had an interest in a national market, in economic modernisation and in national bargaining power in international economic policy would have to support the Hohenzollern monarchy. Even liberals who had been defeated in 1849 by the Prussian counterrevolution entrusted in the 1860s the cause of national unification to the conservative Prussian government. The civil war of 1866 did not raise the deep emotions of the American Civil War of 1861–5. It was of short duration, and the settlement was widely accepted. Austria agreed to the dissolution of the German Federation. Prussia annexed several north German territories and formed in 1871 together with the smaller German states the German empire (*Deutsches Reich*).

THE IMPERIAL NATION-STATE

The German empire of 1871 was widely regarded as the fulfilment of the dream of national unification. Leopold von Ranke, ennobled since 1865, was initially not enthusiastic about the new empire. An ingrained conservative, he thought that the constitution, general and equal male suffrage for the imperial diet, and other democratic elements, yielded too much to the liberal *Zeitgeist*. But as Bismarck, supported by the traditional Prussian military and administrative establishment, ruled Germany with a firm hand, Ranke changed his mind. In 1885, then 90 years old, he remarked that the unification of 1871 was the deepest satisfaction for the German nation. The Prussian monarchy had almost by necessity become the German empire.[35] For a new generation of historians, with Friedrich Meinecke as a prominent representative, the definition of the German nation was now unimpaired by the ambiguities of the early nineteenth century when intellectuals and nationalists had vacillated between cultural nation and political nation, between Austria and Prussia. Under the impact of the new political reality, culture was no longer perceived as an alternative to politics in nation building. Max Weber insisted that the nation was based on political organisation.[36]

Despite the acclaim of prominent historians, the historical legitimacy of the empire of 1871 was doubtful. The new German nation-state excluded several million Germans in the Habsburg empire. On the other hand, it had inherited from Prussian history a large Polish minority in the east, and had acquired a large French minority by the annexation of Alsace-Lorraine. The recent glory of national unification could hardly obscure the fact that Prussia had achieved its dominant position in a persistent struggle against Austria, and against the old German empire. Politicians and intellectuals hurried to weave the glamour and prestige of the old empire, Prussian military power, and German cultural achievements in literature and philosophy, music and the arts into a new national tradition. National symbols and memorials were invented, festivals celebrated and military parades organised to establish a national identity. Imperial Germany is a case in point that national identity is often supported by invented rather than real traditions.[37]

The deficit in historical legitimacy was compensated by economic performance and social policy. According to the first census, Germany had a population of 41 million in 1871. By 1913 the population had increased to 67 million.[38] The industrial revolution changed the structure of production and employment, and transformed Germany from an agricultural to an industrial society. From 1878–9 to 1910–13 the share of labour force in the primary sector decreased from 49 to 35 per cent, while the share in the secondary sector increased from 29 to 38 per cent, and the share in the tertiary sector from 22 to 27 per cent.[39] The founding of the empire was followed by a vigorous economic expansion from 1871 to 1873. The boom ended with the crisis of 1873, which was followed by the Great Depression of 1873–95. Economic growth gained a new momentum around 1895. There was a period of sustained growth, interrupted only by three brief crises in 1900–1, 1907–8 and 1913–14.[40] The average growth rate of real net social product for the long period from 1872 to 1913 was 2.5 per cent, and the growth rate of real net social product per capita was 1.3 per cent.[41]

Germany's economic system was influenced by the liberal doctrine of the time: modern institutions, free trade, and a low level of regulation and government spending. The German constitution of 1871 introduced general and equal male suffrage for the imperial parliament, the Reichstag, though the individual state parliaments could be elected by unequal voting systems. Socialist organisations and publications were prohibited from 1878 to 1890, but socialist politicians could participate in elections and were members of the Reichstag. Tariffs were low, and with the new mark currency which was introduced in 1871 Germany joined the gold standard. The international gold standard of the nineteenth century increased exchange rate stability and reduced the transaction costs of foreign exchange operations.[42]

The Great Depression of 1873–95 led to a change from liberal capitalism to organised capitalism, characterised by economic concentration, the rise of interest groups and increased government intervention.[43] From 1883 to 1889 the government created a modern social security system, with health insurance, work accidents insurance and old age pensions, to offset the negative impact of the suppression of the labour movement and to win the support of the working class.[44] Ideological tensions increased during the Great Depression. The influence of the working class rose with the expansion of the Social Democratic Party and of trade unions after 1890. On the other side, conservative organisations gained influence. A new

anti-Semitism appeared from the late 1870s. The new anti-Semitic movement defined the Jewish minority not as a different culture, but as a different
race. The invention of race made cultural assimilation not only undesirable
but also virtually impossible. According to the new ideology, race was inherited with all the imagined characteristics that were attributed to the Jewish
minority. In retrospect there was an ideological continuity and escalation
from the racist anti-Semitism of the late nineteenth century to the eliminatory racism of the Nazi regime. But at the time, anti-Semites and other
right-wing extremists were never considered a threat to the constitutional
order.[45]

In international economic politics the Great Depression heralded a rise
of protectionism and imperialism. A protectionist tariff was introduced in
1878. From 1884 to 1899, Germany acquired a vast colonial empire in Africa
and in the South Pacific. The potential danger of economic nationalism
and imperialism, however, was neither tariffs nor colonies, but the neo-
mercantilist doctrine that international trade and capital movements were
essentially a closed system in which countries could gain only at the expense of their neighbours. A nation would have to become a world power,
or face decline. The renowned social scientist Max Weber was a prominent advocate of the new doctrine of world power. In 1895 he argued in
his inaugural lecture as professor of political economy that the German
unification of 1871 would be nothing more than a juvenile prank, which
was hardly worth its cost, if Germany did not strive to become a world
power.[46]

The First World War demonstrated the power of national coherence.
Recent research suggests that the national enthusiasm in August 1914 may
not have been as universal as the demonstrations and parades in Berlin
and other big cities suggest. But the vast majority of German soldiers and
workers, of men and women supported to the very end a war in which they
had all to lose and nothing to win.[47] The defeat of the imperial nation-state
was due to Germany's inferiority in soldiers and resources in 1918, not to
the resistance of socialists and pacifists, or to popular defection.[48]

The immediate legacy of the war was death and destruction. It has been
estimated that close to 10 million soldiers died during the war. When the
losses of the civilian population, the Armenian genocide, the Russian civil
war and other consequences of the war are included, the death toll of
the First World War may rise to 20 million people. The economic losses
were also staggering. Large areas were devastated by the war, particularly
in northern France and in Poland.[49] The Russian Revolution of 1917 was
perceived in Germany and many other capitalist countries as a threat to the

bourgeois nation-state. The economic ruin of Europe accelerated the shift of leadership in the world economy from Europe to the United States.[50]

In November 1918 the revolution overthrew the monarchy in Germany and established a socialist government. Elections for a National Assembly were held in January 1919, and in February 1919 a parliamentary government was established. Frightened by the revolutionary situation in Berlin, the National Assembly escaped to the more tranquil Weimar, and there it adopted in August 1919 the constitution for a republican nation. A combination of liberal principles and social demands, the Weimar constitution promised to place the republican nation on a broad consensus. There would be more power for the parliament, the possibility of referendums, equal rights for men and women, co-operation of capital and labour, and an expansion of social policy. Against the nationalistic culture of the imperial nation, the republican nation stipulated a democratic tradition which was based on the democratic movement of the early nineteenth century, the revolution of 1848, and the labour movement.[51]

In June 1919, the Treaty of Versailles was concluded between the Allies and Germany. Germany lost Alsace-Lorraine to France, and a large territory in the east to the new state of Poland. The restoration of the Polish nation-state in 1918 redressed the historical injury of 1795. Smaller border regions were annexed by Belgium, Denmark and the new republic of Czechoslovakia. The city of Danzig became a free city, linked to Poland by a customs union. The Saar region was temporarily separated from Germany as an autonomous territory, controlled by France. The German colonial empire was divided among Belgium, the British empire, France, Japan and Portugal. Germany had to accord unilaterally most-favoured-nation treatment to the Allied countries for a period of five years, and German property in Allied countries could be sequestrated. The treaty obliged Germany to pay reparations as a compensation for war damages. In May 1921 the reparations which Germany had to pay were fixed at 132 billion gold marks. A League of Nations was created to guarantee the new international order.[52]

The republican nation inherited 87 per cent of Germany's pre-war territory. The German population was 63 million in 1919, 6 per cent less than in 1913. Population growth had slowed down since the end of the nineteenth century, and this trend continued during the inter-war period. On the eve of the Second World War in 1939, Germany had a population of 69 million, including the Saar which had come back to Germany in 1935, but excluding Austria and the Czechoslovakian border ('Sudeten') region which were annexed in 1938.[53] Many Germans believed that the peace treaty placed an unbearable burden on the republican nation. The prominent support of John Maynard Keynes has added some credibility to this proposition.[54] And yet the pessimism was erroneous. The colonies had been economically insignificant, and were always a financial loss to the German government. Reparations were a political embarrassment for the Weimar Republic, but not an economic burden. They were financed by capital imports, in large part from the United States. The Dawes Plan of 1924 and the Young Plan of 1930 reduced the amount considerably, and the Lausanne Conference of 1932 put an end to reparations. The territories which Germany ceded to its neighbours were less productive than the rest of the economy. The largest part consisted in backward agricultural regions in the east, and their low productivity was not compensated by Alsatian textile mills or Lorraine iron works in the west.[55] The republican nation was economically more homogeneous than the imperial nation.

The political stability of the republican nation depended upon its economic condition. From 1918 to 1923 the German economy experienced the worst inflation in its history. The inflation temporarily furthered production and employment, and protected Germany against the world economic crisis of 1920–1. But in the end, the inflation ruined the economy and delayed the transition from a war to a peace economy. In November 1923 the mark was stabilised at the impressive exchange rate of 4.2 billion (4.2 thousand milliard) marks to one dollar. In 1924 Germany introduced a new currency, the Reichsmark (RM), and returned to the gold standard at the pre-war exchange rate of 4.20 RM to one dollar.[56] From 1924 to 1928 Germany regained a period of economic stability. Production increased, and in 1927 the real net national product per capita exceeded the pre-war level of 1913. Economic recovery furthered the political stability of the Weimar Republic and its integration into the international system. Economic growth and employment were limited, however, by the deflationary monetary policy which was implemented to defend the gold standard. While workers suffered from high unemployment, entrepreneurs complained about the cost of the welfare state and the power of the trade unions.[57]

From 1929 to 1932, Germany suffered the worst crisis in the history of business cycles. From 1928 to 1932, real net national product per capita decreased by 24 per cent. The number of registered unemployed increased to 6 million in January 1933.[58] The economic crisis eroded popular support for the Weimar Republic, while the conservative elites sought to replace democracy by an authoritarian government. After three chancellors who ruled without popular support by presidential decrees, Heinrich Brüning,

Franz von Papen and Kurt von Schleicher, the government was, in January 1933, transferred to Adolf Hitler, leader of the radically nationalist and anti-Semitic Nationalsozialistische Deutsche Arbeiterpartei (NSDAP). The republican nation-state collapsed after only fourteen years. The attempt to create a new democratic identity and the creation of modern institutions had not provided sufficient popular support to overcome the economic crisis.

THE RACIST NATION-STATE

The Nazi regime declared the seizure of power in January 1933 as the beginning of a national revolution. In August 1934, Hitler boasted before a mass meeting of the NSDAP in Nuremberg that the revolution was now successfully concluded. No other revolution would occur in Germany for the next one thousand years.[59] To contemporaries and historians alike, the Nazi revolution was and is more easily characterised by the social order that it wanted to destroy than by the new social order that it wanted to establish.[60] The conspicuous aims of the Nazi regime were the destruction of democracy, the oppression of the labour movement, an eliminatory anti-Semitism, and the aggressive revision of the international system. The programme for the future was vague, for various reasons. First, the regime presented intentionally a heterogeneous programme to appeal to different classes and interest groups. Second, the Nazi government did not want to reveal its domestic and international objectives before it was firmly established. And third, the regime lacked plans to reconcile the contradictory aims and interests within the party, the government and other institutions.

The different aims and programmes of the Nazi regime converged vaguely in the creation of a new society based on the myth of a superior Germanic 'race'. Organised in a powerful state, the Germanic race would rule over other people and 'races'. The Nazi ideology appealed to nationalist traditions. It appropriated episodes of power, of imperial splendour and military conquests in German history as a traditional legitimation. After the medieval empire, and the second empire of 1871, the 'Third Reich' would be the ultimate triumph of the German nation. But the 'Third Reich' was, nevertheless, a departure from the previous concept of the nation-state. The 'nation' was gradually replaced as an instrument of cohesion by the new concept of a *Volksgemeinschaft*, which can be translated as a 'community of the people'. The *Volksgemeinschaft* suggested more strongly than the nation a programme of social homogenisation, beyond the differences of class and gender. It included all people of the proper ethnicity and mentality but excluded, and finally eliminated, all people who were defined as a different ethnicity, as political opponents, as enemies in general, as weak, as useless.[61]

Economic policy, and the semblance of economic stability, was an important instrument of the Nazi regime to win the support of the people. A hesitant recovery had already begun when the Nazi regime came to power in 1933, and active employment policies were used to accelerate recovery. From 1936 a Five Year Plan directed the economy towards armament and war. In 1938 real net national product per capita, boosted by the armament programme, was 46 per cent higher than it had been in 1929.[62] After years of unemployment the rearmament economy provided full employment. Wages lagged behind the expansion of national income and rationing reduced consumption. But workers were apparently more concerned about employment than about income distribution. Many people, closing their eyes to oppression, murder and concentration camps, were willing to support the regime for its economic performance.[63]

From the national socialist seizure of power in 1933 a direct path led to the Second World War. Even during the early years of the war the Nazi regime tried to maintain a tolerable standard of living in the *Volksgemeinschaft*. It believed to a degree in its own propaganda that the First World War was lost not by military defeat and economic exhaustion, but by the apathy and the frustration of the civilian population, an atmosphere that was easily exploited by national socialist agitators.[64] For this or other reasons, the *Volksgemeinschaft* demonstrated during the Second World War even more cohesion than the imperial nation-state during the First World War. The war effort found desperate supporters until the cities lay in ruins and the Allied armies met in the centre of Germany. Parallel to the transition from armament to war, there was a direct path from the early anti-Semitic outrages, which began as soon as the Nazis were in power, to the extermination camps. This was the darkest time in the history of the German nation-state. There were hundreds of thousands of perpetrators, millions of bystanders who knew about the crimes, and distressingly few people who protested.[65] It has been estimated that 42 million people died in Europe as a consequence of the Second World War, and more than 6 million people died in the genocide of Jews and other victims.[66]

PARTITION

Liberation in 1945 came as an occupation. After the capitulation of the German *Wehrmacht* in May 1945, the four Allies took over the government of Germany. The administration of Germany was divided into four

occupation zones, and an Allied Control Council of the four military governors was installed as a joint administration. In the Potsdam Protocol of
August 1945 the Allies fixed the Oder and Neisse as Germany's provisional
eastern frontier. East Germany was to be annexed by Poland, except the
northern part of East Prussia which was occupied by the Soviet Union. The
definite settlement of Germany's frontiers was deferred to a peace treaty,
but there was no doubt that, in fact, the new frontier was final. The Soviet
Union and Poland expelled, with the consent of the Western Allies, the
German population from East Prussia, Pomerania and Silesia.[67]

None of the four Allied powers planned to divide Germany into two
states. The Allies agreed in the Potsdam Protocol to treat Germany as a unit,
and the occupation zones were regarded as an administrative device of a
temporary nature. But the economic crisis in post-war Germany, the diverging occupation policies of the three Western Allies and the Soviet Union,
and the cold war led to a partition which appeared to many observers in
retrospect as inevitable. The Allied Control Council held its last session in
March 1948. In the three Western occupation zones a capitalist market economy was restored in 1948. The European Recovery Programme of 1948–52
reintegrated the West German economy into Western Europe, and into the
world market.[68] In East Germany the Soviet Union and the German administration established a Soviet-type state socialism. As a counter-move to
the European Recovery Programme the Soviet Union and its East European
satellite states created in 1949 the Council for Mutual Economic Assistance.
In September 1949 the Federal Republic of Germany was founded. In reaction, the Soviet Union transformed its occupation zone in October 1949
into the German Democratic Republic.[69] In the second half of the twentieth century, Germany returned to the ambiguous situation 'between unity
and dissociation' which had irritated Ranke, and other intellectuals, in the
first half of the nineteenth century.

For twenty-three years both German states claimed to represent the
German nation. In the Federal Republic of Germany, unification by
peaceful and democratic means was mandated by the constitution. Until 1972 the West German government contested the legitimacy of the East
German state. The German Democratic Republic also insisted on unification, though on its own terms. A new constitution which was adopted
in 1968 defined the German Democratic Republic as a 'socialist state of
German nation'.[70] In 1972 both German governments agreed to acknowledge the reality of two German states. In West German understanding the
official recognition of East Germany as a sovereign state did not remove
the constitutional option of a future unification by democratic agreement.

The German Democratic Republic, however, broke with the common national tradition of the two German states after the agreement of 1972 and sought to establish a separate national identity. In 1971 the Sozialistische Einheitspartei Deutschlands (SED), the official state party, had already declared that the different socio-economic systems of the two German states had led to the formation of two different nations. The German Democratic Republic had become a new 'socialist nation', while the Federal Republic of Germany was a 'bourgeois nation'.[71] The new constitution which was adopted in 1974, six years after the last revision, defined the German Democratic Republic as a 'socialist state of workers and peasants' without reference to a common German national tradition.[72]

As in the Austrian–Prussian rivalry of the early nineteenth century, economic performance was an important instrument when the two German nation-states of the late twentieth century competed for the consent of the people. The Federal Republic of Germany was the larger competitor. The population increased from 49 million at the end of 1949 to 62 million in 1989. After the mid-1960s, population growth slowed down. A declining birth rate and rising life expectancy changed the age structure of the population.[73] West Germany's economic system was described as a 'social market economy'. It combined a capitalist market economy with a modern welfare state. High economic growth during the 'golden age' from 1950 to 1973 supported the stability of the new democracy.[74] In 1953 real net national product per capita increased above the level of 1938, and economic recovery turned into an unprecedented process of economic growth.[75] From 1950 to 1973, real gross domestic product per capita increased by an average rate of 4.9 per cent.[76] Unemployment, which was still high in the early 1950s, decreased. By 1960 practically full employment was reached, with an unemployment rate of only 1 per cent.[77] After the crisis of 1974–5 economic growth slowed down and unemployment increased. From 1973 to 1989 the average growth rate of gross domestic product per capita was 2.0 per cent. The unemployment rate increased to 9 per cent in 1988.[78] Economic growth changed the structure of the Federal Republic from an industrial to a post-industrial nation. In 1990, only 3 per cent of the labour force were occupied in the primary sector, 39 per cent in the secondary sector and 58 per cent in the tertiary sector.[79] High economic growth created the preconditions for an expansion of government services and social security. Since the late 1970s, the welfare state has shown slower economic growth, rising unemployment and increasing welfare costs. Yet the social market economy remained an essential element of national identity.[80]

The German Democratic Republic claimed to represent the vanguard of historical change. According to the official Marxist-Leninist ideology, a socialist society must necessarily triumph over any outmoded capitalist society. The class structure was transformed by nationalisation of the means of production. East Germany was in many respects a more egalitarian society than West Germany, but it was also a less dynamic society. The population of 19 million at the end of 1949 soon decreased to 17 million and remained at that level until 1989.[81] A large number of East Germans moved to West Germany until the frontier was closed in 1961. East Germany was an advanced industrial country, but the planned economy was much less efficient than West Germany's social market economy. Problems, which were never solved, were the inflexibility of bureaucratic planning, deficits in motivation, and a slow pace of technological innovation.[82] The East German economy remained more conservative in its economic structure than the West German economy. In 1989 11 per cent of the labour force were still in agriculture, 47 per cent in the secondary sector and only 42 per cent in services.[83]

There is general agreement that economic growth was much slower in East Germany than in West Germany. However, the quantitative description of the growth path of the East German economy is difficult, and still controversial among scholars. The problem is not only the difference in national accounting and the poor quality of many East German statistics, but also the different product and price structure of the planned economy. According to Albert Ritschl, there was a period of high growth from 1950 to 1973, when the growth rate of real per capita income in East Germany was between 3.2 and 4.7 per cent. In the 1970s, economic growth slowed down, similar to the West German experience. From 1973 to 1989, the average growth rate of real per capita income was between 1.3 and 3.2 per cent per year. On the eve of reunification, from January to September 1990, the average productivity of the East German economy was between 40 per cent and 60 per cent of the West German level.[84] This estimate does not take into account differences in the design or quality of goods and services. If the productivity of the East German economy is measured by the prices which East German products fetched on capitalist markets, it may have been as low as 14 to 20 per cent of the West German level.[85] The poor economic performance was not the only cause of discontent, but it contributed to the decline of the experimental 'socialist nation' from historical vanguard to historical episode. When the 'silent revolution' of October 1989 overthrew the East German regime, the requests for reform turned soon into a demand for reunification.

A NEW NATION-STATE

The unification of October 1990 created a new German nation. The institutional framework of the new nation was provided by West Germany and to many casual observers, in Germany and abroad, the new Federal Republic of Germany looked like an enlarged old Federal Republic of Germany. Yet behind the façade of continuity from Bonn to Berlin there was a reality of two different societies growing together. The historian Gerhard A. Ritter described the German nation of the 1990s as 'two societies within one state'.[86]

In the dramatic transition period from October 1989 to October 1990, it was estimated that the political unification might be completed within five years by an economic and social unification. That was far too optimistic.[87] The population of the new Federal Republic of Germany increased slowly from 80 million in 1990 to 82 million in 2000. The population increase was due to the rising share of foreign residents in German society. There were 7 million foreign residents in 2000, a share of 9 per cent of the total population. Germany continued its path towards a post-industrial economy. In 2000 the primary sector employed 3 per cent of the labour force, the secondary sector 29 per cent and the tertiary sector 68 per cent. Economic growth was slower in the new nation than it had been in West Germany. From 1991 to 2000 real gross domestic product per head increased by an average rate of 1.3 per cent. Unemployment remained high, with an unemployment ratio of 8 per cent in 2000.[88]

The economic gap between West Germany and East Germany narrowed but did not vanish during the 1990s. While the new market in East Germany led to a short 'unification boom' in the West German economy in 1990–1, the East German economy plunged into a deep transformation crisis. The core of the problem was the low productivity of the East German economy. In 1991, average productivity in East Germany was only 33 per cent of the West German level.[89] After 1993 the East German economy recovered gradually. Yet there remained a considerable gap in productivity, income and employment. Huge public transfers from the West to the East were needed, and will still be needed in the future, to maintain adequate social standards in East Germany (see table 3.1).

As the twentieth century turned into the twenty-first century, European integration and economic globalisation have reduced the importance of the German nation-state. European institutions and international markets limit the scope of the national government in economic policy, fiscal policy, monetary policy and social policy. However, the nation-state remains the

Table 3.1 *Germany, 1871–2000*

	Area (1,000 km²)	Population (million)	GDP (billion marks)	GDP per capita (marks)
Germany 1871	541	41	14	342
Germany 1925	469	62	67	1,066
FRG 1989	249	62	2224	35,877
GDR 1989	108	17	(260)	(15,318)
Germany 2000	357	82	3976	48,371

Notes: The income in the German Democratic Republic in 1989 is the national income.
FRG = Federal Republic Germany; GDR = German Democratic Republic.
Sources: Hoffmann et al. *Das Wachstum der deutschen Wirtschaft*, pp. 172–4, 825–6;
Statistisches Bundesamt, *Bevölkerung und Wirtschaft*, p. 90; *Statistisches Jahrbuch der DDR, 1990*, pp. 1, 101: *Statistisches Jahrbuch BRD* 2001, pp. 654–5; ibid. 2002, p. 44.

ultimate source of democratic, legitimate governance from which all other political activities are derived.[90] As long as that is so, the nation-state will continue to use cultural identity, institutional advantages and economic performance as means to win the consent of the people.

NOTES

1. Leopold von Ranke, 'Über die Trennung und die Einheit von Deutschland' (1832), in *Sämmtliche Werke*, Vols. XLVIII and XLIX (Leipzig, 1887), p. 134.
2. James J. Sheehan, 'Nation und Staat. Deutschland als imaginierte Gemeinschaft' in Manfred Hettling and Paul Nolte (eds.), *Nation und Gesellschaft in Deutschland* (Munich, 1996), pp. 33–45.
3. Ranke, 'Über die Trennung und die Einheit', p. 172.
4. Ernst Schulin, 'Universalgeschichte und Nationalgeschichte bei Leopold von Ranke' in Wolfgang J. Mommsen (ed.), *Leopold von Ranke und die moderne Geschichtswissenschaft* (Stuttgart, 1988), pp. 37–71; Helmut Berding, 'Leopold von Ranke' in Hans-Ulrich Wehler (ed.), *Deutsche Historiker*, Vol. I (Göttingen, 1971), pp. 7–24.
5. Leopold von Ranke, *Geschichten der romanischen und germanischen Völker von 1494 bis 1514* (1824) in *Sämmtliche Werke*, Vols. XXXIII–XXXIV (Leipzig, 1874), pp. v–xv.
6. Leopold von Ranke, 'Die großen Mächte' (1833) in *Sämmtliche Werke*, Vol. XXIV (Leipzig, 1872), pp. 1–40.
7. Schulin, 'Universalgeschichte und Nationalgeschichte', p. 60.
8. Friedrich Meinecke, *Weltbürgertum und Nationalstaat. Studien zur Genesis des deutschen Nationalstaats* (1907) in *Werke*, Vol. V (Munich, 1962).
9. Dieter Langewiesche, 'Reich, Nation und Staat in der jüngeren deutschen Geschichte', *Historische Zeitschrift*, 254 (1992), 361–4.

10. Otto Dann, *Nation und Nationalismus in Deutschland 1770–1990* (Munich, 1993); Otto Dann (ed.), *Die deutsche Nation. Geschichte – Probleme – Perspektiven* (Vierow, 1994); Harold James, *Deutsche Identität 1770–1990* (Frankfurt, 1991); Jürgen Kocka, 'Das Problem der Nation in der deutschen Geschichte, 1870–1945' in Kocka, *Geschichte und Aufklärung* (Göttingen, 1989); Dieter Langewiesche, 'Nation, Nationalismus, Nationalstaat: Forschungsstand und Forschungsprobleme', *Neue Politische Literatur*, 40 (1995), 190–236.

11. John Breuilly (ed.), *The State of Germany: the National Idea in the Making, Unmaking and Remaking of a Modern Nation-State* (London, 1992).

12. Peter Mora, 'Reich' in Otto Brunner, Werner Conze and Reinhart Koselleck (eds.), *Geschichtliche Grundbegriffe*, Vol. V (Stuttgart, 1984), p. 454.

13. Eric Hobsbawm, *Nations and Nationalism: Programme, Myth, Reality* (Cambridge, 2000).

14. Detlef Rogosch, 'Das Heilige Römische Reich Deutscher Nation und die Entstehung des deutschen Nationalgefühls' in Heinz Timmermann (ed.), *Die Entstehung der Nationalbewegung in Europa 1750–1849* (Berlin, 1993), pp. 15–28.

15. Charles Tilly, *Coercion, Capital, and European States, AD 900–1990* (Oxford, 1990); Andrew Vincent, *Theories of the State* (Oxford, 1987).

16. Wolf D. Gruner, *Die deutsche Frage in Europa 1800 bis 1990* (Munich, 1993); Hagen Schulze, 'In der Mitte Europas: Ein normaler Nationalstaat' in Josef Becker and Günter Kronenbitter (eds.), *Wiedervereinigung in Mitteleuropa. Außenpolitik und Innenansichten zur staatlichen Einheit Deutschlands* (Munich, 1992), pp. 159–73.

17. Gruner, *Die deutsche Frage in Europa*, pp. 48–60; James, *Deutsche Identität*, pp. 48–74. Langewiesche, 'Reich, Nation und Staat', pp. 343–5.

18. Benedict Anderson, *Imagined Communities: Reflections on the Origin and Spread of Nationalism* (London, 1993).

19. Karl Marx and Friedrich Engels, *Manifest der Kommunistischen Partei* (1848) in *Werke*, Vol. IV (Berlin, 1969), p. 479.

20. Ruth R. Pierson, 'Nations: Gendered, Racialized, Crossed with Empire' in Ida Blom, Karen Hagemann and Catherine Hall (eds.), *Gendered Nations: Nationalisms and Gender Order in the Long Nineteenth Century* (Oxford, 2000), p. 53.

21. Jürgen Kocka, *Weder Stand noch Klasse. Unterschichten um 1800* (Bonn, 1990), p. 45.

22. Wolfgang Köllmann, 'Bevölkerungsgeschichte 1800–1970' in Hermann Aubin and Wolfgang Zorn (eds.), *Handbuch der deutschen Wirtschafts- und Sozialgeschichte*, Vol. II (Stuttgart, 1976), p. 10; B. Bolgnese-Leuchtenmüller, *Bevölkerungsentwicklung und Berufsstruktur, Gesundheits- und Fürsorgewesen in Österreich 1750–1918* (Vienna, 1978), p. 1.

23. Hans-Ulrich Wehler, *Sozialdemokratie und Nationalstaat. Nationalitätenfragen in Deutschland 1840–1914* (Göttingen, 1971), p. 103.

24. Friedrich-Wilhelm Henning, *Die Industrialisierung in Deutschland 1800 bis 1914* (Paderborn, 1973), p. 25.

25. Walther G. Hoffmann, Franz Grumbach and Helmut Hesse, *Das Wachstum der deutschen Wirtschaft seit der Mitte des 19. Jahrhunderts* (Berlin, 1965), pp. 172–3, 827.
26. David Ricardo, *On the Principles of Political Economy and Taxation* (1817) in *Works and Correspondence*, Vol. I (Cambridge, 1971), p. 136.
27. Paul Bairoch, *Commerce extérieur et développement économique de l'Europe au XIXe siècle* (Paris, 1976).
28. Robert A. Mundell, 'A Theory of Optimum Currency Areas', *American Economic Review*, 51 (1961), 657–65.
29. John Stuart Mill, *Principles of Political Economy* (1848) (2 vols., Toronto, 1965), Vol. II, pp. 625–6.
30. Richard H. Tilly, *Vom Zollverein zum Industriestaat. Die wirtschaftlich-soziale Entwicklung Deutschlands 1834 bis 1914* (Munich, 1990).
31. Carl-Ludwig Holtfrerich, 'The Monetary Unification Process in Nineteenth-Century Germany: Relevance and Lessons for Europe Today' in Marcello De Cecco and Alberto Giovanni (eds.), *A European Central Bank? Perspectives on Monetary Unification after Ten Years of EMS* (Cambridge, 1989); Theresia Theurl, *Eine gemeinsame Währung für Europa. Zwölf Lehren aus der Geschichte* (Innsbruck, 1992); Wim F.V. Vanthoor, *European Monetary Union since 1848: a Political and Historical Analysis* (Cheltenham, 1996).
32. Wolfram Siemann, *Die deutsche Revolution von 1848/49* (Frankfurt, 1985).
33. Heinrich von Treitschke, *Deutsche Geschichte im neunzehnten Jahrhundert*, part 4 (1889), 8th edn (Leipzig, 1923), p. 379.
34. Hans-Ulrich Wehler, *Deutsche Gesellschaftsgeschichte*, Vol. III (Munich, 1995), p. 251.
35. Ranke to Hermann Heiberg, 1 April 1885. Leopold von Ranke, *Das Briefwerk* (Hamburg, 1949), pp. 590–1.
36. Max Weber, *Wirtschaft und Gesellschaft* (Tübingen, 1922), pp. 619–30.
37. Eric Hobsbawm, 'The Nation as Invented Tradition' in John Hutchinson and Anthony D. Smith (eds.), *Nationalism* (Oxford, 1994), pp. 76–83; Klaus von Beyme, 'Deutsche Identität zwischen Nationalismus und Verfassungspatriotismus' in Hettling and Nolte (eds.), *Nation und Gesellschaft*, pp. 80–94.
38. Statistisches Bundesamt, *Bevölkerung und Wirtschaft 1872–1972* (Stuttgart, 1972), p. 90.
39. Hoffmann et al., *Wachstum der deutschen Wirtschaft*, p. 35.
40. Margrit Grabas, *Konjunktur und Wachstum in Deutschland von 1895 bis 1914* (Berlin, 1992).
41. Hoffmann et al., *Wachstum der deutschen Wirtschaft*, pp. 172–4, 827–8.
42. Gerd Hardach and Sandra Hartig, 'Der Goldstandard in der internationalen Währungsdiskussion', *Jahrbuch für Wirtschaftsgeschichte*, 1 (1998), pp. 125–41.
43. Hans Rosenberg, *Grosse Depression und Bismarckzeit. Wirtschaftsablauf, Gesellschaft und Politik in Mitteleuropa* (Berlin, 1967); Wehler (ed.), *Deutsche Gesellschaftsgeschichte*, Vol. III, pp. 924–38, 977–90.
44. Johannes Frerich and Martin Frey, *Handbuch der Geschichte der Sozialpolitik in Deutschland*, Vol. I (Munich, 1996).

45. George L. Mosse, *The Crisis of German Ideology: Intellectual Origins of the Third Reich* (New York, 1964); Shulamit Volkov, 'Nationalismus, Antisemitismus und die deutsche Geschichtsschreibung' in Hettling and Nolte (eds.), *Nation und Gesellschaft*, pp. 208–19.
46. Max Weber, 'Der Nationalstaat und die Volkswirtschaftspolitik' (1895) in *Gesammelte politische Schriften* (Tübingen, 1958), p. 23.
47. Georges-Henri Soutou, *L'or et le sang. Le buts des guerre économiques de la Première Guerre mondiale* (Paris, 1989).
48. Gerd Hardach, *History of the World Economy in the Twentieth Century, Volume II: The First World War, 1914–1918* (London, 1977).
49. J.M. Winter, *The Great War and the British People* (London, 1985), p. 75.
50. Gerd Hardach, 'La prima Guerra mondiale e la ricostruzione (1914–1924)' in Valerio Castronovo (ed.), *Tra espansione e recessione. Storia dell'economia mondiale*, Vol. IV (Rome, 2000), pp. 437–60.
51. Ulrich Kluge, *Die deutsche Revolution 1918/19* (Frankfurt, 1985).
52. Hardach, *History of the World Economy, Volume II*, pp. 237–48.
53. Statistisches Bundesamt, *Bevölkerung und Wirtschaft*, pp. 90, 102.
54. John Maynard Keynes, *The Economic Consequences of the Peace* (1919) in *Collected Writings*, Vol. II (London, 1971).
55. *Das deutsche Volkseinkommen vor und nach dem Kriege*, Einzelschriften zur Statistik des Deutschen Reiches 24 (Berlin, 1932), p. 75.
56. Carl-Ludwig Holtfrerich, *Die deutsche Inflation 1914–1923* (Berlin, 1980).
57. Gerd Hardach, 'Endogenous Versus Exogenous Causes of Stabilization and Crisis in Germany, 1922–1932' in Marta Petricioli (ed.), *Une occasion manquée? 1922: La reconstruction de l'Europe* (Berne, 1995).
58. Hoffmann et al., *Wachstum der deutschen Wirtschaft*, pp. 172–4, 827–8; *Konjunkturstatistisches Handbuch 1936* (Berlin, 1936), p. 16.
59. Reinhard Kühnl (ed.), *Der deutsche Faschismus in Quellen und Dokumenten* (Cologne, 1975), pp. 242–3.
60. Ludolf Herbst, *Das nationalsozialistische Deutschland* (Frankfurt, 1996); Ian Kershaw, *The Nazi Dictatorship: Problems and Perspectives of Interpretation* (London, 1993).
61. William Sheridan Allen, 'The Collapse of Nationalism in Nazi Germany' in Breuilly (ed.), *The State of Germany*, pp. 141–53; Jost Dülfer, 'Hitler, Nation und Volksgemeinschaft' in Dann (ed.), *Die deutsche Nation*, pp. 96–116.
62. Hoffmann et al., *Das Wachstum der deutschen Wirtschaft*, pp. 172–4, 827–8.
63. Werner Abelshauser, 'Germany: Guns, Butter, and Economic Miracles' in Mark Harrison (ed.), *The Economics of World War II: Six Great Powers in International Comparison* (Cambridge, 1998), pp. 122–51.
64. Abelshauser, 'Germany', pp. 151–69; R.J. Overy, *War and Economy in the Third Reich* (Oxford, 1994).
65. Christopher R. Browning, *Nazi Policy, Jewish Workers, German Killers* (Cambridge, 2000); Raul Hilberg, *Täter, Opfer, Zuschauer. Die Vernichtung der Juden 1933–1945* (Frankfurt, 1992); Arno J. Mayer, *Der Krieg als Kreuzzug. Das Deutsche Reich, Hitlers Wehrmacht und die 'Endlösung'* (Reinbek, 1989).

66. Herman van der Wee, *Der gebremste Wohlstand. Wiederaufbau, Wachstum, Strukturwandel 1945–1980. Geschichte der Weltwirtschaft im 20. Jahrhundert*, Vol. VI (Munich, 1984), p. 15.
67. Gunther Mai, *Der Alliierte Kontrollrat in Deutschland 1945–1948. Alliierte Einheit – deutsche Teilung?* (Munich, 1995).
68. Gerd Hardach, *Der Marshall-Plan. Auslandshilfe und Wiederaufbau in Westdeutschland 1948–1952* (Munich, 1994).
69. Hans Karl Rupp, *Politische Geschichte der Bundesrepublik Deutschland* (Munich, 2000); Dietrich Staritz, *Geschichte der DDR* (Frankfurt, 1996).
70. Hermann Weber (ed.), *DDR. Dokumente zur Geschichte der Deutschen Demokratischen Republik* (Munich, 1968), p. 299.
71. Jürgen Hoffmann, *Ein neues Deutschland soll es sein. Zur Frage nach der Nation in der Geschichte der DDR und der Politik der SED* (Berlin, 1989), p. 251.
72. Weber (ed.), *DDR*, p. 345.
73. *Statistisches Jahrbuch für die Bundesrepublik Deutschland 1999*, p. 44.
74. Wendy Carlin, 'West German Growth and Institutions, 1945–90' in Nicholas Crafts and Gianni Toniolo (eds.), *Economic Growth in Europe since 1945* (Cambridge, 1996), pp. 455–97. N.F.R. Crafts, 'The Golden Age of Economic Growth in Western Europe, 1950–1973', *Economic History Review*, 48 (1995), 429–47; Ludger Lindlar, *Das missverstandene Wirtschaftswunder. Westdeutschland und die westeuropäische Nachkriegsprosperität* (Tübingen, 1997).
75. Hoffmann et al., *Wachstum der deutschen Wirtschaft*, pp. 172–4, 827–8.
76. *Statistisches Jahrbuch BRD 1999*, pp. 44, 665–6.
77. Statistisches Bundesamt, *Bevölkerung und Wirtschaft*, p. 148.
78. *Statistisches Jahrbuch BRD 1999*, pp. 44, 120, 666.
79. *Statistisches Jahrbuch BRD 1992*, pp. 112–13.
80. Herbert Giersch, Karl-Heinz Paqué and Holger Schmieding, *The Fading Miracle: Four Decades of Market Economy in Germany* (Cambridge, 1992).
81. *Statistisches Jahrbuch der Deutschen Demokratischen Republik 1990*, p. 1; *Statistisches Jahrbuch BRD 1999*, p. 44.
82. Gernot Gutmann and Werner Klein, 'Herausbildungs- und Entwicklungsphasen der Planungs-, Lenkungs- und Kontrollmechanismen im Wirtschaftssystem' in Materialien der Enquete-Kommission, *Aufarbeitung von Geschichte und Folgen der SED-Diktatur in Deutschland*, Vol. II (Baden-Baden, 1995); André Steiner, *Die DDR-Wirtschaftsreform der sechziger Jahre. Konflikt zwischen Effizienz- und Machtkalkül* (Berlin, 1999).
83. *Statistisches Jahrbuch DDR 1990*, p. 125.
84. Albert Ritschl, 'Aufstieg und Niedergang der Wirtschaft der DDR: Ein Zahlenbild 1945–1989' in *Jahrbuch für Wirtschaftsgeschichte*, II (1995), pp. 11–46.
85. Oskar Schwarzer, *Sozialistische Zentralplanwirtschaft in der SBZ/DDR. Ergebnisse eines ordnungspolitischen Experiments, 1945–1989* (Stuttgart, 1999), p. 217.
86. Gerhard A. Ritter, *Über Deutschland. Die Bundesrepublik Deutschland in der deutschen Geschichte* (Munich, 1998), pp. 194–250, at p. 194.

87. Dieter Grosser, *Das Wagnis der Währungs-, Wirtschafts- und Sozialunion. Politische Zwänge im Konflikt mit ökonomischen Regeln. Geschichte der Deutschen Einheit*, Vol. II (Stuttgart, 1995).

88. *Statistisches Jahrbuch BRD 2001*, pp. 126, 654–5; ibid. 2002, pp. 44, 65, 108–9, 632–3.

89. Sachverständigenrat zur Begutachtung der gesamtwirtschaftlichen Entwicklung, *Wachstum, Beschäftigung, Währungsunion – Orientierungen für die Zukunft. Jahresgutachten 1997/98* (Stuttgart, 1997), p. 334.

90. Rüdiger Voigt, 'Der neue Nationalstaat. Deutschland zwischen Nationalisierung und Globalisierung' in Rüdiger Voigt (ed.), *Der neue Nationalstaat* (Baden-Baden, 1998), pp. 333–78.

CHAPTER 4

The harmony liberal era, 1845–1880: the case of Norway and Sweden

Göran B. Nilsson

INTRODUCING THE THEME

E.J. Hobsbawm has designated the years 1848–75 as 'The Age of Capital'; they might as well be characterised as 'The Harmony Liberal Era'. Not least so in Scandinavia, where the capitalistic breakthrough was accomplished with a minimum of those internal class struggles and internal–external national struggles that accompanied the general European development.

This relatively smooth outcome depended in the final analysis on circumstances that gave nationalism and economic liberalism – the two dynamic ideologies *en vogue* at the time – a less militant and problematic appearance in Scandinavia than elsewhere. As for nationalism, both Norway and Sweden could boast of an ancient domestic culture united by a common enough language spoken by a homogeneous population with few and small ethnic minorities (Lapps, Finns and Gypsies). A dogmatic view of economic liberalism (the 'Manchester' or 'classical' variant) was immediately confronted with hard Scandinavian facts that made atomistic individual freedom on the market seem unrealistic, at any rate in the short run. Norway and Sweden were both poor, sparsely populated and vast countries, circumstances which – from a nationalistic view – called for co-operation and for active intervention or guidance from the comparatively resourceful national state. The result was – to borrow Professor Rune Slagstad's pregnant wording – 'a liberalism chastened by the State', busy in 'staging capitalism'.

Economic growth resulting in national prosperity played a key role in the political programme of the Scandinavian harmony liberals. For them economic progress was not only good in itself but also seen as the prerequisite for all other types of individual and national progress, moral, political and social. Their case was yet further strengthened by their optimistic belief in mankind's almost fated progress towards an ever higher degree of civilisation. The Scandinavian harmony liberals thus had a strong programme and a strong will, and they also knew how to obtain strong political positions in a climate which, especially after the February revolutions of 1848, had become more favourable to new solutions that avoided both the old conservative mistakes and the new ghost of communism.

I will start to develop the above outlined theme in its diverse facets by taking a closer look at six of the harmony liberal era's leading national strategists. From Norway: Frederik Stang (1808–84), Anton Martin Schweigaard (1808–70) and Ole Jacob Broch (1818–89), and from Sweden: Carl Fredrik Bergstedt (1817–1903), Johan August Gripenstedt (1813–74) and André Oscar Wallenberg (1816–86). It will be appropriate to begin with the three Norwegians. First, because Norway had good reasons to make an earlier start, and second, because all three Norwegians were skilled scholars, well experienced in formulating coherent views and arguments, whereas the Swedes generally expressed their theoretical views in connection with actual politics.

THREE NORWEGIANS

Nation building had been an urgent concern for all Norwegian politicians since 1814, when Norway as a gift from above had become a free country, a constitutional monarchy with the most democratic parliament in Europe. The price for this unexpected national success had been amazingly low: a compulsory personal union with Sweden (1814–1905), with both countries sharing the same king, who was designated to be the triumphant French newcomer, Maréchal Jean-Baptiste Bernadotte, followed by his heirs. As the union was a personal one, the only severe restriction of Norwegian sovereignty concerned foreign policy which had to be administered through the Swedish Foreign Department.

The first generation of politicians in Norway, 'the Patriots', had been busy mastering a poor economy and defending their newly won rights against disappointed Swedes in general and King Carl Johan in particular, who soon discovered that he had been too generous in handing over power to his new people. But the strained situation had come to an end already before the king's death in 1844. The new monarch, Oscar I, immediately signalled appeasement in union matters, which was to last for some thirty years.

The time was ripe for a new and young generation of Norwegian politicians, who in the 1830s had gathered in Christiania under the name of 'the Intelligence'. In 1845 their first representative, *Frederik Stang*, was appointed minister for the brand new Home Office. He immediately established a forceful political leadership that lasted until his resignation from the office of prime minister in Christiania in 1880, the beginning of the disastrous end for the regime which J.A. Seip termed 'The Civil Servant's State' (*Embedsmannsstaten*).

Stang had laid the ideological foundations of this bureaucratic state in the 1830s as professor in law at the university (founded in 1811). His contribution was original in not praising the traditional virtue of bureaucratic government and its passive, objective impartiality. On the contrary, Stang stressed the need for active intervention, for 'this powerful, leading influence from the Government, which is the prerequisite for comprehensive and systematical progress'. Such a leadership had to be based on expert knowledge, knowledge of new truths and possibilities constantly being discovered and opened up by (positivistic) science and technology.

In 1845, Stang went from words to deeds, eagerly implementing this programme of 'scientifical reformism' (R. Slagstad). Modernising expertise was used in national organisation of communications (public highways, railroads), of medicine and educational systems, all of which needed 'a powerful, regulating power from above'.

There is no need to go into further details here, but I will give a single example showing Stang's pragmatic handling also of a purely economic question, namely the exploitation of the Norwegian forests. In the late 1850s forestry experts had shown that a continued *laissez-faire* policy here would cause disastrous (forest-eradicating) effects in the future. A Public Administration of Forest was then promptly created in 1860 and in 1863 a new law made it possible for the state to buy forests. This was 'the only remedy against human thoughtlessness and selfishness', Stang remarked, thereby denying the market mechanisms and favouring the national state's interest in long-time progress in a sphere where 'money grows faster than forests'.

Stang here, as usual, was acting in close political companionship with *Anton Martin Schweigaard*, Stang answering for the government and Schweigaard managing the approval by parliament. As a professor of law, political economy and statistics, Schweigaard had a professional duty to make clear the harmony liberals' theoretical standpoint *vis-à-vis* the teachings of radical liberal economists. And he solved this intricate question in an impressive way in his 'Lectures on Political Economy' ('Forelesninger over den politiske økonomi'), held at the university in 1847. Already then Schweigaard had begun a brilliant parliamentary career (ending with his death in 1870), and his lectures, consequently, should be read as a scientific programme for his own political future.

Schweigaard rejected the radical ideas of *laissez-faire* and the night-watch state propagated by what Schweigaard termed 'the English school'. He did so on many grounds which, however, can be summarised thus: radical economic liberalism was not feasible because it presupposed the existence of material and immaterial infrastructures, which were as yet absent in Norway and which only could and should be brought about by the state. As for creating material infrastructures such as railways and highways, actors in a free market were too unreliable, unco-ordinated and shortsighted in comparison with the national state which was stable, co-ordinated and planning for eternity. The state (Schweigaard maintained in 1857) was 'a company which will have to take the distant future into consideration', i.e. it could and should make economically fruitful investments even if they did not pay off directly and immediately.

But the duty of the state to 'awaken and develop the productive forces' also had an important immaterial aspect: the need to create a better morality in the Norwegian people. In other words, the good circle of economic progress could be started only if the actors were educated to be better actors in the socio-economic market. In that respect they would have to learn to refrain from living only in the present and instead be taught to take enlightened responsibility for their own (and preferably the country's) future, something that 'more than anything else gives economic security to society'. For this education the state had to take responsibility through investments in public schools and other educational activities. A corollary for Schweigaard (as for Stang) was the need to take up a public fight against the widespread abuse of alcohol, a moral 'national evil' *per se* but also an important obstacle to economic progress.

But even if Schweigaard was convinced of the Norwegian people's desire to be educated from above in its true interests, he was well aware of the need also to give the ordinary man a solid starting point for his moral betterment, 'a piece of cooked pork'. Only from a citizen who had something to lose could you await the civilised virtue of restriction (birth control and money saving), which was the prerequisite for starting the good circle of economic progress. Such a measure fits well with Schweigaard's view that the national state also had to pay some (unspecified) attention to the need for a just distribution of resources among its inhabitants, socially and geographically. For this reason Schweigaard could not accept the economists' talk of the need to 'increase national wealth'; the question was instead how to 'extend common prosperity'.

In passing it should be mentioned that Schweigaard also had an open eye for the need of betterment also of the scientific infrastructure. The dom- inating classical studies had to make more room for the more progressive study of science and technology. In particular statistics had to be promoted as in England: 'it is from the English statistics that the political economists have gathered the most complete, reliable and valuable facts, from which their theories have been abstracted'.

Statistics was undoubtedly one of the most dynamic disciplines of the time, providing theoretical and practical service to economically progressing society and even promoting a couple of professors in Sweden and Norway to the rank of cabinet minister. The Norwegian professor was also a prominent politician, *Ole Jacob Broch*. Already in 1847 the young professor of applied mathemathics had begun to apply mathematics also in society, founding and leading the first modern insurance company of Norway (Gjensidige). In 1851 he was elected member of the board of Hypoteksbanken (Norwegian Mortgage Bank), which was established then to supply Norwegian agriculture with long-term capital. This was an infrastructural undertaking, which was accordingly favoured with economic aid from the state and controlled by parliament and government. In 1853–5, Broch was appointed by Stang to prepare the new Public Board of Telegraphy, which was to supply the whole of Norway with the blessings of what Broch called 'the greatest triumph of experimental science'. And in 1857 Broch was one of the promoters of the first big private bank in Norway (Creditbanken, DNC).

Broch was a jack of many trades, but his main occupation from 1854 to 1864 was as chief administrator of big public investments in railway building and operation. Already in 1851 Broch had made press propaganda for the building of the first railway (Mjøsbanen), whose usefulness he proved with statistics. His railway articles also made clear what Broch had identified as the prime mover in progressing the economy.

We are a nation with few sources of livelihood. In order to develop and multiply these sources it is necessary to improve our means of communication. – We are a nation with few inhabitants. In order to maintain a bigger population it is necessary to improve our means of communication. – We are a nation with scarce industry. In order to expand our industry it is necessary to improve our means of communication. – And of all improvements of communication, Mjøsbanen is the most important.

Belief in railways, however, was only one part of Broch's belief in communications, a belief that – as his biographer J.A. Seip has put it – amounted to something of a gospel. And, continues Seip, this was indeed a central theme for the 'ideology of the time', where the concept of communication had a richer meaning than nowadays. For in the eyes of the harmony liberals the desired development was a product of interaction; therefore communication was a prerequisite for progress... To break isolation, to further the intensity of living together was accordingly the cultural task in its shortest formula. And this applied both materially and immaterially. Increased prosperity was depending on increased exchange of goods, and cultural progress was depending on free access to and free exchange of ideas. Both resulted in the same practical political programme: to facilitate the external conditions for communication. Both the economic task and the cultural task was first of all a communication problem.

In his later years Broch dedicated much of his vigour to a great project worthy of his capacity as scientist and politician: the international standardisation of measures (length, weight, volume) and of currency. This infrastructural undertaking was supported by statisticians as a means of furthering scientific communication but aimed, first of all, at facilitating national and international exchange of goods. Most ambitious was the striving towards a global economy through establishing the gold standard in every country (or at least in Western Europe and the USA). In that connection Broch went even further, seeking to establish the golden French ten-franc coin as the universal one.

Broch's contributions won international recognition, peaking in his appointment as chief for the Bureau International de Poids et Mésures (in Sèvres outside Paris) from 1879. And on the national arena he was the man behind Norway's approval of the gold standard and the decimal system as early as 1875.

When Sweden followed close upon Norway in these matters, this was due to the companionship Broch had formed with Sweden's representative, A.O. Wallenberg, in 1867 at the first international conference in Paris. These twin souls immediately formed a close personal and political friendship which lasted until Wallenberg's death in 1886. Broch then regretted this 'loss for all Scandinavia' and remarked that their twenty years of friendship never had seen 'any feeling of discord or even any difference of opinion'. Indeed, even if this was a special case and the empirical working out of reforms differed between Norway and Sweden, there is a striking resemblance in the leading harmony liberals' strategical thinking in both countries.

AND THREE SWEDES

In Norway the need for building a new nation had become an imperative necessity in 1814. But also old-established Sweden had about the same time been confronted with the urgent task not of organising but of reorganising the nation. The loss in 1809 of Finland, one-third of the realm, had made unrealistic all dreams of Sweden regaining its ancient status as a great power. Dreams of military glory had to be replaced with dreams of peaceful, economic glory. The question for Sweden from now on – the famous Swedish poet Esaias Tegnér was compelled to admit – was to 'reconquer Finland *within* our (new) boundaries'.

The necessary change in mentality took its time, however, and still in 1851 the young assistant professor in Greek at Uppsala University, *Carl Fredrik Bergstedt*, complained about the 'common disrespect of productive work, of technical innovations, of economic speculation, a contempt that almost taught the productive classes to despise themselves'. This he wrote in an article about 'The Moral Importance of Trade and Industry', where Bergstedt maintained that 'prosperity is the most dangerous enemy of immorality'. Here spoke a Swedish Schweigaard but with a yet more striking contrast between high idealistic goals and crass economic means. And when Bergstedt pointed out that 'eased communications are one of our foremost vital questions' he certainly had much more than railways in his mind: 'What an enormous moral weight should not be laid on easing correspondence by means of a low rate of postage and numerous post offices!'

Bergstedt soon went on from his academic chair to become chief editor of the leading Swedish liberal newspaper, *Aftonbladet*. Later on he combined political journalism and literary criticism with management of iron mills and landed property, also making a séjour in the upper house of the Swedish parliament. Bergstedt has been characterised as 'the sharpest political pen in his contemporary Sweden' and a leading representative for middle-class liberalism. In the article cited above Bergstedt certainly pinned his faith to the 'middle class, which is the core of the population and the soul of the government' – so it was in England and so it should be in Sweden.

Bergstedt's opinion was shared by another harmony liberal, *Johan August Gripenstedt*, a mighty minister of finance, who in the ten years from 1856 stood out as the leading statesman in Sweden. His greatest achievement was perhaps the carrying through of the free-trade system, which peaked in the Commerce and Shipping Treaty of 1866 between France and Sweden-Norway (not least benefiting the upsurge of the Norwegian merchant navy). Another triumph was the realisation of a Swedish railway system, where the state took all responsibility for building and operating the main trunk-lines. In that connection, in 1857, when parliament had to be convinced of the necessity of raising huge foreign loans, Gripenstedt gave a couple of famous (and contested) speeches, known as his 'flower paintings'. In these speeches he praised Sweden's progress since 1834, when the country had stabilised its currency by adopting the silver standard: 'Everything has improved! And I greet with pleasure that day, when you little by little shall see how one class of society after another rises and takes part of the privileges, spiritual as well as material ones, which we more well-favoured, unfortunately enough, almost alone have enjoyed.'

Everyone was welcome to join the race of social progress into the privileged classes. This was hard stuff for the conservative listeners in the House of the Nobility. And they were yet more disturbed when Gripenstedt – once an artillery officer – denied the old military ideals and praised peaceful exchange and the new middle-class hero, the tradesman. This frequently scorned profession, Gripenstedt stated, was on the contrary of immense importance for the progress of civilisation compared with the military system of violence and conquest, on which old-time politics was based and whose

aim was the plundering and oppression of the weaker ones. Not only was this system basically unrighteous and hostile to all true humanity. It inevitably led to hatred and separation between the different countries of the world, free trade relations, on the contrary, aiming at mutual advantage, forming ties of friendship and of common interests . . . Once more, therefore: glory be to the magnificent profession of trade, working for the benefit of mankind!

Gripenstedt's belief in peaceful progress was not shared by conservative noblemen but, at that time, they formed a shrinking minority in the House of Nobility. A more dangerous adversary existed, however, in the royal house, which had great constitutional influence over foreign policy and where especially Charles XV (king in 1859) cherished fantastic dreams of restoring ancient Swedish glory and power. So during the Crimean War, Gripenstedt went to the extreme of mounting an anonymous newspaper campaign in order to thwart the monarchy's plan of involving Sweden-Norway in the war (to recapture Finland); likewise in 1863, when King Charles worked hard to engage Sweden-Norway on Denmark's side in the imminent Danish–German war of 1863–4. On both occasions Gripenstedt's deep concern had economic reasons: in the first case, it would be madness to jeopardise the unprecedented economic boom for neutral Sweden-Norway and, in the second case, it would be madness to declare a Scandinavian war against Germany when Sweden was busy on the German market, taking up large long-term loans for investments in farming and railway-building.

In these matters Gripenstedt received whole-hearted support from the Norwegian government but also from an ardent Scandinavianist, the Swedish banker, politician and journalist, *André Oscar Wallenberg.*

Gripenstedt and Wallenberg had gradually formed a close political companionship reminiscent of the Stang–Schweigaard team, with Gripenstedt managing the government and Wallenberg answering for the Estate of Burghers (which took up a key position in the Swedish four-estate parliament). Their main achievement was the establishment of a modernised and rapidly expanding private banking system in the 1860s, modelled on Wallenberg's innovative Stockholms Enskilda Bank of 1856.

Thrift and industriousness were always emphasised as the cardinal socio-economic virtues by A.O. Wallenberg: outwardly, because they secured the independence of the nation; inwardly, because they were instrumental in the protracted but ultimately successful struggle against human misery. Thus spoke Wallenberg at the height of his power in 1876: 'if a whole nation strives to obtain an ever more improved economic position through honest work and judicious thrift, then in each new generation the number of the children of destitution will diminish ... But beware of confusing this with what in everyday speech is called charity and which belongs to a different chapter.'

Charity was indeed a different chapter, which ought to be written by private philanthropy and not by the state. On the other hand the harmony liberals' striving to minimise public poor relief was accompanied by their positive endeavour to forestall poverty by erecting institutions easing the ordinary citizen's duty to provide for his own future, such as insurance companies and banks. Wallenberg was engaged in both branches but it was, above all, through the private banking system that he could kill two birds with one stone, first, because the modernised private banks opened their accounts for savings from the middle class, and second, because new job opportunities were created in expanding Swedish industry through their lending the acquired capital to productive enterprises.

In securing the success of this doubly beneficial system, Wallenberg allowed for public intervention to a remarkable extent that astonished his more radical liberal colleagues in Europe. To give a single example: every Swedish private bank was obliged to report an extract of its balance sheet at regular intervals (first quarterly, then monthly) to the Department of Finance, where from 1868 a public officer continuously saw to it that the banks followed the rules laid down in public legislation. Throughout his journalistic life Wallenberg published and commented critically upon these reports. For him public control was a forceful means of inducing the public to entrust the private banks with their savings.

Even though this was a special case, it highlights a general concern of the Scandinavian harmony liberals: the need for public intervention in creating a reliable structure of confidence on the anonymous national market. As Rune Slagstad has pointed out, the old system of personal acquaintance and trust had to be replaced or completed with legal institutional arrangements, which promoted predictability and thereby confidence on larger markets.

The economic success of the Swedish private banking companies could be seen as a further success for two other ideals of the harmony liberals: their belief in the power of associations and in science and technology. 'The association is a chief pillar of higher civilisation,' Aftonbladet maintained in an editorial of 1857. And indeed, voluntary association was the liberals' standard rejoinder to conservative critique of the dissocial consequences of atomistic, individualistic freedom. On the contrary, voluntary associations would more than fill the void left by abolished compulsory institutions such as the guild system. They would make possible big, risky undertakings of service to society and so lessen the need of public intervention (as Schweigaard pointed out in his lectures). And of course, such undertakings were beyond the power of the individual who, said Gripenstedt, 'isolated and left only to his own power is incredibly poor and helpless'. He accordingly went on to open the doors for a flood of associations of a new and progressive kind, the companies with *limited* responsibility. They had certainly been allowed by law already in 1848, but the application by the Swedish government had been very restrictive before Gripenstedt's appointment as minister of finance in 1856.

As to science and technology neither Gripenstedt nor Wallenberg had enjoyed the same thorough scientifical schooling as their Norwegian counterparts. Nevertheless (or perhaps exactly for that reason) both appeared as ardent believers. Gripenstedt's use of the French 'harmony economist' Frédérique Bastiat as his household god is well known and, as to Wallenberg, he made profitable use of J.W. Gilbart's textbook wisdom in developing the Scottish banking system and adapting it to the requirements of Sweden (cf. Palgrave 1873). Wallenberg often maintained a thesis, which he brought before the Estate of Burghers in 1854, propagating the abolition of the old legal provision concerning maximum interest on loans: 'What is all practical life other than a utilising of what Theory has discovered being true and useful?' So 'if therefore a free rate of interest is theoretically correct, it also must be practically beneficial'.

SUCCESSES AND FAILURES

The leading harmony liberals of Norway and Sweden gladly registered the predicted successes of their programme, as we have already seen for

Gripenstedt's part in 1857. In the Norwegian parliament Schweigaard, two years later, boasted of how his generation had done twenty, nay fifty times more than its ancestors had done in two hundred years. Equally so on the local level, bragged Wallenberg in 1881, when he dwelt upon 'the well-known fact, that during the last two decades more had been done than during as many preceding centuries for the development of Stockholm's institutions in general, for the capital's embellishment and of expensive work exclusively aiming at furnishing health and comfort for the inhabitants'.

The improvement included the majority of the people, Wallenberg had written in 1861 to his future wife and active feminist, Anna von Sydow. As a pleasant proof he noted the considerable growth of deposits in the Stockholms Enskilda Bank, 'and more than 2,000 women have deposited money with us. They turn out to be punctual in lifting their interests and in accumulating their savings. It is a good sign.' In 1865, Schweigaard likewise pointed out a gratifying change in Norwegian mentality inasmuch as the individual nowadays 'comprehended that ultimately his own interests are inevitably connected with the interests of society. In such an idea rests the future of this country.'

Broch, finally in 1873, proudly registered how the 'colossal expansion in the system of communications', by causing substantial growth in international trade and intercourse in particular and ongoing material and immaterial progress in general, had made 'our age an epoch in the history of the world'.

The successes of harmony liberalism in Norway and Sweden were confirmed also by a famous contemporary outsider, Arthur de Gobineau, when he took up his duties as French minister in Stockholm in 1872. Coming from a distressed France ravaged by external and internal wars, de Gobineau was overwhelmed by the idyll of a welfare state:

You cannot imagine how pleasant it is here, how prudent, industrious and intelligent this people is. No revolution, no question of barbaric outrages from the mob. You live and let live... True independence and personal freedom shine through everything. No class-hatred exists here; the nobility lives free and easy together with the burghers and the people.

Yet the years around the Franco-Prussian war can be denoted as the beginning of the end of the harmony liberal era also in Sweden-Norway. The European experience of the victorious, aggressive German nationalism and the reawakened ghost of communism in France made its impact felt in Scandinavian public debate, and with regards to Broch's and Wallenberg's pet project, the universal coin, the French defeat meant a death blow.

For these two men the compensation through the Scandinavian monetary union of 1873–5 appeared as an unworthy half-measure (in spite of the fact that this monetary union – which held good until 1914 – was to be the most successful one up to the present).

The ultimate failure of the harmony liberal programme in Sweden-Norway can be said to have been partly a consequence of its success. 'It would certainly be better to give the countryman a bushel of barley or a barrel of potatoes than to entitle him to vote in municipal affairs,' Schweigaard had said in 1851. But he then disregarded the risky fact that the satiated and educated countryman of the future would be able to reserve more time and energy for active *political* work aiming at replacing the Stang–Schweigaard 'democratic elitism' (Slagstad) with parliamentarism and democracy from below.

The freeholders had a more traditional than liberal outlook in their economic views and they held a strong political position. After the Swedish representational reform of 1866, the Farmers' Party (Lantmannapartiet) thus dominated the House of Commons (second chamber) in the new two-chamber parliament. Nevertheless the plutocratic first chamber was – as Torbjörn Nilsson has shown – still able to resist radical assaults and to a certain extent promote economic modernisation in the interests of the big entrepreneurs. In Norway, however, no such counterweight existed. The Norwegian freeholders had disposed of the potential majority in the parliament right from the beginning, and they began to make full use of it in the late 1860s, when the leftist party (Venstre) was organised under the astute leadership of the lawyer Johan Sverdrup.

The emergence of disciplined parties was another setback for the harmony liberals. In their view political decisions ought to be the result of open, enlightened discussions (furthered by a free press) where the best, scientifically founded argument would prevail. 'The public opinion', wrote Bergstedt in 1851, 'shall gradually become the true legislator in society.' But this was the case neither in Norway nor in Sweden, where the Farmers' Party year after year turned a deaf ear to Wallenberg's and Gripenstedt's irrefutable arguments against identifying the notes of the State Bank (Riksbanken) with real coins.

The new situation led to a political deadlock in Sweden, where Wallenberg constantly but in vain urged the passive bureaucratic government to show the same energy and power of initiative as in the good old Gripenstedt days. For similar reasons Broch left the Norwegian government in 1872, leaving Stang to carry on an ill-judged defensive struggle against the mighty parliamentary pretenders of power. (When they, in

1880–4, succeeded in seriously encroaching upon the powers of the king, who also was king of Sweden, this entailed a serious deterioration in union matters, peaking in the dissolution of the Swedish–Norwegian union in 1905.)

The political weakness in the harmony liberal programme was made plainer in Norway. The same could be said of the *economic* weakness in the long-run perspective, but the acute crisis became more violent in more industrialised Sweden, when the first Great Depression reached the countries with the acute crisis in 1878–9. Indeed the question of depressions or long-term business cycles was non-existent for the harmony liberals who believed in permanently ongoing progress. It is true that they had learnt to accept the existence of short-term crises and to handle such a crisis with temporary public measures aimed at restoring rational confidence in a market seized by irrational panic. And such an occasional measure – a temporary loan from the state – in 1879 indubitably helped to rescue Stockholms Enskilda Bank from bankruptcy after its over-optimistic engagements in private railway building and industry during the 1870s.

One could not expect more from a harmony liberal state but this was, at the same time, too little and too much for the growing working class and its radical spokesmen: too much in saving Stockholms Enskilda Bank and its distrusted leader A.O. Wallenberg from a defeat, which ought to have been the logical and lawful consequence of market rules, and too little in doing nothing else for the jobless workers than oppressing the first big strikes in Sweden.

One of the strikes in 1879 occurred at the biggest and most modern saw-mill in Sweden, Skutskär, which was owned and managed by a Norwegian entrepreneur, H.R. Astrup (financed by his friend Wallenberg but otherwise a prominent member of the Norwegian leftist party). Things had certainly changed since 1877, when Astrup and his workers had made common cause in cursing the 'damned' ice that was delaying a new season of profitable export. In 1879, Astrup stood alone in cursing the 'damned' European slump, the workers now meeting him with 'howlings and scornful laughter'.

Also for the employers' and the farmers' part discontent was rapidly growing and to an ever-increasing extent resulting in strong demands for a new, protectionist policy instead of the devastating free-trade system. Not least, the situation of the Swedish freeholders deteriorated rapidly in the 1880s, the country being flooded with cheap grain from the USA and Russia. Time had indubitably ripened for new men and new ideologies to take charge of the never-ceasing building of the nation.

CONCLUSION

For small, poor and culturally homogeneous states like Sweden and Norway after 1809–14 it was most natural for politicians on the given and un-contested national arena to further nation building by concentrating on economic growth. All the more so, as the risks of foreign aggres-sion and invasion were small and had been still more reduced by the Swedish–Norwegian union (no doubt its greatest benefit).

It was less natural, though, that the national goal of economic growth was to be sought through liberal means. The harmony liberals were, sure enough, constantly confronted with (natural or ideological) conservative suspicion, condemning liberalism as a cosmopolitic doctrine, whose ad-herents deserted the interests of their native country. This resistance gives a partial explanation to the leading harmony liberals' frequent confessions and concessions to the interests of the nation. As they were all astute politi-cians their behaviour was more pragmatic than dogmatic. And – as Øystein Sørensen points out in his analysis of Schweigaard – it was a pragmatism on principle: you had to take into account conservative resistance (with 'Courage, Patience and Understanding'). Wallenberg brought out the same analysis in his biographical sketch of the late Gripenstedt (in 1874):

His goal was the solution of big questions and when he appeared to linger it was only in order to mark time...When he thought the time was ripe, he devoted himself with the whole strength of his soul and unusual capacity to reach his goal. Delay and compromise was then out of the question, now was the time for breaking a lance and fighting out the battle. Firm resolution and indomitable courage were the outstanding features of Gripenstedt as a political character.

Economic liberalisation meant of course in Sweden and Norway, as elsewhere, deregulation, abolishing privileges and establishing freedom of trade, in order to give every man of age (formally) equal freedom in pursuing economic activities. It is also evident that public intervention – as Francis Sejersted has stressed – was viewed with horror with regard to the monetary system, where the silver (and later gold) standard was apprehended as the objective foundation of the capitalist system. It is also feasible to make valid quantitative estimations of economic growth during the harmony liberal era in both countries.

Nevertheless, I have refrained from discussing these well-known aspects in order to shed light on the less observed but yet important one of positive public intervention. The effects of these interventions from the national state are almost by definition impossible to quantify as they, generally speaking, aimed at staging the market through shaping better

94 GÖRAN B. NILSSON

infrastructures for individual and collective economic activities. And who is capable of quantifying the short-term losses and long-term benefits of, for example, introducing the metric system in Norway in 1875 and in Sweden in 1876? (A closer investigation would have been welcomed by the radical farmer-politician J. Pehrsson, who in the second chamber characterised the reform as 'the biggest misfortune that has met Sweden since 1809').

Yet more difficult to estimate are the material effects of the harmony liberals' reforming activities as regards immaterial infrastructure, more schools and less brandy, being thought of as leading to increased national prosperity. On the other hand, one can say that the difficulty of giving a scientifically valid estimation of the worth of infrastructural measures was exactly what the scientifically minded harmony liberals needed to give free rein to their commonsense and determined will to give a political helping hand to the progress of civilisation.

It is conceivable that Stang, Schweigaard, Broch, Bergstedt, Gripenstedt and Wallenberg would reluctantly agree to this analysis. But it is inconceivable that they would admit the notion of 'immaterial infrastructure'. It ought to be current nowadays. But for the past harmony liberals the immaterial infrastructure, on the contrary, was a superstructure. Economy was certainly all-important but only as the most effective instrument for attaining higher moral goals.

SELECTED BIBLIOGRAPHY

D. Andreae, *Liberal litteraturkritik: J.P. Theorell, C.F. Bergstedt* (Gothenburg, 1940).
O. Gasslander, *J.A. Gripenstedt: Statsman och företagare* (Lund, 1949).
E. Hobsbawm, *The Age of Capital* (London, 1975).
G.B. Nilsson, *André Oscar Wallenberg 1816–1886* (3 vols., Stockholm, 1984–94).
  Banker i brytningstid: A.O. Wallenberg i svensk bankpolitik 1850–1856 (Stockholm, 1981).
T. Nilsson, *Elitens Svängrum: Första kammaren, staten och moderniseringen* (Stockholm, 1994).
  'Schweden 1848 und danach – Unterwegs zu einem "Mittelweg" ' in D. Dowe, H.-G. Haupt and D. Langewiesche (eds.), *Europa 1848: Revolution und Reform* (Bonn, 1998).
I. Palgrave, *Notes on Banking in Great Britain and Ireland, Sweden, Denmark and Hamburg; with Some Remarks on the Amount of Bills in Circulation, both Inland and Foreign, in Great Britain and Ireland; and the Banking Law of Sweden* (London, 1873).
A.-L. Seip, *Vitenskap og virkelighet: Sosiale, økonomiske og politiske teorier hos T.H. Aschehoug* (Oslo, 1975).

J.A. Seip, *Fra embedsmannsstat til ettpartistat* (Oslo, 1963).
  Ole Jacob Broch og hans samtid (Oslo, 1971).
  Politisk ideologi: Tre lærestykker (Oslo, 1988).
F. Sejersted, *Demokratisk kapitalisme* (Oslo, 1993).
  Demokrati og rettsstat (Oslo, 1984).
R. Slagstad, *De nasjonale strateger* (Oslo, 1998).
Ø. Sørensen, *Anton Martin Schweigaards politiske tenkning* (Oslo, 1988).

CHAPTER 5

Nationalism in the epoch of organised capitalism – Norway and Sweden choosing different paths

Francis Sejersted

THE DISSOLUTION OF THE UNION – NATION BUILDING OR MODERNISATION?

In 1905, the union between Norway and Sweden was dissolved. Although, formally, the two nations had been equal partners in the union, Norway had been forced into the union with Sweden in 1814. Sweden had always been the dominant state, and the joint king had always been Swedish. From the Norwegian point of view, the dissolution of the union therefore represented national liberation and independence, and the national rhetoric flourished. It is also relevant that the dissolution of the union came about as the result of a unilateral, actionistic, political move on the part of the Norwegians. The situation was tense, and the prospect of war loomed large. However, in the end, the conflict was settled peacefully, and for the most part, the traditionally good relations between Sweden and Norway were restored.

The problem is, however, that the union had not generally been regarded as negative from the Norwegian point of view. Norway had enjoyed a relatively large degree of autonomy, and the union years had been a period of growth in terms of the economy, culture and political democracy. In the latter area, Norway had come further than Sweden, whereas in terms of economic and cultural development, the two nations were pretty much on a par. Otherwise, there are many obvious parallels in the two countries' development during this period. The harmony liberal era, as it is described by Göran B. Nilsson in chapter 4 of this volume, which lasted from approximately 1845 to 1880, saw parallel liberal reforms in both countries, at the same time as both countries had a strong central government that was used as an instrument in the national modernisation strategy. There was at that time a tendency towards a closer political union. The two countries also constituted a common free-trade area, which had a positive effect on economic growth in both countries. In this same period there was also a not insignificant movement called *skandinavismen*, which to a certain degree served as an alternative to the nationalism in each of the Scandinavian countries. In short, there was a political entity on the Scandinavian peninsula (Norway and Sweden), and it was about to be 'filled with economic and political meaning', to use Gerd Hardach's expression in chapter 3 of this volume. But contrary to what happened in Germany, this development was reversed and ended with the dissolution of the union.

Much of the explanation for this lies in the fact that Norwegian nationalism turned out to be the stronger in spite of *skandinavismen*, although the union was most beneficial in economic terms. The creation of a national identity turned out to be a process relatively independent of economic modernisation. The union, which Norway had been forced into, was felt by many to be humiliating. So the problem is rather why there was suddenly such absolute national consensus concerning the dissolution of the union in 1905 – for this had not been the case previously, as a large part of the political elite had been in favour of the union.

According to Rolf Danielsen, it was, for many Norwegians, not national independence or getting Norway out of the union that was the real goal. Their ultimate aim was to be able to strike the issue of the union off the Norwegian political agenda once and for all, so that the nation could concentrate on more pressing issues, such as modernisation and, in that context, the battle against social radicalism.[1] In the context of the union, that is, in the context of a lack of national independence, nationalism was an obstacle to policies aimed primarily at promoting economic and social development. The result was the paradox that, in order to clear the way for a politically governed economic and social development, national liberation movements had to be allowed to run their course. The economically most viable unit, the Scandinavian peninsula, had to be sacrificed in order to promote economic development. At the risk of oversimplifying the matter: modernisation was the goal, national liberation was the means. Or, to put it slightly differently, the people for whom national independence was a first-order goal had to be satisfied first so that efforts could be concentrated on modernising society.

However, the strategists' purpose with this national consolidation went beyond satisfying the demands of patriots. The nation-state was historically linked to modernisation in the nineteenth century and well into the twentieth century. The very concept of a nation-state was based on the idea that it would act as a functional unit in relation to the modernisation project; and if it did not, then it was not viable.[2] There would certainly not have been a dissolution of the union had not the Norwegian elites

felt strong enough to fill the independent national unit with economic
meaning. What is demonstrated by the dissolution of the union in 1905
is the dialectical relationship between nation building and modernisation.
They are separate and occasionally conflicting projects. In the long run,
however, they interact so as to strengthen each other.

DIFFERENT SYSTEMS OF AUTHORITY

Economic development was not something that happened by chance. In
recent research in Sweden and Norway, there has been a clear tendency
to emphasise that the modernisation process that started at the beginning
of the nineteenth century was a form of 'state-initiated capitalism'.[3] The
concept of the passive 'night-watchman' form of government does not
work as a general description. The state – that is, the nation-state – was
the most important basis for those actors who wanted to initiate social
and economic development, while the free market was one of the most
important institutions, but it was subordinate to a purpose beyond itself.
In order to grasp the dynamics of this kind of political thinking, not to
mention the differences in the political possibilities between these two
countries, we need to understand what we can call the systems of authority.
What was it that legitimised the exercising of political power?

We have already mentioned the parallel developments in Sweden and
Norway in the so-called harmony liberal era. However, there were a number
of differences in the underlying structures that would come to determine
the subsequent developments. Norway had hardly had any nobility to talk
about in modern times, and the few aristocrats who survived had lost all
their privileges in 1814. Similarly, what little there had been of a real bourgeois upper-middle class had suffered huge losses during the crisis after
the Napoleonic Wars. Norway was a nation of small freeholders and had
a highly localised petty bourgeoisie. The Norwegian constitution of 1814
was the most democratic of its kind in Europe. By contrast, Sweden had
developed a strong aristocracy, and in 1809 it introduced a system that
was described as an 'elitist aristocratic constitutionalism' with a traditional
assembly of estates, which in 1866 was transformed into a two-chamber parliament. The first chamber came to serve as a political power base for an economically progressive haute bourgeoisie.[4] This structure was undermined
by the late introduction of parliamentarism around 1920. Nevertheless, it
is clear that by the beginning of the age of organised capitalism at the end
of the nineteenth century, Norway had come much further than Sweden
in terms of democratic development. As far as economic development is

concerned, this relationship was inverted. There is doubtless a connection here.

These matters entail that the systems of authority in society were different in Sweden and Norway. Norway nurtured strong democratic norms, and it was therefore correspondingly difficult to legitimise large concentrations of private economic power. Thus, business was a 'junior partner to government'.[5] In Sweden, by contrast, society was burdened with a heritage from the estate society that made it much easier to legitimise a strong financial and industrial bourgeoisie. Or, to quote Jan Glete: 'In democratic Sweden, the big businessmen have retained their legitimacy as the holders of economic power. In this way, they have also managed to retain that part of the political power that appears to protect the economic forces from attacks by the political forces.'[6] In Sweden, then, the tendency is more that business and government operate as independent and equal spheres of power. This means that Sweden already had a traditional foundation that made it easier to organise capitalism at the dawning of the age of organised capitalism at the end of the nineteenth century. In Norway, there was no such foundation and scarcely any organised capitalism in what was the classical period for this type of organisation elsewhere.

Organised capitalism is characterised by the emergence of financial capital and the development of large financial units with their own internal bureaucracies which, by means of trustification and other strategies, build up market force. During this period, the class struggle also assumed organised forms. The most commonly cited, classic examples of organised capitalism are Germany and the USA from the end of the nineteenth century onwards. By virtue of organised capitalism, these two countries took the lead in the economic development at the time. Sweden is also a typical example of this kind of development, whereas Norway retained much of its dominant small-scale structure from the preceding era. This was a structure that had worked well until then, and there was no political desire to break with this tradition. In Norway, what Jeffrey R. Fear calls 'public attitudes towards bigness' were quite simply negative.[7] There was no legitimising basis for large financial units in the national culture.

ORGANISING FINANCIAL CAPITAL

The differences between Norway and Sweden are perhaps most clearly demonstrated in the economic growth of the two nations. In the period 1870 to 1910, the per capita income in Norway had risen by 61 per cent, while in Sweden it had risen by 131 per cent.[8] These figures are perhaps slightly misleading, as at the beginning of the 1870s, Norway probably had a larger per capita income than Sweden, but nevertheless, during these forty years, Sweden caught up with and overtook Norway. It is difficult to prove the connection between structural change and economic growth because growth that is rooted in structural change must necessarily come after change in time. However, there is much to indicate that the most important cause of the boom in Sweden was institutional systems that go back further than 1870. In this context, we are thinking primarily of the organisation of financial capital.

In chapter 4 Göran B. Nilsson writes about the bank founder A.O. Wallenberg and the minister of finance J.A. Gripenstedt that 'Their main achievement was the establishment of a modernised and rapidly expanding private banking system in the 1860s modelled on Wallenberg's innovative Stockholms Enskilda Bank of 1856.' In Norway, there were attempts at similar moves, most notably in the establishment of Den Norske Creditbank in 1857.[9] However, it hit rough times during a local crisis in the 1860s and never grew to fulfil the expectations for it. At the same time (in 1864), Skandinaviska Banken was founded in Sweden and grew quickly to become one of the leading banks in Sweden. At the end of the 1860s, it had formed associations with twelve provincial banks, which meant that even as early as this, things had come a good way towards the establishment of nationwide banks that could become large precisely because they served the entire nation.[10] In Norway, there was no similar development, and banks remained relatively small, local, commercial banks. (It was not until the 1980s that political licences were granted allowing nationwide banks in Norway.) It is then perhaps not so surprising that the Swedish Skandinaviska Banken dominated the issue of both Swedish and Norwegian government loans from the 1870s on. Stockholms Handelsbank and the Wallenberg family's Stockholms Enskilda Bank were soon in fierce competition for this lucrative market. The latter came to play a particularly important role in the mediation of large international loans both to the central government and to private industrial enterprise, in Sweden and also in Norway.

During this period, Stockholms Enskilda Bank, under the brothers Knut A. Wallenberg and Marcus Wallenberg, and Stockholms Handelsbank, under Louis Fraenckel, developed into successful issuing houses that created and ran industrial enterprises and bore a close resemblance to the German system. However, one major difference was that, according to Swedish law, banks were not allowed to perform these kinds of activities. The banks circumvented this obstacle by having the heads of the banks and their close associates personally buy shares, which were generally financed with loans from the bank against security in these same shares.[11] The fact that the banks could be used in this way gave the key actors enormous financial clout and the opportunity to do big business. The system functioned so smoothly partly because of the great skill of the central actors, but also partly because, in reality, the authorities applauded these issuing activities. In Sweden, the authorities were 'willing to bestow favors on large firms, especially national champions', to quote Fear.

So, why did this kind of system not also emerge in Norway? We have already mentioned the general democratic scepticism towards large units. Norway was also less centralised than Sweden and had a well-developed system of local banks, which consisted for the most part of savings banks that were tailored to the needs of the expansive, local, small-scale business activities in the nineteenth century. It is probably also significant that the Swedish commercial banks had been able to build themselves up at an early stage by issuing banknotes, while this activity was reserved for the central, semi-public, note-issuing bank in Norway. The central bank thus represented a formidable competitor to the first frail commercial banks in Norway. The fact that Riksbanken in Sweden withdrew from the direct market at an earlier point (in the 1890s) than in Norway is also related to the fact that it was 'inclined to sacrifice its liberty as a commercial bank, in order to be able to buy the exclusive rights to issue banknotes', to quote Sven Brisman.[12]

In this connection, there is one additional factor that also played an important role. What we are looking for is the degree to which the consideration of the economic development can explain the national consolidation through, for example, the development of the national infrastructure. It goes without saying that the banking sector is an integral part of this infrastructure, and the development of the banking sector was followed with great interest by the political authorities. However, in some areas, and not least in the economic field, there was, as we have already indicated, a tendency to consider not the nation, but the union as the unit that was to be consolidated. The union was a free-trade area, and there were full reciprocal establishment rights and the right to acquire real property in the other country – all other 'foreigners' needed special permission. As we have seen, the Swedish banks, which were developed under more favourable conditions than their Norwegian counterparts, also operated in the Norwegian market and even mediated government loans to the Norwegian government. Thus, the Norwegian commercial banks had to compete not only with the Norwegian note-issuing bank with all its special privileges, but also with the stronger Swedish commercial banks.

Some banks tried to brave the competition and enter the market. In 1899, several local commercial banks in the rural districts of Norway merged to form Centralbanken for Norge. The driving force behind this project was Nicolai Kielland-Torkildsen, the 'Norwegian Norwegian' as the Wallenbergs ironically nicknamed him. Centralbanken was a very large bank by Norwegian standards,[13] but it did not receive any help from the central Bank of Norway when it ran into difficulties in the 1920s, and in the end, it had to be wound up. The general Norwegian scepticism regarding anyone who had aspirations to grow big probably also played a certain part in this respect. For example, at this time, a parliamentary committee stated that 'It is not sound policy that it is too easy for the largest banks to set up branches that will allow them to stretch their tentacles across the whole country and draw in revenues from every corner of the nation, taking them away from the places that ought to benefit from them.'[14] These kinds of views had no foothold in Sweden.

Why are the banks such important institutions in this context? The very definition of organised capitalism is that financial capital is separated out as an institutional sphere of its own. In this way, it can become a basis for ordering activities on an intermediate level independently of the existing businesses. This was particularly important in order to be able to exploit the possibilities for industrial renewal inherent in the technology based on science that sprang forth from the second industrial revolution, such as electro-technology and chemistry. This role that was ascribed to financial capital around the end of the nineteenth century and the beginning of the twentieth century has been described by many people, and not least during the era itself; for example, Rudolf Hilferding and Joseph Schumpeter. Olle Gasslander, the author of the classic work on the many initiatives and involvements of the Wallenberg family in Sweden and Norway around the turn of the century, *Bank och industrielt genombrott* (Banking and the Industrial Breakthrough), concludes his presentation by placing these activities in Schumpeter's scheme from 1912. In order to generate processes of renewal in the technical-industrial development, it was, according to Schumpeter, important to have a system of credit that made it possible to detach the means of investment from the old forms of production: 'a means to dictate the new direction for production'. The bank sector becomes 'the headquarters of the capitalist economy whence the orders are issued to the individual parts'. In Norway, there were no such 'headquarters'.[15] As we have seen, this is partly because of the traditionally determined structures of authority, but also partly because the union had ascribed this function to the Swedish banks.

THE STRUGGLE FOR THE NATIONAL RESOURCES

So, then, it was important to have an institutional system and a solid financial basis beyond the individual companies. That was one side of the issue; the other consisted of the spirit or the norms that determined action within the business world. 'German businessmen, right from the start of the country's industrial development, have been influenced in some measure by considerations of collective economic policy,' writes Andrew Shonfield in his classic work, *Modern Capitalism*. And he continues with special reference to the big banks: 'They saw themselves essentially as the grand strategists of the nation's industry.'[16] This system and mentality were precisely what had been built up in Sweden, which explains to a great extent why Sweden experienced such a surge of economic growth in this period and developed such a solid industrial basis with several large industrial groups that were oriented towards the international market, while Norway did not.[17]

In Norway, too, there was an industrial revolution of sorts. The Great Depression had a devastating effect on the old outward-oriented businesses, such as the timber industry, fish exports and shipping, with the result that the GDP fell slightly from 1875 to 1885 (in contrast to Sweden). Below the surface, however, a number of initiatives were undertaken on the basis of the new technology of the period and, from the mid-1890s, there was quite considerable growth in Norway. First, there are grounds for emphasising that the old system of small, locally based, industrial enterprises that had functioned so well before the Great Depression was still viable in Norway and was able to reap significant benefits from the new technology. This is particularly well illustrated when electricity became the most important source of energy in the twentieth century. Although trustification and the nurturing of larger units were the framework around the most dynamic sectors of industry, this view of the large corporations as the most progressive organisational form was also a bit of a fad. Both at the time and in retrospect there has been a tendency to overlook the dynamic, small and medium-sized businesses and possibilities to test new technology that are afforded by what has since been called 'flexible specialisation'. This was the path that Norway 'chose' to follow.[18]

Of course, there were signs of a tendency towards organised capitalism in Norway too. Kielland-Torkildsen's attempt to challenge the Wallenberg dynasty has already been mentioned. This attempt was not a complete failure, but it was not a huge success either. Knut Sogner has also demonstrated an example of what he calls 'associative capitalism'. He studied the Solberg and Kiær families, both of whom had firm roots in the traditional

timber industry and who further consolidated their position through in-
termarriage. They managed to co-ordinate their myriad activities under a
single, overall strategy that represented substantial financial stamina. By
far the most important part of their activities was concentrated around
modernising and structuring the wood-processing industry. This involved
considerable direct overseas investments, which in one sense made the group
less 'national' than the Wallenbergs in Sweden. In general, the group had a
very focused international orientation and drew support from its banking
partners beyond Norway and Sweden. However, after the First World War,
it lost its competitive edge and its ability to act as a strong unit.

The most important aspect of organised capitalism was the direct investment in Norway from abroad. The bait was Norway's vast supply of
natural resources and in particular the seemingly endless reserves of hydroelectric power. In this group of actors, we also find the Wallenbergs, who
established a good foothold in Norway before the dissolution of the union
in 1905. But there were many others too, most of whom appeared around
this time. Both Sweden and Norway were important capital importers in
this breakthrough period. As a result of these different systems outlined
above, another, central difference between the two countries arose, which
Gasslander pointed out in the conclusion of his book: while in Sweden the
general pattern was domestic equity capital and foreign loan capital, the
tendency in Norway was for both to come from abroad. In 1909, overseas
investors owned 39 per cent of the total share capital in Norwegian industry as a whole, and a staggering 85 per cent in the chemical industry and
80 per cent in the mining industry.[19]

The dissolution of the union in 1905 seems to have kindled a new lease
of life in the processes of industrialisation and modernisation in both
Norway and Sweden. It has been said that for Sweden 'The years 1905
to 1907 can be described as the era of the breakthrough of Swedish industrial nationalism.'[20] This also rings true for Norway, where this period is
usually designated 'the new working day'. In other words, the Norwegian
strategists behind the dissolution of the union seem to have been right, in
so far as it *was* beneficial for the country as a whole to settle the union
issue once and for all and allow the politicians to move on to deal with
other questions. In Norway, the dissolution of the union was regarded as a
national victory, whereas in Sweden it was more of a national defeat. In this
light, it is perhaps peculiar that it had the same effect in both countries.
But it did. Both parties were interested in furthering their nation – whether
it was to take advantage of the new opportunities that were unfolding or
to compensate for a loss. It is also important to remember that this era

of organised capitalism in Europe was a time of nurturing 'industrial nationalism as a development ideology', to quote the German historian Hans Ulrich Wehler.[21] In this context, then, the dissolution of the union simply reinforced a general trend.

NATIONAL REACTIONS

In Sweden and in Norway alike, this nationalism in trade and industry was linked to the exploitation of hydroelectric power, Scandinavia's 'white coal', which was the new form of energy for the modern age and with which both countries were relatively well endowed. Norway had roughly twice as much exploitable water power as Sweden, and it was also generally much more easily accessible. Without going into details of the intricate legislative regulations concerning the exploitation of water in rivers and lakes, we can state summarily that in general it was easier to get authorisation to exploit rivers for power generation in Norway. Sweden had at the outset quite comprehensive regulations that limited the possibilities for building power stations. These rules and regulations were, however, modified in stages until they were co-ordinated by the introduction of the Water Act in 1918, which finally established a system that was compatible with the development of the power industry and industry in general.

The central government's involvement was important in this respect. The decision that the state itself would develop and run the enormous power station on the state-owned waterfall Trollhättan was significant.[22] This plant opened for production in 1910, when the wholly state-owned hydroelectric power company, Vattenfall, was also established. This company played an important part in the subsequent developments. It is symptomatic of the national strategy pursued by organised capitalism in Sweden that Vattenfall entered into a close partnership that positively discriminated to the advantage of the Wallenbergs' electrical engineering group, ASEA. During this period, ASEA grew into an international group to be reckoned with and made a major contribution to Sweden, becoming a net exporter of electrotechnical products.[23] According to Svenbjørn Kilander, it is typical of the Swedish version of organised capitalism that the borders between private and public undertakings were somewhat fuzzy.[24]

In Norway, there was on the one hand a much larger supply of unexploited resources and on the other a more reluctant government and no strong financial and industrial ruling class to organise development. Furthermore, since there was less legislation regulating the development of waterfalls, there was – as we have seen – a veritable invasion of foreign buyers and developers of waterfalls. This then led to a nationalistic reaction with demands that Norwegian natural resources must be safeguarded for Norwegian interests. In contrast to the situation in Sweden, where the threat posed by foreign investors was scarcely a topic for debate at all, in Norway a period of limiting the possibilities for the exploitation of hydroelectric power now ensued. In 1906, the so-called 'panic laws' were drafted and approved at breakneck speed. They were subsequently followed up by new laws. The new legislation entailed that all foreign companies and all Norwegian companies with limited liability had to apply for a licence in order to acquire rights in natural resources. In addition, a number of specific conditions were laid down linked to the use of these resources, and the government was given extended authority to intervene and regulate their use. Perhaps most remarkable of all was the clause laying down that the waterfalls, hydroelectric power plants and other installations would automatically become the property of the Norwegian state without remuneration after a maximum of ninety years. The new laws also laid down that foreigners were not entitled to buy forests at all. Even for Norwegian citizens, acquisition of forestland was hedged in with such stringent statutory conditions that, according to Even Lange, it was generally believed to be prohibited.[25] The provisions in these laws not only illustrate 'industrial nationalism as a development ideology', they also bear witness to an anti-industrialisation ideology that was manifesting itself in a reluctant state.

General concerns had been voiced on both sides of the border since the end of the nineteenth century about the social problems that followed in the wake of the change to an industrial society. However, it seems that this attitude was more common in Norway than in Sweden. In Norway, this anxiety was inextricably intertwined with the strong democratic norms and the ensuing widespread scepticism towards the large economic amalgamations that we have already mentioned and with a strain of nationalism that was more closely linked to traditional lifestyles than in Sweden. In this light, it is typical that as late as in 1908, the Norwegian labour party regarded it as one of its tasks to build blockades to curb the growth of the giant capitalistic corporations in collaboration with the traditional anti-capitalist movements rooted in traditional agrarian society.[26] At this time, the Swedish labour movement was progressive in an entirely different way, regarding organised capitalism as positive and representing a step on the way to socialism.

It is important to be aware of the fact that nationalism did not necessarily point to industrialisation and economic growth. It can also, as we have seen, constitute an obstacle to modernisation in so far as national

identity is linked to traditional values. We have also seen that the mobilisation of nationalist feelings in the debate concerning the union during
the last phase of the union did indeed present such an obstacle, as is illustrated by the renewed sense of optimism and enthusiasm in Norway
after the union was dissolved in 1905. In general, it seems that we can
safely say that techno-romanticism and the fascination with the possibilities afforded by technology constituted an independent and at least equally
strong driving force behind industrialisation as the moves to accommodate
the national pride in an economic race against other countries. But the
techno-romantics needed the nation as a sphere of action in order to realise
their dream of the technological society, and so they built the nation. For
it is clear that even though there was a great deal of scepticism towards
the new industrial society, especially in Norway, it was the vision of the
future inspired by technology that won in the end. The controversies surrounding the licensing laws continued in Norway; or rather, there was a
tug-of-war as to whether they should be outright anti-capitalist or merely
protect the national interests. In the end, the latter school of thought won.
The 1918 licensing laws, which laid the foundation for what would later
become the Norwegian system, was a means to gain national control over
the industrialisation process, not an attempt to prevent it.

THE LABOUR MOVEMENT AND MODERNISATION

The labour movement has played an important role in the Nordic
countries – both in the political arena and in the field of workers' rights –
and at the end of the nineteenth century, it had developed national organisations in Sweden and Norway.[27] The movement was (naturally enough)
greatly inspired by socialism. This meant that it was anti-nationalistic at the
same time as it was progressive in terms of economics and technology. In
Sweden, as in large parts of Europe, the political right was associated with
and represented nationalism and the national symbols, but in Norway, the
situation was somewhat more complex as a result of the union with Sweden.
In Norway, nationalism and radicalism went hand in hand, and it was this
that made it such a pressing concern for the right wing to remove the union
issue from Norwegian politics once and for all (see above). However, the
socialism-inspired labour movement stood on the sidelines on this issue to a
certain degree, as it – in keeping with the international socialist movement –
was extremely sceptical towards the growing nationalistic tendencies.

The socialist labour movement was by definition anti-capitalist, but with
an important reservation. Progressive capitalism could play a positive role

in a certain phase of the movement towards socialism. The socialists were
thus in many ways actually positive towards organised capitalism and its
potential to modernise society.

As a result of structural differences in the economies of Sweden and
Norway, there were also some characteristic differences between the labour
movement's attitude towards the economic development in the two countries. We have already mentioned that as late as 1908 the Norwegian labour
party supported the traditional anti-capitalist tendencies with a basis in the
agrarian society. At this time, the Swedish labour movement was more progressive, in that it was actually lending a degree of legitimacy to successful
Swedish capitalists. Of course, they had to be controlled and disciplined
by strong trade unions, but at no cost were they to be robbed of the
opportunity to play a historical role. Naturally, the Norwegian labour
movement was also to become as progressive as its Swedish counterpart.
The problem in Norway was that the capitalists did not play their role
in the same way as they did in Sweden. This is perhaps one explanation for
the fact that the Norwegian labour movement was more radical than the
Swedish one. It was more critical of the established system and called more
loudly for modernisation by means of political intervention. The capitalist
process of maturation had to be speeded up, if necessary by means of forced
mergers of private companies under strict social control.

What is particularly striking about the labour movement's ambivalent
attitude towards capitalist development is, first, the degree to which it
demonstrates that the two countries had 'chosen' different routes. This
'choice' is the result of different structural and cultural restraints in the two
nations. None the less, there was an element of choice, in that there were
always alternative paths that could have been followed. Alternatives were
formulated on the political level, both in respect of banking policy in the
second half of the nineteenth century and in respect of the protracted political confrontations over the licensing laws in Norway after the dissolution of
the union. Sweden led the way in the development of organised capitalism;
in Norway, there was a much more prominent feeling of scepticism.

Second, the labour movement illustrates very clearly how the ideology
of modernisation led its own life independently of nationalism. On this
point, bourgeois techno-romanticism and progressive socialism tended to
merge.

Third, we see how the state, as the agency of the collective, is invoked as a
supreme initiator of modernisation when the market and/or the capitalists
do not behave as expected. Initially, the socialists were sceptical towards
using the 'bourgeois' state as an instrument. Later on, however, as they

gained political status and strength, they became more willing to employ this kind of tactic. The interesting point here is how this process also renders the social democrats bourgeois, in the sense that they too start to think in terms of national interests and national concerns. This was demonstrated particularly clearly in the 1930s when they started to employ the conventional national symbols. In many contexts, the red flag of socialism was replaced by the national flag; they accepted the monarchy and took part in the Independence Day celebrations, etc.[28] Thus the capitalist order was consolidated within the national framework.

CONCLUSION

Nation building and modernisation through industrialisation should be analysed as two separate phenomena having different historical roots. They are however interacting and, generally speaking, they have mutually reinforced each other in the period we have looked into. National considerations have deeply influenced economic initiatives by the state as well as by private entrepreneurs, as purely economic considerations have strengthened the nation-state. The nation-state not only was the natural unit within which to build the necessary infrastructure; the nation-state was consolidated and the national identity strengthened by the process of modernisation. As Joan Robinson has said, 'The very nature of economics is rooted in nationalism.'[29] There are, however, important exceptions. As Hobsbawm reminded us, the nation-state has to be economically viable. Not every nation-state could serve as the natural basis for economic modernisation, neither could the most viable unit be developed into a nation-state. The case of Norway reminds us of this last point. Even if the union with Sweden was the most viable solution from an economic point of view, it was not chosen. On the other hand, we have seen how the dissolution of the union between Sweden and Norway nudged both countries in the direction of bolstering their industrial nationalism as a development ideology.

In international circles, Scandinavia or the Nordic countries are often regarded as a single unit or at least as a group of nations that have a great deal in common. People talk about the Scandinavian or Nordic model. However, as demonstrated above, it is important to underline that in some areas there are quite major differences between the Nordic countries. This is particularly true in a comparative study of Sweden and Norway from our current perspective. Sweden was a textbook example of a successful organisation of capitalism in the age of organised capitalism. Norway, by contrast, retained much of the structure from the classic period of industrial capitalism before the Great Depression in the 1870s. Norway did not have its economy organised by a nationally minded financial and industrial bourgeoisie, as was common elsewhere at this time. The structure remained marked by small companies that kept one another at arm's length. However, as time passed, and especially once the labour party Arbeiderpartiet had established itself as the hegemonic ruling party after the Second World War, the central government was ascribed a key role as the facilitator and adapter of the overall structures in society. We could say that it was only then that Norway entered the era of organised capitalism.

The national style that permeates the organisation of the economy is thus quite different in Sweden and Norway. Perhaps it is not so very surprising then that the ongoing globalisation of capitalism that marks developments today is causing greater concern in Norway than in Sweden. One of the main characteristics of this development is the limitation of the role played by the state as an economic actor in relation to the powerful strategists in the business world. In this respect Sweden is better equipped than Norway.

There is a clear connection between the unique structural traits and the national identity with roots in traditional society, on the one hand, and the fact that Norway is the only country that has had the opportunity to join the European Union and turned it down, on the other. Nevertheless, the Norwegian structure and identity have been challenged by the emergence of a large-scale oil industry based on huge finds of oil and gas on the Norwegian continental shelf in the North Sea in the 1970s. Ironically, it was only because of this oil industry that Norway was able to choose to remain outside the European Union and to continue to nurture its own national idiosyncrasies. This is then yet another example of how the economy shapes the nation. How much longer we can continue to stand outside, however, is another question altogether. There are many signs that indicate that Norway will have to follow Sweden into Europe sooner or later.

NOTES

1. Rolf Danielsen, *Det Norske Storting gjennom 150 år* [150 Years of the Norwegian Parliament], Vol II (Oslo, 1964), pp. 370f.
2. Eric Hobsbawm, *Nations and Nationalism since 1780* (Cambridge, 1990), p. 32: 'Self-determination for nations applied only to what were considered to be viable nations: culturally, and certainly economically (whatever exactly viable meant).'
3. Rune Slagstad, *De nasjonale strateger* [The National Strategists] (Oslo, 1998), p. 60.

4. Torbjørn Nilsson, *Elitens svängrum. Första kammaren, staten och moderniseringen 1867–1886* [The Arena of the Elite. The First Chamber, the State and Modernisation 1867–1886] (Stockholm, 1994).

5. This expression is taken from Louis Galambos and Joseph Pratt, *The Rise of the Corporate Commonwealth* (New York, 1988) p. 257.

6. Jan Glete, 'Ägarekonsentrationen och den politiska demokratin' [The Concentration of Owners and Political Democracy] in Rolf Eidem and Rolf Skog (eds.), *Makten över företagen* [Power over Companies] (Stockholm, 1991), p. 238.

7. Jeffrey R. Fear, 'Constructing Big Business: the Cultural Concept of the Firm' in Alfred D. Chandler, Franco Amatori and Takashi Hikino (eds.), *Big Business and the Wealth of Nations* (Cambridge, 1997), pp. 546–74, at p. 549.

8. Lennart Jörberg, 'The Industrial Revolution in the Nordic Countries' in Carlo M. Cipolla (ed.), *The Fontana Economic History of Europe, Volume IV(2): The Emergence of Industrial Societies* (London, 1973), p. 386.

9. Jens A. Seip, 'Assosiasjon og konkurranse: en bankhistorie' [Association and Competition: the History of a Bank] in Jens A. Seip (ed.), *Tanke og handling i norsk historie* [Ideas and Actions in Norwegian history] (Oslo, 1968), pp. 72–89.

10. Ulf Olsson, *I utvecklingens centrum* [At the Centre of Development] (Stockholm, 1997), p. 49.

11. Ibid., pp. 113–19.

12. Sven Brisman, *Sveriges Riksbank 1668–1918: bankers tillkomst och verksamhet*, Volume III: *Den stora reform perioden 1860–1904* (Stockholm, 1931), p. 213.

13. Francis Sejersted, Review in *Historisk Tidsskrift*, 47, 2 (1968), 149–72, at p. 166, of Gunnar Jahn et al., *Norges bank gjennom 150 år* [150 Years of Norges Bank] (Oslo, 1966); N. Kielland-Torkildsen, 'Centralbanken for Norge, den tilblivelseshistorie' [The History of Centralbanken for Norge] in *Ekonomiska Studier tilägnade Marcus Wallenberg* [Economic Studies Dedicated to Marcus Wallenberg] (Stockholm, 1914), pp. 77–109.

14. Cited from Sverre Knutsen, 'Bank, Samfunn og økonomisk vekst' [Banking, Society and Economic Growth] (Master's thesis, Oslo, 1990), p. 197.

15. Olle Gasslander, *Bank och industrielt genombrott* [Banking and the Industrial Breakthrough] Vol. II (Stockholm, 1959), p. 416.

16. Andrew Shonfield, *Modern Capitalism: the Changing Balance of Public and Private Power* (Oxford, 1965), p. 261.

17. Harm G. Schröter, 'Small European Nations: Cooperative Capitalism in the Twentieth Century' in Chandler et al. (eds.), *Big Business*, pp. 176–204. Schröter mentions twelve large Swedish industrial groups, but only two Norwegian ones: Norsk Hydro and Statoil. Indeed, for a long time, Hydro was alone in the Norwegian context; Statoil was only founded as a wholly state-owned oil company in the 1970s when Norway suddenly became an oil-producing nation.

18. Francis Sejersted, *Demokratisk kapitalisme* [Democratic Capitalism] (Oslo, 1993).

19. Trond Bergh, Tore Hanisch, Even Lange and Helge Pharo (eds.), *Norge fra U-land til I-land* [Norway from a Developing Country to an Industrialised Country] (Gyldendal, 1983), p. 158.

20. Mats Fridlund, *Den gemensamma utvecklingen* [The Common Development] (Stockholm, 1999), p. 41.

21. The expression in German is: 'Wirtshaftsnationalismus als Entwicklungsideologie'. Cf. Hans-Ulrich Wehler, 'Der Aufstieg des Organisierten Kapitalismus und Interventionsstaates in Deutschland' in Heinrich August Winkler (ed.), *Organisierter Kapitalismus – Voraussetzungen und Anfänge* (Göttingen, 1974), pp. 36–57.

22. Eva Jakobsson, *Industrialisering av Älvar. Studier kring svensk vattenkraftutbyggnad 1900–1918*. [Industrialisation of Rivers. Studies of the Development of Hydroelectric Power Plants in Sweden 1900–1918] (Gotherburg, 1996).

23. Fridlund, *Den gemensamma utvecklingen.*

24. Svenbjørn Kilander, *Den nya staten och den gamla. En studie i ideologisk förändring* [The New State and the Old. A Study in Ideological Change] (Uppsala, 1991).

25. Even Lange, *Fra Linderud til Eidsvold Værk*, Volume IV: *Treforedlingens epoke 1895–1970* (Oslo, 1985), pp. 72–5.

26. Christine Myrvang, *Sosialistiske produksjonsidealer – 'dagen derpå'* [Socialistic Ideals of Production – 'The Morning After'] TMV report series no. 18 (Oslo, 1996), p. 32.

27. Francis Sejersted, 'Capitalism and Democracy: A Comparison between Norway and Sweden in Haldor Byrkjeflot, Sissel Myklebust, Christine Myrvang and Francis Sejersteol (eds.), *The Democratic Challenge to Capitalism: Management and Democracy in the Nordic Countries* (Bergen, 2001), pp. 87–119.

28. Hans Fredrik Dahl, *Fra klassekamp til nasjonal samling* [From Class Struggle to National Unification] (Oslo, 1969).

29. Joan Robinson, *Economic Philosophy* (London, 1962), p. 117.

CHAPTER 6

Economic development and the problems of national state formation: the case of Spain

Clara Eugenia Núñez and Gabriel Tortella

Spanish schoolchildren have long been taught that Spain is one of the oldest nations in Europe, since its geographical unity dates from the late fifteenth century with the union of the kingdoms of Castile, Leon, Aragon, Granada and Navarre, carried out by marriage and conquest by that remarkable couple, Ferdinand and Isabella (commonly designated as the 'Catholic Monarchs' in Spain); real national identity, however, may have been longer to form, although this is subject to considerable discussion.

BIRTH OF A NATION?

It is well known that all these different kingdoms (to which Portugal was added from 1580 to 1640) were governed as separate entities for centuries and that Spanish writers of the sixteenth and seventeenth centuries advised that 'the kingdoms must be ruled and governed as though their common king were only king of each one of them'.[1]

So it was only slowly – and in incomplete fashion – that a Spanish identity came to be shaped through the centuries. In fact the Spanish case resembles in this respect more the British one than that of Portugal, Holland, or even France, to name other states which became political units in the early modern period. As in Britain, the Spanish state was a 'united kingdom'; the old idea of some medieval Iberian monarchs had been the unification of the whole peninsula on the strength of a common Roman and Visigothic past, and of a similar experience of Christian defeat in the eighth century and then slow reconquest from the Muslims in the next centuries, culminating in the surrender of Moorish Granada in 1492. The addition of Navarre in 1512 put all land south of the Pyrenees, Portugal excepted, under the rule of the Spanish king: but could he be called Spanish? As has been pointed out, the purpose of the Catholic Monarchs had been to incorporate Portugal, but repeated attempts at an alliance only came to fruition three generations later as their great-grandson, Philip II, claimed the Portuguese throne and gained it by force of arms. Yet peninsular unity lasted only sixty years.

The geographical unity of the peninsula had been evident to observers since antiquity. The peninsula had been called Hispania and Iberia since Roman times, if not before. And it was still known as Hispania in the late sixth century by Saint Isidore of Seville in his *Laus Hispaniae* (Praise of Spain), later on under the Muslim kingdom(s), and in the early twelfth century *Poema del Cid*, the earliest epic poem in the Castilian language. The word 'Spanish' (*Español*), however, appeared later. Apparently the first 'Spaniards' were those emigrants from south of the Pyrenees who established themselves in the Languedoc in southern France in the early Middle Ages, presumably escaping from the Moors, and were so called by the Languedocine inhabitants. The word *'Español'* then entered Spain with the French pilgrims coming to Santiago in the late Middle Ages and appears in documents and poems already in the late twelfth century.[2] And yet, there have been several problems with Iberian or even Spanish unity. In spite of being almost an island,[3] Iberia has internal mountain chains almost as impassable as the Pyrenees, and this explains the numerous separated political units which sprang up in the Middle Ages with different languages, religions and cultures. Thus the union under Ferdinand and Isabella was a conglomerate of conglomerates.

In the Castilian civil war of 1474–6, two women were competing for the Castilian throne; the winner, Isabella, was married to the heir to the kingdom of Aragon; the loser, her niece Juana, was married to the king of Portugal; both husbands and their respective kingdoms played very active roles in the war. It was obvious that one or the other state (Aragon or Portugal) was going to be united to Castile, the central peninsular kingdom. Isabella and Aragon won; but although Isabella and Ferdinand always considered themselves and their respective kingdoms equal, in fact there was no equality. Ferdinand thought of himself, acted, and was recognised as king of Castile; Isabella never considered herself or was accepted as queen of Aragon, except as consort. Having its king as the more powerful of the two monarchs, however, did not work to the advantage of Aragon, because Ferdinand in fact paid more attention to Castile and to foreign affairs than to his original fief. There were, basically, two reasons for this: Castile was the stronger and more prosperous political unit; it was also easier to govern, being more integrated and unified. Thus, while each Aragonese kingdom had its own Cortes, laws and traditions, all of Castile had only one Cortes, and, in spite of its larger size both in terms of territory and of population, was more unified in language and customs, and royal authority was stronger.

Both kingdoms had been wrecked by civil wars which had defied royal authority. In Castile, nevertheless, the war had ended with clear-cut victory for Isabella and Ferdinand (in the battle of Toro, 1476) and their authority had never again been in question. In the Aragonese kingdom of Catalonia a bitter and complicated social war, in which urban and rural conflicts were mixed with dynastic dissensions (*guerra dels remences*), raged for most of the fifteenth century and was only solved in 1486 (*Sentencia de Guadalupe*), with a resounding victory for the peasants and farmers against the nobility. The *Sentencia* was to become the basis of a prosperous agriculture in the centuries to come, but Catalonia remained ravaged and debilitated by war for a long time. Its weakness, furthermore, had originated in the crisis of the fourteenth century, which had decimated Catalonia with special cruelty. Malthusian mechanisms seem to have been at work in fourteenth-century Catalonia, since the ravages of the plague were preceded by famines, especially that of 1333 (*lo mal any primer*, 'the first bad year' in Catalan tradition). The population of Barcelona fell precipitously from around 50,000 in 1340 to around 20,000 in 1477, and the population of Catalonia, the most highly populated of the Aragonese kingdoms, had fallen from around 550,000 in 1340 to 278,000 in 1497. In total, Aragon had some 900,000 inhabitants by the end of the fifteenth century, probably fewer than one century and a half earlier. By contrast, the Castilian population was around 4.5 million.[4]

Castile was not only larger, it was more prosperous. It had been less seriously affected by the plague. Its agriculture was mediocre, but low population density in the southern half permitted the transhumant grazing of sheep which provided it with its main export staple, merino wool, which had become the basis of a flourishing textile industry in numerous towns of the interior (especially Segovia, Ávila, Burgos, Zamora, Toledo and Cuenca) and of a thriving export trade through Bilbao and Santander. The active trade in wool had given rise to a network of fairs in northern Castile (Burgos, Medina del Campo, Medina de Rioseco, Villalón), to the development of an incipient financial sector and to specifically mercantile corporations and courts, such as the *consulados*. There were *consulados* and important banks – the *Taulas del Canvi* – in Catalonia too. Trade had also been very active in Aragonese ports (Barcelona, Valencia, Majorca), but the fourteenth-century crisis had hit it harder than northern trade. As a consequence of all this, during the reign of the Catholic Monarchs and of their Habsburg successors, Castile clearly had the upper hand.

This meant that as long as things went well and as long as Aragonese traditions were respected, the very slow unification of the kingdoms into a single political and social unit could proceed. When fortunes were reversed the correlation of forces changed and dissension ensued. This is what happened in the seventeenth century and came to a head in the fateful year of 1640.

Evidence of the diversity of the different Spanish kingdoms is shown by the fact that the recently discovered American colonies were adjoined to Castile alone. This was made explicit several times and implied that Aragonese and Navarrese subjects were treated as foreigners in Spanish America. A heavy price was paid for this exclusiveness both by the excluded kingdoms, which thereby lost the American markets and outlets, and by the American colonies, which were provided for by a narrower range of suppliers than would have been the case if all the Spanish kingdoms had had access to America. Furthermore, the monopoly of transatlantic trade was vested in the *Casa de Contratación* in Seville, which made trade with other regions more expensive, even that with the Castilian ports of Santander, Coruña or Bilbao, since their ships were required to report and register in Seville, which considerably prolonged their voyages.[5]

The unity of the peninsula in one sole kingdom was finally achieved under Philip II in 1580, but only after he invaded Portugal and obtained recognition by the Portuguese parliament. Might and right were not the only reasons for the relative ease with which Philip achieved victory and Portugal accepted the annexation: there were powerful economic motives which on this occasion overcame Portugal's traditional mistrust of Castile. For one thing, Philip was at the time 'the most potent Monarch of Christendome, who in his own hands holds the Mines of the War's sinews – money – and hath now got a command so wide, that out of his Dominions the Sunne can neither rise nor set'.[6] The 'Mines of the War's sinews' were at full swing by the end of the sixteenth century, and their silver was essential to European trade. Europe had a structural balance of trade deficit with the East, which had to be paid in silver. European silver output was clearly insufficient, and American silver bridged the gap.[7] For Portuguese merchants operating in the East, securing a steady supply of silver was essential, and only the Spanish American empire could offer it. It was also felt that, since both Portugal and Spain had enormous overseas empires, joint management, administration and defence might bring about economies of scale. Furthermore, both domestic economies were growing more complementary and interdependent, with increasing numbers of common ventures and overland trade.[8]

But peninsular unity was not to last long: as the economic tide ebbed for the Spanish empire its constituent parts tended to secede. From 1560

Spain had been warring with nascent Dutch nationalism, and what to Philip II had been the nuisance of his mischievous subjects from the Low Countries soon became the open wound that bled the Spanish empire of its resources and led it to bankruptcy. The war effort caused a growing deficit in Spain's (national) budget, and an upset in the traditional Iberian division of economic power. As war expenditures mounted, tax revenues faltered, especially in the seventeenth century.[9] There were a series of flaws in the Spanish fiscal system, the most important of which was over-taxation, which ruined the Castilian economy.[10] This view was already held by contemporaries and has been confirmed by modern researchers. The flourishing sixteenth-century Castilian textile industry was priced, taxed and regulated out of competitiveness. Furthermore, inflation (the falling price of silver) ate into the revenues of the Spanish crown.

The climax of disaster arrived under Philip IV, who acceded to the throne in 1621, the year when the truce in the Netherlands ended. To strengthen his army the new king immediately had recourse to all the means at his command. He availed himself of many expedients, but the easiest and cheapest was to issue inflated copper money. All in all, according to Hamilton, some 41 million ducats of copper were issued between 1599 and 1626. In spite of all these measures the crown's straits were such as to cause serious political difficulties. The king lacked the means to make the customary travel of new kings to Catalonia to swear the oath and receive homage from his vassals; as a consequence, the legitimacy of his rule in Catalonia was much in dispute there and his person unpopular, circumstances which contributed to open rebellion in 1640. On top of all this, or maybe as a consequence, the government suspended payments in 1627 and proclaimed a new unilateral reduction of debt (there had been several of those under Philip II). The irritation of the Genoese bankers, at the time the main creditors of the Spanish state, was such that they threatened political reprisals.[11]

In times of difficulty the inequities in the distribution of the fiscal burden became glaring. It was evident that Castile paid a disproportionate share of the crown's revenues and the opinion spread in government circles that the imbalance ought to be redressed not so much on ethical grounds as on those of necessity: Castile was exhausted and impoverished and the time had come for other kingdoms (Aragon, Portugal, the Basque provinces) to lend a hand. The champion of this idea was Philip IV's prime minister, the Count-Duke of Olivares, who, since its basic aim was to strengthen common defence, called the project Union of Arms (*Unión de Armas*). Of course this was not a popular project outside Castile. Since Castile was the obvious leader, as political decisions were being made in Madrid and since she had kept the Indies and their remittances for herself, in the opinion of the other kingdoms it was fair that she should bear the burden of taxation. On ethical grounds the discussion could be endless. On purely political grounds it was obvious that Olivares was right. The grandiose imperial policies of the Habsburgs had ruined Castile and could not be carried on – if at all – without additional support from the other kingdoms. He miscalculated, however, on the degree of inter-regional solidarity. The attempt to put the Union of Arms into practice provoked an explosion of unprecedented dimensions. In 1640 both Catalonia and Portugal rebelled and seceded from Castile. Even in Andalusia there was a (failed) conspiracy to secede in 1641. It took twelve years to subdue Catalonia. Portugal gained definitive independence, confirmed by the Treaty of Lisbon in 1668. For Catalonia the war of 1640–52 became a symbol of national independence.

THE STRAINS OF MODERNITY: THE PAINFUL BIRTH OF A STATE

The year 1640 marked the effective end of Spain's world power ambitions but not of its internal problems. Castile and Aragon remained separate political units as Philip IV felt compelled to promise that nothing would change, so as to attract his rebellious Catalan subjects to the fold. The relative peace that ensued witnessed a certain economic recovery. The War of the Spanish Succession at the beginning of the eighteenth century, however, brought about a renewal of regional war: while Castile supported the French pretender (Philip of Anjou), Catalonia and Valencia supported the Austrian candidate (the Archduke Charles). As usual, dynastic, regional and class considerations were intertwined. Philip won after a long war, and started a process of gradual unification. He was not bound by any promise, and was adept at French-style centralisation in government, which is why the Catalans had fought him.[12] In 1716 he issued the *Decretos de Nueva Planta*, in which many of the Catalan legal and political traditions were abolished. Aragonese and Valencian traditions had been even more radically obliterated in 1707, before the war had ended. Catalan organs of government were put on a par with those of the other regions, i.e. the top echelons were appointed from Madrid. While most Catalan private law was respected, the tax system was radically overhauled and, although it was different to that of Castile, it was set up so that the tax burden would be equivalent. As a matter of fact, the main tax, based on a *catastro*, was called *equivalente*; being more modern, however, it turned out to be fairer and more efficient than that of Castile.

The Seville monopoly was gradually replaced by cautious liberalisation of American trade. One advantage for Catalonia in being assimilated was that it was no longer excluded from transatlantic trade, and it thoroughly profited from these new opportunities. The *flota* system (whereby, for reasons of safety, there were only two annual naval commercial expeditions to all of Spanish America) was abolished in 1735 and in 1765 several Catalonian ports, including Barcelona, were authorized to trade directly with the Americas. Finally, in 1778, general freedom of trade with the Americas was proclaimed. This did not entail free trade, since stiff tariffs, prohibitions and other barriers to commerce subsisted. All this contributed to economic prosperity on both sides of the Atlantic, but Catalonia probably was the region that benefited most. Its agriculture thrived and its industry (especially cotton textiles which, in spite of timid commercial liberalisation in other branches, enjoyed government protection) grew remarkably, thanks in part to Castilian and American markets. An unmistakable sign of progress was the fact that Catalonia was the first Spanish region to undergo demographic transition; its birth rate soared during the eighteenth century, as the economic bonanza stimulated younger marriages. The Catalan population was 7 per cent of the Spanish total in 1717, and 11 per cent in 1857, although its proportion stagnated thereafter.[13]

After the relative tranquillity of the eighteenth century, the early nineteenth century put serious strains on the political and social fabric of Spain (as it did in other European countries and in the Americas).[14] The French invasions and the colonial wars unleashed centrifugal forces. As the war against the French formally implied a rebellion against the state (i.e. King Joseph Bonaparte), the country broke into a series of provincial juntas and committees operating independently and clandestinely, which eventually coalesced in a Cortes (where Spanish America was also represented) meeting in Cadiz. In spite of geographical fragmentation, the Napoleonic War generated a remarkable patriotic upsurge in which all regions and groups (save a small minority of *afrancesados*) fought against the invader. Once the war was over, however, profound divisions surfaced. The most glaring was between *liberales* (a word coined at the Cortes in Cadiz during the war) and conservatives (*serviles*, according to the liberals). After the triumph of the latter with the help of Ferdinand VII, who assumed absolute power through a *coup d'état* in 1814, the liberals recovered power following the death of Ferdinand in 1833, and civil war ensued. The absolutists rebelled in the name of Ferdinand's younger brother, Don Carlos (hence their name, *carlistas*), against the reforms proposed by the liberals, which aimed at constitutional monarchy, parliamentary government, equality before the law, fiscal reform, disentailment of church and public lands, universal schooling and other freedoms. Perhaps surprisingly, Carlism gathered most support among Basque, Navarrese and Catalan peasants, although it also drew diffuse backing from other agricultural areas and, of course, almost unanimous support from the clergy. Carlism was an anti-modern, reactionary movement, which in many ways paralleled the *miguelista* party in Portugal and the *chouannerie* in France. It was in favour of absolutism, clerical religion and a host of rather mythical ancient regional traditions (*fueros*), and its main economic interest was in low taxes paid in kind (a return to the tithe). After losing the war through an armistice in 1839, Carlism remained an extreme right-wing movement which resorted to armed struggle whenever the opportunity arose. The liberals in power, meanwhile, split into *progresistas* and *moderados*, and fought for power by fair means and foul, mostly the latter.

Carrying through the liberal programme met with serious obstacles, which were rooted in economic backwardness. The crisis of the early nineteenth century had profoundly shaken the old structures. Although no longer a leading world power, Spain had a very large colonial empire at the end of the eighteenth century and its economy was in many ways dependent upon imperial finances. Liberal Spain found itself in the 1830s largely bereft of empire, in the middle of a civil war, burdened with a crushing war debt, with an archaic, inefficient fiscal system, full of regional exceptions and anomalies and, of course, deprived of the imperial remittances. Fiscal reform was vital to its survival and was fought tooth and nail by the Carlists. Although the reform was enacted some years after the war (the so-called Mon-Santillán reform of 1845), chronic budget deficits were one of the plagues of the Spanish economy during the nineteenth century (as was the case in Portugal and in Italy). The burden of debt and of very large military expenditure crippled the modernisation of the state (its very tax-assessment mechanisms were gravely impaired by lack of funds), hampered social capital formation and crowded out private enterprise. Low public credit ratings were a serious obstacle to capital imports and even to domestic borrowing.[15] Perennial shortage of funds limited investment in infrastructures, in education and in public health. Compulsory primary schooling was decreed in 1813, but remained unenforced until well into the twentieth century.[16] The same was true of early vaccination programmes, as a result of which infant mortality remained very high and did not start falling until early in the next century.[17] As a whole, the Spanish population remained traditional, and its transition to demographic modernity only started in the 1890s.

Public finances could have been better managed. Agriculture's problems were even less tractable, because physical conditions (the aridity of a large part of the country's soil) were a serious obstacle to the kind of productivity revolution which was spreading in northern Europe. The largest share of Spanish agricultural land was devoted to cereals, with very low yields due to aridity and primitive techniques.[18] Given the conditions of the time (insufficient and expensive transportation, lack of refrigeration), shifting to other products, better suited to the soils (fruits and vegetables), was out of the question. The only viable alternatives, the vine and the olive tree, were expanded, but there were also physical limitations. Agriculture, the main sector in terms of output and employment, stagnated during the nineteenth century, and with it the economy and society as a whole. Industry was hampered by scarcity of capital, entrepreneurship and qualified manpower, as well as by shallow markets due to the stagnation of agriculture. The usual vicious circles of backwardness operated in nineteenth-century Spain. Low per capita output limited savings and investment; low investment limited productive capacity.

Economic backwardness in turn had serious political repercussions. Liberal attempts to modernise the state and make it more democratic failed because of a lack of effective support. The Spanish populace was too divided between an apathetic and illiterate peasantry and a firmly entrenched upper class of landowners and bureaucrats, who accepted the semblance of a parliamentary system as long as it did not threaten their privileges. The lack of vigorous industry and commerce was the cause of the weakness of the middle classes who could have bridged the gap between these two groups. In these conditions not even a limited system of suffrage could function. During most of the nineteenth century governments were very often renewed by *pronunciamiento* and elections were grossly manipulated. As the political system malfunctioned, popular pressures were channelled through sporadic violence and rebellion rather than through organised day-to-day action, a typical trait of backward societies.

In these conditions the national state developed haltingly. The slow pace and incomplete expansion of a cheap and efficient transport system hampered interregional trade and communication. This was made evident by the lack of price convergence during most of the century. Spain has no river or canal transportation possibilities, but the road and railway networks were built slowly due to the factors already referred to: capital scarcity, technical backwardness and, in the long run, relative lack of effective demand, due to low population density and purchasing power. The weakness of the transport network, plus the incomplete introduction of universal education made for only tenuous social cohesion and the persistence of local sentiment.

During most of the nineteenth century, however, the only clear local or regional dissidence was that of the Carlists. Large cities, such as Barcelona, the only industrial city in Spain until the very end of the nineteenth century, were centres of liberalism. The Barcelona liberals were strongly protectionist in the tradition of the cotton manufacturers since the eighteenth century. Catalan protectionism was double-edged. On the one hand, it was formulated in conjunction with Spanish nationalism: the slogans were 'a national market' and 'national work and labour'. On the other hand, the threat of separatism (and of worker rebellion) was wielded as an instrument of pressure by Catalan industrialists and politicians. Catalan cultural movements had developed during the century, centred upon a renaissance (*la Renaixença*) of the language, which during the early modern period had been reduced to being used in the countryside almost exclusively. Catalonia's position within the Spanish nation was awkward. It was more economically developed and prosperous, and this, plus the language, was the 'differential fact' (*fet diferencial* in Catalan) so frequently bandied about. At the same time, Spain's market was the natural outlet for Catalonia's output, precisely because Catalan industry found no competition there. Catalonia manipulated Spanish politics to obtain tariff protection and, in order to do this, it had to handle the *fet diferencial* with care. The Catalans coalesced with the Castilian wheat growers in lobbying for protection, and for this entente anti-Castilian expressions had to be repressed; but, on the other hand, whipping up anti-Castilian sentiment was an effective way of rallying support in protectionist meetings. Protectionism and Catalanism became almost synonymous, while protectionism appealed to a Spanish 'national market'. As Vicens Vives has shown in his masterpiece *Industrials i polítics*, Catalonia largely shaped nineteenth-century Spanish nationalism and politics, while at the same time a vocal minority of Catalans painted Catalonia as a victim of 'centralism'.[19]

ECONOMIC DEVELOPMENT AND NATIONAL FERMENT

Political instability reached its climax with the 1868–74 revolution. During this period, Cuba rebelled, the Carlists took up arms, and a 'Cantonalist' (republican–federalist–anarchist) rebellion raged for a whole year (1873) in Andalusia and the eastern Mediterranean provinces. Faced with all these military challenges and with generalised tax evasion, the revolutionary governments ran huge deficits and borrowed in large amounts, while their credit deteriorated badly. In spite of this desperate situation, not all was negative about the 1868 revolution. It introduced universal (male) suffrage, lowered tariffs, liberalised the economy, and carried out monetary reform, establishing the peseta as the currency unit. Many of the institutional innovations introduced by the revolution were preserved by the ensuing Restoration (1875–1923), and other improvements, at first abolished, were reintroduced later.

The Restoration was a period of peace and a semblance of order. Political life was rife with rigged elections (*pucherazos*) and rotten boroughs (*caciquismo*), though both liberals and conservatives shared power. With peace and low tariffs there was some economic growth. Exports of minerals, wine, fruit and even some light industrial products (cork manufactures, canned preserves, shoes, textiles) stimulated production, investment and capital imports. Especially notable at this time was the industrialisation of the Basque country, spurred by iron ore exports. Soon the iron producers joined wheat growers and textile manufacturers in demanding higher tariffs. Protectionism triumphed in 1891.

Economic growth brought about renewed social strains. Catalonia and the Basque country attracted southern emigration and this produced an intensification of regional-national feeling in these areas, an impulse of self-affirmation in front of (and hostility towards) the newcomers. Meanwhile, new political parties appealed to new voters. Republicans, socialists and anarchists, after a brief appearance in 1868–74 and a twenty-year lull thereafter, stirred again and found a following in the expanding mass of urban workers.

The Restoration system was sorely tested after the defeat in the Spanish-American war of 1898, where Spain was militarily and diplomatically humiliated and lost its last overseas colonies (except for some bridgeheads in Africa). The loss of Cuba, Puerto Rico, the Philippines and some smaller islands produced a far stronger revulsion in 1898 than the loss of Spanish America had done in 1824. The inferiority complex that the '*desastre*' produced was turned in many quarters into rabid nationalism, while in saner minds what developed was the desire for radical reform or *regeneración*. In Catalonia and the Basque country the 'disaster' caused a wave of anti-Spanish sentiment: the birth of Catalan and Basque nationalism as viable political movements can be dated to 1898.

There were some reformers or '*regeneracionistas*' in the old traditional parties (conservatives and liberals) but they tended to group themselves in the new *Reformista* party, or among republicans and socialists. Most of them were critical of the Spanish 'centralist' state. Their dissatisfaction was widely shared, and popularised by a remarkable group of writers and novelists who became known as 'the generation of 98'. Critics pointed out the deficiencies of the Spanish national state. Its lack of legitimacy was universally decried: *caciquismo* and *pucherazos* put the levers of power in the hands of a clique of corrupt professionals who used this power to enrich themselves, their relatives and their cronies. From this derived a rigid, insufficient fiscal system, taxing the poor and the middle classes and spending in favour of the rich. As a consequence, general education was abysmal, public health was so mismanaged that Spanish death rates were among the highest in Europe, public works were insufficient for the needs of the country. The Spanish economy remained backward, in particular agriculture, which was plagued by very low yields and productivity due largely to the ignorance of farmers, to the uneven distribution of land ownership and to the lack of irrigation works. Economic failure was symbolised for many by the precipitous fall of the peseta which, never on the gold standard, had seriously depreciated during the Cuban war (1895–8). However, the most glaring and scandalous example of the state's inefficiency and corruption was in the armed forces. The problem was that, short of revolution, it was the corrupt and inefficient political system that had to reform itself. In the best of cases, this would take time.

The only reform the conservatives carried out was the Villaverde stabilisation plan, which balanced the budget after 1899, solved the public debt problem and stabilised the peseta.[20] This may not seem much when compared with the huge demands put out by the reformists, but the economy was greatly favoured. Fiscal responsibility brought about renewed capital inflows, and the Spanish economy started to develop a more complex industrial sector: alongside the traditional consumer goods industries, heavy chemicals and metallurgy appeared, the building trades developed with urban renewal. The banking sector grew and became more modern, helped by increased savings, capital imports, emigrant remittances, and industrial and commercial demand. This development was especially perceptible in the Basque country and Madrid, while in Catalonia the banking sector stagnated (many Catalans blamed 'centralism', symbolised by the Bank of Spain, for this). Even agriculture, retrenched behind high tariff walls, inched ahead in yields and productivity. But this was hardly noticed by public opinion.

Social tensions increased. Strikes and violence, especially in Barcelona, during the First World War and after, created an atmosphere of ungovernability which reached its climax in 1923. That year General Primo de Rivera dissolved the Cortes and inaugurated a dictatorial government which lasted until 1930, and was soon after replaced by the Second Republic.

The republic was seen by a majority as an opportunity to redress all wrongs. It is remarkable how far it went in accomplishing the reformist programme when one considers that its normal life extended for five years and three months, and that of these, two years and two months were spent under conservative, anti-reform governments. Through electoral reform the corrupt voting practices of the Restoration were abolished and suffrage was extended to women. Land reform was finally enacted, the armed forces were overhauled, an ambitious public works programme was approved and initiated, educational reform, already under way since 1902 and widened by the dictatorship, was effectively furthered, and autonomy statutes were granted to Catalonia, the Basque country, and even to Galicia, where nationalist agitation had begun to stir after the First World War. To this must be added advanced social legislation and another old aspiration of the left: clear-cut separation of church and state. All this availed little to the republican regime, or perhaps its ambitious reform programme brought about such hatred from conservatives and soldiers that political dissension combined with economic problems led to civil war.

It would be a mistake, however, to think that the failure of the republic and the tragedy that ensued were due to economic backwardness pure and simple. In the first place, figures show that Spain was one of the European countries least affected by the Great Depression. Second, this first third of the twentieth century was a period of strong economic growth for Spain, with an average annual rate of per capita income growth well above 1 per cent, much higher than in earlier periods and notable also when compared with its European neighbours. The failure of the republic may have been attributable more to the strains of growth and institutional change, combined with a turbulent international situation, than to retardation and inertia.

DICTATORSHIP AND DEMOCRACY

The victory of Franco's rebellion against the legitimate republican government meant the triumph of extreme nationalism. Regional-nationalists were accused of separatism, hence of treason against the fatherland, and severely repressed. The emblem of Falange, the Spanish fascist party, was the yoke and arrows, a symbol used by Ferdinand and Isabella to represent the unity of their five kingdoms: Castile, Leon, Aragon, Granada and Navarre. The Franco regime systematically referred to the glorious reigns of the Catholic Monarchs and of their sixteenth-century successors as the models it intended to follow. But in the long run the repressive franquist policies of extreme Spanish nationalism backfired.

Economic growth continued under Franco after a notoriously long interruption due to the effects of the civil war, the Second World War and the inept economic policies of early franquism, which had self-sufficiency, or autarchy, as its avowed aim. From the mid-1950s, and especially after the stabilisation plan of 1959, whereby a fair measure of liberalisation was introduced in the Spanish economy, growth rates were remarkable: agriculture was rapidly modernised, while industry and the tertiary sector developed rapidly. Economic development solved many problems that had seemed intractable at lower income levels. After the restoration of constitutional monarchy in 1977, old items in the reformists' programme seemed definitely something of the past. Fast growth had produced remarkable social mobility so that, together with the fiscal reform enacted in 1978, more equality prevailed and the old revolutionary, utopian, equalitarian ideas of left-wing republicans also saw their appeal diminished.

Regional nationalisms, however, re-emerged stronger than ever. In Spain at least, these nationalisms do not seem to stem from poverty, but rather the reverse. Catalan and Basque nationalism grew when these regions developed economically (in fact, economic development and industrialisation seem to have transmuted backward, agrarian Carlism into more modern-sounding, urban-industrial nationalism in Catalonia and the Basque country – especially in the latter); furthermore, nationalism has sprouted in Spain's more developed regions. Franquist repression was, of course, a potent tonic for these nationalisms: they could pose as victims of the dictatorship, and also of 'Spanish nationalism' and 'centralism', which became dirty words in the political vocabulary after 1975. So much was the value scale reversed that many considered regional nationalisms as the only legitimate ones.

As a result of all this the new constitution of 1978 recognised the right of 'historical communities and nationalities' to autonomy and self-government. The map was redrawn and Spain divided into seventeen 'autonomous regions', many with little historical, geographical or economic justification. The problem was that (paraphrasing Orwell's *Animal Farm*) all regions were autonomous but some regions had the right to be more autonomous than others. This created invidious, unhealthy competition. 'Non-historical national communities' wanted to have the same degree of autonomy and special treatment as Catalonia and the Basque country. These, in turn, maintain that they should be more autonomous than the others because of their 'historical' rights. Let us make clear that the present degree of autonomy attained by Catalonia and the Basque country (especially the Basque country, which had never been an autonomous political unit), let alone the other fifteen regions, has no historical precedent.

Nevertheless, and contrary to the expectations of the politicians in 1978, more autonomy has brought about more, not fewer demands. Those who demanded, and obtained, autonomy, now demand self-determination. One reason is clear: the autonomous governments have gained control of education, and have used it to issue curricula that have emphasised nationalist values and interpretations. The anti-centralist interpretation of history, the build-up of regional-nationalist mythology and, above all, the imposition of teaching in the regional-national language have been turned into the backbone of education in these communities. Regional-nationalist governments also have an ample share of control of the media in their communities, and make use of it for their purposes. All this has tended to accentuate, not mollify, regional-nationalist demands. It is only logical. Nationalist politicians in power have a vested interest in cultivating this nationalist revindicative spirit, since it is the simplest way of gaining voters. But it is not a question of politicians only: many professionals and public servants gain a competitive edge from regional nationalism. If only Catalan (or Basque) is spoken in the courts, Castilian-speaking lawyers cannot compete with native Catalans (or Basques). The same applies in teaching, the clerical professions, even in business. Nationalism thus becomes one more mechanism to restrain competition. From the nineteenth-century call to preserve the 'national market', regional nationalists have moved to the establishment of their own exclusive markets.

CONCLUSION

Spanish capitalism has a long tradition of corporatism and rent-seeking. We have seen this to have been the case with tariff protection. Spain has been one of the most protectionist countries in Europe. It has a long tradition of mercantilism, already decried by Adam Smith, but able to show more longevity than the Scottish philosopher. Direct state intervention is not the only problem: corporatism has pervaded Spanish society with complex networks of local, professional, customary privileges.[21] After a moderate tide of liberalism in the 1868–91 period, protectionism, corporatism and interventionism returned in force in the twentieth century, and reached their zenith under Franco.[22] Even under Franco, however, the imperatives of economic growth dictated a scaling down of the autarchistic tendencies and some liberalisation after 1959. Spain's full integration into the European Union has taken away from the state many of those traditional levers of control. Tariffs, subsidies (although subsidies granted by national states are still a bone of contention, and although the Brussels bureaucracy has successfully replaced the national states as an intrepid commercial warrior and a largesse-giver), monetary policies, etc., are no longer in the hands of national authorities. For those who want this kind of protection other barriers are needed, and the regional-national states can increasingly dispense them. Micro-nationalism, as a Catalan politician[23] has called it, has a great future.

NOTES

1. E. Belenguer, *Fernando el Católico. Un monarca decisivo en las encrucijadas de su época* (Barcelona, 1999), p. 19.
2. A. Castro, *Sobre el nombre y el quién de los Españoles* (Madrid, 1973), pp. 32–41, 72–86. The word *Español* is the only national designation in Spanish ending in 'ol', a desinence common in Catalan or Provençal.
3. S. Barton, 'The Roots of the National Question in Spain' in M. Teich and R. Porter (eds.), *The National Question in Europe in Historical Context* (Cambridge, 1996), pp. 106–27, at p. 106.
4. A. González Enciso et al., *Historia económica de la España moderna* (Madrid, 1992), pp. 15–17; J. Vicens Vives, *Manual de historia económica de España* (Barcelona, 1959), ch. xv
5. F. Soldevila, *Historia de España*, Volume III (Barcelona, 1954), pp. 93–103.
6. Cited in G. Parker, *Philip II* (Chicago and La Salle, Ill., 1995), p. 159.
7. Whether it was the European demand for Asian commodities or the Asian demand for silver that predominated, as stated by D. Flynn and A. Giráldez, 'China and the Spanish Empire,' *Revista de Historia Económica*, 14, 2 (1996), 309–38 is immaterial to this argument. The fact is that exporting silver to Asia was a very profitable endeavour for European merchants.
8. A. H. de O. Marques, *History of Portugal, Volume I: from Lusitania to Empire* (New York, 1972), pp. 306–17.
9. On seventeenth-century financial problems, see A. Domínguez Ortiz, *Política fiscal y cambio social en la España del siglo XVII* (Madrid, 1984); Domínguez Ortiz, *La sociedad española en el siglo XVII*, Volume VII (Madrid, 1963); J.E. Gelabert, *La Bolsa del rey. Rey, reino y fisco en Castilla (1598–1648)* (Barcelona, 1997); I. Pulido Bueno, *La real hacienda de Felipe III* (Huelva, 1996); F. Ruiz Martín, *Las finanzas de la Monarquía hispánica en tiempos de Felipe IV (1621–1665)* (Madrid, 1990); J.A. Sánchez Belén, *La política fiscal en Castilla durante el reinado de Carlos II* (Madrid, 1996); J. L. Sureda Carrión, *La hacienda castellana y los economistas del siglo XVII* (Madrid, 1949). See also E.J. Hamilton, *El florecimiento del capitalismo y otros ensayos de historia económica* (Madrid, 1948); J.H. Elliott, *Imperial Spain 1469–1716* (New York, 1963); M. Ulloa, *La hacienda real de Castilla en el reinado de Felipe II* (Madrid, 1977); A. García Sanz, 'Desarrollo del capitalismo agrario en Castilla y León en el siglo XIX. Algunos testimonios, algunas reflexiones y un epílogo' in B. Yun Casalilla (ed.), *Estudios sobre capitalismo agrario, crédito e industria en Castilla (siglos XIX y XX)* (Salamanca, 1991); G. Tortella

and F. Comín, 'Fiscal and Monetary Institutions in Spain (1600–1900)' in M. Bordo and R. Cortés Conde (eds.), *The Legacy of the Western European Fiscal and Monetary Institutions for the New World: Seventeenth to Nineteenth Century* (Cambridge, 2001).

10. According to García Sanz, 'Desarrollo del capitalismo', pp. 17–18, fiscal pressure in Castile went from 5 per cent around 1500 to 10 per cent around 1600, and then on to 15 per cent in the first half of the seventeenth century. Then it went down to around 5 per cent in the eighteenth century. See also A. García Sanz, *La ganadería española entre 1750 y 1865: los efectos de la reforma agraria liberal* (unpublished report, 1994), esp. p. 424.

11. Hamilton, *El florecimiento del capitalismo*, pp. 60, 70; Elliott, *Imperial Spain*, esp. p. 154.

12. After 1640 the Catalans had sought French support and some assimilation; the repulsion the French embrace had produced among the Catalans was a relevant factor in weakening their resistance to Castilian troops.

13. R. Nicolau, 'La población española' (Doctoral thesis, University of Barcelona, 1989); J. Benavente, 'La minva de la fecunditat a Catalunya' in F. Cabana i Vancells (ed.), *Història econòmica de la Catalunya contemporània*, Vol. II (Barcelona, 1990); P. Vilar, *La Catalogne dans l'Espagne moderne. Recherches sur les fondements économiques des structures nationales*, 3 vols. (Paris, 1962); J.K.J. Thomson, *A Distinctive Industrialization: Cotton in Barcelona, 1728–1832* (Cambridge, 1992). All this may support Mancur Olson's contention that losing wars is economically healthy: M. Olson, *The Rise and Decline of Nations: Economic Growth, Stagflation, and Social Rigidities* (New Haven, Conn., 1982).

14. For the broad lines of nineteenth- and twentieth-century political and economic developments, see R. Carr, *Spain 1808–1975* (Oxford, 1984); G. Tortella, *The Development of Modern Spain. An Economic History of the Nineteenth and Twentieth Centuries* (Cambridge, Mass., 2000).

15. Tortella and Comín, 'Fiscal and Monetary Institutions', pp. 161–7.

16. C.E. Nuñez, *La fuente en la riqueza. Educación y desarrollo económico en la España contemporánea* (Madrid, 1992), ch. 6.

17. V. Perez Moreda, 'Spain's Demographic Modernization, 1800–1930' in N. Sánchez-Albornoz (ed.), *The Economic Modernization of Spain, 1830–1930* (New York, 1987), pp. 13–41.

18. J. Simpson, *Spanish Agriculture: the Long Siesta, 1765–1965* (Cambridge, 1995), pp. 16–25; P.K. O'Brien and L. Prados de la Escosura, 'Agricultural Productivity and European Industrialization, 1890–1980,' *Economic History Review*, 2nd series, 45, 3 (1992), 514–36.

19. J. Vicens Vives and M. Llorens, *Industrials i politics del segle XIX* (Barcelona, 1961).

20. For a short description of economic policies and events around 1898 and thereafter, see G. Tortella, 'The Role of Banks and Government in Spanish Economic Development, 1850–1935,' in R. Sylla, R. Tilly and G. Tortella (eds.), *The State, the Financial System, and Economic Modernisation* (Cambridge, 1999), pp. 158–81.

21. P. Fraile, *La retórica contra la compentencia en España (1875–1975)* (Madrid, 1998), esp. Part II.

22. For a recent description, see G. Tortella and S. Houpt, 'From Autarky to the European Union: Nationalist Economic Policies in Twentieth-Century Spain' in A. Teichova, H. Matis and J. Pátek (eds.), *Economic Change and the National Question in Twentieth-Century Europe* (Cambridge, 2000), pp. 127–49.

23. A. Vidal-Quadras, 'Los viejos muebles de la familia (una mirada escéptica sobre la fantasía onírica conocida como la Europa de los Pueblos)' in G. Gortázar (ed.), *Visiones de Europa. Análisis de una controversia política* (Madrid, 1994), pp. 107–22.

PART II

CHAPTER 7

The state and economic development in Central and Eastern Europe

David F. Good

INTRODUCTION

The sizeable economic lag of the former Eastern bloc within Europe was a central theme of the cold war and seemed to offer proof of communism's failure as an economic system. Not surprisingly, the collapse of communism over a decade ago sparked euphoria and high expectations that the economic gap soon would begin closing, and then gave way to a more sober recognition of the monumental task confronting post-communist societies.

While some observers are inclined to see the persistence of the economic gap through the 1990s as a legacy of communism, historians of the region know that the issue is far more complicated. When the communists came into power, they inherited economies with already low income levels compared with the West. Indeed, the origins of the region's lag stretch far back into the past, most likely well into the early modern period. However big the gap was in the sixteenth century, it probably did not widen substantially until after the Napoleonic era when economic development accelerated in Britain and other parts of Europe, and Central and Eastern Europe fell increasingly behind. Precisely how much it fell behind and how the gap changed in the century that followed is unclear.

At a deeper level, we understand even less why the lag persisted throughout the twentieth century. Most explanations, at least implicitly, are rooted in an enduring view about the region's political economy: that the economies of Central and Eastern Europe have languished under top-heavy state structures as a legacy of the region's *Sonderweg* or special path to modernisation. Despite a growing body of research against it, this view has remarkable staying power. In this chapter, I present comparative evidence on long-term economic growth and state building in the region for the period 1870 to 1989 that challenges the conventional wisdom on the region's political economy. I conclude by sketching out an alternative explanation for the region's persisting economic lag over the past century that stresses the importance of the discontinuities rather than the continuities in its institutions of political economy.

THE TRADITIONAL VIEW ON STATE AND ECONOMY IN CENTRAL AND EASTERN EUROPE

Older narratives of the region's economic history prior to the First World War focused on the region's fundamentally agrarian structure, the low level of its productive forces, and its increasing lag behind the rest of Europe, especially Prussia and later Germany, as a result of centuries under Habsburg and Ottoman rule.[1] This negative view softened somewhat after the Second World War but still persisted.[2] The older historiography on the inter-war years is equally pessimistic. In the wake of the First World War, the world-wide decline of commodity prices and the Great Depression, the region allegedly suffered from economic instability and stagnation with little change in its fundamental agrarian character and technological lag behind Western Europe.[3] Despite unprecedented rates of growth in the Eastern bloc during the cold war, pessimistic assessments still dominated discussions of economic performance under state socialism.[4] Most centred on the findings that actual growth rates derived from standard (Western) national income accounting methodology were far below the official growth rates reported by planners, not to mention the target rates embedded in the central plans themselves. In addition, observers focused on the early signs of a growth slowdown that spawned the reform movement in the 1950s, and then accelerated in the 1970s.

The older historiography on the economic history of Central and Eastern Europe parallels the much larger and better-known literature on the region's alleged abnormal path to modernisation.[5] According to the traditional view of state building, state structures in early modern Western Europe gradually grew out of and complemented a self-generating socio-economic transfor-mation that ultimately led to the emergence of modern economic growth. In Eastern Europe, the same kind of self-generating socio-economic trans-formation was missing. In order to survive within international competi-tion, states in Eastern Europe were forced to adopt aggressive strategies of modernisation within highly rigid, hierarchical societies. These strategies in turn passed on a legacy of top-heavy state structures that made these societies prone to authoritarian rule. In this sense, the traditional view of state and society in Central and Eastern Europe resembles strongly the older and much-debated notion of Germany's *Sonderweg*. As in Germany, modernisation in Central and Eastern Europe allegedly deviated from the normal path towards democracy and capitalism taken by Britain, France and the United States.[6]

In the Habsburg lands, top-down modernisation seemingly began in earnest with the reforms of Maria Theresa and Joseph II in the eighteenth century.[7] The absence of a successful bourgeois-led social revolution in 1848 represented a missed opportunity to reverse this pattern of political change and led instead to a new round of reforms from above in the 1850s.[8] In the Balkans, too, the newly formed independent states of Bulgaria, Romania and Serbia had sizeable, modern-looking state structures that dominated traditional socio-economic structures.[9] In the inter-war era, the tasks of building new states from the ashes of the First World War, of bringing about post-war economic reconstruction, and of forging national integration demanded a level of state involvement in economic life that transcended the restricted role reserved for it by the prevailing liberal orthodoxy in Western Europe. In the wake of the Great Depression, the state intervened even further as fascist, authoritarian governments supplanted fledgling, conflict-ridden democracies.[10] Through the lens of this *Sonderweg* view, the experience of the former Eastern bloc under state socialism represents the most recent and most rigid incarnation of this long-term pattern of top-down modernisation. Political power was concentrated in the top echelons of the Communist Party, which developed and implemented its strategies for economic and social modernisation within the formal structure of central planning.[11]

The striking parallels in these narratives of economic and political development encourage scholars to link them together, that is, to search for the source of the region's long-term lag behind slow growth and stagnation in its *Sonderweg*. Except for the era of state socialism, this argument has not been articulated in any systematic way, but the general outlines are clear. From the middle of the eighteenth century, the state in Central and Eastern Europe became an instrument of modernisation, but its effectiveness was limited because its sheer size dominated the market economy and tended to snuff out its vitality.

According to this view, before the First World War policies of modernisation promoted economic growth, but the 'primacy of politics' reduced their effectiveness. In the Habsburg empire, for example, the high cost of carrying out the empire's diplomatic and military role as a 'European necessity' in international relations and the growing conflict among the different nationalities meant that political factors rather than economic rationality tended to drive economic policy.[12] In the inter-war period, fascism was capable of producing rapid recovery from the Great Depression, for example, in Nazi Germany, but the primacy of politics ultimately led to irrationalities and inefficiencies.[13] Daniel Chirot argues that the economies of Eastern Europe may have actually performed rather well, but that neo-liberal, less-interventionist policies would have served the region even better.[14] In the communist period, most observers agree that the primacy of politics was especially burdensome. The major source of economic failure in the Eastern bloc lay in the institutional mechanisms of state planning even in its reformed versions. The central plan failed to provide incentives for 'positive-sum' productivity-raising behaviour and was rigid in face of changing external circumstances.[15]

Over the past three decades, a substantial body of research suggests the need for a far more nuanced view of state building and economic development in Central and Eastern Europe than is suggested by the standard literature.

The evidence on economic performance

In this section I draw on collaborative work undertaken with Tongshu Ma[16] to answer two basic questions about the long-term economic development of Central and Eastern Europe: how fast did the economies of Central and Eastern Europe grow over the past century or so? In what sense do the observed rates of growth constitute poor economic performance? Based on a comparative analysis, I conclude that in the era of unusually rapid growth from the late nineteenth century to the present, the economies of Central and Eastern Europe grew impressively, but fell short of their potential.

All international comparisons of income involving historical data confront two main problems – how to convert data from national currencies to a common base to ensure comparability and how to assure reliability in earlier time periods. Angus Maddison's handling of these problems has made his country-level estimates of GDP per capita a staple in such international comparisons and accordingly provide the basis for the data set we used.[17]

These problems are compounded by features that are unique to Central and Eastern Europe. Generating long-term data on national income in the region is especially difficult for the pre-First World War era, when most of it was under imperial (largely Habsburg) rule. To provide firmer foundations, Tongshu Ma and I expanded on my earlier adaptation of a technique that is widely used when national income type data are poor but a wide range of other socio-economic data are available to estimate GDP per capita before the First World War on the territories of the present-day states of the region.[18]

The post-1945 communist era poses a very different kind of problem. The methods used by central planners in the former Eastern bloc greatly overstated actual rates of growth because their output measures involved double counting, exaggerated quality improvements and reflected political influences to a greater degree than was true in the West.[19] We use Maddison's data, which in turn rely on the most thorough reworking of the official data using standard national income methodology.[20]

It is not known how rapidly the economies of Central and Eastern Europe grew from the early modern period through the middle of the nineteenth century, but the Good and Ma data show unequivocally that the region's lag was well entrenched by 1870. In the following discussion, I place the region in a larger comparative context that includes not only the rest of Europe, but also Latin America, which, much like Central and Eastern Europe within Europe, has lagged persistently in the New World behind the United States and Canada.

According to the data in table 7.1, GDP per capita in the region approached levels in north-western Europe only on the territory of present-day Austria[21] and, to a lesser extent, former Czechoslovakia. Moving south and east along the economic gradient, income levels were lower in Hungary, lower still in the Yugoslav lands and in the former Habsburg portions of present-day Poland, Ukraine and Romania, and in the independent state of Bulgaria. In addition, based on the data for 1910, income levels were generally higher in Central and Eastern Europe than in Latin America, except for Argentina whose income level was exceeded in Europe only by the United Kingdom, Switzerland and Belgium.

How rapidly did the economies of Central and Eastern Europe grow after 1870 and how does this performance compare with the rest of Europe and the economies of Latin America? To answer this question, we estimated the growth rates over the entire period 1870–1989 and within three sub-periods set off by the two world wars of the twentieth century: 1870–1914, 1920–38 and 1950–89, the standard periodisation scheme in modern European economic history.

If we take the thesis of economic failure at face value, the estimates of table 7.2 suggest that rates of economic growth in Central and Eastern Europe were surprisingly fast. The region certainly did not stagnate because rates of growth were positive in all three periods. Moreover, in all three periods and over the entire period, the states of the region grew at the European

Table 7.1 *GDP per capita in Europe and Latin America, 1870–1989 (in 1990 Geary-Khamis dollars)*

	GDP per capita					
	1870	1910	1920	1938	1950	1989
North-west						
United Kingdom	3,263	4,715	4,651	5,983	6,847	16,288
Belgium	2,640	3,978	3,878	4,730	5,346	16,299
Netherlands	2,640	3,684	4,117	5,122	5,850	16,024
France	1,858	2,937	3,196	4,424	5,221	17,457
Germany	1,913	3,527	2,986	5,126	4,281	18,015
Switzerland	2,172	4,070	4,256	6,302	8,939	21,381
Nordic						
Denmark	1,927	3,564	3,840	5,453	6,683	17,620
Finland	1,107	1,852	1,792	3,342	4,131	16,676
Norway	1,303	2,052	2,529	3,945	4,969	16,675
Sweden	1,664	2,980	2,802	4,725	6,738	17,593
Mediterranean						
Italy	1,467	2,281	2,530	3,244	3,426	15,650
Portugal	1,085	1,366	902	1,707	2,132	10,355
Spain	1,376	2,096	2,309	2,022	2,397	11,752
Greece	NA	NA	NA	2,727	1,951	10,262
Central/East						
Austria	1,891	3,016	2,428	3,583	3,731	16,305
Czechoslovakia	1,508	2,497	1,933	2,971	3,502	8,729
Hungary	1,180	2,194	1,709	2,655	2,480	6,787
Poland	946	1,690	676	2,182	2,447	5,685
Romania	930	1,661	831	1,242	1,182	3,890
Yugoslavia	864	1,524	1,054	1,360	1,546	5,917
Bulgaria	1,132	1,455	909	1,595	1,651	6,217
East Germany	NA	NA	NA	5,364	3,128	12,530
Latin America						
Argentina	1,311	3,822	3,473	4,072	4,987	6,655
Brazil	740	795	937	1,291	1,673	5,139
Mexico	710	1,435	1,555	1,380	2,085	4,893
Chile	NA	2,472	2,430	3,139	3,827	6,347
Peru	NA	981	1,331	1,757	2,263	3,228
Venezuela	NA	886	1,173	4,144	7,424	7,928
Colombia	NA	NA	NA	1,843	2,089	4,804

Notes: NA: No data available or not applicable.

The GDP per capita data are for the states in their post-1945 boundaries with the following exceptions for the period 1870–1910 only: the data for Bulgaria are for the state in its pre-First World War boundary; the data for Poland and Romania are for the territories of the present-day states that were in the Habsburg empire.

Sources: For north-western, Nordic and Mediterranean Europe, and for Central and Eastern Europe (including Austria) for the period 1920–38 and the periods after the Second World War, the data are from Angus Maddison, *Monitoring the World Economy 1820–1992* (Paris, 1995), Table D-1a. For Central and Eastern Europe, including Austria, for the period 1870–1910 only, the data are revised estimates by Good and Ma, 'New Estimates of Income Levels in Central and Eastern Europe, 1870–1910' in Franz Baltzarek, Felix Butschek and Gunther Tichy (eds.), *Von der Theorie zur Wirtschaftspolitik-ein Österreichischer Weg. Festschrift zum 65. Geburtstag von Erich Streissler* (Stuttgart, 1998), table 7.3, which replace earlier estimates by Good, 'The Economic Lag of Central and Eastern Europe: Income Estimates for the Habsburg Successor States, 1870–1910', *Journal of Economic History*, 54 (1994), 869–91, table 7.3. For Latin America, the data in all periods are from Maddison, *Monitoring the World Economy*, Table D-1d.

Table 7.2 *Long-term economic growth in Latin America and in four regions of Europe, 1870–1989*

	Annual rate of growth in GDP per capita (per cent)			
	1870–1910	1920–38	1950–89	1870–1989
Europe	1.23	2.00	3.23	1.92
North-west	1.19	1.51	2.75	1.64
Nordic	1.32	2.76	3.04	2.12
Mediterranean	0.89	1.97	4.24	2.09
Central/East (A)	1.37	1.99	3.18	1.99
Central/East	1.40	2.22	3.10	1.94
Latin America I	1.55	1.89	1.70	1.76
Latin America II	1.55	0.22	2.40	1.76

Notes: Central/East (A) includes Austria; Central/East excludes Austria. Latin America I includes Argentina, Brazil and Mexico only. Latin America II includes all countries for which data are available.

The regional growth rates and measures of the growth slowdown are calculated from the simple averages of the individual countries in each region.

average. Considering the pessimistic implications of the conventional wisdom and the dramatic changes in the region associated with the two world wars, this seems to be a significant achievement.

Before the First World War, growth may actually have exceeded the average. According to table 7.2, Central and Eastern Europe grew from 1870 to the First World War at a rate that was exceeded only by Latin America[22] and matched in Europe only by the Nordic economies. These results confirm work in the 1970s and 1980s by quantitative economic historians for the lands under Habsburg rule that challenged the received wisdom on the region's economic failure in the pre-1914 period.[23] Between the two world wars, the economies of Central and Eastern Europe grew at the European average: slower than the Nordic, about the same as the Mediterranean, but faster than both the north-west and Latin America. There has been no recent analysis of growth in the region during the inter-war period, but these results, which are based on Maddison's estimates of GDP per capita, are consistent with Chirot's rather positive assessment of growth in the region based on his reading of published data on industrial and agricultural production.[24] Under state socialism, GDP per capita in the region also grew at the European average: slower than the Mediterranean, somewhat faster than the Nordic and the north-west, and considerably faster than Latin America.

Comparing actual rates of economic growth in Central and Eastern
Europe is not an unambiguous standard for judging the region's economic
performance. Growth at the European average from 1870 to 1989 implies
that the region's relative position within Europe remained essentially un-
changed over the long run, which is confirmed by the data on income levels
over time in table 7.1.[25] Both economic theory and economic history suggest that the persisting lag of the region's economies behind higher income
economies gave them the potential to begin closing the gaps and to grow
faster than average. To the extent that they did not grow at this potential,
it can be argued that they performed rather poorly.

A sizeable literature in economics suggests that the scarcity of capital
and low levels of technology in low income economies may enable them to
grow faster than high income economies in a temporary period of catch-
up, which would allow for income levels across regions and nations to
converge over time.[26] Similarly, among economic historians Gerschenkron
has argued that certain advantages of backwardness may have permitted
low income economies in nineteenth-century Europe to engineer a 'great
spurt' of industrial growth, but that a sustained catching-up was in no
way inevitable.[27] Another body of literature suggests that economies may
temporarily experience unusually rapid growth after a sustained period
of slower growth or a sharp downturn in economic activity.[28] Crafts and
Toniolo have applied this kind of analysis to post-1945 growth in Western
Europe, and Dumke has demonstrated econometrically that the size of
shocks induced by the Second World War and the subsequent recoveries
from them account for much of the difference in growth rates among
sixteen OECD countries in the post-1945 era.[29]

In summary, the literature suggests that two key factors should be
taken into account in assessing the long-term economic performance of
economies in a comparative context. All things being equal, economies
that start at lower income levels and experience greater shock-induced declines in output have the potential for temporarily growing faster than
economies that have higher income levels and experience smaller shock-
induced output declines. Table 7.3 shows that as a group the economies of
Central and Eastern Europe did in fact have consistently low income levels
(the lowest of all regions in 1938, and the lowest except for Latin America
in 1870 and 1910) and experienced greater shock-induced output declines
(the steepest of all as a result of the two world wars, and the steepest except
for Latin America in the case of the Great Depression). To the extent that
the region did not exhaust its potential for higher than average growth,

Table 7.3 *Levels of GDP per capita and the severity of shocks in four regions of Europe and in Latin America, 1870–1989 (in 1990 Geary-Khamis dollars)*

	GDP per capita						Shock variables		
	1870	1910	1920	1938	1950	1989	WWI	GD	WWII
Europe	1,643	2,657	2,466	3,586	4,026	13,096	0.89	0.88	1.10
North-west	2,414	3,819	3,847	5,281	6,081	17,577	1.01	0.86	1.14
Nordic	1,500	2,612	2,741	4,366	5,630	17,141	1.05	0.94	1.29
Mediterranean	1,309	1,914	1,914	2,324	2,477	12,005	0.96	0.95	1.05
Central/East (A)	1,207	2,005	1,363	2,227	2,458	8,258	0.65	0.83	1.00
Central/East	1,093	1,837	1,185	2,001	2,277	7,108	0.63	0.84	0.99
Latin America I	920	1,732	1,817	2,518	3,478	5,571	1.14	0.79	1.35
Latin America II	920	2,017	1,988	2,248	2,915	5,562	1.06	0.80	1.34

Notes: Central/East (A) includes Austria. Central and East excludes Austria. Latin America I includes Argentina, Brazil and Mexico only. Latin America II includes all countries for which data are available. The regional levels of GDP per capita are calculated as the simple averages of the individual countries in each region.

The severity of the shocks are calculated as the simple averages of the individual countries from time-series data in the sources described in table 7.1. The measures are defined as follows: WWI: The ratio of GDP per capita in 1920 to 1910; GD: The ratio of GDP per capita in the trough of the Great Depression to the peak of the previous boom; WWII: The ratio of GDP per capita in 1950 to 1938.

then growth at the average with no change in relative income levels seems rather unremarkable.

Ma and I used formal statistical analysis to test whether actual rates of growth in Central and Eastern Europe fell short of the potential as we have defined it.[30] For the pre-First World War era, the analysis shows that the slightly higher than average measured growth from 1870 to 1910 was consistent with the potential inherent in its relatively low incomes in 1870. After accounting for differences in income levels, growth rates were no different in Central and Eastern Europe than elsewhere. By contrast, the results for the inter-war period show that the measured rate of growth in Central and Eastern Europe, which was at the European average, represents a kind of missed opportunity for the region. The region grew below its potential, that is, the rate that was consistent with its income level in 1910 and the output declines associated with both the First World War and the Great Depression. In the post-1945 era, the states of the Eastern bloc grew very rapidly at or near the European average, but this period, too, represents an even more decisive missed opportunity. Growth in the Eastern bloc was well below the rate that was consistent with its low income levels in 1938 and the large declines in output associated with the Second World War.[31] These results for the era of the cold war conform to the pattern for the entire period 1870–1989. Over the long run, Central and Eastern Europe grew below the potential inherent in its low income levels in 1870 (see table 7.4).

In summary, depending on the standard we use to judge growth rates in Central and Eastern Europe, the glass is either half full (the economies grew at the European average in all three periods) or half empty (the economies only grew at their potential before the First World War, that is, at rates that were consistent with their low income levels and steep drops in output in the wake of major shocks). On balance, however, the overly harsh judgements about the region's long-term economic performance that tend to dominate the traditional literature do not seem justified.

The evidence on the Sonderweg thesis

Similarly, recent work by social and political historians has challenged simplistic notions that the absence of the bourgeoisie-led social and political transformations that had occurred in England, France and the United States endowed Central and Eastern Europe with a built-in propensity for authoritarian rule. This newer work shows that state building in the modern sense did not precede socio-economic modernisation in Central and Eastern Europe, but, as in the West, grew along with it. The differences lay in the timing and the cultural context of these changes. Compared with the West, the dual transformation in the East began much later and was more compressed in time, and it occurred in a multinational setting. An important implication is that the tendency towards authoritarian rule in Central and Eastern Europe in the twentieth century, and especially after the Second World War, represents a qualitative break rather than a simple extension of pre-First World War trends.

The key to understanding the new view, according to Diana Mishkova, is to reject typologies of state-building and economic modernisation in Europe that rest on stark qualitative distinctions between West and East.[32] To be sure, state-building and economic development in Europe was marked by regional differences within an overall pattern of broad similarities. Specialists on Europe, of course, tend to focus less on the similarities and more on the differences because they typically have strong regional or national specialisations and rarely do comparative work that includes non-European parts of the world. But if one steps back and compares Europe with most of Asia, Africa and South America, the differences within it seem

Table 7.4 *Long-term economic growth in Europe and Latin America, 1870–1989*

	Annual rate of growth in GDP per capita (per cent)			
	1870–1910	1920–38	1950–89	1870–1989
North-west				
United Kingdom	0.98	1.55	2.13	1.22
Belgium	1.00	0.78	3.07	1.38
Netherlands	0.80	1.48	2.68	1.45
France	1.22	1.32	3.22	1.81
Germany	1.54	2.02	3.35	1.80
Switzerland	1.59	1.89	2.07	2.19
Nordic				
Denmark	1.59	2.10	2.70	1.89
Finland	1.37	3.23	3.57	2.32
Norway	0.96	2.84	3.34	2.19
Sweden	1.37	2.87	2.56	2.09
Mediterranean				
Greece	NA	NA	4.57	NA
Italy	0.96	1.17	3.82	2.00
Portugal	0.65	3.54	4.32	2.36
Spain	1.07	1.19	4.23	1.90
Central/East				
Austria	1.22	0.62	3.77	2.26
Czechoslovakia	1.30	1.59	2.49	1.79
Hungary	1.53	1.87	2.69	1.68
Poland	1.53	4.69	2.53	1.80
Romania	1.42	1.09	3.14	1.59
Yugoslavia	1.35	0.86	4.10	2.10
Bulgaria	1.26	3.20	3.62	2.69
East Germany	NA	NA	3.11	NA
Latin America				
Argentina	2.71	0.38	1.30	1.23
Brazil	0.13	1.59	3.33	2.28
Mexico	1.81	−1.31	2.57	1.79
Chile	NA	1.40	0.94	NA
Peru	NA	2.74	1.31	NA
Venezuela	NA	6.53	0.19	NA
Colombia	NA	NA	2.26	NA

Notes: NA: No data available or not applicable. The growth rates for the individual countries are estimated from a regression of the log of GDP per capita on time that relies on all available data points in the time-series rather than the two end points.
Sources: See table 7.1 for data sources.

rather small and the paths followed by its major regions appear as minor variations on the same theme. As Eric Jones states it:

> Europe was a mutant civilisation in its uninterrupted amassing of knowledge about technology... Despite internal differences in the timing of change, it shared the fact of change and must be treated as an interconnected whole... Nothing is clearer than that the fires of modernisation and industrialisation, once lighted in Britain and Belgium and the Rhineland, burned quickly to the fringes of this European system. Even Russia and the Christian colonies of the Ottoman empire smouldered [and] at the asbestos edge of the Muslim sphere the fires abruptly died.[33]

Although West and East did share the fact of change,[34] due to the relative isolation of Central and Eastern Europe from the full force of the commercial revolution in the late medieval and early modern periods, the peoples of the region entered the modern era not only at low levels of socio-economic development, but also, contrary to the *Sonderweg* narrative, with relatively weak state structures. Without the pull of commercialisation and urbanisation, large peasant populations lived and laboured under the authority of landlords who wielded local power under the 'second serfdom' as part of large-scale, tribute-taking imperial structures. This apparent stability began to erode in the early modern period as imperial authorities found themselves having to compete in a world of increasingly concentrated political and economic power. To ensure survival, they had to institute policies of modernisation along Western European lines.[35]

Partly in response to these policies but also independent of them, a process of increasing social differentiation unfolded in the Habsburg lands from the late eighteenth century to the First World War.[36] As a result of proto-industrialisation in both rural and urban areas in the late eighteenth and early nineteenth centuries, the north-west European pattern of family and household systems – late age of marriage, high incidence of servants, the dominance of nuclear as opposed to the joint family system – prevailed in the western lands of the empire. By contrast, the East European pattern of large household size and fewer joint families dominated the eastern regions, but even here Habsburg border areas seem to have tilted more towards the Western European pattern than neighbouring regions in the Ottoman empire.[37]

These micro-level changes in society form the foundation for the subsequent growth and vitality of civil society, and middle-class politics in the Habsburg lands, especially at the local level, 'says much about a broad process of political modernization in imperial Austria and a gradual democratization of segments of policy-making and administration'.[38] Furthermore, these popular political parties and interest groups had significant impact on policies of the central government during the late imperial period. Both local political elites and ministerial elites tried to figure out how to work with each other either in parliament or in other political settings.

The growth of civil society means that the often-maligned Austrian *Rechtstaat* (state ruled by laws) should not be viewed as an abnormality within Europe. It 'not only served to facilitate the monarchy's transition to the basic forms of modern economic, social, cultural, and political life, but [also] provided an element of stabilizing continuity for the change this process involved'.[39] By embodying both Enlightenment ideas and the time-honoured institution of monarchy, it served to bridge the modern and traditional in state and society and therefore contained the ambiguity that the ruler was both above and subject to the law. This ambiguity and the shifting balance between the modernising and traditional foundations of the *Rechtstaat* are seen in all the major interventions of the state in modern Habsburg history such as the reforms of the mid-eighteenth century and after 1848, and the Compromise of 1867. They are also present in the need for state officials to accommodate the demands of an increasingly mobilised population to achieve the goal of centralising and bureaucratising administrative and fiscal machinery.

State building along modern lines and modern economic growth came even later to the Balkan lands under Ottoman rule than to the lands under Habsburg rule. Mishkova points out that political modernisation in the Balkans started more or less from scratch.[40] Once they came into power, modernising elites in the newly created independent Balkan states looked to the West for institutional models for centralising administrative structures and broadening political participation. The subsequent growth in the state apparatus was enormous, so by the end of the nineteenth century the gap between the Balkans and the countries of Western Europe was much smaller in the case of political modernisation (as measured by the size of the labour force in the public sector, the public sector's taxing capacity, and popular electoral participation), than in the case of economic modernisation. But political modernisation had to precede economic modernisation because the latter depended on the kind of institutional change and developmental infrastructure that only a strong state could provide. In short, if the newly independent Balkan states were to survive, the strategy of 'politics as development' was a matter of necessity not choice.[41]

The second difference between West and East in the dual transformation towards modern state building and modern economic growth is that in the East it occurred in a multinational setting. Some older and newer works on nationalism[42] stress that nation building was inextricably tied to economic and political modernisation. Economic development brings changes in social structure (new classes), the sectoral and spatial composition of production (movement of capital and labour out of agriculture into industry and services, from rural areas into urban areas, from existing industries into new ones), and increased literacy. In the context of late nineteenth-century Central and Eastern Europe, these changes spawned shifting coalitions of economic, political and cultural elites around state-formation and nation-building agendas, and mobilised increasingly large segments of the population around national symbols. Reflecting the different interests of elites and the populations they wished to influence, national identities became strongly contested not only among different national groups but also within the same national group.[43] Because economic development emerged unevenly across regions, national identities were strongly shaped by the socio-economic disparities that accompanied uneven development. These gave rise to explicit strategies and policies of nationalism, which were designed to enhance the power of the nation *vis-à-vis* those who were perceived as outsiders.

In the multinational Habsburg context, of course, vigorous interest group politics was a potentially destabilising force as national identities began to compete with and transcend imperial, regional and social class identities. Perhaps the most visible manifestation of grass-roots political mobilisation in the empire lies in the emergence of self-conscious nation-building agendas after mid-century. A key point to keep in mind is that recent scholarship has dealt a severe blow to the longstanding view that the intense and growing conflict among the subject nationalities in the late Habsburg empire had pushed it to the brink of collapse even before the start of the First World War.[44] Most nationalist leaders spent far more time and energy trying to redistribute income within the empire in favour of their own national group than in developing strategies for dismantling it. On the eve of the First World War, there were no signs of a revolutionary situation that would be a prelude to its imminent collapse.[45] Even during the First World War, the Habsburg military and imperial structure held together remarkably well considering how ill-prepared the empire was for war in 1914 and the brutal and protracted nature of the war itself.[46] In the end, the nationality conflict actually demonstrates the fundamental modernising character of the *Rechtstaat*; the most widely discussed solutions to the nationality problem called for changes in the constitution not radical political change.[47]

Based on this recent research, the path to modernisation in most of Central and Eastern Europe up to the First World War was in large measure 'normal' in the sense that the growth of modern state structures went hand in hand with a profound transformation in economy and society. What made it different was the relatively late appearance of both state building and economic modernisation and its multinational context. It is true, too, that much in the resulting legacy was negative. Many of the post-1919 successor states of the Habsburg empire, for example, inherited sizeable agrarian sectors that were burdened with large inequalities in landholding and low levels of productivity that caused immense economic problems and social conflict after 1919. Levels of income per person in many of them fell below the European average. In addition, the successor states inherited strong traditions of bureaucratic and state centralism that contained some propensity towards authoritarian rule in the region.

But the negative features cannot be viewed in isolation because much of the legacy was positive. As noted earlier, most of the successor states inherited Habsburg territories that had experienced considerable economic growth in the late nineteenth century. None of these societies was by any stretch of the term 'modernised', but in all of them the values and institutional infrastructure associated with modern economic growth were beginning to form – a responsiveness to market opportunities, increasing levels of education, evolving capital markets, etc. The same holds for the political legacy. As Cohen argues, the Habsburg successor states inherited a 'political culture of strong partisan loyalties, vigorous electoral politics, and in many areas the intensive engagement of popular interests in municipal and regional or provincial governmental bodies'.[48] Although these had to compete with and function within bureaucratic traditions of state centralism, this inheritance still provided some foundations for modern political life after the First World War.

Of course, the subsequent history of the region tells us that the positive political legacy was largely dissipated after the First World War as two waves of authoritarian rule swept over much of the region: fascism in the 1930s and communism after 1945. An important implication of the pre-1914 history of the region is that the prevalence of authoritarian rule in Central and Eastern Europe in the twentieth century, and especially after the Second World War, represents a qualitative break rather than a simple extension of pre-First World War trends.

THE EVIDENCE ON THE STATE AND ECONOMIC DEVELOPMENT

The underlying premise of a *Sonderweg* explanation for the persisting economic lag of Central and Eastern Europe within Europe seems to be that authoritarian political regimes promote economic growth less effectively than do democratic regimes. This premise seems to be highly problematic in the light of studies by political scientists. From a theoretical standpoint, the relationship between politics and economic growth can go either way.[49] Regimes under popular control may promote growth more effectively than authoritarian regimes because democratic institutions constrain the predatory behaviour of the state in siphoning off resources for non-productive uses. But autocratic or bureaucratic regimes may actually be more growth-promoting if they insulate decision makers from the kind of rent-seeking behaviour of special interest groups that is typical of democracies or if they can suppress popular demands for current consumption to foster high rates of investment. Using the large amount of data that are available for the post-1945 period, political scientists have tested statistically whether democratic or authoritarian regimes promote growth more. After reviewing eighteen of these studies, Przeworski and Limongi argue that the empirical evidence is inconclusive; it seems clear that political institutions 'do matter for growth' but a continuum running from democracy to authoritarianism 'does not seem to capture the relevant differences'.[50]

In a much more informal way, the Good and Ma growth rate estimates for Central and Eastern Europe and crude generalisations from the region's political history are useful for examining whether the nature of political regimes mattered for economic growth. I characterise states as having stronger or weaker regimes and make comparisons both across and within periods, and both in Central and Eastern Europe, and between the region and the rest of Europe. In judging economic performance, I use two standards: actual rates of economic growth and potential rates of economic growth as defined above. Like the results of Przeworski and Limongi, the evidence here seems inconclusive. Over the past century, there seems to be no systematic relationship between the nature of political regimes in the region and their economic performance.

In the Habsburg lands, the evidence on the growth of civil society and on the importance of market forces rather than the state in economic development[51] suggests that the state was relatively weak before the First World War. By contrast, in the period between the wars the losses and physical destruction of the war, the creation of successor states out of the ruins of imperial collapse, the persistence of pre-war social conflict into the 1920s necessarily called forth an increasingly interventionist state.[52] The post-1945 era saw the emergence of the strong regimes in face of their weak civil societies and centrally planned economies.

If we compare the region's growth rates across these periods, the evidence seems to support the virtues of a stronger rather than a weaker state. Growth was slowest (1.4 per cent) in the Habsburg era of the weak state, fastest (3.1 per cent) in the communist era of strong authoritarian rule, and modest (2.0 per cent) in the inter-war era of the interventionist, but not dominant state. By contrast, a comparison of growth rates in the region with the rest of Europe across these same periods, suggests the benefits of a weaker rather than a stronger state. Although the states in the region grew more or less at the European average in all three periods, the Good and Ma analysis shows that they grew at the potential inherent in their lower income levels in the era of the weak state before 1914, but lower than its potential in the eras of the interventionist state between the world wars, and the authoritarian state after 1945.

If we examine the relationship between the character of political regimes and economic growth within Central and Eastern Europe, the evidence is just as inconclusive. After 1867, the Habsburg empire was composed of two relatively autonomous states, Austria and Hungary, which were bound together in the person of the emperor as a customs and monetary union with a common military and foreign policy. Of the two, the Hungarian state was in some sense stronger because its civil society was less developed, and its economic policy was shaped by the Hungarian elites who dominated both state agencies and Parliament at the expense of the relatively weak non-Hungarian nationalities.[53] By contrast, the Austrian state was weaker because its civil society was more developed, and its economic policy less purposeful as a product of intense bargaining among the three main national elites, the Germans, the Czechs and the Poles. Between 1870 and 1910, Hungary grew at 1.45 per cent and Austria at 1.25 per cent, which suggests the virtue of a stronger rather than a weaker state. The advantage disappears, however, if we take into account Hungary's relatively low income levels. Hungary's more rapid growth compared with Austria may not be the result of its more activist state, but simply a function of its relatively low income levels, which gave it greater inherent potential for catch-up.

With the exception of Czechoslovakia, all of the newly formed successor states gravitated towards authoritarian rule in the 1930s. Judging from the gap between actual and potential growth, the region's more interventionist states may have been harmful. Within the region, however, a less interventionist state in Czechoslovakia brought no apparent advantage to the economy. Its rate of growth from 1920 to 1938 (1.59 per cent) stood at the median of seven countries in Central and Eastern Europe: faster than Austria (0.62 per cent), Yugoslavia (0.86 per cent) and Romania (1.09 per cent), but slower than Poland (4.69 per cent), Bulgaria (3.20 per cent) and Hungary (1.87 per cent). Also, with respect to achieving its potential,

Czechoslovakia did relatively better than Austria, Romania and Yugoslavia, but worse than Poland, Hungary and Bulgaria.

Within post-Second World War Central and Eastern Europe, there was considerable variation in the extent to which states adhered to the Soviet model. Austria, at the heart of Central Europe before the Second World War, was not in the communist orbit at all so, despite its sizeable state sector and *Proporz* democracy, its civil society was far less dominated by the state than any country in the Eastern bloc.[54] Within the Eastern bloc, Poland, Yugoslavia and Hungary tended to be more reformist and deviated most from the rigid Soviet model, while Czechoslovakia, Romania and Bulgaria adhered more to the Soviet model.[55]

As in the case of inter-war Europe, the countries of the Eastern bloc grew in the post-Second World War era at the European average, which suggests that their strong states were not a drag on economic growth, but they also grew below their potential, which suggests that they hindered growth. Comparative growth rates within Central and Eastern Europe, especially if the region is defined to include Austria, are just as inconclusive. The Good and Ma data show no systematic relationship between regime type and economic growth. In the period 1950–73, 'Stalinist' Bulgaria (5.14 per cent) actually stood at the top of the growth league while reformist Yugoslavia (4.79 per cent) and market-oriented Austria (4.48 per cent) ranked second and third respectively. Not far behind was Stalinist Romania (4.66 per cent), reformist Hungary (3.60 per cent) and reformist Poland, with Stalinist Czechoslovakia (3.24 per cent) last. If we examine actual performance relative to potential, only democratic Austria actually grew at least as fast as the potential inherent in its 1938 income level and its output decline in the Second World War, while the countries of the Eastern bloc did not. Within the Eastern bloc, however, Bulgaria and Romania (strong regimes) and reformist Yugoslavia grew closer to potential than did reformist Hungary and reformist Poland, which fell way short of the potential inherent in their 1938 levels of income and sharp drops in output during the Second World War.

RETHINKING STATE AND ECONOMY IN CENTRAL AND EASTERN EUROPE

At the heart of the traditional view on state building in Central and Eastern Europe is the idea that strong states are constants in the region's history. To some extent, this is true and it is useful to focus on this continuity, but it is also very misleading. For the twentieth century, the striking thing about the region's history is not the continuity of the region's political and economic institutions but their vulnerability in the wake of major shocks. The impact of the two world wars went far beyond the destruction of human life, capital equipment and infrastructure that typically follows military clashes. These shocks led to large-scale efforts by elites to reinvent institutions and ideology that were far more profound in Central and Eastern Europe than elsewhere. Prior to the First World War, local elites in the region used ethnic symbols and appeals to mobilise local populations in the context of uneven economic development but, at least in the lands under Habsburg rule, political mobilisation occurred within a largely stable set of institutional arrangements. After the First World War, the Paris peace treaties fundamentally redrew the map of the region, which brought disruptions in financial and labour markets, and in legal structures, as new states came into existence. Elites spent the next two decades adapting existing institutions to the new set of international realities.

The Second World War resulted in institutional discontinuities of a different kind. As in the case of the First World War, institutional arrangements were disrupted by some territorial realignments, but this occurred on a relatively modest scale. The major shock to institutions was an indirect result of the war, that is, occupation by the Soviet Union. By 1950, modernising elites were promoting state socialism on the Soviet model as an answer to the discredited models of development in inter-war Europe – fascism and liberal capitalism. They spent the next three decades implementing and fine-tuning this systemic transformation in the context of the cold war. After 1989, the erosion and sudden collapse of the Soviet Union launched a new era of institutional change whose scale and scope matched the previous post-1945 systemic transformation to communism.

A growing literature in political science and economics suggests that the costs of these frequent large-scale, ongoing transformations in Central and Eastern Europe were large.[56] First, the uncertainty surrounding them would have created disincentives for individuals and economic elites to undertake productivity-raising investments in physical and human capital and to respond flexibly to rapid change. Second, resources that would have gone directly into production would have gone towards restructuring or creating new institutional arrangements. Third, the contested nature of each new order would have led to rent-seeking behaviour by elites around competing models of economic and political modernisation. After each successive regime change, new institutional arrangements and the policies of modernisation they supported fostered much of the impressive growth that occurred in the wake of these shocks, but the dramatic shifts in the nature of these regimes as much as flaws in the regimes themselves may account for the failure of the states in the region to grow at their potential and begin catching up with the rest of Europe.

CONCLUSION

In the light of research over the past three decades, this chapter has challenged the traditional view of state building and economic development in Central and Eastern Europe. It ends by sketching out an alternative approach for explaining the persistence of the region's economic lag. There are three main conclusions. First, how we judge long-term economic performance in Central and Eastern Europe depends on the standards we use. In the era of unusually rapid growth among the now developed economies from the late nineteenth century to the present, the economies of Central and Eastern Europe grew impressively, but fell short of their potential. Second, contrary to the *Sonderweg* view, state building in the modern sense did not precede socio-economic modernisation in Central and Eastern Europe, but, as in the West, grew along with it. The differences between East and West lay in the timing and the cultural context of these changes. Compared with the West, the dual transformation in the East began much later and was more compressed in time, and it occurred in a multinational setting. An important implication is that the prevalence of authoritarian rule in Central and Eastern Europe in the twentieth century, and especially after the First World War, represents a qualitative break rather than a simple extension of pre-First World War trends. Third, from a theoretical point of view, both democratic and autocratic regimes are capable of promoting economic growth. The historical evidence on growth in Central and Eastern Europe confirms studies by political scientists on the post-1945 period. Over the past century, there seems to be no systematic relationship between the nature of political regimes in the region and their economic performance.

The key to understanding the persistence of the region's economic lag lies in the discontinuities as much as in the continuities of the region's history. The shocks of the two world wars and the Great Depression of the twentieth century led to more profound changes in political and economic institutions in Central and Eastern Europe than elsewhere in Europe. New institutional arrangements and the policies of modernisation they supported account for much of the impressive growth that occurred in the wake of these shocks, but the periodic shifts in the nature of these regimes as much as flaws in the regimes themselves may account for the failure of the states in the region to grow at their potential in the twentieth century. At this point, my argument remains a hypothesis that deserves careful scrutiny.

NOTES

The author wishes to thank the German Marshall Fund of the United States for the fellowship that supported the creation and analysis of the data set used in this chapter.

1. See, for example, Friedrich Hertz, *Die Produktionsgrundlagen der österreichischen Industrie vor und nach dem Kriege, insbesonders im Vergleich mit Deutschland* (Vienna, 1917); Oscar Jaszi, *The Dissolution of the Habsburg Monarchy* (Chicago, 1961); David Mitrany, *The Effect of the War in Southeastern Europe* (New Haven, Conn., 1936).

2. See Eduard März, 'Die wirtschaftliche Entwicklung der Donaumonarchie im 19. Jahrhundert. Gedanken zu einem neuen Buch von David F. Good', *Wirtschaft und Gesellschaft*, 11, 3 (1985), 367–92, and Wilhelm Weber, *Österreichs Wirtschaftsstruktur: gestern, heute, morgen* (Berlin, 1961), but also the more widely read works of Alexander Gerschenkron, *Economic Backwardness in Historical Perspective: a Book of Essays* (New York, 1962) and *An Economic Spurt that Failed: Four Lectures in Austrian History* (Princeton, 1977); and W.W. Rostow, *The Process of Economic Growth* (New York, 1962).

3. See Leo Pasvolsky, *Economic Nationalism of the Danubian States* (London, 1928); Iván T. Berend and György Ránki, *Economic Development in East-Central Europe in the Nineteenth and Twentieth Centuries* (New York and London, 1974); Doreen Warriner, *Economics of Peasant Farming* (London, 1964); Paul N. Rosenstein-Rodan, 'Problems of Industrialisation of Eastern and South-Eastern Europe', *Economic Journal*, 53, 210/11 (1943), 202–11; Mitrany, *The Effect of the War in Southeastern Europe*.

4. Typical of these studies are Abhijit V. Banerjee and Michael Spagat, 'Productivity Paralysis and the Complexity Problem: Why Do Centrally Planned Economies Become Prematurely Gray?', *Journal of Comparative Economics*, 15 (1991), 646–60; Abram Bergson, *Productivity and the Social System: the USSR and the West* (Cambridge, Mass., 1978); Peter Murrell, *The Nature of Socialist Economies: Lessons from Eastern European Foreign Trade* (Princeton, 1990).

5. For an excellent summary of these views, see Diana Mishkova, 'Modernization and Political Elites in the Balkans before the First World War', *East European Politics and Societies*, 9, 1 (1995), 63–89.

6. On Germany, see David Blackbourn and Geoff Eley, *The Peculiarities of German History: Bourgeois Society and Politics in Nineteenth-Century Germany* (Oxford, 1984). In the case of Habsburg Central and Eastern Europe, see Gary B. Cohen, 'Neither Absolutism nor Anarchy: New Narratives on Society and Government in Late Imperial Austria', *Austrian History Yearbook*, 29, 1 (1998), 37–61; Pieter Judson, *Exclusive Revolutionaries: Liberal Politics, Social Experience, and National Identity in the Austrian Empire, 1848–1914* (Ann Arbor, 1996); James Shedel, 'Fin de Siècle or *Jahrhundertwende*:

Modernization and the Austrian Sonderweg' in Steven Beller (ed.), *Rethinking Vienna 1900* (New York, 1995), pp. 80–104.

7. John Komlos, *Stature, Nutrition, and Economic Development in the Eighteenth-Century Habsburg Monarchy: the 'Austrian' Model of the Industrial Revolution* (Princeton, 1990); Herbert Matis (ed.), *Von der Glückseligkeit des Staates. Staat, Wirtschaft und Gesellschaft in Österreich im Zeitalter des aufgeklärten Absolutismus* (Berlin, 1981).

8. On the failure of 1848, see Jaszi, *The Dissolution of the Habsburg Monarchy*; A.J.P. Taylor, *The Habsburg Monarchy 1809–1918* (Chicago, 1948); Erich Zöllner, *Geschichte Österreichs: von den Anfängen bis zur Gegenwart* (Vienna, 1979). On the reforms of the 1850s, see Herbert Matis, *Österreichs Wirtschaft. Konjunkturelle Dynamik und gesellschaftlicher Wandel im Zeitalter Franz Josephs I* (Berlin, 1972); Eduard März, *Österreichische Industrie- und Bankpolitik in der Zeit Franz Josephs I* (Vienna, 1968).

9. John Lampe and Marvin Jackson, *Balkan Economic History 1550–1950: From Imperial Borderlands to Developing Nations* (Bloomington, Ind., 1982); Gale Stokes, *Politics as Development: the Emergence of Political Parties in Nineteenth-Century Serbia* (Durham, N.C., 1990).

10. G. Ránki and J. Tomaszewski, 'The Role of the State in Industry, Banking and Trade' in M.C. Kaser and E.A. Radice (eds.), *The Economic History of Eastern Europe 1919–1975* (Oxford, 1985).

11. Iván T. Berend, *Central and Eastern Europe 1944–1993: Detour from the Periphery to the Periphery* (Cambridge, 1996); Paul Johnson, *Redesigning the Communist Economy: the Politics of Economic Reform in Eastern Europe* (Boulder, Colo., 1989).

12. On international relations, see Thomas Huertas, *Economic Growth and Economic Policy in a Multinational Setting* (New York, 1977), pp. 36–50; Paul Kennedy, *The Rise and Fall of the Great Powers* (New York, 1987), pp. 162–6. On the impact of national conflict, see Gerschenkron, *An Economic Spurt that Failed*.

13. Charles Maier, *In Search of Stability: Explorations in Historical Political Economy* (Cambridge, 1987), pp. 70–120.

14. Daniel Chirot, 'Ideology, Reality, and Competing Models of Development in Eastern Europe Between the Two World Wars', *East European Politics and Society*, 3, 3 (1989), 378–411.

15. See, for example, Murrell, *The Nature of Socialist Economies*.

16. David F. Good and Tongshu Ma, 'The Economic Growth of Central and Eastern Europe in Comparative Perspective, 1870–1989', *European Review of Economic History*, 3, 2 (1999), pp. 103–37.

17. Angus Maddison, *Monitoring the World Economy 1820–1992* (Paris, 1995). Maddison starts with 1990 estimates of income per capita, which, following the methodology of the International Comparison Project (Irving Kravis, Allan Heston and Robert Summers, 'Real GNP Per Capita for More than One Hundred Countries', *Economic Journal*, 88 (1978), 215–42; Irving Kravis, 'The Three Faces of the International Comparison Project', *Research Observer*, 1

(1986), 1–26; Robert Summers and Alan Heston, 'A New Set of International Comparisons of Real Product and Price Levels: Estimates for 130 Countries, 1950–1985', *The Review of Income and Wealth*, 34 (1988), 1–25), relies on purchasing power parities rather than exchange rates to convert GNP in different national currencies into a single currency, and then creates a time-series by projecting these levels back at growth rates derived from the work of country specialists.

18. David F. Good, 'The Economic Lag of Central and Eastern Europe: Income Estimates for the Habsburg Successor States, 1870–1910', *Journal of Economic History*, 54 (1994), 869–91; David F. Good and Tongshu Ma, 'The Economic Growth of Central and Eastern Europe in Comparative Perspective 1870–1989' (unpublished paper, 1998); Good and Ma, 'The Economic Growth of Central and Eastern Europe'. Along the lines of N.F.R. Crafts (Crafts, 'Gross National Product in Europe 1870– 1910: Some New Estimates', *Explorations in Economic History*, 20, 4 (1983), 387–401), we used data for seven benchmark years between 1850 and 1910 and for twelve European countries with reasonably good national income data to estimate a structural equation where Gross Domestic Product per capita is a function of several proxy variables. Assuming that this structural equation holds for Central and Eastern Europe, we used its coefficients to estimate incomes from proxy data for the Habsburg regions and successor states, and for the independent Balkan states for key benchmark years.

19. Maddison, *Monitoring the World Economy*; Paul Marer, Janos Arvay, John O'Conner, Martin Schrenk and Daniel Swanson, *Historically Planned Economies: a Guide to the Data* (Washington, DC, 1992), p. 264; Frederic L. Pryor, 'Growth and Fluctuations of Production in OECD and East European Countries', *World Politics*, 37 (1985), 204–37.

20. Thad P. Alton, 'Economic Growth and Resource Allocation in Eastern Europe' (Washington, DC, 1974); Alton, 'East European GNPs: Origins of Product, Final Uses, Rates of Growth, and International Comparisons' (Washington, DC, 1985); Alton, 'East European GNP by Origin and Domestic Final Uses of Gross Product, 1965–1984', Research Project on National Income in East Central Europe (Washington, DC, 1985).

21. Austria clearly belonged to Central and Eastern Europe under Habsburg rule and in the inter-war era. We provide two sets of estimates for income levels and growth rates in Central and Eastern Europe: one that includes and one that excludes Austria in the three periods. In the formal analysis of growth rates, I include Austria in Central and Eastern Europe in the pre-First World War and inter-war periods, but not after 1945. Austria's '*Anschluss*' with Germany between 1938 and 1945 and its evolution outside the Eastern bloc until 1989 in no small measure overwhelmed the longstanding cultural, political, social and economic ties that bound it inextricably to the region prior to the Second World War.

22. Based on data available for three countries only, two of which – Argentina and Mexico – experienced exceptionally high growth.

23. David F. Good, *The Economic Rise of the Habsburg Empire, 1750–1914* (Berkeley, Calif., 1984); John Komlos, *The Habsburg Monarchy as a Customs Union: Economic Development in Austria-Hungary in the Nineteenth-Century* (Princeton, 1983); Richard Rudolph, *Banking and Industrialization in Austria-Hungary* (Cambridge, 1976). Scholarship on the independent Balkan states adopts a more pessimistic view of economic growth in that part of the region; see John Lampe and Marvin Jackson, *Balkan Economic History 1550–1950: From Imperial Borderlands to Developing Nations* (Bloomington, Ind., 1982); Michael Palairet, *The Balkan Economies c. 1800–1914: Evolution without Development* (Cambridge, 1997). Also, Schulze's recent estimates of growth in GDP per capita for pre-First World War Austria and Hungary using national income methodology lead to somewhat lower estimates of growth compared with those of Good and Ma, which are based on the proxy method; see Max-Stefan Schulze, 'Patterns of Growth and Stagnation in the Late Nineteenth Century Habsburg Economy', *European Review of Economic History*, 4, 3 (2000), 311–40.

24. Chirot, 'Ideology'.

25. The rest of this section draws on Good and Ma, 'The Economic Growth of Central and Eastern Europe'. See original source for details.

26. Robert Solow, 'A Contribution to the Theory of Growth', *Quarterly Journal of Economics*, 70, 1 (1956), 65–94; Robert J. Barro, *Determinants of Growth: a Cross-Country Empirical Study* (Cambridge, Mass., 1997).

27. Gerschenkron, *Economic Backwardness in Historical Perspective*.

28. The idea is inherent, of course, in business cycle theories, but also in theories that posit cycles of a longer-term nature. See Nikolai D. Kondratieff, 'The Long Waves in Economic Life', *Review of Economics and Statistics*, 17, 6 (1935), 105–15; Simon Kuznets, *Economic Growth and Structure: Selected Essays* (New York, 1965), pp. 1–8, 328–78; Joseph A. Schumpeter, 'The Analysis of Economic Change', *Review of Economics and Statistics*, 17, 4 (1935), 2–10.

29. Nicholas Crafts and Gianni Toniolo (eds.), *Economic Growth in Europe since 1945* (Cambridge, 1996); Rolf H. Dumke, 'Reassessing the Wirtschaftswunder: Reconstruction and Postwar Growth in an International Context', *Bulletin of Economics and Statistics*, 52 (1990), 451–90.

30. We specified a formal model in which the rate of growth in GDP per capita in a given time period is a function of three variables – the relative economic lag, the severity of shocks, and a 'dummy' variable that tests for regional effects – and used regression analysis to estimate it for economies in both Europe and Latin America. The sign and significance level of the coefficients on each regional variable indicate whether the region's rate of economic growth differed significantly from that of the countries in north-western and Nordic Europe given its relative income levels and the relative severity of shocks.

31. The Good and Ma results differ from those in Frederic L. Pryor, 'Growth and Fluctuations of Production', which concludes that after accounting for differences in initial levels of income, growth rates in post-1945 Eastern European economies were not slower. Apart from differences in underlying data, his results are not strictly comparable with ours. His sample of Western countries

included all OECD countries, not just European members, and his sample of Eastern European countries included the Soviet Union. Also, he did not include a war shock variable in his regressions.

32. Mishkova, 'Modernization and Political Elites'. For the older view, see Andrew Janos, 'The Politics of Backwardness in Central Europe, 1780–1945', *World Politics*, 41, 3 (April, 1989), 325–58; Peter Sugar, 'Continuity and Change in Eastern European Authoritarianism: Autocracy, Fascism, and Communism', *East European Quarterly*, 18, 1 (1984), 1–23.
33. Eric L. Jones, *The European Miracle* (Cambridge, 1981), pp. 45–6.
34. Mishkova, 'Modernization and Political Elites'.
35. Komlos, *Stature, Nutrition, and Economic Development*; Herbert Matis (ed.), *Von der Glückseligkeit des Staates*.
36. James O. Brown and Markus Cerman, 'The Social History of the Family in the Territories of the Austrian Monarchy', *Austrian History Yearbook*, 29, 1 (1998), 265–88.
37. Karl Kaser, 'The Balkan Joint Family', *Social Science History*, 18, 2 (1994), 243–69.
38. Cohen, 'Neither Absolutism nor Anarchy', p. 55. See in particular, Gary B. Cohen, *Education and Middle-Class Society in Imperial Austria* (West Lafayette, Ind., 1996) on the growth of education; John W. Boyer, *Political Radicalism in Late Imperial Vienna: Origins of the Christian Social Movement, 1848–1897* (Chicago, 1981) and *Culture and Political Crisis in Vienna: Christian Socialism in Power, 1897–1918* (Chicago, 1995) on the Christian Social movement in municipal-level politics in Vienna; Pieter Judson, *Exclusive Revolutionaries: Liberal Politics, Social Experience, and National Identity in the Austrian Empire, 1848–1914* (Ann Arbor, 1996) and Lothar Höbelt, *Kornblume und Kaiseradler. Die deutsch freiheitlichen Parteien Altösterreichs 1882–1918* (Munich, 1993) on associational life and local-level politics among German liberals and nationalists; and Catherine Albrecht, 'Pride in Production: the Jubilee Exhibition of 1891 and Economic Competition between Czechs and Germans in Bohemia', *Austrian History Yearbook*, 24 (1993), 101–18; Catherine Albrecht, 'The Rhetoric of Economic Nationalism in the Bohemian Boycott Campaigns of the Late Habsburg Monarchy', *Austrian History Yearbook*, 32 (2001), 47–67; T. Mills Kelly, 'Taking it to the Streets: Czech National Socialists in 1908', *Austrian History Yearbook*, 29 (1998), 93–112; Claire E. Nolte, ' "Every Czech a Sokol!": Feminism and Nationalism in the Czech Sokol Movement', *Austrian History Yearbook*, 24 (1993), 79–100; and Keely Stauter-Halstead, 'Patriotic Celebrations in Austrian Poland: the Kosciuszko Centennial and the Formation of Peasant Nationalism', *Austrian History Yearbook*, 25 (1994), 79–95, on national movements and national politics.
39. Shedel, '*Fin de Siècle*', pp. 97–8.
40. Mishkova, 'Modernization and Political Elites'.
41. Ibid. The term 'politics as development' is Gale Stokes, *Politics as Development*.
42. See, for example, Karl Deutsch, *Nationalism and Social Communication* (Cambridge, Mass., 1966); Ernst Gellner, *Nationalism* (New York, 1997).

43. Albrecht, 'Pride in Production'; Albrecht, 'Rhetoric of Economic Nationalism'; Kelly, 'Taking it to the Streets'; Nolte, ' "Every Czech a Sokol!" '; Stauter-Halstead, 'Patriotic Celebrations'; Pieter Judson, ' "Not Another Square Foot!" German Liberalism and the Rhetoric of National Ownership in Nineteenth-Century Austria', *Austrian History Yearbook*, 26 (1995), 83–97.

44. See especially, Jaszi, *The Dissolution of the Habsburg Monarchy*; Taylor, *The Habsburg Monarchy*.

45. Samuel R. Williamson, jr., *Austria-Hungary and the Origins of the First World War: the Making of the twentieth Century* (Basingstoke, Hampshire, 1991); Istvan Deak, *Beyond Nationalism: a Social and Political History of the Habsburg Officer Corps* (Oxford, 1990), pp. 190–204; Alan Sked, *The Decline and Fall of the Habsburg Empire, 1815–1918* (London, 1989).

46. Deak, *Beyond Nationalism*, pp. 190–204.

47. Shedel, 'Fin de Siècle', pp. 23–4.

48. Cohen, 'Neither Absolutism nor Anarchy', p. 45.

49. Adam Przeworski and Fernando Limongi, 'Political Regimes and Economic Growth', *Journal of Economic Perspectives*, 7 (1993), 51–69.

50. Ibid., 51.

51. See Scott Eddie, 'Economic Policy and Economic Development in Austria-Hungary, 1867–1913', *The Cambridge Economic History of Europe*, Volume VIII (Cambridge, 1989), 814–86; Komlos, *The Habsburg Monarchy as a Customs Union*; Thomas F. Huertas, *Economic Growth and Economic Policy in a Multi-national Setting: the Habsburg Monarchy, 1841–1865* (New York, 1977).

52. Chirot, 'Ideology'; Alice Teichova, 'East-Central and South-East Europe, 1919–1939', *Cambridge Economic History of Europe*, Volume 8 (Cambridge, 1989), ch. 13, 887–983; Ránki and Tomaszewski, 'The Role of the State'.

53. On civil society in Hungary, see András Gerö, *The Hungarian Parliament, 1867–1918: a Mirage of Power* (Boulder, Colo., 1997); Gerö, *Modern Hungarian Society in the Making: the Unfinished Experience* (Budapest, 1990). On elites, see Eddie, 'Economic Policy'.

54. Anton Pelinka, *Austria: Out of the Shadow of the Past* (Boulder, Colo., 1998).

55. See discussion in Derek H. Aldcroft and Steven Morewood, *Economic Change in Eastern Europe since 1918* (Aldershot, 1995); Berend, *Central and Eastern Europe*; Paul Johnson, *Redesigning the Communist Economy*.

56. Clemens L.J. Sierman, *Politics, Institutions, and the Economic Performance of Nations* (Cheltenham, and Northampton, Mass., 1998).

CHAPTER 8

Concepts of economic integration in Austria during the twentieth century

Ernst Bruckmüller and Roman Sandgruber

THE ECONOMY AND THE NATIONAL PROBLEM OF THE LATE HABSBURG EMPIRE

In Austrian history a particularly contradictory development can be observed. On the one hand, the various provinces of the Habsburg monarchy became part of one economy in the course of the nineteenth century. On the other hand, nationalist movements, based mainly on common language or national consciousness, arose about the same time. They strongly ran counter to the collective consciousness of belonging to a common state. Although these movements were not always disloyal to the monarchy, they developed very different ideas about the economy that only partly went along with the existence of the customs union of 1850.[1] For example, the Hungarian Independence Party called not only for sovereignty of the Hungarian state, but also for economic independence, which mainly meant protective duties for Hungarian industry and a separate Hungarian customs area.[2] Also Austrian agriculturists demanded a customs division between Austria and Hungary, in order to protect themselves against the strong competition of Hungarian agriculture.[3]

Nevertheless, the customs union had existed before and continued to exist after the Austro-Hungarian Compromise of 1867. Therefore, trade agreements were negotiated and signed by the common imperial and royal foreign ministry. The *Zoll- und Handelsbündnis* (customs and trading union) and the monetary union obviously were in the interest of the dominant economic and social groups of the 1860s, which consisted of Hungarian agrarian big business and Austrian industry (mainly German-Bohemian, German-Moravian and Lower Austrian).[4] As the customs and trading union was not part of the unchangeable articles of the two laws of the Compromise it had to be renegotiated every ten years.[5] The negotiations about renewals were usually accompanied by fervent discussions, since not only economic issues were at stake, but also 'the quota', i.e. the amount which both parts had to pay for their common affairs in the following decade (about 95 per cent of which was for the army).

The Austro-Hungarian Compromise of 1867 did not manage to appease nationalist thinking in politics and trade. Only the radical Hungarian Independence Party lost its importance for some time. Most of the Slavic people of both halves of the empire were disappointed by this agreement, in particular the Czechs. Their programme of the late 1860s, the *Fundamentalartikel*, did not contain any special economic separation from the rest of the monarchy.[6] However, certain economic activities, for example the foundation of industrial and agricultural credit co-operatives, were considered to be a programmatic part of a particular 'national' movement since the 1870s. These credit co-operatives were usually founded in a language-national context. Economic progress was considered to be part of national emancipation.[7] As nationalism was becoming ever more radical in the 1880s and 1890s new slogans soon predominated: '*Kauft nur bei Deutschen!*' – '*Kauft nur bei Tschechen!*' – '*Jeder zu den Seinen!*' – '*Sv ůj k svému*' (Everyone to his own kind). This meant that a Czech should only have economic contact with a Czech, a German with a German, a Slovenian with a Slovenian and altogether they should not have any contact with Jews.[8] These requests were, of course, only partly followed. Still, such slogans symbolised the beginning of economic and social segregation of the rising national communities within the monarchy, which clearly saw a radicalisation after the Badeni riots in 1897.[9]

The economic impact of these movements of economic nationalism is still a matter of debate.[10] Contemporaries often claimed that national discordance was a hindrance to economic growth. Also difficult to prove is the validity of Stephan Koren's observation that ethnic and cultural diversities led to differing patterns of demand,[11] which tended to obstruct mass production on a larger scale. In various Slavic countries people became convinced that Viennese capital was 'foreign' capital. This is evidence of a growing mental disintegration between the nationalities, which began to influence the economy as well.

COMMON MARKET AND NATIONAL (DIS-)INTEGRATION

It is unclear whether the common market led to economic integration. On the one hand, we see trends towards an equalisation of prices in different parts of the monarchy.[12] On the other hand, we get the impression that peripheral regions such as Dalmatia, Croatia, Galicia or the Bukovina could not benefit from the economic growth of the developed and central regions. And the latter were unable to integrate the mass of agricultural population leaving the peripheral regions. Most of them finally emigrated to Germany or to the USA.[13] It seems that there was not enough impetus in the centres to develop the periphery of the empire. This observation contrasts remarkably with the reality that the Habsburg monarchy was relatively little integrated into the world market, because the economic areas of the monarchy complemented each other.[14] Indeed, the export of Hungarian agricultural products was directed to the western part of the monarchy, and this orientation increased in the course of time.[15] Hungary itself was the preferred market for Austrian capital exports, which were largely responsible for the notable economic growth in Hungary from the 1880s.[16]

It is ascertainable that economic integration of both parts of the monarchy was increasing continuously until 1900. At the same time, however, symptoms of social segregation between self-integrated national communities appeared. Entrepreneurs often warned of integral nationalism and disapproved of appeals to boycott each other.[17] On the German side admonitions appeared to avoid an intensification of national conflicts.[18] Would a higher degree of development of 'national' economies inside the Habsburg monarchy (which existed neither in theory nor in statistics, but were developing in reality) have had a positive impact on supra-regional division of labour? This question cannot be answered, because the monarchy broke apart in 1918.

ECONOMIC PLANNING AS A REMEDY AGAINST NATIONAL DISINTEGRATION

Around 1900 the Habsburg monarchy was facing two complexes of problems: Hungary's Independence Party was becoming stronger at the same time as tendencies towards economic separation from Austria spread.[19] Concurrently the results of the Badeni riots led to national radicalisation of new and unseen dimensions in Austria.[20] Both phenomena challenged the monarchy's foundations in 1897, when the customs and trading union had to be renewed again, which required two corresponding laws of both parliaments. As both Austrian houses of parliament had, in fact, been unable to work since 1897, the provisional renewal of the Compromise was brought about by emergency decrees of the emperor until the law at last passed parliament in 1907. The fact that the Hungarians did not take advantage of this situation shows the importance of the Austrian market for Hungarian agricultural producers. Big agriculture remained the core of the Hungarian economy, although industry was growing very fast.[21]

While the problem of the economic compromise was dragging on for years as a provisional arrangement, the Austrian prime minister, Ernest von Koerber, presented a bigger plan for the rebuilding of the infrastructure in the years 1900 to 1904. Gerschenkron stresses that Koerber hoped to increase the economic competitiveness of the western part of the monarchy (Cisleithania). Thus the *Koerber-Plan* was 'nothing less than a programme for economic development'[22]: 'The main goal was to engineer a radical shift in political emphasis away from the highly divisive nationality problem and toward a common concern that would unite, coalesce, and integrate all the nationalities of Cisleithania. That "concern" was to be the economic interests.'[23]

The improvement of the economic infrastructure should also further social integration. Koerber, a high-ranking civil servant, was also a very capable politician, full of determination and self-confidence. Appointed to the post of prime minister in 1900, he proposed a bill concerning the construction of new railways. When this bill did not pass parliament, he dissolved the Reichsrat.[24] But the elections of 1901 were won by the radical nationalist parties as a result of the intensified national conflicts of the years before. Confronted with these electoral results, Koerber tried to lead the parties back to parliamentary work by proposing various bills.

One central point of the so-called *Koerber-Plan* was the reconstruction of the harbour of Trieste.[25] Important industrial regions such as the Czech Lands, however, used other seaports, such as Hamburg, for their overseas trade. Therefore Koerber encouraged the planning of new railways as well as a network of canals to connect the 'Hinterland' with the Adriatic Sea.[26]

The two houses of the Austrian parliament – 'in an atmosphere of considerable enthusiasm' – voted for two bills, serving the investment for the construction of railways and inland waterways (canals and river irrigation).[27] The Slovenes, expecting to profit from the railways in Carniola and in Gorizia, voted for the plan. Also the allied Czechs supported Koerber's initiative.[28] Economic interests obviously were stronger than nationalism.[29] In May 1902, the budget was passed according to constitutional procedures for the first time since the Badeni crises. As Gerschenkron stresses, in spring 1902 Koerber 'had reached the acme of his success and influence'.[30]

It is self-evident that the *Koerber-Plan* was of great importance for the construction of a network which led to a considerable increase in the transport of goods and especially persons. Alpine railways linked Salzburg, Carinthia and Carniola with Trieste. Railway construction and the upgrading of the harbour of Trieste led to an increasing demand for investment goods, such as iron, steel, rails and steam engines. Thus, the *Koerber-Plan* contributed significantly to economic growth during the first decade of the twentieth century.[31] The plan for the extension of the railway lines was fulfilled to a relatively high degree, whereas the plans for a network of waterways never reached the phase of realisation.[32]

But the central question about the success of the *Koerber-Plan* is not an economic one. It is doubtful whether the *Koerber-Plan* managed to encourage social integration and to decrease national divisions. It ought to be stressed that the regions concerned were primarily the Alpine regions where Germans or Slovenians were the dominant nationalities, and Trieste itself had an Italian majority and a Slovenian minority. It cannot be proved whether – as a result of the *Koerber-Plan* – these three nationalities would have developed a greater understanding of one another. Indeed, in 1910, when a population census took place, national disturbances in Trieste reached a new climax.[33]

We can only quote Frederick Hertz: 'As soon as national passions reach a certain level, there is no more place in the heads for a dispassionate acknowledgement of economic advantages offered by a multinational state.'[34]

THE DISSOLUTION OF THE HABSBURG MONARCHY

Historians tend to see an interrelation between political dissolution and economic failure and, automatically, they attribute economic backwardness to unstable political conditions. This line of argument is repeatedly applied to the Habsburg monarchy, which was sometimes described as Europe's China or as 'the ill man at the Danube' by contemporaries.[35]

There is no doubt that the Habsburg monarchy, on the whole, was still scarcely developed during the nineteenth century and its economic performance did not reach the level of Western Europe. Only at the end of the nineteenth and the beginning of the twentieth century did an economic spurt set in. Yet, the GNP per capita in the area of present-day Austria reached the average of Germany. However, people usually do not think in terms of GNP and the German-speaking Austrians felt that their incomes had decreased. As a result, the German-speaking Austrians who formed the Austrian Republic after 1918 had developed a dual consciousness of being German as well as Austrian. Symbolically, they identified themselves both with 'German culture' and with the Habsburgs and the Austrian state.[36]

From 1918 onwards the German-speaking Austrians wanted to be 'Germans' in the first place. The German Reich, despite the severe territorial losses resulting from the Versailles Peace Treaty, still remained a great power, whereas the Austro-Hungarian monarchy had lost its existence. However, before we can turn to the economic and mental effects of this shock, the dissolution itself has to be briefly discussed.

As outlined above, the monarchy was much weaker economically than the German Reich, France or Great Britain. Yet, it survived the first three years of the First World War in economic conditions even better than Russia or Italy. By the last year of the war the economy was totally exhausted and a continuation of warfare seemed impossible.[37] Far worse than in the war industries was the situation as regards food supplies. It is remarkable that it was not the military situation at the front but the lack of food from 1915 onwards which destroyed the loyalty towards the monarchy.[38] Beginning in 1917 a terrible famine spread across the country. The last remains of loyalty among the non-German and non-Hungarian peoples were erased by military absolutism, which increasingly showed anti-Slav and anti-Roman traits: thus, for instance, Slav officers were observed by military intelligence and no longer promoted to higher ranks in the last year of the war.[39]

By the beginning of October 1918 the situation of the Central Powers had become hopeless. On 16 October Emperor Charles tried to transform the western part of the monarchy into a federation of nation-states, but failed. Instead of a federation a series of new independent states was established from 28 October onwards in realisation of national dreams: the new nation-states of Czechoslovakia, the State of Serbs, Croats and Slovenes (later Yugoslavia), Hungary, (German-) Austria, and (Great-) Romania formed a body of succession states. Although an armistice was in force since 4 November 1918, some of the succession states declared themselves as belligerent powers on the side of the Entente.

For that reason the political dissolution was paralleled by economic separation. The new states underlined their independence by currency separation, i.e. by stamping their banknotes.[40] The Peace Treaty of St Germain with Austria of 10 September 1919 provided the possibility of reciprocal relations regarding the customs regime, but it was not put into practice. On top of that, the menace of reparations, which the small Austrian Republic was expected to pay for the sins of the monarchy, questioned the viability of the republic entirely.

THE TRAUMA OF NON-VIABILITY AND NATIONAL CONSCIOUSNESS OF GERMAN AUSTRIANS

As *Deutschösterreich* could 'not exist geographically, economically and industrially independently on its own', secretary of state Otto Bauer explained in a memorandum in December 1918, it should be integrated into 'a part of a bigger federation of states'. As Bauer realised that a federation of the countries of the former monarchy was not feasible, a union with Germany seemed to be the only alternative.[41] A union with Germany meant for him not only the 'union with socialism', but also preventing French plans concerning Central Europe (*Mitteleuropa*) as well as a Danubian Confederation under Habsburg rule.[42]

The dismemberment of the Habsburg monarchy marked the biggest crisis of identity for Austria. This crisis was, undoubtedly, of a political nature, but was primarily discussed on an economic basis. The member of the Austrian delegation to Paris, Hans Loewenfeld-Russ, stated that Germany, although defeated, had remained a great power, whereas Austria had become 'a nobody and beggar'.[43]

Austria's economic viability after the First World War became a topic of discourses. While contemporaries were convinced of Austria's non-viability, recent historical interpretation comes to a different conclusion: Austria had indeed 'inherited' substantial assets. The Austrian Republic's national income was higher than the average national income and its industrialisation was more advanced compared with former Cisleithania. With less than one-quarter of Cisleithania's population Austria produced more than one-third of its GNP. The Austrian Republic had an advanced electrical industry, a highly developed trade and transport system, a dense banking sector and infrastructure, an excellent educational system and an outstanding standard in science and research. And could the loss of the eastern, agriculturally dominated and underdeveloped regions not also be interpreted as an advantage?

A burdensome and problematic heritage was the ammunitions, automobile and aircraft industry in the area of Wiener Neustadt, which had expanded during the war. The Treaty of St Germain demanded a complete dismantling of the military industrial complex and some regions in Lower Austria and Styria became centres of unemployment during the inter-war years. In terms of economic balance problems arose because Austria inherited over 80 per cent of Cisleithania's automobile and locomotive industries, over 50 per cent of bicycle production and 35 per cent of iron production, but only 6.3 per cent of coal mining and 4.7 per cent of sugar refinery. Austria received about one-quarter of the cotton spinning capacity but had hardly any weaving mills. In agriculture Austria remained dependent on imports. On the other hand, civil servants were over-represented, numbering 12.8 per cent of all employees.[44] The railway network of the former Habsburg monarchy had approximately 46,000 km, of which about 5,800 km came to the Austrian Republic. In the past the north–south direction had been of great importance, now the east–west traffic's importance increased but was hindered by the existence of only an awkward and partly single-track main line from Vienna to Innsbruck via Zell am See. Very specific circumstances were to be found in the new province of Burgenland, a former part of western Hungary, where only skeleton-lines repeatedly crossed the new national boundaries.

THE TRAUMA OF HYDROCEPHALIC VIENNA

After 1918 Austria was confronted with an extremely inhomogeneous territorial structure. More than half of the overall population lived in Lower Austria and Vienna and one-third lived in Vienna. The structural tensions between the capital and the provinces were intensified by political tensions between 'red' Vienna and the 'conservative' *Länder*.

The capital, Vienna, with its highly developed service industries, had provided the whole Habsburg monarchy with managers, merchants, technicians, academics, civil servants and officers. In return Vienna received earnings from the entire territory of the former Austro-Hungarian monarchy. From this perspective, the question of Austria's viability was primarily reduced to that of Vienna's.[45] The first Czechoslovak prime minister, Karel Kramář, declared that Vienna had to give up 'living as a pensioner from the labour of others'.[46] Post-war Vienna, no matter how sophisticated its intellectual life and how impressive its municipal services were, from that point of view had lost the most. The Austrian provinces grew self-confident whereas many upper-class Viennese, like in one of Joseph Roth's novels, lamented the 'forestation of Vienna' (*Verwaldung Wiens*) and thought Austria ruled by 'Christian Alpine imbeciles'.[47]

It was generally believed that disaster could only be averted if Vienna no longer remained a hydrocephalic capital of an impotent miniature state, but became one of the numerous commercial centres that prospered in the large German Reich.[48] There was a failure to notice that Vienna's problem was not a matter of size but a matter of economic adaptation.

NON-VIABILITY AND AUSTRIAN IDENTITY

Many Austrians believed that the solution to the structural problems lay in a union with the German economy. 'Understanding Austria's economic outlook means understanding the movement in favour of the *Anschluss*,' State Chancellor Karl Renner wrote in 1945.[49] The Conservative Party (Christlichsoziale Partei), in danger of being separated into an urban and a rural wing, was much less enthusiastic about a union with a socialist, Protestant or even revolutionary Germany: 'Being... one province among other provinces under Prussia's reign' was not an option which Chancellor Ignaz Seipel envisaged for Austria. Also Joseph Schumpeter stated that

Austria after an *Anschluss* would at best function as a 'limited partner' 'in the larger German company'.[50] After 1919 the *Anschluss* movement was favoured mainly by Vorarlberg, Tyrol, Salzburg, Upper Austria and Styria against 'red' Vienna.

Even the expansion of Alpine electrical power supply was seen as an act of resistance against central government and as an expression of federal independence. Semi-public companies, partly owned by the *Länder* and supported by foreign capital, furthered electrification. However, the expansion programme lost momentum when foreign coal again was available. The big banking industry, which kept shares of Czech coal mining, was much more interested in coal consumption than in financing Austrian hydraulic-power plants.

Tourism became a 'matter of survival' for the Austrian Republic, but was very much affected by business cycles and political crises. Investments were made to improve the infrastructure, such as the electrification of railways, the expansion of roads, mountain railways and cable cars. The opening ceremony of the Großglockner Hochalpenstrasse in August 1935 was the highlight of Austrian self-confidence; the metaphor of Austria's function as a bridge between orient and occident was emphasised. The Großglockner Hochalpenstrasse became the symbol of a new Austria in the middle of Europe.[51] Its model also influenced Austria's presentation at the Paris World Exhibition in 1937. In an unpublished typescript the author of the exhibition's catalogue, Friedrich Schreyvogel, wrote: 'Now as Austria's light focuses on a much smaller space, some matters have been rediscovered.'[52]

THE *ANSCHLUSS* TRAUMA

Ever since 1918, many Austrians considered the *Anschluss* to Germany as unification with an advanced economy. Therefore, they welcomed the *Anschluss* of 1938. National socialism was successful in overcoming the unemployment crisis by initiating modern industrial plants mainly in Upper Austria. The expansion was financed by deficit spending and Austria's economy was integrated into German economic warfare. As a result of the findings of several research projects, the story of an economic miracle as a consequence of the *Anschluss* has to be doubted: 1938 did not have such far-reaching consequences as assumed.[53] Between 1938 and 1945 even the name Austria did not exist. The transformation into the Ostmark was 'legalised' by two laws.[54] Only a few companies kept the name Austria during the Nazi regime; the capital of the former Holy Roman Empire was 'denatured into a German provincial town' (Thomas Mann).[55]

The Nazi authorities did not favour Vienna's leading position. A plan to establish a central chamber of commerce which was to be in charge of the total Ostmark was strongly criticised by different *Gauleiters*, arguing against 'racially corrupted Vienna'.[56] The *Gaue* came under direct control of Berlin and in contrast to Berlin, Hamburg, Nuremberg, Munich and even Linz, the 'Führer's city', Vienna remained in the shadow of economic expansion. Plans to build a harbour and to connect the Danube by a waterway system to the North Sea and the Baltic failed as well as the construction of modern motorways and industries. Alternatives, such as the emphasis on Vienna's position as a fashion metropole[57] and 'cultural missionary' were resisted, for such plans provoked envy with the central authorities.[58]

The 'de-provincialisation' of the province, the adaptation of different economic and cultural levels, of life's opportunities and of political influence of the western provinces to the former metropolis Vienna, though levelled down, was undoubtedly supported by the new administrative structure. Still, a process of urbanisation and a rural migration began. The concept of the 'de-provincialisation of the province' was formulated as an anti-urban position as well as a project of modernisation. The strengthened *Gaue* themselves became ambitious to establish a political and economic dependency of marginal regions. After the occupation of Yugoslavia in 1941 Oberkrain and the former Untersteiermark were integrated into Carinthia and Styria, respectively and their Germanisation was forcefully implemented. Consequently the economic resources of these Slovenian settlement areas were wasted on purpose.

After the *Anschluss*, the northern part of the Burgenland, and after the Munich Agreement (30 September 1938), parts of south Moravia, southern Bohemia and Slovakia were integrated into Lower Austria/Lower Danube. These areas were considered as a 'border *Gau*', a 'stronghold against the east' as well as the 'ancestors' *Gau*' of the Führer. In July 1938 Krems was made the new capital of this *Gau*, though only symbolically, as Vienna remained the official and administrative seat of the *Gau* leaders. For the future the *Gauleiter* planned to make Brno the worthy capital of a Germanised greater *Gau* in the Lower Danube.[59]

The new territorial repartition brought no economic advantages to these regions.[60] None of the national socialist industrial centres was founded either north of the Danube or in the recently acquired regions. The South Bohemian–South Moravian economic area, which showed a lack of infrastructure, had to endure further losses during the national socialist regime.[61] Small craft-enterprises and small-sized industry decreased. The Linz office's policy of 'aryanisation' was aimed at favouring the Germanisation of the

Protectorate. The economic area of Bohemia and Moravia was to be disintegrated and Prague, like Vienna, was to be transformed into a provincial town.[62] Linz was to become the new centre of the south, an idea that was not at first supported by the Berlin authorities for reasons of the war economy.[63]

The expansion of the provinces was based on territorial claims and economic imperialism. The reorientation of east Austria towards the Danube area and the Balkans, according to the imperialistic concepts of establishing a German-dominated Central and South-east Europe, was not realised.[64] But what had so far been extremely provincial could now see itself as part of the German Reich and member of the future central power of Europe.[65]

RECONSTRUCTION AND AUSTRIAN INTEGRATION

The economic disintegration into many regional 'islands' in 1945, which had already begun at the end of the war, was increased by the establishment of the four occupation zones (British, French, American and Soviet) and the nearly complete breakdown of the transport system.[66] Until the Second Control Agreement of 28 June 1946 the economic affairs of the four occupational zones were more or less hermetically sealed off from each other and the trading of essential goods was reduced to the so-called 'inter-zone compensation trade'. Therefore Austria's integration into a homogeneous economy had been particularly at risk. In February 1946 the first steps towards a relaxation of the demarcation lines had been taken in Judenburg, where the representatives of the *Länder* and the government agreed on a transition from individual counter-trade deals to a global quota.

Nevertheless the economic development of the Western and the Soviet zones was increasingly drifting apart. As a result of the war the starting positions of the individual regions were different and the various policies of the occupation forces increased the economic imbalance even more, favouring the western part of Austria. The major structural damage to Austrian industry (71 per cent) had occurred in Lower Austria where the armament industry had been concentrated. In the western part of Austria, on the other hand, hardly any industrial production facilities had been bombed. The situation of the electrical power supply and of transport was clearly worse in the east than in the west, where hardly any of the traffic routes had been damaged and electrical power was available from water-power. Furthermore, less livestock had been lost in west than in east Austria.

During the last weeks of the war, investments, raw materials and supplies had been transferred from east to west Austria, which meant further improvement of west Austria's initial position. Just to name a few examples: the operating equipment of the Steyr group was transferred from its Polish factories to Upper Austria, parts of Steyr's aircraft production were moved from Budapest and Vienna to Upper Austria and Salzburg, and the nearly completed aluminium factory near Hainburg was moved to Linz.

A dramatic reduction of machinery occurred between April 1945 and January 1946, mainly caused by Soviet forces dismantling factories. Eastern Austria was affected most as 60 per cent of Austria's industrial capacity was then to be found in east Austria, the Soviet occupation zones.[67] The policy of the Soviets was not only to satisfy their reparation claims, but also to reduce Austrian industry to a pre-war level. This became evident in the 'Soviet economic programme for Austria', which demanded that the Hermann-Göring factories in Linz be dismantled.[68] Industrialists from eastern Austria as well as from foreign countries and entrepreneurs who had been expelled from the Sudetenland, tended to migrate to west Austria because of the unstable situation in eastern Austria. A boom in founding enterprises immediately after the war was initiated by refugees, expellees and enterprising people seeking prosperity.[69] The transfer of factories and assets of enterprises, the sufficient labour force represented by refugees and the different strategies of the Western occupation forces created a comparably favourable situation for further economic development.[70]

The resources of the Marshall Plan (ERP) were distributed to the individual occupation zones according to the strategic aim of increasing the value of the economy in the western zones and of reducing their dependence on the eastern zone. Thus ERP funds were not distributed to the eastern zone unless it was proved that the produced goods were not delivered to the Soviet Union or any other Eastern European state.[71]

Trade with eastern neighbouring countries, which had accounted for one-third of total exports during the First Republic, had by 1951 been reduced to an export ratio of 13 per cent and an import ratio of 11 per cent. When the Council for Mutual Economic Assistance (Comecon) was founded in 1949, an isolated bloc was formed at the eastern border of Austria and it soon became evident that all hopes for a swift restoration of trading with Eastern European countries were quite unrealistic. Goods traditionally imported from Eastern Europe were substituted by ERP-deliveries. Austria participated in the economic progress of Western Europe but was deprived of its former trading partners in the east by the foundation of the Comecon. Thus, eastern Austria had to face further disadvantages in comparison to west Austria.[72]

In 1947–8 the Americans developed the so-called 'neutralisation plan' in order to counteract the economic policy of the USSR in Austria and to shift the centre of Austrian industry to the west. The economic significance of the USIA (Uprawlenje Sowjetskim Imuschestwom w Awstrij, i.e. Administration of Soviet Assets in Austria) combine was to be decidedly diminished and its economic viability eventually undermined.[73] This plan harboured the danger of the country being divided and thus found little support from the Austrian government. The intention to diminish the economic power of the USIA can clearly be seen in the small amount of ERP funds being distributed in the eastern part of Austria, while in the western occupation zones replacement production was taken up.[74]

The orientation towards the West, which had been started by the *Anschluss* and was furthered by investments during the war, became evident after 1945. When the Iron Curtain was erected and West European economic growth increased, the economic centre of Austria shifted further to the west.[75] The transfer of the industrial centre is clearly illustrated by the distribution of large-scale enterprises with more than a thousand employees. In 1930, thirteen of these concerns comprising a total of 20,500 employees existed in Lower Austria and had increased to only fifteen, comprising a total of 28,000 employees, by 1959. In Upper Austria, however, the number of these enterprises had increased from three, comprising 3,400 employees, to fifteen, comprising 43,000 employees within the same period. The relative significance of the medium and large-scale enterprises had altogether increased.[76]

NATIONALISATION, INDUSTRIALISATION AND THE IDEA OF AN AUSTRIAN NATION-STATE

The ideology of the post-war economy in Austria has been influenced by several characteristics: the nationalised industry, which served as a flagship of the Austrian economy; the so-called *Sozialpartnerschaft* (the informal institution representing the relations between representatives of employers and employees), which served as an instrument for economic development; and the idea of Austria's function as a bridge between East and West. The success of the Austrian *Sozialpartnerschaft* was the result of a high degree of concentration and centralisation of the Austrian system of representation of interests. Thus differences were solved by advisory committees of the *Sozialpartnerschaft*. Furthermore, the representatives of the *Sozialpartnerschaft* were closely connected with the political parties, and lastly, the state was greatly involved.[77] This high degree of co-operation (corporatism) was of great help in avoiding labour disputes and in realising the often-cited Austrian climate of 'social peace'.

After 1945 Austria aimed at a market system in which the public sector was to receive great influence. For the Socialist Party's position in this matter the aspects of full employment and the intention to reinforce central administration were crucial. The Austrian experience with heavy industry during the inter-war period led the workers' party to reduce industrialists' political influence, which before the war had been used to combat labour unions and the ideas of democracy in general. After 1945, the Socialist Party's left wing favoured a certain degree of planned economy and a more equal distribution of income associated with the principles of the welfare state.[78] 'Our country's future undoubtedly belongs to socialism,' State Chancellor Karl Renner wrote to Stalin.[79] This statement was probably motivated by diplomatic tactics to appease the Soviets, but justifiably can be seen as an example that the victory of socialism was a widely held belief.

In budgetary matters, the left wing of the Austrian People's Party (ÖVP = Österreichische Volkspartei) was influenced by Karl Lueger, the mayor of Vienna in the late 1890s. Lueger pleaded for a transfer of 'local socialism' to a national level. The 'programmatic principles' of the conservative ÖVP of 1945 were in tune with state intervention in the economy, as long as 'socialisation and communalisation of vital enterprises' were carried out 'with circumspection, i.e. respecting socially and economically tolerable limits'.[80]

Swift economic recovery seemed more easily achievable with government intervention. Additionally, bringing industry into the state's orbit served as an effective barrier against reparation claims aimed at German property. Claims for reparations had been approved by the Allies at the Potsdam Conference in July 1945. Another object of Austrification was to prevent foreign financial control over Austrian assets as it had existed between 1922 and 1936. The anti-foreigner argument convinced even staunch privatisers to regard nationalisation as a possible solution. Approximately one-fifth of Austrian industry was nationalised accordingly in the wake of the first law of nationalisation of 26 July 1946, which was followed by the second law of 26 March 1947 when all electrical supply concerns exceeding a certain scale were nationalised. Towards the end of the 1950s, at the height of its power, state-owned industry employed about 130,000 people and produced about 30 per cent of Austria's exports.[81] In the following years not only were public enterprises caught up in a whirlpool of pretensions of the two big political parties (*Proporz*) but from the 1970s onwards they were also made use of to influence Austria's economic growth and the state's employment policy within the framework of Keynesian theory. The state-owned industrial combines reacted to the economic crash in 1975 by maintaining a high level of investment, by concentrating on the production goods industries and by investing in employment and regional policy programmes. Consequently the employment rate was even raised – but the necessary structural adjustments were not undertaken.[82]

Austria saw its opportunity as mediator between the two existing economic blocs, namely, the liberal bloc of the Marshall Plan states and the bloc of the Comecon states. At the world exhibition in Brussels in 1958, where the Austrian pavilion was designed by the famous Austrian architect Karl Schwanzer, the metaphor of a bridge was used. This was clearly underlined by the following quotation taken from the catalogue of the exhibition: 'The idea of an Austrian state is best to be compared with a bridge. Austria, located in the centre of Europe, has always been a link between the peoples and cultures of this continent.'[83] Austria was epitomised as a 'bridge between past and future, between tradition and modern spirit, a bridge to trade cultural and actual goods between north and south, east and west'. The bridge was a 'symbol for the idea of the Austrian state'. Because of the internationalisation of the economy and of scientific research, a small state like Austria was hardly able to 'accomplish outstanding achievements', which may be regarded as exclusive ones, therefore the focus of representing Austria was put on Austria's cultural history, which had cosmopolitan features. Austria was to be presented to the world 'by cultural achievements, by its complaisant and optimistic mentality and by its ability to balance opposites', instead of by 'nuclear reactors, missiles and supersonic aircraft' as was argued in the catalogue. Therefore the exhibits included historical documents of international treaties from the Congress of Vienna to the foundation of the International Atomic Energy Authority in 1958. Furthermore Austria represented itself as a fast-industrialising country which was illustrated by the exhibits of raw materials and primary products that were shown on the ground floor.

THE 'ISLAND TRAUMA'

The metaphor of a bridge was gradually replaced by one of an island. On the one hand, Austria is afraid of international competition and of losing market share; on the other hand, its people fear being overrun by immigrants, and thus losing jobs. Once Austria was fully industrialised people were afraid of more developed economic systems, which were more productive. In the 1960s they were afraid to join the European Economic Community (EEC) and its competitive market, especially the German one, which could upset the Austrian market. Furthermore there were grave doubts about such a step because of Austria's neutrality.

In addition to the fear of competition there is Austria's inclination to wait for external wonders and the clandestine hope that foreigners will be able to solve the country's problems. This attitude was quite common in the years after the First World War, when the belief was widespread that Austria could not cope unless help from the larger foreign countries, Germany or the League of Nations was forthcoming. The tendency to refer to external pressure to gain greater acceptance for internal political decisions can still be perceived in the course of the entry into the European Union (EU), when measures long overdue were justified with EU directions.

Thus it is not surprising that Austrian politicians tend to sell combines, in which the state holds interest, preferably to foreign companies. They have rarely aimed at national solutions. The foreign manager is expected to do wonders. Thus the trained Austrian reacts the more offended if these optimistically expected foreigners do not give or do not want to give anything away for free.

In the 1990s the fundamental political consensus of the Second Austrian Republic started to be questioned. This development was the result of the impossibility of carrying on neutrality in the traditional way after the fall of the Iron Curtain. Austrian full membership in the European Union, achieved after a plebiscite in 1995, implied the duty to fulfil certain obligations towards the new partner states. Already before that, the dismemberment of the former Soviet bloc fundamentally altered Austria's political and economic status. Opening up the borders towards the East gave the Austrian economy the chance to re-establish traditional links to the new democracies in the Danube basin and beyond. However, this happened at the cost of having to abandon the old and comfortable position of an uncommitted neutral bystander. As the former satellites of the USSR lined up for membership in NATO (and in the EU, as far as economic integration was concerned) Austria was confronted with the challenge of making new strategic choices for its future.[84]

CONCLUSION

Apart from the changes in Austria's position in the world it became obvious that the eonomic development of the Second Republic went along with the confirmation and stabilisation of a distinct Austrian national consciousness. The levelling of regional differences during the long period of considerable growth (from 1953 to the 1970s) contributed to the social homogenisation of the population and definitely discarded theories of Austrian economic non-viability. The State Treaty of 15 May 1955, the Declaration of Neutrality of 26 October 1955 and, among others, the widely shared pride in the beauty of the Alpine regions, or in the resounding names of important industrial enterprises, have been symbols of Austrian consciousness to this day.

NOTES

1. Rudolf Sieghart, *Zolltrennung und Zolleinheit* (Vienna, 1915); Alexander von Matlekovits, *Die Zollpolitik der österreichisch-ungarischen Monarchie von 1850 bis zur Gegenwart* (Budapest and Vienna, 1877).
2. Iván T. Berend and György Ránki, 'Economic Factors in Nationalism: the Example of Hungary at the Beginning of the Twentieth Century', *Austrian History Yearbook*, 3, 3 (1967), 163–88, at 170 f. : 'By 1900 the issue of the independent Hungarian customs area was very nearly the most crucial issue in Hungarian politics... However, the superficiality of the economic literature dealing with the subject and neglect of the economic aspects of the issue when political compromises were made show that the main reasons for the Hungarian desire for an independent customs union were of a political and nationalist nature.'
3. Ernst Bruckmüller, *Landwirtschaftliche Organisationen und gesellschaftliche Modernisierung* (Salzburg, 1978), p. 193.
4. David Good, *The Economic Rise of the Habsburg Empire 1750–1914* (Berkeley-Los Angeles, 1984), p. 110 (citing Scott Eddie). Belonging to the 'Zoll- und Handelsbündnis', cf. Ákos Paulinyi, 'Die sogenannte gemeinsame Wirtschaftspolitik' in A. Wandruszka and P. Urbanitsch (eds.), *Die Habsburgermonarchie 1848–1918*, Vol. I (Vienna, 1973), pp. 567–604.
5. Edmund Bernatzik (ed.), *Die österreichischen Verfassungsgesetze mit Erläuterungen*, 2nd edn (Vienna, 1911), p. 441.
6. Otto Urban, *Die tschechische Gesellschaft 1848–1918* (Vienna, 1994), Vol. I, p. 368.
7. Bruckmüller, *Landwirtschaftliche Organisationen*, p. 145.
8. Berthold Suttner, 'Die politische und rechtliche Stellung der Deutschen in Österreich 1848 bis 1918' in Wandruszka and Urbanitsch (eds.), *Die Habsburgermonarchie 1848–1918*, Vol. III, part 1 (Vienna, 1980), pp. 154–339, esp. p. 212. About this theme a young Czech scholar, Barbara Hofmannová, wrote an excellent text for the author's (Bruckmüller's) seminar in the summer semester of 2000.
9. Berthold Sutter, *Die Badenischen Sprachenverordnungen von 1897, ihre Genesis und ihre Auswirkungen vornehmlich auf die innerösterreichischen Alpenländer* (2 vols., Graz and Cologne, 1960–5).
10. Scott M. Eddie, 'Economic Policy and Economic Development in Austria-Hungary, 1867–1913' in Peter Mathias and Sidney Pollard (eds.), *The Cambridge Economic History of Europe*, Vol. VIII (Cambridge, 1989), pp. 814–86, at p. 822: 'Comprehensive statistics in sufficient details to allow a thorough assessment of the economic dimensions of the nationality problem do not exist for either Austria or Hungary.'

11. Stephan Koren, 'Die Industrialisierung Österreichs' in Wilhelm Weber (ed.), *Österreichs Wirtschaftsstruktur gestern – heute – morgen*, Vol. I (Berlin, 1961), pp. 223–549, at p. 305.
12. Good, *Economic Rise*, p. 111.
13. Heinz Fassmann, 'Einwanderung, Auswanderung und Binnenwanderung in Österreich-Ungarn. Eine Analyse der Volkszählung 1910', *Österreichische Osthefte*, 33 (1991), 51–67; Ivo Nejašmić, 'Hauptmerkmale der kroatischen Auswanderung 1880–1991', *Österreichische Osthefte*, 37 (1995), 343–53; László Katus, 'Über die wirtschaftlichen und gesellschaftlichen Grundlagen der Nationalitätenfrage in Ungarn vor dem ersten Weltkrieg' in Peter Hanák (ed.), *Die nationale Frage in der österreichisch-ungarischen Monarchie 1900–1918* (Budapest, 1966), pp. 149–216.
14. Nachum T. Gross, 'Die Stellung der Habsburgermonarchie in der Weltwirtschaft' in Wandruszka and Urbanitsch (eds.), *Die Habsburgermonarchie 1848–1918*, Vol. I (Vienna 1973), pp. 1–28, at pp. 19 ff.
15. Julianna Puskas, 'Gestaltung der landwirtschaftlichen Produktion in Ungarn und der Markt der Monarchie (1870–1914)' in *Die Agrarfrage in der österreichisch-ungarischen Monarchie 1900–1918: Mitteilungen auf der Kanferenz der Geschichtswissenschaftler, Budapest, 4–9. Mai 1964* (Bucharest, 1965), pp. 173–232, at pp. 218 ff, tables 14, 15 and 16.
16. George Barany, 'Hungary: the Uncompromising Compromise', *Austrian History Yearbook*, 3, 1 (1967), 234–59, at p. 254; Berend and Ránki, 'Economic Factors', 172–3 f.; John Komlos, *The Habsurg Monarchy as a Customs Union: Economic Development in Austria-Hungary in the Nineteenth Century* (Princeton, 1983), pp. 190 ff.
17. Hans Peter Hye, 'Bürgerlichkeit im Spiegel des Vereinswesens am Beispiel der nordböhmischen Stadt Aussig [Ústí nad Labem]', *Österreichische Osthefte*, 36 (1994), 85–108, at 91, 97.
18. Cf. also Janez Cvirn, *Trdnjavski trikotnik. Politična orientacija Nemcev na Spodnem Štajerskem (1861–1914)* [The *Festungsdreieck*. The Political Orientation of the Lower Styrian Germans 1861–1914] (Maribor, 1997), pp. 255–6.
19. Berend and Ránki, 'Economic factors', pp. 170–1: 'By 1900 the issue of the independent Hungarian customs area was very nearly the most crucial issue in Hungarian politics...'
20. Sutter, *Badenische Sprachenverordnungen, passim*.
21. Paulinyi, 'Wirtschaftspolitik', p. 579.
22. Alexander Gerschenkron, *An Economic Spurt that Failed: Four Lectures in Austrian History* (Princeton, 1977), p. 25.
23. Ibid., p. 23.
24. Alfred Ableitinger, *Ernest von Koerber und das Verfassungsproblem im Jahre 1900* (Vienna, 1973).
25. Stenographische Protokolle des Abgeordnetenhauses des Reichsrates, XVII. Session, Beilagen.
26. Roman Sandgruber, *Ökonomie und Politik. Österreichische Wirtschaftsgeschichte vom Mittelalter bis zur Gegenwart* (Vienna, 1995), pp. 306 ff.
27. Gerschenkron, *Economic Spurt*, p. 71.

28. Ibid., p. 82.
29. Ibid., p. 83.
30. Ibid., p. 84.
31. Fulvio Babudieri, *Industrie, commerci e navigazione a Trieste e nella Regione Giulia dall'inizio del settecento ai primi anni del novecento* (Milan, 1982), p. 192.
32. Gerschenkron, *Economic Spurt*, pp. 85–121, showed that the minister of finance, Eugen von Boehm-Bawerk, himself was the 'anti-hero' who hindered the canal plan.
33. Emil Brix, *Die Umgangssprachen in Altösterreich zwischen Agitation und Assimilation* (Vienna, 1982), pp. 194 ff. The increasingly aggressive language of the Germans in the Slovenian parts of Styria testifies to a new dimension of national divergence. Cf. Cvirn, *Trnjavski trikotnik*, pp. 315 ff.
34. Frederick Hertz, *The Economic Problems of the Danubian States: a Study in Economic Nationalism* (London, 1947).
35. Ernst Hanisch, *Der kranke Mann an der Donau. Marx und Engels über Österreich* (Vienna, 1978).
36. Ernst Bruckmüller, *Nation Österreich. Kulturelles Bewußtsein und gesellschaftlich-politische Prozesse*, 2nd edn (Vienna, 1996), pp. 286 ff.
37. Robert J. Wegs, *Die österreichische Kriegswirtschaft 1914–1918* (Vienna, 1979); Manfried Rauchensteiner, *Der Tod des Doppeladlers. Österreich-Ungarn und der Erste Weltkrieg* (Graz, Vienna and Cologne, 1993).
38. Hans Loewenfeld-Russ, *Im Kampf gegen den Hunger. Aus den Erinnerungen des Staatssekretärs für Volksernährung 1918–1920*, edited by Isabella Ackerl (Vienna, 1986).
39. Franz Rueh, *Moj dnevnik 1915–1918* [My Diary 1915–1918] (Ljubljana, 1999), p. 222. Rueh was a lieutenant of the reserve within the Austro-Hungarian army who felt himself to be Slovenian. As a 'Slovenian nationalist' (in September 1918) he was transferred into the 'Festungsbaudirektion' in Vienna.
40. Alice Teichova, *Kleinstaaten im Spannungsfeld der Großmächte. Wirtschaft und Politik in Mittel- und Südosteuropa in der Zwischenkriegszeit* (Vienna, 1988), pp. 113 ff.
41. Arnold Suppan, 'Zur österreichischen Außenpolitik 1918/19' in A. Suppan (ed.), *Außenpolitische Dokumente der Republik Österreich 1918–1938 (ADÖ), vol. I: Selbstbestimmung der Republik*, eds. Klaus Kock, Walter Rauscher and Arnold Suppan (Vienna, 1993), p. 40.
42. Arnold Suppan, 'Österreich im Schatten von St. Germain' in *ADÖ*', *Vol. II: Im Schatten von St. Germain*, eds. Klaus Koch, Walter Rauscher and Arnold Suppan (Vienna, 1995), p. 10.
43. Walter Rauscher, 'Die österreichische Außenpolitik unter Karl Renner und Michael Mayr' in *ADÖ, Vol. III: Österreich im System der Nachfolgestaaten*, eds. Klaus Koch, Walter Rauscher and Arnold Suppan (Vienna, 1996), p. 13.
44. Hertz, *The Economic Problems*; Friedrich Hertz, *Ist Österreich wirtschaftlich lebensfähig?* (Vienna, 1921); Friedrich Hertz, *Zahlungsbilanz und Lebensfähigkeit Österreichs*, Schriften des Vereins für Sozialpolitik (Berlin, 1925), p. 167;

Gustav Stolper, *Deutschösterreich als Sozial- und Wirtschaftsproblem* (Munich, 1925); Eduard März, *Österreichische Bankpolitik in der Zeit der großen Wende 1913–1923. Am Beispiel der Creditanstalt für Handel und Gewerbe* (Vienna, 1981), pp. 275 ff.

45. Stolper, *Deutschösterreich*, p. 115.
46. Suppan, 'Zur österreichischen Außenpolitik 1918/19', p. 42.
47. Joseph Roth, *Die Kapuzinergruft* (Amsterdam and Cologne, 1972), p. 176.
48. Gustav Stolper, 'Unsere wirtschaftliche Zukunft', *Der Volkswirt*, 8 (23 November 1918).
49. Karl Renner, *Denkschrift über die Geschichte der Unabhängigkeitserklärung Österreichs und die Einsetzung der provisorischen Regierung der Republik* (Vienna, 1945), pp. 18–19.
50. Quoted in Herbert Matis, 'Wirtschaftliche Mitteleuropa-Konzeptionen in der Zwischenkriegszeit. Der Plan einer Donaukonföderation' in Richard G. Plaschka, Horst Haselsteiner, Arnold Suppen, Anna Drabek and Brigitte Zaar (eds.), *Mitteleuropa-Konzeptionen in der ersten Hälfte des 20. Jahrhunderts* (Vienna, 1995), pp. 229–55, at 251–2.
51. Georg Rigele, *Die Großglockner-Hochalpenstraße. Zur Geschichte eines österreichischen Monuments* (Vienna, 1998), pp. 184 ff.
52. Ulrike Felber, Elke Krasny and Christian Rapp, *Expositionen. Österreich auf den Weltausstellungen 1851–1992* (manuscript), p. 131.
53. Josef Moser, *Oberösterreichs Wirtschaft 1938 bis 1945*, Studien zur Wirtschaftsgeschichte und Wirtschaftspolitik 2, edited by H. Matis and R. Sandgruber (Vienna, 1995); Otto Lackinger, *50 Jahre Industrialisierung in Oberösterreich: 1938–1988; 1945–1995* (Linz, 1997).
54. Ernst Hanisch, *Der lange Schatten des Staates* (Vienna, 1994), pp. 363–4.
55. Ernst Hanisch, *Gau der guten Nerven. Die nationalsozialistische Herrschaft in Salzburg 1938–1945* (Salzburg, 1997), pp. 9 ff.; Ulrich Weinzierl (ed.), *Österreichs Fall. Schriftsteller berichten vom 'Anschluß'* (Vienna, 1987), pp. 161–2.
56. Minutes of a conference of the 'Gauwirtschaftsberater' with Rafelsberger in Vienna, 19 September 1938, quoted after Horst Schreiber, *Wirtschafts- und Sozialgeschichte der Nazizeit in Tirol* (Innsbruck, 1994), p. 25.
57. Gloria Sultano, *Wie geistiges Kokain…: Mode unterm Hakenkreuz* (Vienna, 1994), pp. 119 ff.
58. A diary entry of Goebbels in 1942 formulated the aim to break Vienna's cultural hegemony as well: 'He [Hitler] does not want the Reich to have two rivalling capitals. Vienna should above all not maintain a hegemonic position in comparison to the Austrian *Gaue*… The *Führer* approves of the cultural policy I adopted with regard to Vienna and he is pleased that I help him to shift the focus of our cultural care from Vienna to Graz and above all Linz'; quoted after Klaus Amann, 'Die Brückenbauer. Zur "Österreich"-Ideologie der völkisch-nationalen Autoren in den dreißiger Jahren' in K. Amann and A. Berger (eds.), *Österreichische Literatur der dreißiger Jahre* (Vienna, 1985), pp. 60 ff., at p. 72.
59. Maren Seliger, 'Wien und Niederösterreich' in Emmerich Tálos, Ernst Hanisch and Wolfgang Neugebauer (eds.), *NS-Herrschaft in Österreich* (Vienna, 1988),

p. 406; Petr Nemec, 'Gauleiter Dr Hugo Jury und sein Wirken im Protek-
torat Böhmen und Mähren' in Th. Winkelbauer (ed.), *Kontakte und Kon-
flikte. Böhmen, Mähren und Österreich. Aspekte eines Jahrtausends gemeinsamer
Geschichte* (Horn, 1993), pp. 469 ff.

60. Both regions, Krumau/Český Krumlov and Kaplitz/Kaplice, which had mainly
    a German-speaking population, were economically oriented towards the
    Danube area in the eighteenth and nineteenth centuries. In 1918 the German
    delegates of the Bohemian provinces and the Austrian Privy Council planned
    to integrate the German-dominated judicial counties of Kaplitz, Krumau,
    Prachatitz, Bergreichenstein and Neuer as 'German South Bohemia' to Upper
    Austria. The improved economic situation of the recently founded Czechoslo-
    vakia diminished the options for Austria. Without a referendum the state treaty
    of St Germain assigned the region to Czechoslovakia. After 1918 the east–west
    link became, as in Austria, the main economic connection of Czechoslovakia.
    The north–south link lost its significance. South Bohemia, like the Austrian re-
    gion north of the Danube, was marginalised. But in the regions of Kaplitz and
    Krumau the economic situation was better than in the rest of the Sudetenland
    or in the neighbouring Mühlviertel.

61. Michael John, 'Südböhmen, Oberösterreich und das Dritte Reich. Der Raum
    Krum(m)au – Kaplitz/Český Krumlov-Kaplice als Beispiel von internem Kolo-
    nialismus' in Winkelbauer (ed.), *Kontakte und Konflikte*, pp. 447 ff.

62. Quoted after John, 'Südböhmen, Oberösterreich und das Dritte Reich', p. 465.

63. Ibid., p. 466.

64. Robin Okey, 'Central Europe/Eastern Europe: Behind the Definitions', *Past
    and Present*, 137 (1992), 102–33.

65. Jörg K. Hoensch, 'Nationalsozialistische Europapläne im Zweiten Weltkrieg'
    in Richard G. Plaschka, Horst Haselsteiner, Arnold Suppan, Anna Drabek
    and Brigitte Zaar (eds.), *Mitteleuropa-Konzeptionen in der ersten Hälfte des 20.
    Jahrhunderts* (Vienna, 1995), pp. 307–25; Václav Kural, 'Von Masaryks "Neuem
    Europa" zu den Großraumplänen Hitler-Deutschlands' in Plaschka et al. (eds.),
    Mitteleuropa-Konzeptionen, pp. 351–7.

66. *Monatsberichte Wirtschaftsforschungsinstitut* (1946) 10, 7 (1947), 142.

67. Felix Butschek, 'Der Arbeitsmarkt in der Zeit der großen Koalition',
    Österreichisches Jahrbuch f. Politik (Vienna, 1989), 123.

68. Wilfried Mähr, *Der Marshall-Plan in Österreich* (Graz, 1989), p. 96.

69. *Monatsberichte Wirtschaftsforschungsinstitut*, 7 (1947), 142.

70. Thus about the foundation of the Iweg-Machine Works Ltd. in Ried we can
    read: 'The basis of the company was only some machines transferred from a
    Viennese factory, which stood dismantled in an unsatisfactory space and for
    which neither work nor construction plans were available.' Lackinger, *50 Jahre
    Industrialisierung*, p. 143.

71. Günter Bischof, 'Der Marshallplan in Österreich', *Zeitgeschichte*, 17 (1990),
    467; Arno Einwitschläger, *Amerikanische Wirtschaftspolitik in Österreich
    1945–1949* (Vienna, 1986), p. 110; Otto Klambauer and Ernest Bezenek, *Die
    USIA-Betriebe in Niederösterreich* (Volume V of H. Feigl and A. Kusternig

(eds.), *Studien und Forschungen aus dem niederösterreichischen Institut für Landeskunde*) (Vienna, 1983), pp. 68, 73; William Lloyd Stearman, *Die Sowjetunion und Österreich 1945–1955* (Bonn, 1962), pp. 120 ff.

72. Rudolf G. Ardelt and Hanns Haas, 'Die Westintegration Österreichs nach 1945', *Österreichische Zeitschrift für Politikwissenschaft*, 4 (1975), 379 ff.; Fritz Breuss, *Österreichs Außenwirtschaft 1945 bis 1982* (Vienna, 1983), pp. 365 ff.

73. Einwitschläger, *Amerikanische Wirtschaftspolitik*, pp. 45 ff.; Mähr, *Der Marshall-Plan in Österreich*, p. 100. Above all they mainly thought of gradually suspending all deliveries of raw materials, energy, industrial products and investment goods from the west.

74. Einwitschläger, *Amerikanische Wirtschaftspolitik*, pp. 61 ff.; Mähr, *Der Marshall-Plan in Österreich*, p. 100.

75. Stephan Koren, 'Die Industrialisierung Österreichs – Vom Protektionismus zur Integration' in W. Weber (ed.), *Österreichs Wirtschaftsstruktur gestern – heute – morgen*, Vol. I (Berlin, 1961), pp. 336 ff.; Kurt W. Rothschild, 'Wurzeln und Triebkräfte der österreichischen Wirtschaftsstruktur' in Weber (ed.), *Österreichs Wirtschaftsstruktur gestern – heute – morgen*, Vol. I, pp. 105 ff., 111.

76. Franz Mathis, *Big Business in Österreich*, Vol II (Vienna, 1990), pp. 140 ff., 147–8, 170 ff.; Rothschild, 'Wurzeln und Triebkräfte', pp. 111–12.

77. Emmerich Tálos and Bernhard Kittel, 'Sozialpartnerschaft. Zur Konstituierung einer Grundsäule der Zweiten Republik' in Reinhard Sieder, Heinz Steinert and Emmerich Tálos (eds.), *Österreich 1945–1995. Gesellschaft – Politik – Kultur* (Vienna, 1995), pp. 109 ff.

78. Sandgruber, *Ökonomie und Politik*, pp. 458–9.

79. Eva-Marie Csáky, *Der Weg zur Freiheit und Neutralität. Dokumentation zur österreichischen Außenpolitik 1945–1955* (Vienna, 1980), p. 35; Hanisch, *Der lange Schatten*, p. 403.

80. Sandgruber, *Ökonomie und Politik*, pp. 458–9.

81. Edmond Langer, *Die Verstaatlichung in Österreich* (Vienna, 1966) pp. 113 ff., pp. 254 ff.; Fritz Weber, '1946–1986. 40 Jahre Verstaatlichte Industrie' in: *ÖIAG – Journal* (1986), 1 ff.

82. Gunther Tichy, 'Wirtschaft und Wirtschaftspolitik' in Wolfgang Mantl (ed.), *Politik in Österreich. Die Zweite Republik: Bestand und Wandel* (Vienna, 1992), p. 713; Fritz Weber (ed.), *Austro-Keynesianismus in Theorie und Praxis* (Vienna, 1993), p. 88.

83. *Österreich. Katalog zur Weltausstellung Brüssel 1958* (Vienna, 1958).

84. Gordon Brook-Shepherd, *The Austrians: a Thousand-Year Odyssey* (London, 1996), pp. 448–9.

CHAPTER 9

The economy and the rise and fall of a small multinational state: Czechoslovakia, 1918–1992

Václav Průcha

The Czechoslovak Republic was founded on 28 October 1918 as one of the successor states to Austria-Hungary, and comprised the Czech Lands, Slovakia and the easternmost Subcarpathian Ruthenia annexed in 1919.[1] From the Habsburg monarchy Czechoslovakia inherited 21 per cent of the territory and 25 per cent of the population. After stabilising its frontiers the new state had a population of 13.5 million.

Over the seventy-four years of its existence (until its division into two republics on 1 January 1993) Czechoslovakia went through far-reaching economic and social changes and experienced considerable shifts in the nationality structure of its population. The multinational pattern of the population, typical of the inter-war period, was simplified in the course of the Second World War and soon after the end of that war owing to the tragic fate of the Jewish population, the annexation of Subcarpathian Ruthenia to the Soviet Union, the expulsion of Germans, the exchange of the population with Hungary, and the return of emigrated Czechs and Slovaks from various countries of the world. According to the 1930 census, 66 per cent of the population (9,689,000) were Czechs and Slovaks; by 1948 that percentage had risen to 95 per cent (11,584,000) and did not undergo any more substantial changes over the following decades.[2]

The Czech Lands, a part of Cisleithania in Austria-Hungary, enjoyed a considerably higher economic and cultural standard than Slovakia, which had been part of Hungary (Transleithania). The economic and social heterogeneity of the various regions, even within the Czech Lands and Slovakia, proved to be fatal to the new multinational state both socially and politically. Apart from the understandable problems of founding a state out of the generally obtaining post-war chaos, ill effects made themselves felt particularly in the aggravated economic situation in the 1930s, when the Nazi regime in Germany began to foment discontent among the different nationalities using social unrest and disorders for its own aggressive ends.

The economic structure of the Czechoslovak Republic was determined by the western regions of the country, which were generally more developed and considerably larger with respect to area and population. In 1930 the Czech Lands had 72 per cent of the whole population of the country, but 92 per cent of the industrial production. In 1910 more people in the Czech Lands were earning their living by working in industry than in agriculture; in Slovakia that shift had not been achieved until the late 1950s. In the inter-war period Slovakia – not to mention Subcarpathian Ruthenia – remained mostly an agrarian country, with agriculture manifesting a highly extensive character (on 10 hectares the output was approximately equivalent to the 4 hectare output in the Czech Lands).

In 1918, the Czechs, who had long been a subordinate nation, became a state-forming nation in newly founded Czechoslovakia. Supported by the Slovaks in the early years of the new state the Czechs created the idea of one Czechoslovak nation comprising two ethnic branches speaking two closely related Slavonic languages, Czech and Slovak. The Czechs, with the limited participation of the Slovaks, were gradually able to gain control of the most important economic positions (thanks to favourable circum-stances brought about by the land reform and the nostrification of joint stock companies). The large German minority lost its former hegemony in the sphere of high-level state administration and the military and was further weakened as far as its aristocratic and big bourgeois components were concerned. It however managed to maintain its economic positions, which were more than proportionate to its share of the population of the republic.

Czechoslovakia had a democratic system in which, apart from the Czech and Slovak political parties, minorities were also represented in their own political parties, including participation in government. The democratic regime proved its viability and resilience as the only one in Central and South-East Europe, and unlike the neighbouring fascist and authoritarian regimes survived until 1938, when it was destroyed by brutal foreign inter-vention. It was in no way by a mere chance that Czechoslovakia became the Mecca for political *émigrés* from the countries suppressing the democratic rights of their citizens.

The linking of Slovakia with the Czech Lands brought the Slovak nation considerable benefits in the sphere of politics, national independence and culture, and demographic structure. The pressure of Magyarisation, which had been a real threat to the very existence of the Slovak nation for decades, was followed by regeneration and flourishing of the nation's potential. This development was accompanied by gradual democratisation of political and public life, which proved to be a definite step forward, despite a number

Table 9.1 *Nationality and social structure of the population of Czechoslovakia, 1930 (percentages)*

Nationality	Total	Self-employed and tenants	White-collar workers	Manual workers[a]
Czechs[b]	49.9	35.2	19.8	45.0
Slovaks[b]	15.9	51.4	12.4	36.2
Ukrainians, Ruthenians and Russians	3.7	66.2	3.8	30.0
Germans	21.9	34.2	18.0	47.8
Hungarians	4.7	50.0	8.5	41.5
Poles	0.6	19.6	16.8	63.6
Jews	1.3	68.8	18.0	13.2

Notes: [a] Including day labourers and apprentices.
[b] In the census the nationality was given as Czechoslovak. In the first line, Czechs and Slovaks in the Czech Lands and in Ruthenia; in the second line, Slovaks and Czechs in Slovakia. Foreigners and the nationalities not quoted in the table accounted for 2 per cent of the population.
Source: Československá statistika: Pramenné dílo [Czechoslovak Statistics: a Source Book], Volume 116 (Prague, 1935), pp. 12–16.

of conflicts, in contrast to the former aristocratic, clerical and bureaucratic Hungarian regime. There was a particularly marked improvement in social policy, education, enlightenment of the population, art, and in the overall educational level of the young generation. However, the dynamism of the Slovak national movement gradually came into conflict with the prevailing state ideology which did not recognise the independent identity of the Slovak nation.

In the economic sphere, grave problems arose in Slovakia after 1918. The adjustment of the Slovak economy to the new situation was far from easy under the conditions of the competitive prevalence of Czech capital, which led to numerous economic and social collisions. Until 1938, Slovakia – and the extremely underdeveloped Subcarpathian Ruthenia – to a large extent, supplied the Czech Lands with raw materials and foodstuffs. In the 1920s some parts of Slovakia were even hit by de-industrialisation. But starting in the late 1930s Slovakia enjoyed faster economic growth than the Czech Lands and this process lasted until the 1980s.

Czechoslovakia had a very mixed population from the point of view of individual nationalities, which were socially structured quite differently and participated in a different manner in the various branches of social activity. (See tables 9.1 and 9.2.) According to the 1930 census, Czechoslovakia's population was 14,730,000 (including 250,000 foreigners).

Table 9.2 *Occupational distribution of the nationalities of Czechoslovakia, 1930 (percentages)*

Nationality	Sector					
	A	B	C	D	E	F
Czechs[a]	26.9	39.1	7.0	7.6	5.7	13.7
Slovaks[a]	59.8	19.0	5.1	4.2	3.5	8.4
Ukrainians, Ruthenians and Russians	82.1	6.2	1.9	0.8	2.1	6.9
Germans	23.0	45.5	4.0	8.9	4.3	14.3
Hungarians	63.8	16.9	2.6	3.8	3.8	9.1
Poles	16.2	55.6	6.0	3.1	2.3	16.8
Jews	13.1	22.2	3.6	42.6	6.6	11.9

A Agriculture, forestry and fisheries.
B Mining, manufacturing industry, building industry and crafts.
C Transport and communications.
D Trade and banking.
E Public services and liberal professions.
F Other branches.
Note: [a] See table 9.1, note b.
Source: See table 9.1.

As far as the Czech population was concerned, the industrial component was very numerous, and the majority were workers in the manufacturing industry or low-grade clerical workers. This was even more marked among those of German and Polish nationality. Among the Slovaks, Ukrainians, Ruthenians and Hungarians, the number of those engaged in agriculture was clearly the highest, and this was reflected in the high percentage of 'self-employed persons'. The proportion of agricultural labourers in the total workforce was larger in the eastern part of the republic than in the Czech Lands. Jews, or those who claimed to be of Jewish nationality, were mostly linked with trade, commerce and finance, and very few of them were workers, farmers or peasants. The rate of employment of women declined towards the east, regardless of nationality.

Large differences could be seen in the cultural level of the population of various nationalities, which was reflected in both the structure of skills of the workforce and the cultural standard of work. Considering the elementary indicator, literacy, in 1921 7.4 per cent of people were illiterate in the whole Czechoslovak Republic, less than 3 per cent among the Czechs and the Germans in the Czech Lands, and 6 per cent among the Poles, whereas among the Slovaks and Czechs living in Slovakia (and also among

Jews throughout the whole republic) this percentage was 16, and among Hungarians it was 11. An extreme 61 per cent of illiterate people was recorded among the Ukrainians and Ruthenians living mostly in the easternmost regions of the Czechoslovak Republic – in Subcarpathian Ruthenia. The differences reflect the unequal standards of the systems of education in the western and the eastern parts of Austria-Hungary, and were also caused by Magyarisation which had hindered the non-Hungarian population in Slovakia and Subcarpathian Ruthenia in acquiring education.

As compared with the year 1913, Czechoslovakia recorded above-average economic growth in the 1920s in relation to all the countries of Europe, in particular in comparison with Germany, Austria and Hungary. The favourable economic and social situation contributed greatly towards pacifying nationalistic antagonisms. In Slovakia autonomistic tendencies were confined practically to the Catholic-oriented Slovak People's Party, whereas the Slovak representatives of the politically most influential Czechoslovak parties, the agrarian and the social democratic parties, were in close collaboration – like the Slovak Protestants – with the governmental line-up of Czech politicians (Milan Hodža, a Slovak politician, was Czechoslovak prime minister in the years 1935–8).

The German minority, too, had its members in the Czechoslovak government and the co-operation between the economic representatives of the two nationalities was quite satisfactory. A proportion of the Germans and also Magyars were unable to rid themselves of the nostalgia for the times when they were the ruling nations. The Polish minority, pained by the post-war boundary disputes, calmed down gradually and the Ruthenians were still passing through a stage of seeking their own national identity.

The economic crisis of the 1930s was deeper and of longer duration in Czechoslovakia than in most European countries, which resulted in far-reaching social, political and nationalistic consequences. The agrarian crisis weighed heavily upon small producers and the poor country population, i.e. upon the classes among which Ruthenians, Hungarians and Slovaks were extremely numerous. In spite of the fact that after 1918 the situation of these nations in the Czechoslovak state improved, their living standard was relatively low and the crisis hit them very painfully. To make matters worse, the USA and some other countries changed their immigration policies so as to minimise the influx of foreigners, thus limiting the possibilities of social emigration, which had operated as a release valve of agrarian overpopulation since the end of the nineteenth century.

The crisis brought about the collapse of foreign trade. Czechoslovak exports fell from 21.2 billion Czechoslovak korunas to 5.9 billion in 1933 (in current prices), and in 1937 the level (12 billion) was still substantially below the pre-crisis level.[3] The crisis also exposed the vulnerability of the structure of both exports and industrial production. Owing to the Austria-Hungarian heritage and the structural inertia of the 1920s the manufacturing industry was extensively represented by export-oriented branches of light industry, whereas the share of the progressive branches of heavy industry (with the exception of the booming armaments industry) was comparatively lower.

In 1936–8 heavy industry, concentrated mainly in regions inhabited by the population of Czech nationality, was recovering relatively fast and, after surmounting the peak of depression, managed to exceed the 1929 level. That is to be accounted for by the growing armaments industry and also by the orientation towards technologically advanced products – from steel, cement and electricity to electrical engineering and transport. That development contributed among other things towards improvement of the social standing of the Polish minority concentrated in the main Czechoslovak region of coal mining, metallurgy and some branches of engineering.

In contrast, such typical export-oriented branches as the textile, glass and china porcelain industries, the manufacture of toys, musical instruments and imitation jewellery, and lace-making had by 1938 not been able to make up for the critical decline during the depression. This situation was aggravated by the fact that the branches of industry mentioned above were those with a particularly large share of labour, which resulted in high rates of unemployment. A considerable part of the capacity of light industry was located in the border regions of the Czech Lands – thus in regions mainly inhabited by a German-speaking population.

The general impoverishment of the population caused by the depression stirred up nationalistic sentiment. In Slovakia autonomists were gaining ground and the number of Slovaks willing to accept the thesis of one Czechoslovak nation was gradually decreasing. In spite of a certain revival of the Slovak economy, which resulted, above all, from the newly increased capacity of the armaments industry, the expansion of the shoe company Baťa to Slovakia and the accelerated construction of the transport infrastructure, a systematic policy leading to the enhancement of the eastern part of the country was absent. Not until 1937 was such a policy conceived which was to link industrialisation with general progress of civilisation. By then it was too late and it could not have been brought to fruition. Also in Subcarpathian Ruthenia voices demanding autonomy were more frequent than before: they usually contained reproaches to the effect that the promise given at the time of the inclusion of the territory into the Czechoslovak Republic had not been fulfilled.

Of the greatest complexity was the situation in the regions settled by the German-speaking population after the Nazi takeover in Germany. The social consequences of the crisis, whose course was prolonged in the Czech borderland owing to the historically conditioned structure of industry, were presented as a failure of Czechoslovak policy. At the same time, the nationalistically oriented political party Sudetendeutsche Heimatsfront (whose name was changed to Sudetendeutsche Partei) openly propagated Nazi ideology and the German approach to the solution of economic and social problems. Under the slogan 'Heim ins Reich' it steered into anti-Czechoslovak waters and extended and intensified its demands. Like the German minorities in Poland, Lithuania, Yugoslavia and other countries, the major part of the German minority in Czechoslovakia became an active tool of Hitlerite expansionist policy and an actual fuse of the Second World War. As early as in the elections of 1935 the Sudeten German Movement polled 15.2 per cent of the votes,[4] that is more than all the other political parties (for the Czech and the Slovak votes were split owing to the greater number of Czech and Slovak political parties). In 1938, when that movement was oriented clearly towards the disintegration of Czechoslovakia, its support within the German minority was estimated at 90 per cent. The fascist ideology was gradually also adopted by the majority of the 'Carpathian Germans' living in Slovakia.

The events of the years 1938–9 resulted in the disintegration of Czechoslovakia and the integration of the separated territories into the sphere of interest of Nazi Germany (South Slovakia and Subcarpathian Ruthenia were annexed to Hungary). The Czech borderland, the Protectorate of Bohemia and Moravia, and the Slovak Republic became part of the German *Grossraumwirtschaft*. In the occupied Czech Lands, in contrast to Slovakia, the features of discontinuity were much more marked and the militarisation of the economy caused much graver structural deformation. In the Czech Lands the output of the industries that were not involved in armaments production fell considerably.

In Slovakia, by contrast, the output of all the important branches of industry rose although increments varied from industry to industry (which must also have been partly due to production having been started in plants the construction of which had begun before 1939). Despite the fact that Nazi Germany exploited Slovakia systematically, particularly as far as mineral resources, foodstuffs, timber and the usage of communications were concerned, the exploitation did not reach such drastic dimensions as in the Czech Lands.

After 1938 the trends in Slovak society continued as before, if the tragic fate of the Jewish population is not taken into account.

German capital, which controlled key positions in the Slovak economy, did not deny the Slovak entrepreneurial class the possibility of prospering economically. This fact was also greatly enhanced by 'aryanisation', which transferred smaller Jewish businesses as well as Jewish-owned land into the hands of 'aryanisers' of Slovak nationality. But the greater proportion of Jewish real estate was placed into German hands (while in the Protectorate of Bohemia and Moravia Jewish property was acquired exclusively by German nationals).

Czech society at this time was characterised by descending social mobility. All Czech universities were closed in autumn 1939, and the network of secondary and vocational schools was greatly reduced, resulting in an interruption of the reproduction of skilled and qualified labour. Whole groups of the population were persecuted or forbidden to continue their occupations. This applied to the politicians active during the period of the pre-Munich Czechoslovak Republic, officers of the Czechoslovak army, diplomats, university lecturers and professors, workers in research and cultural institutes, etc. The Czech monied class of businessmen was weakened both in number and also as far as the disposability of their capital was concerned. Small tradesmen's businesses and carrier and training firms were forcibly closed in several waves. A large number of workers and technicians were hit by the loss of their qualifications. The patterns of factory teams changed radically because the original workforce was replaced by people from outside the working classes, such as housewives and school-leavers. In addition, great numbers of Czechs were ordered to work as labourers in Germany.

After the expected victory the Nazis intended to solve the Czech problem definitively by 'total Germanisation of the space and the population' – a combination of Germanisation of the 'racially acceptable' Czechs, expatriation, massacring ('*Sonderbehandlung*' – execution without trial) and German colonisation.[5]

In the Czechoslovak Republic, re-established in 1945, the number of the members of minorities was radically reduced owing to the Holocaust, expatriation of a greater part of the Germans and annexation of Subcarpathian Ruthenia (now Transcarpathian Ukraine) to the Soviet Union. According to the 1950 census Czechoslovakia was still inhabited by a scattered minority of 165,000 Germans, 68,000 Ruthenians, the latter mostly in north-east

Slovakia, and 73,000 Poles concentrated in the Cieszyn region – a region of intensive construction of industrial plants and an influx of new population which resulted in a decline of the Polish share in the population of that part of the country. Poles were mostly employed in industries where wage levels were above normal. The number of Germans had fallen as low as 61,000 by 1980, which was primarily caused by the high share of old Germans who remained in Czechoslovakia after the expatriation of the greater part of the German minority, and also by their extensive emigration in the 1960s and 1970s. The Magyars were the most numerous minority (half a million) compactly settled in the south of Slovakia.[6] The majority of them were peasants, whose living standard was relatively high, because the regions inhabited by ethnic Magyars were among the most fertile regions of the country.

As far as relations between Czechs and Slovaks are concerned, in the Košice government programme of 5 April 1945 the old concept of a single Czechoslovak nation with two 'branches' and two official languages was replaced by the concept of the Slovak nation being regarded as sovereign and endowed with the same rights as the Czech nation. That programme also guaranteed the existence of specific Slovak organs of administration, which did not have their counterparts in the Czech Lands. An asymmetrical model of the state had thus been created that existed until the establishment of the federation in 1968. Apart from the National Assembly of the representatives of the Czech and the Slovak nations and the central government, Slovakia had its own legislative organ (the Slovak National Council) and its own executive organ (the Corps of Commissioners). Foreign relations, defence, finance and foreign trade remained within the competence of the central government, which had twenty-four members in 1945, nine of whom were Slovaks. In these circumstances, the Slovak ministers were in control of the affairs of the Czech Lands, but in Slovakia their competence was curbed by the Corps of Commissioners – a kind of 'little Slovak government'.

In 1945 it was already considered inevitable that a programme of gradual economic and social equalisation of the two parts of the republic would have to be realised. In the election campaign of May 1946 great emphasis was placed on this issue by all Slovak political parties, the Czech Communist Party and the Social Democratic Party. After the victory of the left in the Czech Lands industrialisation of Slovakia became an important part of the government programme as well as the Two-Year Plan of Post-War Reconstruction of the Economy (1947–8). In addition to the newly constructed plants, Slovakia became the location of a number of industrial plants that were moved and reallocated from the Czech borderland regions. These plants gave employment to about 25,000 workers at the same time as a large number of workers from Slovakia found jobs in the Czech Lands, particularly in agriculture, forestry and mining. A number of Slovaks settled in the Czech Lands as owners of homesteads.

The two-year plan started a qualitatively new period of expansion of the Slovak manufacturing industry. That period became part of the process usually referred to as 'socialist industrialisation'. The equalisation of the economic differences between Slovakia and the Czech Lands was one of the priorities of the economic policy of the central government until the mid-1980s and was incorporated into the tasks set out by all the following five-year plans.

In the period of the first five-year plan (1949–53) the Soviet system of planning and management of the national economy was embarked on in Czechoslovakia and it managed to survive, with minor corrections, until the 1980s. The strengthening of the effect of centrally made decisions, the introduction of a system of directive and detailed planning, the concentration of resources in the hands of the economic centre and the allocation of these resources to preferred sectors were the tools also ensuring a more rapid economic development of Slovakia in comparison with the Czech Lands. However, the excessive centralisation greatly enhanced the risks of incorrect and inadequate decisions owing to both the centre's poor familiarity with local conditions and the concessions granted to various lobbies.

In the early 1950s the centralisation of management led among other things to an imposition of a restraint on the power of the Slovak national organs in favour of the Prague-based centre. This process also hit the Communist Party of Czechoslovakia itself, where the autonomous position of the Slovak communists was greatly weakened. The opponents of the drive aimed at curtailing the authority of the Slovak national organs of power were accused of 'bourgeois nationalism' and a number of them were framed and convicted on fabricated charges in politically motivated trials. Further curtailments of the competence of the Slovak organs and cancellation of part of that competence were enacted by the new constitution of 1960.

The growing discontent fomented by excessive centralisation of control over the national economy and other sectors of life and society was one of the causes of the political crisis of the 1960s, which resulted in the reform process which reached its peak in 1968. The programme of reforms drawn up by the 'Prague Spring platform' aimed at a transition from the centrally planned command economy to a market economy, but it did not include any mass privatisation of state enterprises. Planning was to have been based on long-term scientific prognoses, and targets were to have been achieved with the help of purely economic instruments.

One of the key principles of the reform movement was the federalisation of the republic, which proved to be a complex problem, particularly as far as the economic sphere was concerned. The division of responsibilities in the newly structured state had to be defined in a situation where the forces of integration were gaining ground world-wide and where the Czechoslovak economy had for long decades been built up as an integrated system. It was no wonder that a wide range of points of view, including extremes threatening the country with destabilisation, should have appeared when a compromise was being sought between meeting the Slovak demands and ensuring the continuation of the process of integration.

Negotiations concerning the model of the Czechoslovak federation were started in April 1968 and they continued after 21 August, when the military intervention of the five countries of the Warsaw Pact put a stop to the process of democratisation. The new federal arrangement was enacted by a constitutional Act of Parliament on 27 October 1968, effective from 1 January 1969. As of this date new legislative bodies, governments and other organs of the Czech and the Slovak Socialist Republics came into existence. Some of the articles of this constitutional act, however, were soon amended (in 1970), and some of the responsibilities of the two republics were transferred to the federation, the reason being 'the reinforcement of the integrating function of the federation'.

The formalisation of many of the responsibilities of the republics, as well as of the lower organs of state administration and enterprise management, was realised by the restoration of the directive system of planning and management of the national economy effected in the course of 1969–70. The reforms of the 1960s oriented towards a gradual transition to a market economy were abandoned, not only in Czechoslovakia but also in Hungary and in other countries, including the Soviet Union itself. In this anti-reform climate the long-term programme of economic integration of the Comecon countries adopted in July 1971 had no chance of success.

Despite some swings in the political situation the economic levels of the two parts of the republic were gradually approximating each other. This is evident from table 9.3. Differences still survived in the 1980s, which could partly be accounted for by such facts as the greater share of young people in the Slovak population, or by the larger share of less fertile land in Slovakia which, of course, tended to decrease the productivity of labour.

From table 9.3 it should be evident that the national income used in Slovakia was steadily approximating the Czech level more than the national

Table 9.3 *The level of Slovakia correlated with the Czech Lands, 1948–89*
(Czech Lands = 100)

Indicator	1948	1960	1970	1980	1989
National income created[a]					
per inhabitant	61.2	74.4	78.8	85.2	85.7
per active member of the workforce	58.9	87.2	91.2	92.1	95.1
National income used					
per inhabitant	70.9	83.1	90.7	94.1	92.4
Personal consumption					
per inhabitant	81.0	82.3	85.5	91.4	91.6
Fixed assets in the material sphere					
per inhabitant	57.9	80.2	85.8	95.1	98.3
Fixed assets in the non-material sphere					
per inhabitant	53.3	64.3	70.8	80.8	82.6
Industrial output[b]					
per inhabitant	48.4	64.5	76.6	89.0	89.0
per worker in industry	95.4	107.3	106.1	108.3	109.8
Agricultural output[c]					
per inhabitant	98.7	109.4	100.3	99.3	94.6
per worker in agriculture	59.4	65.5	74.8	77.8	79.5
per hectare of agricultural land	69.8	74.0	77.2	82.0	83.7
Average monthly wages	91.6	96.7	98.2	98.2	98.5

Notes: [a] Excluding foreign trade.
[b] Gross industrial output.
[c] Gross agricultural output. Periods: 1948, averages 1956–60, 1966–70, 1976–80, 1985–89.
Sources: Historická statistická ročenka ČSSR (Prague, 1985); *Statistická ročenka ČSFR* (Statistical Yearbook of the CSFR) 1991, 1992 (Prague, 1991, 1992), various pages. Mostly calculated from absolute data.

income created. In view of the weakness of the Slovak economy and the absence of foreign capital, the success of the programme of equalisation of the historically conditioned differences depended to a great extent upon the transfer of material and financial resources from the Czech Lands to Slovakia. In a centrally managed economy quantification of this transfer is however rather difficult.

The data in table 9.4 confirm that the Czech and the Slovak patterns of employment by various branches of the national economy were gradually coming closer to one another. The increments of the workforce in the non-agricultural branches of the economy were ensured mainly due to the transfer of labourers from agriculture and the employment of housewives. In Slovakia the growth of the rate of employment in the non-agricultural sectors was invariably higher than in the Czech Lands, and in some of the

Table 9.4 *Occupational distribution of the Czech and Slovak workforce in the principal sectors and its dynamic, 1948–89*[a]

Indicator	Country	Percentage distribution					Index[b]
		1948	*1960*	*1970*	*1980*	*1989*	*1989*
Agriculture (excl. forestry)	C	33.1	20.3	14.6	10.9	9.4	38.4
	S	60.6	36.1	23.5	14.8	12.2	33.1
Manufacturing industry and	C	38.8	48.9	48.6	47.9	47.4	165.7
building industry	S	20.8	34.5	40.8	43.9	43.8	347.7
Transport	C	4.3	4.8	5.3	5.2	5.0	159.6
	S	3.8	5.2	5.5	5.3	5.2	229.7
Communications	C	1.1	1.2	1.5	1.4	1.4	177.3
	S	1.5	1.2	1.3	1.2	1.2	418.4
Trade[c]	C	8.4	7.8	8.5	9.7	9.8	158.2
	S	4.7	6.1	7.5	9.3	9.6	335.5
Banking and insurance	C	0.9	0.5	0.5	0.5	0.5	72.3
	S	0.3	0.4	0.4	0.4	0.4	215.6
Science and research	C	0.4	1.8	2.5	2.3	2.3	855.9
	S	0.2	1.2	1.5	2.1	2.4	1868.1
Education and culture	C	2.6	4.3	5.5	6.7	7.4	377.3
	S	1.5	4.7	6.7	7.3	8.3	910.0
Health service and social	C	1.9	2.9	3.6	4.5	5.0	366.5
care	S	0.8	2.6	3.9	4.5	5.4	1085.0
Administration and justice	C	2.5	1.6	1.6	1.6	1.5	79.7
	S	1.8	1.6	1.6	1.6	1.4	131.3
Other[d]	C	6.0	5.9	7.8	9.3	10.3	230.9
	S	5.0	6.4	7.3	9.6	10.1	332.3
Total of those employed	C	3,984	4,450	4,923	5,148	5,402	135,6
(in thousands)	S	1,514	1,555	1,948	2,288	2,498	165,1
Percentage of female	C	36.5	43.7	46.5	45.8	45.8	–
employees	S	39.7	38.7	42.8	44.6	45.5	–

C: Czech Lands, S: Slovakia

Notes: [a] Excluding the armed forces, women on maternity leave, 1980 and 1989 including secondary-job workers.
[b] Index of the absolute number of the workforce, 1948 = 100.
[c] Home trade, foreign trade and purchase of agricultural products.
[d] Forestry, water provision, geological and designing activities, publishing, housing, services to tourism, municipal, commercial and technical services, and other activities.
Sources: Historická statistická ročenka ČSSR, pp. 429, 460–3, 630, 661–4 (1948–70); *Statistická ročenka ČSFR,* pp. 51, 67, 194–5 (1980–9). Mostly calculated from absolute data.

branches of the tertiary sector the workforce even rose nine- to eighteen-fold.

From the mid-1970s onwards a gradual shift in economic policy could be observed in official documents and in plans and prognoses of the national economy attenuating the emphasis placed on the economic equalisation of Slovakia with the Czech Lands in favour of a demand for some substantial contributions by the two republics towards higher economic effectiveness. This resulted in stronger pressure to deal with long-neglected problems such as the relatively backward state of the tertiary sector and the environment. Although after 1975 economic growth of the country went into a long-lasting decline in both parts of the federation, the planned rate of growth of Slovakia continued to be higher than that of the Czech Lands. In April 1985 it was officially announced (by the federal premier L. Štrougal on the occasion of the fortieth anniversary of the Košice government programme) that the process of equalisation of the two republics had reached its target. In 1989 Slovakia's share in the principal economic indicators equalled 30 to 34 per cent, with 33.7 per cent of the total population of the federation.

There is no doubt that in the whole post-war period up to 1989 economic development exhibited greater dynamism in Slovakia than in the Czech Lands. However critical our attitude to the economic development of a country under the communist regime may be, and even though great reservations about the method of industrialisation of Slovakia may be voiced, the reduction of the economic and social differences between the two parts of the country in the course of several decades is an undisputed fact, which was also reflected in the social consciousness of that time. Public opinion polls undertaken in the 1970s and 1980s and also in the post-communist period show that the population of Slovakia judged post-war economic and social developments much more favourably than the Czechs, and that until the end of 1989 the Slovaks were more optimistic about the country's future prospects.

The fact that during the communist era the previously existing deep contrasts between Slovakia and the Czech Lands were greatly mitigated as far as both the economy and the structural indicators, education and the living standard are concerned, casts considerable doubt on the hypothesis seeing the main cause of the disintegration of the republic in the economic and social development before 1989. It should of course not be ignored that the stagnation of the economy in the late 1970s and 1980s established an atmosphere of growing discontent whose possibility of amelioration was also seen in the reform of the relations between the two republics, recession from centralism and new division of competency.

Soon after the fall of the communist regimes all the three multinational federal states disintegrated. The comparison of the USSR, Yugoslavia and Czechoslovakia shows that these states disintegrated regardless of the differences of their previous economic development. In the USSR and Yugoslavia, in contrast with Czechoslovakia, the economic inequality even survived and deepened. Estonia and Latvia generated a national income three times higher (per inhabitant) than some of the central Asian republics of the USSR. And Slovenia's national income was five times higher in the 1970s, and approximately seven times higher at the time Yugoslavia disintegrated, as compared with Kosovo and its enormous population boom.

Too little time has so far elapsed for the causes of the disintegration of Czechoslovakia to be fully clear. The information that has so far been published is rather incomplete and will probably remain so for quite a long time. On the whole, we are able to reconstruct the polarisation of the nationalistic standpoints and the process of dismantling the federation by the Czech and the Slovak political representation including the rejection of the referendum on the fate of the common state quite reliably,[7] and can confirm the different reaction of the majority of the Czech and the Slovak population to the economic policy of the Czech liberals, who took up the reins in that case; but the still hidden interior, exterior, international political, economic and military context can only be surmised.

NOTES

1. From the historical point of view the Czechs had regained independence after 300 years.
2. *Historická statistická ročenka ČSSR* [Historical Statistical Yearbook of the ČSSR] (Prague, 1985), p. 62.
3. Ibid., p. 862.
4. *Dějiny Československa v datech* [History of Czechoslovakia in Dates] (Prague, 1968), p. 467.
5. The same aim is formulated e.g. in the memorandum issued by K.H. Frank, secretary of state and deputy Reichsprotektor, on 28 September 1940, approved by A. Hitler on 12 October 1940. It was before the Munich Conference that an analogous goal had already been formulated in a classified document of the Sudetendeutsche Partei entitled '*Grundplanung O. A.*': 'The Czech language must be completely repressed. Its complete disappearance is in the German interest... The final goal must be: decay of the consciousness of Czech nationality, settlement of the territory by Germans, transformation (partly by re-settlement) of the Czech nation so as to be embraceable by Germany.' (Archives of the Ministry of the Interior, *The Office of the Reichsprotector*, and Annex No. 234 to the Indictment against K.H. Frank of 1946).

6. *Historická statistická ročenka ČSSR*, p. 62. In the 1950 census 368,000 people opted for Hungarian nationality and in 1961 this number rose to 534,000. One can only judge that a number of Magyars claimed a nationality other than Hungarian in the year 1950.

7. According to the public opinion poll undertaken in autumn 1992, one-fifth of the population (a bit more in the Czech Republic than in Slovakia) were in favour of the division of the republic, though great differences existed as far as the form of the state was concerned. However, a vast majority were resigned, claiming that preparations for the division had already gone too far to be stopped and for the end of the common state to be prevented.

CHAPTER 10

Economic retardation, peasant farming and the nation-state in the Balkans: Serbia, 1815–1912 and 1991–1999

Michael Palairet

Government is concerned with the exercise, projection and defence of its power. In the Balkans, the checks and balances which subordinate state power to the rule of law in a modern democracy were honoured more in rhetoric than in practice. Ruling elites in the Balkans tried to minimise the risks arising from the plurality of political challenges by linking personal power to dependence on government. Therefore governments tried to foster cohesion within the political class around their own objectives.

The problems of governing a nation-state differed fundamentally from those which confronted government in a multinational empire or federation. By a nation-state (within the South-East European context) I would understand a state built upon the assent of a numerically predominant people sharing a common language and religion. In such a state, the political interests of minorities have been subordinated, if necessary by force, to those of the dominant nation. In the historical context of the nineteenth and twentieth centuries, Balkan nation-states include Serbia (1804–1918), Montenegro (1858–1914), Greece (since 1825), Bulgaria (since 1878), Albania (since 1912) and Serbia, as the Federal Republic (FR) of Yugoslavia, since 1991.[1]

There have been three counterpart multinational entities in the Balkans: the Habsburg and Ottoman empires, and Yugoslavia (in its first and second creations). None of these states could achieve stability by the same means as the nation-states, because as mass consciousness of national identity grew, the suppression of pluralism, though often tried, proved impossible to sustain.

The Balkan nation-states, thanks to their intrinsic cohesion, have survived and prospered politically. Of these, only Montenegro disappeared as an independent entity, and it may well reappear. All the nation-states have been trounced in disastrous foreign wars, more often than not initiated by themselves: Serbia in 1876, 1885, 1915, and (arguably) in 1991, twice in 1995, and again in 1999; Bulgaria in 1913, 1918 and 1945; Greece in 1898,

1922 and 1941. However they possessed sufficient internal cohesion to re-emerge, sometimes shorn of territory, either as nation-states or, in the case of Serbia, as the dominant entity within the first Yugoslavia. On the other hand, none of the four multinational entities survived, nor is any of them likely to be reconstituted.

The advantage of intrinsic national cohesion in a nation-state offered no guarantee that the nation would cohere around its ruling elite. However, governments knew that their heartlands, where the numerical dominance of the state-nation was not in doubt, were never in danger of permanent loss, no matter what external danger they courted. In the Balkans, where real or imagined minorities of the state-nations dwelt beyond national frontiers, their existence created irridenta for the external projection of power, and as a force for internal national cohesion. Therefore the nation-states tended to be expansionist, while the multinational states were more concerned to maintain their control over existing territory, and to curb the aspirations of their neighbours. If the opportunity occurred to annex territory they would exploit it, but the war aims of nation-states have always been irridentist. (This was true of Serbia in 1914, even though that war was not of its own making).[2] Nation-states therefore expected, periodically, to go to war. As their governments wanted their armies to fight whole-heartedly, it was imperative to mobilise a consensus behind their war aims. They did not, therefore, want significant sections of the nation to be alienated by pluralistic distractions.

This basic difference between the nation-state and the multinational state would have repercussions in the economic field. The multinational states were confronted by political pluralisms, which could not be repressed by appeals to patriotism, so they learned to bid for the loyalty of their subjects. This could mean intervening in the economy. The promotion and diffusion of economic development to counter separatism was far from absent from the political thinking of Vienna. The development plans, costing upwards of 500 million crowns, of Prime Minister Koerber in 1900 were laid precisely with this aim. Even though his project failed,[3] the remarkable economic dynamism of the Habsburg core was diffused among the outlying provinces, and into Hungary. Ease of access to Austrian capital and technology facilitated Hungary's industrialisation.[4] Within Hungary efforts were made to implant industries into Slovakia, where Hungarians were in the minority.[5] Croatia and Dalmatia also shared in the economic growth of Austria-Hungary.[6] The most striking example of diffusion was in Bosnia-Hercegovina, where Austro-Hungarian administrators bade for the allegiance of the Muslims by pursuing economic policies which would induce well-being in the province. Bosnians would then be convinced that their prosperity resulted from membership of the Habsburg community.[7]

In the first Yugoslavia, the relatively advanced areas were those of minority nations (Slovenia and Croatia) so diffusing prosperity meant transferring resources towards the Serb political heartland rather than away from it. Regional policy therefore worked against the grain of cohesion, as it always will when economically advanced territories are subordinated to a backward political core. Still, vigorous efforts to stimulate development were made by Stojadinović's government in 1935–9, with more success than its quest for a stable *modus vivendi* between Belgrade and Zagreb.[8]

The communist rulers of the second Yugoslavia (which was not, during the lifetime of Tito, under Serbian political dominance) were committed to economic convergence policies for building a cohesive Yugoslav state. Huge transfers were arranged in the 1950s and early 1960s for advancement of underdeveloped territories to which Slovenia had to pass on 'up to one third of its income'.[9] After 1965, pressures from the northern republics caused a reduction in inter-regional assistance. Because of defective implementation, the resources passed southwards were insufficient to narrow the gaps in regional development, so these became more rather than less pronounced. (In 1952 Kosovo's per capita social product was 44 per cent of that of Yugoslavia, but by 1988, it was down to 27 per cent.) The apparent waste of development resources[10] therefore fostered division rather than unity. Nevertheless, Yugoslavia's development policies required the promotion of economic growth and structural change, and a grudging acceptance of the political pluralism which accompanied this.

Nation-states would also intervene in economic matters, but for different reasons. The nation-state did not have to buy cohesion through economic development and its regional diffusion. It wanted industrialisation for the enhancement of state power. But welfare-promoting economic changes were only encouraged in so far as they were compatible with higher political ends. Change caused political pluralisation, and threatened the *status quo*. So the governments of nation-states, despite their avowed radicalism, favoured social and economic policies which would minimise structural change and pluralism, and they subordinated economic development to political stability.

The focus of this study is the case of Serbia, both in its nineteenth-century creation, and in the period since the break-up in 1991 of the second Yugoslavia. It will be argued that the economic policies and outcomes in these two incarnations of Serbian state power share certain parallels. Both Serbian states resisted economic and social change, for fear of creating uncontrollable pluralism. In both cases their policies were economically retardative – and in the latter case frankly disastrous. Both before 1914 and post-1990, economic performance depended heavily on the agricultural sector, but, as will be argued, over-fixation by government (and, indeed, by economic historians[11]) on the supposedly dynamic role of the 'modern' industrial sector to the detriment of farming inhibited development. Serbia, despite its conspicuous political success, was probably poorer and less productive in 1912 than it had been in 1862. Also, since 1990, the present territory of Yugoslavia has suffered the most dreadful immiseration in its history.

The only period of sustained progress towards prosperity occurred between the mid-1950s and the early 1970s, when Serbia participated in the growth of the economy of Tito's Yugoslavia. This was a state whose economic policies Serbia did not control, and the liberalising (and therefore pluralising) economic reforms of the 1960s, which induced prosperity, and those of the 1980s, which sought to restore it, were resisted and aborted by the Serbian political elite.

PRE-1914 PEASANT POLICY

Emergent Serbia under Karadjordje in 1804–14 was effectively a confederation headed by powerful local notables (the *knezevi*). If left undisturbed, the *knezevi* would have implanted feudal institutions, because land was so abundant that only the coercion of peasant labour could valorise it as an investment. After destruction by the Ottomans of Karadjordje's Serbia, the Serbs of the Belgrade *pašaluk* (province) rose for a second time in 1815 under the leadership of Miloš Obrenović. In the 1820s the *knezevi* tried to amass land and to demand labour services from the peasants,[12] but Miloš was determined to prevent the emergence of a territorial elite which might challenge his autocratic authority. He therefore posed as protector of peasant rights to check incipient opposition power. In 1833 he suppressed the feudal right of *spahiluk* (small territorial fief of feudal cavalrymen), and in 1835 abolished the right of territorial administrators to demand corvée of their peasants.[13] These measures prevented the emergence of large-scale landed estates, so the Serbian state came to rest on small-scale peasant landownership. Miloš compensated himself financially by bringing foreign trade under a system of permits and controls, selling export licences to favoured businessmen.[14] As a result emergent capitalistic wealth tended to be exported, in search of better returns than could be secured domestically.[15] Concern by his government lest peasants be displaced through usury as owners of the land led in 1836 to the protection of homesteads from sequestration for debt repayment.[16]

Excluded from the perquisites of both landownership and commerce, his political opponents drove him from power in 1839 and remained in control till 1859. They abolished controls over foreign trade, and they scrapped the homestead law. The effects on agrarian structure were probably minimal, though concern about the emergence of rural debt led after restoration of the Obrenović dynasty in 1859 to enaction of a new homestead law in 1861. No subsequent attempt was made to reverse this disposition.

The law's practical effect was to deprive the peasants of credit other than on usurious terms, since they could offer no collateral because most peasant land had been rendered inalienable. This law became the cornerstone of a raft of policies which have been described as the 'tutelage of the peasantry'. The authorities wanted to maintain rural Serbia within a self-sufficient subsistence framework, and to minimise the market forces to which agriculture was exposed. The peasants must pay their taxes, and to this object they should export livestock (mainly pigs and cattle) to the Habsburg lands. Since livestock raising was conducted on a purely extensive basis, the gradual clearance of the forests diminished the capacity of the peasants to raise and export livestock, so by the 1860s the production of grain for surplus and export became unavoidable. The authorities deprecated the burgeoning export of grain, for they thought it threatened peasant solvency and self-sufficiency. They did not interfere directly with it, but they repeatedly took measures to minimise peasant access to exchange goods. They believed that by containing peasant demand for merchandise, they would minimise the risk of agrarian debt.[17]

In this they were abetted by the *čaršija*, the urban artisans and merchants, who wanted to stifle competition for the custom of the rural market. Under Miloš, village shops required licences, which were only grudgingly awarded. Their trade was restricted to necessities, and the few shops that opened were highly taxed.[18] The 1863 census showed that villages even in fertile provinces had hardly any shops or even taverns, but during the export boom years of the late 1860s, the number of village shops expanded.[19] Urban interests complained of the diversion of trade. Petty craftsmen were pressed by increasing import competition, as Serbia's commercial isolation was eroded. They won support from local administrators, who regarded the acquisition by the peasants of 'trifles' as thoroughly undesirable. In 1870, village shops were barred from selling imported goods, and were restricted to a minimum of 15–18 km from the nearest town. The *čaršija* pressed for their total suppression. It never achieved this objective, but it secured a law in 1891 to restrict sales in village shops to a specified list of products. This prevented incentive goods, even sugar, from being legally sold by them. This law was enforced up to 1914. Village shops were not the only means by which the peasants came into contact with exchange goods, so the attack on rural commerce was extended by a string of laws, in 1859, 1879 and 1889. These restricted the trade carried out at country fairs, and led to their decline. Pedlars were banned in 1850, and the law against their activities was repeatedly strengthened.[20]

As late as 1863, 93 per cent of Serbia's population was rural. So, by its policy of peasant 'tutelage', government choked off indigenous sources of economic dynamism. This was no less apparent in other fields. Communications were rudimentary, yet the army, fearing the impact railways might have on security, and the *carsija*, fearful of import competition, blocked all proposals for building any.[21] When, in 1881, Serbia began to build her main trunk line, it was as a result of compulsion under the Berlin Treaty of 1878. Thereafter, the railway question came to be viewed almost wholly in strategic terms, and government only started building branch railways in 1908. Until then it had blocked all private projects of this nature.[22]

Human capital formation was also minimal. In 1866, 95.8 per cent of the population (and 98.4 per cent of rural dwellers) were illiterate. This had improved somewhat by 1900, when literacy had reached 20.3 per cent of the population as a whole. Even so, education was accorded a low priority. In 1878, social reformer Francis Mackenzie tried to establish schooling for refugee children, but faced a bureaucracy unable to comprehend any purpose in educating such people. His later efforts at establishing educational establishments likewise led to conflict with the authorities.[23] Education, in the eyes of administrators, was needed by urban business and for the formation of future state officials – but was wasted on peasants.[24] No rural initiatives offset this lack of urban concern, for peasants exhibited little interest in supporting schools.[25]

Though state policy harmed the development of agriculture, it was not intentionally repressive towards the peasantry. Over time, the tax burden was shifted increasingly on to the urban dweller, mainly by imposing excises and monopolies upon commodities of which peasants made sparing use.[26] However the diminution of peasant direct tax burdens probably decelerated the monetisation of produce, because in a weakly integrated market with high transactions costs, it was the availability of subsistence goods rather than of exchange products which determined a peasant family's welfare.

Agriculture remained technologically stagnant and subsistence-orientated. Non-agricultural economic activity was also stunted. Neither proto-industry nor intensive farming (both of which flourished in late Ottoman Bulgaria) could gain a hold. Therefore the emergence of enterprise culture was feeble, and the demand for exchange goods was curtailed. The small urban sector, guild-ridden and fearful of competition, provided small stimulus.

It is not possible to quantify the extent to which obstructing railway development, distancing the peasant from incentive goods and withholding trade finance from the village community caused the retardation of rural commerce, and consequently of wider economic development. However, a heavy price was to be exacted for agricultural stagnation. Population expanded from 15 per sq. km in 1820 to 29 in 1860 and 61 by 1910. As most demographic increase was reabsorbed by the villages, as late as 1910, small communities still comprised 89 per cent of the population. Farming still accounted for 57 per cent of GDP, and only 38.4 per cent of farm output went to market. Growth in farm-based exports per capita of the rural population decelerated from the 1860s onward and turned negative by the 1900s. My own estimate is that the per capita output of farm products by the farm population declined by 24.5 per cent between 1863/72 and 1903/12, and that growth in other sectors of the economy was not robust enough to compensate. Economic decline may have set in as early as the 1830s, and between 1863 and 1910 Serbia's per capita GDP probably declined further by 15–20 per cent.[27]

Though its agrarian institutions were counter-developmental, government in Serbia wanted modernisation and industrialisation. The state built up a public sector industry complex, and industrial concession laws were established in 1873 and strengthened in 1898. These were designed to attract capital from abroad, but this inflow would have been larger were it not for the repulsive forces of official xenophobia and corruption.[28] Resources were also lavished upon the capital city, whose Europeanisation stood in contrast to the semi-oriental stagnation of the provincial towns.[29] In all, modernisation was superficial, because it had no domestic roots to draw on, thanks in part to state policy towards the rural population.

SERBIA-YUGOSLAVIA UNDER MILOŠEVIĆ

In 1991 Serbia re-emerged as a nation-state in all but name from the wreck of former Yugoslavia. Yugoslavia had been expected to perform better than the former Soviet bloc countries as its economy was more open, its productive equipment was mainly imported from the West and planning distortions were thought to be milder. Yet the economic consequences of Slobodan

Milošević's 'conservative' rule on the Serb-Montenegrin rump left this then physically unscathed country in worse economic disorder than any other Yugoslav successor state, or ex-Soviet satellite.[30] Officially measured social product, already in decline during the 1980s,[31] contracted by 44 per cent between 1990 and 1998,[32] and the reality was still worse. Per capita national expenditure provisionally recalculated from the household expenditure surveys (which should pick up the black economy) indicates a fall from 3,909 dinars of 1994 value in 1990 to 1,456 in 1998. (All amounts are in dinars of 1994 value when the dinar stood at an exchange parity of one German mark.) Neither measure takes account of the decline over the same period of the country's capital stock. Over the same period, the volume of road and rail freight traffic, a sensitive indicator of business activity, fell to 26.9 per cent of its former level. The impact on popular well-being was extreme. Real monthly earnings of the employed workforce in Yugoslavia had already dropped from a peak of 1,243 dinars in July 1978 to a low of 622 dinars in September 1988. In 1988, Milošević exploited the consequent dissatisfaction by promising the Serbian public a 'Swedish' standard of living by 2000,[33] but real earnings collapsed from 491 dinars in December 1991 to around 200 dinars per month, at which they remained stable between mid-1994 and October 1998. In long-term perspective, mid-1994–1998 earnings levels fell to less than 30 per cent of those of 1914.[34] Officially recognised unemployment rose in 1997 to 25.9 per cent.[35]

    This chapter is primarily concerned with agriculture. However, we need to understand the causes of rump Yugoslavia's economic descent in order to set the context for agricultural development. It is helpful to understand why the Milošević regime conducted its economic policies in the way it did. Milošević took power primarily by exploiting Serbia's national concerns over Kosovo, but the take-over was also accompanied by a so-called 'anti-bureaucratic revolution'. This was a conservative response to the threat of economic liberalisation. By the mid-1980s, it had become apparent that Edvard Kardelj's reforms in the 1970s had entangled the enterprises in a complex of contractual undertakings and cartels which so undermined incentives to rationality that urgent restructuring was needed to allocate resources efficiently. Reform was not, however, costless. From the standpoint of Belgrade, it could be represented as a northern-inspired attack on Serbia's interests. As the existing political structure decayed in the 1980s, nationalism was the obvious vehicle for re-establishing power within an increasingly fluid political environment. In an economic context, nationalism meant resistance to structural adaptation. Therefore Milošević's 'anti-bureaucratic revolution' was about conserving the existing structure of economic and political power, and subordinating pluralist competition. The inheritance to be conserved differed from that inherited by Yugoslavia from pre-1914 Serbia, because of industrial expansion in the communist era. Therefore Milošević's regime built its political power base around the 'big systems' – the heavy industry combines – while taking care to avoid antagonising the increasingly important farming sector.

Ideologically, the 'big systems' were supposed to act as the 'locomotives' of socialist development. Their directors, and those of the state banks, which financed them, were closely knit into the structures of political power. Unfortunately, the 'big systems' were economic albatrosses. They had been built up on the basis of dubious planning decisions. They were heavy loss-makers and bad debtors. By pouring 'fresh money' into the banking system to roll over their escalating losses in the 1980s, the authorities fuelled galloping inflation. The 'big systems' would have no obvious role to play in a reformed economic system.

The 'big systems' directors therefore saw economic reform as a threat to their power and perquisites, while their mass workforces feared for their jobs. The need for reform in the 1980s became so pressing that Ivan Stambolić, Milošević's predecessor as leader of the ruling party in Serbia, admitted in 1987 that one of Serbia's proudest giants, the MKS steel complex at Smederevo, was a 'rock on the shoulder of Serbia, and . . . a significant factor in its economic backwardness'. The threat to close or downsize MKS and similar enterprises caused Milošević to pose as their protector, and for nationalists to represent restructuring as a Croat–Slovene conspiracy to weaken Serbia. Milošević acted from the outset in support of the Serbian 'big systems', and remained consistent in his support.[36] Indeed, during the years of war and sanctions, the regime maintained the 'big systems' intact as the basis for future regrowth and reinvestment, even though their activity was redundant to present needs.

The catastrophic shrinkage of real pay rates and gradual shedding of labour should have reduced industrial losses and eased the cash-flow pressures on enterprises and the banks. This did not happen. A mild recovery in industrial output between 1994 and mid-1998 caused no improvement in conditions, because priority was given to restoring production in the 'big systems'. As these were massive value-subtractors, their recovery merely intensified the burden on the rest of the economy. In 1991 'uncovered' enterprise losses amounted to 100 billion current dinars (roughly 10 billion dinars of 1994).[37] In 1996, despite the now paltry wages disbursed, net losses for the 'economy' as a whole amounted to 8.59 billion dinars, and in 1997, to 13.41 billion.[38] The 200 largest enterprises employed 468,000 workers in 1996 and 464,000 in 1997. Their losses in 1996 ran at 11,821 dinars per employee and in 1997 at 22,465 dinars,[39] sums which far exceeded what they paid in wages (7,904 dinars in 1996 and 9,782 dinars in 1997).

The simplest way to cover the cash-flow deficits would have been to monetise them, but this could destabilise an already shaky currency into a new hyperinflation. Though Milošević's state had survived a hyperinflation already, it feared the consequences of creating another, so alternative means of carrying the corporate losses had to be found. The state banks carried representatives of their biggest debtor enterprises on their boards, especially enterprises headed by high party comrades (as they were still called). They knew these clients were insolvent but, if they were wise, they looked to 'higher places' for guidance as to which of them deserved further support. Bankers were expected to align themselves with JUL, Mira Marković's elite political movement.[40] Disobedient banks risked losing their licences.[41]

To absorb these losses, the banks set extremely wide margins between their borrowing and lending rates of interest. For January–August 1998, during which time annual price inflation was 44.8 per cent, the big banks paid (an annualised) 19 per cent on deposits. Beogradska Banka (the largest) lent at 122 per cent, plus multifarious fees for 'bankers' services'. Since 'privileged' borrowers could not repay, whatever the interest rate, their demand for credit was insensitive to interest levels. Propping up the 'big systems' crowded out the viable business borrower.[42] As the banks could not attract personal savings, they needed continuous central bank assistance to alleviate their chronic illiquidity. This continuously forced up the money supply. Price controls proliferated in response, deepening corporate deficits. The dinar remained incurably weak. The new currency of January 1994, which had been given limited Deutschmark (DM) convertibility at 1:1, traded on the street in December 1999 at less than 5 pfennigs.

The commitment of available resources to cover the trading losses of the 'big systems' left little funding for investment, so enterprises were unable to make good their depreciation provisions, and their assets wasted away. Formerly modern installations (as of 1987) were, a decade later, obsolete, while the products they made became old fashioned and unexportable. As table 10.1 shows, from 1988 to 1997 the fixed capital stock of the economy diminished at an accelerating pace to fall by 8.2 billion dinars (or DM) of 1994 value. Even then, only assets currently in commission were depreciated and this excluded the approximately 50 per cent of industrial capital stock which stood idle. Financial exigency also led to the run-down of merchandise inventories, which declined by 31 per cent by 1997 from the already dangerously low level of 1991 (when the series first appeared).[43]

Table 10.1 *Fixed investment and depreciation Yugoslavia/FRY, 1987–97 (in billion dinars of 1994)*

Year	Investment	Depreciation	Net investment
1987	12.6	11.0	1.6
1988	10.7	11.0	−0.3
1989	11.2	11.1	0.0
1990	9.2	10.0	−0.8
1991	7.9	8.4	−0.5
1992	5.5	6.0	−0.5
1993	3.5	3.9	−0.5
1994	3.0	3.9	−0.8
1995	2.9	4.1	−1.1
1996	2.8	4.4	−1.7
1997	2.8	4.7	−2.0

Source: Calculated from *Statistički godišnjak Jugoslavije* [*SGJ*], 1995, p. 142; 1998, pp. 124, 163; 1999, pp. 124, 165. Depreciation = social product − *dohodak* (net output).

Obsolescence affected not only manufacturing. Infrastructure decayed. Forced to produce at far below cost, the electricity system staggered from crisis to crisis with less than minimal repairs. Between 1991 and 1995, it invested about $300 million, less than one-fifth the rate attained in 1981–5. So too with water supplies. Want of funds (in 1997) caused maintenance of supply networks to be neglected, and equipment cannibalised. The roads also deteriorated, as maintenance spending per kilometre declined by 89 per cent between 1990 and the mid-1990s. The mean age of vehicles rose from seven years in 1990 to eleven years in 1998.[44] So in 1991–8 both the capital stock of the enterprises and the infrastructure were eroded. Discussing the modest nominal economic revival of 1994 economist D. Marsenić warned that 'statistical growth' was illusory, for the productive capacity of the economy had diminished, while increased current output had been achieved by running down inventories.[45] This process was to accelerate.

Financial insolvency in the 'big systems', and consequently in the banks, did not result simply from the misallocation of funds. The Yugoslav carcass provided rich pickings from which the 'deserving' elite and its criminal associates rewarded themselves. The 'big systems' were exploited by their directors who, after a mass sacking of independent directors in 1989/90, were predominantly allied to the ruling party.[46] Their gains were largely siphoned offshore. The hyperinflation in 1992 and 1993 was caused largely by the printing of banknotes to sell on the street for hard currency, and it yielded about 6 billion DM in offshore deposits. The hard currency extracted from the impoverished population was laundered in Cyprus and about 30 per cent of the proceeds 'went into the pockets of the political establishment'.[47] Stabilisation in January 1994 required a diminution in currency dumping, but in 1994–6, the state periodically manipulated the black market to raid citizens' hard currency holdings.[48]

The 'big systems' bosses also bled their enterprises and exported the proceeds as hard currency. They created monopolistic intermediaries to interpose themselves between the factories, their suppliers and their customers, especially where import and export transactions were concerned.[49] (These also gave rise to economic rents through privileged access to foreign exchange at official exchange rates.[50]) Supporters of the system justified the use of privileged intermediaries on the grounds that 'a single purchaser' should supply the products of a 'single producer', since producer and the purchaser 'know each other excellently'. These rackets were a 'mass phenomenon',[51] and economist Ljubomir Madžar demonstrated that they were integral to the survival strategy of the regime.[52]

Because of the consequently inflated input costs and artificially low realisations of the enterprises, it was small wonder they lost money and needed permanent assistance from the banks. Remittance of the proceeds offshore caused Yugoslavia to suffer a permanent foreign exchange crisis, which could only be alleviated (as it was to some extent in 1997) by selling assets to foreign investors. When asset sales were diminished by the reimposition of financial sanctions in 1998, the upper bound for economic activity set by the availability of foreign exchange for importing input materials for industry contracted, and depressed the economy still further.

AGRICULTURE

In Tito's Yugoslavia, agricultural performance had been plagued by policy and ideological constraints which depressed its performance. In 1985 agricultural output was only double that of 1939. After the productive disaster caused by forced collectivisation in 1949–51, the authorities let the collectives collapse in 1953, but restricted peasant holdings to a maximum of 10 hectares. Even then, 'large' holdings were so heavily taxed as to speed up the rate at which these holdings were subdivided.[53] The number of private holdings (in Serbia and Montenegro) remained remarkably constant, 1.26 million in 1952, 1.18 million in 1991. In 1969, the average peasant property disposed only 3.3 hectares, and even this was fragmented into

Table 10.2 Dohodak *(net output) and payroll value for industry and agriculture, Federal Republic of Yugoslavia, 1990–7 (in billion dinars of 1994 value)*

Year	Net output			Payroll	
	Total	Industry	Agriculture	Industry	Agriculture
1990	35.9	13.4	4.2	7.3	3.8
1991	32.1	11.5	4.6	5.1	3.5
1992	23.2	8.9	3.8	3.8	3.0
1993	16.3	5.4	3.7	n.d.	n.d.
1994	16.9	5.5	3.9	2.6	3.1
1995	17.9	5.8	4.1	2.4	3.4
1996	18.9	6.2	4.1	3.1	3.7
1997	20.3	6.8	4.4	2.7	3.3

Sources: Dohodak: SGJ, (1998), p. 124; (1999), p. 124. Payroll data are given each year, at current prices, in *SGJ* (1992–9), tables of social product and material costs by types of ownership.

6.5 parcels. In order to keep them dependent on the socialised sector, peasants were deprived until 1967 of the right to purchase new machinery. There was no advance upon 1930s output levels until 1957, and despite modest growth to 1976, the labour productivity of Yugoslav agriculture (in 1976–8) was no higher than that of Pakistan. From 1976 to 1990, agricultural output in Serbia stagnated entirely. Despite the participation (in 1981) of 29 per cent of the population in agriculture, Yugoslavia was from 1970 onwards a consistent net importer of farm products.[54] The unfailing record of plan under-performance in agriculture was in 1989 to result in the abolition of the maximum of 10 hectares per holding and, effectively, of the long-term commitment of the state to the eventual socialisation of agriculture. However, few farmers expanded their holdings, and farming remained fragmented: 3.81 million persons were directly dependent on agriculture in 1991, and 95.5 per cent of holdings were of 10 hectares or less.[55]

The collapse of industry in rump Yugoslavia between 1990 and 1993 caused agriculture, merely by holding output stable, to reassume dominance in the country's economic life. This is not immediately apparent from the official statistics. Figures for *dohodak* (output, after deduction of official depreciation provisions) of industry and agriculture are displayed as columns 3 and 4 of table 10.2. They appear to indicate the continued predominance of industry, but *dohodak* included corporate and turnover taxes. This distorts comparison between sectors because taxes embedded in agricultural product prices were very low. *Dohodak* also included surpluses for accumulation. As there was no surplus (rather a huge deficit) the only non-tax element in net output (*dohodak*) was wages. For agriculture, predominantly peasant farming, 'wages' are defined as subsuming 'that share of income of private producers disposable for personal consumption'.[56] The serials for *dohodak* at constant price do not break it down into its components, so in order to show the value in constant dinars of the wage element in the industrial and agricultural sectors, I have taken the annual breakdowns at current price, and have applied the proportions in these attributed to wages to the *dohodak* figures in table 10.2, columns 3 and 4. This procedure creates columns 5 and 6. On average, 'wages' amounted to 46.5 per cent of the net output of industry and 83.0 per cent of that of agriculture. On a 'payroll' basis, therefore, agriculture became by 1993 or 1994 a significantly more important contributor to total output than industry.

Agriculture also absorbed more labour than industry. In 1995, industry employed 870,000 persons, including those on 'compulsory holiday', while in 1996, 838,000 persons were active in private agriculture.[57] (Socialised agriculture employed a further 93,000 persons.)

From 1991 onwards rump Yugoslavia raised a net surplus for international trade. But there was no revival in agricultural production, rather a collapse in the domestic demand, caused by mass impoverishment. Food sales held up better than those of industrial products, for in 1993 some 54.3 per cent of all household income had to be spent on foodstuffs.[58] Immiseration between 1990 and 1994 caused a 34 per cent contraction in the retail sale of fresh meat and poultry, and a 35 per cent contraction in the sale of animal fats.[59] Similar falls affected milk products, eggs, rice and fish. Thus, while in 1990 the country exported the equivalent of DM 676 million of food and in 1992, 682 million, food imports shrank from 1,168 million dinars to 461 million.[60] With the partial post-war revival of demand, the balance sank once more into deficit. By 1996 imports and exports roughly balanced and in 1997 bad harvests caused agricultural exports to sink to $396 million while imports rose to $695 million.[61]

The peasants, who in 1994 farmed 84.4 per cent of the cultivable land, produced 79.7 per cent of agricultural output.[62] There remained, especially in the Vojvodina, a substantial state farm and collective sector. These deficit-ridden giants were no model for emulation. They came to specialise in crop farming, while gradually abandoning the raising of livestock. In 1989, they held 18.7 per cent of the livestock, in 1997, 8.2 per cent of a total herd which had diminished in aggregate by 20.0 per cent.[63] During the period 1989–96, their social product fell 44 per cent from 1,412 million dinars of 1994 to 790 million, while private peasant agricultural product (according to the official statistics) rose slightly from 3,634 million to 3,731 million.[64] This was partly because socialised farms lost labour, land and livestock more rapidly than did private farming. However, the land they lost, mainly under a programme for the return of property confiscated after the Second World War, was weed-choked and out of cultivation; as such it stayed.[65]

Agriculture could not be unaffected by the collapse of industry. Private farming had to contend with a disastrous fall in the use of mineral fertiliser, insecticides and fungicides. As early as 1991, (former) Yugoslavia's consumption of fertiliser per hectare had fallen below that even of Albania.[66] Fertiliser use declined from 1.45 million tons (556,000 tons of active material) in 1985 to 291,000 in 1994, and 379,000 in 1997. Private farmers virtually ceased to use it, for after deducting social sector fertiliser consumption, private consumption collapsed from 938,000 tons in 1985 to 126,000 in 1994 and 110,000 in 1997.[67] The problem lay partly on the supply side. In March 1999, only two of seven fertiliser factories were in production, because the industry lacked the funds to import raw materials and natural gas.[68] The decline in the use of fungicides and insecticides by peasant farmers was almost as dramatic. In 1985, 15,396 tons were applied, and in 1997, 3,409 tons; in 1997 private farmers used only 19.5 per cent of the supply, though in 1991 they had used 30.0 per cent of it.[69] The undersupply of inputs exacted a creeping toll on output per hectare. In 1987–91, wheat yielded 4.18 tons per hectare, in 1992–5, 3.38 tons; maize yielded 4.01 and 3.38.[70] Land whose yield had collapsed through under-fertilization gradually fell out of cultivation.

Agricultural fixed investment declined by 48 per cent between 1990 and 1994,[71] but in 1994, private farming invested 246 million dinars, against depreciation of 240 million.[72] The stock of tractors actually rose – from 391,000 in 1990 to 425,000 in 1998.[73] However, sales of new tractors at retail collapsed from 13,905 in 1990 to 198 in 1996, sales of ploughs from 13,851 to 1,971.[74] As a result, in December 1998 the national stock of tractors and combines was of an average age exceeding sixteen years.[75] As there was an acute shortage of spare parts to maintain these antiques, cannibalisation of machines was routine.[76]

The livestock sector faced equally serious problems. While in 1991 Serbia had 850,000 breeding cows, it is claimed that their number had fallen to about 500,000 in 1998. By this time, allegedly, Yugoslavia was the lowest per capita meat consumer in Europe, even behind Albania.[77] The general

Table 10.3 *Structure of peasant production
and consumption, Serbia, 1986–98*

	Farm output self-consumed (%)	Income consumed as food and drink (%)
1986	49.0	39.6
1987	53.8	40.6
1988	55.7	43.1
1989	57.3	43.7
1990	55.5	40.5
1991	61.5	41.0
1992	60.9	49.5
1993	69.7	58.1
1994	65.3	53.5
1995	62.7	53.3
1996	63.1	50.3
1997	63.8	49.6
1998	62.0	49.5

Sources: SGJ (1988–98), tables of houshold consumption by agricultural and mixed households.

contraction of incomes held meat prices down to levels that did not justify production costs, especially the cost of fodder, which had a significant import content.[78] So farmers were forced to shift out of livestock towards cereals. About 70 per cent of crop production was normally grown as animal feed, causing livestock raising to be regarded as 'the locomotive of the development of crop production'.[79] Conversely, its diminution diminished agricultural efficiency.

For all their difficulties, farmers fared better during the collapse of the 1990s than did the economy as a whole. Their incomes were taxed more lightly than those of employees, and their exposure to indirect taxation was reduced by their taking a high and rising proportion of their output as subsistence goods. In 1991, agricultural households spent (and self-consumed) some 76.6 per cent as much as households as a whole, but in 1995, 101.8 per cent. In 1995, 43.4 per cent of the income of farming households was taken as self-consumption.[80]

The annual household consumption surveys show this trend to self-consumption. They are imprecise because of the small size of the samples. Table 10.3 shows the structure of income of households in Serbia and Vojvodina in which at least one household member engaged full time in private farming, i.e. agricultural and 'mixed' households. I have excluded

Kosovo because sampling there collapsed in the 1990s because of passive resistance by the Albanians.

As peasant agricultural production rose slightly over this period, it appears that peasants consumed an increasing amount of their own produce, not only in relative terms but also in absolute quantity, while compensating with diminished consumption of exchange goods. In 1986–90, the peasants marketed 45.7 per cent of their produce, but in the years following the hyperinflation, 1994–7, they marketed only 36.3 per cent of it. (During the hyperinflation of 1993, the figure fell temporarily to 30.3 per cent.) In 1992, a poor harvest year, dissatisfaction with the price of grain offered by the state, the sole purchaser, caused peasants to reorientate towards satisfying their needs in kind, to minimise produce marketing and to hold surpluses for seed and for 'black days' ahead. This process was accompanied by deterioration in agricultural technique. Risk aversion caused peasants to cut back spending on agrotechnology while deterioration was also remarked in seed selection. This reflected farmers' reluctance or inability to spend money and their increasing orientation to subsistence provision. This was a long-term trend, not a short-term response to transiently unfavourable market conditions.[81]

The regime did little to insulate the farmers from distress. In 1993, the government promised them the equivalent of DM 240 per ton for the wheat harvest, but, having deferred payment in the rapidly depreciating currency, eventually gave them an effective DM 20.[82] Nor were farmers immune to the criminal depredations of the Milošević *garnitura*.[83] However, by reorientating towards subsistence, peasants were insulated from the deterioration of popular welfare and were kept politically quiescent. Rural areas were subject to a 'media blockade' of all but government-supporting information flows. Rural Serbia remained an electoral bastion of the ruling party, but this may have owed something to the fear of rural voters that the authorities would know how they voted.

In structural terms, rump Yugoslavia's economy was reconverging upon that of Serbia in 1910. The most marked difference lay not in the structure of what was produced, but in the proportion of total income levied by government. But even in this respect, the peasants remained largely insulated from bearing the cost of the state, thanks to the high subsistence component of their output and the low level of taxation on their income. Yet, as in Serbia before 1914, the price of rural quiescence has been high. By the beginning of 1999 it became an anguished question as to how long food output could be maintained in the face of the depletion of soil fertility, the attrition of available machinery, and the inability of farmers to maintain their herds and flocks. An article of February 1999, warning of a 'meatless year' approaching, reported that 30,000 pig sties stood empty.[84] According to another article headed 'Shortage of Money Empties the Stables', meat products were vanishing from the food shops. In April–December 1998, deliveries of beef animals were down 34 per cent on the same period of 1997, deliveries of pigs 12 per cent and the slaughterhouses worked at below one-third capacity. The farm lobby attributed the crisis to fertiliser shortages and bank interest rates of 450 per cent.[85]

As farming reverted to subsistence, the cities were (in spring of 2000) confronting an unprecedented food supply crisis. The progressive weakening of the link between the peasant sector and the rest of the economy can only be reversed by the far-reaching structural reforms needed to eliminate the loss-making propensities of the socialised sector, and the parasitism upon it which prevents economic recovery.

CONCLUSION

The experience of Serbia as a nation-state both in 1815–1912 and again since 1991 presents a paradox. In South-Eastern Europe, the nation-state has proved far more viable politically than the multinational alternative: it is what is left when multinational states inexorably fall apart. On the other hand, the economic experience of Serbia as a nation-state has varied from the disappointing to the disastrous, when contrasted with the economic record of the multinational states. At bottom, this may be traceable to the facility with which governments in an immature nation-state could suppress pluralism, and pursue counter-developmental economic strategies which minimised competition for political power. This was in contrast to the multinational states of the Balkan area, on which a significant measure of pluralism was forced by their ethnic diversity.

Minimising pluralism meant, for pre-1912 Serbia, holding society within the framework of a mass smallholding peasantry by obstructing the development of the rural market. This was a formula for long-run decline in per capita farm output, which was not offset by growth in the non-farm sector. Domestic capacities for non-farm capital formation and industrialisation were minimal, state policies retarded railway development, while state xenophobia and corruption discouraged foreign investment.

Re-emergent Serbia under Slobodan Milošević underwent not stagnation but dramatic economic shrinkage. Again, this is traceable in underlying terms to its ability to suppress pluralism. Because of the industrial collapse, the new state became almost as heavily dependent on mass peasant agriculture as had Serbia before 1912. As then, peasant farming acted as a population sink giving a minimally adequate livelihood in an environment of mass unemployment. The priority given to maintaining intact the parasitical 'big systems' stifled the spontaneous forces for restructuring the economy.

The immiseration suffered by the citizens of the Balkan nation-states is so intense, however, that the trend away from the multinational state may yet be reversed. Throughout South-Eastern Europe people long to escape the shackles of domestic economic failure by integration in the political institutions of the West. However, it remains to be seen if the corrupt and unstable structures of the European Union will be better able to integrate these nations than were the corrupt and unstable multinational states of their recent past.

NOTES

1. The 'federalism' of FR-Yugoslavia is largely fictitious. It has behaved for most purposes as the nation-state of Serbia's Serbs.
2. John R. Lampe, *Yugoslavia as History: Twice There Was a Country* (Cambridge, 1996), pp. 100–1.
3. Alexander Gerschenkron, *An Economic Spurt that Failed* (Princeton, 1977).
4. John Komlos, 'Growth and Industrialization in Hungary, 1880–1913', *Journal of European Economic History*, 10 (1981), 5–46.
5. David F. Good, *The Economic Rise of the Habsburg Empire, 1750–1914* (Berkeley, Calif., 1984), pp. 136, 143.
6. David Good, 'Austria-Hungary' in R. Sylla and G. Toniolo (eds.), *Patterns of European Industrialization in the Nineteenth Century* (London, 1991), p. 230.
7. Peter F. Sugar, *Industrialization of Bosnia-Hercegovina, 1878–1918* (Seattle, 1963); M.R. Palairet, 'The Habsburg Industrial Achievement in Bosnia-Hercegovina, 1878–1914', *Austrian History Yearbook*, 24 (1993), 133–52; Ivo Banac, *The National Question in Yugoslavia* (Ithaca, N.Y., 1988), p. 360.
8. Lampe, *Yugoslavia*, pp. 177–85.
9. F.E. Ian Hamilton, *Yugoslavia: Patterns of Economic Development* (London, 1968), p. 348.
10. M.R. Palairet, 'Ramiz Sadiku: a Case Study in the Industrialization of Kosovo', *Soviet Studies*, 44 (1992), 897–912.
11. See William Ashworth's critique of the Gerschenkron approach in 'Typologies and Evidence: Has Nineteenth Century Europe a Guide to Economic Growth?', *Economic History Review*, 30 (1977), 140–58.
12. John R. Lampe, 'Financial Structure and the Economic Development of Serbia, 1878–1912' (Unpublished Ph.D. thesis, University of Wisconsin, 1971), p. 27.
13. Danica Milić, *Trgovina Srbije 1815–1839* (Belgrade, 1959), pp. 54, 58–9.
14. Lampe, 'Financial Structure', p. 78.

15. V. Stojančević, *Miloš Obrenović i njegovo doba* (Belgrade, 1966), p. 447.
16. On the homestead laws see Nikola Vuco, *Polozaj seljastva i. Eksproprijacija od zemlje u XIX veku* (Belgrade, 1955).
17. Michael Palairet, *The Balkan Economies c. 1800–1914: Evolution without development* (Cambridge, 1997), p. 110.
18. Tihomir Djordjević, *Srbija pre sto godina* (Belgrade, 1946), p. 150.
19. Palairet, *Balkan Economies*, p. 121.
20. The principal source used on interference with rural commerce is Nikola Vuco, *Raspadanje esnafa u Srbiji*, Vol. I (Belgrade, 1954), pp. 278–82, 294–300, 332, 335–7. See also Joel Halpern and Barbara K. Halpern, *A Serbian Village in Historical Perspective* (Prospect Heights, Ill., 1986), p. 61.
21. D. Arnaoutovitch, *Histoire des chemins de fer Yougoslaves, 1825–1937* (Paris, 1937), pp. 38–54; London Public Record Office. FO. 78 2237. No. 4 comm. of 16 May 1868.
22. Palairet, *Balkan Economies*, pp. 328–30.
23. Michael Palairet, 'God's Property Developer: Francis Mackenzie of Gairloch in Serbia (1876–1895)' in P. Henry (ed.), *Scotland and the Slavs: the Glasgow-90 East–West Forum* (Nottingham, 1991), pp. 87–113.
24. Holm Sundhaussen, 'Von der traditionellen zur modernen Rückständigkeit' (conference paper, Bad Homburg.)
25. Sreten Vukosavljević, *Istorija seljačkog društva, III, Sociologija seljačkih radova* (Belgrade, 1983), p. 374.
26. M.R. Palairet, 'Fiscal Pressure and Peasant Impoverishment in Serbia before World War I', *Journal of Economic History*, 39 (1979), 719–40.
27. Palairet, *Balkan Economies*, pp. 307, 323, 366–7.
28. Ibid., pp. 330–9.
29. J.R. Lampe, 'Modernization and Social Structure: the Case of the pre-1914 Balkan Capitals', *Southeastern Europe*, 5 (1979).
30. *Ekonomska politika* (Belgrade) [*EP*] (19 Oct. 1998), 19–20.
31. Work in progress for a forthcoming book on the economics of growth, decline and decay in Yugoslavia, 1945–1999.
32. *Ekonomist magazin* (28 Feb. 2000), 58.
33. *EP* (20 July 1998), 6.
34. For real wages between 1914 and 1993 see M. Palairet, 'Real Wages and Earnings in Long-Run Decline: Serbia and Yugoslavia since 1862' in P. Scholliers and V. Zamagni (eds.), *Labour's Reward: Real Wages and Economic Change in Nineteenth and Twentieth Century Europe* (Aldershot, 1995), pp. 76–86.
35. Statistički godišnjak Jugoslavije [SGJ] (1998), p. 99.
36. Michael Palairet, 'Metallurgical Kombinat Smederevo 1960–1990: a Case Study in the Economic Decline of Yugoslavia', *Europe-Asia Studies*, 49 (1997), 1093–4.
37. *EP* (18 May 1992), 11.
38. *EP* (23 Nov. 1998), 14.
39. *EP* (9 Nov. 1998), 8, 9; (2 Nov. 1998), 8.
40. *EP* (21 Sept. 1998), 7.
41. *EP* (27 July 1998), 24.

42. Calculated from data in *EP* (26 Oct. 1998), 21.

43. *Indeks* (Belgrade), 2 (1995), 8; 1 (1998), 8; 11 (1998), 8.

44. *EP* (22 Mar. 1999), 20–1; (18 Aug. 1998), 17–18; (24 Nov. 1997), 14; (21 Sept. 1998), 16; (12 Oct. 1998), 16; (23 Nov. 1998), 8–11; (16 Nov. 1998), 13; (7 Sept. 1998), 16.

45. Dragutin V. Marsenić, *Ekonomika Jugoslavije* (Belgrade, 1995), p. 532.

46. *EP* (22 Jan. 1990), 21–3.

47. Mladjan Dinkić, *Ekonomija destrukcija. Velika pljačka naroda*, 2nd edn (Belgrade, 1995), especially pp. 143–9, and see p. 75 for his estimate of the value of the hoards.

48. Petar Djukič, *Moč i nemoč ekonomske politike* (Belgrade, 1997), pp. 15–16, 139–40.

49. S. Vuletić, 'Tačke otpora promenama (2)', *EP* (27 July 1998), 23.

50. *EP* (9 Mar. 1998), 10; (2 Mar. 1998), 4; (5 Oct. 1998), 13.

51. *EP* (9 Mar. 1998), 8–10; Slobodan Ostojić, *Sistem u promenama* (Belgrade, 1996), p. 183.

52. Ostojić, *Sistem u promenama*, p. 183; *EP* (5 Oct. 1998), 10–11.

53. On collectivisation and decollectivisation, see Jozo Tomasevich, 'Collectivization in Yugoslavia' in Irwin T. Sanders (ed.), *Collectivization of Agriculture in Eastern Europe* (Lexington, Ky, 1958), pp. 166–92.

54. Dragan Veselinov, *Sumrak seljaštva* (Belgrade, 1987), pp. 35, 110, 195, 197, 200.

55. *SGJ* (1996), p. 210. This is the most recent census date. Also see *EP* (7 Sept. 1992), 21.

56. *SGJ* (1996), p. 114.

57. *SGJ* (1996), p. 84.

58. *SGJ* (1996), p. 133 (excludes drinks and tobacco).

59. *SGJ* (1996), p. 321.

60. *SGJ* (1996), p. 299.

61. *EP* (5 Oct. 1998), 18.

62. *SGJ* (1996), pp. 190, 191.

63. *SGJ* (1998), p. 207.

64. Calculated from data in *SGJ* (1996), p. 191, and (1998), p. 206.

65. *EP* (1 Feb. 1999), 13.

66. At 76 kg of active material per hectare; *EP* (19 May 1992), 24.

67. *SGJ* (1998), pp. 220, 224.

68. *EP* (1 Mar. 1999), 10–11.

69. *SGJ* (1996), p. 204; (1998), p. 220.

70. *SGJ* (1992), p. 196; (1996), p. 179. The identity of wheat and maize yields in 1995 is coincidence, not an error of repetition.

71. *SGJ* (1996), p. 190.

72. *SGJ* (1996), pp. 118, 190.

73. *SGJ* (1998), p. 220.

74. *SGJ* (1998), pp. 337, 323.

75. *EP* (1 Mar. 1999), 10.

76. *EP* (15 Feb. 1999), 10.

77. *EP* (18 Aug. 1998), 11–12.
78. *EP* (20 June 1994), 22.
79. *EP* (27 June 1994), 23.
80. *SGJ* (1992), p. 105; (1996), pp. 127, 132.
81. *EP* (7 Sept. 1992), 20–1.
82. Dinkić, *Ekonomija destrukcija*, pp. 106–7.
83. Robert Thomas, *Serbia under Milošević: Politics in the 1990s* (London, 1999), pp. 274–5, 269–70.
84. *EP* (15 Feb. 1999), 10.
85. *EP* (15 Feb. 1999), 10; (22 Feb. 1999), 16.

National and non-national dimensions of economic development in nineteenth- and twentieth-century Russia

Peter Gatrell and Boris Anan'ich

INTRODUCTION

This chapter examines the interaction of state and 'nation' in the Russian empire and the Soviet Union over the course of two centuries of economic development. It addresses a series of related questions. Given that the doctrine of nationalism assumed major significance in much of Europe and the wider world after the French Revolution, to what extent did it influence economic change in nineteenth- and twentieth-century Russia and the Soviet Union? Alternatively, did non-national or supra-national factors loom larger in the considerations that governed policy-makers in the tsarist empire and the USSR? What impact did state-led economic programmes and policies have on incipient nationalism, amongst non-Russians as well as Russians? Finally, to what extent and how did 'national' ambitions – couched in terms of economic advantage or disadvantage – contribute to the collapse of these political systems?

Economic historians need to engage more than they have hitherto in a dialogue with historians and theorists of nationalism, nation-state formation and national identity. Some elements of the conversation may readily be constructed. The very stuff of much economic history is the scrutiny of economic projects advanced within the framework of the modern nation-state. How did the nation-state come to have 'such a great influence on economic development' in nineteenth-century Europe? Without doubt this question has produced much high-quality work on important aspects of the formulation and impact of government economic policy, as well as on the social and political consequences of economic change in continental Europe.[1]

All the same, the dialogue remains somewhat restricted. Perhaps the reason is to be found in the insistence by many theorists of nationalism upon the primacy of politics or of culture. Yet, notwithstanding the pronounced emphasis upon nationalism as political principle and political process, or upon the practical realisation of a culturally imagined and politically instituted national community, several thinkers have constructed theories of nationalism primarily on the basis of an understanding of economic change. Economic historians have been slow to respond to this challenge.[2]

In this chapter we begin with some general observations, drawing upon the work of two outstanding thinkers, Friedrich List and Ernest Gellner. To summarise crudely, Friedrich List argued that nationalism provided the basis for the state to promote industrialism and to strengthen itself in the process. By contrast, Gellner maintained that industrialism – the transition from a segmented agrarian society to urban mass society – provided the basis for nationalism. The Listian framework has exerted some influence on the economic historiography of pre-revolutionary Russia, whereas Gellner's ideas have yet to make any impact. We then consider aspects of the economic history of Russia and the USSR, in order to demonstrate the interplay of non-national and national dimensions of economic history in this vast land mass, which possessed and continues to possess global significance.

ECONOMIC ACTIVITY AND NATIONALISM: LIST AND GELLNER

Most economic historians are familiar with the classic work of Friedrich List (1789–1846). List was fascinated by the economic and political potential unleashed by the Industrial Revolution and, in contrast to the prevailing mood of romanticism, he believed that every encouragement should be given to the promotion of modern forms of economic activity. He advocated specific government measures as a means to accelerate economic and political progress. These included the protection of a nascent manufacturing sector. Inevitably this would impose costs, but 'the nation must sacrifice and give up a measure of material property in order to gain culture, skill and powers of united production'.[3] Political objectives were never far from the centre of his attention. In List's view, economic endeavour should serve the needs of the modern nation-state. Much of his attention was inevitably devoted to Germany, where the political construction of a unified economic space would undermine regional particularism and pave the way for the political consolidation of the 'nation'.[4] If Germany were to survive in the international economic system it would have to develop industrially. By the same token, its failure to develop would leave the way clear for the United States, France and even Russia to become dominant world powers. It was also an essential part of List's doctrine that states had to be sufficiently large to employ the talents of their population fully: 'a small state can never bring to complete perfection within its territory the various branches of production'. Finally, it is important not to overlook other elements of List's argument, including his insistence that an industrialised society was more likely to encourage personal liberty than its rural counterpart.[5]

List thus gave pride of place in his scheme to the pursuit of national economic objectives, which alone could secure the strength of the nation-state in a world of competing states. His ideas played an important part in Alexander Gerschenkron's classic interpretation of the ideological framework for European industrialisation.[6] As we shall see in the following section, List's ideas also influenced a generation of Russian economic policy-makers as they sought to come to terms with Russia's economic backwardness.

Ernest Gellner (1925–95) was interested not in industrialisation as the product of a 'national' economic strategy, but in the prior emergence of the doctrine of nationalism. What conditions gave rise to this extraordinary principle – according to which the 'political and national unit should be congruent' – which was bound to challenge the established dynastic imperial polities in Europe around 1815, and has continued to influence political action ever since? Gellner regarded nationalism as the product of the broad economic transformation from agrarian to industrial society. Agrarian society was characterised by a small elite which exercised power over isolated peasant communities that possessed little sense of extra-village consciousness. The main effort of the elite was directed towards the extraction of surplus, and thus towards its own reproduction and political supremacy. Within that traditional society a special role was assigned to a specialist stratum that defended the old order. The subsequent shift to industrial society transformed key aspects of traditional society. Industrialism imposed greater uniformity of economic life. It entailed mobility of labour. It emphasised perpetual growth, allied to cognitive development. It instilled an emphasis upon generic training; technical operations had to be understood and communicated. Education became universal, standardised and generic. Different skills, devices and desires emerged. The political consequences were earth-shattering. To become a citizen entailed a choice: either to subscribe to the high culture of the group that dominated the existing political unit, or to change the political unit to ensure that it corresponded to one's own culture. A new patriotic elite articulated a vision of national culture that rivalled and eventually supplanted the existing and exclusionary high culture; 'at the base of the modern social order stands not the executioner but the professor'. 'National' culture has become the standardised locus of collective identity and affiliation. Thus, 'the roots of nationalism [are to be found] in the distinctive structural requirements of industrial society'.[7]

From a European perspective, Gellner's analysis seems particularly helpful in accounting for the challenge of national minorities in the Habsburg empire. What of Russia and the Soviet Union? Did economic change help to crystallise a sense of nationality? How might economic historians engage with Gellner to account for the collapse of empire? And, finally, were those states convulsed by the claims of a patriotic intelligentsia and a mass national movement, or did they – as Gellner himself believed – succumb to other pressures?[8]

ECONOMIC STRATEGIES IN A NON-NATIONAL CONTEXT: TSARIST RUSSIA

Economic policy in the Russian empire was not primarily driven by 'national' considerations. This is not to deny that conscious efforts were at times made to direct economic policy along national lines, nor that legislation discriminated against national minorities, notably Russia's Jews. Nor does it overlook the fact that developmental strategies were sometimes justified by appealing to a 'national idea'. For the most part, however, economic policy reflected non-national or supra-national purposes. The tsarist empire was a politically centralised dynastic state ('united and indivisible', according to the Fundamental Laws of 1906), whose rulers pursued a broad strategy designed to maintain domestic and external security. Its officials were correspondingly preoccupied with the collection of taxes and the conscription of military recruits to underpin those ambitions. It would have seemed strange to many of its statesmen that economic policy should take account of 'national' needs. Such a course of action would have been regarded as intolerably narrow in conception and fraught with political dangers. Geo-politics, not 'national interest', lay at the heart of pre-revolutionary policies. This was as true of economic policy as it was of other spheres of state activity.

The tsarist vision of imperial conquest and administration did not distinguish between Russian and non-Russian elements; all were subject to imperial authority: 'all peoples, Russians included, were the raw material of empire, to be manipulated or dominated as seemed expedient to its unity and strength'.[9] One consequence of this indiscriminate subordination of people to state was a relatively relaxed attitude towards indigenous elites and a toleration of ethnic, religious and cultural difference. Throughout its long history the tsarist state pursued policies that were designed to sustain its territorial integrity and political stability. On the relatively rare occasions when non-Russian ethnic groups rebelled against tsarist rule, the consequences were disastrous for the participants. But the state meted out harsh punishment to anyone who engaged in open revolt, irrespective of nationality.

This strategy was well articulated by one of its leading statesmen, Sergei Witte. Witte categorically opposed any state-led policy of Russification: 'the aim of such an empire cannot be to turn everyone into a "true Russian". Rather than attempt to reach such a goal it would be better to part with our borderlands.' However, Witte went on to proclaim that 'the error of our recent policies toward non-Russian subjects derives from our forgetting that since the days of Peter the Great we have not been "Russia" but "the Russian Empire" (*rossiiskaia imperiia*).'[10] He thus simultaneously drew attention to a shift in government policy towards the end of the nineteenth century, when the traditional vision of a 'multinational' empire had yielded to the affirmation of Russianness as the core of empire. Following the revolution of 1905–6, which erupted with particular bitterness on the imperial periphery, conservatives asserted still more aggressively the virtues of Russian nationalism against the threat from non-Russians. In the liberal camp, too, some spokesmen embraced the 'national idea'.[11]

Let us look a little more closely at this tension. A key moment in the economic history of tsarist Russia occurred during the late 1870s and early 1880s, with the emergence of elite opposition to the reform programme launched two decades previously by Tsar Alexander II. Men such as K.P. Pobedonostsev and M.N. Katkov bitterly denounced what they took to be the westernising direction of government policy, advocating instead a programme of autocratic consolidation and 'national industry'. Basic elements of their programme included the maintenance of a paper currency, tariff protection, support for the landed gentry, close supervision of private enterprise and the preservation of the traditional land commune. Their campaign resulted in the replacement of the liberal-minded minister of finances, N.Kh. Bunge, by the technocrat I.A. Vyshnegradskii, who attempted to steer a course towards 'national industry'. Vyshnegradskii's protégé, Sergei Witte, published a work on List in 1889, in which he denounced 'cosmopolitanism' in economic policy and declared that free trade had inflicted great damage on the Russian economy.[12] Ironically, when he became finance minister, Witte was accused of that very offence; his detractors argued that his policy of tariff protection, increased taxation, the adoption of the gold standard (in 1897) and the import of foreign capital had 'ruined' peasant farming.[13] Witte responded by vigorously defending the need for a strong national economy, a programme that relied upon the support of an emerging entrepreneurial elite whose members depended to a considerable extent upon the patronage of the imperial state.[14]

Meanwhile, other merchants and industrialists consciously espoused Slavophile ideas, which turned on the notion of a distinctive Russian, non-Western path of industrial development, preferably one that relied to the minimum possible extent on the import of foreign capital and entrepreneurship. Indeed many of these men, including F.V. Chizhov and P.P. Riabushinskii, espoused a vision of 'Slavophile capitalism' that hinged upon a fond but outmoded attachment to non-corporate business structures and embraced a wholly romanticised notion of labour relations. But these merchants did not have things their own way. They were in turn countered by an emerging non-Russian national bourgeoisie, whose members were perfectly willing to co-operate with the imperial state in the pursuit of new markets and capital accumulation. Non-Russians' access to positions of economic power provides evidence that economic development cannot be reduced to a single dimension. Data on the ethnic composition of corporate owners and managers in Moscow reveal that, between 1905 and 1914, the proportion of ethnic Russians amongst management fell from 63 per cent to 57 per cent, whereas the proportion of Germans rose from 15 to 17 per cent and the Jewish contingent from 4 to 9 per cent in the corresponding period. Whatever else it meant, Russification did not produce an ethnically homogeneous managerial caste.[15]

There are other issues to consider as well. What did empire imply for the economic development of the 'periphery' and for Russia itself? Did the incorporation of small 'national areas' bring them significant economic benefits? The debate has been couched either in liberal terms, emphasising the gains from international trade between states, or in populist terms, stressing the costs of incorporation and the advantages of national self-sufficiency. A third alternative (the 'imperial view') stresses the advantages conferred on a state by its integration in a larger unit whose dominant political authority enforces the rules of the market, confers political stability, promotes investment and adjudicates in disputes. Forms of patronage include the establishment of a free-trade area, protecting the smaller unit from foreign competition, the creation and maintenance of a modern financial system, a uniform currency, a standard system of weights and measures, and the creation of an appropriate infrastructure. This, ultimately, was Witte's vision: a strong national economy that rested upon the integration of geographically, economically and culturally differentiated sub-units, bringing benefits to each.[16]

ECONOMIC STRATEGIES IN A NON-NATIONAL CONTEXT: SOVIET UNION

The tsarist state was shattered in 1917 although, territorially, a version of the old empire survived for a further three-quarters of a century. It survived, of course, in a new guise. The Bolsheviks aimed to release non-Russian national minorities from what Lenin termed the 'prison-house' of tsarism. The USSR was not a unitary state – still less was it defined in terms of 'Russia' – but rather a federal state, which attached great importance to sub-state national minorities and which assigned 'national' institutions considerable economic, social and cultural significance. Conscious as its leaders were of the claims of non-Russian minorities for autonomy, the state established ethno-territorial administrative units and encouraged the acquisition and preservation of 'national' languages. In the long term, the construction of these units not only promoted a sense of national 'homeland'; they also created proto-states, within which administrative elites carried out a variety of economic, educational and cultural functions.[17]

Supra-national considerations helped to drive Soviet economic strategy, but they were of a quite different kind to those pursued by the tsarist state. At the outset, the basic aim was to promote the interests of an international proletariat and the universal solidarity of the working class and poor peasantry. International revolution, not 'primitive' or 'bourgeois' nationalism, defined Soviet strategy. It did not take long, however, for the dream of international revolution to turn sour. Instead, by the late 1920s, 'socialism in one country' became the slogan for a profound social and political transformation. According to Stalin's vision, rapid industrialisation and mass collectivisation served to create the social underpinning for a new socialist society. But socialism in one country did not equate to socialism in a (Russian) nation-state. Any suggestion of national 'chauvinism' remained anathema to the new Sovietised technocratic elite who articulated the vision of economic revolution.[18]

All the same, Soviet leaders were acutely conscious of the claims advanced by ethnic minorities. One crucial innovative element in the programme of sustaining a sense of loyalty to the new Soviet state entailed overcoming the development gap between advanced and backward parts of the Soviet Union. This took place within the framework of *korenizatsiia* ('nativisation'), that is affirmative action to develop human capabilities at the 'national' level. During the 1920s the new state actively promoted national languages (totalling 192) and the accelerated recruitment of representatives of each ethnic group to administrative, judicial and educational posts. To be sure, these measures resulted in a backlash from Russians who complained that they were being marginalised, particularly in the autonomous regions of the USSR. But at no time did Soviet rulers abandon the principle of ethno-cultural autonomy. Cultural policy affirmed difference. Even at the height of Stalinism, Soviet leaders continued to affirm the national essence of administrative units.[19]

This strategy also had a clear economic dimension, with Listian over-
tones. The Soviet leadership sought to reduce the development gap between
the more advanced and less developed parts of the Soviet Union. The main
plank in this strategy was to encourage rapid growth by means of investment
in production, infrastructure and education. The results were undoubtedly
impressive, at least in terms of accelerating the economic development of
less developed regions such as Central Asia, where new factories, power
stations and transport links were built, along with hospitals, schools and
universities. But these policies themselves produced a nationalist backlash.
In pre-war Ukraine, for example, the Soviet regime faced accusations of
having expanded heavy industry in the eastern region, at the expense of
light industry and agriculture in the ethnically more homogeneous western
parts of Ukraine. These arguments were not dissimilar to those deployed
by members of the patriotic intelligentsia before 1914, but they now formed
part of a debate about the need to locate new factories further from the vulnerable western frontier – a policy that yielded fewer changes than political
and military leaders originally envisaged.[20]

The policy of purposive economic intervention survived until the 1970s,
when the Central Committee of the CPSU declared that equalisation had
been achieved. Thereafter the emphasis switched to 'a general state approach'. In other words, within a unified economic space, the Soviet leadership decided to promote a greater division of labour and to foster inter-
republican economic links. The constituent republics accordingly came
to depend heavily on trade with their neighbours. Nationalist economists
bemoaned this development as well, claiming that economic integration
hindered 'national' economic progress. However, we should distinguish
between membership of the USSR and subordination to an increasingly
sclerotic planned economy, to which that membership obliged them to ad-
here. The ultimate failure of central planning disadvantaged the constituent
republics, not their incorporation in the Soviet Union as such.[21]

INDUSTRIALISM AND NATIONALISM: THE GELLNER QUESTION

Did rapid economic change help to crystallise nationalism in the manner
proposed by Gellner? This is a complex question. In late imperial Russia,
increased population mobility – or, in the case of Russian Jews, restrictions
on mobility – may have contributed to an emerging sense of ethnicity. For
example, the restrictions imposed on the employment of Poles in the so-
called 'western provinces' forced them to find work in the Russian interior.
By 1914, around 15 per cent of the empire's Latvian population lived outside

the Baltic region, the result of a generation of economic development and migration to European Russia. The new industrial settlements of Ukraine, such as Iuzovka, were home to more than thirty different ethnic groups. Migrants were exposed to ethnic difference. In the famous Kreenholm textile factory, accommodation, dining and education were arranged along ethnic lines.[22] Yet we should not press this point too far. Many migrant workers appear to have become 'assimilated' and – more importantly – to have articulated their experience in terms of class rather than ethnicity.[23]

The policies pursued by the tsarist government were probably more important in promoting a sense of ethnic difference. As mentioned above, Russification gathered pace after 1880. Few attempts were made to sustain the image of a multinational state. Following the 1905 revolution – which took a particularly violent form on the empire's periphery – Stolypin 'returned to Russification with a heightened sense of urgency'.[24] Yet, at the same time, the tsarist state did not succeed in curbing the growth of a non-Russian cultural intelligentsia and a politicised bourgeoisie, both of which expressed a wish for greater national autonomy within the tsarist empire, particularly as cultural Russification gathered momentum. Minority groups, such as many Poles and Latvians, educated their children in private and spoke their own language in the home. Their leaders created some space for the elaboration of cultural autonomy. Private initiative led to the formation of numerous organisations – by 1914, for example, there were 860 Latvian farmers' societies, part of 'an infrastructure in the Latvian countryside that called for extensive and continuing interaction between Latvians in their own language'. Choral societies, study circles and co-operative associations flourished. Sixty Latvian newspapers appeared in the vernacular. Such activities were not confined to Latvia. Lithuania boasted an impressive co-operative movement, designed to cater for spiritual as well as material needs. In Ukraine, popular enlightenment (*prosvita*) associations, co-operatives, zemstvo societies, choirs and amateur dramatic clubs constituted havens for national cultural consciousness. Even though 'Ukrainian national life existed on the margins of society', nevertheless a non-Russian patriotic intelligentsia manifested 'an active affection for the region in which they lived, associated with a thirst for knowledge of every new and insufficiently investigated phenomenon'.[25]

However, 'nationality' did not strike deep roots amongst the bulk of the population. Only a minority ever participated in the kind of migration that may have exposed them to ethnic difference. Ethnic identity competed with other kinds of allegiance and consciousness. 'Latvian' peasants maintained a primary affiliation with the local village community, pitting themselves against Baltic German landlords and officials. Much the same could be said of Ukrainian and Estonian peasants. There may have been some sense of ethnic and cultural distinctiveness, but these minorities did not feel part of an incipient Ukrainian or Latvian 'nation'. Russian peasants, too, remained wedded to communal ownership, egalitarianism and mutual responsibility (*krugovaia poruka*). No matter how energetically the Russian intelligentsia articulated a notion of a distinctive Russian national tradition, with the peasantry at its core, the link between patriotic elite and the peasant mass remained a tenuous one. Here too, the popular basis for nationalism remained superficial. What survived was an uncompromising peasant suspicion of the state and of the Russian intelligentsia alike, something that contributed decisively to the collapse of the old regime.[26]

Thus nationalism alone did not determine the configuration of political change in late imperial Russia. True, the tensions that emerged during the First World War, including the deliberate targeting of national minorities (Jews, Poles and Germans) and the mass migration of refugees to the Russian interior, helped to give nationality issues greater prominence. But, as Ronald Suny has shown, the particular combination of ethnic difference with class distinction generated decisive social conflicts in late imperial Russia. Azeri workers attacked Armenian businessmen; Ukrainian peasants attacked Russian landlords. Nationality reinforced class conflicts, which ultimately proved subversive of the old regime. To that extent, Gellner's argument needs to be modified: there was no straightforward link between industrialism and nationalism in imperial Russia.[27]

What implications did economic change have for nationalities in the USSR? Did Soviet-style industrial modernisation help to foster a sense of nationhood? In the early years, of course, the priority was simply to survive. The new state was threatened by peasant guerrilla warfare and by economic collapse. All Soviet citizens, irrespective of nationality, found themselves in dire straits. The rural economy suffered a devastating famine in 1921–2; in the Caucasus famine recurred in 1924. Economic recovery and political stability after 1921 went hand in hand with the restoration of peasant agriculture. This offered, in Gellner's terms, a weak social basis for mass national movements.

Under the New Economic Policy the revival of the rural economy was the *sine qua non* to the eventual recovery of the urban economy. Here, important changes were taking place. Economic progress modified the ethnic character of urban space. Before 1917, it was said of Ukraine that 'the city governs the countryside and the "foreigners" govern the cities'. Thereafter, the ethnic Ukrainian share of the urban population increased from 33 per cent (1920) to 47 per cent in 1926. Ukrainian peasants entered the industrial labour force, enrolled in Ukrainian schools and found jobs in republican administration. In part this reflected deliberate state intervention, under the slogan of *korenizatsiia*. A leading member of the KP(b)U stated that 'we shall not forcibly Ukrainize the Russian proletariat in Ukraine, but we shall ensure that the Ukrainian, when he goes to the city, will not be Russified'. Migration mattered; under the new dispensation, peasants in towns could begin to think of themselves as Ukrainians.[28] Simultaneously, and in a foretaste of things to come, these programmes for 'national' economic transformation reduced the economic role of the non-indigenous groups, who now perceived themselves as victims of 'bullying' by the indigenes: imprisoned in a homeland to which by virtue of ethnicity they did not 'belong'.[29]

The economic counterpart of *korenizatsiia* was freedom for the peasantry to sell their grain under the terms of NEP. The New Economic Policy left alone those food producers in the non-Russian lands, whose form of economic and social organisation bore no resemblance to Bolshevik ideas of modernity. As Kalinin candidly put it in 1925, 'if a project starts with a prayer to Allah and ends in great success – excellent. However, if it starts with the "Internationale" and ends as a failure, then this project is a crime.'[30] But NEP came to an abrupt end in 1928–9, and the death-knell for nativisation was sounded soon afterwards. What mattered now were fast tempos of economic growth, allied to a transformation of social relations. Industrial modernisation and the collectivisation of agriculture brought about massive population migration. Economic upheaval, and in particular the catastrophe of collectivisation and famine, is sometimes said to have fostered mass national consciousness. However, this issue needs to be treated carefully. The depth of national sentiment may have been exaggerated by the Stalinist leadership as a pretext for direct intervention and centralisation of the economic apparatus. To be sure, the hectic pursuit of socialism led eventually to nationalist claims that a gross injustice had been perpetrated. Some historians have also endorsed the view that Stalinist collectivisation represented a deliberate programme of genocide. Many scholars remain unconvinced. These events were part and parcel of a profound social, cultural and political revolution, not a separate story of nationalist assertion and defeat.[31]

In the long run, Stalin's creation bore the hallmarks of a more urban, better educated and more mobile society, precisely the attributes that Gellner identified as central to the crystallisation of nationalism.[32] But again these need to be set in a broader context. Space prevents a proper consideration of the impact of war and post-war economic change upon the nationality factor. A full discussion would have to take account of non-economic developments, including the unhindered efflorescence of nationalism during the 'Great Patriotic War', the deportation of supposedly 'disloyal' nationalities, the subsequent revival of 'national' cultures during the Khrushchev thaw, and the opportunities created by administrative decentralisation for political practice and expression in a 'national' key.[33] From the perspective of economic change, post-Stalinist economic modernisation did not lead to a withering away of nationalities or a reduction in ethnic cohesiveness. Instead, each 'national' republic constituted itself, to a greater or lesser extent, as a real or imagined homeland to its indigenes. Thus, by 1989, all but 4 per cent of Lithuanians, Latvians and Georgians lived in 'their' SSR (at the other extreme, only two-thirds of Armenians lived in Soviet Armenia). Where a 'nation' had union republic status, 83 per cent of its members resided in the respective 'homeland' in 1989, hardly in keeping with the official claim that national republics were becoming less significant ethnically. It also demonstrated that the Soviet development model had not produced the degree of inter-republican ('inter-homeland') migration that it was sometimes thought to have done. Instead, the indigenous population formed a sentimental attachment to their homeland, which offered them ready access to education and employment. They did not wish to disadvantage themselves by relocating to another republic. On the other hand, many Russians appear to have regarded the Soviet Union as their 'homeland', and therefore to have been more disposed to inter-republican mobility. This had profound political and social consequences when the Union collapsed.[34]

The slowdown in economic growth that became apparent from the 1970s helped to encourage nationalist dissatisfaction. The sources of earlier growth – abundant supplies of capital and labour – became exhausted. Ideally, this scenario required the implementation of measures to increase the rate of growth of factor productivity. But systemic inefficiencies could not easily be overcome. Vested interests maintained the old-style administrative-command economy. Some nationalists saw opportunities to profit from secession rather than from continued membership of the Soviet state, regarding independence as a means of escape from Soviet (Russian) domination and exploitation, without necessarily espousing a radically different economic system. From amongst the 'maze' of nationalities came the realisation that tight central control and the imposition of uniform solutions to economic problems had disastrous consequences. Dissatisfaction over the deceleration in economic growth went hand in hand with political opportunism and cultural complaint.[35]

The expectation that ethnic minorities would 'fuse' (the doctrine of *sliianie*) was revealed as a sham. Brezhnev's attempt to generate 'a new historical community of the people, the Soviet nation', came to naught.[36] Attempts to create a sense of Soviet citizenship foundered on an antagonism between minority peoples and Russian political overlords that was sharpened by the economic failings of the party-state. From the point of view of national affiliation, Russia itself was increasingly acknowledged to be a nationality with its own claims on allegiance. Russian nationalists appealed to popular opinion, advocating an end to the imperial 'burden'. This was a complicated and tortuous process, involving a progressive collapse of the Soviet/Russian distinction: 'the Soviet past was becoming progressively more Russian and so were the upper echelons of the Party and state'.[37]

During perestroika, Gorbachev remained loyal to the late Soviet vision of state unity and economic interdependence. Speaking to the Nineteenth Party Conference in 1988, he outlined his view that the 'obsession with national isolation can only lead to economic and cultural impoverishment', and went on to warn his audience that 'those who believe that decentralization is opening up the floodgates for parochialism or national egoism will be making a grave mistake'.[38] Events proved him wrong. The fresh political opportunities created a perfect forum for nationalists to articulate their vision of political and economic independence, which they justified in terms of prolonged economic crisis and environmental damage.

The sudden disintegration of the USSR in 1991 and the creation of a Commonwealth of Independent States meant that 280 million former Soviet citizens were now scattered amongst fifteen sovereign states. In a process of territorial reconfiguration reminiscent of the settlement following the First World War, the Soviet Union became a 'fragmented continent'.[39] The creation of the CIS was not accompanied by any supra-national institutions that could arbitrate between the new states, leaving them to quarrel, negotiate and co-operate as they come to terms with the legacy of Soviet communism. The rupture of inter-republican links poses major problems of adjustment. Some nationalist leaders see this simply as the bitter legacy of decades of Soviet economic policy, although they tend to be coy about their preferred alternative. Others see opportunities to engage in international trade, specialising on the basis of natural resource endowments (and enriching themselves in the process). Economic difficulties are compounded by political uncertainties. The establishment of a sovereign Russian Federation encouraged non-Russian ethnic groups within its borders to press for various 'rights', including claims for compensation for environmental damage, showing again that the 'nationality factor' cannot be divorced from the legacy of economic history. Thus a vocal Siberian lobby, speaking on behalf of 32 million people, demanded that Siberia be given favourable consideration within the Russian Federation. Once more, economic collapse provided an opportunity to formulate solutions in 'national' (or proto-national) terms.[40]

CONCLUSION

This chapter has focused on a large land mass, home to a multiplicity of ethnic groups, whose members have commonly been living in a supranational polity. Here the nation-state, in the sense that Friedrich List would have understood it, has been the exception rather than the rule. Only on rare occasions – for a brief moment in 1918–20 and since 1991 – have nation-states sought to constitute themselves as the dominant political framework. Yet nationality mattered. It impinged on those tsarist officials and merchants who espoused a vision of a Russified national economy and who advanced the cause of Russification. It mattered, differently, to Soviet leaders who denounced Russian chauvinism and tolerated the creation of an ethno-territorial state within which 'national' loyalties contended with Soviet supremacy. When the legitimacy of the supra-national state was questioned (in 1905, 1917 and after 1985), political opposition was expressed at least in part in national terms. But military catastrophe and socio-economic crisis, not 'nationalism' *per se*, were the decisive motors of change.

In response to Gellner, our argument is that economic changes formed part of a broader process of transformation, which allowed national claims to be asserted alongside other claims. Under tsarism, economic change contributed to the creation of national sentiment and allegiance. In the Soviet case, the state sought to mobilise the population towards the goal of socialism, but ultimately many citizens became convinced that nationalism, rather than the pursuit of Soviet-style socialism, offered them better prospects of economic improvement. Generations of Soviet leaders pinned their hopes on economic growth, full employment, educational opportunities and social welfare as sufficient inducements to all citizens, irrespective of ethnic affiliation, to subscribe to the legitimacy of the Communist Party and the viability of the USSR. The Soviet state has important economic, social and cultural achievements to its credit, even if their magnitude has been called into question.[41] Nevertheless, those achievements entailed huge sacrifices, which have been crucial in generating a sense amongst non-Russian minorities that the Soviet economic transformation yielded little benefit. According to an emerging patriotic intelligentsia amongst the non-Russians, the Soviet project failed to eliminate the sense of Russian supremacy and exploitation. Ethnic minorities were deemed to have borne the brunt of collectivisation, famine, industrialisation and environmental degradation. After 1985, many citizens appropriated the rhetoric of nationalism as a powerful device with which to undermine the old regime. The Soviet leadership contributed to its own downfall by promoting national consolidation by territorial-administrative means. When the cupboard was shown to be bare, nationalists promised an escape into sovereignty and freedom from want. But the precise mechanisms for improved growth and welfare, as well as their ideological foundations, remain unresolved.[42]

What was taking place at the end of the twentieth century was the reiteration of national conflict and of the conflicts between different minorities in the borderlands of empire. As in 1917, these were peripheral manifestations of broader calamities, which include a strong element of socio-economic collapse. The demise of the Soviet Union has encouraged ethnic minorities – and ethnic majorities – to rethink their history. In this sense, economic history provides vital clues to the past, present and future of these troubled lands.

NOTES

1. Alan S. Milward and S.B. Saul, *The Economic Development of Continental Europe* (London, 1973), p. 24. The late Sidney Pollard's *magnum opus* on the economic history of Europe, *Peaceful Conquest: the Industrialization of Europe, 1760–1970* (Oxford, 1981), is a rich source of ideas, but it does not seek to examine the association between economic development and the nation-state in any formal sense. See also Arcadius Kahan, 'Nineteenth-Century European Experience with Policies of Economic Nationalism' in H.G. Johnson (ed.), *Economic Nationalism in Old and New States* (Chicago, 1967), pp. 17–30, and Dieter Senghaas, *The European Experience: a Historical Critique of Development Theory* (Leamington Spa, 1985).

2. Ernest Gellner, *Nations and Nationalism* (Oxford, 1983). For another influential account, see also Benedict Anderson, *Imagined Communities: Reflections on the Origin and Spread of Nationalism* (London, 1983). Anderson's theory rests crucially upon the universalisation of a process of 'print capitalism', and demands the attention of economic historians. For a helpful review, see John Breuilly, 'Reflections on Nationalism' in Stuart Woolf (ed.), *Nationalism in Europe, 1815 to the Present: a Reader* (London, 1996), pp. 137–54.

3. Roman Szporluk, *Communism and Nationalism: Karl Marx versus Friedrich List* (New York, 1988), pp. 115, 137.

4. Thus, in Germany, railways and a customs union were conceived as 'Siamese twins, born at the same time, physically attached to one another, of one mind and purpose', which together overcame provincial interests and prejudices. Ibid., p. 112.

5. Szporluk, *Communism and Nationalism*, pp. 125, 140; T.H. von Laue, *Sergei Witte and the Industrialization of Russia* (New York, 1963), pp. 58–62.

6. Alexander Gerschenkron, *Economic Backwardness in Historical Perspective* (Cambridge, Mass., 1962), p. 25. Gerschenkron believed that Listian ideas were fundamental to German industrialisation, whereas Marxism acted as the ideological underpinning for Russian industrialisation.

7. Quotations from Gellner, *Nations and Nationalism*, pp. 34–5, 108n. Note, by contrast, Stalin's utterance that 'villages are the keepers of nationality'; quoted in Yuri Slezkine, 'The USSR as a Communal Apartment, or How a Socialist State Promoted Ethnic Particularism', *Slavic Review*, 53 (1994), 414–52, at p. 423.

8. E. Gellner, 'Nationalism in the Vacuum' in A. Motyl (ed.), *Thinking Theoretically about Soviet Nationalities* (New York, 1992), pp. 243–54.

9. Geoffrey Hosking, *Russia: People and Empire* (London, 1997), p. 39.

10. *The Memoirs of Count Witte* (New York, 1990), p. 373.

11. In 1912, for example, the renowned liberal politician Peter Struve wrote that 'capitalism speaks and will speak Russian, and not Ukrainian'; quoted in Theodore Weeks, *Nation and State in Late Imperial Russia* (DeKalb, Ill., 1996), p. 80.

12. A.P. Korelin and S.A. Stepanov, *S. Iu. Witte: finansist, politik, diplomat* (Moscow, 1998), pp. 314, 346. Pobedonostsev was attracted by the ideas of Thomas Carlyle and Max Nordau, both of whom criticised Western parliamentarianism, whilst the newspaper editor Katkov followed closely Bismarck's campaign to neutralise the fledgling German labour movement. Witte, meanwhile, drew a veil over List's political liberalism. An *émigré* Russian economist detected in the views of N. Mordvinov another inspiration for Witte's programme. See J.F. Normano, *The Spirit of Russian Economics* (London, 1949), p. 59.

13. For a rebuttal of Witte's critics by a modern economist, see Paul Gregory, *Before Command* (Princeton, 1994), chs. 2 and 3.

14. A.J. Rieber, *Merchants and Entrepreneurs in Imperial Russia* (Chapel Hill, N.C., 1982), pp. 134–48, 165–77.

15. T.C. Owen, *Russian Corporate Capitalism from Peter the Great to Gorbachev* (New York, 1995), pp. 69–70, 188. In 1905–14, Russian managers made up less than two-fifths of the total group in the ten major cities of the empire.

16. M. Spechler, 'The Economic Advantages of Being Peripheral: Subordinate Nations in Multinational Empires', *Eastern European Politics and Societies*, 3 (1989), 448–64. Data on industrial production per head of population in different parts of the empire (based upon the 1908 industrial census) put Ukraine and the Urals at around 20 rubles, and Central Asia at 10 rubles per head, compared with a figure of 70 rubles in Russia's north-west and central industrial region. V.Z. Drobizhev, *Istoricheskaia geografiia SSSR* (Moscow, 1973), p. 248.

17. H. Carrère d'Encausse, *The Great Challenge: Nationalities and the Bolshevik State 1917–1930* (New York, 1992). As Gellner pointed out, this 'hierarchic approach to ethnic categories' – in which 'nations' were allowed their own republic, whilst 'nationalities' were provided with autonomous regions – stored up massive problems for the future. Gellner, 'Nationalism in the Vacuum', pp. 252–3. See also Valerie Bunce, 'Subversive Institutions: the End of the Soviet State in Comparative Perspective', *Post-Soviet Affairs*, 14 (1998), 323–54.
18. Initially, technical specialists who remained on Russian soil after the revolution believed the Bolsheviks to be heirs to the statist tradition of modernising 'Russia'. But they yielded to a Stalinist elite after 1928. Szporluk, *Communism and Nationalism*, p. 220.
19. Slezkine, 'The USSR as a Communal Apartment', p. 439. For a discussion of the victims of this strategy, see Terry Martin, 'The Origins of Soviet Ethnic Cleansing', *Journal of Modern History*, 70 (1998), 813–61.
20. W.E.D. Allen, *The Ukraine* (Cambridge, 1940), pp. 366–7; R.W. Davies, Mark Harrison and S.G. Wheatcroft, (eds.), *The Economic Transformation of the Soviet Union, 1913–1945* (Cambridge, 1994), p. 301.
21. Gertrude Schroeder, 'Nationalities and the Soviet Economy' in Lubomyr Hajda and Mark Beissinger (eds.), *The Nationalities Factor in Soviet Politics and Society* (Boulder, Colo., 1990), pp. 43–71.
22. Robert J. Kaiser, *The Geography of Nationalism in Russia and the USSR* (Princeton, 1994), pp. 62–6; T.H. Friedgut, *Iuzovka and Revolution: Life and Work in Russia's Donbass, 1869–1924* (Princeton, 1989); Reginald Zelnik, *Law and Disorder on the Narova River* (Berkeley, 1995), pp. 25–7.
23. Charters Wynn, *Workers, Strikes and Pogroms: the Donbass-Dnepr Bend in Late Imperial Russia 1870–1905* (Princeton, 1992).
24. Raymond Pearson, 'Privileges, Rights and Russification' in Olga Crisp and Linda Edmondson (eds.), *Civil Rights in Imperial Russia* (Oxford, 1989), p. 99.
25. Miroslav Hroch, quoted in Kaiser, *The Geography of Nationalism*, p. 34; A. Plakans, 'The Latvians' in E. Thaden (ed.), *Russification in the Baltic Provinces and Finland, 1855–1914* (Princeton, 1981), p. 272; Bohdan Krawchenko, *Social Change and National Consciousness in Twentieth-Century Ukraine* (New York, 1985), pp. 27–8.
26. Hosking, *Russia*, p. xxvi.
27. R.G. Suny, *The Revenge of the Past: Nationalism, Revolution and the Collapse of the Soviet Union* (Stanford, Conn., 1993); Mark von Hagen, 'The Russian Empire', in M. von Hagen and K. Barkey (eds.), *After Empire* (Boulder, Colo., 1997), pp. 58–72.
28. Shakrai, cited in George Liber, *Soviet Nationality Policy, Urban Growth and Identity Change in the Ukrainian SSR, 1923–1934* (Cambridge, 1992), p. 6; for the other quotation, see Krawchenko, *Social Change*, p. 56.
29. Carrère d'Encausse, *The Great Challenge*, p. 198.
30. Quoted in G. Simon, *Nationalism and Policy toward the Nationalities in the Soviet Union* (Boulder, Colo., 1991), p. 103. See also Yuri Slezkine, *Arctic Mirrors: Russia and the Small Peoples of the North* (Ithaca, N.Y., 1995).

31. On collectivisation as genocide, see Robert Conquest, *Harvest of Sorrow: Soviet Collectivization and the Terror-Famine* (London, 1986). A full account of the famine of 1932–3 remains to be written. For its economic impact, see R.W. Davies, M.B. Tauger and S.G. Wheatcroft, 'Stalin, Grain Stocks and the Famine of 1932–1933', *Slavic Review*, 54 (1995), 642–57.

32. Moshe Lewin, *Russia/USSR/Russia: the Drive and Drift of a Superstate* (New York, 1995).

33. Martin, 'Origins'; Amir Weiner, 'Nature, Nurture, and Memory in a Socialist Utopia: Delineating the Soviet Socio-Ethnic Body in the Age of Socialism', *American Historical Review*, 104 (1999), 1114–55.

34. Kaiser, *The Geography of Nationalism*, pp. 161–70; R.G. Suny, *Looking toward Ararat: Armenia in Modern History* (Bloomington, Ind., 1993), p. 185.

35. There was some truth in nationalist claims that the titular nationalities were at a disadvantage relative to the rest of the population, in so far as the former were more concentrated in low wage sectors. However, this did not apply to Russians in the RSFSR, Armenians in Armenia and Georgians in Georgia. Schroeder, 'Nationalities', pp. 45–6.

36. M. Raeff, 'Patterns of Russian Imperial Policy toward the Nationalities' in E. Allworth (ed.), *Soviet Nationality Problems* (New York, 1971), pp. 22–42.

37. Slezkine, 'The USSR as a Communal Apartment', p. 443.

38. Quoted in Schroeder, 'Nationalities', p. 63.

39. Suny, *Looking toward Ararat*, p. 124; Schroeder, 'Nationalities', p. 45.

40. Roman Szporluk, 'The Imperial Legacy and the Soviet Nationalities' in Hajda and Beissinger (eds.), *The Nationalities Factor*, pp. 1–23.

41. M. Harrison, 'Trends in Soviet Labour Productivity, 1928–1985', *European Review of Economic History*, 2 (1998), 171–200.

42. For a range of ideological viewpoints, see Tim McDaniel, *The Agony of the Russian Idea* (Princeton, 1996).

PART III

CHAPTER 12

Nation without a state and state without a nation: the case of Africa south of the Sahara

Catherine Coquery-Vidrovitch

There exist nations with states, and nations without a state. In Africa south of the Sahara, we sometimes have to face another case: states without nations. This of course implies that first a definition be proposed as regards what is a state, and what is a nation. The question is on the agenda for the African continent; today a large literature exists on the topic in and on Africa. Let us say, to oversimplify, that hypothetically, exactly as anywhere else in the world, also in Africa:

• a state may be defined by its political sovereignty, its territory and state apparatus;
• a nation is a combination of various factors: a common cultural and therefore historical and often linguistic past (as is the case in Europe for Germans), but also a community built on freely recognised institutions, as for example in France those institutions inherited from the French Revolution of 1789, as well as the modern democratic model.

The hypothesis here is that, before independence in Africa – more or less before the 1960s which is very recent indeed – the economy played an important, if not a major part in the making not only of pre-colonial political entities, states and even nations, but also of colonial territories. Therefore, as colonies were to give birth to independent states, these inherited economic forms were decisive and still heavily weigh on the Africa of today.

Ironically, independence reversed the process. Before independence, including in colonial times, economic trends were at least as important as political, ideological and cultural factors. After independence, ideology and political processes took the lead because local national states were economically powerless. Therefore a national process prevailed at the same time as the national economic exigencies were neglected. This explains, at least partly, the present political predicament of most modern African states.

In pre-colonial times, as far as state building is concerned, economic and political life was more intertwined than most anthropological studies suggest. Cultural anthropologists and sociologists have tended to give

239

precedence to religious and military incentives, except for Marxist economic anthropologists, whose school was mainly French-speaking in the
late 1960s and early 1970s (Claude Meillassoux and others).

In the making of states, and even of nation-states, for which the pre-
colonial nineteenth-century history is exemplary, two cases can be made.
The first concerns the rise of large conquering states, based on trade,
frequently internal slave trade and armed conquest. In the case of *jihad*
(Muslim holy wars), ideology and trade went hand in hand. Great religious
men were at one and the same time major entrepreneurs, such as Al-hadj
Umar in western Africa, or Usman dan Fodio in northern Nigeria of today.
Historians usually emphasise religious incentives and the impact of Islam.
They tend to neglect economic motives which were extremely strong in the
making of these empires. Al-hadj Umar, who first settled in upper Guinea,
was a very successful businessman, not only in long-distance trade but also
as a coloniser: thousands of his soldiers became settlers and landowners in
the newly conquered eastern lands (in Mali of today), noticeably in the
Bamana kingdom of Segu previously populated with non-Muslim peasants
and warriors. They drastically transformed the rural landscape, using the
former inhabitants as slaves and cultivators.[1]

Samori was also typical: originally, he was a trader. Like other *dyulas*, or
professional Muslim traders south of Jenne, he traded in slaves, guns, cloth
and other goods between northern and southern Guinea. It is because he
was a trader connecting the middle Niger valley to the Atlantic coast that he
created his empire, based on his trading wealth; as Islam was the prevalent
ideology of the time he proclaimed himself a Muslim leader. However, his
ambitions were stymied by the growing influence of the French and the
British, who progressively pushed him back eastwards. There, he proceeded
to conquer new lands, and new people whom he enslaved. These slaves
became soldiers and kept his army growing. Thus he built a formidable but
fragile empire; fragile because it was based on brutal colonisation. As with
other conquerors of the time, he was defeated by the European colonisers
without having had enough time to start nation building. Instead colonised
Africans rather fomented local revolts and ethnic strife.

This was also the case in eastern Africa, where economics and politics
went hand in hand with the emergence and apex, in the nineteenth century,
of an actual colonial regime organised by the sultanate of Oman. In 1840,
Sultan Said moved his capital city from Arabia to Zanzibar island because
the trade in slaves and cloves that was organised there was extremely profitable. He also supervised large plantations on coastal Africa with the help of
Indian bankers and of Swahili, Arab or Islamised Bantu chiefs who brought

caravans of ivory and slaves from the hinterland. From the tenth or twelfth century onwards a mixed culture and language arising from the encounter of male Arab traders and female Bantu autochthonous people had emerged. Swahili culture reached its climax in the eighteenth century and gave a general unity to the whole, while later competition arose between the Arab Omani rulers and the previous Swahili local aristocracies. Nevertheless, all of them contributed to building a lasting common feeling of belonging to the same whole: their cross-cultural economic interests emanating from the exploitation of the hinterland were reinforced by a common language of communication, which was progressively adopted by local people spreading far into the interior of the continent. Today Swahili is the language spoken mainly in the eastern half of Africa due to the close connection between economics and politics which lasted for centuries. Eventually, at the very end of the nineteenth century, Western colonialism by the Germans and the British was assisted partly by the antagonism among African people and partly by the Swahili aristocracies reacting against the previous Arab colonialism.[2]

Very different is the second case concerning smaller political entities which comprised nation-states, i.e. the existence of political sovereignty, a state apparatus and economic power built on a historical, cultural and linguistic community. These were true nation-states.[3] In their context: they enjoyed local specificities, and their conceptualisation of power was similar to but different from European nation-states. Such were, for example, the small slave-trading coastal kingdoms from the mid-seventeenth century to the mid-nineteenth century: the Abome kingdom (in modern Benin) or the Asante empire (in modern Ghana). The Atlantic slave trade became regular and important only from the mid-seventeenth century, after the Portuguese imported into Brazil's sugar-cane plantations the system of slavery they had first introduced in the Sao Tome islands at the bottom of the Bight of Benin in West Africa as early as the end of the fifteenth century. At the time when trade in slaves became the main Atlantic business, chiefdoms and kingdoms emerged on the African coast where active African businessmen entered the market. Their emergence, rise and decline are coeval with the rise and expansion of Brazilian, Caribbean and American slave sugar (and later cotton) plantations, continuing with the growing use of wage-labour rather than slaves. That is the reason why the history of African slave kingdoms is closely connected with the history of the Atlantic slave trade.

One could multiply examples of small nation-states emerging as early as the eighteenth century. Such were the so-called interlacustrine states which arose in eastern Africa, Rwanda, Burundi, Ankole or Buganda (the core of today's Uganda). Their peoples enjoyed a long common history, using a common language and culture. The kings organised their power in a way similar to that of the slave kingdoms, based on alternating periods: engaged in cultivation during the rainy season, while fighting wars against neighbours during the dry season when passage of armed forces was possible. The king's men were part-time peasants and part-time warriors, benefiting from part of their crops and a share of the booty. They obeyed chiefs of provinces, who themselves were dependent on the king by nomination rather than by kinship for their power and wealth. The state power was hierarchised and controlled, based on the king's ability to prove his power emanating from his wealth which conditioned his generosity. Therefore politics and economics were inextricably connected. A late example of this successful balance of power can be studied in the core of central Congo, where the Bakuba kingdom reached its peak in the first half of the nineteenth century. Closely entangled economic relationships existed between the capital city, where craftsmen created and diffused an elaborated art, and the countryside, where female slaves and dependent peasants fed the city, while long-distance trade, only partially consisting of slave trading, guaranteed the king's power.[4]

The above mentioned examples suggest that people enjoying a common history, language, culture and nationalism could, in the course of time, build nations which survived. But then colonisation occurred, and that was a major turning point. European colonialism either destroyed or accepted and used previous political entities. The so-called colonial imperialism took its rapid course between 1885 (when the European International Conference of Berlin was held) and 1900, when colonisation was completed over nearly all of Africa.

Imperial colonialism openly proclaimed its purpose as mainly economic. In the late 1960s and early 1970s, scholarly discussions took place on the question of whether colonial imperialism was myth or reality. In my opinion, it was rather myth than reality, at least during the first period of conquest and expansion.[5] For Britain colonial expansionism was largely a 'reluctant imperialism',[6] and probably cost as much as it was profitable for the other colonisers of the time, France being the first after Britain. Nevertheless, at least during the first half of the twentieth century, the official and often actual aim of colonialism was openly to be profitable to the mother country. Colonial ideology also explained – and this was partly indeed true – that monetarisation and the inclusion of colonial Africa in a modern capitalist economy would be rewarding not only for the mother countries, but also for colonised people.

Officially, including in South Africa, the basic aim of colonialism was production. It rapidly became the main incentive. Politically, as late as the early 1950s, colonial regimes imposed by the most democratic European nations on African populations were close to dictatorship. Power was exclusively in the hands of white colonisers and settlers, ruling a huge majority of African 'native' people who submitted to native rules and courts. Economically, colonial enterprise had its logic and rationality. For example, the creation of large French federations – FWA (French West Africa) and FEA (French Equatorial Africa) – was an attempt to rationalise economic exploitation and organisation. The Belgian Congo was specifically set up by King Leopold of the Belgians to make money. The Rhodesia Federation, elaborated between 1955 and 1965, was a similar attempt to minimise expenditure and maximise profits.

But ironically, African people, who were often split up between different colonial territories depending on varied mother countries, began, quite early in colonial times, to build a kind of national consciousness inside these given territories. One has to say 'a kind of national consciousness' because one has to take into account the coeval exacerbation of regionalisms known as ethnicities, to a large extent based on their previous broken history. For ethnic groups were just former historical, cultural and, definitely, political entities. During colonisation the concept of 'ethnic group' was biased (when colonisers rather used the term 'tribes'), while former independent and sometimes competing neighbours had to live within the same colonial boundaries claiming regionalisms, which had once been independent nations.

As a matter of fact, forced or not, African people became accustomed to living together for at least two and sometimes more than four generations. Administrative boundaries slowly evolved towards political frontiers. This was so generally accepted that independent states quite freely decided in 1963 – writing it in the OAU (Organisation of African Unity) charter – to maintain and protect colonial boundaries for the new independent states. Of course, it was partly to avoid military conflict as they had so many other vital problems to deal with at the same time. But it also conformed to reality: Francophone, Anglophone, Lusophone areas had been defined for a century or more. In French-speaking Africa territorial reform which began in the early 1950s resulted in isolating and nationalising the varied territories previously bound strictly to one another by a centralised federation. French West Africans were progressively turned into Senegalese, Ivoirian, Guinean citizens. This resulted in nation building in the making which had begun at least a century before. In Senegal, for example, you may be Wolof-speaking, Pular-speaking or Mande-speaking but, except in the south in

Casamance where Diola irredentism grew, now you are a Senegalese Wolof, or a Senegalese Al-pular, or a Senegalese Serer, rather than a Wolof or Tukuloor or Serer Senegalese. Of course, you may feel both, but national consciousness is now very strong. It has become a fact.

The *a contrario* proof of the reality of African nationalisms of today is that all secession wars failed in Africa, except one: Eritrea. Why? Because Eritrea had no common colonial past with Ethiopia. Eritrea was sold as early as 1890 by the Ethiopian Emperor Menelik to the Italians who failed, six years later, to colonise Ethiopia, which remained independent. Eritrea was turned into an Italian colony as late as 1941, when the British military occupied it during the Second World War and then ruled it as a protectorate until 1960. Only then, eighty years after the partition, did the Ethiopian empire recover Eritrea. This was never accepted by Eritreans who, for about three generations, had experienced quite a different process of development. In particular, because of the Second World War, the British launched industrialisation along the Red Sea, and trade unionism developed along with the proletarianisation of thousands of workers. Besides, Eritrea had inherited the northern Abyssinian culture, while Ethiopa was later submitted to the Amhara dynasty and culture of the central province of Shoa. This was quite different from the case of Germany, when both East and West Germany claimed their common past culture. Therefore, when the British negotiated Eritrea's reunification with Ethiopia, Eritreans constantly opposed their return to this medieval remnant of imperial conservatism. This appears in total contrast with Congo, whose multiple ethnicities and important regional diversities, as vivid as they are, nowadays are totally included in a strong common national feeling of being Congolese.

The turning point of the 1950s and 1960s, the so-called decolonisation period, was a decisive moment. In Africa south of the Sahara, sometimes – however seldom – a pre-national liberation war occurred, such as the Mau-Mau revolt in Kenya or the UPC (*Union des Peuples camerounais*) movement in Cameroon led by the radical trade unionist, Ruben um Nyobe. Most of the time, independence was achieved following a transitional period characterised by the emergence of a democratic process: free elections, and even franchise in FWA in 1956, political parties and trade unions, allowed nearly everywhere in French and British Africa after the Second World War. Therefore, a vivid political life and a civil society developed simultaneously.[7] Consequently, for a short while, there occurred a somewhat reasonable equation between the economic purpose (aid and development, a theory born from the Second World War) and the political area, supposed to be adjusted to the democratic models of the mother countries.

Unfortunately, this did not last long. Independence was achieved, which obviously was a political victory, but proved to be an economic disaster. It was a disaster because independence was strictly conceived as *political* independence: namely, the making of a state with a state apparatus – the only model being the European democratic nation-state. However, the economic aims and organisation did not change. Ever since colonial times, and even before that, the economy had been oriented outward, ruled by an international market, located out of reach of African control. It remained the same, globally ruled by a North–South unequal exchange. A gap appeared and widened between the economic system and the internal political strife. Most African states were tiny, in terms of either their dimensions or their populations, or both.

Nevertheless, a few African states could have taken the leadership, such as Nigeria, Congo or even Ethiopia. They are humanly and economically viable; why not politically? Only South Africa offers such a hope. It is a fascinating case because, only a few years ago, all foreign observers thought it would explode. It still might, but for the moment, hopefully, it resists. This is all the more surprising as no nation-state in Africa is more variegated; nowhere will you find so many ethnicities – white or black – so many varied regions – from desert to cornfields to precious mines – and such a diversified economy – from miserable scattered villages to modern highly industrialised metropolises. Nowhere was it less plausible for a state to be built in Africa, still less a nation, given the history and populations of the country. South Africa has become a nation-state, except for tiny minorities still claiming distinct independence: Whites are South Africans, Africans are South Africans, Indians are South Africans, so-called coloured people resulting from world-wide intermingling are South Africans. South African consciousness resulted from the fierce struggle against apartheid and might partly be explained by a seemingly successful balance between economics and politics. The system consists of a close interconnection between, on the one hand, a liberal but controlled modern economy largely immersed in globalisation and, on the other hand, a democratic political system, or at least a strong will and quest for democracy.

Elsewhere in Africa, this conjunction does not yet exist, mostly because of historical factors and heritage. These clearly appear when you look at Congo, former Zaire, former Belgian Congo, and still before that the so-called Free State of Congo, when it was created in 1885 by Leopold II, king of the Belgians, as his private property.

Congo is more or less an enigma for international observers. In spite of apparent similarities, its recent history is the exact opposite to Yugoslavia.

Yugoslavia disintegrated, Congo did not, and, in spite of numerous predictions, is not likely to do so. Most observers cannot understand the reasons for this staying power because they lack the necessary historical knowledge. Congo is by no means the battlefield of 363 tribes, as it is usually described by journalists. Its population consists of 30 million Congolese, who definitely feel themselves to be Congolese. For a relatively long time Congo has been a state and a nation in the making. It developed along the lines of defined economic aims which, alas, only recently disappeared. Moreover, Congolese nationalism was cemented by at least two successive civil wars which decisively failed: history has proved everywhere that nothing can bind a nation more closely together than a war of secession which was, in the end, successfully overcome. Today, Congo is immersed in a political disaster because of the desperate state of its economy rather than the reverse. In the past the model of the state functioned as long as economic issues were dealt with, even though a series of abuses of human rights went along with the colonial regime. The following conclusions can be drawn:

1 During Leopold's autarchy (1885–1907), the economy was reduced to a private business to make as much money as possible from rubber, rightly nicknamed 'red rubber', or bloody rubber by international opinion of the time. Leopold used the profits, among other projects, to turn Brussels into a brilliant capital city. He enjoyed absolute power devoted to his economic ventures.[8]

2 During Belgian colonialism (1907–1960), Congo became a classical model of 'colonial paternalism', aiming to extract the greatest possible amount of profits through mining and industrialisation with minimum welfare and maximum political authority. From the mid-1920s, in particular, the economic policy of the *Union minière du haut Katanga*, the powerful corporation exploiting copper in Katanga, was to shift from a rapid turnover of unskilled workers as used elsewhere, specifically on the South African Rand, to a stable better-paid labour force. A model villagisation occurred around the mines, where workers were married and their children taught by missionaries within a tight association between the state and the Catholic Church – the only condition on access to this improvement in welfare was the requirement of strict obedience to colonial laws. It proved to be harsh but efficient colonialism.[9]

Unfortunately, political independence was unable to recover from nearly a century of these outward-oriented economic streams. Meanwhile, the Congolese were knit together by a common administrative network, but also by common misery. With the advent of independence, and through the following forty years, any kind of reasonable economic framework was neglected and destroyed.[10] The state was reduced to an inefficient political dictatorship at the same time as the nation had emerged. After a few difficult civil wars, Mobutu came to power in 1965, changed Congo into Zaire, and organised the systematic plundering of the nation's wealth for his own profit and to sustain his patrimonial practices, manipulating and reaching compromises with his state's bourgeoisie.[11] Because of the continuing interest of international powers in the extraordinary mineral wealth of the country (gold, diamond, copper, cobalt, etc.), and because of their demand for a stable and strong power, whatever its internal drawbacks might be, Mobutu was protected by the French and maintained by the United States.

Since then the Congolese nation, welded by the melting-pot of the labour market generated by colonisation, has been resisting. Because investments had been high during colonialism, a huge labour force was used to build roads and railways, to open large plantations, and to populate numerous mining compounds. Hundreds of thousands of migrant workers were on the move from the beginning of the twentieth century. Urbanisation grew, cultural syncretisms were at work for years, including christianisation. Ironically, Mobutu himself reinforced Congolese nationalism, founding it on the myth and reality of its founding hero of independence: Patrice Lumumba. Therefore Congo now faces a dramatic separation. From the viewpoint of most Congolese, Congo is a nation without a state; in Kabila's, and most observers' viewpoint, it would rather be a state without a nation.

The Congolese nation without a state generates its own economy, which is informal and a so-called parallel economy. The Congolese have a joke about this: they live on article 14 of the constitution, which in fact consists of only thirteen articles. The fourteenth is the well-known 'debrouillardise' (how to manage with nothing) article. Article 14 stands for the survival of the whole. Therefore, even in this ultimate case, a nation needs, implies and generates an economy to exist. Undoubtedly this is the case in Congo. The official state depends on a dying international market based on minerals; a dying market but with splendid funerals, while the present wars are being entirely financed and conditioned by who controls which mines; meanwhile, the people organise and create new economic strategies, which begin to be scrutinised and studied by international institutions, such as the World Bank and the International Monetary Fund (IMF).

Therefore Congo is, at one and the same time, a nation without a state but with a given economy, and a state without a nation enjoying a separate economy. This dichotomy generates schizophrenic reactions. Unfortunately such a lethal dichotomy cannot be solved at once, i.e. the urgency to reconcile Congolese society with politics, and politics with economics. Many foreseeable trends are emerging: modern social and political movements, an embryonic civil society, and claims of democratisation although with hardly any success yet. The insurrection against Mobutu in 1994 and struggles against Kabila's dictatorship were far from being a total failure, even though the extremely complex situation is augmented by foreign involvement. However, at least one thing appears to be certain: Congo is a state which will not split up. Congolese nationalism is a reality reinforced by African wars around and inside it, when at least six other African foreign states (Rwanda, Uganda, Sudan, Zimbabwe, Angola, Namibia) directly and two others (Burundi and Zambia) indirectly are involved on its frontiers. So far the problem of co-ordinating the Congolese state and the Congolese economy has not been solved. This is the very condition necessary for peace to be achieved.

It is the moment when history and historians may get involved by reacting against the official mood of Afro-pessimism which is a reality of today. It is also an ideology, based on the belief that Africans cannot and, above all, will not manage by themselves. This ideology was born during the slave-trade period, long before modernity. White traders discussed whether Africans were human beings or not; later, colonisers regarded them as children to be educated. Nowadays, the Western world doubts their ability to develop. Surely, for the moment many African economies are bloodless, epidemics are threatening and famines are spreading in a number of areas, etc. This is obvious and tragic, but represents a myopic view. In the short run, we may agree that no real solution can be expected. Nevertheless, Africa is a huge continent, three times as large as America; a number of countries, as different as Botswana, Tanzania or Mali and others, receive little attention from the international media because things do not go so badly there. Africa also possesses obvious assets. Although its quickly growing population is today a drawback, the continent is relatively underpopulated and may become comparable to other continents in the future. For the past fifteen or twenty years, social change has dramatically accelerated, creativity has flourished, a democratic impulse has been launched. Above all, except in a few disaster-stricken areas (Somalia, Liberia, Congo...), productivity and production are rapidly increasing, even though, for the moment, not enough when compared with population growth. A new peasantry has emerged. Just as the peasantry, separated from the state, had opposed colonialism,[12] new peasants, well aware of economic trends, are feeding the cities. Market farming is increasing: potatoes are grown in Rwanda, vegetables everywhere, rice is produced in Ivory Coast, Kenya and elsewhere, although foreign imports (imported wheat versus local millet) appear to be dramatically competitive. Mining and hydroelectric power, among the richest resources in the world, are just being industrially developed. Within two or three generations, things may dramatically evolve and, in the long run, an optimistic view is far from unrealistic. We have to keep in mind that African nations are very young, and that henceforth a number of them are overcoming their tribal heritage. Without doubt, several nations such as South Africa or Ivory Coast – if this one is not overcome, as others, by civil wars – and possibly Nigeria, among others, are ready to struggle by themselves. However, at the present, not surprisingly, most of them are not as yet mature states equipped with efficient economic networks. But these are emerging too. Patrimonial states are not completely negative and corrupted and can also play their part as long as an organised social security and welfare network is not guaranteed. Surely, a number of states in Africa, which are too tiny and underpopulated, are not viable by themselves. But they have to unite to compete. Will the actual boundaries born from colonialism and guaranteed by the Organization of African Unity survive?

In spite of internal struggles and a major war involving the whole of Central Africa, the pan-Africanist ideas, launched in Africa by Kwame Nkrumah, slowly gain support because unity becomes economically and politically unavoidable. More and more African people are conscious that Africa's problems could begin to be solved by building a union similar to that of Europe. This is a vision of the future. But democratisation has begun and a long process is needed to achieve democracy. Given the acceleration of 'universal' concepts and rights resulting from globalisation, it may not take as long in Africa as it took in Europe, where the development of democratic forms needed several centuries and a number of setbacks before it triumphed.

NOTES

1. David Robinson, *The Holy War of Umar Tal: the Western Sudan in the Mid-Nineteenth Century* (Oxford, 1985).
2. Abdul Sheriff, *Slaves, Spices and Ivory in Zanzibar* (Athens, Ohio, 1991); Jonathon Glassman, *Feasts and Riots: Revelry, Rebellion, and Popular Consciousness on the Swahili Coast, 1856–1888* (London, 1995).
3. Basil Davidson, *The Black Man's Burden: Africa and the Curse of the Nation-State* (London, 1992).
4. Jan Vansina, *The Children of Woot: a History of the Kuba People* (Madison, Wis., 1978).
5. Henri Brunschwig, *French Colonialism 1871–1914: Myths and Reality* (London, 1966).

6. John S. Galbraith, *Reluctant Empire: British Policy on the South African Frontier 1834–1854* (Berkeley, Calif., 1963).
7. Richard Joseph, *Radical Nationalism in Cameroun: Social Origins of the UPC Rebellion* (Oxford, 1977); Achille Mbembe, *La naissance du maquis dans le Sud-Cameroun (1920–1960). Histoire des usages de la raison en colonie* (Paris, 1996); Florence Bernault, *Démocraties ambiguës en Afrique centrale. République gabonaise, République du Congo 1945–1980* (Paris, 1996).
8. Adam Hochschild, *King Leopold's Ghost : a Story of Greed, Terror, and Heroism in Colonial Africa* (Boston, 1998).
9. John Higginson, *A Working Class in the Making: Belgian Colonial Labor Policy, Private Enterprise and the African Mineworker 1907–1951* (Madison, Wis., 1989).
10. J. Vanderlinden, *Du Congo au Zaïre 1960–1980. Essai de bilan* (Brussels, 1980).
11. Benoît Verhaegen, 'Impérialisme technologique et bourgeoisie nationale au Zaïre', *Connaissance du tiers-monde*, 10, 18 (1978), 347–80.
12. Goran Hyden, *Beyond Ujamaa in Tanzania: Underdevelopment and an Uncaptured Peasantry* (Berkeley, Calif., 1980).

CHAPTER 13

The economic foundation of the nation-state in Senegal

Ibrahima Thioub

In April 1960, Senegal, like most French African colonies, became independent. The new regime expressed a strong will to build a nation within the borders inherited from colonisation and to promote social and economic development in order to reach the level of Western industrialised societies within a relatively short time.[1] To attain this double objective of economic prosperity and nation building, several political strategies were elaborated on the basis of the doctrine of 'African socialism'.

Basing its legitimacy on a strong belief in these objectives, and supported by a coalition of social forces efficient enough to exert tight control over Senegalese society, the regime, with relative ease, absorbed, neutralised or eradicated any tendency to dissent by a combination of repression and co-option of its opponents. This strategy appeared politically successful with regard to the desire to curb dissent and strengthen central power. Under the pretext of promoting national unity and nation building several new policies were implemented. At the institutional level power was reinforced and stabilised by a single political party and an authoritative presidential regime. On the economic level the state assumed a central position that enabled it to exercise the social control necessary to implement its economic programmes. It extended its control by managing the country's resources and monopolising the sphere of policy decisions.

However, very soon, political tensions arose in the upper sphere of the state, revealing disagreements between Mamadou Dia, President of the Council, and Léopold Sédar Senghor, President of the Republic about the orientation of the regime. The former questioned the distribution of power in the rural areas and advocated a series of radical reforms to promote small and medium-sized producers and to give them more political power. The latter argued in favour of maintaining the socio-political *status quo* in the rural areas; in other words, he accepted the powerful leadership of the heads of religious brotherhoods and rural notability. The crisis was resolved in favour of the President of the Republic in December 1962. This event was

important in the process of stabilisation and consolidation of the regime
and revealed what was at stake in the control of political power and in the
definition of the regime's economic policies.

By the end of the 1970s the project of economic development, supposedly based on the central role of the state, had failed and caused a
crisis whose impact was reflected in the ruptures in government policies.
The state henceforth limited intervention in the economy, kept off the entrepreneurial field and implemented structural reforms that served a double
objective: trade liberalisation and privatisation of an important part of the
state's portfolio,[2] and the creation of a multiparty system with the gradual
enlargement of the public sphere, etc.[3]

However, neither determining the diagnosis nor implementing remedies
could dispose of the multiple symptoms of crisis in the national project
whose economic programme had greatly contributed to jeopardising the
conditions in which nation building was to be achieved.

Numerous studies from various disciplines have attempted to analyse
the trajectories of Senegal as an independent state and its relationship
with civil society. Although most of this research shows remarkably high
scientific standards, the different studies reveal glaring contradictions in
their conclusions. While the authors' analyses acknowledge the failure of
the regime's economic policy there is disagreement on the identification of
its causes.[4]

Economists unanimously draw a rather catastrophic picture of the situation on the basis of the contrasting performances in different sectors of
the economy. Those interested in other aspects of the trajectory of Senegal
as an independent state are generally fascinated by its evolution, often considered as a proof of an exceptional success story. Cruise O'Brien,[5] in a
review of four books on Senegal,[6] gives the best synthesis of the elements
constituting the trajectory of Senegal compared with that of other African
states. Senegal experienced the longest French colonial domination in Sub-
Saharan Africa, and it has since independence been playing a major role
in the French-speaking communities. The following factors constitute the
'Senegalese exception': the relatively long tradition of the Senegalese multiparty system; the success of its nation-building project until the late 1970s;
the original model of linkage between the political and religious spheres
which preserved a secular state, followed by more than 90 per cent of the
population, was shaped; and the existence of a civil regime that had survived since 1960. The absence of religious and ethnic antagonisms as well as
the political elite's tolerance and broad-mindedness had accorded Senegal

a favourable image. This in turn allowed the regime to benefit from substantial international assistance, a sort of bonus for its democratic stability that did not reflect its poor economic performance.

By investigating the relations between the national project and the colonial economy it replaced, this chapter is designed to show that the elements nourishing the success of the hegemonic model set up by the Senegalese ruling class should be linked to the economic failings of the 1960s and 1970s, which were the result of deliberate choices by the interest groups that controlled the state apparatus. The structural constraints inherited from colonisation should evidently also be taken into consideration, but this does not suffice to explain the impact of the choices made by the ruling class. Consequently, the failure and economic hardships caused by the Senegalese regime cannot only be apprehended in terms of disorientation and mismanagement by the central administration. In fact, such an approach underscores the shortcomings of the so-called 'Senegalese exception' which revealed its inconsistencies in the early 1980s.

The exhaustion of economic capacities of the post-colonial model by the government of the 1960s and 1970s became apparent in the increasing segmentation or even atomisation of interest groups whose coalition had reinforced the stability of the ruling power. This was augmented by the subsequent intensification of competition for control over public resources which were frequently used to finance one or the other political clientele. The management of Senegal's economy was governed by the concern for political stability and thus actual economic concerns were neglected to such an extent that the productive capacities of all sectors were drastically reduced. This disrupted the stability of the regional systems, already subjected to internal dissent, and it damaged the perspectives of national cohesion and aggravated negotiations in a period of structural adjustment. Expressions of this development could be seen, on the one hand, in young migrants from the Groundnut Basin escaping the socio-political control of their elders and, on the other hand, in the armed rebellion of the population in the peripheral regions (Casamance) as well as in cultural dissent (Futa).

Unlike in the 1950s, characterised by the rise of nationalism, it is at the present time proving difficult to construct a new hegemonic coalition representing an economic alternative to liberalism able to sustain the construction of a nation-state. Accordingly, the economic orientation chosen by the hegemonic group that negotiated independence has to be seriously questioned.

SOCIAL AND ECONOMIC CONSTRAINTS INHERITED
FROM COLONISATION

Before the proclamation of independence the most urgent economic objective of the Senegalese government was to put an end to the cash-crop
economy, a symbol of colonial exploitation and oppression. This was a goal
that was able to mobilise people to support the newly born state's project
of nation building. The achievement of such an objective was supposed to
be based on a radical questioning of the economic and political structures
inherited from the colonial masters.

In Senegal the cash-crop economy involved only one export product:
groundnuts. Several factors contributed to the process that imposed
groundnut crops on rural producers and enforced their submission to the
forces of the world market. Groundnuts were introduced in Senegal during the slave trade era when they were used as food for the crew during the Atlantic passage. With the abolition of slavery in the nineteenth
century groundnut cultivation under the management of Islamic movements became a means for farmers to become emancipated from the *ceddo*
aristocracy.[7] However, as a consequence of the changes brought about by
the colonial conquest the cash-crop economy no longer served to eman-
cipate farmers. On the contrary, these crops became instrumental in the
exploitation and oppression of their producers.[8]

It was the authoritative nature of the colonial power and not economic
concerns that contributed to the prioritisation of administrative and extra-
economic constraints in the process that imposed the groundnut economy
on Senegal. Compulsory farming under the control of the local administration and taxes to be paid in cash from the income of the sales of crops
were the main causes for Senegal's specialisation in groundnut growing.

However, these causes alone cannot account for the scale, duration and
intensity of groundnut cultivation in Senegal that has led to the complete identification of the country with a groundnut economy. Mbodj
has convincingly demonstrated that the labour time a peasant dedicates
to groundnut farming, in order to get sufficient returns to cover his tax
payments, represents only a small proportion of the total time needed for
groundnut production. Starting from what he calls a 'speculation rate',
defined as the part reserved for groundnut production within the total
area available for cultivation in the 'Groundnut Basin', Mbodj shows how
farmers, through the mechanism of credit, were forced to cultivate crops for
export until, by 1912, groundnuts had become the dominant crop.[9] While
Mbodj's analysis correctly identifies the credit system as the crucial factor

in this development of a monoculture he seems to have overlooked that the year 1912 was, at the same time, a turning point in the pacification of the relationship between the colonial administration and the *marabouts*, leaders of the Islamic brotherhoods. This fact, indeed, confirms his already convincing analysis of this period. The *marabouts* contributed inestimably to the mobilisation of farmers for groundnut cultivation. The friendly relations between the colonial administration and the Islamic leadership reinforced the influence of the brotherhoods on the rural masses usually working on the *marabouts'* farms.

The *marabouts de l'arachide*[10] (groundnut-*marabouts*) became large-scale producers by mobilising more and more disciples to clear and farm new land.[11] Consequently, the administration and the companies which enjoyed a *de facto* monopoly over the groundnut trade profited from the impact of the Islamic leadership, which became an integral part of the system that determined the major economic objectives of the colonial order. Hence, all available measures were taken to consolidate the power of the *marabouts* whose political support and economic contribution remained particularly profitable to them until the eve of independence.[12] By the end of this development, the leaders of the religious brotherhoods in Senegal exerted considerable social control in the 'Groundnut Basin', a region that occupied a central position within the colonial territory, and they thus necessarily became prime collaborators in the implementation of economic policy.

This distribution of social and economic power was to have a decisive impact on the negotiations concerning the economic options of the postcolonial regime, and on the project of nation building. In addition to the protection of local interests linked to Senegal's specialisation in groundnut crops, the independent state, in conformity with the role assigned to it, maintained its support of France by assuring the colonial power supplies of groundnut plants at the lowest possible cost. Considerable resources of the colony were mobilised for this purpose. The groundnut economy, whose profitability has been questioned since the crisis of the 1930s, has survived due to tariff protection of the colonial market, preferential prices, credit for the purchase of seed, logistic assistance to production and extra-economic pressure on farmers in order to preserve the specialisation of the territory's economy.[13]

One of the main characteristics of the colonial cash-crop economy is the non-intervention by the state and by commercial capital in the production in rural homesteads. This had important consequences for the economic cohesion of the territory. The lack of technological support available to farmers prevented a continued quantitative increase of groundnut crops. Under these circumstances, the only way to increase production and profits was by extending the area under cultivation, either by clearing new land or by abandoning food crops, and by reducing the transport costs to ports and oil factories. All steps taken to meet the demands of the metropolis rapidly proved insufficient and by the eve of independence the maximum level of production had been reached. The continuation of the country's speciali- sation in groundnut crops, made possible through the over-exploitation of the rural labour force and the country's natural resources, had left indepen- dent Senegal with an environment generally unfavourable to its project of nation building.[14]

The important role of groundnuts in the economy of colonial Senegal had transformed its central production zone into the economically most important area of the colony, where labour, land and machines were con- centrated. This situation, in turn, led to an imbalance in land management characterised by the marginalisation of the regions not producing ground- nuts, these being either relegated to the role of suppliers of labour, or sim- ply abandoned or isolated. Analysing the causes of the crisis of the 1930s, Edmond Giscard d'Estaing clearly expressed this point of view by affirm- ing the necessity to begin to diversify by concentrating on a small number of activities: 'the dynamic colony', whose efficiency would be maximised. Although the contrast between privileged areas and the rest of the country would be accentuated, 'that would continue its autonomous existence... and slowly obtain economic progress'.[15]

The poor remuneration of the labour force reinforced the imbal- ances, particularly in its demographic aspects, by encouraging rural exodus towards the cities. Launched in the 1920s, the industrialisation of colonial Senegal could not redress these imbalances. While it succeeded in breaking the resistance of the metropolis to question the system of the 'exclusive colonial',[16] the industrialisation process was guided by the strict logic of immediate profit that prevented long-term, sustainable development.[17]

Closely linked with trade, the relatively early industrialisation of Senegal started with the manufacturing of groundnut products (shelling and oil factories). Launched by local colonial traders, industrialisation contributed towards increasing the commercial value of groundnut crops, while sup- plying a home market until then dominated by metropolitan oil producers. The foundation of oil factories clearly indicates a movement guided by the shifts in the trade cycle. It illustrates the fact that neither the financial cap- ital of the metropolis nor the large-scale colonial trade was the key element of industrial investment in French West Africa.

Paradoxically, it was the medium-scale trade that furthered the creation of the main industrial units specialised in groundnut processing. Consequently, inefficient industrial enterprises which relied solely on a protected metropolitan market broke up. Between 1920 and 1948 Senegal had a dozen oil factories, half of which were located in Dakar. Investment in groundnut processing was, in fact, the strategy of the medium-scale trade to counter periods of slumps when low exchange rates and prices made exports of raw materials unprofitable.

Until the end of the Second World War, when the state launched important financial investments in the colonial economy, the major companies had been unwilling to engage in activities other than groundnut processing but, by 1960, these industrial enterprises were fully involved in the manufacturing of alternatives to imported products. However, this industry rapidly proved its shortcomings in terms of its capacity to ensure an integrated economy for the country. It depended on foreign markets for its supplies of raw materials and technological equipment, and the intersectoral links between the different units of the industry remained particularly weak. Furthermore, the industries were concentrated in the region of Dakar in order to optimise immediate profitability.[18]

From this brief survey of the characteristics of the cash-crop economy the following question emerged, a question that had to be answered by the regime: How, on the basis of the structural constraints mentioned above, could an economy be set up capable of sustaining a project of nation-building?

THE CHALLENGE OF INDEPENDENT SENEGAL: BUILDING A NATION ON THE FOUNDATIONS OF THE COLONIAL ECONOMY

Immediately after the formation of the first Senegalese government under a regime of *autonomie interne*, a Comité d'Etudes Economiques was formed and designated to evaluate the industrial and commercial problems of agriculture likely to arise during the economic planning process. The results of the surveys conducted by the committee throughout the country constituted the basis for the first Senegalese plan for economic development.

State-controlled trade economy

The elimination of 'the infernal cycle' of trade was one of the major objectives for the implementation of this plan.[19] New organisational structures were created to attain this goal. After 1960 a large number of organisations were created for assisting and restructuring rural activities throughout the country. In 1960 the co-operative movement consisted of 100,000 farmers belonging to 810 Associations d'Intérêt Rural (AIR – Rural Interest Associations). These associations were expected to recruit new co-operative members, set up new structures and by 'this revolution', turn 'archaic structures into a new order'.[20] During the colonial period numerous co-operatives existed in Senegal, which were in turn preceded by several Sociétés de Prévoyance (SIP – Local Contingency Funds), authorised by the law of 10 September 1947. The SIPs, like the co-operatives after the Second World War, were either set up or controlled by rural notables and religious leaders. Their existence had always been subject to protests from commercial interests.[21] The co-operative movement introduced by the new regime was supposed to be run by local farmers recruited and trained by rural co-ordinators.

The commercialisation of groundnut production was moved from the private sector to a new commercial and industrial public institution, l'Office de Commercialisation Agricole (OCA – Office for Agricultural Commercialisation), in charge of the collection and transport of groundnut crops and the exportation of the surplus that could not be processed locally. The collection of crops from the producers was carried out in two parallel ways: co-operatives, on the one hand, and traders, authorised by OCA, and called Organismes Stockeurs (OS – Organisations of Stokers), on the other. A public credit institution, the Banque Sénégalaise de Développement (BSD) supervised the financing of the commercialisation campaign and of the equipment for farmers. The Centre Régional d'Assistance pour le Développement (CRAD) was responsible for the technical execution of the task.

Concerning the control of rural production, the policy of the plan was clear. By planning to accord substantial resources to rural production and to communication infrastructures, the state implemented a policy of minimising costs by augmenting the quantity of groundnut crops. It was expected that the volume of production would increase by 30 per cent and commercial revenues by 50 per cent.[22] As public organisations (OCA, BSD) controlled the distribution of the expected surplus drawn from increased groundnut production, this surplus could be transferred to the industrial sector in accordance with the objectives of the plan. However, this policy option was detrimental to private trade. The determination of the regime to control the groundnut circuit in order to ensure the realisation of the objects of the economic plan was not limited to the creation of new organisations with vast powers of intervention.

An analysis of the planned investments gives rather accurate indications concerning the economic policy of the new regime. State intervention in investment was clearly divided into public and private spheres. Sectors like agriculture, cattle breeding, forestry, administrative costs, social expenditures (education, health, housing) and transport infrastructure were prioritised by the state at the same time as investments in the commercial sector were almost non-existent and remained quite negligible in tourism and industry.

Paradoxically, the regime relied on the industrial sector to redress the balance in foreign trade, hasten economic growth, augment urban employment and connect the various sectors of the economy. Yet, the state invested the smallest part of its resources in industry. 'The emphasis on industry'[23] was manifested only as an expectation that foreign investors would arrive.

Considering the investment choices outlined in the plan and the reforms implemented, it is undeniable that there was a clear determination to abandon the colonial trade system – at least in its traditional form – and put an end to the dependence on imports of light industrial commodities.[24] But the dependency on foreign capital was not questioned. On the contrary, it was the foreigners' reluctance to invest in Senegal that preoccupied the regime. The planners omitted to analyse uncertain factors and limited themselves to expressing their wishes concerning essential measures for realisation of the plan. They ignored the impact of climatic changes and fluctuations in groundnut prices on the world market which were determining factors for the farmers' choice of crops.

Due to low revenues the Senegalese domestic market could not compensate Senegalese industry for the loss of the West African market emanating from the 'balkanisation' of the continent after independence. The debates which preceded the dislocation of French West Africa clearly point out the failure of 'a co-ordination of industrial policies'[25] that had been expected by the Senegalese regime. This explains the particular attention given to the creation of 'favourable conditions for the injection of private capital',[26] a domain in which the states of former French West Africa were in fierce competition.

The tax system in independent Senegal: privileges for foreign investors

A transitional fiscal regime was passed in 1959, before being repealed on 21 March 1962 when the taxation of enterprises was settled in the new code of investments.[27] This law constituted two special regimes that replaced the 1959 Convention d'Etablissement and the Régime fiscal de longue durée that had guaranteed 'the stability of all or part of the fiscal charges... concerning the basis of taxation, tax collection rules, and the tariff of taxes and dues'. The Convention de l'Etablissement, independent of the Régime fiscal de longue durée, ensured 'liberty in commercial exchanges, facilitating staff recruitment and equality between enterprises'. However, the advantages and guarantees were no longer sufficient to attract the amount of foreign capital required for the realisation of the different objectives for industrialisation in Senegal's first plan of development (1961–4).

In order to reach that objective, the state committed itself to creating conditions favourable to attract enough foreign investment by participating, if necessary, in supplying money for the purchase of seed and taking measures to protect the domestic market in the context of customs agreements between West African countries. Finding a market for the promotion of a national industry has been an ever-present problem for the Senegalese state. A small and poor population and a region consisting of small states in fierce competition with each other constitute the main obstacles for the development of such a market.

Two particular regulations contained in the code of investment of 1962 expressed, in practical terms, the principle that governed the plan: that is, to attract foreign investors to the industrial sector. The law of 21 March 1962 offered potential investors the possibility of choosing the status of a prioritised or an authorised enterprise. The prospect of fast profitability, outlined by the liberal code of investment, was expected to produce a strong motivation for foreign investors. Nevertheless, the sacrifices made by the public treasury to further the profits of industrial investments and the measures taken to reorganise the rural economy did not suffice to meet the expectations of the national planners. The other actors in the economic arena, particularly the native entrepreneurs, suffered from this liberal policy.

The 1960s, marked by economic reorganisation, were also a period of alternating opposition and negotiations between native entrepreneurs and the regime about obstacles to the development of a class of native businessmen with the capacity of becoming an important support in the nation-building project. By their political commitment, businessmen had contributed considerably to the process leading to the independence of Senegal. After independence had been achieved they hoped to see the government conduct a policy to their advantage against the hierarchy which had prevailed on the world market during colonisation. However, the first reform carried out by the state during the regime of *autonomie interne* rapidly put an end to these hopes.

*Relations between local entrepreneurs and the state in the process
of nation building*

Between 1960 and 1980, successive Senegalese governments were confronted
with the question of supporting local businessmen and promoting their
interests as one of the main aspects of the nation-building project. However,
at the end of this period, neither Mamadou Dia's option nor Léopold Sédar
Senghor's government orientation had satisfied the expectations of local
entrepreneurs.

The government of Mamadou Dia: promoting local entrepreneurship
Immediately after the formation of Mamadou Dia's first government, native
businessmen started to voice their demands. On their behalf, the president
of the Transport Workers Union expressed the wish that 'the new African
power' should dedicate itself to the promotion of Senegalese businessmen
in the profitable sector of the national economy by facilitating their access
to bank loans and by Africanising the circuits of the groundnut trade.[28]
But the doctrinal orientation of the regime and the first reforms of the
economic structure of the country disappointed these expectations. The
revolt of native businessmen against the regime persisted until its fall. On
their hostility the head of the government remarked:

Je comprends ... que des hommes d'affaires véreux, qui avaient misé sur un boule-
versement politique, se trouvent désemparés par l'échec de leurs calculs. Je pense,
par contre, qu'il y a place, plus que jamais, et dans des conditions meilleures, pour
tous les autres qui veulent travailler avec nous au développement et à l'essor de
notre pays.[29]

('I understand that the dubious businessmen who expected a political upheaval
are at a loss because they were misled by their false prediction. Unlike them, I
remain convinced that there are enough opportunities for everybody who wants
to work with us for the development and expansion of our country.')

On the basis of purchases made prior to the agreement of 1960, the
former traders from the interior were authorised by the OCA to hold
stocks. Competition between the co-operatives that collected groundnut
crops and the fees collected by the state[30] curbed the profits of these
traders who were obviously and consciously misled by the administration. Besides, the OS disappeared progressively as they were replaced by
co-operatives that collected the crops, and their status was officially cancelled with the 1967–8 *campagne de commercialisation.*[31] As the traders were
eliminated from the process of crop collection, they were converted into
members of the trade co-operatives set up in every region of the country

with the exception of Dakar. But these co-operatives also failed. While native traders with larger-scale enterprises in Dakar had been relatively successful early in this period, they too were soon faced with serious difficulties.

Traders in the capital city became members of co-operatives through a form of joint enterprise between native and former colonial firms. The 'policy of consortiums' was initiated by Abdoulaye Fofana, at that time minister of commerce. The most important of those consortiums were Societé Sénégalaise pour le Commerce et le Développement (SOSECOD), l'Africaine d'Importation et d'Exportation (AFRIDEX) and Societé Nationale d'Industrie et de Commerce (SONIC). Each consortium was sponsored by an important former colonial trade company that contributed to the capital, partly provided by local traders. Societé Commerciale de l' Ouest Africain (SCOA) and Campagnie française de l'Afrique Occidentale (CFAO) were respectively in charge of SOSECOD and AFRIDEX.

Within five years all consortiums went bankrupt. Opinions are divided on the causes of the simultaneous failures of these joint enterprises. One of the motives behind their creation can be found in the determination of the state to put an end to demands for the nationalisation of trade. The minister responsible for this operation confessed at the time that 'in opting for, and facilitating an association of foreign investors, Senegal gave no credit to the demands for nationalisation since the country's interests were preserved through the consortiums'.[32]

In rural as well as urban areas, all measures taken by the government between 1957 and 1962 to promote native investment failed. The hostility of the commercial sector, on the one hand, and the fear among rural and religious notables of the mobilisation of peasants as well as of the progress of the co-operative movement in the rural areas, on the other hand, were detrimental to the government of Mamadou Dia. As a result he lost influential supporters who had brought about the popularity of his party on the eve of independence. The immediate cause of the government's collapse was the disagreement between the President of the Council and the President of the Republic. However, the vote of censure passed against the former by the National Assembly was initiated by twelve Members of Parliament, nine of whom were businessmen.[33] In the 17 December 1962 coup against the President of the Council the participation of business interests introduced a new era in the relations between the traders as a social group and those in control of the state apparatus.

Senghor's policy of rectification: native entrepreneurs again among
the disadvantaged

In 1963, Léopold Sédar Senghor was elected President of the Republic on the basis of a new constitution that conferred enormous powers on him.[34] He immediately abandoned the radical policies concerning rural structures and the mobilisation of peasants initiated by the former government. Furthermore the regime, while still following its socialist doctrine, was once again obliged to reward the support of the religious and rural notables during the crisis of December 1962. Once the regime's control of the rural areas was assured, the next important step was to consolidate urban support by creating various institutions in order to achieve this goal. The organisations in charge of training and supervision in the rural areas, until then conceived as a means of emancipating farmers, were turned into efficient political systems for recompensing the social and political clientele of the regime. The trade community adapted its strategy to this situation while continuing to become more involved in political rivalries. Gigantic and highly centralised organisations of the state had preserved their control over the surplus of groundnut crops after 1962. Henceforth, promotion in business was proportional to the degree of allegiance to the bureaucracy of the state apparatus which controlled the mechanisms of large economic organisations such as l'Office Nationale de Coopération et d'Assistance au Développement (ONCAD) and the Banque Nationale du Sénégal (BNDS). Political cliques stabilised their power base by generously rewarding their clientele of *marabouts* and businessmen.

Climatic changes and the imbalance in the terms of trade unfavourable to African countries have often been evoked to justify the dead end in which African economies found themselves during the first decade of independence.[35] These two elements certainly played a role as independent factors leading to the crisis, but more importantly, they revealed its real causes by disclosing the drawbacks of favouritism as a method of political management in the context of a poor and dependent economy. It is true that the years of drought as well as the unequal relations that governed the world market had negative consequences on the economic achievements of the 1960s and 1970s. None the less, it is also true that economic imperatives were sacrificed on behalf of political stability achieved by distributing resources to a clientele and opening them up to predatory consumption.[36]

The main criticism of the first plan's economic orientation concerned the priority given by the previous government to industry to the detriment of agriculture. This led to the collapse of heavy industry as small units of production were favoured by state investments to support the industrial sector.[37] In addition to this, from 1964, an accelerated programme aimed at the improvement of agricultural productivity was elaborated. Its main objective was the enhancement of rural equipment through the use of horse-driven ploughs with the aim of increasing groundnut crops from 800,000 to 1,000,000 tons per year without extending the area under cultivation. At the same time, Senegal's independence from foreign supplies of agricultural products was to be secured by encouraging millet production. However, the priority given to the development of the rural economy was undermined by an important diminution of its available resources, directly through an increase of taxes and indirectly through the cost of public organisations, particularly the ONCAD. This office, created in 1966, was an enormous administrative structure with numerous functions deriving from the liquidation or transfers of the responsibilities of other interventionist organisations into its own sphere of activities. After fourteen years of existence, despite the monopoly it held on the groundnut trade and the low price policy it practised on a market of rural products where there were no competitors, the office left a debt of 90 billion francs to be cleared by the state, besides a loss of 12 billion due to unaccounted expenditure.[38] The state thus inherited a financial deficit from one of its main instruments of intervention in the rural economy, but it also had to take over a debt of 32 billion francs contracted by farmers in loans from public organisations.

Peasant farmers had undoubtedly also been indebted prior to the control of the groundnut trade by the state, but at the beginning of the 1970s a critical stage was reached. Consumer co-operatives, although denounced by the President of the Republic as sources of corruption,[39] were not the only organisations responsible for the difficulties of rural producers. From 1965 to 1969, the groundnut price compensation fund drew from the rural economy a net profit estimated at 6.5 billion francs which was used to finance public investments during the same period.[40] That might, economically speaking, justify the deficit incurred by the office of commercialisation and the clearance of the farmers' debt by the public treasury. ONCAD cost Senegal and all Senegalese dearly. At all levels fraud, corruption and mismanagement of all kinds occurred. The press, under the control of the state, even described ONCAD as 'très accueillante maison pour tous ceux qui cherchent à placer un protégé'.[41] The regime itself was worried by the extent of the misappropriation of public funds, and by the impunity of the offenders. In 1969, the President of the Republic estimated the loss in income due to fraud at 5 billion francs, and the embezzlement of public funds at 200 million per year, without mentioning bribes in the process of calls for tenders. The services mostly hit were ONCAD, OCAS, Office des Postes et Télécommunication (OPT) and Contrôle Economique.

Embezzlement and theft committed by civil servants were held by the regime to be due to moral decline and a tendency to wasting money.[42] The infernal trade cycle that led the state to take control of the groundnut trade was thus replaced by the whirlwind of illegal wealth acquisition by the state bureaucracy and its allies, to the detriment of the national economy.

The diagnosis that established mismanagement or misguided orientation as the source of the failure of public power often ignored the socio-political structure of the control of economic activity by the state. In so doing, it prevented a clear understanding of the root causes of the national project's failure in the 1960s and 1970s.

CONCLUSION: THE ECONOMIC ROOTS OF THE NATIONAL
PROJECT'S FAILURE

By the end of these two decades of development, the economic situation of Senegal had seriously deteriorated, affecting the living conditions of the most vulnerable groups of the population: the rural masses and urban workers. In the agricultural sector, the groundnut economy was most severely hit by complete stagnation or even decrease in its productivity. The 1980s also witnessed a long stagnation in the industrial sector.

The severe criticism of the regime by politicians went beyond blaming climatic changes or the adversity of external factors (deterioration of the terms of trade). One of the forms of the public sector's expansion had been the multiplication of semi-public organisations. Today it is widely acknowledged that these bodies did not meet the optimistic expectations they aroused at the moment of their creation. In fact, it was hoped that state enterprises would be the spearhead of modernisation and technological innovation, and that they would favour public savings with which to revitalise investment and economic growth.

According to Cheikh Hamidou Kane, Senghor's *ministre du Plan* at the time, the entrepreneurial public sector was the victim of 'unfocused orientations and careless management'.[43] Faced with growing difficulties in maintaining stability in its public finances, the regime resorted to financial institutions which were increasingly obsessed with the imperatives of re-paying the debts incurred during the 'golden years' of the mid-1970s, when the state was carrying out a generous policy of loan accessibility. Mamadou Touré, at the time *ministre de l'Economie et des Finances*, argued that the problem of the country's heavy debt was created in the years between 1974 and 1979, a favourable period that could have been used as an opportunity to restructure the declining groundnut economy.[44] The economic crisis was one of the phenomena that revealed the failure of the national project in the 1960s. Consequently, its main champion and theoretician, L.S. Senghor, voluntarily resigned from the presidency of the republic, thus opening the field to profound changes that affected the entire political personnel with the arrival and subsequent domination of technocrats in the political leadership of the state.[45] In so doing, he made way for the implementation of structural adjustment policies in the country.

The consequences of the economic crisis and the attempted solutions compromised, to a large extent, the foundations of nation building. The solution to the crisis was seen in the pursuit of the colonial project, based on the country's specialisation in groundnut crops and on a substitute industry for imported products in the context of scarce market opportunities. This furthered the interests of the ruling social groups: the intellectual elite, an emerging bureaucratic bourgeoisie and its allies, the leaders of brotherhoods, and the urban or rural traditional notables. The first, while exerting direct control over the state apparatus, remained bogged down in the mire of a clientele rationale which constitutes a major obstacle to nation building. Six months after he was elected president, on 29 June 1981, Abdou Diouf, successor to Léopold Sédar Senghor, passed a law against 'illicit enrichment'. The law was ineffective. Only a few people were used as scapegoats to satisfy public opinion. Scandals in the press revealed that huge amounts of money had been embezzled by leading civil servants and by the party in power. Some cases of mismanagement and misappropriation of public funds, such as by Loterie Nationale Sénégalaise (LONASE) or Croix Rouge Sénégalaise, went unpunished. In his speech to the cadres of his party, the head of state urged those who had transferred their bank savings abroad to repatriate the money, while assuring them that by doing so they would not run any risks at all.

For the various factions of this group, the politico-administrative apparatus functioned like a doorway to enrichment thoroughly divorced from economic productivity. In such a situation political allegiance was the basis of wealth distribution. Consequently, these groups were unable to have a clear understanding of the meaning of national economic development. Above all, the *marabouts*, who exerted the most effective socio-political influence on the rural masses, suffered from such a handicap. In order to reward these religious leaders for their support, politicians accorded them important economic privileges which were reinvested in symbols of religious power.[46] Until the 1980s, the religious leaders had concentrated their efforts on their brotherhoods and on the groundnut economy.

The study of the socio-economic rationale followed by the intellectual elite and the group of *marabouts* whose alliance had stabilised the Senegalese political regime has shown their inability to promote nation building and economic development as defined in the project of the 1960s.

To summarise: the two decades of the implementation of the national project considerably accentuated regional disparities and inequalities,[47] and reinforced dependence on foreign investment, which caused a deficit in the supply of foodstuffs and generated regional dissent that stymied territorial unity in Senegal and led to armed rebellion in Casamance.[48]

NOTES

The translation of this text owes much to Gilbert Diatta, Badara Sall and Ingrid Smette. They have all done more than merely translating the text. Through their questions and comments to clarify the translation, I reshaped and expressed my ideas more clearly. My thanks go to all of them for the invaluable assistance they gave me.

1. Léopold Sédar Senghor, political leader and theoretician of the regime, stated that the project was to be concluded by the year 2000.

2. Ibrahima Thioub, Momar Coumba Diop and Catherine Boone, 'Economic Liberalisation in Senegal: Shifting Politics of Indigenous Business Interests', *African Studies Review*, 41, 2 (1998), 63–89.

3. Momar Coumba Diop and Mamadou Diouf, *Le Sénégal sous Abdou Diouf. État et sociétés* (Paris, 1990), p. 436.

4. See Samir Amin, *L'Afrique de l'Ouest bloquée. L'économie politique de la colonisation, 1880–1970* (Paris, 1971), p. 322; Elliot Berg, 'Adjustment Postponed. Economic Policy Reform in Senegal in the 1980s', Report prepared for USAID/Dakar (October 1990), p. 253 and appendices.

5. Donald B. Cruise O'Brien, 'The Senegalese Exception', *Africa*, 66, 3 (1996), 458–64.

6. Andrew F. Clark and Lucie Colvin Phillips, *Historical Dictionary of Senegal*, 2nd edn. (New York and London, 1994); Momar Coumba Diop (ed.), *Senegal: Essays in Statecraft*, trans. Ayi Kwei Armah (Dakar, 1993); Anthony Kirk-Greene and Daniel Bach (eds.), *State and Society in Francophone Africa since Independence* (London 1995); Leonard A. Villalon, *Islamic Society and State Power in Senegal: Disciples and Citizens in Fatick* (Cambridge, 1995).

7. The *ceddo* aristocracy is the ruling class that originated in the Atlantic slave trade and took an active part in the military organisation of political power in Wolof states. See Boubacar Barry, *La Sénégambie du XVe au XIXe siècles: traite négrière, Islam et conquête coloniale* (Paris, 1988).

8. Mohamed Mbodj, 'Sénégal et dépendance: le Sine-Saloum et l'arachide, 1887–1940' in C. Coquery-Vidrovitch (ed.), *Sociétés paysannes du Tiers-Monde*, (Lille, 1980), pp. 139–54.

9. Ibid.

10. J. Copans, *Les marabouts de l'arachide* (Paris, 1980).

11. Paul Pélissier, *Les paysans du Sénégal. Les civilisations agraires du Cayor à la Casamance* (Saint-Yriex, 1966), p. 939.

12. The colonial power is indebted to the *marabouts* for their massive vote in favour of the 'yes' position during the referendum of 28 September 1958. (See Gerti Hesseling, *Histoire politique du Sénégal. Institutions, droit et société* (Paris, 1985), p. 170.

13. For an analysis of the various forms of public support to the groundnut economy, see, among others, the following studies: André Vanhaeverbeke, *Rémunération du travail et commerce extérieur, essor d'une économie paysanne exportatrice et termes de l'échange des paysans Sénégalais* (Louvain, 1970), p. 253; Bernard Founou-Tchuigoua, *Fondements de l'économie de traite au Sénégal (la surexploitation d'une colonie de 1880 à 1960)* (Paris, 1981); Jacques Marseille, *Empire colonial et capitalisme français. Histoire d'un divorce* (Paris, 1984), p. 462.

14. Founou-Tchuigoua, *Fondements de l'économie*.

15. Financial inspector in the colonial administration, Edmond Giscard d'Estaing, sent on a mission in French West Africa, produced an informative report on the causes of the 1930s economic crisis. Archives nationales de France, Aix-en-Provence, Carton 539, Edmond Giscard d'Estaing, 'Rapport de mission au ministre des Colonies', 18 April 1932, p. 80.

16. The system called *exclusif colonial* obliges the colonies to supply their market exclusively from the metropolis industries and to convey their exported products by metropolis boats.

17. Amin, *L'Afrique de l'Ouest bloquée*.

18. Institut des Sociétés Economiques Appliquées (ISEA), *Les industries du Cap-Vert, analyse d'un ensemble d'industries légères de l'Afrique occidentale* (Dakar, 1964), p. 79.

19. République du Sénégal, *Premier plan quadriennal de développement pour la période de 1961–1964 (Loi n° 61–32 du 13 mai 1961)* (Rufisque, 1962), p. 16.

20. Mamadou Dia, *Réflexions sur l'économie de l'Afrique noire* (Paris, 1960), p. 125.

21. M.F. Etile, 'Les sociétés indigènes de Prévoyance au Sénégal 1910–1940', Mémoire de Maîtrise, Université Paris 7 (1976), p. 117.

22. République du Sénégal, *Premier plan quadriennal*, p. 43.

23. Ibid., p. 93.

24. In 1960, Senegal imported 80–90 per cent of its consumption in industrial foodstuffs. See République du Sénégal, *Premier plan quadriennal*, p. 11.

25. Ibid., p. 94.

26. Ibid., p. 18.

27. République du Sénégal, *Journal Officiel de la République du Sénégal* (Rufisque, 1962).

28. Private archives, Syndicat Patronal de l'Ouest Africain, letter from El Hadji Amadou Lamine Niang to Mamadou Dia, President of the Council, 1957.
29. Dia, *Réflexions sur l'économie de l'Afrique*, p. 161.
30. For each kilogram collected, they received 2 francs from which 1 franc was deducted to be shared between the weighers and OCAS. Included in the sum of 1,700 francs for each ton of peanuts bought were 200 francs for bagging charges and 800 francs as deposit.
31. Régine Van-Chi-Bonnardel, *Vie de relations au Sénégal. La circulation des biens*, Mémoires de l'IFAN 90 (Dakar, 1978), p. 628. *La campagne de commercialisation* is the period when groundnut crops are authorised for sale. The dates of this period are determined by the administration and the sale of crops before and after this period is prohibited.
32. 'Le Sénégal à l'heure de l'industrie', special issue of *Moniteur Africain* (8 Feb. 1962).
33. G. Blanchet, *Elites et changements en Afrique et au Sénégal* (Paris, 1983), p. 263.
34. Boubacar Barry, *Le Sénégal 1960–1980: arachide, bourgeoisie bureaucratique et sécheresse*: Paper presented to a symposium at the University of Zimbabwe, 8–11 January 1985: *Les indépendances africaines: origines et conséquences du transfert du pouvoir 1956–1980*, p. 32.
35. Léopold Sédar Senghor, *Rapport de politique générale au VIᵉ Congrès de l'UPS* (5–7 January 1968) (Rufisque, 1968), p. 30.
36. Gilles Duruflé, *L'ajustement structurel en Afrique (Sénégal, Côte d'Ivoire, Madagascar* (Paris, 1988), pp. 28–9.
37. Senghor, *Rapport de politique générale*, p. 44.
38. N. Caswell, 'Autopsie de l'ONCAD. La politique arachidière au Sénégal', *Politique Africaine* (14 June 1984), 39–73.
39. Senghor, *Rapport de politique générale*, p. 102.
40. Amin, *L'Afrique de l'Ouest bloquée*, p. 36.
41. Caswell, 'Autopsie de l'ONCAD'.
42. Senghor, *Rapport de politique générale*, pp. 152–6.
43. Cheikh Hamidou Kane, 'La nouvelle politique de développement économique et social', Communication au Conseil National du Parti socialiste, Dakar, 26 April 1986, p. 21.
44. Mamadou Touré, 'Politique d'ajustement économique et financier', Communication au Conseil National du Parti Socialiste, Dakar, 11 May 1985, p. 21.
45. Diop and Diouf, *Le Sénégal sous Abdou Diouf*, p. 440.
46. Generally, with the money they receive from politicians, the *marabouts* strengthen their social and religious influence by constructing mosques and other places of worship, etc.
47. Diène Dione, 'Région périphérique et région centrale au Sénégal: approche géographique des disparités régionales', *Annales de la Faculté des Lettres de l'Université Cheikh Anta Diop*, 18 (1989), 125–40.
48. Dominique Darbon, *L'administration et le paysan en Casamance (Essai d'anthropologie administrative)* (Paris, 1988), p. 222.

CHAPTER 14

From the Jewish national home to the state of Israel: some economic aspects of nation and state building

Jacob Metzer

The nurturing of ethno-nationalism, and the building of nations and states, although being primarily political and socio-cultural processes, are obviously not devoid of economic aspects. While we may question whether, and to what extent, economic factors have affected the creation of nations and states, it seems indisputable that economic means and actions, let alone their outcomes and implications, have constituted a significant element in any ethno-national pursuit and state formation.

Noticeable in this respect are, on the one hand, moves of a consolidating nature, which have typically been supportive of economic growth within the state's borders, such as the institution of common currencies, the establishment of unified monetary and fiscal systems, and the integration of internal markets. On the other hand, ethno-nationally induced restrictions on the access of 'others' to certain markets, as well as constraints imposed on trade and factor mobility, which by their very nature are output-reducing and income-redistributing, have often accompanied the creation of states and their 'growing up' patterns. Such modes of behaviour have usually been externally aimed, but in ethno-nationally heterogeneous states (or states in the making) they have also played a role in frequently emerging internal ethno-national conflicts concerning collective rights, political hegemony and the nature of the states' nation-ness. Likewise, various self-perceived 'modernising' and 'catching-up' goals, affecting the industrial structure of production, have been a common feature of national economic policies in newly established states.

In addition to the basic task of identifying the collective objectives and means of these various expressions of nation building, a number of questions, raised by their versatility, can and should be addressed in specific historical instances. For example, the question of whether individuals and groups can be made to comply 'voluntarily' with the economic 'requirements' of nationalism, or need to be coerced to do so, is of particular importance and interest, given the public good properties of nationalism and their distributive implications. Moreover, taking that some coercion is indeed required for the implementation of the economic agenda of state building – certainly in ethno-nationally divided societies but likely in others as well – a natural question that follows regards what it implies for the public–private mix in the economic lives of the societies concerned.[1]

The Jewish-Israeli story provides an illuminating case for addressing these and related questions, and a rather distinct one in at least four respects. First and foremost, it should be emphasised that the evolvement of the Jewish immigrating settlers' community and polity in Palestine differed substantially from the 'standard' patterns of nation building. While in the latter, territorially based ethno-national communities have typically established their nation-states, or opted for self-determination, in the territories of their actual being, in the former, the very creation of a territorially identified people was a major component of the nation-building process itself.

Relying on world Jewry as a source of people and capital, the Zionist endeavour was expected to produce in Palestine, under the auspices of the British Mandate, a just, self-ruled community, facilitating economic growth and prosperity, while providing its members with advanced public and social services. Building the Jewish national existence on such solid foundations should have attracted, according to the Zionist 'blueprint', a continuous flow of immigrants and capital, thereby securing the viability of the Jewish National Home (and possible future state) in Palestine.

In return, the Diaspora Jews were to benefit from the unifying symbol of national identity and potential safe haven with which an autonomously thriving Jewish community was to provide them. This mutually beneficial 'exchange' was expected to shape and continuously nurture the ties of the Jews to their ethno-national outpost in Palestine, and eventually motivate a good number of them to become, by way of migration, full members of the Jewish territorial nation in the making.

It is in this context that the financial support of world Jewry, on which the Zionist 'nation-building' activity was to be heavily dependent, was conceptualised in wide Zionist circles as a kind of 'national tax'. This voluntarily self-imposed tax should have facilitated, at least partly, the 'production' of the 'public good' of Jewish nationhood in Palestine, which was supposed to be 'consumed' by the Jewish people all around the world. Note that drawing on immigration and partly on Jewish financial aid continues to be a 'work in progress' of nation building in Israel to this date.[2]

A second noticeable feature of Jewish territorial-nation building, which is still very much with us, has been the sharp ethno-national divide between

Arabs and Jews. Naturally, the national aspirations of the, mostly indigenous, Palestinian Arabs were diametrically opposed to those of the immigrating Jewish settlers, and reflected in part their response to the Jewish
build-up and to the (League of Nations-granted) British Mandate facilitating it.

The quantitative dimensions of this build-up were impressive, indeed.
The Jewish population grew from about 75,000 people in early 1922, or
10 per cent of the entire population of Palestine (741,000) at the time,
to 630,000 by the end of 1947, making for 32 per cent of the country's
1,970,000 inhabitants, with immigration accounting for 73 per cent of this
growth. Likewise, the Jewish share in Palestine's total production rose from
17 per cent to 57 per cent, and their land possession from less than 3 per cent
to more than 11 per cent of the entire non-desert land area of Palestine
between these two years.[3]

Thirdly, we should draw attention to the fact that the Zionist executive, although officially recognised by Britain (and the League of Nations)
as the Jewish Agency representing the Jewish people (and community in
Palestine) for matters concerning the National Home, did not enjoy the
coercive power of a government. Hence the means it could use for turning public objectives into private actions were extremely limited. These
constraints had certain implications for the *modus operandi* of the Zionist
national institutions and for the 'division of labour' between them and various specialised and sectoral institutions (prominent among them was the
General Federation of Jewish Labour, the Histadrut) in promoting national
objectives in the economic scene.

A fourth appreciable characteristic of our story, raising interesting questions of continuity and change, is its progression through different phases.
It takes us from the pre-statehood build-up through the creation of Israel
and the aftermath of the 1948 war, to the state's formative years prior to
the war of 1967. The story, however, does not end there; it has continued
to unfold in the post-1967 era, which in some respects may be perceived as
yet another formative phase in Israel's evolvement as a nation-state.

Reference is here primarily to two interconnected issues. One concerns
the nature and spatial dimensions of Palestinian self-determination in the
territories captured by Israel in the 1967 war, and, by implication, the
boundaries of its territorial sovereignty. And the other has to do with
the unsettled position and ambiguous self-identity of the Arab citizens of
Israel as members of an ethno-national minority in the Jewish state. This
issue, defining a good deal of the 'Israeli dilemma' since statehood, has
rendered the question of nation-ness, and the distinction between nation

(building) and state (building) rather problematic in our case.[4] The recent establishment of a Palestinian autonomy in Gaza and the West Bank may have added a new, and possibly complicating, factor to this dilemma.

It is against this background that some of the economic dimensions of the Jewish nation and state building are discussed in the rest of this chapter. The discussion commences on the Mandatory period, moves next to pre-1967 Israel, and concludes with some observations on the post-1967 era.

JEWISH NATION BUILDING IN MANDATORY PALESTINE

The Zionist national economic 'design' consisted of three specific elements: collective acquisition and ownership of land; an industrial structure of employment (and production) dominated by manual labour and material production, primarily in agriculture; and Jewish labour self-sufficiency. These were regarded in mainstream Zionism as essential components of a consistent structural and operational system on which a territorially based Jewish nation was to revive in Palestine and lead eventually to self-determination and statehood.

Palestine's land regime allowed effectively for private property rights on about 85 per cent of the country's non-desert land area. This made purchases from existing landowners (most of them Arabs) the main channel by which Jews (or anybody else) could acquire land and exercise on it any property rights. It is within this context that the idea of public acquisition and perpetual national possession of land became a basic tenet of Zionist ideology and policy.

The Zionist Organisation had created already in 1901 a fund-raising organ – The Jewish National Fund (JNF) – for the purpose of purchasing land in Palestine and making it available to Jewish settlers on a leasehold basis. The leaseholders could, with the consent of the JNF, subcontract or transfer their holdings in certain circumstances, but only to Jews. Since the JNF's charter forbade the selling of land, its acquisitions secured the Zionist collective ownership of a rising portion of Jewish-held land in the country (reaching about 50 per cent by the end of the Mandate). This national landownership, and the safeguard it provided against selling Jewish land to non-Jews, should have approximated, according to Zionist thinking, the realisation of the collective rights of the Jewish people to the land of Israel. As such, nationally owned land was to be both a necessary precondition for the future implementation of Jewish territorial self-determination, and a substitute for its lacking under the British Mandate.[5]

Having said that, it should be emphasised that the basic Zionist norm of not selling land to non-Jews was adhered to by private Jewish landowners as well. This suggests that either a 'taste' for Jewish nationalism, reflecting deep ideological conviction, at the individual level, or group pressure, or scarcity of selling opportunities, or some combination of the three, may have provided a check on the sale of Jewish land across ethno-national lines. Accepting this inference, one may wonder whether the national control of land may not have been a somewhat redundant requirement in this respect.[6]

In other respects, though, the control of land supplied the Zionist authorities with a partial substitution for governmental fiscal and regulatory powers by providing them with some economic and administrative means, albeit of limited capacity, for turning collective wants into individual behaviour. For example, the generous financial terms of the lease contracts offered by the JNF (coupled with further financial support from the Zionist institutions) on the one hand, and their stipulated requirements for in-residence farming and for the exclusion of non-Jewish hired labour on the other hand, should have induced potential settlers to follow the Zionist territorial and ethno-national directives in settling on national land and tilling it.

It was precisely this kind of settlement that the Zionist leadership advocated. Since farming was expected to create strong emotional bonds between settlers and land, agricultural settlement (typically by self-employed communal and co-operative groups in kibbutzim and moshavim) was perceived in Zionist ideology and practice to be the major determinant of the spatial contours of the Jewish territorial nation in the making, and a guarantor of its viability.

Furthermore, agriculture was designated in the Zionist programme to be a prime immigration-absorbing industry. By providing gainful employment to a growing number of incoming Jews within a short time of their arrival, farming was to be instrumental in shifting the service-leaning occupational structure of Diaspora Jews towards material production. Agriculture was thus assigned in the making of the Jewish territorial nation an analogous role to that of manufacturing in newly developed and newly created (postcolonial) states. In both cases the promoted industry was expected to lead the evolving nation to converge on the economic structure of established states.[7]

It is in this context that the concept of an ethno-nationally segregated market for manual labour enters the scene as an instrumental component of the economics of Jewish nationalism. Note that, other things being equal, the presumed comparative advantage of Arab workers in manual labour, and their low supply reservation wage (due to their poor earning domestically) made them an attractive hire for Jewish employers. Their exclusion from the Jewish labour market was therefore expected to serve two national objectives. One was to secure employment opportunities at sufficiently high wages for Jewish workers, thereby providing material incentives to potential immigrants to move to Palestine (and to those who had done so already, to stay on) and be absorbed there in agriculture and other blue-collar pursuits. The second objective was to prevent a colonialist-type Jewish farming sector, employing 'cheap' indigenous labour, from developing and threatening the national character and the legitimacy of Jewish settlement in Palestine as a nation-building endeavour.[8]

The ethno-national segregation of the labour market would have, obviously, benefited the Jewish workers at the expense of the Jewish employers (as well as at the expense of the Arab labourers), and its implementation would therefore call for collective action (of which the, above discussed, JNF lease contracts were an instrumental tool). Furthermore, it is the potential gains to the workers, in addition to its national and social ideology, that made the General Federation of Jewish Labour (Histadrut) – the institutional flagship of the Zionist labour movement – lead the campaign for Jewish labour self-sufficiency. But although this campaign was conducted quite forcefully, resorting to persuasion as well as to more assertive means of demonstration and picketing, its success, beyond the confines of the settlements on national land, was very limited.[9]

Note, however, that the attempts to bar Arab labour from the Jewish economy, futile as they may have been, were just one example of the emerging co-operation and 'division of labour' between the Jewish Agency and the Histadrut in collectively promoting the economic objectives of Zionism. The Histadrut, which was established in 1920, was by itself an all-inclusive labour organisation, with membership reaching 75 per cent of all Jewish wage earners. In addition to its functioning as a well-co-ordinated trade union and provider of employment services, it supplied its members with an elaborate system of health, social and cultural services, and became, as a Workers (holding) Company, an organisational setting for the 'labour economy', which consisted of a wide array of productive establishments. Some of these establishments, mainly in construction, manufacturing, distribution and financial intermediation, were owned by the Workers Company (i.e. by the entire Histadrut membership). Others, such as the large bus-transportation co-operatives and the productive establishments of the communal and co-operative settlements, while being organisationally part of the Workers Company, were not owned by it.

In providing its members and their households (covering more than half of the Jewish population) with an extensive basket of health and other services, the Histadrut became actually responsible for a substantial portion of the collectively supplied social services in Palestine's Jewish community. Moreover, the employment-generating objectives of the labour economy's enterprises (which took precedence over profit maximisation) made them a participatory organ in this socio-economic arena, as well.

Apart from that, the Histadrut enterprises were regularly summoned by the Zionist authorities to undertake 'national projects' – carrying low private returns and often high risks – in constructing infrastructure installations in transportation, public utilities, defence and other areas. It may thus be concluded that the Histadrut was an integral and essential component of the Zionist autonomously functioning public sector in Palestine, a role that grew in importance from the 1930s onward, with Labour-Zionism becoming the leading political force in the Zionist Organisation and in the Jewish Agency.[10]

We may ask at this stage, where did all this lead to in terms of the desired public–private mix in the Jewish economy? The national objectives calling for collective action in activities such as land acquisition, spatial dispersion of settlements, the promotion of agriculture and of Jewish labour self-sufficiency, and development-oriented investments, made a 'strong case' in Zionist thinking for substantial public involvement in economic life. Working in the same direction was the emphasis in the Zionist nation-building 'blueprint' on public (although not free) education, and on modern social services in, and for, the Jewish community, as well as the mistrust in which Labour-Zionism held the allocative and distributive mechanisms and consequences of the (free) market.

However, one should not be inclined to conclude that the private sector, operating in a market environment, was devoid of any designated national role in the prevailing Zionist attitudes. Liberal-Zionism (which led the Zionist Organisation in the 1920s), for example, endorsed private enterprise as a national objective in itself. Underlying this viewpoint was the presumption that the main reservoirs of people and capital for Jewish colonisation were the *petit bourgeois* and middle classes of Diaspora Jewry, who required a free market environment in order to be attracted, and commit their resources, to the Jewish national endeavour in Palestine.

The mainstream of Labour-Zionism with all its distaste for the 'market' did not actually contest this point of view and even adhered to it in practice if not in ideology. The resulting outcome was that of a mixed economy. The Zionist quasi-governmental public sector (financed largely by contributions from Diaspora Jews) and the Histadrut labour economy coexisted, mostly amicably, with a substantial private sector (accounting probably for about 80 per cent of Jewish production) functioning in an essentially free market environment, in which the intervention of the Mandatory government was minimal.

Was the Zionist economic plan successfully implemented in this environment? In some very important respects it certainly was. The collective action of the Zionist Organisation played a pivotal role in acquiring land and in extending the boundaries of the Jewish national polity by encouraging the establishment of agricultural outposts at the frontiers of settlement and continuously supporting them. This pioneering, and at times risky, activity was made the omen of the Zionist national ethos for years to come.

In other respects, however, the Jewish economy did not evolve according to the Zionist design. Besides the failed attempts to maintain labour self-sufficiency already mentioned, it should be recalled that the Zionist vision of an economy based on self-employed agriculture and other industries of material production did not materialise either. The Jewish community remained primarily urban (74 per cent of the Jewish population of Palestine lived in urban localities in the 1930s and 1940s), with about half of its labour force employed in services, which accounted for 55–62 per cent of Jewish output in the inter-war period. These failures, however, must not mask the foremost achievement of the Zionist movement: crystallising and leading an autonomous and extremely fast-growing modern Jewish community under British rule, while laying the necessary institutional and operational foundations for statehood.[11]

THE BUILDING OF A (JEWISH) NATION-STATE: ISRAEL, 1948–1967

The war of 1948, the massive, largely involuntary, exodus of Arabs and the enormous influx of Jewish immigrants left the state of Israel (created on 14 May 1948) by the end of 1952 in control of about 76 per cent of the territory of former Mandatory Palestine, with a population of 1.6 million, of whom 1.4 million (89 per cent) were Jews and only 179,000 (11 per cent), Arabs.[12] These extraordinary developments presented Israel in its infancy with major challenges, over and above those expected in any transition from colonial subordination to sovereignty.

The new state needed, of course, to establish a workable structure of legislative, judiciary and executives branches of government, and create an operative fiscal system and a credible monetary apparatus (the latter became a particularly acute need following the expulsion of Palestine from the sterling block in early 1948). At the same time Israel had to fight an extremely tough war, cope with the problems of feeding, sheltering and providing employment to an unprecedented inflow of immigrants, while striking some balance between the immensity of the needs and the scarcity of the resources.

Meeting these challenges was undoubtedly crucial for the existence and stabilisation of the state. And although the literature is still debating whether some of the economic policies and regulations designed to do exactly that (such as the exchange rate stuck to, the price controls and the administered means of austerity and rationing which led to compressed inflation) were the 'correct' ones to use at the time, or for the duration they remained in effect, it is widely agreed that Israel met its immediate challenges rather success-fully. This achievement should be attributed, not least, to the operational legacy of the British wartime economic policies, to the institutional and operational experience of Jewish self-governance in the Mandate period, and to the measures that the organised Jewish community took between 1945 and 1948 in anticipation of statehood.[13]

Apart from these urgent tasks, early statehood amidst the massive terri-torial and ethno-national changes raises some additional issues concerning the economic dimensions of the Jewish-Israeli nation and state building and their pre-state legacy. To some of these issues I turn now, starting with the national economic agenda set by the government for the newly born state.[14]

The labour movement, which dominated the government of Israel up to 1977, kept the main economic building blocks of Zionist, now turned Israeli, nationalism pretty much in place, with immigration and spatially dispersed agricultural settlement continuing to play centre stage. Likewise, the financial assistance of Diaspora Jewry continued to be intensively sought by Israel and similarly rationalised as done by the Zionist fund-raising bodies in the pre-state days.

Free Jewish immigration was, and continues to be, the *raison d'état* of Israel as a Jewish state. Hence, actively encouraging Jewish immigration and successfully assimilating the newcomers into Israel's economy and society remained a major institutional responsibility, as well as a national strategic means of strengthening and consolidating the new state *vis-à-vis* the heavily populated Arab world.

Analogously, the dispersion of (Jewish) population and frontier settle-ment retained their functions as guarantors of territorial integrity, and were regarded as vital instruments, alongside the security forces, of border control in Israel's early years. Note in addition that the settling of Jews in internal regions populated mainly by Arabs (primarily the lower Galilee) was also considered a national objective calling for state promotion. The 'Judaisation of the Galilee' was aimed at preventing the crystallisation of Arab regional enclaves and ethno-national aspirations concerning their status from developing. As such it justified (in the eyes of the government and mainstream public opinion) even the use of disputable means of land confiscation to bring it about.

Another related task was the agricultural settlement of immigrants on lands mostly abandoned by the Arab refugees (see below). This was supposed to achieve three major objectives: first, enabling speedy economic absorption of immigrants in an easily expandable industry; second, raising the supply of foodstuff badly needed by the extremely fast-growing population; and third, populating as quickly as possible the vacant Arab lands, thereby establishing a new, politically consequential reality in the area.

Only towards the end of the first decade of statehood was this national-economic agenda modified. Following the exhaustion of the opportunities for further expansion of agriculture (given the resource constraints of water and land and the fast productivity advances in the industry), the government made the establishment of new (development) towns, based on labour-intensive manufacturing (primarily textile), its main promotional objective. It was this new urbanism that became the principal mode for population dispersion in the late 1950s and early 1960s, and manufacturing, the industry to focus on in the development drive of the growing Israeli economy.

Targeting manufacturing as a leading industry made the industrial structure aimed at by the government of Israel converge on the structural objectives of economic nationalism typically observed in new, post-colonial states that came into being after the Second World War (see above). Pursuing policies of state-led industrialisation, in which domestic, import-substituting, manufacturing enterprises were established and sheltered from foreign competition by heavy subsidisation, protective tariffs and quantitative trade restrictions, was perceived by the governments of these states – Israel included – as a necessary prescription for modern economic development and growth. Furthermore, vigorous inducement of manufacturing should have enabled the new developing states, according to this school of thought, to catch up fast with the advanced industrial countries, which was regarded by itself as a sign of national economic maturity.[15]

Another cornerstone of Jewish economic nationalism that was carried over from the pre-state era was the principle of national landownership.

Following the massive Arab exodus and the takeover of their abandoned property by the government, nationalisation was now applied to about 93 per cent of Israel's total land area (or to 84 per cent of its non-desert area). These lands, defined by the basic land legislation of 1960 as 'Israel Lands', became a perpetual public domain, not to be sold, donated or otherwise transferred, with the governmental 'Israel Land Administration' managing them since that year.

About four-fifths of the 'Israel Lands' were in the early 1960s state owned. Of these lands, 85 per cent consisted of the inherited Mandatory state domain, and the remainder (around 2 million dunams), mainly of expropriated Arab land (most of it formerly owned by the refugees fleeing the country in 1948, but some was the previous property of Arabs living in Israel). The other one-fifth of the 'Israel Lands' (3.6 million dunams in total) was the property of the Jewish National Fund (JNF). Note that only a quarter of the JNF lands were acquired before statehood, while at least two-thirds of them were also abandoned Arab lands, which were sold to the fund immediately after the war by the Israeli government.

Limiting the use of the country's lands to leasehold only has been regarded by all Israeli governments as an essential supplement to (and not just a pre-state necessary substitute for) the regulatory and fiscal powers of the state for turning collective objectives into individual behaviour in the spatial arena. In the state's early days the 'spatial' tasks of the leasehold contracts had concentrated on securing the stability of new agricultural settlements on frontier and vacant lands, and on guaranteeing the attachment of the immigrants-turned-farmers to the soil, avoiding both consolidation and excess fragmentation of holding.[16]

In the course of time these objectives widened and diversified. From the late 1950s onwards we observe the government offering entrepreneurs in various manufacturing and service industries the use of public lands at extremely generous terms (in combination with other legislative and administrative incentives) in order to encourage and lead dispersed economic activity according to its predetermined spatial priorities.

The policies outlined so far are a clear manifestation of Israel's self-perceived identity as a Jewish state, fully subscribing to the Zionist ideology and economic agenda of nation building. As such, they ran the (realised) danger of being incompatible with the principle of equal rights and treatment, to be applied to all its citizens (Jews and non-Jews alike), to which Israel as a self-declared egalitarian democracy has been formally committed since day one of statehood. Note, however, that the Law of Return, granting automatic citizenship to immigrating Jews (who so wish), does maintain a constitutionally entrenched inequality between Jews and non-Jews, but only as citizens-to-be at the port of entry.

Being aware of the problem, the government utilised various legislative and administrative means to minimise overt discrimination of the Arab minority or its appearance, and to justify such discrimination, when exercised, on security grounds and implications (such as in the case of various benefits that are conditional upon military service to which the Arab citizens were never drafted).[17] Another basic device that enabled Israel to manoeuvre between its Jewish nation-ness and the rights of the Arab citizenry was the functional differentiation of the state's official organs from the national-Zionist institutions.

The latter, whose government-type functions became redundant by statehood, continued to advance Israel's national Jewish causes and interests, and in the early 1950s were granted by law a formal status as non-state institutions operating in that capacity. The World Zionist Organisation (WZO)–Jewish Agency retained its fund-raising role among Diaspora Jewry and its responsibility in the areas of Jewish immigration, absorption and settlement. Likewise, the memorandum of the JNF, approved by the Ministry of Justice under the JNF law of 1953, reinstated the company's goal to possess and acquire land (in the state of Israel or in any area controlled by the government of Israel) for the purpose of settling Jews on it.

The practical implications of the reconfirmed national mission of the JNF was that the abandoned Arab lands, most of which, as indicated above, were sold to the fund by the government, were available, as long-run leasehold, only to Jews, hence effectively preventing Israeli Arabs from expanding their rural landholdings. It is in this respect that the distinction between state lands, to the use of which no overt ethno-national discrimination could be legally applied, and the lands owned by the JNF (and administered by the Israel Land Administration) was of crucial importance. Thus, by enabling Israel to get around some of its nation versus state dilemmas in the Arab–Jewish arena (although only legalistically), the Zionist institutions retained their usefulness as promoters of Jewish nation building also under statehood.

The Histadrut fulfilled a similar role. While otherwise being gradually relieved of its national functions in the economic scene, it maintained, during Israel's first decade, its position as a protector of Jewish labour. Throughout the 1950s the Histadrut admitted only Jewish workers as full members, enrolling Arabs into a separate subsidiary union, and its labour exchanges served, practically, only Jewish employment seekers.

Considerations of security, stemming from the uncertainty regarding the attitudes of the Israeli Arabs to the unsettled conflict with the outside Arab world, and the sensitivity of the matter in the aftermath of the 1948 war, were another factor distinguishing the Arab minority from the Jewish majority. Their immediate manifestation was the military administration imposed on the Arab population in 1948 and lifted only in 1966. However, the restrictions on the Arabs' free movement, which were the gist of the military administration, were used in the 1950s not just for security reasons but also, and probably mainly, in order to prevent them from competing with the newly arrived Jewish immigrants in a unified labour market. Consequently, the first decade of statehood saw a continuation, and even intensification, of the pre-state nationally motivated patterns of economic separation between Jews and Arabs – now being largely enforced by the state.

Towards the end of the decade, though, things started to turn around. The rising labour supply of the fast-growing Arab population, exerting pressure on its limited land resources, met a Jewish demand for manual workers, which, due to the slowdown of immigration and the growth of the economy, was rapidly increasing as well. In 1959 the Employment Service Law was enacted, requiring that all the employment services be handled on a non-discriminatory basis by state labour exchanges. Likewise, Arab workers were admitted to the Histadrut as full members. These developments, which resulted in about half of the Arab employed persons being employed by Jews already in the early 1960s, marked the onset of their incorporation into the vigorously expanding Israeli economy.

But this dynamic did not altogether remove ethno-national distinction from the economic scene. By suffering from uneven allocation of government resources (mainly based on criteria such as military service, and/or on preferential treatment of regions, localities and industries for nationally designated development goals), Arabs were at a disadvantage in so far as capital resources, public services and transfer payments were concerned. Furthermore, effective barriers constraining entry to a good number of employment categories, partly for security reasons, left non-negligible elements of ethno-national segregation in the labour market intact.

We may therefore conclude that the Arab–Jewish economic coexistence was transformed from nationally induced and state-enforced separation in the early days to 'compartmentalised integration' of the differentially treated Arab citizens into the Israeli economy later on. This dynamic has made the

Arab minority a participatory beneficiary of the secularly rising output and living standard in Israel, but has nevertheless left it in an economically inferior position *vis-à-vis* the Jewish majority.

The economic attributes of state and (Jewish) nation building that Israel pursued in its formative years were guided primarily by national objectives. Considerations of efficiency were typically subordinated to these objectives, although policy-makers often (wrongly) took the two to be consistent with one another (as, for example, in the early industrialisation drive when import-substituting industries were sheltered from foreign competition by highly protective trade policies).

The tasks of nation building, involving policy directives and constraints on non-governmental economic actors, besides direct public entrepreneurship, provided the government (backed by the electorate) with strong incentives for, and self-proclaimed justification of, a good part of its extensive intervention in economic life. Note, though, that whereas heavy governmental intervention in the economy fitted well with the 'traditional' Labour mistrust of the market, the Likud conservative government, coming to power in 1977, continued to embrace this basic étatiste approach (at least until the mid-1980s), despite some initial steps towards economic liberalisation.[18]

A major instrument for directing and regulating economic activity, apart from the ownership of land, was the government's virtually complete control of the capital market, facilitated not least by its being the institutional destination for most of the country's capital imports. These inflows, which comprised mainly unilateral transfers made by World (mostly American) Jewry, loans and grants in aid provided by the US government, and German reparations, were the major source of capital facilitating domestic investment. The government used part of these resources for public investments in infrastructure and housing, and another part for initiating and guiding private investments according to its sectoral, locational and industrial preferences.

Economists and economic historians have by and large accepted the notion that the enormous tasks of the early years of statehood necessitated at the time a 'command economy', and that the continuing burden of defence has required a sizeable public sector ever since. On the other hand, it has also been widely agreed that the resource misallocation and the incentives for rent-seeking and political manipulation, created by the massive economic interventionism of the government, made its economic heavy hand, at least since the mid-1970s, long overdue.[19] This observation leads us, naturally, to the post-1967 period, the final leg of our nation- and state-building journey, on which some closing remarks are offered next.

A NEW PHASE OF NATION BUILDING: ISRAEL AFTER 1967

Two processes relevant to our discussion have marked the post-1967 period. One has to do with changes in the domestic economic regime, and the other with Israel's attitudes and policies concerning the areas captured in the 1967 war.

The most pronounced domestic economic development has been the slow retreat of the government, primarily in the past fifteen years, from its excessive economic interventionism. This process, although neither all-inclusive nor complete, has been noted by the liberalisation of foreign trade and exchange, by control-lifting reforms in the capital market, and in general, by gradual substitution of universally applied rules for bureaucratic discretion in the economic and social scene. A case in point demonstrating these changes is the government's conscious decision to rely heavily on the market for the absorption of the massive influx of immigrants from the former Soviet Union in the late 1980s and early 1990s.[20]

These patterns have signalled, on the one hand, a maturing phase that Israel's political economy reached in the late 1980s after passing through the infancy and adolescence stages of nation building in the earlier years. On the other hand, they reflected the effects of world-wide changes in economic attitudes and policies, enhancing openness, unrestricted movement of capital (and to a large extent of labour as well), free trade and privatisation.

As for the occupied territories, their capture in 1967 required the Israeli government to make a number of major policy decisions in the economic arena.[21] Separately administering the West Bank and the Gaza Strip with their 1 million or so Arab inhabitants (in the early 1970s) as occupied territories, the government decided pretty soon after the war to base Israel's economic relations with them on customs free trade of goods and services (including labour services). In doing so Israel made it abundantly clear that it did not contemplate a return to the pre-state and early statehood postulates of economic separation between Arabs and Jews.

None the less, considerations of economic nationalism were not absent from Israel's economic policies towards the occupied territories. For years the Israeli administration imposed various administrative restrictions on their industrialisation in order to prevent competition with its own manufacturing industry. Similarly, in applying to the territories the same protective regulations governing the import of agricultural produce as to its other trade partners, Israel actually prevented the territories from fully exercising their comparative advantages in agricultural production (mainly of vegetables) in their bilateral trade.

However, the major policy issues concerning the territories were not those of trade but the ones that had to do with land and Jewish settlement. In securing possession of all the state lands in the territories, and in attempting to extend their area to the possible legal limits, the Israeli government has utilised the land under its control primarily for encouraging and supporting (at least *ex post facto*) Jewish settlement. Likewise, the JNF, in accordance with its above-mentioned mission (to acquire land for the purpose of Jewish settlement in any area controlled by the government of Israel), resumed with government backing its pre-state activity of purchasing private Arab lands now in the occupied territories (and so did some other Jewish NGOs and private developers), thus widening the options for Jewish settlement there.

In executing these policies of colonising penetration into the occupied territories in an attempt to establish a Jewish-Israeli national existence there, and thereby a claim for future sovereignty, Israel has turned, essentially, full circle back to the 'old' Zionist pre-state means of nation building. However, judging from (post-Oslo) recent history and from nowadays history in the making, these government-led (or agreed to) attempts at substantial territorial expansion, via Jewish settled presence on lands captured in the 1967, war may turn out to be less successful than their pre-state forerunner.

NOTES

I wish to thank Stanley Engerman, Patrick O'Brien and the participants of the Pre-Congress Conference in Vienna for their helpful comments.

1. Interesting discussions of these issues can be found in Harry G. Johnson (ed.), *Economic Nationalism in Old and New States* (Chicago, 1967) and Albert Breton, Gianluigi Galeotti, Pierre Salmon and Ronald Wintrobe (eds.), *Nationalism and Rationality* (Cambridge, 1995).

2. For more elaborate discussions of Zionist economic vision and plans, see Jacob Metzer, 'The Concept of National Capital in Zionist Thought 1918–1921', *Asian and African Studies*, 11 (1977), 305–36; Metzer, 'Economic Structure and National Goals – the Jewish National Home in Interwar Palestine', *Journal of Economic History*, 38 (1978), 101–19; Metzer, *The Divided Economy of Mandatory Palestine* (Cambridge, 1998).

3. Metzer, *The Divided Economy*, pp. 1–27, 85–6.

4. For an insightful overview, see Yoram Ben-Porath, 'Israeli Dilemmas: Economic Relations between Jews and Arabs', *Dissent* (Fall 1984), 459–67.

5. See Metzer, 'Economic Structure'; Metzer, *The Divided Economy*, pp. 85–94.
6. For a (speculative) claim that the yield superiority of land in Jewish use was sufficiently large to make its resale price prohibitively high for Arab potential buyers, see Yakir Plessner, *The Political Economy of Israel* (New York, 1994), pp. 66–70.
7. Metzer, 'Economic Structure'.
8. Metzer, *The Divided Economy*, pp. 123–33, 149, 190–6.
9. See Zvi Sussman, 'The Determinants of Wages for Unskilled Labour in the Advanced Sector of the Dual Economy of Mandatory Palestine', *Economic Development and Cultural Change*, 22 (1973), 95–113; Anita Shapira, *Futile Struggle: Hebrew Labour, 1929–1939* (in Hebrew) (Tel Aviv, 1977).
10. Zvi Sussman, *Wage Differentials and Equality within the Histadrut* (in Hebrew) (Ramat Gan, 1974); Ephraim Kleiman, 'The Histadrut Economy of Israel in Search of Criteria', *The Jerusalem Quarterly*, 11 (1987), 77–94; Metzer, *The Divided Economy*, pp. 3–7, 190–6.
11. See Metzer, *The Divided Economy*, pp. 9, 196–9, 219, 240.
12. *Statistical Abstract of Israel* (Jerusalem, 1999), tables 1.1, 2.1.
13. For recent analyses of economic policies in early day Israel, see Haim Barkai, *The Beginnings of the Israeli Economy* (in Hebrew) (Jerusalem, 1990); Nachum Gross, 'Israeli Economic Policies, 1948–1951: Problems of Evaluation', *Journal of Economic History*, 50 (1990), 67–83; Plessner, *The Political Economy*, pp. 1–176; Ephraim Kleiman, 'The Waning of Israeli *Etatisme*', *Israel Studies*, 2 (1997), 146–71.
14. The following discussion of the economic dimensions of nation building in Israel's formative years draws partly on the analyses of Yoram Ben-Porath, 'Patterns and Peculiarities of Economic Growth and Structure', *The Jerusalem Quarterly*, 10 (1986), 43–63 and Kleiman, 'Israeli *Etatisme*'.
15. Johnson, *Economic Nationalism*, pp. 1–16, 124–42.
16. Avraham Granott, *Agrarian Reform and the Record of Israel* (London, 1956), pp. 85–163; David Kretzmer, *The Legal Status of the Arabs in Israel* (Boulder, Colo., 1990), pp. 49–76; Sandy Kedar, 'Majority Time, Minority Time, Land Nation, and the Law of Adverse Possession in Israel' (in Hebrew), *Law Review*, 21 (1998), 665–746.
17. The following discussion concerning the socio-economic state of the Arab minority as affected by Israel's (Jewish) nation-building policies draws on the following studies: Yoram Ben-Porath, *The Arab Labour Force in Israel* (Jerusalem, 1966); Ben-Porath, 'Israeli Dilemmas'; Kretzmer, *The Legal Status*; Noah Lewin-Epstein and Moshe Semyonov, *Patterns of Ethnic Inequality* (Boulder, Colo., 1993); Zeev Rosenhek, 'The Origin and Development of a Dualistic Welfare State: the Arab Population in the Israeli Welfare State' (Ph.D. thesis, The Hebrew University of Jerusalem, 1995); Kedar, 'Majority Time'.
18. Yoram Ben-Porath, 'The Conservative Turnabout that Never Was – Economic Policy and Ideology Since 1977', *The Jerusalem Quarterly*, 8 (1983), 3–10.
19. See particularly Plessner, *The Political Economy*, and Kleiman, 'Israeli *Etatisme*'.

20. Kleiman, 'Israeli *Etatisme*'.
21. The following remarks draw on Ben-Porath, 'Israeli Dilemmas'; Jacob Metzer, 'What Kind of Growth? A Comparative Look at the Arab Economies in Mandatory Palestine and in the Administered Territories', *Economic Development and Cultural Change*, 40 (1992), 843–65; Ephraim Kleiman, 'Some Basic Problems of the Economic Relationships between Israel and the West Bank and Gaza' in Stanley Fischer, Dani Rodrik and Elias Tuma (eds.), *The Economy of Middle East Peace: Views from the Region* (Cambridge, Mass., 1993), pp. 305–33.

PART IV

CHAPTER 15

Economic change and the formation of states and nations in South Asia, 1919–1947: India and Pakistan

B.R. Tomlinson

This chapter deals with events that took place in British India during the first half of the twentieth century, and resulted in the transfer of power in August 1947 to independent governments in India and Pakistan. Both these new regimes claimed legitimacy as nation-states, with clear ideologies based on a spiritualised secularism in India and a distinctive Islamic identity in Pakistan. These events have spawned a large literature of exposition, explanation and recrimination. The sheer size and complexity of this literature may be daunting to non-specialists, but it provides an excellent foundation for an investigation of the relationship between economic change and the formation of nation-states in the modern world.[1]

The historical process that led to the creation of India and Pakistan had a number of distinctive features caused by the nature and purposes of British colonial control. In the first place, the new states replaced an existing imperial administration which had recruited heavily from the local population. Thus, while new nations were formed in 1947, they inherited much of their state structures from the past. Most members of the bureaucracy, judiciary, police and army in the new states had held similar positions under the colonial regime. In an important sense, what happened in 1947 was that an existing colonial state structure was given a post-colonial legitimacy by the transfer of power to the elected representatives of new nations. The question of whether the 'nation' (as expressed through the political process) has controlled the state (represented by a continuing tradition of bureaucratic authoritarianism) since independence, or vice versa, remains a disputed issue for historians and political scientists.[2] Secondly, the nation-states that were created out of the wreckage of the Raj had drawn on 'primordial' and 'constructed' identities of nationalism to contest colonial control.[3] The new national leaders of India, represented in the Indian National Congress, claimed to represent a broad church of primordial groups that had been constructed into a nation by the mechanisms and rhetoric of the freedom movement. The Muslim League, which campaigned intensively for a separate state in the 1940s and inherited power in Pakistan in 1947, promoted an Islamic nationalism based on the 'two-nation' theory of Indian society and culture which was, in part at least, a political construct used instrumentally by the leadership of the separatist movement for their own ends.[4]

An older tradition of historical explanation based on an imperial perspective still views the process of decolonisation in South Asia as a relatively smooth transition from a paternalist-imperial regime to its liberal-nationalist heirs.[5] However, many analyses of decolonisation and its consequences have stressed the disruptive effects of the death-throes of the Raj, and the shortcomings of the successor regimes that sought to impose their own hegemony on the states that they inherited in the name of national identity through deliberate programmes of 'nation building'. The history of the subcontinent since 1947 has certainly revealed imperfections in the intellectual and emotional foundations of both states, and many accounts of it are dominated by critiques of their claim to speak for nations, and their ability to operate as just and effective states. The Indian National Congress, by far the largest political movement in the subcontinent, which dominated the politics of independent India for over twenty years after independence, claimed legitimacy from shared values and cultural identity – but this apparent inclusiveness concealed widespread problems of exclusion or alienation from the political, cultural, moral and economic community of colonial nationalism. The Muslim League's rhetoric of exclusive Islamic identity was foreign to the social and material lives of many Indian Muslims, and did not provide a firm foundation of national unity in the difficult years following partition.

Partition itself imposed external boundaries on the new states that caused significant internal divisions within them, and was accompanied by a process of dislocation that cost many lives and much human tragedy. The complex political processes of 1946–7 resulted in Pakistan being created with two entirely separate geographical areas – in the north-west and north-east of the old Indian empire. The two major administrative units of these regions – Punjab and Bengal – were internally divided in the summer of 1947, leading to riots that cost over 200,000 lives. By 1951, the Muslim population of British India was divided roughly in three – one-third in India, one-third in West Pakistan and one-third in East Pakistan – with over 14 million of the population of both countries classed as 'displaced persons'.[6] Thereafter strong regional and sectional identities remained imperfectly integrated into the new regimes, especially in Kashmir and East Pakistan (which split away to become Bangladesh in 1971) with disruptive effects that are still felt today. While the Congress was able to capture state power effectively in India, and to maintain its role as the dominant political institution that mediated between the state and the nation for the next twenty years, the foundations of the League's position were less secure, resulting in political instability that culminated in the imposition of military rule and martial law in 1958. The endemic tensions between the western and eastern wings of the country – separated by a thousand miles of Indian territory – played a large part in this. Despite the avowed secularism of the Indian government, and the strand of liberal Muslim opinion represented by the first-generation League political leadership in Pakistan, the primordialist legacy of the 1940s has remained not far beneath the surface, breaking through in campaigns of Islamisation, *Hindutva*, and other constructions of cultural identity around exclusivist doctrinal and ritual symbols.[7]

The social and economic record of the independent states of South Asia that were created in 1947 has also been widely attacked as inadequate, especially in their failure to create stable and inclusive civil societies, and their inability to achieve economic development. The process of agricultural and industrial development has been relatively slow compared with other Asian economies, which has done little to solve the serious welfare problems – measured by income levels, life expectancy, literacy, infant mortality and access to basic needs – that were an important legacy of the years of British rule. As a result, large groups of the population have often been excluded from the (highly imperfect) growth dynamics over the past fifty years – notably marginal agriculturists, tribal communities, small-scale industrial and handicraft workers, and many in the informal service sector.[8]

In the 1970s and 1980s a number of accounts of the political economy of South Asia identified particular elite groups in society with substantial material interests that profited from current policy, and whose dominant position in the state was linked to their control of agriculture and industry in the late colonial period. Such groups were identified from a neo-Marxist perspective as the emerging 'national bourgeoisie' of dominant peasants, industrialists and public sector employees who spear-headed the national movement before independence, and who have determined the nature of development policy since then. For analysts working within a neo-classical framework, the same groups have been labelled 'rent-seekers' who have secured rewards for the ownership of scarce factors of production and privileges (land, capital, industrial licences and education), rather than from their productive employment. Both approaches also point to internal contradictions of economic interest within these 'hegemonic' classes which have caused political instability while preventing thorough-going revolutionary change or structural adjustment.[9]

The problems of human and material development in contemporary South Asia can be linked back to internal flaws in the process of national mobilisation that appeared during the first half of the twentieth century. Much of the classic debate on the process of decolonisation and state formation in colonial India has been concerned to reconstruct the *realpolitik* of late colonialism, identifying the economic costs and benefits of imperial rule to Britain, and showing the links between the nationalist movements and powerful political and socio-economic interests (such as educated elites, dominant groups of land-controllers, and urban merchant networks) that were based on the control of informal mechanisms of power and influence, often at a provincial or local level. These approaches have also stressed the circumstances that constrained the actions of national leaders, and limited their ability to impose their ideologies or to control events, unless these were in the interest of powerful sub-national groups. While many such interpretations concentrate on the ability of privileged groups to control the formal process of constitution-making for their own political ends, others have broadened out the analysis to demonstrate a wider class basis of Indian nationalism, identifying the emergence of the post-independence 'national bourgeoisie' as a dominant force in the socio-economic structures of colonial India in the decades before decolonisation.[10]

It is fair to say that these interpretations of the political economy of nationalism and the post-colonial state have provided a more plausible explanation of events in India than in Pakistan. While the political and economic problems of Pakistan have often been presented in terms of the dominance of a relatively small elite of rural and urban magnates with close links to state power, there is, as yet, no satisfactory socio-economic explanation of the 'two-nation' theory that fully accounts for the separation of Muslim from Hindu identity in twentieth-century South Asia. This weakness is significant because such doubts about the links between political mobilisation and cultural identity based on socio-economic determinism have now spread from studies of the Muslim separatist movement to many other aspects of elite and mass politics in the late colonial age.

The current literature on twentieth-century South Asia has moved a long way beyond a simple analysis of the anti-colonial freedom movement as the construction of elites, and the focus of research has shifted from the political economy of nationalism to its socio-cultural foundations. Here the stress has been on the politics of identity, rather than the politics of interest. Much historical work in this field has tried to write the history of modern India 'from the bottom up', and has stressed the importance of the internal history of the many 'subaltern' (subordinate) groups who took part in the struggle against colonialism, but whose wants and needs were not integrated into nationalist ideology. Such studies have continued the deconstruction of nationalist rhetoric, demonstrating how partial and particular were the symbols that the formal political process employed in its representations of the nation. Stressing the diffuseness and fragmentation of society and culture in the subcontinent has provided a useful further corrective to the grand narrative of imperialism and nationalism. However, the very diffuseness of such studies and their willingness to give equal privilege to every cultural experience have made it difficult to use them to explain the dramatic events of decolonisation, partition and state formation that shaped the lives of so many people in South Asia – dominant groups and subalterns alike – in the middle decades of the twentieth century.[11] The theoretical underpinnings of this research, and its conclusions about the political process, also downplay the impact of structural socio-economic change in the history of state formation and nation making, and ignore the economic context in which these events took place.

In considering the history of both state and nation in South Asia, there is a danger of becoming imprisoned by hindsight. If we focus our attention solely on the events of 1947, it is easy to explain the increasing mistrust between communities, and the final crisis of the riots, massacres and mass movements of population, in terms of primordial identities of religion that determined the construction of both nations and states. But such simple explanations distort a much more complex and fragmented reality. The problem, rather, is to explain why so many identities at this time became constructed in primordial terms, using categories of religious observance to distinguish between 'us' and 'them'. Had the complex and multi-stranded process of political and social mobilisation and evolving cultural identity not been truncated by the crisis of public order that led to the sudden establishment of rival nation-states in 1947, then the subsequent history of the region might have been very different. The short-term causes and consequences of decolonisation, and the problems of establishing and maintaining viable and relatively stable state structures, marked a significant break in the chain of historical causation, giving new opportunities to particular individuals, groups and interests to establish their position against internal and external rivals. But we need to ask why the chain was broken at this point – did the links snap simply because they were subjected to insupportable strain, or had they already been corroded to a point of critical weakness?

If political and social ideology and action is understood in terms of 'imagined' or 'invented' communities, with shifting identities that determine variable and conflicting patterns of mobilisation, we need to explore the boundaries to that imagination and invention, and to uncover the material factors that may have influenced their parameters. Here it can be argued that economic change played a significant role in undermining existing socio-cultural structures, and in creating fresh political imperatives, and this needs to be reintegrated back into any general explanation. By doing so we can deepen accounts of social and political history that stress the varied nature of the ideological and cultural responses to colonial rule, and the very imperfect nature of colonial nationalism as a foundation for broadly based structures of political legitimacy and social integration. Once the complex links between the economic history of the Indian subcontinent and the transition from colonial to post-colonial states are fully investigated, we can also replace the out-dated attempt to identify a functional relationship between economic and political power based on interest groups or dominant classes with more sophisticated explanations.

The remainder of this chapter will set out, briefly, the main events that led to decolonisation and partition, and then relate these to the uncertainty and fragmentation of material life.[12] Imperial rule in India was always profoundly divisive in its refusal to accept any concept of Indian identity or of the legitimacy of nationalism, and in its consistent attempts to create alternative political structures based on the rights of minority communities and the rulers of the Princely States. As the threat to imperial control of India's resources increased during the first half of the twentieth century, so British efforts to maintain their rule by dividing their subjects intensified. After the First World War India's imperial masters imposed a new structure of governance (the 1919 Government of India Act) that was designed to win political support while maintaining the integrity of the colonial state and its ability to meet its 'imperial commitment' – to manage Indian affairs in such a way as to ensure a market for British goods in India, the availability of the Indian army as an imperial strike-force, and the payment of the 'Home Charges' (debt payments and other charges that fell due in London and were met from Indian revenues). This was achieved by extending the use of the two crucial tactics for political manipulation that the British had introduced into India in the late nineteenth century – the creation of elected self-government institutions with limited financial and executive powers, and the identification of heterogeneous and immiscible social and cultural groups within the electorate – based on caste, religion and race – that required special and distinct representation. The British regarded the

Muslims as the most important of these groups, and the policy of separate electorates had been initiated in 1907 to meet the fears of some members of the Muslim elite of northern India (expressed through the Muslim League, founded to make the case for special franchise arrangements in 1906) that their privileged status in education and employment would be compromised by the coming of electoral politics.

The 1919 Act created representative provincial legislatures and administrations in which Indian ministers would have responsibility for matters of local concern – such as education, industrial policy and local self-government. Other more important matters, such as land revenue, and law and order at the provincial level, were still under the control of the bureaucracy; there was also an elected Central Legislative Assembly, which could discuss government policy but had no executive powers. These reforms established a 'free market polity' in which Indians would select their own representatives by direct election (from a very restricted franchise), but with significant limitations. The 1919 Act continued the British policy of denying the existence of a unified Indian political nation by maintaining 'separate electorates' for the new assemblies with reserved seats for minorities and special interests.

Formal political opposition to British rule in India was most effectively and self-consciously organised by the Indian National Congress, which had been founded in 1885 to challenge the right of the colonial bureaucracy to manage the affairs of India without restraint. By the early 1920s the Congress had built itself up into a pluralist political movement, under the leadership of Mahatma Gandhi, that provided an alternative structure of institutions, and a rival political ideology and source of moral legitimacy, to those of the colonial state. During the great mass campaigns of the post-war years (the Rowlatt *satyagraha*, the *Khilafat* movement and the Non Co-operation campaign) Gandhi managed to draw on a wide range of support – spanning most regions, many classes and all communities – for an alternative political vision of India unified by symbolic acts of protest that demonstrated rejection of the moral authority of British rule triggered by the Jallianwallah Bagh massacre. Inevitably, it was far easier to orchestrate such expressions of moral alienation than to compose them into a coherent and universally acceptable programme of action, and Non Co-operation was suspended in 1922 once Gandhi's personal control of the campaign seemed threatened.

By the early 1930s the wheel of Indian political reform had turned once more. The British government now committed itself to extending the process of devolution by creating fully responsible elected provincial governments, and eventually conceding some powers at the centre to Indian ministers responsible to an elected legislature. These events gave Congress the chance to reassert its role as the vehicle for alternative constitutional reform by organising inter-communal opposition to separate electorates, a demand for *purna swaraj* (complete independence) in December 1929, and a fully blown agitational campaign of civil disobedience to secure it – beginning with Gandhi's Salt March in April 1930. These events resolved themselves into the passing of a new Government of India Act in 1935 which set up responsible, representative provincial governments, and proposed a federal structure for central government in which guaranteed representation for the Indian princes and other 'minority interests' would provide a check to nationalist power, with mechanisms to ensure that essential matters of imperial interest (in defence, foreign policy and monetary policy) remained under official influence or control. As part of the process of constitution-making, the British government identified in 1932 a long list of special interests that required statutory protection in electoral politics – Muslims, Sikhs, Indian Christians, Anglo-Indians, Europeans, women, representatives of commercial, landholding, labour and university interests, and 'backward areas'. Of the total of 1,575 seats in the new provincial assemblies, 48.7 per cent were to be contested from special electorates, and a further 9.6 per cent reserved within the general constituencies for Depressed Caste candidates. The largest protected group was the Muslims, with 482 seats overall (30.6 per cent of the total, significantly higher than the Muslim percentage of the total population).

The Congress response to the political opportunities provided by the 1935 Act (against Gandhi's advice and wishes) was to contest the elections for the new provincial governments that were held in 1936 under new franchise qualifications that allowed 13 per cent of the adult population to vote. This campaign was spectacularly successful, with the Congress winning 45 per cent of the seats available, making it by far the largest single party represented in the new legislatures. In selecting candidates for the elections and planning the campaign, Congress organisers were able to combine the appeal of their previous sacrifices in the name of nationalism, and the backing of an active and enthusiastic canvassing organisation, with a careful and sophisticated selection of candidates who brought with them substantial personal support, or symbolic strength as representatives of powerful local interest or identity groups (of caste, language, etc.). Only in Bengal, the Punjab and Sindh did Congress fail to win at least a third of the seats in the new legislatures. In 1937 Congressmen formed governments in six of the eleven provinces of British India – Madras, Bihar, Orissa, the Central

Provinces and the United Provinces (where they held a simple majority of seats) and Bombay (where they held 49 per cent of the total). Over the next two years the Congress became increasingly powerful in all arenas of Indian politics; by 1938–9 it had a membership of over 4.5 million, making it by far the largest voluntary political organisation in the world. The Congress now operated as both a national movement and a political machine, a forerunner of the 'party system' of the post-independence decades.[13] As a result, both support for and opposition to the Congress ministries were often expressed within the party's institutions. Congress ideology remained inclusive, incorporating both right-wing and left-wing activists in a rather uneasy unity, although some of the symbols used in the process had greater emotional resonance for Hindus than for other communities.

The 1936 election results and the formation of Congress ministries in 1937 dismayed the colonial authorities, who had not expected the nationalists to be able to capture power so easily. British plans to neutralise Congress influence in a future central administration were also frustrated by the refusal of the princes to agree terms to join a federal government and give up the privileges of their individual treaty arrangements with the British crown. In September 1939 the viceroy, Lord Linlithgow, declared the Indian empire to be at war with Germany without consulting Indian opinion. This provided the Congress 'High Command' (the group of all-India Congress leaders led by Jawaharlal Nehru and Vallabhbhai Patel who borrowed Gandhi's moral authority to try to impose central direction on the freedom movement) with the excuse to force the Congress ministries to resign. Normal political activity remained effectively suspended until the end of hostilities, and the Congress-governed provinces were placed under direct rule by the bureaucracy. The Congress attempted to retain its moral leadership by launching very limited campaigns of individual *satyagraha* in 1940 and 1941, finally launching the much more threatening 'Quit India' movement in 1942, following the Japanese invasion of South-East Asia and the failure of the British government to satisfy their demands for post-war independence in the negotiations surrounding Stafford Cripps' mission to India in April 1942. The 'Quit India' movement that began in August 1942 was by far the largest direct challenge to British control of India since the 'Indian Mutiny' of 1857; it was suppressed ruthlessly by mass arrests and military action – for the last three years of the war almost all of the top leadership of the Congress was in jail.

By refusing to compromise with British rule during the war, the Congress leaders opened the way for others to establish their credentials as representatives of the various political nations that the British still expected to find in India. The most obvious beneficiary was the Muslim League, led by Mohammed Ali Jinnah, which succeeded in establishing itself as the spokesperson for an alternative national identity based on Islam. The self-appointed leaders of the Muslim 'political nation' after 1930 had found many advantages in the new constitutional arrangements that seemed to guarantee them some influence at the provincial level, but this did not necessarily strengthen the position of the League. In the 1936 elections, a number of small regional parties contested the polls in the Muslim minor-ity provinces to bolster their position for special treatment by government agencies, and the attempt by the All-India Muslim League to co-ordinate a unified nationwide political response to the new constitutional arrange-ments was largely unsuccessful; the League won just over a fifth of the Muslim seats available in the 1936 elections. In Punjab and Bengal the parties that formed ministries in 1937 – the Unionist Party in Punjab and the Krishak Praja Party, in coalition with the Muslim League, in Bengal – represented some Muslim interests, but also relied on support from other communities.

With the unexpected and sweeping Congress victory in 1936, the sit-uation for Muslim political leaders changed dramatically. Now their best chance of influencing events was to appeal to the British-held centre, rather than to the Congress-dominated provincial arena. Although the Congress maintained its credentials to represent all Indians during the ministry pe-riod, local difficulties and complex rivalries often prevented established Muslim politicians from outside the Congress moving within its ranks. Jinnah and his allies had succeeded in establishing themselves as an impor-tant voice for the political establishment of the Muslim minority provinces by 1939. With the outbreak of war, and the possibility of further constitu-tional advance at the centre after the end of hostilities, the League seized the chance to identify itself as the spokesperson for the entire community. The famous 'Pakistan Resolution', adopted by the Muslim League as its political creed in February 1940, broke new ground in two important re-spects. First, the League now asserted the unity of India's Muslims on the basis of a shared cultural identity of Islam; second, the League asserted that this Islamic identity meant that there was no possibility for compromise with non-Muslim nationalist organisations – Muslim interests could only be protected in a separate, Islamic state. In the 1946 elections, held under the same franchise as before, the League won 439 of the 494 seats reserved for Muslims, including almost all of those in Punjab and Bengal.

The last months of British rule in India were a time of desperate games played for high stakes at a time of great instability. There is no space here to set out the complex series of events that began with the reopening of negotiations with Indian leaders in August 1945, and culminated in the partitioning of the subcontinent into two independent successor states in August 1947. Detailed investigations of the uncertainties and dislocations of 'high politics' during the end-game of the Raj have revealed that much of the posturing of politicians and officials may have been tactical – with the British seeking a way to retreat in good order, the League trying to maximise their representation within a federal structure in a united India, and the Congress weighing the advantages of uncontested power within a partitioned successor state against the disadvantages of power-sharing in a larger unit.[14] However, while the godfathers of decolonisation may have been in charge of events, they were not always in control. Many studies of political mobilisation from below have suggested that social, cultural and political identities in large parts of northern, north-western and north-eastern India in the 1940s were expressed through language, signs and symbols that denied the possibility of reconciliation between communities. From the 'Great Calcutta Killing' of August 1946 to the riots and massacres of the Punjab in the summer of 1947, actions on the ground made it increasingly difficult, and finally impossible, to prevent the succubus of communal identity from giving birth to the monster of partition.

These political events and actions, both at the top and on the ground, were played out in the last three decades of British rule against a background of increasing economic difficulty. Both the great Congress agitational campaigns of the inter-war period – Non Co-operation in 1920–2 and Civil Disobedience in 1930–1 and 1932–3 – took place at times of severe external economic shocks which had serious effects on the Indian economy, especially on agriculture. The inflationary conditions of 1919–20 raised prices much faster than wages, especially for deficit food-producers in the rural economy who had to sell their labour to supplement their agricultural activities. The severe deflation of prices for primary products from 1929 onwards had even more serious effects; the Indian rural economy was suffering from a liquidity crisis by 1928, which damaged internal mechanisms for the supply of rural credit and the sale of agricultural produce for the home and export markets. As rural discontent increased, it found expression in no-rent and no-tax campaigns, and in attacks on indigenous bankers, rural money-lenders, landlords and their agents. Even so, participation by Muslims in the disturbances of Civil Disobedience was much less than it had been during Non Co-operation; partly this was because the latter campaign lacked the explicitly Islamic symbolism of the *Khilafat*, and partly because much of the rural agitation was organised by *kisan*

sabhas (peasant leagues) that used Hindu revivalism as one of their emotional foundations. By contrast, the most violent rural protests of the early
1930s occurred in eastern Bengal where Muslim tenants and small farmers
rebelled against the predominantly Hindu landlords and money-lenders
whose domination had become oppressive with the collapse of agricultural
profits.

   The Second World War brought further major disruptions to established
patterns of market and customary relations in the domestic economy. India's
role as a major supply-base for the Allied war effort after 1941 had serious
implications for production and consumption, and for the social relationships based on markets for goods and services. Defence expenditure during
the war exceeded Rs. 34.7 billion (£2.6 billion), as against a normal peacetime expenditure of less than Rs. 400 million (£30 million). About half
of this sum was billed to the British government, following the Defence
Expenditure Agreement of 1940, and was credited to the Indian sterling
balances in the form of treasury bills held in London, but all the supplies
consumed had to be paid for in India from taxation, loans and expansion
of the money supply. The result was inflationary: wholesale prices tripled
between 1939 and 1947 (despite rationing and 'fair-price' schemes introduced in 1944); total money supply increased by more than 700 per cent
between August 1939 and September 1945. Increased demand for war materials boosted some Indian industries, so far as supply problems would
allow, and built up the profits and capital reserves of a number of leading
Indian business groups. Inflationary finance skewed demand for labour,
food and raw materials, and caused major disruptions and shortages within
the civilian economy. Problems of securing adequate supplies of food in
an unstable market helped to fuel the peasant protests that accompanied
the 'Quit India' campaign. By December 1943 the price of rice stood at 9.5
times its 1939 level. Following the tragedy of the Bengal famine in 1943,
which caused the premature death of more than three million people, an
extensive rationing and requisitioning system was introduced, mainly to
feed the ever-growing population of the cities and industrial centres. This
was often ineffectual – the state found it very hard to command the stored
surplus of peasant producers – but it extended the role of government
considerably, and led to corrosive tensions between officials and producers
throughout the rural economy.

   The unprecedented civil disturbances that precipitated and accompanied
partition expressed in the language of conflicting communal identity also
had their roots in the socio-economic uncertainties of the late colonial
age. The devolution of the apparatus of the colonial state at local and

provincial level to Indian control during the 1930s and 1940s led some elite groups to identify communal threats to their position. In the United Provinces many members of the established Muslim elite of service gentry, who had built a mutually supportive alliance with the provincial colonial administration to ensure access to influence, employment and education, calculated that such protection could better be ensured in the future by supporting the demand for Pakistan. In Bengal the Hindu *bhadralok* elite similarly found communalist politics (expressed by the Hindu Mahasabha) a useful way of defending their access to public education and employment against demands from formerly excluded – largely Muslim – competitors. In Punjab and Bengal the effect of government intervention during the war to control the production and distribution of the agricultural surplus convinced many peasant proprietors and tenants that their interests could best be defended against landlords and the state by a political ideology that stressed shared values within the village community, rather than by socially inclusive parties which relied on landlords and urban interests for support.[15] These examples are crucial, because the three regions of UP, Punjab and Bengal provided the cockpit of sectarianism that determined the events of partition.

Finally, the imperatives of creating post-colonial states in South Asia during the confused and difficult period of national and international re-construction after 1945 required considerable state economic intervention to establish distribution mechanisms, control foreign exchange and re-pair regional networks torn apart by partition. The international context of uncertainty over currency and trade regimes, the rise of ideologies of import-substituting industrialisation, and the impact of the cold war in shaping new relations between potential patrons and possible clients for development and defence also all had an effect. Against this background, the formation of nation-states in South Asia was followed by the creation of inward-looking national economies, accompanied by considerable cen-tralisation and the imposition of bureaucratic planning. The creation of economic control regimes was as much the result of the difficult circum-stances of reconstruction as of ideological predisposition, but the result was to bind states, nations and markets together more firmly than was necessary or desirable.[16]

In colonial South Asia 'community' (in secular as well as religious terms) was partly determined by material issues, as well as by the power of other symbols – of religion, nationality, regional identity, caste and so on. Eco-nomic networks and connections permitted or encouraged certain identities (for tenants, industrial labourers, landowners and trading groups, for example) but prevented others. Vertical and horizontal connections developed through market structures were important here, but the imperfect nature of such markets – for land, labour, capital and knowledge – and their asymmetrical nature caused by imperfect access to social and political power limited their effectiveness. The middle decades of the twentieth century saw considerable market failure, with significant disruptions to international and inter-regional networks of production and exchange. In agriculture, especially, difficult economic circumstances resulting from the Great Depression and the wartime supply crisis provided an opportunity for those holding social and political power to increase the inter-linking of markets for rural labour and credit on which the material life of much of the population depended. By contrast, developments in the industrial and urban economies strengthened certain community linkages (in the emergence of a new business elite in India, for example), while increasing competition and uncertainty for some sections of the urban professional and working classes. In general, slowly emerging patterns of market integration that had provided the basis for networks of material identity in the late nineteenth and early twentieth centuries were subjected to new strains and disruptions, and lacked the resources to provide rewards that could sustain alternative communities of interest and imagination. Such changes destabilised existing socio-economic networks of production and exchange, and also gave a boost to some groups of 'surplus' peasants and businessmen who supplied the domestic market for food and consumer goods, and who were now able to dominate internal supply networks more directly. These powerful interests, by and large, supported nationalism, but they were not alone in this. The collapse of the colonial regime in the 1940s produced further dislocations and market failures, with many of the institutional mechanisms of production and distribution dependent on increased state intervention – an intervention that was also clearly signalled during the war as the best hope for economic development after 1945. Finally, the market failures of the period of reconstruction required state intervention and the replacement of missing markets by public institutions that were controlled by state agencies. Thus the last stage of the political conflict between the British Raj and its would-be successors, and between the Congress, the League and other political and social movements that sought to be represented in the new regimes, was a battle for control of the economic functions of the state. Definitions of the nation were shaped and moulded as part of this process.

The long-term underdevelopment of the Indian economy under colonial rule undermined the foundations of any material culture around which new social or ideological connections could be built. The 1920s, 1930s and 1940s were a period of great economic uncertainty and disruption, which lacked any strong forces of economic growth to mitigate conflicts over the scarce resources of land, food, capital and employment. Even on optimistic assumptions, *per capita* food supply in India declined during the last three decades of British rule, while *per capita* income and domestic product stagnated. The isolated pockets of growth that existed around export-orientated agriculture in the 1920s, and domestic industry for the protected home market in the 1930s, were relatively small, and were disrupted by the depression of 1929–33 and the problems of the wartime economy after 1939. More widespread economic growth began in the 1950s and 1960s, but from a very low base and with continued difficulties of distribution. These events largely determined the aims and agenda of the British rulers of India, and the timing of their decisions about constitutional change and imperial retreat. They also underpinned the strength of post-colonial state structures that employed the rhetoric of nationalism which had gained currency during the 1940s, while constraining the activities of political and social movements to empower subordinate groups. Seen in this way, the history of South Asia can provide useful comparisons with that of Europe, Asia, Africa and Latin America in the nineteenth and twentieth centuries, by allowing us to identify the relationship between the context of material life and the networks of political, cultural and social identity that have shaped the history of nations and states in the modern world.

NOTES

1. Excellent introductions to this literature are provided by four recent bibliographic essays: Robin J. Moore, 'India in the 1940s', pp. 231–42, and Ian Talbot, 'Pakistan's Emergence', pp. 253–63, in Robin W. Winks (ed.), *The Oxford History of the British Empire, Volume V: Historiography* (Oxford, 1999); Sugata Bose and Ayeesha Jalal, *Modern South Asia: History, Culture, Political Economy* (London, 1998), pp. 250–81; and Mushirul Hasan (ed.), *India's Partition: Process, Strategy, Mobilization* (Delhi, 1993), pp. 427–34.
2. See, for example, Ayeesha Jalal, *Democracy and Authoritarianism in South Asia: a Comparative and Historical Perspective* (Cambridge, 1995).
3. On these terms, see Alexander J. Motyl, *Revolutions, Nations, Empires: Conceptual Limits and Theoretical Possibilities* (New York, 1999), chs. 4–6.
4. On the issue of instrumentalism in Muslim politics, see Paul Brass, 'Elite Groups, Symbol Manipulation and Ethnic Identity among the Muslims of South Asia', pp. 35–77, and Francis Robinson, 'Islam and Muslim Separatism', pp. 78–112, in David Taylor and Malcolm Yapp (eds.), *Political Identity in South Asia* (London, 1979).

5. For an account along these lines, see Judith M. Brown, *Modern India: the Origins of an Asian Democracy* (Oxford, 1984). For an alternative perspective that stresses the contested and constructed nature of nationalism, see Bose and Jalal, *Modern South Asia*.

6. Joseph E. Schwartzberg (ed.), *A Historical Atlas of South Asia* (Chicago, 1978), pp. 92, 231.

7. On Hindu nationalist politics in India, see Christophe Jaffrelot, *The Hindu Nationalist Movement in India* (New York, 1996).

8. For a summary of the wide-ranging literature on the Indian economy since 1947, see B.R. Tomlinson, *The Economy of Modern India, 1860–1970*, New Cambridge History of India III:3 (Cambridge, 1993), pp. 156–218, 229–31.

9. For convenient statements of these views, see Pranab Bardhan, *The Political Economy of Development in South Asia* (Oxford, 1984) and Deepak Lal, 'Ideology and Industrialization in India and East Asia' in Helen Hughes (ed.), *Achieving Industrialization in East Asia* (Cambridge, 1988), pp. 195–240. On state and class relations in Pakistan, see Hamza Alavi, 'The State in Post-Colonial Societies: Pakistan and Bangladesh' in K.P. Gough and H.P. Sharma (eds.), *Imperialism and Revolution in South Asia* (New York, 1973).

10. See John Gallagher, Gordon Johnson and Anil Seal (eds.), *Locality, Province and Nation: Essays on Indian Politics, 1870–1940* (Cambridge, 1975) and D.A. Low (ed.), *Congress and the Raj: Facets of the Indian Struggle, 1917–47* (London, 1977).

11. Typical work includes Gyanendra Pandey, 'The Prose of Otherness' in David Arnold and David Hardiman (eds.), *Subaltern Studies VIII: Essays in Honour of Ranajit Guha* (Delhi, 1994), pp. 188–221, and Partha Chatterjee, *The Nation and Its Fragments: Colonial and Postcolonial Histories* (Princeton, 1993). For an exposition and critique, see 'AHR Forum on Subaltern Studies', *American Historical Review*, 99 (1994), 1475–545, and D.A. Washbrook, 'Orients and Occidents: Colonial Discourse Theory and the Historiography of the British Empire' in Winks (ed.), *Oxford History of the British Empire, Volume V*.

12. The line of interpretation follows that in B.R. Tomlinson, *The Indian National Congress and the Raj, 1929–1942* (London, 1976) and *The Political Economy of the Raj, 1914–1947: the Economics of Decolonization in India* (London, 1979).

13. Myron Weiner, *Party Building in a New Nation: the Indian National Congress* (Chicago, 1967); Stanley A. Kochaneck, *The Congress Party in India: the Dynamics of One-Party Democracy* (Princeton, 1968).

14. Asim Roy, 'The High Politics of India's Partition: a Revisionist Perspective', *Modern Asian Studies*, 24 (1990), 385–415, reprinted in Hasan (ed.), *India's Partition*.

15. See Joya Chatterji, *Bengal Divided: Hindu Communalism and Partition* (Cambridge, 1994) and Partha Chatterjee, 'Bengal Politics and the Muslim Masses, 1920–47', *Journal of Commonwealth and Comparative Politics*, 20 (1982), 25–41 on Bengal; Lance Brennan, 'The Illusion of Security: the Background to Muslim Separatism in the United Provinces', *Modern Asian Studies*, 18 (1984), 237–72 on UP; and Ian A. Talbot, 'The Growth of the Muslim League in

the Punjab, 1937–46', *Journal of Commonwealth and Comparative Politics*, 20 (1982), 5–24 on Punjab. These last three articles are all reprinted in Hasan (ed.), *India's Partition.*
16. B.R. Tomlinson, 'Historical Roots of Economic Policy' in Subrato Roy and William James (eds.), *Foundations of India's Political Economy: Towards an Agenda for the 1990s* (Delhi, 1992), pp. 274–302.

CHAPTER 16

State transformation, reforms and economic performance in China, 1840–1910

Kent G. Deng

The period immediately after the Opium War (1840–2) marked the first stage of state transformation and economic reforms in modern China. During this period, the age-old socio-political and socio-economic structures and equilibria ended and new structures gradually took shape. Despite political hiccups, including the erosion of China's sovereignty, the market worked its own way out and modern growth began.

CHINA'S EARLY SUCCESS AND A CHANGE IN THE RULES OF THE GAME

China's superiority

China was a success story of pre-modern economic growth. Its socio-economic structure was flexible enough to expand across four time zones and 10 million km², reaching the physical limits for an agrarian civilisation. Its economy was productive enough to generate the surplus to finance Confucian education, science and technology, a bureaucratic machine controlling more than a thousand counties, an army of one million men and gigantic public works (e.g. the Great Wall and Grand Canal), and to sustain a remarkable degree of urbanisation, a nationwide market and extensive foreign trade.

In terms of inventions and innovations, the Chinese almost certainly held the world record by the eve of the European Renaissance with a long list of claims including metallurgy, gunpowder, the compass, stirrups, silk, porcelain, paper-making and paper currency, block printing, mechanical clocks, examinations to recruit civil servants, to name just a few.

China's production capacity was reflected by its export pattern. Until the end of the eighteenth century, China remained the main supplier of porcelain wares to the rest of the world.[1] Up to the end of the nineteenth century China was the main supplier of silk and tea to the world market. To facilitate foreign trade, by the end of the nineteenth century China had more than 10,000 compradors, with an aggregate wealth of 18,400 tons of silver, averaging 1.84 tons per head of the group.[2] Chinese diasporas spread far and wide in Asia with sophisticated trading networks long before the Europeans.[3]

China's wealth was crystallised by its possession of the largest reserves of monetary silver in the world.[4] Having the large quantities of monetary silver for such a long period not only enabled China to establish a silver standard but also caused a price revolution.[5]

Behind its deliberately preserved extravagant and mighty façade, the 'Confucian state' was small and cheap with limited devices for and influence on the economy.[6] The functions of that state were to, first, promote Confucian values for social stability, second, promote and regulate economic activities for tax revenue, and third, provide public goods: national defence and internal law and order, key infrastructure (such as the Grand Canal and public granaries) and emergency relief (against famine and violent price fluctuations). The underlying financial policy of the Chinese state was a balanced budget. The government revenue was merely 1–2 per cent of China's total GDP.[7] Even so, the Qing suffered a chronic shortfall of 15 per cent of its revenue target.[8]

Understandably, as China seemed to reach a Pareto optimum, the opportunity costs for a change in production function were too high. Until the nineteenth century, any such change could cost China's long-held supremacy.

A change in the rules of the game

The conflict between the Qing state and the West occurred as the former struggled to maintain its grip on China's exports established in 1760. The corner-stone of this monopoly was the employment of 'chartered maritime merchants' at Canton. Huge sums were yielded for the empire.

As China's door for trade was never closed but monopolised, the West had two hurdles to overcome: its own trade deficits and the Qing monopoly. It was a hopeless task until opium was discovered as an equaliser in trading with China. Soon, China's tea export was offset by opium instead of silver. Not only that, in 1817–19, for the first time, China had a trade deficit with Britain and India. From then on, China's hard-earned silver began to flow out at a greater speed than that at which the metal had been imported during the previous periods. The Canton-Cohong system, which was characterised by trade monopoly of the Qing state, tumbled as trade surpluses were no longer guaranteed.

The response of the Qing state was to ban the opium trade. It was a passive measure trying to stifle opium trade at home rather than enhancing China's monopolistic supply overseas. As Britain had too much to lose from the opium sales, the ban triggered invasion by British gun-ships.[9] The rules of the game were unilaterally changed by the West from peaceful market exchange (in which the West had some limited comparative advantage) to armed confrontation (in which the West possessed *force majeure*).

The gamble paid off. In 1842, the Nanking Treaty was signed. Opium was legalised. The British had free access to China's market with their property rights protected. As the icing on the cake, China was also made to pay crippling reparations as punishment for being the loser.[10] The two hurdles were cleared for good.

The benefit from the change of rules was so great that resorting to force to settle a dispute with China became the norm. Japan became addicted to it and waged more wars against China than all the other powers put together.

THE NANKING TREATY REFORM AND STATE TRANSFORMATION

Regardless of the brutality of the Opium War, a reform was swiftly carried out which can be called the 'Nanking Treaty Reform' (NTR). Mercantilistic in nature, many changes took place and some were revolutionary.

First, China's jealously guarded domestic markets were systematically opened up with forty-four main ports for foreigners.[11] Foreign dominance in China's foreign trade and investment in railways became reality (tables 16.1–16.3).

Second, the political control of the state began to crack as foreign spheres of influence functioned as alternative power centres. It was no accident that a decade after the Opium War rebellions such as the Taiping so seriously challenged the Qing rule that the Beijing government only survived with financial and military assistance from the West (see table 16.4). In the final twist, the treaties made the state pro-Western.

Third, with the decline of the agricultural sector as the dominant revenue-earner and the rise in importance of commerce, the old tax structure became obsolete (see tables 16.5 and 16.6). Unlike taxes from the agricultural sector, which were dictated by fluctuations in population and farming land, the revenue from customs duties was determined by trade

Table 16.1 *Shares of import and export tonnages in China, 1873–1910*

Year	Foreign (I) %	Chinese (II) %	I:II
1873	98	2	49.0
1882	73	27	2.7
1892	79	21	3.8
1902	83	17	4.9
1910	84	16	5.3
Mean	83.4	16.6	5.0

Source: Based on Tang Xianglong, *Zhongguo Jindai Haiguan Shuishou He Fenpei Tongji* [*Statistics of Customs Revenue and its Distribution in Modern China*] (Beijing, 1992), p. 21.

Table 16.2 *Investment shares in Chinese railways, 1888–1946*

Sector	Total	Foreign (I)	Chinese (II)	(Private)	(Government)	I:II
No. Projects	90	76	14	(10)	(4)	5.4
% of total	100.0	84.5	15.5	(11.1)	(4.4)	
Sum[a]	1,398,235,438	1,078,932,172	319,303,266	(299,681,530)	(19,621,736)	3.4
% of Total	100.0	77.2	22.8	(21.4)	(1.4)	

Notes: [a]Converted with period exchange rates.
Source: Based on ZTBZ (Zhongguo Tielushi Bianji Yanjiu Zhongxin [Research Center of History of Railways in China]) (ed.), *Zhongguo Tielu Dashiji, 1876–1995* [*Main Events in the History of Chinese Railways, 1876–1995*] (Beijing, 1996); Yang Yonggang, *Zhongguo Jindai Tielushi* [*A History of Railways in Modern China*] (Shanghai, 1997).

Table 16.3 *Foreign control over Chinese railways, c. 1918*

Powers	Length (in km)	% of total
Western	13,980	88.6
Asian	1,792	11.4
Total	15,772[a]	100.0

Note: [a]This is at least 90 per cent of China's aggregate railway length. (See Yang. *A History of Railways in Modern China*; cf. Angus Maddison, *Chinese Economic Performance in the Long Run* (Paris, 1998), p. 51.
Source: Based on ZTBZ, *Main Events in the History of Chinese Railways*; Yang, *A History of Railways in Modern China*.

Table 16.4 *Chinese government foreign debts, 1861–98*

Year	Purpose	Sum (in silver liang)	Debtor	Annual interest (%)
1861–6	To counter Taiping rebellion	1,609,925[ab]	Foreign merchants in Jiangsu, Fujian and Guangdang	?
1867–8	To counter Muslim rebellion	2,200,000[a]	Foreign merchants in Shanghai	18.0
1874	Taiwan defence	2,000,000[c]	British bank	8.0
1875	To counter Muslim rebellion	3,000,000[c]	British banks	10.5
1877–78	To counter Muslim rebellion	6,750,000[c]	British bank	15.0
1883–85	Coastal defence	13,602,300[c]	British bank	9.0
1886	Naval updating[d]	980,000[c]	German bank	5.5
1887–8	Flood control	1,968,800[ab]	British bank	7.0
1893–5	Coastal defence	42,090,000[ce]	British and German banks	6.0–7.0
1895–6	War reparation to Japan	200,000,000[e]	French and Russian banks	4.0–5.0
Total		274,201,025 (10,227.7 tons)		

Notes: [a]Loans for 2 years.
[b]Loans for 2–5 years.
[c]loans for 6–19 years.
[d]Fund abused for the Summer Palace.
[e]Loans for 20 years and over.
Source: Based on Tang, *Statistics of Customs Revenue*, pp. 34–41.

performance. A rapid increase in duties marked an unmistakably intensive, market-driven growth. A turning point was reached in 1903–4 when for the first time in Chinese history customs duty revenue surpassed revenue from taxes on agriculture. This ushered in an era of mercantilism as the state increasingly relied on commerce to maintain its function.

ECONOMIC PERFORMANCE UNDER THE NTR

Market-driven growth

First of all, with the forty-four main trading ports open to foreigners, the savings were enormous. Under the Canton–Cohong system, tea produced in Fujian had to travel some 1,400 kilometres south before being exported.

Table 16.5 *Old Chinese tax structure (in silver liang), 1652–1766*

Type	Land and Poll	Grain[a]	I	Salt	Customs	Other	II	I:II
1652	21,260,000	8,430,000 (5,620,000 *shi*)		2,120,000	1,000,000	–		9.52
Share in total	*64.80%*	*25.69%*	*90.49*	*6.46%*	*3.05%*	–	*9.51*	
1682	26,340,000	9,510,000 (6,340,000 *shi*)		2,760,000	2,000,000	–		7.53
Share in total	*64.86%*	*23.42%*	*88.28*	*6.80%*	*4.92%*	–	*11.72*	
1766	32,910,000	12,476,700 (8,317,800 *shi*)		5,740,000	5,400,000	4,490,000		2.90
Share in total	*53.93%*	*20.45%*	*74.38*	*9.41%*	*8.85%*	*7.36%*	*25.62*	

Notes: (I) Percentage share in the total tax revenue extracted from the agricultural sector. (II) Percentage share in the total tax revenue extracted from trade. [a]In the seventeenth and eighteenth centuries, the average price of rice was 0.94–2.18 liang per *shi* in the Yangzi Delta and 1.03–1.93 liang per *shi* in Guangdong and Guangxi (Yie-chien Wang, 'Secular Trends of Rice Prices in the Yangzi Delta, 1639–1953' in T.G. Rawski and L.M. Li (eds.), *Chinese History in Economic Perspective* (Berkeley, Calif., 1992), pp. 40–7; R.B. Marks, 'Rice Prices, Food Supply, and Market Structure in Eighteenth-Century South China', *Late Imperial China*, 2 (1991), 102.) Hence, a mean value of 1.5 liang per *shi* is used for estimation.
Source: Based on Zhou Boudi, *Zhongguo Caizheng Shi* [*A History of State Finance in China*] (Shanghai, 1981), pp. 419–21, 426.

The cost of inland transport accounted for one-third of the free on board price. The opening of Fujian allowed an astonishing total saving of 600,000 liang of silver (22.4 tons) per year for the buyers from the annual 150,000 *dan* tea trade.[12]

Second, foreign trade rapidly proliferated across the empire. Most noticeable were that, first, around 1899 opium imports dropped from the early high of 44.5 per cent to 13.8 per cent of China's total imports in value (partly because after the opium trade was legalised, home-grown supply of the drug substituted imports);[13] and second, China's tea and silk exports rocketed (see figure 16.1).

In terms of the total volume and value of foreign trade, the increase was spectacular. According to the Nanking Treaty, the ceiling for the customs duties was set at 5 per cent. Although this rate was re-endorsed by the 1858 Tianjin Treaty, with numerous concessions and duty-free treatments, the actual rate after 1858 was only 3 per cent.[14] Thus, it is safe to use the ceiling 5 per cent to estimate the total value of trade with the formula $V_i = \frac{C_i}{r}$, where V_i is the total value of goods traded during period i; C_i, the aggregate customs duties paid during period i; and r, the ceiling duty rate

Table 16.6 New Chinese tax structure (in silver liang), 1820–1910

Year	I Agricultural taxes[a]	Index	II Customs duties	Index	I:II	Tax-payers (no.)	Index	Farming land (in mu)	Index
1820	30,206,144	100	2,932,796[b]	100	10.3	353,377,694	100	779,321,984	100
1825	—	—	—	—	—	379,885,340	108	—	—
1830	—	—	—	—	—	394,784,681	112	—	—
1835	—	—	—	—	—	401,767,053	114	—	—
1840	—	—	—	—	—	412,814,828	117	—	—
1845	30,213,800	100	—	—	—	421,342,730	119	—	—
1850	—	—	—	—	—	429,913,134	122	—	—
(1851	—	—	—	—	—	—	—	756,386,244	97)
1855	—	—	—	—	—	318,845,752	90	—	—
1860	—	—	—	—	—	—	—	—	—
1865	—	—	8,245,394	281	—	260,697,717	74	—	—
1870	—	—	10,041,826	342	—	271,793,461	77	—	—
(1873	—	—	11,257,824	384	—	—	—	756,631,857	97)
1875	—	—	12,893,471	440	—	305,014,000[c]	86	—	—
						368,063,232	*104*		
1880	—	—	14,692,208	501	—	288,559,000[d]	82	—	—
						368,153,866	*104*		
1885	32,356,768	107	14,056,914	479	2.3	295,881,000[e]	84	—	—
						358,036,060	*101*		
(1887	32,792,627	109	16,411,544	560	2.0	377,636,000	107	911,976,606	117)
1890	33,736,023	112	19,100,657	651	—	333,242,000[f]	94	—	—
						380,717,468	*108*		
1895	—	—	20,694,712	706	—	332,336,000[g]	94	—	—
						379,682,395	*107*		

(1898	—		22,976,817	783	—	319,719,000[h]	90	—)
						367,324,219	*104*	
1900	—	—	24,456,571	834	—	—	—	—
(1903	28,086,771	93	27,659,313	943	1.0	—	—	—)
(1904	—	—	28,132,456	959	—	—	—	—)
1905	—	—	30,965,612	1056	—	—	—	—
1910	—	—	35,340,714	1205	—	—	—	—
(1912	—	—	—	—	—	368,146,520	104	—)

Notes: Entries in parentheses are supplementary to show continuation of the data. Italicised numbers are estimates weighted to include the missing provinces. (Mean values are applicable to Anhui (6.30%), Shaanxi (4.66%), Gansu (2.71%), Fujian (4.40%), Guangxi (1.32%), Yunnan (2.04%) and Guizhou (0.49%), Jilin (0.09%) and Xinjiang (0.10%) are based on the limited statistics from one year. Taiwan is excluded due to the absence of data. The formula is: $P'_i = \frac{P_i}{(1-n)}$. Where $P'i$ is the estimate for the period i; Pi, the incomplete aggregate for population of the period i; n, the combined share of the missing provinces in China's total.)

[a]Including the Land–Poll Combined Tax, Grain-to-Cash Conversion (*liangzhe*) and Silver Loss Discount (*haoxian*).

[b]Estimated figure based on the highest share of the customs duty revenue (8.85%) during 1652–1766.

[c]No data for seven provinces (Anhui, Shaanxi, Gansu, Xinjiang, Taiwan, Guangxi and Yunnan).

[d]No data for nine provinces (Jilin, Anhui, Shaanxi, Gansu, Xinjiang, Fujian, Taiwan, Guangxi and Yunnan).

[e]No data for eight provinces (Anhui, Gansu, Xinjiang, Fujian, Taiwan, Guangxi, Yunnan and Guizhou).

[f]No data for six provinces (Anhui, Gansu, Xinjiang, Taiwan, Guangxi and Yunnan).

[g]No data for six provinces (Anhui, Gansu, Xinjiang, Taiwan, Guangxi and Yunnan).

[h]No data for eight provinces (Jilin, Anhui, Gansu, Xinjiang, Fujian, Taiwan, Guangxi and Yunnan).

Source: Based on Liang Fangzhong, Zhongguo Lidai Huko Tiandi Tianfu Tongji [*Dynastic Data of China's Households, Cultivated Land and Land Taxation*], (Shanghai, 1980), pp. 10, 253–4, 256–7, 264–7, 380, 400, 401, 414–18, 426; Tang, *Statistics of Customs Revenue*, pp. 126–8.

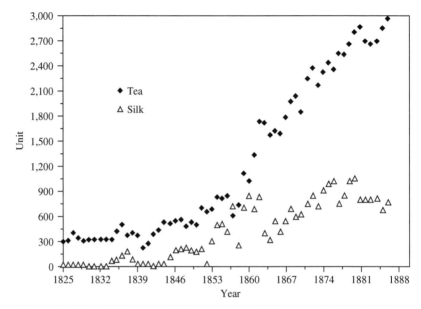

Figure 16.1 Rise in China's tea and silk exports, 1825–88 (based on Lin, 'China's Silver
Outflow', pp. 30–5).

(2.8 per cent before 1842[15]). The following result is derived from the data in
table 16.6.

Year	Value in silver liang	(in tons)	Value index
1820	104,742,714	(3,906.9)	100
1861	110,465,280	(4,120.4)	105
1871	215,676,120	(8,044.7)	206
1881	301,694,420	(11,253.2)	288
1891	402,676,620	(15,019.8)	384
1901	437,310,820	(16,311.7)	418
1910	706,814,280	(26,364.2)	675

There was also a hidden factor. With the rise of the opium trade, a rapid
silver drain from China caused severe deflation in the early nineteenth
century. In 1838, the exchange rate of one liang of silver rose from the
previous official par of 1,000 bronze coins to 1,600. It rose further to 2,300
coins in 1845 and 4,000 coins in 1899 with the average deflationary rate of
1.4 per cent over the period of a century.[16] Thus, the real growth index for
the total volume of foreign trade has to be much greater than the value
index:

Year	Volume index (1820 price)
1820	100
1861	187
1871	418
1881	672
1891	1,031
1901	1,287
1910	2,362

Even so, the estimate is conservative as the actual duty rate was lower with the practice of a duty-free regime. Any such increase means a higher degree of commercialisation.

Third, geographically, the importance of Guangzhou (Canton) in foreign trade was surpassed by Jiangsu, where the new trading centre, Shanghai, was located. Foreign trade also penetrated into China's interior (see table 16.7). The whole development was dictated by the market itself.

In addition, the shares of customs duties suggest differences in market conditions in different zones. Conditions in the West-influenced south were far more favourable than in the Russia and Japan-affected north. This pattern is revealed further in the East China Sea coast: after Japan colonised Taiwan in 1895 and extended its influence in on-shore Fujian, Fujian's foreign trade plunged by 50 per cent (as at 1910).

Fourth, as foreign trade multiplied, a new pattern of a balance of payment developed. China no longer held its position as a net goods exporter (see table 16.8). This is a clear sign that China gradually assimilated to and synchronised with the world economy.

Fifth, there was a clear trend of railway-induced investment in new industries (see figures 16.2 and 16.3). The railways effectively shifted the centre of industrial gravity from the east coast and the Yangzi reaches to a vertical belt with a clear bias towards heavy industry (see table 16.9).[17] Traditional workshops were gradually replaced by modern factories. For example, by 1894 Chinese private modern filatures in Guangzhou and Shanghai employed 13,600 workers and supplied about 70 per cent of China's total silk exports.[18] During the same period, private cotton-textile factories hired some 6,500 workers, able to produce 96,300 rolls a year for marketing.[19] Chinese private investment also found its footing in matches, paper, printing, shipbuilding, engineering and machinery. Overall, in 1894, the private sector employed at least 28,000 factory workers, about one-third of China's modern workforce.[20] China's modern industries progressed so efficiently in Asia that Japan had to capture them by force later to eliminate competition.[21]

Table 16.7 *Percentage shares of Chinese customs duties by province, 1861–1910*

	I	II			III					IV				
Year	DB	HeB	AH	JS	ZJ	FJ	GD	HuB	HN	JX	GX	SC	YN	Total
1861	–	1.81	–	41.66	7.41	18.28	30.84	–	–	–	–	–	–	100.00
1865	2.10	4.16	–	31.49	5.14	26.70	13.45	10.78	–	6.18	–	–	–	100.00
1870	2.67	4.17	–	32.69	7.18	22.42	12.07	13.39	–	5.41	–	–	–	100.00
1875	1.88	2.85	–	33.40	6.33	22.67	14.05	13.28	–	5.54	–	–	–	100.00
1880	2.08	2.96	0.31	35.00	4.81	21.68	13.52	14.57	–	5.07	–	–	–	100.00
1885	2.21	3.08	0.46	32.78	5.23	21.91	14.75	14.06	–	5.52	–	–	–	100.00
1890	2.09	3.18	2.16	30.83	5.51	17.45	23.26	10.20	–	5.13	0.01	–	0.18	100.00
1895	0.68	4.18	1.88	38.44	5.98	10.78[a]	18.26	12.74	–	4.98	0.03	1.60	0.45	100.00
1900	2.91	3.94[b]	4.19	37.36	5.32	8.65	17.88	12.14	–	3.74	1.22	1.88	0.77	100.00
1905	2.81	9.55	3.26	42.27	4.07	6.04	14.15	10.92	0.39	2.12	1.73	1.79	0.90	100.00
1910	5.59	9.22	1.67	36.39	3.81	4.98	17.02	13.37	0.74	2.15	2.04	2.24	0.78	100.00

Notes: I) Far North (Manchuria). II) Northeast. III) Southeast coast. IV) Southwest and South inland. Abbreviations for provinces: DB–Dongbei (Manchuria), HeB–Hebei, AH–Anhui, JS–Jiangsu (predominantly Shanghai), ZJ–Zhejiang, FJ–Fujian including Taiwan until 1895, GD–Guangdong (Guangzhou only), HuB–Hubei, HN–Hunan, JX–Jiangxi, GX–Guangxi, SC–Sichuan, YN–Yunnan.
[a]Point of decline in trade after Japanese colonisation of Taiwan.
[b]Decline due to the Boxer Rebellion.
Source: Based on Tang, *Statistics of Customs Revenue*, pp. 69–78.

Table 16.8 *Chinese trade performance (in 10^6 silver yuan), 1871–1911*

Period	Total value traded	Index	Import (I)	Index	Export (II)	Index	I–II
1871–3	216 (216)	100 (100)	106 (106)	100 (100)	110 (110)	100 (100)	+4 (+4)
1881–3	234 (276)	108 (128)	126 (148)	119 (140)	108 (139)	98 (126)	−18 (−9)
1891–3	386 (525)	179 (243)	219 (298)	207 (281)	167 (227)	152 (206)	−52 (−71)
1901–3	784 (1,223)	363 (566)	473 (738)	446 (696)	311 (485)	283 (440)	−162 (−253)
1909–11	1,272 (2,213)	589 (1,025)	702 (1,221)	662 (1,152)	570 (992)	518 (902)	−133 (−229)

Note: Figures in parentheses are at the 1871 constant price.
Source: Based on Tang, *Statistics of Customs Revenue*, p. 23.

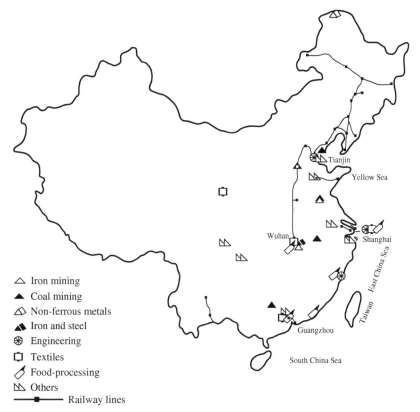

△ Iron mining
▲ Coal mining
◁ Non-ferrous metals
◢ Iron and steel
⊛ Engineering
▯ Textiles
⟋ Food-processing
⋈ Others
━■━ Railway lines

Figure 16.2 Railways and modern industries in China, c. 1906. Contemporary China is taken as a proxy for the empire (based on Chi-Keung Leung, 'China: Railway Patterns and National Goals', Research Paper No. 195, Department of Geography, University of Chicago (1980), p. 36; Chen Dunyi and Hu Jishan (eds.), *Zhongguo Jingji Dili* [*Economic Geography of China*] (Beijing, 1983), p. 21).

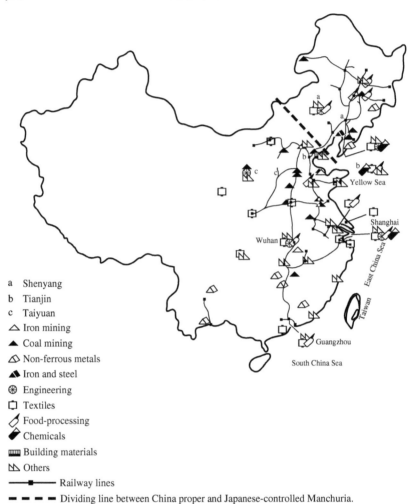

a   Shenyang
b   Tianjin
c   Taiyuan
△ Iron mining
▲ Coal mining
◬ Non-ferrous metals
◣ Iron and steel
✹ Engineering
▢ Textiles
⟋ Food-processing
◤ Chemicals
▦ Building materials
⋈ Others
━━■━━ Railway lines
▬ ▬ ▬ ▬ Dividing line between China proper and Japanese-controlled Manchuria.

Figure 16.3 Expanding railways and modern industries in China, *c.* 1937. Contemporary China is taken as a proxy for the empire (based on Leung, 'China: Railway Patterns and National Goals', p. 61; Chen and Hu, *Economic Geography of China*, pp. 23, 322).

Evaluation: was China simply a victim?

One of the most visible outcomes of the NTR was the key role played by foreign traders and foreign investors (railways and loans being examples) in China's market (see tables 16.1–16.2, 16.7–16.8). To Marxist–Maoists and

Table 16.9 *Distribution of Chinese Industrial Workers in regions and sectors*

	Workers	% of all workers
Region		
Shanghai	36,220	46.4
Hanko	13,350	17.0
Guangzhou	10,300	13.2
Tianjin	4,180	5.4
Fuzhou	3,240	4.1
Nanjing	1,000	1.3
Jiujiang	1,000	1.3
Shantou	600	0.8
Xiamen	500	0.6
Other	7,700	9.9
Total	78,090	100.0
Sector		
Heavy industry[a]	51,700	52.7
Light industry	42,800	43.6
Other	3,600	3.7
Total	98,100	100.0

Note: [a]Given that the capital–worker ratio is much higher in heavy industry, the investment share for this sector must be much higher.

nationalists alike, this is the most upsetting sign of foreign imperialism. However, foreign control over trade and investment alone does not automatically justify the claim that China was a victim of external exploitation. Two questions will have to be asked: (1) Given the importance of the customs revenue, who paid most of the customs duties and by how much? (2) Were the foreigners the sole beneficiaries of the revenue?

From table 16.10 as well as table 16.1, it is obvious that foreigners paid most of the customs duties.[22] The data reveal the fact that foreign traders were the main contributor to a 'second budget' for the Qing. As shown earlier in table 16.6, by the turn of the twentieth century, revenue from the customs duties matched that from the agricultural sector. Although small in number, foreign traders had as much fiscal weight as several hundred million farming Chinese.

Another common illusion is that since the Qing state mortgaged China's customs duties to the West, the duty revenue never benefited the Chinese. Quite the opposite. In conjunction with table 16.10, figure 16.4 shows that the lion's share of the income from customs duties was controlled by the

Table 16.10 *Duties at Shanghai customs, 1861–1910*

Year	Total[a]	By foreigners	%	By Chinese	%
1861	1,500,507	1,500,507	100.0	0	0.0
1866	1,080,148	1,080,148	100.0	0	0.0
1871	2,143,110	2,143,110	100.0	0	0.0
1873	1,982,361	1,976,134	99.7	6,227	0.3
1878	2,175,779	1,990,595	91.5	185,184	8.5
1883	2,357,503	2,135,413	90.6	222,090	9.4
1888	3,658,811	3,348,224	91.5	310,587	8.5
1893	3,674,996	3,288,984	89.5	386,012	10.5
1898	4,820,657	4,445,212	92.2	375,445	7.8
1903	7,198,990	6,768,598	94.0	430,392	6.0
1910	7,405,551	6,900,372	93.2	505,179	6.8

Note: [a]Including both import and export duties, in silver liang.
Source: Based on Tang, *Statistics of Customs Revenue*, p. 21.

Qing state and distributed among seven earmarked funds. The priority was given to national defence and internal peace-keeping as one-third of the total income was allocated to the military, equivalent to the combined shares for the custom duties, foreign debt repayment and war reparations. The moneys kept for the central administration and the royals were rather trivial, and certainly not sufficient for excessive rent-seeking by the state.

It is obvious that the new revenue from the customs duties was milked from foreigners but used by the Qing state for legitimate purposes.

Now it is easy to assess the Maoists' claim that 1840 marked the beginning of a 'semi-colonial' China, although the term itself has never been clearly defined. The closest thing was the Japanese puppet regimes of the 1930s and 1940s in Manchuria and north-east China proper. Thus, China's semi-colonial status occurred much later and did not last long.

It is worth noting that foreign powers came to China with very different purposes. As the Westerners approached China to trade for profit, the Russians and Japanese, like opportunistic scavengers, came to loot China after it was badly injured. This is clearly reflected by their appetite for China's plentiful territory and wealth. By 1911, Russia and Japan had grabbed in all 3 million square kilometres, or 15 per cent of the Qing territory. In 1895 Japan demanded an astronomical war reparation of 230 million liang of silver (8,580 tons), a sum over ten times greater than all the previous reparations from China put together.[23] If anything, in its entire modern history, China fell victim primarily to Russo-Japanese colonialism.

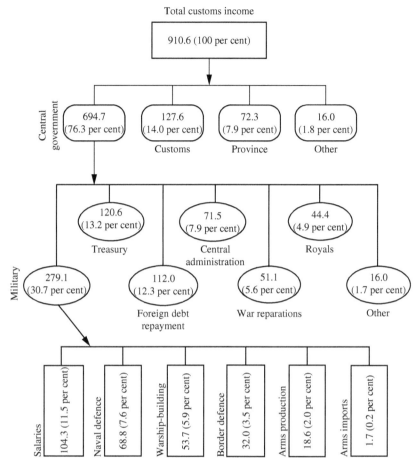

Figure 16.4 Distribution of total income from customs duties in China, 1861–1910, in million liang of silver. Figures in parentheses are percentages of the total (based on Tang, *Statistics of Customs Revenue and its Distribution in Modern China*, pp. 126–9, 139–44, 170–3).

OTHER REFORMS AND THE DEMISE OF THE QING

Voluntary reform: the 'Westernisation Movement'

Despite China's humiliating experience with Western demands, the NTR represented the first step of a long line of reforms in post-Opium War history. The most influential one was the 1870–95 'Westernisation Movement', aimed at rebuilding China's military strength and thus sovereignty. By now, with newly established confidence and financial resources, the Qing state appeared proto-Gerschenkronian as it dismantled remaining trade barriers, promoted modern industries and initiated technological dissemination.

With the priority being to build a modern arms industry with naval hardware, between 1861 and 1910, a quarter of the Qing military expenditure was invested in the arms industry (totalling 72.3 million liang of silver or 2,696.8 tons). Western technicians were hired and capital goods imported. The first modern gunboat was built in 1868, which marked a new era of import-substitution industrial (ISI) growth.[24] By 1890, the number of government-sponsored ordnance factories had grown to nineteen with a workforce of 11,000, some 10 per cent of China's workforce in modern industries.[25] Between 1867 and 1894, the Shanghai Arsenal received a total investment of 2.92 million liang of silver (108.8 tons) and developed into a huge complex of thirteen divisions with 2,821 workers.[26] It was the largest in East Asia and one of the largest in the world at that time.[27] By 1894, this arsenal alone had produced in all 561 heavy machines, 15 ships, 585 cannons, 563 torpedoes, 51,285 rifles, 158,250 bullets, 1,201,900 shells, 411,023 artillery shells and 4,081,469 pounds of explosive.[28]

In addition, a modern naval academy was established in 1867 in Majiang to train officers under several dozen French instructors. Four more were founded in Tianjin (1880), Guangdong (1887), Nanjing (1890) and Yantai (1903).[29] The standard four-year courses included English, geography, mathematics, geometry, physics, chemistry, astronomy, meteorology, cartography, steam engines, hydromechanics, calculation of longitude and latitude, reckoning, pilotage, artillery and surveying.[30] Schools were also established to train seamen with skills such as the use of cables and knots, handling of sails, steering, use of the compass, rowing, swimming, and use of firearms and swords.[31] Moreover, from 1876 onwards, naval cadets were sent to foreign naval academies and shipyards in Western Europe, mainly Britain and France, to learn the latest technology and craft.[32]

The result of the government efforts was impressive. By 1875, China had a new navy with two modern fleets, equipped with modern ships and Western training and management.[33] There were also provincial naval forces in Fujian and Guangdong Provinces, under the command of the Southern Sea Minister. By the time of the Sino-Japanese War in 1894–5, the total displacement tonnage of the Northern Sea Fleet alone had reached 53,394 tons.[34] Such progress was closely followed by Western observers. In 1872, they reported that 'Chinese military power was vastly different from what it had been in 1860', 'the output of factories and shipyards

Table 16.11 *Employment pattern in the modern sector, foreign vs Chinese investment*

Investor	Workers employed	% in total
Foreigners	34,000	34.3
Chinese	65,000	65.7
Private	28,000	28.3
State	37,000	37.4
Total	99,000	100.0

Source: Sun, *Materials on Modern Industries in China*, p. 1201.

was impressive', and 'Chinese-built warships would soon equal the highest European standards'.[35]

State involvement in modern industry was not limited to arms. In 1884, another 26,000 workers were on the government payroll, producing coal, copper, gold, silver, iron, steel and textiles which made the state the largest employee in the modern sector (see table 16.11). Thanks to the state initiatives, foreign control was not as overwhelming as in the railways.

The Japanese invasion and the 'One-Hundred-Day Reform'

The fruit of the Westernisation Movement was brutally destroyed by the Japanese invasion of mainland Asia in 1894 as the very symbol of the Westernisation Movement – the Northern Sea Fleet – was defeated in a close match with heavy losses on both sides. The following 1895 Maguan Treaty pushed China back to square one and the pattern associated with the Opium War repeated itself. This time, 'later industrialisers' – Japan, Germany and Russia – came in for the kill, as seen in the 1896 Beijing (Peking) Treaty, the 1898 Fuzhou Concession Agreement, the 1898 Jiaozhou Bay Concession Treaty, and the 1898 Lü-Da Concession Treaty.

The Chinese radical, idealistic elite responded to this regression with the 'One-Hundred-Day Reform'. Instead of rebuilding China's military strength, the aim of this reform was to modernise the state itself after the British model of constitutional monarchy to facilitate capitalist industrialisation. With the direct involvement of Emperor Guangxu (r. 1875–1908), the reformers masterminded a range of institutional changes including appointing reformers to replace old mandarins in the government;

abandoning the traditional Imperial Examination for bureaucrat recruitment; encouraging entrepreneurship and private investment in mining, manufacturing, transport and telecommunications; establishing a central bank; modernising state budgeting; streamlining the armed forces; upgrading modern education; and experimenting with freedom of speech and freedom of travel overseas. With hindsight, these reforms were too far ahead of their time as these revolutionary changes have yet to be fully accomplished in contemporary China.

The reform created such a stir in the old establishment, that groups with vested interests under the banner of Dowager Empress Cixi (1835–1908) launched a military coup with the support of China's gentry class, who were threatened with being made outcasts. The clock was then reset: China had no reform until 1911 when, *à la* the French 1789 model, Dr Sun Yat-sen's revolution ended the Qing monarchy.

CONSEQUENCE OF THE REFORMS AND STATE TRANSFORMATION

Reforms and state transformation in Qing China originated from the trade of humble, contraband opium which triggered a long chain reaction for a century. Until 1910, the mercantilistic NTR was reasonably achieved. The Qing state benefited at least from the second budget, while the Chinese economy was boosted by the 'Ricardian gains' – the 'vent for surplus' type – an increase in overseas trade and foreign capital, the intake of Western technology and the rise in modern industries. Such gains certainly eased the pain of the erosion of China's sovereignty. The proactive, quasi-developmental Westernisation Movement marked a systematic attempt at ISI which demonstrated how far the state had been transformed. Heavy public spending on industrial projects was justified by the need for and fetish of modern arms.

However, these two reforms did not come about without problems, some fatal. The NTR was never popular among the public who saw the Qing state as incompetent in keeping foreign powers at bay, especially Japan, which China always despised culturally, politically and economically.[36]

This resentment was refuelled by two marked consequences of rampant foreign trade. First, China's terms of trade steadily deteriorated (see figure 16.5). Second, there was chronic deflation of China's silver currency. These two factors doubly discounted the relative price per unit of China's exports. Thus, the mounting income from customs duties meant that much

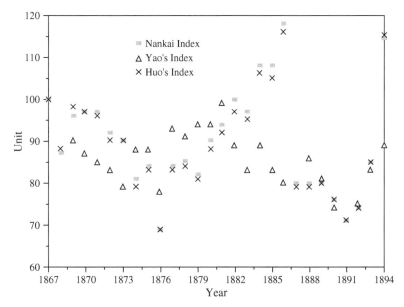

Figure 16.5 Changes in China's terms of trade, 1867–94 (based on Wang Jingyu, 'Qianyi Jindai Zhongwai Jingji Guanxide Pingjia Wenti' ['On Evaluation of Sino-Foreign Trade Relationship'], *Jindaishi Yanjiu* [*Study of Modern History*] 1 (1991), 1–27).

more domestic produce was required for exportation to make up the same revenue, let alone an increasing one (see table 16.6).

Moreover, despite the creation of a second budget, the reforming state did not touch the old tax system. Although the nominal rate remained constant (see table 16.6), as deflation worsened, ordinary households had to sell more in exchange for the same amount of cash to pay the tax. Thus, in the end, the real burden of the Land and Poll Combined Tax must have increased some threefold. Now the very tax regime which helped China's commercialisation earlier began to work against the state. In addition, during the post-Opium War period, extra surcharges were common which broke the political taboo against imposing a heavy tax burden. The Percentage Toll (*lijin*, or *likin*) – originally imposed in 1853 as a temporary measure for suppressing the Taiping rebels – was the most hateful of all. Hungry for funding, the Westernisation Movement activists only institutionalised the new taxes which proved counter-productive for the embryonic 'developmental state'. The erosion of the state's political and moral authority was shown by mass rebellions such as the anti-Manchu Nian (1852–68) and pro-Christian, anti-Confucian Taiping (1851–64) rebellions.

There was a financial explanation. By 1910, state access to China's total GDP had increased from the early 1–2 per cent to 16 per cent,[37] unprecedented in Chinese history but still not enough to overturn China's old economic structure in the given time. The 16 per cent was however not always guaranteed. Sweeping fifteen farming provinces, the Taipings firmly controlled the most affluent southern region of the empire – much of Anhui, Jiangsu, Zhejiang, Fujian, Hubei and Jiangxi. Meanwhile, the Nians haunted eight farming provinces in the north. The Taiping core area alone easily cost the Qing Treasury 34 per cent of its agricultural revenue (as at 1849) and 49 per cent of its customs duties (as at 1865, excluding Shanghai). The 'Dagger Society' (*xiandaohui*), a close ally of the Taipings, captured Shanghai in 1853–4, which jeopardised another one-third of the Qing customs duties.[38] To survive, the state then became increasingly reliant on new taxes despite the mounting political risks and pursued Western assistance in a dangerous liaison. This in turn alienated the state further from society. By 1910 there was a consensus among the masses that the Qing state was a traitor to China and its people.

As the 'top-down' reformers increasingly concentrated in a few cities with their agenda more and more isolated from that of the rest of the population, the 1898 'One-Hundred-Day Reform', critical for fully fledged modern state-hood, was aborted. This downfall was not because of external interference but due to internal crises accumulated gradually right from the beginning of the NTR as the benefits of reforms did not trickle down enough to enrich citizens at the grassroots level, especially in rural China. Not surprisingly, there was no public outcry against Cixi's reactionary coup to end the 'One-Hundred-Day Reform'.

Although China achieved some noticeable growth in the market during this period, its state transformation of the first round failed. But the Qing 'state failure' did not result from 'institutional sclerosis' but from the reforms' negative externalities regarding socio-economic stability (currency deflation and tax burden) and national security (law and order, sovereignty and territorial integrity), so much so that the 'social costs' for the majority exceeded the 'social benefits' from changes, a problem which haunted China for decades to come.

NOTES

1. See Quan Hansheng, 'Lielun Xinhanglu Faxianhoude Zhongguo Haiwai Maoyi' ['On China's Overseas Trade after the Discovery of a New Asia–Europe Sea Route'] in Zhang Bincun and Liu Shiji (eds.), *Zhongguo Haiyang Fazhanshi*

Lunwenji [*Selected Essays on the Maritime History of China*], Vol. V (Taipei, 1993), pp. 11–12; C.J.A. Jörg, *Porcelain and the Dutch China Trade* (Lange, 1982), chs. 1 and 3 and Appendix 11.

2. See Huang Qichen, 'Mingqing Guangdong Shangbang' ['Merchant Groups in Guangdong during the Ming–Qing Period'], *Zhongguo Shehui Jingjishi Yanjiu* [*Studies of Chinese Economic History*], 4 (1992), 36; Yen-P'ing Hao, 'A "New Class" in China's Treaty Ports: the Rise of the Compradore-Merchants', *The Business History Review*, 4 (1970), 446–59; Yen-P'ing Hao, *The Compradore in Nineteenth-Century China: Bridge between East and West* (Boston, Mass., 1970).

3. W.L. Schurz, *The Manila Galleon* (repr., Manila, 1985), pp. 63–4; Gungwu Wang, *China and the Chinese Overseas* (Singapore, 1991), ch. 9.

4. Immanuel Wallerstein, *The Modern World-System* (New York, 1974), p. 338; Anthony Reid, *Southeast Asia in the Age of Commerce, 1450–1680* (New Haven, Conn., 1993), p. 27.

5. Gang Deng, *Chinese Maritime Activities and Socio-economic Consequences, c. 2100 BC–1900 AD* (London and West Port, Conn., 1997), Appendix C.

6. Gang Deng, *Development versus Stagnation: Technological Continuity and Agricultural Progress in Premodern China* (London and West Port, Conn., 1993), pp. 19–20 and Appendix 1.

7. Dwight Perkins, 'Government as an Obstacle to Industrialization: the Case of Nineteenth-Century China', *Journal of Economic History*, 27 (1967), 478–92; cf. Albert Feuerwerker, 'The State and the Economy in Late Imperial China', *Theory and Society*, 13 (1984), 300; Gang Deng, *The Chinese Premodern Economy – Structural Equilibrium and Capitalist Sterility* (London and New York, 1999), Appendix 7.

8. Liang Fangzhong, *Zhongguo Lidai Huko Tiandi Tianfu Tongji* [*Dynastic Data of China's Households, Cultivated Land and Land Taxation*] (Shanghai, 1980), pp. 391, 394, 397, 398, 401, 414–19.

9. Arnold Toynbee (ed.), *Half the World: the History and Culture of China and Japan* (London, 1973), ch. 11.

10. From 1842 to 1901, China signed in all twenty-six treaties for seventy-three concessions with twelve foreign powers including unilateral most-favoured-nation treatment for trade, consular jurisdiction, free access to the interior, permanent residency for foreigners, the right to deploy foreign armed forces, war reparations and territorial cessions. See Zhao Dexin (ed.), *Zhongguo Jingjishi Cidian* [*Dictionary of Chinese Economic History*] (Wuhan, 1990), pp. 874–80. Between 1842 and 1900, China's war reparation premiums totalled 713 million liang of silver (26,600 tons), equivalent to 22 times the Qing annual revenue from agricultural taxes of the same period (Zhao, *Dictionary of Chinese Economic History*, pp. 874–80; Tang Xianglong, *Zhongguo Jindai Haiguan Shuishou He Fenpei Tongji* [*Statistics of Customs Revenue and its Distribution in Modern China*] (Beijing, 1992), p. 33; Liang, *Dynastic Data*, pp. 387, 397–8, 401, 415–16). China was broke and its geo-political landscape was changed as the country became 'zoned' by foreign powers. See Hermann Kinder and Werner Hilgemann (eds.), *The Penguin Atlas of World History* (London, 1978), p. 90.

11. Tang, *Statistics of Customs Revenue*, pp. 54–60.

12. Lin Manhong, 'Zhongguode Baiyin Wailiu Yu Shijie Jinyin Jianchan (1814–1850)' ['China's Silver Outflow and Decline in Gold and Silver Outputs in the World (1814–1850)'] in Wu Jianxiong (ed.), *Zhongguo Haiyang Fazhanshi Lunwenji* [*Selected Essays on the Maritime History of China*], Vol. IV (Taipei, 1991), pp. 234–6.

13. Chen Ciyu, 'Yi Zhong Yin Ying Sanjiao Maoyi Wei Jizhou Tantao Shijiu Shiji Zhongguode Duiwai Maoyi' ['Study of Nineteenth-Century Sino-Foreign Trade based on the Trade Triangle of China, India and Britain'] in Editing Committee for *Maritime History of China* (ed.), *Zhongguo Haiyang Fazhanshi Lunwenji* [*Selected Essays on the Maritime History of China*], Vol. I (Taipei, 1984), pp. 156–7.

14. Yan Zhongping (ed.), *Zhongguo Jindai Jingji Tongji Ziliao Xuanji* [*Selected Statistical Data for Modern China's Economy*] (Beijing, 1953), p. 60.

15. Before the Opium War, the stated export duty was 4 per cent and import duty 1.6 per cent, which made an average rate of the duties of 2.8 per cent. See Sun Xugang (ed.), *Jianming Zhongguo Caizhengshi* [*A Compact History of Finance of Premodern China*] (Beijing, 1988), p. 190.

16. Sun, *Compact History of Finance*, p. 204.

17. As at 1894, based on Sun Shutang, *Zhongguo Jindai Gongyeshi Ziliao* [*Materials on Modern Industries in China*] (Beijing, 1957), p. 1202.

18. Sun, *Materials on Modern Industries in China*, pp. 969, 1195.

19. Ibid., pp. 1068, 1197.

20. Ibid., p. 1201.

21. Kaoru Sugihara, 'Intra-Asian Trade and East Asia's Industrialisation, 1919–1939', London School of Economics and Political Science, Working Papers in Economic History 44 (1998), pp. 25–57.

22. The data in the tables relate to Shanghai. By 1855, this city had become China's leading trading port whose total export value to Britain was nearly seven times that of Guangzhou. See Cao Tunyu, 'Ningbo Shanghaigangde Lishi Guiji Yu Xiandai Fazhan Qushi' ['Developmental Trend of Port Ningbo and Port Shanghai, Past and Present'], *Zhejiang Shehui Kexue* [*Social Sciences in Zhejiang*] 6 (1995), 93.

23. Tang, *Statistics of Customs Revenue*, pp. 32–3.

24. Hao Peiyun, *Zhongguo Haijun Shi* [*A Naval History of Modern China*] (Beiping, 1929), pp. 8–9.

25. Sun, *Materials on Modern Industries in China*, p. 1188.

26. Ibid., p. 279.

27. M.C. Wright, *The Last Stand of Chinese Conservatism* (Stanford, 1957), p. 212.

28. Ibid., p. 293.

29. Hao, *A Naval History of Modern China*, pp. 17, 65, 71, 167.

30. Anon., *Regulations of the Northern Sea Fleet*, pp. 179–97.

31. Ibid., pp. 199–204.

32. Hao, *A Naval History of Modern China*, pp. 13, 20, 45, 159, 170–1.

33. Xia Zhengnong (ed.), *Cihai* [*Encyclopaedia*] (Shanghai, 1989), pp. 157, 382.

34. Anon, *Regulations of the Northern Sea Fleet*, pp. 1–118.
35. Wright, *The Last Stand of Chinese Conservatism*, p. 220.
36. In effect, in post-Opium War China, most mass protests and revolutions were in one way or another related to Japan's aggressions.
37. The traditional share was 1–2 per cent. The tax in cash with silver deflation made up an extra 6 per cent and the growth in customs revenue another 8 per cent (see table 16.6).
38. Liang, *Dynastic Data*, p. 415; Tang, *Statistics of Customs Revenue*, pp. 69–78.

CHAPTER 17

Japan's unstable course during its remarkable economic development

Hidemasa Morikawa

INTRODUCTION

Japan had become a nation-state by the end of the twelfth century, and has remained one ever since. It is true that between 1895 and 1945, Japan absorbed Taiwan, as it did Korea between 1910 and 1945. Both territories were treated as colonies, however, and their non-Japanese populations (the Taiwanese and Koreans) were not given the rights of Japanese. Thus, no change in Japan's status as a nation-state occurred as a result of those ventures into colonialism. Japan also compelled the Ainu people of Hokkaido and the people of the Ryukyus (now Okinawa Prefecture) to become Japanese, but their numbers were too small to lead one to deny that Japan was and is a nation-state.

Japan's administrative structure has, of course, changed at various stages since the twelfth century, but its status as a nation-state has not. Several reasons for its being able to survive as a nation-state over the centuries may be adduced.

First, Japan, an island nation lying off the farthest reaches of East Asia, was thereby insulated from invasions that might have produced loss of ethnic unity. Similarly, until 1894, Japan was incapable of sending military forces to subjugate other countries. (The attempt by Toyotomi Hideyoshi to invade Korea, between 1592 and 1597, ended in failure.) In this respect, Japan differs from Britain: while both are island nations, the Straits of Dover are far narrower than the Tsushima Strait between Japan and Korea.

Second, the centuries during which Japan's national exclusion policy was in effect (1633–1859), closing Japan to almost all trade or other contact with other countries, did more than withdraw Japan from international society. It also prevented Japan from conquering, or being conquered by, other countries.

The third reason is that the Soviet Union did not participate in the occupation of Japan that followed upon its defeat in 1945. As a result, Japan avoided being split into two states, as Germany was.

Japan, then, has consistently been a nation-state, and its achieving that status was not the effect of economic change. Rather, I would argue that its integrity as a nation-state has had an impact on economic change in Japan. Therefore, addressing a topic that is a slight twist on the theme of this volume, I will discuss the relationship between economic change in Japan and its integrity as a nation-state.

STABILITY OF THE NATION-STATE AND INSTABILITY OF THE ECONOMY

Japan has maintained its integrity as a nation-state since the twelfth century. It might appear that the arrival of European ships, the expansion in overseas trade, and the introduction of Roman Catholicism between the mid-sixteenth century and the latter half of the seventeenth caused change. The Shogunate's institution of national seclusion policies to close Japan to almost all contacts with other countries, however, sheltered the Japanese nation-state from international society.

In 1859, however, Japan did finally open, under pressure from Western states, and launch itself on a course to modernisation. The Western impact was reinforced by unequal treaties which, by denying Japan control of its own tariff levels and granting foreigners extra-territoriality, threatened Japan's independence. To preserve its independence as a nation-state, Japan had to stand on its own feet economically. To reach this goal, it had no alternative to introducing technologies and systems of the standard already reached by the United States and the European states.

Japan's integrity as a nation-state was sufficiently firm to enable the central government authorities to pursue that process. Prior to the Meiji Restoration (1868), the Tokugawa Shogunate had functioned in many ways as the central government, but it had direct control only over its own lands; the rest of the country was divided into dozens of *han* (domains) under the semi-autonomous rule of their respective *daimyo* (lords). Under the impact of the West, however, that nation-state was forged into one of more powerful integrity. To succeed in modernisation and industrialisation, Japan in the Meiji Restoration rejected both the Tokugawa Shogunate and the *daimyo* with their *han*, and built a strong, fully developed central government.

Economic development of that nation-state under the direction of the central government and with the support of the people was swift and successful. This may give the impression that, over the decades between 1868 and the 1980s, Japan's economic growth was also highly planned and stable. The reality is quite the opposite.

The course of economic growth in Japan was, in fact, quite unstable. What, then, was the connection between its integrity as a nation-state and its far from smooth history of economic development? That is the question this chapter addresses.

Any capitalist nation will experience periods of economic expansion and contraction. Such fluctuations are an essential characteristic of capitalist economies, and Japan is no exception in experiencing them. What is exceptional about fluctuations in the Japanese economy, however, is the extremely rapid pace at which the ups and downs occur. As a result, the course of Japan's economic development gives the impression of being extremely unstable when compared with the development process in Europe and the United States.

Perhaps the best example of these drastic fluctuations is the contrast between the rapid economic growth that Japan achieved after the oil shocks of the early 1970s, its booming prosperity after the 1985 Plaza Agreement, and the extended recession that began in the autumn of 1990 and which, as of 1999, showed no signs of ending.

What causes this instability? To answer this question, I shall first introduce two historical examples of quite unstable economic fluctuations in Japan. One is the contrast between Japan's great prosperity during the First World War and its rapid economic decline after the war ended. The other is the example mentioned above: the contrast between Japan's prosperity and decline in recent years.

JAPAN'S ECONOMY AND THE FIRST WORLD WAR

The First World War, in which Japan did not participate directly, provided Japan with unprecedented wartime demand resulting in economic expansion. The outbreak of the war in July 1914 did not, however, touch off an economic boom; the immediate reaction was stagnation in response to uncertainty about the war's implications for the future of the economy. In February 1915, however, the war-induced shortage of materials sent prices soaring on the world market and Japanese enterprises began responding to the opportunities presented by the war.

Not everyone waited to see what the war would bring. As early as November 1914, when others regarded the outlook as uncertain, Suzuki Shôten, based on information from employees stationed overseas, predicted that the war would cause an extreme shortage of goods. Acting on that prediction, the company issued simultaneous orders to all its branches in Japan and abroad to buy.

Suzuki Shôten was a Kobe-based trading company that had put together a trading network overseas and had invested its trading profits in building up a diversified group of industries. Since Suzuki Shôten's founder had died in 1894, when his son and heir was only twelve years old, management of the firm was entrusted by the Suzuki family to a salaried manager, Kaneko Naokichi. Kaneko was an extremely able manager who exercised autocratic leadership, developed aggressive policies and expanded Suzuki Shôten.

It was, of course, Kaneko who directed all branches of the firm to buy in November 1914. Kaneko hoped to use the opportunity presented by the wartime boom to enable Suzuki Shôten to catch up with the giant *zaibatsu* (groups of diversified businesses exclusively owned and controlled by a single family or an extended family) such as Mitsui and Mitsubishi. In a statement issued in 1917, Kaneko said, 'We can make big profits from this war and pull ahead of Mitsui and Mitsubishi. Or, if that is not possible, we can divide up Japan's business world three ways with them. That's the goal we all, as Suzuki Shôten employees, have, and we wouldn't begrudge sacrificing five or ten years of each of our lives to achieve it.' Kaneko's statement was intended to raise employees' consciousness and morale.

Kaneko was not bluffing when he talked about overtaking the major *zaibatsu*. In 1917, Suzuki Shôten's annual turnover was ¥1.54 billion, far outstripping Mitsui Bussan's ¥1.1 billion. It was also far ahead, in 1919, in volume of shipping on sea routes to Europe: Suzuki Shôten had thirty ships with a total capacity of 220,000 gross tonnes, compared with Mitsui Bussan's fourteen ships totalling 100,000 tonnes.

Suzuki Shôten aggressively bought up metals, machinery, foodstuffs and other essential war materials throughout the world, sold them at highly appreciated prices and secured vast profits. Ships were a particularly profitable investment as war transport needs tend to drive up demand for ships. During the First World War, as German submarines were indiscriminately sinking Allied shipping, the shortage of ships was severe, and shipbuilding and sales (or chartering) became a powerful money-spinner. Suzuki Shôten worked to increase the number of ships in its fleet, including both its own ships and those it chartered. To do so, it bought two shipyards in Japan.

While Suzuki Shôten led the way in the First World War boom, many *zaibatsu* and other large-scale enterprises, attracted by the prospect of high profits, followed. Increased activity in the maritime industries was particularly conspicuous, with new firms entering the field and existing players expanding their operations. The Kuhara *zaibatsu*, the Kawasaki Shipbuilding Company and the Asano *zaibatsu* were among the outstanding examples.

Kaneko Naokichi of Suzuki Shôten, Kuhara Fusanosuke of the Kuhara *zaibatsu*, Matsukata Kôjirô of Kawasaki Shipbuilding and Asano Sôichirô of the Asano *zaibatsu* all scored major successes by taking advantage of the wartime boom. These four had several points in common: they all had dictatorial power over their enterprises (apart from Kaneko, who was a salaried manager, they were all owner-managers), they were all charismatic personalities, and their operations were all largely dependent on borrowed funds. Their successes could not, however, be sustained for long.

THE ECONOMIC ENVIRONMENT AFTER THE FIRST WORLD WAR

The First World War ended in November 1918. But the situation did not end simply with contraction of the war-driven demand, falling prices and the collapse of the boom. Beginning in the spring of 1919, after the armistice was signed, speculation based on nothing more than optimistic predictions of European recovery erupted on a global scale. The result was a speculative boom with no basis at all in real demand, and the Japanese economy was embroiled in it as well. The enterprise groups led by the four heroic figures introduced above were no exception: responding positively to the boom, they encouraged further expansion of trading and manufacturing activities built up during the war in anticipation of a rosy future.

Eventually, of course, the illusory nature of the post-war boom became obvious. In February 1920, the global speculative bubble burst, and many Japanese enterprises that had hitched a ride on the speculative boom went bankrupt. The enterprises described above were again a striking example. In fact, even after February 1920, Kawasaki and Asano continued to act on an optimistic prognosis and maintained their aggressively positive policies. As a result, the four enterprise groups took a bad fall, with the following results:

• Kuhara Trading: recorded a loss of ¥100 million (against a capital of ¥10 million). The Kuhara *zaibatsu* collapsed, and Kuhara Fusanosuke withdrew from its management.

• The Asano *zaibatsu*: its Oriental Steamship Company's international routes and the ships that sailed them were transferred to NYK (Nippon

Yûsen Kaisha), Japan's largest shipping company, and the company's capital and scale of operations were reduced. Its steel making, shipbuilding and trading companies also subsequently failed.

- The Kawasaki Shipbuilding Company: an oversupply of ships, a legacy of its stock boat production method, a contraction of military demand after the war (Kawasaki had also built naval vessels) and a recession in oceanic shipping led to the company's ceasing operations in 1928. Thanks to support from the navy, it avoided bankruptcy, but its heroic leader at the helm, Matsukata, was deposed.
- Suzuki Shôten: it escaped bankruptcy from major losses suffered after the war, but only by living on bank loans. Its indebtedness to banks built up (as of the end of 1926, it owed one bank, the Bank of Taiwan, ¥ 360 million, compared with paid-up capital of ¥50 million) to the point when Suzuki Shôten finally sank into bankruptcy under its weight in April 1927.

The four cases deserve explanation in detail, but space constraints lead me to stop at these brief descriptions. We should also note that other enterprises also went bankrupt, while others recorded huge losses. Even major *zaibatsu* such as Mitsubishi and Furukawa did not avoid losses in the post-1918 environment.

The end of the wartime boom and collapse of the post-war speculative bubble are not sufficient, however, to explain the failure of major firms. Counter-examples of enterprise groups that sustained stable, sound operations despite facing the same disadvantageous environment also exist: the Mitsui and Sumitomo *zaibatsu*.

The Sumitomo *zaibatsu*, thanks to the cool judgement and prudent decision making of its top managers, did not establish a trading company and avoided losses in the post-war environment. The decision not to set up a trading company was made in January 1920; had Sumitomo decided the other way, it would unquestionably have been embroiled in the collapse of the bubble in the following month.

Mitsui Bussan (the Mitsui *zaibatsu* trading company) was founded in 1876 and had a great depth of experience in international trade. Its top management conducted affairs by consultation among highly trained salaried managers promoted from within, a system developed over the firm's long history. Mitsui Bussan had also built an information-gathering network on a global scale. Armed with those organisational resources, its top salaried managers predicted, first of all, the end of the war five months before the armistice was actually reached, at which point they gave orders to cut back on operations. Moreover, they concluded that the economic boom that began in the spring of 1919 was speculative in nature. Acting with foresight, just as they had in anticipating the end of the war, they kept the brakes on trading. Mitsui Bussan is unique among the major trading companies in not having recorded a single net loss in any year since 1914. After the First World War it surged ahead of its competitors to earn high profits and the nickname 'globe-spanning Mitsui Bussan'.

Discovering new business opportunities and promptly investing in them is the road to high profits. Naturally, attracted by the high profits the pioneer earns, many other enterprises will follow into the same field. The result is economic expansion, growth and prosperity.

The problem in this process lies in the number of followers. If far too many firms join in the search of the same opportunity for high profits, supply will expand to the point of excess, and the marginal return on investments in this opportunity will shrink and vanish. A surfeit of followers can be prevented by the existence of sound enterprises, such as the Mitsui Bussan and Sumitomo *zaibatsu* and their strategy after the First World War. They had well-developed information-gathering networks, a wealth of data, the capacity to exercise cool judgement, and an established process of prudent consultations and discussions instead of dependence on the inspirations of an autocratic leader. The more firms with those qualities there are in the nation's business community, the more its growth can be kept on a stable path. Without them, growth tends to be unstable.

BOOM AND RECESSION IN JAPAN'S ECONOMY SINCE THE 1980S

The Japanese economy, during and immediately after the First World War, experienced instability – swift, steep ups and downs – from an inrush of firms hoping for high profits from wartime demand and post-war reconstruction. More settled, thoughtful large-scale enterprises, such as Mitsui Bussan and the Sumitomo *zaibatsu*, however, performed a stabilising role. In the contemporary Japanese economy, from the 1985 Plaza Agreement until today, no such stabilisers exist. The result is the long drawn-out, grinding recession Japan is currently experiencing.

In utter contrast to the First World War period, the Japanese economy at the end of the twentieth century is managed jointly by the government and business, by the bureaucrats of the central government and managers of business enterprises. Above all, the co-operation between the Ministry of Finance (MoF) and financial institutions is solid. 'Co-operation' may not be quite the right term, for it is not co-operative action between equals; Japan's financial institutions are under the rigid control and direction of the MoF.

This financial system was set up in the late 1930s, when it was necessitated by Japan's war with China, and was maintained with the consent of the Occupation Forces even after Japan's defeat in the Second World War. It functioned to promote Japan's economic recovery and rapid economic growth. Amazingly enough, that same system exists today and is an important feature of the Japanese economy. In fact, it is this MoF-dominated financial system that set off the economic fluctuations Japan has experienced since 1985.

The Plaza Agreement of September 1985 (reached at a meeting of the finance ministers and central bankers of the 'Group of Five' nations at the Plaza Hotel in New York) was to force the yen and Deutschmark to appreciate against the US dollar, on the assumption that undervalued Japanese and West German currencies were injuring the US economy. (The following discussion concerns only the US–Japan side of the situation.)

The United States demanded, first of all, that Japan liberalise its financial system. One argument was that deregulation would strengthen international demand for Japan's currency and thus lead to appreciation of the yen – whether that argument holds up is a question I leave to the economists. Second, the United States demanded that Japan mobilise fiscal measures to expand domestic demand. The attempt was to shield Japan from the deflationary effects of a stronger yen by shifting the Japanese economy to a domestic-demand-driven policy.

Japan's MoF, however, rejected both those demands. In fact, Japan's prime minister, Nakasone Yasuhiro, had promised President Ronald Reagan that Japan would liberalise its financial sector. The MoF, however, rejected liberalisation in 1985, claiming that implementation would be premature. Subsequently the MoF took only fragmentary and intermittent measures towards deregulation, delaying full-scale implementation until Prime Minister Hashimoto Ryûtarô's November 1997 announcement of Japan's Big Bang. There are several conceivable reasons why implementation was delayed, but the most important was that the MoF did not want to give up its controlling authority over Japan's financial sector.

Furthermore, the MoF's rigid attachment to its traditional sound fiscal policies led to its refusal to use fiscal measures to expand domestic demand. So wedded were MoF bureaucrats to that inflexible posture that they even employed the duplicitous artifice of indicating, in statements directed overseas, that they would mobilise fiscal means, while denying it in statements for domestic consumption. Miyazawa Kiichi, who was then minister of finance, was aware of that ruse and tried to counter it, but had to give in to the MoF bureaucrats.

Table 17.1 *Year-end values of equities and real estate in Japan, 1985-9 (in trillion yen)*

	1985	1989	Ratio
Equities	242	890	3.68
Real estate	1,049	2,189	2.09
GDP	320	400	1.25

Source: Japanese government statistics.

Rejecting fiscal means, the MoF employed monetary means to try to expand domestic demand and counter the deflationary effects of the shift to a stronger yen. To do so, it pressured the Bank of Japan to implement ultra-low interest rate policies. Beginning in January 1986, the Bank of Japan reduced the official discount rate five times in about one year, pushing it down to 2.5 per cent. The MoF, furthermore, directed banks to expand their lending aggressively. These moves, combined with the effects of the Bank of Japan's foreign exchange market operations to boost the yen, ensured that the Japanese economy was awash in a flood of excess liquidity.

The business opportunities during the First World War period arose from a market phenomenon, i.e. the war-induced shortage of goods. In contrast, business opportunities since 1985 have arisen from the MoF's dogmatism on policy measures. Under MoF direction, the funds surging out of the banks increased by 10 per cent or more annually, but the money was not invested in productive facilities or used for individual consumption. It was spent on stocks, land, paintings, golf-club memberships and speculative purchases of goods expected to rise in value in the future. The most popular speculative investment was land – just as ships were in the First World War boom.

Between 1986 and 1990, share prices and land prices soared, as can be seen from table 17.1. People have labelled this phenomenon 'Japan's bubble', and many influential voices condemned the unsoundness and risk-taking of what was happening. None the less, the MoF made no efforts to rein in the 'bubble'. In fact, it welcomed it as a means of expanding domestic demand through monetary policy and also of increasing tax revenues.

With the MoF's encouragement, banks actively provided funds for spec-ulating in stocks and real estate. Not wanting to lose out in the competition between banks for profits, the banks aggressively accepted applications for loans without performing adequate credit checks, whether they were ex-tending credit to a real estate company or a construction company to buy land or whether the borrower had land as collateral.

The banks themselves became agents of speculation. They cajoled and badgered owners of small plots of residential land to borrow with their land as collateral and build condominia, making verbal promises that the investment was sure to be profitable. When at length the bubble burst and the borrowers discovered that the prices of condominium units were plummeting and tenants were non-existent, the banks took no responsibility, the lending officer involved often having been transferred to another post. Ignoring complaints from borrowers and asserting that no evidence existed that banks had guaranteed profits to their borrowers, the banks simply acted to recover the funds they had lent by force, as allowed by law. Such behaviour – which amounted to a form of fraud – was widespread.

In March 1990 land prices began to fall. That October, stock prices also plummeted. The bubble had definitely burst. None the less, Japan recorded a 5 per cent economic growth rate that year, and the MoF, taking an optimistic view of prospects for economic expansion, developed no measures to cope with plunging land and stock prices. Meanwhile, speculative investments were failing generally, producing an outbreak of non-performing loans.

What we must remember here is that land prices and stock prices could not continue to rise indefinitely. At some point, prices had to fall and more speculative investments had to fail. But, closing their eyes to what was common knowledge, both individuals and business firms flocked to buy stocks and land – and the banks kept extending them credit, especially if there was land as collateral for loans. Furthermore, after the bubble had burst, the MoF, although its brief included exercising total control over the financial system, developed no measures to deal with the situation.

The example that made the greatest impression concerned what are known in Japanese as the 'jusen', non-banks specialising in housing loans, set up in the 1970s under the MoF's guidance with capital participation of all financial institutions. Bubble-period speculative investments having failed, the *jusen* were saddled with non-performing loans. Over a year after the bubble had burst, between 1991 and 1992, the MoF's on-the-spot investigations of the *jusen* determined that they had ¥6.4 trillion in non-performing loans (38 per cent of their total outstanding loan balance). None the less, the MoF took no measures whatsoever to deal with the situation until August 1995. It simply let it ride.

In the three or four years during which the MoF ignored the *jusen* problem, the non-performing loans in the seven *jusen* companies' portfolios had grown to ¥8.1 trillion. How that happened is a conundrum yet to be solved. But one thing can be said: the MoF, Japan's most prestigious bureaucratic institution, for whatever reason, failed to do what it should have done and when it should have intervened. The result has been the extreme severity of the problems of non-performing loans and recession that are the after-effects of the collapse of the 'bubble'.

LESSONS FROM TWO EXAMPLES: THE PERIODS FROM 1914 TO 1930 AND FROM 1985 TO 2000

The difference between the fluctuations that Japan has experienced in the two periods (from 1914 to 1930 and from 1985 to the present) lies in the fact that, in the latter case the MoF officials, who have wielded huge power over the economy, have repeatedly erred and procrastinated, leading the economy into a severe recession. The MoF rode over the general public's opposition to its plan for disposing of the *jusen* non-performing debt, instead pouring in ¥685 billion in public funds – taxes the people have paid – to rescue the *jusen*. Then, having jumped to the conclusion that, with the *jusen* problem solved, the economy would recover, it immediately forced through increases in indirect taxes, health insurance fees and medical costs, thereby restraining individual consumption. With scandals in its dealings with private sector firms also coming to light, criticism of the MoF grew heated. As a result, it had no energy to spare to make adequate preparations in advance of Prime Minister Hashimoto's November 1996 proclamation of Japan's Big Bang. These blunders have increased the oppressive weight of the recession.

In addition to the MoF's authority, the nature of Japan's large-scale enterprises has become a major destabilising factor in the economy. In the First World War period Japan had large-scale enterprises such as Mitsui Bussan and the Sumitomo *zaibatsu* that did not join the rush to grab large profits but made decisions coolly, based on ample stores of information. At the present time, no such enterprises exist.

Most of those making use of the MoF-led ultra-low interest rate policies and ultra-liquidity to embark on speculating in land and stocks were, not surprisingly, large-scale enterprises in the financial, real estate, construction and related sectors. Not too many major firms in the manufacturing sector were directly caught up in the 'bubble' and its collapse. None the less, some did try to participate in the benefits of the bubble in the form of investing surplus cash in what are called fund investment trusts (investments left up to the discretion of the trust bank, for the duration of the trust period). Even firms that were not involved in the speculation fever were often taken in by the illusion that the bubble-induced boom signified real expansion in the domestic market and, therefore, increased their capital investments. As a result they ended up saddled with excess productive capacity, such as Toyota, Nissan and other car manufacturers, or Hitachi, Matsushita and other electrical equipment manufacturers – the examples are legion.

At any rate, even these large-scale manufacturing firms, with their vaunted world-class organisational capabilities, did not manage to make cool projections and decisions amidst the bubble fever. That lack of the stabilising effect of prudent large-scale enterprises is an extremely important element distinguishing the recent fluctuations from those that occurred during and after the First World War.

CONCLUSION

I should point out what the situations in the two periods we are considering had in common as well as how they differed. What they did have in common is a pattern in which, once a business opportunity arose, a concentrated rush to embrace it was touched off. Instead of setting their own courses, in both cases we see enterprises thronging together to set off down the same course and run it in the same way as all the others. In the First World War case some individual action was involved: some enterprises anticipated the end of the opportunities presented by the wartime boom and scaled back more quickly. In the case of the end of the twentieth century, however, everyone suffered from the 'bubble's' collapse.

A facile explanation for this phenomenon of proceeding in lockstep, not deviating from what the others are doing, is often offered in terms of Japan's uniquely group-oriented culture or a national character in which individualism has yet to take root. It is, however, difficult to provide adequate, data-based support for such explanations.

Moreover, the 'group-oriented, lockstep mentality' hypothesis cannot be accounted for by what I have argued is a key factor in the situation of financial institutions in Japan after the Second World War: their being under the powerful control of the MoF and, in a real sense, not permitted to compete freely. That element of government control did not exist in the first World War case. Furthermore, while the MoF did during the recent 'bubble' give instructions to financial institutions on investing the excess liquidity they were awash in, financial institutions' speculations in stocks and real estate were not controlled. Non-financial-sector firms were even less constrained by MoF interference to embark on speculation. Thus, the existence of the MoF's regulatory powers does not in itself provide a sufficient explanation of behaviour by Japanese enterprises, financial or otherwise.

It is my view that the answer lies in how investment opportunities are perceived. Both before and after the Second World War, investment opportunities in Japan have been remarkably restricted. I mean 'restricted' in a deliberately skewed sense: both enterprises and individuals that had funds to invest perceived only a restricted set of investment opportunities to exist, even though actual opportunities were not limited. Therefore possibly, when a really obvious opportunity did appear – as, for examples, 'shortages in wartime mean rising prices' in the First World War or 'rising stock and land prices' from 1985 on – investors responded with a concentrated rush to take advantage of it.

Why, however, did potential investors regard investment opportunities as restricted? Since the Meiji Restoration (1868), investors in Japan had, under the direction of the central government, concentrated their resources on investing in industries that were needed to achieve economic independence for the nation-state – to make Japan able to stand on its own feet. Those industries were managed by large-scale enterprises that could rely on relatively large, stable demand. They were also given government protection. Japanese investors had a focus on the large and government-connected enterprises which were characteristic of the early stages of industrialisation, during which modern technology and the large-scale factory system were being introduced from the West.

In the twentieth century, as modern industries developed in Japan, the scope of large-scale enterprises expanded. Their growth meant an expansion in investment opportunities, but although the supply of money to be invested was also increasing, the perceived restrictions on investment opportunities as a whole did not cease.

Breaking out of that bind would require altering the pattern by which investors perceived large-scale enterprises and nation-state-oriented industries. Given Japan's almost excessive integrity as a nation-state, however, there was little confidence in the long-term growth and prosperity of industries that were less strictly oriented towards building the nation-state. Smaller manufacturers setting up enterprises to meet the needs of consumers were seen as peripheral to the great task of industrialisation, and the custom of businesses and individuals with capital to invest putting it into such smaller enterprises – the basic form of capitalism in the West – did not take root.

The result was that smaller manufacturers in Japan consistently suffered from a shortage of capital to expand and develop, even though they had superb technologies, as the examples of Japanese textile producers and automobile parts manufacturers reveal. It can be argued that Japan needed to concentrate all available resources on large-scale enterprises, to press ahead rapidly with modernisation and industrialisation. The capital that might have been invested in small manufacturers was absorbed by the government and by large-scale enterprises in the form of taxes, bank deposits, stocks and government bonds, and then used to fund large-scale enterprises. With investment opportunity equated to investing in a large-scale enterprise, the pattern was set. Awareness of what is common knowledge in Europe or the United States, namely that potential investment opportunities existed all around in every aspect of life, did not penetrate.

General acceptance of the concept of 'restricted investment opportunities' meant that when an obvious business opportunity did show up, there was a concerted rush to invest in it, 'in lockstep', among the businesses and individuals with capital they dearly hoped to increase. And, inevitably, the opportunity would disappear, the investments would fail, and businesses and individuals would go bankrupt. That perception of restricted opportunities and concentrated drive to utilise the few that appear is why the fluctuations in the Japanese economy have been so extreme and why its path to economic development has been so unstable. The need for rapid industrialisation from the Meiji era on was related to Japan's powerful integrity as a nation-state, which had taken shape through its long and unbroken history as a nation-state. That, I would conclude, is why the unique pattern of investment that produced the instability and fluctuations described above developed.

NOTES

Since almost none of the sources of the data I relied on in writing this chapter have been translated, introducing them to my colleagues who do not read Japanese would not be meaningful. I have therefore not included them.

The following English-language publications were not direct sources of data for this paper but would be useful references in reading it.

Hidaka Chikage and Kikkawa Takeo, 'The Main Bank System and Corporate Governance in Postwar Japan', Paper presented to the 5th Anglo-Japanese Business History Conference, held in Tokyo, in 1998.

Hidemasa Morikawa, *Zaibatsu: the Rise and Fall of Family Enterprise Groups in Japan* (Tokyo, 1992).

J. Hirschmeir and Yui Tsunchiko, *The Development of Japanese Business, 1600–1975* (Cambridge, Mass., 1975).

PART V

CHAPTER 18

The state and economic growth in Latin America: Brazil and Mexico, nineteenth and early twentieth centuries

Carlos Marichal and Steven Topik

If one were looking for historical evidence to support a liberal economic policy, Brazil and Mexico in the period of 1870–1910 would seem to be good cases. During these four decades Latin America's two most populous countries experienced a deepening of capitalist market relations and substantial economic growth while being guided by liberal statesmen who largely believed in the advantages of *laissez-faire* policies, particularly free trade and foreign investment. Indeed, according to numerous historians, this was the period of economic 'take-off' in the two nations. Conventional wisdom holds that in both cases a fundamental cause lay in dismantling the remnants of colonial mercantilist patrimonial regimes by reducing state intervention.

This chapter will take a different stance by arguing that from the 1870s the states in Brazil and Mexico, guided by pragmatic considerations, in fact played substantial and *growing roles* in forging economic growth and indeed in creating propitious market conditions for domestic and foreign entrepreneurs.[1] Export-led growth in the private sector contributed to the economic transformation of both countries but equally important were active state roles in securing property values, reducing transaction costs through the adoption of new financial and monetary policies and spurring growth of key economic sectors by promotion of state enterprises.

By 1910 governments in these two nations exercised large roles in the export commodity and currency markets as well as in banking, railways and ports. Both states, fully committed to capitalist development, were among the most interventionist in what would after the Second World War be called the 'Third World' – not despite their liberalism but rather because of their liberalism. Demands of the international economy and of diverse domestic actors meant that, even while ostensibly committed to *laissez-faire* liberalism, governing elites in Brazil and Mexico – almost despite themselves – set the groundwork for the consolidation of the interventionist, populist state of subsequent decades.

At the same time, it is important to emphasise that, while we do argue that there was convergence in economic strategies of both states in the late nineteenth and early twentieth century, the respective national experiences differed markedly as to origin, evolution and impact of specific policies. In order to identify parallels as well as contrasts, in this chapter we analyse what we consider to be the key areas in which the state exercised a major role: international trade and commercial policy; the tax systems and tariff policies; external finance and international debt policy; foreign investment and government development strategies; and, finally, monetary and banking systems. It should be noted, however, that in all cases there was a reciprocal dynamic: state regulations and policies had an impact on economic actors and markets, but simultaneously economic forces influenced the development of state administrations and strategies. In fact, it could be argued that it was a particular confluence of international financial and commercial forces in the latter part of the nineteenth century which led states as dissimilar as Brazil and Mexico almost inevitably to adopt parallel economic strategies in various realms.

In sum, by 1900, in what has been described as an early golden age of economic globalisation, Mexican and Brazilian governing elites adopted the discourse of economic liberalisation but, at the same time, pushed the state to actively promote economic development. A century before, in 1800, this result could hardly have been predicted as it would have been difficult to find two societies more different than those of Brazil and Mexico. The explanation of subsequent convergence therefore inevitably makes it essential to briefly consider colonial and post-independence legacies before analysing the trajectories of state and economy in both nations in later decades.

COLONIAL LEGACIES AND THE DIFFERENT PROCESSES OF STATE BUILDING IN NINETEENTH-CENTURY BRAZIL AND MEXICO

The contrasts between the historical experiences of Brazil and Mexico in the prolonged process of *nation building* and state modernisation are striking. They therefore help to illustrate why it is not possible to think of Latin America as one, homogeneous social, economic or political whole. To begin with, their colonial legacies were fundamentally dissimilar. At the beginning of the nineteenth century Brazil was a rural, slave-based plantation society (half the population being of African origin) with an agrarian export economy, a colonial administration and church which were relatively weak in so far as they had little control over the vast territories under their nominal sovereignty. In contrast in late colonial Mexico both state and ecclesiastical administrations were imposing structures which held sway over a predominantly Indian population which resided in 4,000 peasant towns (called 'repúblicas de indios') and in several hundred haciendas; paradoxically, despite the secular importance of agriculture, the Mexican economy depended most heavily on its small but productive silver mining sector which made it the jewel of the Spanish empire.

The result of these differing colonial legacies was that the transition to independent states proved to be very different. Bourbon Mexico, which was similar – in institutional terms – to a European *ancien régime* society composed of estates (nobles, ecclesiastics, merchants, artisans and peasants), operated within the framework of the geographically vast but well-integrated Spanish empire. When the absolutist monarchy of Charles IV was overthrown by Napoleon, the metropolitan crisis led to the breakdown of the colonial administration of New Spain and to a prolonged civil war. The Mexican wars of independence, which lasted from 1810 to 1820, were the bloodiest in the hemisphere and eventually provoked the collapse of the wealthiest and most highly centralised colonial government in Latin America. Subsequently, a federalist republic was established in 1824 but regional forces almost tore the new country apart. Certainly, it would be a mistake to speak of the construction of a solid nation-state in the early nineteenth century in Mexico, which indeed suffered more internal and external conflicts than any other country in the Americas. The United States invasion of 1847 led to loss of huge northern territories and the French occupation (1863–7) – known as the Empire of Maximilian – once again painfully demonstrated the military and financial weakness of the Mexican central administration. Indeed it would not be until the last third of the nineteenth century that the Mexican government consolidated and modernised, making it possible to speak of a true nation-state.

Independence came to Brazil in a very different way. It was in a flotilla of royal ships bound for Brazil that the Portuguese king, João VI, abandoned Portugal in 1808 as a result of the Napoleonic invasion of his country. Rio de Janeiro hence became an imperial capital for more than a decade. On the return of the king to the motherland in 1822, his son Pedro I became the first head of the now-independent imperial Brazilian government, avoiding the wars that plagued most other Latin American states. A restricted, constitutional monarchy proved to be a source of political stability and allowed for the development of a relatively efficient civil administration that benefited from an expanding slave-based coffee export economy. The stability and prosperity of the Brazilian state long stood in sharp relief to the instability and fiscal poverty of the Mexican republic. While Brazil did participate in two regional wars in South America in the first half-century of independence, these did not debilitate but rather strengthened the government, army and navy. Hence, already from mid-century the Brazilian state was able to begin promoting and financing a variety of economic development projects which were essential to subsequent expansion.

None the less, the contrast between the relative stability and unity of the Brazilian imperial government and the instability in the Mexican republic (caused by civil wars and foreign invasions in the decades before 1870) does not explain economic policy. The contraposition provides an essential historical context, but in order to delve more deeply it is essential to analyse and compare specific arenas of economic activity and government regulation.

FROM DIVERGENCE TO CONVERGENCE: EXTERNAL TRADE TRENDS IN THE NINETEENTH CENTURY

During the first three quarters of the nineteenth century the Brazilian and Mexican states faced quite different conditions in their relationship to the world economy, viewed by numerous authors as the key to growth and development.[2] In 1800 Mexico – which then had a population of 5.2 million – enjoyed the highest volume of total trade of all the New World colonies with a value of approximately 60 million pesos per year or US$11.54 per capita.[3] In the same year Brazil had about 3.5 million inhabitants and a trade of some £5.5 million sterling (roughly US$50 million) or approximately US$14 per capita.[4] After ten years of wars of independence in Mexico, trade recovered slowly and actually stagnated for more than half a century. By 1870 Mexico's foreign trade had barely reached US$75 million, a figure that indicates the extremely slow growth rates of the external sector of the economy. Meanwhile, population had only reached 9 million inhabitants, indicative of a depressed demographic trend. Brazil, on the other hand, grew faster: its foreign trade had tripled by 1870 (standing at about US$150 million) and therefore was now twice Mexico's, while the Brazilian population also grew faster, having surpassed 10 million.[5]

One of the reasons that explains the difference between Brazil's substantial export growth as opposed to the very slow expansion of Mexican trade can be found in the type of export commodities. Throughout the first three quarters of the nineteenth century Mexico continued to depend on its classic colonial export, silver, for almost two-thirds of all foreign exchange income. Thus, independence brought few changes to Mexican external trade which not only stagnated but also continued to depend basically on one sector of the economy (silver mining) that produced a high-unit value commodity but which employed few people. Unfortunately after 1873, world demand for silver slackened, causing a 28 per cent drop in price. By 1888 Mexico had relinquished her previously unchallenged position as the world's greatest silver producer to the United States.

One of the keys to the economic success in subsequent decades would be the ability to diversify away from dependence on silver. Silver declined from 71 per cent of total exports in 1880 to 29 per cent in 1910 as industrial ores (such as copper and lead) and agricultural goods (such as henequen and coffee) took up the slack.[6] But this forced diversification was a mixed blessing. In the 1890s, in particular, the fall in the price of silver weakened Mexico's terms of trade, undercut foreign credit and sharply restricted government revenues. Railway construction ground almost to a halt, and there was a combined agrarian and financial crisis in 1893, which led to restrained foreign borrowing and limited state spending. And it would not be until the turn of the century, as the Mexican export economy again picked up speed, that foreign investment flows and loans were renewed. At the same time, the continuing crisis of silver mining was dramatically underlined by the adoption of the gold standard in 1905.

In contrast to Mexico, in the decades immediately following independence Brazil's external sector consistently prospered through its ability to profit from growing world demand and high prices for tropical luxuries and industrial raw materials. These trends were particularly noticeable as international commerce grew with unprecedented and unimagined speed after 1840. Brazil was able to outcompete the rest of the world in two of the most dynamic and sought-after products in the world economy: coffee and rubber.[7] Thus, even though all of Latin America combined provided only 3.4 per cent of world commerce in 1889, Brazil dominated two important markets, furnishing half of the coffee and 90 per cent of all rubber.[8] Together these two commodities accounted for three-quarters of the country's shipments abroad.[9]

The divergent paths followed by the two countries after independence meant that for a half-century Brazil benefited from a cosmopolitan export economy while Mexico failed to fully enjoy the commercial boom brought on by the industrial revolution. By the last quarter of the century, however, the trajectories of both economies were moving towards convergence because of Mexican export diversification. From the 1870s Mexico's exports accelerated while Brazil experienced a slump in the 1880s. Between 1888 and 1910 real exports of both nations grew rapidly; Mexico's exports expanded 150 per cent and Brazil's 178 per cent. None the less, by 1910 the two economies were still at quite different levels. Although foreign trade represented about 18 per cent of GDP in both countries, Brazil still had more than twice Mexico's total exports and 43 per cent more in per capita terms.[10]

The greater dynamism of its export economy allowed Brazil's per capita income to be perhaps 40 per cent greater than Mexico's in 1888. While the roughly US$38 (in current prices) that the average Brazilian earned a year was tiny by United States or Western European standards, it was quite substantial compared with most of the world. It is doubtful that any other 'Third World' country, with the exception of the three Southern Cone countries and Cuba, surpassed this figure.[11] In terms of per capita income Brazil was about at the level of some Eastern European countries such as Hungary and Russia and considerably ahead of the Ottoman empire and Japan. By 1910, Brazilian income per capita had almost doubled. Meanwhile, although Mexico's GDP had increased, on a per capita basis it was still 40 per cent less than Brazil. This was striking testimony to the material difference the early nineteenth century had made as Mexico and Brazil now switched places in terms of wealth while converging in economic policy.

TAXATION POLICY: A SIMILAR RELIANCE ON TRADE

Throughout the nineteenth century and up until 1930, international commerce provided the lifeblood of both regimes. Both states had turned to taxing foreign commerce after independence because they had been forced by their liberal revolutions to abandon mercantilist state monopolies and enterprises, which had formerly contributed large amounts to the treasury. For both national governments, with underdeveloped bureaucratic apparatuses, international trade was the easiest source to tax since import and export taxes merely required the establishment of customs houses in ports and on the land frontiers. Moreover, the goods assessed had knowable value (unlike much land or subsistence production), and their owners had liquid funds with which to pay and could pass the cost on to the final consumers.

Thus, throughout most of the nineteenth century, the treasuries of Mexico City and Rio de Janeiro both earned between half and two-thirds of their revenue from import and export duties. Reliance on international commerce to pay for the machinery of government prevented adoption of a complete free trade policy since the state's interest in collecting revenue was more important than maintaining the purity of the principal of comparative advantage. At the same time, duties could not be prohibitively high on important commodities or else goods would cease entering and customs income would decline drastically.

In addition to circumscribing tariff policy, indirect taxes on external trade had the additional drawback, from a political economic perspective, of taxing the most economically active and efficient producers, i.e. exporters, while leaving relatively untouched subsistence and self-sufficient producers. It was a taxation policy based on convenience and fiscal exigencies, not a means of stimulating development. Indeed the respective governments' abilities to collect sufficient revenue by attacking foreign commerce allowed them to avoid measures that would have required fiscal reform and possibly significant political reforms. The emphasis on taxing international trade rather than land or capital also brings into question the extent to which the landowning oligarchy crafted state policy. But, at the same time, and perhaps paradoxically, it is clear that by making public revenues rely so heavily on foreign trade, both the Brazilian and Mexican states became inextricably wedded to export-led models of growth.

The collection of customs and export duties reveals the greater extractive efficiency of the Brazilian state. The Brazilian central government in 1888 had perhaps 2.5 times the per capita income of the Mexican federal treasury and three times the global income. The comparative prosperity of the Rio treasury was not simply a result of slicing from a larger pie; tax agents took a second helping of that larger pie: the Brazilian administration absorbed about 15 to 24 per cent of GNP (typically pre-industrialised states took 10 to 15 per cent of the national product) while Mexico stood at only half that, 7.5 per cent.[12]

The Mexican government had much greater difficulties during the first three quarters of the nineteenth century in fully asserting its legitimacy and capacity to collect taxes nationwide, which is, after all, one of the most distinguishing marks of sovereignty. Tax collection cost approximately 10 per cent of revenues – a fairly high figure – but in addition the system had great leakage. This was closely related to the fact that Mexico also faced a greater propensity to smuggle because of porous, extended borders. The Atlantic and Pacific coasts as well as the extremely long frontier with the United States were open to contraband trade while in Brazil commerce could reach significant population centres only through the Atlantic seaboard. To discourage contraband, Mexican authorities had to charge lower duties.

Consequently, Mexico's duties reached only 30 per cent of imports in 1888 even though the state was in desperate need of more funds.[13] Brazil's import duties stood at 46 per cent of total imports.[14]

A comparison of tariff policies suggests, however, that after the turn of the century, there emerged some broad similarities with regards to state tariff policies, particularly as a result of protectionist policies applied to stimulate the burgeoning textile industries in both nations. According to Stanley Stein, in Brazil the period after the establishment of the new tariff of 1900 could be considered the 'Golden Age' of protection in that country, a fact that would seem to be confirmed by the doubling of domestic Brazilian textile production at a time of intensified international competition in that key manufacturing sector.[15] In Mexico tariff rates were raised for many manufactured goods in 1892, 1893 and 1896, although effective protection tended to decline because of the fall in value of the silver peso. However, after 1902 imports began to be appraised in their silver currency value and this – together with another customs revision in 1906 – caused the protection level to rise by one-third. By 1909 a US Congressional investigator reported that the Mexican tariff on cotton goods was one of the highest in the entire world.[16]

Overall, by 1910 real per capita federal government income in Brazil was still twice Mexico's total. Considering that the Brazilian state was decentralising, with states capturing an ever greater share of public revenues (from 19 per cent in 1863 to 27 per cent in 1886 to 39 per cent in 1907–10), while Mexico was centralising (states and municipalities went from 38 per cent of total revenues in 1895–9 to 31 per cent in 1903–6), it is surprising to see the Brazilian federal government so much richer than the Mexican.[17] This is related to the fact that Brazil became ever more dependent on international trade. Import duties, which had supplied 52.3 per cent of federal revenues in Brazil in 1890, rose to 64.8 per cent in 1910 while they fell in Mexico from 55 per cent to 43.7 per cent over the same years. It would seem that, at least by some measures, state building and export orientation were compatible.

BRAZILIAN COMMODITY REGULATION VERSUS MEXICAN
LAISSEZ-FAIRE

The importance of international trade made both economies subject to the impact of fluctuating world prices, but Brazil was particularly vulnerable. This is reflected in the fact that far more workers, probably two to three times as many, were directly employed in Brazil's coffee and sugar plantations and rubber fields than in Mexico's mines.[18] As a result, the Brazilian government was obliged to take an interest in the regulation of the export economy's cycles.

The best-known example of the Brazilian government's actions was the defence of the price of coffee. Beginning with the valorisation of coffee in 1906 and ending up with the Institute for the Permanent Defence of Coffee in the 1920s and finally the Departamento Nacional de Café in 1933, the Brazilian federal and state governments came to finance much of the world's coffee trade, and hold most of its visible stocks. Coffee regulation thus set the precedent that OPEC and other raw material producers would later follow. It also transformed the Brazilian state's role in the domestic economy. By the end of the First Republic in 1930 the Brazilian state was responsible for much of the finance, warehousing, transportation and sales of coffee and controlled one of the world's largest commodity markets.[19] As we shall see, the defence of coffee impelled the state to intervene in monetary and financial markets and oversee the transportation infrastructure.

Mexico did not intervene as effectively in export markets. Most of its agricultural and forest exports such as rubber, coffee and chicle occupied either a small share of the world market or, as with vanilla and chicle, small markets. State interventions were not promising under these conditions. In the case of Mexico's other major agricultural export, henequen, the lack of co-ordination between political leaders in the nation's capital and the Yucatan economic elite, which owned the plantations, led state officials to seemingly conspire with foreign importers, such as the US International Harvester Company, to drive *down* the price of henequen rather than, as in coffee, prop it up.[20]

Among mineral exports, Mexican copper and lead represented a growing percentage of world production, but nothing comparable to Brazilian coffee, and any attempt to manipulate the market in these commodities was condemned beforehand to failure. Even in the one market in which Mexico truly competed well, that of silver production, conditions were not appropriate for state action. The United States had surpassed Mexico as the leading world silver producer in the 1870s. Moreover, for domestic and international political reasons, the USA and other countries traditionally on a bimetallic standard switched to the gold standard in the last quarter of the nineteenth century. And, although Mexico joined with the USA and China (the world's largest silver consumer for coinage) in various international conferences designed to attempt to stabilise the world prices of silver, they had limited success.[21]

INTERNATIONAL DEBT POLICY: THE STATE'S ROLE IN
ATTRACTING FOREIGN CAPITAL

As we have seen there were broad similarities in the tax policies of Brazil
and Mexico but important differences in commodity regulation during the
nineteenth and early twentieth centuries. If we look now to their experience
with regard to foreign debt it is possible to conclude that while for decades
policies were radically different, by the turn of the century finance ministers
in both countries came to adopt almost identical strategies and discourses.

Brazil was long considered by foreign bankers to be the most credit-
worthy of Latin American nations. From the time of independence, the
imperial government of Brazil turned to London to borrow funds, beginning with two loans in 1824 and 1825, followed by additional loans in
the 1860s, 1870s and 1880s.[22] The respect of European bankers for Brazil's
monarchy, which punctually repaid loans (largely because of the capacity
of Rio's tax collectors to collect a steady and large stream of taxes), was
sufficient to allow for loans even at times of distress. Brazil's prospering export economy produced impressive trade surpluses, which averaged US$5.8
million annually in 1886–90. With increased trade and customs revenues,
European capitalists were generous; they showered Brazil with more overseas loans than any of its Latin American neighbours, except Argentina.
Consequently, its foreign debt in 1888 was one of the largest in the Third
World, US$136 million. This amount seems insignificant by today's gar-
gantuan standards. But it may have represented the equivalent of five or six
years of national savings for Brazil.[23]

Following the domestic financial crisis of the early 1890s known as the
'encilhamento', foreign bankers – led by N.M. Rothschild and Sons of
London – decided to support the global restructuring of Brazilian foreign
debt. The 1898 Funding Loan allowed the Brazilian republic – after a decade
of unorthodox monetary policies and foreign discredit – to return to or-
thodox policies. Indeed, the Brazilian treasury enjoyed the double good
fortune of earning greater income at home while at the same time being a
welcomed guest in the financial markets of London and the Continent. By
1910 the foreign debt had grown more than fourfold to US$627 million.
Because of a long record of punctually repaying the loans and its close relationship to the House of N.M. Rothschild of London, Brazil was able to
secure loans on terms comparable to those for European borrowers at 4.5 to
5 per cent interest and discount rates of only 3 to 5 per cent.[24]

The option to obtain funds abroad permitted politicians some freedom
of manoeuvre *vis-à-vis* civil society since funds were readily available that

did not require the immediate acquiescence of taxpayers. Moreover for both administrative and political reasons, abruptly raising taxes internally was hardly an option. Thus overseas loans strengthened the central government's relative autonomy from civil society (before 1888 no province or municipality borrowed abroad) while at the same time increasing its dependence on foreign lenders. The demands of servicing the foreign debt, however, circumscribed monetary, fiscal and tariff policy. European capitalists' willingness to open their wallets to the Brazilian finance minister afforded him the resources for some economic innovations, but mostly permitted him to cover current administrative expenses and the servicing of previous loans. In 1890, 61 per cent of the federal budget was spent on administrative costs and a quarter on debt (foreign and internal) payments. That left only 11 per cent for investments and another 4 per cent for transfer payments.[25] By 1910 administration had fallen a little to 51.3 per cent of spending while investments grew somewhat to 18.2 per cent.

In stark contrast to Brazil, the failure of debt policies in Mexico was intimately related to the fact that for half a century it was a militarily weak, politically unstable and debt-ridden state. As early as 1828 Mexico suspended payments on its early 1824 and 1825 loans and did not renew debt service for decades. In 1862 the non-payment of the old English debt and the infamous 'Jecker' bonds provided the excuse for intervention by a tripartite European military force, followed by occupation of Mexico by 30,000 French troops. After the collapse of the French-supported Mexican empire of Archduke Maximilian in 1867, President Benito Juárez once again placed a moratorium on debt repayment. All these events made Mexico an international pariah for foreign bankers during much of the nineteenth century.[26] And this was not strange considering the fact that there was, in fact, an effective suspension of payments on the early British loans for six entire decades (from 1828 to 1886), the longest moratorium of any nation in modern history.

Only in the 1880s did the Mexican government begin to restore its credit by reaching an agreement with British bondholders in 1886 and then organising the great £10.5 million conversion loan of 1888. The latter loan 'met with great success' by pledging considerable guarantees and granting a 21.5 per cent discount.[27] Not only past history, but continuing trade deficits (which averaged US$3.5 million in the 1880s) tarnished Mexico's credit. In 1888 Mexico's foreign debt stood at US$70.8 million, about one-half of Brazil's. But because of lower exports, it required a marginally larger share of national exports to service it. Debt repayment was momentarily less important for the Mexican treasury because some debts were still under negotiation and not being repaid. Hence debt servicing only consumed 11 per cent of the budget. That total jumped to one-quarter of the budget once debt servicing was normalised two years later and remained at about that level for the next two decades, approximately the same share as in Brazil. Increasingly after 1890, foreign loans were contracted not just to refinance former debt but to finance building projects such as the Tehuantepec railway and port, the port at Veracruz and the draining of Mexico City. Thus while they were not listed as capital investments, in good part they truly were and therefore reflected growing state participation in the economy.

Convergence between Brazilian and Mexican foreign debt policy became manifest at the end of the century as shown by a comparison of two major and almost simultaneous financial operations: the Brazilian Gold Conversion Loan of 1898 and the Mexican Gold Conversion Loan of 1899. In both cases, the bulk of outstanding foreign debts were converted into 4 per cent gold bonds which allowed for substantial savings but also paved the way towards subsequent adoption of the gold standard, as we shall later see.

THE STATE-LED DRIVE TO ATTRACT FOREIGN DIRECT INVESTMENT

Contrary to some arguments in the traditional 'dependency' literature, it is our view that the adoption of a debt policy consistent with the interests of foreign investors and bankers was also essential to attracting foreign direct investments. In this regard, the financial policies of the states were important instruments in attracting foreign capital not only for the public but also for the private sectors. This can be judged by reviewing some data on foreign direct investment in both countries.[28]

Brazil and Mexico would become two of the largest recipients of foreign capital in the world. Estimates for foreign investment are notoriously unreliable. Foreign long-term investment in Brazil was probably between US$300 million and US$400 million in 1888, probably five-sixths of it coming through London (though often held by continental investors). Different estimates for Mexico put the total at between US$250 million and US$500 million.[29] North Americans and Englishmen controlled most of Mexico's major railways and a great number of its mines. Wholesale commerce fell to German, French and Spanish merchants who soon exercised a dominant role in the first banks. The French and Spanish dominated Mexico's largest bank, the Banco Nacional de México, while British and later French investors held major stakes in the Banco de Londres y México.

Foreign capital also began to be invested in agriculture, land and public utilities, although not yet on a large scale. If we estimate gross national and gross domestic capital stock by applying Simon Kuznet's calculation it generally equalled between 11 and 22 per cent of GNP for developed nineteenth-century European countries. However, he recognises that in developing countries, before they industrialised, the ratio was considerably lower, maybe only 2 per cent. Since Mexico in 1888 was closer to an *ancien régime* than an industrialising economy, we can estimate foreign capital's share of total capital to be quite possibly greater than one-third.[30]

In the years 1897–1910, more interventionist, nationalistic state policy transformed the nature of foreign investment in Mexico. After 1900 European investments continued but were dwarfed by the inflow of North American capital. The new funds were placed mostly by large corporations in direct investments, being impelled by the banking and industrial cartels that came to dominate the United States economy. Until the depression of 1907, Mexico became a major battleground for international finance capital, receiving half of all US foreign portfolio investment and trailing only Argentina as the largest recipient of foreign investment in the Third World with between US$1.7 billion and $2 billion.[31] Nowhere else in this period did such prominent members of the haute bourgeoisie as the French and British Rothschilds, the Guggenheims, the Speyers, J.P. Morgan, Bleichroeder, and John D. and William Rockefeller invest risk capital on a large scale. Now, state policy privileged national and international financiers and large-scale corporations rather than bourgeois entrepreneurs as formerly and sought, at the same time, to increase central control of the economy.

Foreign investors also took great interest in Brazil, although almost exclusively European, principally British, French, German and Belgian. Government borrowing was the largest single share of external investment, comprising more than a third but less than half of the total which reached almost £350 million by 1914 (US$1.7 billion).[32] Railways were the major recipient of foreign risk capital but most of the main coffee-carrying lines belonged to Brazilians or the government. There were several sizeable British-owned mines, but nothing on the scale of Mexico. French and English capitalists initiated several ill-fated central sugar mills as well. British and Portuguese investors controlled several of the leading banks and together with Germans and French dominated wholesale commerce. Indeed, although foreigners were instrumental in financing exports through commercial credit, they rarely invested directly in export production.[33] At the turn of the century foreign direct investment in Mexico was somewhat greater than in Brazil (and much more important in relation to GDP) and would remain so until 1910 when the Mexican Revolution erupted.

So far we have argued that in the last quarter of the nineteenth century it is possible to observe a noticeable convergence in the economic roles of the central government in Mexico and Brazil with regard to integration into the world economy, including the promotion of export economies, the negotiation of public loans with foreign bankers and the attraction of a growing stream of foreign direct investment. But national political elites clearly also had the goal of promoting national integration and economic development. Another way to put this is that politicians and bureaucrats sought to defend national sovereignty and the country's position in the world economy, while at the same time encouraging increased and interlinked capital accumulation without jeopardising the functioning of a specific class-based social system. By the last part of the nineteenth century state building, nation building and economic development had become complementary projects.

The forging of capitalist relations and national markets were primary goals. In this regard, it should be kept in mind that despite centuries-long incorporation into the world economy and the fundamental importance of the export sectors, Brazil and Mexico still had in large part pre-industrial self-sufficient economies. After all, 70 to 80 per cent of economic activity was outside of international trade.[34] Internal markets in both countries were dynamic but had quite different structures. Differing urbanisation patterns meant that Mexico had thriving local markets, some important regional markets and international markets but no national market. Movement from one region to another, especially before the railway, was difficult. Brazil, on the other hand, had less vigorous local markets, but healthy regional ones. However, the locations of Brazil's major cities reflected their dependence on the international economy: all of Brazil's ten largest cities were ports except São Paulo, which stood at the railhead connecting the plateau to the port of Santos. This coastal and outward-looking structure of the largest Brazilian markets also implied that regional markets could be linked by relatively inexpensive maritime freight. In contrast, in Mexico the only port among the ten largest cities was Veracruz, a fact that perhaps explains why its merchant marine was remarkably underdeveloped.

In terms of integration of internal markets probably the single most important vehicle for tying together the peoples of Brazil and Mexico was the railway. Brazil's first line was built in 1854. Tellingly, it connected the court with the emperor's summer residence in the mountain city of Petropolis. In the 1860s and 1870s railways of greater economic import began snaking out from the major port cities of Recife, Salvador, Rio de Janeiro and Santos in search of exports in the hinterlands. The 1880s saw the most intense railroad building of the nineteenth century and the second greatest decade of construction in Brazil's history. By 1888 Brazil had the largest rail system in Latin America. Its 9,583 kilometres of track ranked it twelfth in the world behind nine European and North American countries and two colonies: India and Australia. It had a larger rail system than all Africa combined and twice the size of all Asia outside of India.[35]

Surprisingly, fully one-third of the Brazilian system was state owned, the lines often being initiated and planned by the central government. None the less, in 1888 nowhere had rail moved more than two hundred miles from the coast. The various regions of the country also had not been integrated. The unplanned and dispersed nature of the network was mitigated by the fact that the various hubs were ports (or in the case of São Paulo, connected to the port of Santos). Consequently coastal shipping lines, which also expanded enormously in the 1880s, linked them. As a result, total Brazilian shipping, coastal and overseas, grew more than 400 per cent between 1843 and 1883 while exports fell from one-quarter of that freight to 16 per cent.[36] Domestic maritime trade was growing faster than international shipping.[37]

After 1889 railways grew rapidly so that in 1910 the national total was 21,325 kilometres. Initially that growth was due to foreign companies which not only established new companies, but also took over some important state lines. But economic crises in the beginning of the twentieth century, provoked by the fall of the price of coffee, led the federal government, and to a lesser degree, provincial governments, to take over and run bankrupt companies. By 1930 two-thirds of the national system was publicly owned and half publicly run.[38] The system integrated the country as the great majority of the traffic was for internal consumption, not exports, and ran through the population centres.

Mexico was slower in creating a modern transport system. Before 1880 only one important line was built, connecting Mexico City and Veracruz; begun under Maximilian by Mexican and British capitalists it was concluded in 1873 and facilitated the prosperous import/export trade conducted through Veracruz but did not contribute markedly to the expansion of internal markets. This situation changed in the early 1880s as furious building of track from the United States south led to the establishment of three great trunk lines linking Mexico to the dynamic economy of its northern neighbour. Thus, by 1888 Mexico had almost as large a railway system as Brazil.

In contrast to Brazil, however, none of the early railway lines in Mexico was owned by the government. The Mexican authorities preferred to adopt a system of state financial subsidies to stimulate foreign investors (United States and British) to build the principal lines. The complex and expensive system of subsidies – among other factors – led to repeated fiscal and financial crises in 1885, 1890 and 1893, but they did contribute to the completion of a broad and modern transport network which stimulated both foreign trade and the expansion of domestic markets. In a classic study, John Coatsworth calculated that half of the freight on the major railways was international commerce but recent studies have shown that a greater share was in fact for domestic purposes.[39]

In the 1890s the Mexican government began to participate more directly in the promotion of railways and other major infrastructure projects. Large contracts were signed preferentially with one great British engineering firm, headed by the entrepreneur Sir Weetman Pearson, which took charge of constructing the railway across the isthmus of Tehuantepec, the modernisation of the port of Veracruz and the huge drainage works in the Central Valley of Mexico City.[40] In all these cases, the Mexican government issued a steady stream of silver bonds to the contractors in order to guarantee the work and thereby ended up holding a major stake in all of these great public works projects.

Thus despite an initial preference for indirect participation in railways, the Mexican state gradually came to take a more direct interest, the most important event being the nationalisation in 1908 of several of the principal trunk lines connecting Mexico to the United States. Historians have debated the reasons for this early nationalisation and have placed emphasis on the financial distress of foreign companies, which apparently drove the state into rail ownership. But concern with US rail trusts impinging on national sovereignty and the need to integrate the country to mobilise troops quickly were also key motives in the nationalisation.

Despite a similar increase in the role of the state in railways, a sector which – it should be emphasised – contained the largest modern enterprises in both Brazil and Mexico, by 1910 there were important contrasts between the two national rail systems. Despite being close to the same length, Brazil's companies carried twice as much freight and had four times the gross profits.[41] Mexican railways, on the other hand, were high-debt and low-profit enterprises, a fact which was clearly linked to the mountainous topography of the nation and to continuing obstacles to regional integration of markets.

Despite the increasingly activist economic role of the Mexican government particularly in railways and port works, it should also be noted that difficulty in collecting revenue and borrowing on favourable terms severely hindered the state's activities.[42] In a vicious cycle, fiscal poverty undermined the institutional foundations necessary for restoring prosperity. The relatively small cadre of state employees that he could afford to employ shortened Porfirio Diaz's reach from the capital into the distant corners of Mexico. It appears that Mexico had only half Brazil's number of public employees on the national, provincial and local level. And, because of the tradition of violence, over half of the lower-ranking public employees in Mexico were members of the armed forces; in absolute numbers Mexico's soldiers and sailors were double Brazil's military contingent (33,226 to 16,800), leaving a civilian bureaucracy one-quarter the size of that of Brazil.[43] These proportions were reflected in the budgets. The Mexican armed forces consumed 38 per cent of the 1888 federal budget while their Brazilian counterparts took just 18 per cent. This situation, however, reflects the greater tranquility in Brazil rather than a different style of governance since the Brazilian military had previously also dominated spending; it had been responsible for fully 56 per cent of all expenditures between 1835 and 1888.[44] It comes as no surprise, then, that only 5 per cent of the Mexican central government's budget was dedicated to fixed investments in 1888. That translated, in absolute terms, to only one-ninth the amount of central government funds invested in Brazil.[45] That amount almost doubled to 9.2 per cent in 1910, but Brazil's fixed investments' share grew at a similar rate so that the Brazilian state was investing twice as large a share of revenues which, on a per capita basis, were already twice as large.

THE ROLE OF THE STATE IN DOMESTIC MONETARY AND BANKING SYSTEMS

While it is clearly our argument as elaborated so far that the role of the state in Brazil and Mexico became increasingly important from the late nineteenth century in the fields of trade, taxes, debt and economic integration, attention should also be directed to its influence in the realms of the respective monetary systems and early banking structures. Once again, it seems worthwhile emphasising that while divergence was marked in the first three quarters of the nineteenth century, convergence gained strength by the turn of the century, both with regard to the establishment of similar monetary and exchange policies and in the field of banking regulation.

It is often affirmed that money is the emblematic symbol of national sovereignty. In so far as this is true, it would appear that to trace the history of monetary systems can provide an important guideline to political history, or more specifically the history of states. In the case of Latin America this is certainly true, but it should be noted that each of the nations of the subcontinent experienced quite different monetary trajectories after independence. The cases of Mexico and Brazil reflect the diverging trends in the early part of the century.

The monetary system of post-independence Mexico was to all intents and purposes identical to that which had been current during three hundred years of colonial rule. As the leading silver producer in the world, the basis of monetary circulation in Mexico was quite simply silver coin, with a small, complementary volume of copper coin for small transactions. During the colonial period, the minting of silver was a royal privilege, which could only be exercised by the royal mint at Mexico City. After independence, this mint remained important and was under control of the central government, but there also emerged regional mints, which were under the administration of state governments, a fact which is not surprising, given the federal structure of the new republic. None the less, the fundamental determinants of the volume of circulating currency were not government (central or local) but rather the cycles of silver mining production. Thus the 'state' could not effectively regulate monetary circulation despite its claim to monetary sovereignty. And this situation would become increasingly complicated in the 1880s when, at long last, a banking system emerged in Mexico, which meant that, apart from silver coin, paper currency – in the shape of banknotes – also began circulating.

The struggle among various banks in the last decades of the nineteenth century forced the Mexican government to begin to regulate monetary and financial markets, beginning with the Commercial Codes of 1884 and 1889, followed by the National Banking Law of 1897. This law established common rules for the entire banking system and reduced the privileges of the most powerful bank, the Banco Nacional de México, which had served as virtual banker to the government since 1884. Hence, by regulating, the state helped domestic financial markets operate more freely and efficiently.

Brazil offers a noticeable contrast to Mexico with regards to its early monetary history. During the first half of the nineteenth century, the Brazilian economy suffered from a pronounced scarcity of metallic currency except for the small amounts of gold produced in the region of Minas Gerais and the foreign currency obtained from foreign trade. As a result, there was a strong demand for alternative monetary instruments. It was logical that paper money should begin to circulate from an early date, beginning with the creation of the first Latin American bank, the Banco do Brasil, in 1808. After the failure of this early bank in 1828, however, paper currency did not disappear: rather, the government continued to print paper money and also allowed the first private, commercial banks to circulate notes. As a result, Brazil had a rather more complex monetary system than most other Latin American nations at the time.

In the 1860s and 1870s there was a considerable debate in Brazil on the virtues of free banking versus a state monopoly of issue.[46] In fact, the Brazilian state allowed for a curious combination of both in so far as in some years commercial banks were encouraged to issue their banknotes to meet commercial demand, while at other times the state took the dominant role – in conjunction with the new Banco do Brasil – in the issue of paper money to finance public deficits.

In the 1880s and early 1890s an extraordinary economic expansion, accompanied by a banking boom, led to increased monetary expansion and, finally, to a major financial crisis. As a result, by the end of the century the Brazilian political and financial elites had resolved that it was necessary to institute a series of reforms in order to counteract the effects of monetary instability, inflation and unbridled banking rivalry. With the support of British bankers, plans were put into practice to consolidate the public debt (accomplished through the Funding Loan of 1898) and to stabilise and regulate the banking system, basically through the establishment of the reformed Banco do Brasil in 1905. It should be added that although the government participated directly in the bank, this did not conflict with liberalism, as it did not receive any specialised legislated privileges.[47]

As can be seen, broadly similar policies came to be adopted by both the Brazilian and Mexican governments with respect to banking and financial policies. But in addition it should be noted that shortly after the turn of the century, both states decided to adopt a gold exchange standard, which was as close as they could get to a full-fledged gold standard.[48] The Mexican government ratified a monetary reform (1905) which officially recognised the 50 per cent depreciation of the price of silver and effectively demonetised silver to prevent further declines. At the same time, to ensure the repayment of foreign loans taken out to prop up the price of coffee, the Brazilian government established the Caixa de Conversão (1906), which issued convertible notes at better than market rates in return for gold-backed currency.[49] It was thus, at this same point in time, that in both Brazil and Mexico the liberal state affirmed its monetary sovereignty by adopting that pre-eminent symbol of the free market system at the turn of the century, the gold standard.

CONCLUSION

During the first half of the nineteenth century, the direct role of the state in the respective economies of Brazil and Mexico was relatively limited except in the realms of fiscal and public debt policies but, subsequently, in the late nineteenth and early twentieth centuries governments (on national, provincial and even municipal levels) began to take a more active part in a large number of areas. This was related to the increased capacity of the states to act because of a rise in revenues available as the export economies expanded and as a result of access to a larger volume of international capital. However, care should be taken to note that a more activist state, which simultaneously promoted political and economic modernisation, did not imply an abandonment of liberal ideology. On the contrary, from the second half of the nineteenth century down to 1930 (even after the Mexican Revolution), liberalism and the ideal of the parliamentary state were the predominant guideposts of elites in Brazil and Mexico as well as the rest of Latin America.

In summary, states in Brazil and Mexico, while guided by the theory of liberalism, in fact played central roles in economic development. Links to the international economy paradoxically forced some interventionist policies such as participation in commodity markets, tariff protection and nationalisation of the railways. Officials were not driven simply by ideology, and their actions changed over time. National sovereignty and political peace were as compelling as the balance of payments and per capita GNP. Markets did not run on their own; they required states' guidance.

NOTES

Steven Topik would like to thank UC Mexus and the Humanities Center of the University of California, Irvine for funding this research.

1. In the case of Mexico, however, it should be noted that after the outbreak of the revolution in 1910 such market conditions deteriorated dramatically and did not recover until the early 1920s.
2. For example, see Victor Bulmer Thomas, *The Economic History of Latin America* (Cambridge, 1994).

3. The figure is the sum of exports and imports based on statistics provided by the Consulado de Veracruz, Balanza del Comercio Exterior, reproduced in Miguel Lerdo de Tejada, *México en 1856: El Comercio Exterior de México* (1856; repr. Xalapa, 1985).

4. Mircea Buescu, *Evolução Econômica do Brasil* (Rio de Janeiro, 1979), p. 96.

5. Brasil, IBGE, *Séries Estatísticas Retrospectivas*, Vol. I (Rio de Janeiro, 1986), pp. 3, 68.

6. El Colégio de México, *Estadísticas Económicas: Comercio Exterior* (Mexico, 1965), pp. 96, 154, 390, 457, 458.

7. Michael George Mulhall, *Dictionary of Statistics*, 4th edn (London, 1899), pp. 129, 130.

8. Ibid., p. 129.

9. Diretoria Geral de Estatística. *Anuário Estatístico 1939/1940*, (Rio de Janeiro, 1940), p. 89 based on the average for 1886–1890.

10. John H. Coatsworth, 'Economic and Institutional Trajectories in Nineteenth-Century Latin America' in John H. Coatsworth and Alan M. Taylor (eds.), *Latin America and the World Economy Since 1800* (Cambridge, Mass, 1999), pp. 31, 33, 35. Angus Maddison in the *Journal of Economic History*, 43, 1 (1983), 27–41, also finds Brazil overtaking Mexico in the nineteenth century.

11. Paul Bairoch, in *The Economic Development of the Third World since 1900* (Berkeley, 1975), p. 193 shows Latin America's per capita GDP as two-and-a-half times Asia's in 1900 and almost twice Africa's 1960 figure.

12. James Wilkie, in 'Changes in Mexico since 1895,' *Statistical Abstract of Latin America*, Vol. 24 (Los Angeles, 1984), p. 875, using the Banco de Mexico's GDP data, arrives at an even lower 4.5 per cent in 1900. For more data, see Steven Topik, 'The Economic Role of the State in Liberal Regimes: Brazil and Mexico Compared, 1888–1910' in Joseph Love and Nils Jacobsen (eds.), *Guiding the Invisible Hand: Economic Liberalism and the State in Latin America* (Westport, Conn., 1988), pp. 117–44.

13. Calculated from El Colégio de México, *Estadísticas Económicas del Porfiri-ato: Fuerzo de Trabajo y Actividad Económica por Sectores* (Mexico City, 1965), p. 206 and *Estadísticas Económicas del Porfiriato: Estadísticas Comerciales Exterior de México, 1877–1911* (Mexico City, 1965), pp. 205–6.

14. Liberto de Castro Carreira, *História Financeira e Orçamentária do Império no Brasil*, Vol. II (repr. Rio de Janeiro, 1980), passim; DGE, *Anuário Estatística 1939–1940* (repr. Rio de Janeiro, 1980), p. 68.

15. Stanley Stein, *The Brazilian Cotton Manufacture: Textile Enterprise in an Underdeveloped Area* (Cambridge, Mass., 1957), p. 99, and Steven Topik, *The Political Economy of the Brazilian State* (Austin, 1987), p. 142.

16. Daniel Cosío Villegas, *La Cuestion Arancelaria en México* (Mexico, 1932), p. 54; Stephen Haber, *The Industrialization of Mexico, 1890–1940* (Stanford, 1989), p. 39; William A. Graham-Clark, 'Cuba, Mexico, and Central America' in *Cotton Goods in Latin America*, part 1 (Washington, DC: Government Printing Office, 1909), p. 38.

17. M.J.F de Santa-Anna Nery, *Le Brésil en 1889* (Paris, 1889), p. 450; Brazil, DGE, *Anuário Estatístico, 1939–1940*, pp. 1409, 1412, 1418; México, Secretaría de Fomento, *Anuário Estadístico de la República México, 1906* (Mexico City, 1907), pp. 221, 222; Secretaría de Fomento, *Cuadro Sinóptico, Año de 1900* (Mexico City, 1900), pp. 70–3.

18. Estimate calculated from data from Alfredo Ellis Júnior, *A Evolução da Economia Paulista e Suas Causas* (São Paulo, 1937), p. 225. Mexican data from Comision Monetária reported in its *Actas de las Juntas a Ellas Anexos* (Mexico City, 1904), p. 40. According to the Colégio de México, *Estadísticas Económicas del Porfiriato*, p. 131, Mexico in 1898 had 89,072 miners. The state of São Paulo alone had more coffee workers than that.

19. Topik, *The Political Economy of the Brazilian State*, ch. 3. For a comparison of Brazilian and Mexican state roles in export markets – coffee and henequen – see Topik, 'L'état sur le marché: approche comparative du café bresilien et du henequen mexicain', *Annales, Economies, Societies, Civilisations*, 46, 2. (March–April 1991), 429–58.

20. Topik, 'L'état sur le marché'.

21. It was curiously enough the United States that took the lead in proposing an international bimetallic standard as can be seen in *Proceedings of the International Monetary Conference in Paris* (Washington, DC, 1887).

22. For information on Brazilian foreign loans, see appendices in Carlos Marichal, *A Century of Debt Crises in Latin America: From Independence to the Great Depression* (Princeton, 1989).

23. For more on Brazil's foreign debt servicing, see Topik, *The Political Economy of the Brazilian State*.

24. Brazil, Agency Letter Book 4, N.M. Rothschild's archive, London; Castro Carreira, *História Financeira*, vol. II, pp. 714–16. The low discount was 89 per cent in 1883, but the 1875 loan was at 96.5, the 1886 at 95 and the 1888 at 97 per cent.

25. Anníbal Villela and Wilson Suzian, *Política do Governo e Crescimento da Economia Brasileira, 1889–1945* (Rio de Janeiro, 1979), p. 414.

26. On Latin American borrowing, see Marichal, *A Century of Debt Crises*.

27. Council of the Corporation of Foreign Bondholders, *Report for 1888* (London, 1988), p. 112. Apparently the loan did worse in Berlin. German Minister to Mexico Wangenheim wrote to Von Bülow, Mexico, Oct. 1905 (Reichsamt des Innern 4384, Deutsches Zentralarchiv Potsdam) that the interest rate in 1888 was 8.01 per cent and the discount 58.76 per cent.

28. For a compilation of recent studies on the history of foreign investments in Latin America in this period, see Carlos Marichal (ed.), *Las inversiones extranjeras en América Latina, 1850–1930* (Mexico City, 1995).

29. Irving Stone, 'British Direct and Portfolio Investment in Latin America before 1914', *Journal of Economic History*, 39 (Dec. 1979), 695; J. Fred Rippy, *British Investments in Latin America, 1822–1949* (Hamden, 1959), pp. 25, 37, 68; Rippy, *The United States and Mexico* (New York, 1926); *New York Times*, 7 Jan. 1888 and 5 Sept. 1888; Nicolas D'Olwer, 'Las Inversiones Extranjeras', in

Daniel Cosío Villegas (ed.), *Historia Moderna de México* (Mexico City, 1965), pp. 1161–3.

30. Simon Kuznets, 'Capital Formation in Modern Economic Growth (and Some Implications for the Past)' in Kuznets, *Population, Capital, and Growth: Selected Essays* (New York, 1973), pp. 126, 162.

31. *Mexican Herald*, 5 Sept. 1897, p. 1; Barbara Stallings, *Banker to the Third World* (Berkeley, 1987), p. 125; Naomi R. Lamoreaux, *The Great Merger Movement in American Business, 1895–1904* (Cambridge, 1985), p. 1; W. Arthur Lewis, *Growth and Fluctuations, 1870–1913* (London, 1978), p. 163; Jean Bouvier and Rene Girault (eds.), *L'imperialisme français d'avant 1914* (Paris, 1976), pp. 9, 309; Steven Topik, 'The Emergence of Finance Capital in Mexico' in Virginia Guedea and Jaime Rodriguez (eds.), *Five Centuries of Mexican History/México en el medio milenio* (Mexico City, 1992), pp. 227–42.

32. For a detailed analysis, see 'Tableau des principales valeurs brasiliennes' (1914), Paribas Bank Archives, Conteneur 368, vol. 5.

33. Stone, 'British Investment', 695; Rippy, *British Investments*, pp. 25, 37, 68; Marshall Eakin, *British Enterprise in Brazil: the St. John d'el Rey Mining Company and the Morro Velho Gold Mine, 1830–1996* (Durham, N.C., 1989), pp. 17–19. It has been estimated that in 1888 $200 million of British commercial credit was extended to people in Brazil.

34. This is subtracting from the GNP all export and one-half of imports (to compensate for the value added of commerce and transportation).

35. Mulhall, *Dictionary of Statistics*, pp. 495, 496.

36. Calculated from DGE, *Anuário Estatístico, 1939–1940*, pp. 49, 86, 87.

37. We arrived at this conclusion by assuming that imports, whose value accompanied that of exports, also had a relatively steady ratio in terms of weight. It is true that as the price of coffee doubled, the same bulk of coffee purchased twice as much in the way of imports. However, sugar fell 30 per cent in price and imports contained ever greater labour so that their ratio of weight to value declined.

38. Julian Duncan, *Public and Private Operations of Railways in Brazil* (New York, 1932), p. 87.

39. John Coatsworth, *Growth Against Development: the Economic Impact of Railroads in Porfirian Mexico* (De Kalb, Ill., 1981). But see Sandra Kuntz, *Empresa Extranjera y Mercado Interno. El Ferrocarril Central Mexicano, 1880–1907*, (Mexico City, 1995).

40. Priscilla Connolly, *Weetman Pearson: el Contratista de Don Porfirio* (Mexico City, 1998).

41. Mulhall, *Dictionary of Statistics*, p. 496.

42. See Marcello Carmagnani, *Mercado y Estado, Historia de la Hacienda Publica en México, 1857–1910* (Mexico, 1994), passim.

43. Peter Smith, *The Labyrinths of Power* (Princeton, 1979), p. 41, gives 71,834, something more than the 63,777 found in *Secretaria de Fomento, Curadro Sinoptico y Estadísticao de la Republica Mexicana ... ano de 1900* (Mexico City, 1901), p. 61 and the 59,553 in 1895 in *El Colegio de México, Estadísticas Económicas*

del Porfiriato: Fuerza de Trabajo y Actividad por Sectores, 1877–1911 (n.p., n.d.), pp. 54, 56. For Brazil, we arrived at 129,000 (Contadoria Geral da República, *Resumo do Orçamento da Receita e Despeza para o Exercício de 1893*; [Rio de Janeiro, 1893]; the Estrada de Ferro Central do Brasil, *Relatório, 1893* (Rio de Janeiro, 1893) table D1; and Topik, *Political Economy*, p. 21. The ratio between the two was probably closer in 1888 because the Brazilian state bureaucracy grew by probably one-third in the subsequent twelve years while there is evidence that the Mexican staff stagnated. The Brazilian armed forces in 1888, according to José Murilo de Carvalho, 'As Forças Armadas na Premeira República', in Boris Fausto (ed.), *Historia Geral da Civilizaçaõ Brasileira*, Vol. IX (Rio de Janeiro, 1977), p. 201, was 16,800 while Mexico's in 1895 was 33,226.

44. Castro Carreira, *História Financeira*, Vol. II, pp. 614, 657; Carlos San Juan Victoria and Salvador Velásquez Ramírez, 'El Estado y las Políticas Económicas en el Porfiriato' in Ciro Cardoso (ed.), *México en el Siglo XIX (1821–1920); Historia Económica y de la Estructura Social* (Mexico City, 1980), p. 308.

45. El Colégio de México, *Estadísticas Económicas del Porfiriato: Fuerzo de Trabajo* pp. 305, 311, 323. Michael J. Twomey, 'Patterns of Foreign Investment in Latin America in the Twentieth Century' in Coatsworth and Taylor (eds.), *Latin America and the World Economy*, p. 123 shows that Brazil not only had substantially more foreign investment than did Mexico in 1913–14, but a much greater share of it was portfolio capital.

46. For a discussion of banking debates in Brazil and other Latin American nations at mid-century, see Carlos Marichal and Pedro Tedde (eds.), *La Formación de la Banca Central en América Latina: Antecedentes Históricos*, Vol. I. (Madrid, 1994), pp. 131–50.

47. Topik, *The Political Economy of the Brazilian State*, p. 40.

48. For a brief discussion, see Carlos Marichal and Daniel Diaz, 'The Origins of Central Banking in Latin America, 1900–1930' in Jaime Reis (ed.), *The Origins of Central Banking: Essays in Comparative Economic History* (Cambridge, in press).

49. Steven Topik, 'Los Lazos que Ataron: Brasil y Méjico en la Economia Mundial, 1880–1910' in *America Desarrollo y Dependencia*, Diputación Provincial de Granada and the Sociedad de Historiadores Mexicanistas (Granada, Spain, 1990), pp. 181–215.

CHAPTER 19

Building the Brazilian nation-state: from colony to globalisation

Domingos A. Giroletti

The Brazilian state played an essential role in the formation of its own country. In fact, Brazil is a creation of the Portuguese state. Our territorial unit is also a creation of the state. The state articulated all efforts to face the challenge of industrialisation and to make it possible. Once a basic productive infrastructure had been installed, favourable conditions were created for the completion of the construction of a national social plan.

Celso Furtado.[1]

INTRODUCTION

In Brazil, the building of a nation-state, as an exogenous process, began as a result of the emergence of European states, capitalist world expansion and colonial conquest after the great discoveries. The two constitutive elements of the modern state, territory and people,[2] were constructed from outside until its independence. Brazil's demographic growth as a Portuguese colony followed the occupation process and the settlement and exploration of its territory. Production of sugar was the *raison d'être* of the economy leading to the growth of population in the sixteenth and seventeenth centuries in the north and north-east regions. The discovery of gold and other precious metals was the main factor promoting population growth in the central hinterlands towards the west during the eighteenth century.[3]

Mineral exploitation was an important factor in building Brazilian unity as a continental state. The rush for gold and other precious metals in Minas Gerais (1690 to 1760) and Goiás and Mato Grosso made these the economic powerhouse in the hinterland of Brazil. In consequence there was a massive shift of population from São Paulo, Bahia and Pernambuco to the mineral extraction areas. These transformations can be evaluated by the amount of gold produced in Brazil that represented around 50 per cent of total world production during the eighteenth century.[4] Gold and diamond exploration created a large internal market leading to economic integration among all

Brazilian regions. Gold and precious metal production stimulated trade as it could be used as currency; its exploitation led to the growth of towns in Minas Gerais and other mining provinces, as well as the development of craftsmanship, manufactured products and the organisation of commerce and banking. Rio de Janeiro grew in importance as a port and as the new capital.[5]

Portuguese government administration was transferred from Salvador to Rio de Janeiro in 1763 in order to protect the gold mines and trade from smuggling and foreign infiltration. During the peak of the gold cycle, between 1690 and 1776, the Brazilian population increased more than sixfold, from 300,000 to 1.9 million inhabitants, with the main concentration in Minas Gerais, Rio de Janeiro and São Paulo. Minas Gerais was the centre of the largest nationalist and independence movement in Brazil, the 'Inconfidência Mineira' (1789). Here, as everywhere else, political unification has a dialectical relation with market formation. Market unification reinforces the consolidation of political power and vice versa.

The transfer of the Portuguese court to Brazil in 1808, making Rio de Janeiro the capital city of the whole Portuguese empire, furthered the building of the Brazilian state. As liberal measures were introduced (opening the Brazilian ports to direct trade with other countries, revoking restrictions on production and trade in the colony and lifting restrictions on the establishment of manufacturing enterprises, etc.), Brazilian colonial ties with Portugal were, in practice, severed. Improvements in urban infrastructure and facilities consequent upon the presence of the Portuguese royal family in Rio de Janeiro stimulated growth, and reinforced its political position as the capital city and as the main focus of economic activity.[6] All these changes helped set the scene for Brazil to become an independent state in 1822. D. João VI returned to Portugal in 1821, leaving his son D. Pedro I as the regent prince of Brazil. The proclamation of independence in 1822 was a peaceful movement led by the regent prince with the support of the elite and without popular participation. The development of Brazilian sovereignty came after independence as an endogenous process.

The three decades following independence constituted the most crucial period in the consolidation of Brazil's state power: the central government had to approve the Brazilian Constitution (1824), create the state structure, accommodate the internal conflicts between Portuguese and Brazilians, transfer the government (1831) from D. Pedro I to his son, D. Pedro II, and overcome several serious provincial revolts in order to stabilise the new monarchy.[7] By 1845 the Brazilian unitary state and the imperial government had already consolidated its power. Externally the Brazilian government negotiated its independence between 1824 and 1826. At same time, Brazil defined its external boundaries with neighbouring countries, a task carried on during the empire and peacefully concluded before the First World War.

The following sections describe the role of economic and political processes in the building of the Brazilian state with special emphasis on more recent periods. In conclusion, the chapter considers some aspects of present dilemmas in completing the Brazilian nation-state building process.

THE FIRST MODERNISING MEASURES

Brazilian industrial development began during the second half of the nineteenth century with the import-substitution process. The adoption of the first protectionist measures in 1844–5, increasing the duties on imported goods from 15 to 30 per cent *ad valorem*, decisively affected later industrial development.[8] In 1860 the Brazilian government decided to increase duties up to 50 per cent. In the early years of the twentieth century duties fluctuated between 75 to 100 per cent *ad valorem*.[9] The majority of Brazilian entrepreneurs strongly supported protectionism. For example, the future viscount Mauá, the greatest Brazilian trader, decided to move from import and export trade to industrial and banking activities in 1845 and became the biggest native industrialist and banker.[10]

Further, the suppression of the slave trade, imposed by the Brazilian government in 1850, liberated great sums of capital, which were applied to new agricultural, commercial and financial ventures, and the protectionist law encouraged entrepreneurs to invest their gains in industrial projects. Concurrently, private, foreign and public investment flowed into improvements in transport. The opening of railways, roads, urban and coastal transport were important modernising initiatives.[11] The Brazilian government, for security and economic reasons similar to contemporary Russian policy,[12] adopted a policy of incentives to build railways throughout the country. The expansion of transport stimulated the development of a national engineering industry, the incorporation of new technologies (railway equipment and steam engines), the emergence of national entrepreneurs and a skilled workforce. This contributed to the modernisation of the agricultural, industrial and service sectors.[13] The end of slavery (1888) and immigration policy (after 1870) were further Brazilian state initiatives to improve the capitalist economy, industrialisation and urban society.

Another policy to stimulate industrial development was the 'Taubaté Agreement' signed in 1906 by the presidents of the three main provincial coffee producers, São Paulo, Minas Gerais and Rio de Janeiro. This ensured that the Brazilian state and the three provincial governments controlled coffee production and trade, keeping prices high in domestic and international markets. This policy was maintained throughout the first half of the twentieth century with positive effects on public finances and on the economy as a whole. It helped the government during the 1929 world economic crisis and enabled it to support industry after 1930.[14]

Until independence in 1822 almost all industrial goods consumed in Brazil were imported. In 1907, the import coefficient of industrial goods was 44.6 per cent, falling to 28 per cent in 1919 and to 20 per cent in 1939.[15] This significant decrease indicates the success of the import-substitution process in Brazil initiated after the second half of the nineteenth century.

THE 1930 REVOLUTION: POLITICAL CHANGE AND INDUSTRIAL POLICY

There is general consensus that the 1930 revolution was a major turning point in the history of Brazil, in its development strategy and in the organisation of state and society. Important changes took place in its colonial economy.

In the first place, the 1929 world crisis worsened the fragility of the Brazilian economy and its external dependence. The government and part of the Brazilian elite perceived that the country could no longer rely on being primarily an agricultural producer; neither could it accept a subordinate role relative to more industrialised economies. After 1930 the emphasis was changed from exporting primary products to industrial activities and the internal market. Capital raised from agricultural exports was applied to industrial projects. The government promoted greater integration among the former economic sectors ('islands of prosperity') which had developed before 1930[16] and strengthened programmes of state intervention in the economy, becoming a more active agent in promoting industrial and urban development. From then on, the industrialisation of the country became synonymous with national aims and hopes.

In the second place, the old oligarchic order was eroded. While the proclamation of the republic in 1889 changed only the government and the political regime, it did not lead to the disintegration of the elitist monarchical order as in the French Revolution.[17] D. Pedro II had lost political support after abolishing the slave system because he did not provide any financial compensation to landlords. The new regime only introduced a more decentralised administration from 1889 to 1930, giving power to regional oligarchies, which caused many political distortions in governing the country. Provincial power reinforced 'cornelismo' in towns. Thus presidents of the main provinces (São Paulo, Rio de Janeiro and Minas Gerais) were more powerful than the central government. The 'religious question' affected the power and influence of the Catholic Church in society and the state. An attack on the church came from the new elite of civilian freemasons, republicans from the army and positivists with strong influences on public opinion and the state bureaucracy. From the discovery of Brazil until the end of empire, the Catholic Church was the official religion of the country and part of the state, supporting colonial ties and slavery. However, after independence many priests were republicans and supporters of independence movements.[18] The separation of church and state after 1889, the reduction of the former's social prestige and authority and the lack of official state support created scope for a deep-seated process of secularisation of culture. The 'Modern Art Week', organised in São Paulo in 1922 to celebrate the centenary of Brazil's independence, was its strongest expression. It was a political and cultural movement looking for the true Brazilian national identity based on more secular values and Brazil's best historical and cultural traditions. The government strengthened the secularisation process after 1930 at the same time as its public policy aimed at gaining support for developing urban society and industrialisation.[19]

In the third place, the old oligarchic political order changed. The 'agrarian coffee export complex elite' lost its political hegemony after the 1930 revolution. The new government was based on a wider social constituency, such as the dissident coffee and agrarian elites engaged in services, industrial plant and the domestic market in all provinces. Part of the middle class, including liberal professionals, intellectuals and junior officers, supported a more liberal national outlook. Industrial and urban workers organised in labour unions or in liberal and communist parties. The central core of the new poliarchic political structure was formed by several regional ruling classes. The new government absorbed part of the intellectual middle ground, which played an important role in modernising public services, improving educational and cultural institutions and building new national development programmes.[20]

In the fourth place, the heritage of slavery, the previously dominating sector, began to crumble. Under the new government of President Vargas (1930–45) Brazilian workers were publicly recognised as citizens, wealth creators and as 'persons' with their own values. Workers' claims were no longer viewed as a matter for police action. Workers' rights were a subject of specific labour legislation to be managed by the new Ministry of Work, Industry and Commerce. Labour conflicts were to be investigated by the

Work's Justice, a special branch of the judiciary responsible for dealing with labour and capital questions. The 'populist state', adopted in many Latin American countries after 1930, was based on the mass participation of industrial and urban workers in politics.[21] This social and political recognition was not only symbolic but accompanied by real measures and benefits. Doors were opened to full citizenship.

In the fifth place, changes occurred in state administration and the formulation of policy. The new government adopted a more centralised model. During the transitional period (1930 to 1933), President Vargas dismissed the old provincial presidents and selected new governors from among his allies, including several army officers. The new national constituent assembly approved the constitution of 1934 and confirmed Vargas as president. However, in 1937, following upon internal and external unrest, President Vargas imposed an authoritarian regime with fascist characteristics called 'Estado Novo' (1937–45), disbanding the National Congress, forbidding political parties, promoting a new constitution (1937), censoring the press and radio, and persecuting left- and later right–wing politicians and trade union leaders. Concurrently, President Vargas introduced policies of modernisation, reflecting important changes in the direction of a more industrial and urban society and, for the first time, a more independent policy for external relations.[22] Substantial progress was made in the industrial field: in 1938 industrial production surpassed agriculture for the first time. Industrial establishments increased threefold from 1919 (13,336) to 1939 (40,938).[23]

THE DEMOCRATIC PERIOD FROM 1946 TO 1964

Participation of Brazil in the Second World War (1942–5) and the victory of the Allies created conditions for change from an authoritarian to a more democratic regime (1946–64), endorsed in the constitution of 1946.

Relationships between state and society in Brazil were becoming more complex as a result of urbanisation and industrialisation. The appearance of new classes and new political leaders brought pressure, especially from the lower classes, for the democratisation of society and the creation of a more pluralistic state. Thus the state appeared not simply as an instrument of domination of one class over others but as an expression of support of broader sections of society and an instrument of its democratisation. In this historical period the promotion of industrialisation ceased being reactive and defensive (as it was after the 1930 revolution through Brazilian economic fragility) and became more proactive. Development was adopted as the main state policy and different studies and economic plans were prepared as a counterpart to the liberal view that development occurs spontaneously through the interplay of free market forces.

Initiatives were launched between 1950 and 1954 in which public finance was employed in four main areas: electrical energy, transport, nutrition and education. In 1951 the Brazil–United States Economic Commission was created, responsible for ambitious studies on Brazilian economic evolution and planning to be backed by national and international resources. Three main areas were selected: transport (railways, ports, coastal shipping and motorways), electrical energy (generation and transmission), and economic diversification (in agriculture and industry). The commission did not formulate any detailed proposals but provided the best studies on the Brazilian economy, used later in specific projects. It supported the creation of the Banco Nacional de Desenvolvimento Econômico (BNDE – National Bank of Economic Development) in 1952 (still working today as BNDES). This made a great contribution to the development of the country, above all, in infrastructural and industrial projects.

The most ambitious economic planning project was the 'Plano de Metas' introduced by President Juscelino Kubitschek (JK) (1956–61), concerned with five areas: energy, transport, agricultural diversification and industrial modernisation, and education. JK also supported the construction of Brasilia, a very important initiative to gratify the central and western hinterland. All these planning initiatives show convergence, indicating consensus on the main economic and social problems. Another important point of the JK government was the political decision to attract more foreign investment. Rule 133 (1957) of SUMOC (Bureau of Currency and Credit) provided incentives for the establishment of industrial plant in Brazil, leading to the rapid growth of foreign investment in industrial schemes.[24]

PETROBRAS, the strongest national company, set up in 1953 during the second government of President Vargas (1950–4), was responsible for petroleum exploration, refining and distribution, supporting the growth of the automotive industry initiated in 1956. Its production grew from 2 million barrels per year in 1955 to 43 million in 1961, then representing 43 per cent of the crude oil consumed in the country. ELETROBRAS was created in 1962 to plan and co-ordinate the Brazilian electrical system. New railway and motorway links were planned to converge on the new capital of Brasilia.[25]

The Brazilian import-substitution plan was given governmental priority. Its results were impressive: external dependence on import of capital goods was 59 per cent in 1947 falling to 12.9 per cent in 1962, at the same time as there was a reduction of imports of consumer goods from 10 per cent in 1947 to 1.1 per cent in 1962. A further indicator of progress in industrialisation was the increased rate of economic growth, which was 6 per cent per year from 1947 to 1962; however, considering only the 1956–61 period, the annual rate of growth amounted to 7.8 per cent. Between 1947 and 1961 agricultural production grew 87 per cent and industrial production 262 per cent.[26] Despite progress in the modernising process, the central left coalition was coming to an end.

THE MILITARY REGIME, 1964 TO 1985

The *coup d'état* in 1964 halted the democratisation process of society and state but not the import-substitution strategy.[27]

Beginning in 1960, the struggle for active citizenship spread to the rural areas, an expansion which prompted a process of intense mobilisation for land reform and against the 'latifúndio' – the large rural estates which maintained mechanisms of private control very similar to those of the slavery days. The right also joined the process of political radicalisation, at a moment when the Cuban Revolution aggravated the latent conflict of the cold war. In this context, it was not a hard task to link the political mobilisation of popular urban and peasant segments to the imminence of a socialist revolution. The radicalisation of forces appalled the centre and created the atmosphere for an alliance between right and centre. When that happened, the road was open for the 1964 military *coup*, which was funded by national and multinational business with direct support from the United States. This alliance politically supported the military regime until its end.

The results of the *coup* are well known. A right-wing, pro-American, anti-communist, anti-popular military administration was installed. The popular segments and the left were violently repressed. Press censorship was imposed, and rights such as freedom of movement, assembly and speech were curbed. Sectors of the left embraced armed struggle. It took twenty years for a reshaped Brazil to emerge freed from military dictatorship. During this time, the 'frente democrática' (democratic front) emerged, which took responsibility for the transition from a military to a civilian regime. During its creation, the centre-left alliance was gradually rebuilt. The Movimento Democrático Brasileiro (MDB) gradually became the host of all opposition segments of Brazilian society. It was through MDB that political positions in the formal domains of government – local, state and federal, executive and legislative – were achieved.

Simultaneously, popular movements grew, helped by the struggle for amnesty and, in 1984, by the 'Diretas-já!' (Direct elections now!) movement. The strengthening of these forces led to the break-up of army unity, to the isolation of the military from the rest of society, to the divorce between military and civil forces that supported the regime and to the loss of political initiative by the military administration. It meant, once again, the appeasement of left and centre, which was the essence of the successful strategy to move from a military to a civilian-democratic regime. On the one hand, the return to the rule of law, the promulgation of a new constitution (1988), freedom of association and speech, and the full functioning of democratic institutions (such as free elections and activities of political parties) restored active citizenship and the democratisation of state and society. On the other hand, the processes of establishing democracy and active citizenship were stalled by the persistence and growth of poverty.

In contrast to earlier initiatives of state intervention in the economy the military government furthered the entry of foreign capital and of exports. This was in keeping with the anti-communist and pro-American policy of the regime and began to form part of its development strategy. Direct foreign investment, which between 1965 and 1969 amounted on average to US$84 million annually, increased to US$1 billion annually between 1973 and 1976. Foreign loans increased more than ten times in the same period. Average annual loans, which had been US$604 million from 1965 to 1969, increased to US$6.5 billion from 1973 to 1976.[28]

Beginning in 1973, with the first oil crisis, a new situation occurred in the Brazilian economy with important consequences for the model of development by import-substitution. The oil crisis provoked deep economic reforms in the industrial model dating from the Second World War based on large industrial complexes. A new economic strategy was put in place based on electronic technologies, small productive plants, flexible and decentralised processes and more horizontal management, which encouraged worker participation in the planning and execution of production. This was introduced during the government of the third military president, Gen. Ernesto Geisel (1974–9), when the country was experiencing a period of accelerated economic growth. Due to the opposition of the civil and military right wing, the transition to a democratic regime could be better served by economic growth. In this context, the Brazilian government decided to improve the Second National Development Plan (II PND) (1975) with three basic objectives: (1) to avoid recession by implementing a policy of economic growth; (2) to accelerate the strategy of development by import-substitution, expanding and diversifying exports; and (3) to attract more capital from international banks to finance it. In practice, the II PND was helped by public companies providing the greater part of investment in new industries (steel, aluminium, copper, fertiliser and petrochemical products) and infrastructure (electrical and nuclear power, alcohol production, transportation and communication). Private firms established the capital goods industries with private and public funds provided for the most part by BNDES. Brazil was attempting to achieve self-sufficiency in power and to increase its competitive advantages in other industrial sectors.

Economic growth was the result of investment generated by the II PND at an annual rate of 7 per cent until the end of the 1970s. Industry continued to grow at an average rate of 7.5 per cent, just above the GDP rate. Sectors stimulated by the plan performed best: chemical, metal and paper products, engineering and electrical machinery. The effects made themselves felt in terms of import-substitution as a result of investments in 1975 and 1976. Comparing import data of certain intermediate products from 1973 to 1981, it is possible to see positive results: paper imports dropped from 22 to 8 per cent; cellulose from 16 to 1 per cent; steel from 25 to 5 per cent; aluminium from 54 to 14 per cent. For the capital goods sector, the foreign dependency coefficient was 66 per cent in 1973, dropping to 40 per cent in 1981.[29] These data reveal the structural changes brought about in Brazil during the military regime. But, paradoxically, the success of the import-substitution process, providing more autonomy, independence and sovereignty to Brazil, brought about increasing external dependency due to the growth of the foreign debt caused by oil imports and as a result of internal policies established by the authoritarian military regime. In 1973, at the time of the first price shock, Brazil imported 80 per cent of the oil consumed. With the crisis, the prices in international markets quadrupled and the cost of imports rose from 11.5 per cent in 1973 to 25 per cent of the total of Brazilian exports in 1974. The oil imports cost US$6.2 billion in 1973, rising to US$12.6 billion in 1974. The current account deficit rose from US$1.7 billion in 1973 to US$7.1 billion in 1974.[30] The new stage of industrial development was basically financed by international loans because internal savings, taking into account the oil bill, were insufficient. There was the expectation that by intensifying import-substitution and by increasing exports, trade balance surpluses might be achieved. However, with the world-wide decline in international trade after the first oil crisis, this policy failed.

The Brazilian external debt accelerated after the oil crisis. During the 1960s indebtedness was controlled. The debt started to increase in 1967, when the military regime opted for a development strategy related to international capital. From 1967 to 1978, the debt grew by an average of 25 per cent per year, from US$3.3 billion to US$12.6 billion. The public debt, as a result of loans contracted by state companies, federal and state entities, increased from 51.7 per cent in 1973 to 63.3 per cent in 1978.[31] Since the greater part of the loans were contracted in 1973, when petrodollars were abundant in the international market and interest rates relatively low, the cost of the debt was initially tolerable: 13.4 per cent in 1974, 5.9 per cent in 1975 and 6.9 per cent in 1976. From 1979 it started to grow exponentially to 63 per cent due to the second oil crisis and as a result of the increase in flexible rate loan interest by private banks. In 1982, debt service represented 83 per cent of exports and the interest alone absorbed 52 per cent.[32] The consequences of this indebtedness abroad and of this dependency have been the worst possible: recession, return of inflation, unemployment and poverty. This excessive foreign indebtedness compromised Brazilian economic development and the democratisation process of society, and stymied the state's sovereignty.

FINAL CONSIDERATIONS

In the course of this chapter, the constitution of the Brazilian government and society has been presented as a result of an exogenous and endogenous process and was analysed through its three formal elements: the territory, the people and the achievement of sovereignty. By occupying and settling territory, the Portuguese and Brazilian state and government created the people, an amalgam of three races that is still in progress. The structural changes in the economy and society resulting from the relative success of development by import-substitution are still in force. Brazilian society today is more complex as the result of urbanisation, industrialisation and the secularisation of culture. New classes and new actors in politics, urban middle classes and the mass of the population were involved in the struggle for social, political and civil rights.

The democratisation of the Brazilian state and society today depends on maintaining the process of development in the new global world and the success of the country in resolving its problems of internal and external debt. Brazilian prospects are not very rosy due to growing dependence on foreign capital and on technology and as a result of the new forms of neo-colonialism in the relations among developed and underdeveloped countries. The Brazilian policy of opening the Brazilian economy unilaterally, initiated in 1990 by former President Fernando Collor (1990–2) and continued by President Fernando Henrique Cardoso in his first (1995–9) and second governments (1999–), increased foreign indebtedness through more imports and by growing difficulties of increasing and diversifying exports, because of the low competitiveness of Brazilian products, over-valuation of the real, and the direct and indirect protection measures adopted by other countries, individually or as blocs. The continuous Brazilian trade balance deficits aggravate the burden of foreign debts and the cost of servicing it. Government reform, constitutional change and privatisation plans do not help to resolve the problem of foreign dependence. On the contrary, they have worsened it. Funds for the amortisation of domestic and foreign debt are hardly able to meet interest charges. The fragility of the economy after the privatisation programme meant that many medium-sized Brazilian firms are passing into multinational control. The debt will increase with the transfer of profits, payment of royalties, importation of foreign technology and the payment of salaries to foreign technical and management personnel. Government reforms, privatisation, wages reduction and growth of unemployment curtailed the domestic market, another cornerstone of development by import-substitution.

The Brazilian people ended the nineteenth century with the feeling of having succeeded in their task of occupying their territory, but they did not feel same in relation to building their country's independence. During the twentieth century, the Brazilian people did well and worked towards the same goal: the conquest of their country's national autonomous development as the condition of its independence. Brazil changed greatly during the twentieth century: it is more modern, urban and industrial, but it is not possible to hide another frustration because the general result is not what was expected. The country invested in its economic independence and in its national autonomous development project but ended up with more external dependence and the loss of control of many national and private companies. The feelings of the Brazilian people about the future of their country are not so positive as they were at the end of the nineteenth century. Internal and external debt, economic globalisation, increasing mergers of multinational companies, the denationalisation of the Brazilian economy and the political option for the model of dependent capitalistic development adopted by President Cardoso [33] made secondary what was built upon the past: the natural and human resources of the country, its continental size and its diversified internal market.

The Brazilian people are no longer sure about the future of their country and the best way to improve its development. Two main strategies seem possible: the dependent capitalist model (which has incorporated many characteristics of the neo-liberal model), supported by the centre-right coalition still in government; and the national autonomous model, which was supported by a set of heterogeneous opposition forces from the right to left wing.[34] In summary, this is the national and global context where and when Brazil must build its nation-state during the twenty-first century. To make the most of these challenges it is necessary to reinvent relationships among communities, market and state.

NOTES

1. C. Furtado, 'Há Risco de uma Ingovernabilidade Crescente' in A. dos Santos Mineiro et al. (eds.), *Visões da Crise* (Rio de Janeiro, 1998), pp. 20–1.
2. These two elements are already known. For more details, see D. Ribeiro, *O Povo Brasileiro e o Sentido do Brasil* (São Paulo, 1995).
3. C. Prado Júnior, *Formação do Brasil Contemporâneo (Colônia)* (São Paulo, 2000); C. Furtado, *Formação Econômica do Brasil*, 27th edn (São Paulo, 2000).
4. Baer, *Economia Brasileira*, trans. E. Sciulli (São Paulo, 1996), p. 31.
5. A.B. Castro, *7 Ensaios sobre a Economia Brasileira*, 2nd edn (2 vols. Rio de Janeiro, 1975).
6. J.O. Rodrigues, *Aspirações Nacionais, Interpretação Histórico Política*, 4th edn (Rio de Janeiro, 1970).
7. F. Iglésias, *Trajetória Política do Brasil, 1500–1964* (São Paulo, 1993), part 3; R. Faoro, *Os Donos do Poder, Formação do Patronato Político Brasileiro* Vol. I, 10th edn (São Paulo, 2000), chs.7–8.
8. E.V. Costa, 'Introdução Estudo da Emancipação Política' in C.G. Mota, *Brasil em Perspectiva* (São Paulo, 1974) pp. 105–8. According to 1845 data, collected by the author in 'Minutes of the Manchester Commercial and Industrial Association', Brazil was at that time the largest importer of English textiles in the world.
9. A. Fishlow, 'Origens e Conseqüências da Substituição de Importações no Brasil' in F.R. Versiani and J.R.M. Barros (eds.), *Formação Econômica do Brasil, a Experiência da Industrialização*, 1st edn (São Paulo, 1978), pp. 15–16; Baer, *Economia Brasileira*, p. 41.
10. J. Caldeira, *Mauá, Empresário do Império* (São Paulo, 1995); A. Marchant, *Viscount Mauá and the Empire of Brazil: a Biography of Irineo Evangelista de Souza, 1813–1889* (Berkeley, 1965).
11. S. Topik, *The Political Economy of the Brazilian State, 1889–1930* (Austin, 1987).
12. M. Tugan Baranowski, *The Russian Factory in the 19th Century* (Ontario, 1970).
13. D. Giroletti, 'A Modern Transport Network and the Industrial Development of Brazilian Southeast, 1850 to 1890' in *Anais da 2a Conferência Anglo-Brasileira de Negócios* (Belo Horizonte, 1999), pp. 39–54; C.M. Lewis, 'Railways and Industrialisation: Argentina and Brazil , 1870–1929' in C. Abel and C.M. Lewis (eds.), *Latin American Economic Imperialism and State: the Political Economy of the External Connection from Independence to the Present* (London, 1985).
14. C. Furtado, *Formação Econômica*, pp. 191–207.

15. Baer, *Economia Brasileira*, p. 41, 56, 94.
16. R.R. Aguiar (ed.), *C. Furtado, Obra Autobiográfica de Celso Furtado* (3 vols., Rio de Janeiro, 1997), Vol. I, pp. 165–6.
17. J.M. Carvalho, *A Formação das Almas, o Imaginário da República no Brasil* (São Paulo, 1990); Faoro, *Os Donos do Poder*, Vol. II, ch. 14.
18. R.D. Cava, 'Igreja e Estado no Brasil do Século XX: Sete Monografias Recentes sobre o Catolicismo Brasileiro, 1916/64', *Estudos CEBRAP*, 12 (1975), 7–52.
19. H.C. Lorenzo and W.P. Costa (eds.), *A Década de 1920 e as Origens do Brasil Moderno* (São Paulo, 1997).
20. B. Fausto, *A Revolução de 1930, Historiografia e História* (São Paulo, 1970).
21. J.G. Castañeda, *Utopia Desarmada, Intrigas, Dilemas e Promessas da Esquerda Latino-americana*, trans. Nepomuceno (São Paulo, 1994).
22. Faoro, *Os Donos do Poder*, Vol. II, ch. 15; L. Sola, 'O Golpe de 37 e o Estado Novo' in C.G. Mota (ed.), *Brasil em Perspectiva*, 5th edn (São Paulo, 1974).
23. See Baer, *Economia Brasileira*, pp. 52–9; Iglésias, *Trajetória Política do Brasil*, pp. 250–7; Rodrigues, *Aspirações Nacionais*, pp. 141–59.
24. Iglésias, *Trajetória Política do Brasil*, pp. 252–3.
25. Rodrigues, *Aspirações Nacionais*, pp. 138–59.
26. Baer, *Economia Brasileira*, p. 79.
27. H. Jaguaribe et al., *Brasil, Sociedade Democrática* (Rio de Janeiro, 1985).
28. Baer, *Economia Brasileira*, p. 93.
29. Ibid., p. 106–7.
30. Ibid., p. 104.
31. Ibid., p. 107–8.
32. Ibid., p.108–17.
33. *O Presidente segundo o Sociólogo: Entrevista de Fernando Henrique Cardoso a Roberto Pompeu de Toledo* (São Paulo, 1998).
34. See the essays in Santos Mineiro et al. (eds.), *Visões da Crise*.

CHAPTER 20

The role of nationhood in the economic development of the USA

Gavin Wright

In the study of American economic history, it is not standard to ask whether national political independence was essential for the remarkable economic development of the nineteenth and twentieth centuries. In accounts of US economic performance, one may read about entrepreneurship, about technological innovation, about resource abundance, inter-regional trade and migration, perhaps even about policy initiatives in transportation, banking and education; but American writers rarely stop to ask whether these sources of dynamism would have been as effective if the revolution of 1776 had not occurred. To be sure, the constitution of 1787 normally comes in for its share of praise as a guarantor of order, property rights and the inviolability of contracts; but here too the economic record of the nineteenth century is seldom reviewed with an eye towards contingency. A reader of the economic history literature might feel justified in concluding that only 'economic fundamentals' really mattered for America's rise to world leadership, and hence that the only essential role for the nation-state was to step aside and allow these forces full sway. This antiseptic economic history is curious, because political theorists regard the founding of the USA as a pioneering early example of nation building and the rise of national consciousness.[1]

The goal of this chapter is to reopen consideration of this neglected topic. Because my intention is to offer an affirmative answer to the question of association between nationhood and economic development, some disclaimers at the outset may be appropriate. To suggest that independent nationhood was essential for American development is by no means to propose a universal formula or even a correlation for economic history generally. It is easy to imagine circumstances where political independence has adverse economic consequences, if for example the independent state comes under the control of powerful interests with an obstructionist agenda. In any particular instance, one has to ask: political independence for whom? Full political autonomy for large numbers of small nation-states might well

be economically perverse, if it fosters military rivalries and local protectionism, and thereby limits the scope for scale economies in production and in
the generation of knowledge. Thus, this chapter offers neither a recipe nor
a general interpretation of history, only an examination of one important
historical case.

As we shall see, US national development was in many ways special and
quite possibly non-reproducible, an arrangement in which *limitations* on
the nation-state roles of the member states were as important as any active
policies pursued by the centre; yet at the same time they were free to pursue
active pro-development agendas, and did so with a vengeance. Whether
such an edifice of federalist machinery can be consciously engineered in
very different historical settings is questionable. But it is also questionable
whether this structure would have emerged under British colonial status,
at least within the next century.

WHAT IS TO BE EXPLAINED?

According to the best current estimates, some time between 1790 and 1840
the rate of growth of US income per capita accelerated from its colonial level
of no more than 0.5 per cent per year, to its modern average between 1.5 and
2.0 per cent per year.[2] This acceleration might seem to constitute a *prima
facie* case for the beneficial effects of independence and the constitutional
arrangements put into operation in 1789. But the available data do not allow
a precise statement of the timing of growth within this period, and the
interpretation of such estimates would in any case be subject to debate, in
light of the political and economic turbulence touched off by the European
wars that prevailed almost continuously between 1793 and 1815. For these
reasons, many economic historians are inclined to date the US take-off
from approximately 1815, a full generation removed from the state-building
events of the 1780s.

Whatever the deficiencies of quantitative evidence, if our *explicandum*
were to be limited to the standard indicator of per capita income, and
if the question at hand were limited to whether the residents of these
territories would have experienced high and rising incomes in the absence
of political independence, we could spare ourselves further exertion. We
know that the answer is positive, because British colonial North Americans
already enjoyed living standards among the highest in the world before the
revolution. The technologies and market opportunities emanating from the
industrial revolution would surely have spread to British North America
in the first half of the nineteenth century, as they did to many other areas

that were politically and institutionally receptive to them. As part of the same broad cultural heritage and demographic pool, Americans would have shared in these new possibilities under virtually any conceivable political regime.

It seems, therefore, that we should set the bar somewhat higher. Growth in per capita income barely scratches the surface of the global significance of American economic development in the nineteenth century. Historians of the industrial revolution now tell that story less in terms of per capita income and real wage growth, and more in terms of the capacity of the British economy to support a larger population at a standard no lower than previously. By analogy, it is appropriate to consider the expansion in size of the American economy as a whole as part of the history that we hope to explain. An exclusive focus on relative per capita growth rates severely understates the American productive achievement of the nineteenth century, because one of the features of US performance was mass immigration from abroad. In this way, the 'American standard of living' was shared by large numbers of newcomers, the bulk of whom came from countries with much lower average incomes. Thus for many purposes the growth of US population and the size of the US economy are also legitimate objects of historical study.

It follows that we should also direct attention to the emergence of a viable US manufacturing sector in the nineteenth century, since this was the economic destination for the majority of immigrants. In turn, it follows that American technological developments should also be part of the record to be explained, not only those in manufacturing directly, but also in sectors such as internal transportation, marketing and mining, which complemented and facilitated productivity growth in manufacturing and agriculture. Long before assuming leadership in per capita income, the USA effectively *acted* like a leader rather than a follower country, by carving out distinctive national approaches to technology, economic organisation and distribution. Here too standard economic measures understate the significance of the US record, because the 'American system' in time spread to other parts of the world, as an alternative to European models and methods. As with the industrial revolution, some part of the global acceleration of growth over the past two centuries may be seen as an indirect consequence of US development, albeit an unknown and probably unknowable portion. All of this multifaceted history forms the corpus of what is to be explained, with specific reference to the role of political independence.

One can begin to see why the subject is neglected. The full implications of American economic development were not manifest until the twentieth century, at which point the revolution was a distant memory, and American independence taken for granted. But political independence in the 1770s was by no means inevitable, and given independence, it was by no means inevitable that US nation building should have taken the shape that it did after 1787. This chapter sets out to explore the economic consequences of these political developments. For reasons of practicality, the focus is on the first half of the nineteenth century, but in truth these consequences go well beyond that era.

THE NATURE OF AMERICAN NATIONHOOD

Historians have long debated whether the American Revolution was an economic phenomenon at bottom. Without doubt, disputes over taxes and money were among the flashpoints that led to the escalating political conflicts of the 1770s. But that is not the same as saying that immediate economic issues and interests were uppermost in the minds of the signers of the famous declaration of July 1776. Rather, it seems that chronic contention with Parliament and the king finally persuaded prominent colonials that their long-term political and economic interests would be better served by separation. Independence as a remedy came on the scene late in the game, and its full implications could not have been foretold with confidence in 1776.

There are several reasons why direct economic conflict is now downplayed as a factor in the onset of the revolution. The external commerce of the colonies had long been tightly regulated under the Navigation Acts and other statutes; but these regulations offered benefits as well as costs, and were not a main centre of dispute. Parliament's prohibitions (in the Currency Acts of 1751 and 1764) on the issuance of paper money by colonial legislatures had more political bite and potential economic impact. But the underlying issues there had mainly to do with political authority as opposed to economic principle, and on this matter they had been largely compromised by the 1770s. In contrast, attempts by Parliament to impose taxes on the colonies (the Stamp Act of 1765, the Townshend duties of 1767) led to mass popular protest. But Egnal and Ernst show that political responses to the tax issue were inconsistent.[3] In their view, protests were largely driven by the interests of urban merchants threatened by import duties but also by periodic crises of indebtedness and excess inventories. The Tea Act of 1772 – not a revenue measure but a bailout of the British East India Company at the expense of colonial merchants – convinced this important interest group to give up on Parliament as protector.

Although these economic conflicts contributed to the coming of the revolution, political independence did not really settle them. The new state and national governments still had to deal with issues of taxation and its legitimacy. They still had to confront periodic financial crises, including the penchant of state legislatures to issue paper currency as a means of alleviating the plight of debtors. The non-decisiveness of the revolution similarly applies to the one issue on which we might identify a true difference in economic interests between Britain and the colonies, namely the desire of farmers, trappers and land speculators to settle and 'develop' what they took to be the unoccupied lands to the west. Acutely conscious that continued migration would generate costly conflict with Native American tribes, the British ministry announced as an emergency measure the Royal Proclamation Line of 1763, prohibiting settlement or land purchase on lands west of the Appalachian mountains. Intended as temporary, the policy appeared to become permanent with the Proclamation of 1774 and the Quebec Act of the same year. These restrictive acts may have helped bring on the revolution.[4] But after independence, the same divergent interests reappeared between the financially strapped centre and the expansionist frontier, the new federal government now assigned the role formerly played by Parliament.

Not only were the economic problems and issues much the same, but the new central government was in a far weaker position to deal with them, under the Articles of Confederation and Perpetual Union, the country's governing document between 1777 and 1789. The Articles gave the federal government only those powers that the colonies recognised as belonging to king and Parliament, and these were precious few. It had no power to tax and no power to limit the states' rights to collect customs duties. It had the power to establish post offices and collect postage (its only revenue source), to set standards for weights and measures, and to coin money, but no power to limit the states' issuance of paper money. Each state had one vote, and nine votes out of thirteen were required on important matters such as treaties, borrowing money, raising armed forces, or appointing a commander-in-chief. In the absence of sanctions, raising funds through requisitions from the states worked as poorly as one would expect. Unable to borrow money, to negotiate trade agreements or to settle disputes on the frontier, the new nation was hardly a nation at all. We might well conclude that political independence *per se* was not a positive contributor to American economic progress.

And yet, in the midst of the chaos of the 1780s, developments in two key areas helped to lay the basis for the events of the nineteenth century.

The first of these was the market for land. Although land sales and land speculation had long been features of American colonial life, these activities were freshly invigorated when the new state constitutions swept away most remaining feudal restraints on inheritance, subdivision and alienation of land.[5] These abolitions are often downplayed as merely the ratification of pre-existing *de facto* reality, but the new clarity with respect to property rights in land was sufficiently salient to encourage investments in schemes to raise land values. Rothenberg reports that beginning in the decade of the revolution, estates of decedents in Massachusetts came to include shares in such enterprises as bridges, turnpikes, canals and aqueducts.[6] These enterprises were typically sponsored by groups of landowners with a shared interest in the value of property in a particular area. Well before the ambitious state-sponsored canal projects of the nineteenth century, turnpike companies were 'crisscrossing the northern and middle states with a network of moderately improved toll roads'.[7]

The commodification of land extended to the western territories. Though jealously clinging to their rights in monetary affairs, one by one the states ceded their western land claims to the federal government, giving the nation a collective possession of millions of acres. By 1786, Congress was in possession of all the land south of Canada, north of the Ohio, west of the Alleghenies and east of the Mississippi. The southern states followed suit in the 1790s, Georgia being the last to fall into line by 1802. The Land Ordinance of 1785 established what was to be the basis for American public land policy until the Homestead Act of 1862. It provided for a rectangular survey of public lands and a division into townships six miles square, each to consist of thirty-six sections of 640 acres each. Land offices were to be established at convenient points, and lands sold in orderly progress at a price of not less than one dollar an acre. Four sections of every township were to be set aside for the federal government, and one section reserved for the maintenance of public schools. This economic legislation had a political counterpart in the Northwest Ordinance of 1787, which provided for the organisation of the new areas, first into territorial status, and then into statehood as an equal partner with the original members, when sufficient population had been attained.[8] Having come through the revolution, Congress had no desire to play the part of the mother country in a replay of the colonial drama.

Although Congress was certainly hoping to raise revenue through these policies, they none the less constituted acts of nation building that both reflected and helped to define national identity. It was crucial that settlers entered new territories under national rather than state aegis, so that the standardised land system operated to reinforce their sense of American nationality, as opposed to attachment to one of the states. Had these territories been the object of competing state claims (as they had been in colonial times), the effect of migration on the sense of identity might have been quite different. Land policies were articulated as representations of the values thought to be implicit in the revolution itself. And in typical American fashion, these values offered opportunities both to individual family farmers and to huge, ambitious land companies hoping to make a profit from real estate development. From this early point, in other words, American nation building was a commercial proposition.

AMERICAN NATIONHOOD AND FREE LABOUR

The Northwest Ordinance proclaimed, 'There shall be neither slavery nor involuntary servitude in said territory', a proactive measure of prime significance for the economic development of that region. Abolition of slavery in the northern states was clearly a consequence of the revolution, a response to the glaring inconsistency between the rhetoric of freedom and equality on the one hand, and the fact of human bondage on the other. These state-level measures, begun in the 1780s and completed just after the turn of the century, are not normally identified as important *economic* policy shifts, because they are seen mainly as confirming slavery's marginal significance in these states. Such a dismissal is misleading, not only because slave-owners in states like New York and New Jersey fought long and hard to maintain their property rights in slaves, but because opening the north-west territory to the importation of slaves would have changed the course of history in dramatic fashion. The post-war emancipations set the ideological context for the Ordinance, which in turn set the terms for territorial settlement.

Despite the proscription in the Ordinance, there were slaves and strong pro-slavery forces in Ohio, Indiana and Illinois, and the issue was not definitively settled until the 1820s. Only the need to gain Congressional approval for statehood led the legislature of the Indiana territory in 1810 to prohibit the introduction of new slaves or servants.[9] The Illinois territory, which split off from Indiana over the slavery issue, had a proslavery majority as late as 1818; again, only the threat of Congressional rejection deterred Illinois from attempting to enter the Union as a slave state. From the viewpoint of distant would-be land developers, property rights in labour always seemed to be the quickest and surest way to develop empty lands. These people undoubtedly underestimated the speed and enthusiasm with which free family farmers would soon fill up the territory (with dramatic effects on land values); but if the pro-slavery forces had had their way politically, that free farm settlement might never have occurred, and the entire pace and pattern of regional development would have been unrecognisably different.

Several things are notable about the exclusion of slavery from the northern territories. The first is that it would not have happened in the absence of political independence.[10] The British anti-slavery movement barely existed prior to the American Revolution, achieving its first goal of ending the African slave trade only in 1807 – the same year in which the US ended the African trade, with the acquiescence (indeed with active support in some cases) of the slave South, by then aware of the potential for profit in appreciating slave values. Abolition of slavery in the British empire had to wait until 1833. Thus the hypothetical settlement of the American north-west by slave-holding planters might really have occurred had the revolution been avoided.

Second, articulation of the basis for excluding slavery was an aspect of nation-building, which had broad consequences for defining the concept of freedom and the operation of labour markets. Throughout the northern states and territories, slaveholders tried to evade the law by claiming that their servants had voluntarily signed long-term labour contracts. The result was to create a powerful legal presumption against the validity of such contracts, as a denial of fundamental human rights. One of the legal disputes arising in the new state of Indiana (the case of Mary Clark, a woman of colour) led to the following sweeping judicial statement in 1821:

It may be laid down as a general rule, that neither the common law nor the Statutes in force in this State recognize the coercion of a specific performance of contracts ... Such a performance, if enforced by the law, would produce a state of servitude as degrading and demoralizing in its consequences, as a state of absolute slavery; and if enforced under a government like ours, which acknowledges a personal equality, it would be productive of a state of feeling more discordant and irritating than slavery itself.[11]

The statement defines 'a government like ours' in what are recognisably nationalist terms, yet in such a way that the slave South does not fit in. Thus, a corollary of American nation-building was that the slave South came to seem like an alien land to northerners, notwithstanding its participation in the revolution and in the democratising trends of the early nineteenth century.

Once the slavery issue was settled, the northern states threw their energies into projects oriented towards raising the value of land: by improving transportation, opening markets, building towns and recruiting new settlers. Growth as real estate development is often seen as the typically American style, but it only makes economic sense in a region where there are well-established fee-simple property rights in land, and property rights in labour are not permitted. Northern abolition thus helped to channel economic activity in these regions.

THE US CONSTITUTION AND THE CAPITAL MARKETS

To explain the timing and magnitude of economic change, however, we have to return to the national constitutional situation as it stood in 1787. The convention that met in Philadelphia in that year was emphatically an exercise in nation building, perhaps the canonical case. Officially the delegates had no authority to undertake such a sweeping project in institutional design, having been appointed by Congress only to recommend possible revisions to the Articles of Confederation. But the assembled group quickly agreed that more drastic alterations were required, in effect a new national beginning. Among the delegates, there was near consensus on the federal government's need for an independent revenue source and clearer authority in matters pertaining to foreign trade, the army and the territories. It is far from clear that this consensus was broadly shared among the politically active population in the member states – as the bitter struggle over ratification confirmed. Thus these events count as a true turning point, without which subsequent history (economics included) would have been very different.

To understand the basis for the ratification debates, one must appreciate the context of the 1780s. Although it is mainly studied historically as an example of inflationary war finance, the revolution itself had significant effects on economic activity. Indeed, the war may be viewed as the first step in the long turn inward towards the opportunities of the domestic economy, as booming markets for farm produce generated new interest in inland transportation.[12] The end of the war disrupted this new internal trade, but without restoring access to British imperial markets. The resulting distress caused considerable political turbulence, leading to demands for the remedy with which the colonial legislatures were long familiar – unbacked paper money as a form of debt relief. Seven states pursued this course in the 1780s, striking terror in the hearts of domestic creditors. Among the primary goals of many at the convention was thus not just to empower the federal government, but to *dis*empower the states from paper money and other forms of mischief. Benjamin Rush wrote in 1788: 'If the new Constitution held forth no other advantages [than] that [of] a future exemption from paper money and tender laws, it would be eno' to recommend it to most men.'[13]

It is significant, therefore, that the constitution gave the federal government *exclusive* authority over money, over foreign and inter-state commerce, and over the territories (including relations with the Native Americans). These powers, and their exclusivity, were given credibility by the simultaneous creation of a federal executive branch and an independent judiciary, to enforce the constitution as the 'Supreme Law of the land... anything in the Constitution or laws of any State to the contrary notwithstanding' (Art. VI, § 2). The states retained extensive powers in such areas as banking, transportation, taxation and education. But American nation building was simultaneously a creation of sovereign powers combined and an abrogation of major aspects of sovereignty by the states; as much a chapter in nation-state restraint as in nation building.[14]

In one important respect, however, the history of the USA was not fundamentally different from that of European nations, in that financial policies were dictated by the fiscal needs of governments. On this count the constitution of 1789 left much unsaid, giving the federal government access to tax revenue only implicitly through its control over customs. Of equal importance in defining the US nation-state was the federalist programme enacted during George Washington's first term of office (1789–92), under the leadership of Secretary of the Treasury Alexander Hamilton. Hamilton's reports on the public credit, on the Bank of the United States and on manufactures are classics of US political economy and national definition. With the exception of the report on manufactures, virtually the entire plan was backed by the president and promptly voted into law by Congress. The immediate results included a sweeping assumption of debt by the federal government ('funding at par' the long-depreciated war debts of the states), launching of a banking system based on liabilities convertible into a specie base, and a dramatic improvement in the status of US federal government debt in the capital markets of Europe. The long-term effects are more subject to interpretation, but potentially include US territorial expansion, creation of a national securities market, and facilitating the large inflow of foreign capital into the country during the first half of the nineteenth century.[15]

The debts of the Confederation Congress were valued at 15 to 25 cents on the dollar in 1789. When Hamilton's new US securities first appeared in late 1790, they were valued at 30 to 70 cents on the dollar. By August of 1791, they were selling above par in London and Amsterdam. 'Our public credit', wrote Washington, 'stands on that ground, which three years ago

it would have been considered as a species of madness to have foretold.'
Ten years later, when President Thomas Jefferson offered France US $7.5
million for the Island of New Orleans – an essential outlet for the products
of western farms – Napoleon countered with a proposal to sell the entire
Louisiana territory for $15 million. Of this amount, $11.25 million took the
form of new federal securities, for which the French found ready buyers in
Holland. The transaction doubled the country's land area, and would have
been inconceivable under the Articles of Confederation.

Research by Richard Sylla and collaborators shows that trading in US securities was active in American cities far earlier than previously appreciated,
in markets displaying depth and geographic integration even in the 1790s.
As in the 'financial revolution' of eighteenth-century Europe, prudent management of government debt contributed to the institutional evolution of
the capital market, widening opportunities for public and private agents
to raise funds for ambitious new projects. Among the first to respond were
state-chartered banks, whose securities were second only to those of the
government as objects of investment and trade. The constitution deprived
the states of the power to issue money, but not the power to charter banks,
an indirect means of expanding the money supply (through note issue) and
gaining revenue (or credit on favourable terms) for the state. The number
of banks increased from 3 in 1790 to 28 in 1800, 102 in 1810, 327 in 1820, and
584 by 1835.[16] Thus, from the near-absence of financial institutions in the
1780s, the USA developed a sophisticated network of banks and securities
trading by the early nineteenth century. Hamilton's nation-building measures were essential to this development; but so too were the (constrained)
efforts by the states to promote economic activity and gain revenue.

Similar complementarities between private and state motives pervaded
the active state developmental programmes that were popular between
1815 and the 1840s, chiefly in the form of state-sponsored or subsidised
improvements in transportation. The underlying constituencies for these
programmes were coalitions of urban merchants competing for trade, and
landowners hoping for capital gains on their property. Geographically, these
interests did not coincide very closely with state boundaries. But the states
were the political and institutional vehicles, because their taxing powers
allowed them to offer the 'loan of the state's credit' to investors. Beginning with New York's spectacular success with the Erie Canal (begun in
1817 and completed in 1825), state governments committed some $300 mil-
lion to internal improvements by 1850, in cash or credit. The great bulk
of the funding was supplied by overseas investors, who purchased bonds
from state-owned or (more commonly) state-subsidised canal companies.

Although the federal government played little active role in promoting development during this phase of history, there were clear historical links between this inflow of foreign capital and the structuring of US national institutions in the 1780s and 1790s. Indeed, the peculiarities of American federalism led to some consternation among foreign investors in the 1840s, when nine of the states defaulted on debt payments (including some repudiations), and the federal government was unwilling to take responsibility for these obligations. But by then the US 'transportation revolution' was well underway, and this episode did no long-term damage to American credit in world markets.

THE RISE OF AMERICAN INDUSTRY

Hamilton proposed to fill out the nation-building agenda with an active federal programme to promote American manufacturing; but this plan had little appeal to the nation in the 1790s. If this negative political view had prevailed for the next century, the USA would still have experienced prosperity and economic growth. Indeed, the acceleration of productivity growth between 1790 and 1840 was primarily an agricultural phenomenon, necessarily so because of the predominance of farming in the national economy at that time. But in the absence of a dynamic manufacturing sector, the USA would not have become the world's leading economic nation. And the historical record suggests that US industry would not have been launched on its road to modernity in the absence of national unity and government encouragement; and these policies in turn required the constitutional structure of 1789.

Individual states might, of course, have pursued industrial protection policies on their own. Some of them did: in the 1780s, tariffs on foreign goods were enacted by New York, Massachusetts, Pennsylvania, Rhode Island and New Hampshire.[17] But these were not fully effective for either revenue or protective purposes, because the tariffs were not uniform among the states. Thus, state-level duties on 'foreign' goods inevitably generated pressure for taxes on goods coming in from other states, as some alleged was happening in that decade. Tariff policies by individual states would have been a different economic animal indeed. The USA escaped the adverse consequences of protectionism chiefly because of the large size of the national domestic market. Again, we see the contribution of the constitution in restraining state actions as much as in enabling federal action.

How then did the country move from the indifference of the 1790s to a policy of industrial protection in 1816? In briefest summary, through a path-dependent course of events in which nationhood was crucial. When the European wars escalated after 1793, American ports and shippers were able to prosper from the nation's neutrality, by supplying shipping services and transshipments of goods to both sides. Until 1807, the north-eastern seaboard enjoyed a unique period of mercantile prosperity, a stimulus to urban and financial development, but certainly not to US manufacturing activity. This open-economy world changed virtually overnight into a closed-economy antithesis, with the imposition of Jefferson's embargo in December 1807. To make a short story even shorter, one may regard the embargo–non-intercourse–wartime period of 1808–15 as almost a textbook experiment in the sudden shutoff of trade with the outside world. For the seaboard shippers, the results were devastating. But alongside their suffering, the years of isolation stimulated a remarkable expansion of internal trade, including rapid growth of manufactures. The most dramatic example was cotton textiles, but hothouse factories also sprang up in such activities as metals and machinery, iron and chemicals. In Philadelphia, the carpet and glass industries enjoyed an unprecedented boom.[18]

Of course, most of these wartime operations were flimsy and inefficient, and quickly closed with the return of British imports in 1816. But not all failed, and not without a struggle to survive through political as well as economic means. Out of the turbulence came the tariff of 1816, traditionally identified as the nation's first protective tariff. Even the staunch free trader Frank Taussig allowed that this duty might have been justifiable as a temporary measure, in light of the severe problems of post-war adjustment.[19] Justifiable or not, under this tariff and its successors, the US cotton textile industry enjoyed almost complete protection against cheap Indian imports, and a substantial competitive advantage in the domestic market relative to Great Britain, the undeniable world leader in that industry. Further, not all of the adjustments were political. Some lasting technological innovations date from precisely this transition period, such as the 'life-saving' development of the power loom by Francis Cabot Lowell and Paul Moody.[20]

To what extent was the tariff essential to the success of US industry in the nineteenth century? We do not know the answer to this question with any precision. Economic historians have tended to focus on the retrospective policy question of whether tariff protection could be justified by standard criteria, such as learning effects and externalities. Studies of late nineteenth-century protection tend to reach negative conclusions, arguing that US tariffs by that point were too high and indiscriminate to have had net benefits for the economy. For the antebellum period, only protection of cotton textiles has been carefully examined. For that case, the most careful study finds, not that protection was necessarily justifiable, but that American labour costs were such that the vast majority of firms in the industry required protection for survival.[21] This finding does not necessarily imply, however, that protection had only adverse effects on US industrial development. By allowing an expansion of the *scale* of US cloth-making, tariff protection made possible the rise of specialised producers of textile *machinery*; the textile machinery industry, in turn, was one of the main early loci of the machine-tools industry that propelled American industry into world-class status by the end of the century. As early as the 1830s, machine shops that were initially attached to textile factories began to diversify their product lines into steam engines, turbines, locomotives and other machine tools. Through a process that Rosenberg calls 'technological convergence', a common national body of metalworking and mechanical knowledge came to be applied to a diverse range of industries.

Would all this have happened, if it had not been for the embargo of 1807 and the tariff of 1816? Intricate counterfactuals such as this are inherently unanswerable, at least not at the level of rigour to which quantitative economic historians now aspire. The precise effects of tariff legislation are perhaps less essential than an appreciation of the positive interactions that were at work, between nation building in the broad sense, political support for economic development, and the evolution of an indigenous national technological community. Although this was a decentralised process, it amounted to a process of collective learning, because American engineers and mechanics were engaged in adapting what were originally European innovations to an American environment that was distinctive in its resource base, in its conditions of factor supply, and in the scale and character of its product markets.[22]

CONCLUSION

This chapter has endeavoured to show that these characteristic American patterns of economic development would not have been possible in the absence of the institutional arrangements that emerged from the 1780s and 1790s. And these in turn would not have occurred, at least not at that time and in that way, if there had not been an American Revolution in 1776. The remaining task is to compare this US record with that of other broadly comparable nations in Europe and the Americas.

One of these comparisons should be with the divergent path of the American South. The slave South was a full participant in the revolution, in the design of the constitution, and even in the acceleration of economic growth in the first half of the nineteenth century. But essential features of the American nation-building experience were not shared by the South. Although the southern states also pursued development schemes, the region lagged in population growth, infrastructure investment, territorial settlement, urban development and education – in short, in most of the components of what we now take to constitute 'economic development'. In essence, the failure was in nation building. If the slave states had separated in 1789 and formed a separate nation – as they tried to do unsuccessfully in 1861 – that entity might have been better able to define and implement a national agenda more suited to a slave-holding republic. The deeper problem, however, was that the slave-based economy did not generate the same symbiosis between profit seeking and nation building that formed the core of the American experience for the rest of the country.

NOTES

1. Liah Greenfeld maintains that American nationalism is the second oldest in the world, deriving directly from the original English nationalism, turning English ideals into reality. See her 'The Origins and Nature of American Nationalism', in Knud Kraku (ed.), *The American Nation – National Identity – Nationalism* (New Brunswick, N.J., 1997). pp. 21, 25. See also Benedict Anderson's chapter 'Creole Pioneers' in his *Imagined Communities*, rev. edn (London, 1991; First pub. 1983), pp. 47–65.
2. For the most recent review of national income statistics for this period, see Paul A. David, 'Real Income and Economic Welfare Growth in the Early Republic or, Another Try at Getting the American Story Straight', *Discussion Papers in Economic and Social History*, 5 (Oxford, 1996).
3. Marc Egnal and Joseph A. Ernst, 'An Economic Interpretation of the American Revolution', *William and Mary Quarterly*, 3rd series, 29 (1972), 3–32.
4. See Marc Egnal, *A Mighty Empire: The Origins of the American Revolution*, (Ithaca, NY, 1988).
5. Willi Paul Adams, *The First American Constitutions* (Chapel Hill, N.C., 1980), pp. 194–6. The classic account is J. Franklin Jameson, *The American Revolution Considered as a Social Movement*, Chapter II.
6. Winifred Rothenberg, *From Market-places to Market Economy* (Chicago, 1992), pp. 120–2.
7. Carter Goodrich, *Government Promotion of American Canals and Railroads 1800–1890* (New York, 1960), p. 21.
8. In providing for new states, the Northwest Ordinance fulfilled earlier statements of Congressional intention, in the 1780 Resolution on Public Land and the Ordinance of 1784. The 1787 Ordinance also explicitly established fee simple ownership in the territories. See Douglass C. North and Andrew R. Rutten, 'The Northwest Ordinance in Historical Perspective' in David C. Klingaman

and Richard K. Vedder (eds.), *Essays on the Economy of the Old Northwest* (Athens, Ohio, 1987), pp. 22–3.

9. Paul Finkelman, 'Evading the Ordinance: the Persistance of Bandage in Indiana and Illinois', *Journal of the Early Republic*, 9 (Spring 1989), 21–51, at 39.

10. Counterfactual scenarios are explored by David Brion Davis, in 'American Slavery and the American Revolution' in Ira Berlin and Ronald Hoffman (eds.), *Slavery and Freedom in the Age of the American Revolution* (Charlottesville, Va., 1983), pp. 262–80.

11. Quoted in Robert J. Steinfeld, *The Invention of Free Labor* (Chapel Hill, N.C., 1991), p. 144.

12. Curtis P. Nettels, *The Emergence of a National Economy, 1775–1815* (New York, 1969; first published 1962), pp. 43–4.

13. Quoted in Gordon S. Wood, 'Interests and Disinterestedness in the Making of the Constitution' in Richard Beeman, Stephen Botein and Edward C. Carter III (eds.), *Beyond Confederation* (Chapel Hill, N.C., 1987), pp. 69–109, at p. 108.

14. Federalism as a basis for US economic development is emphasised in Peter Temin, 'Free Land and Federalism', *Journal of Interdisciplinary History* 21 (1991), 371–389. The political economy of constrained inter-state competition is analysed by Barry Weingast, 'The Economic Role of Political Institutions: Market-Preserving Federalism and Economic Development', *The Journal of Law, Economics and Organization*, 11 (1995), 1–31.

15. This section draws on Richard Sylla, 'Shaping the US Financial System', 1690–1913: the Dominant Role of Public Finance' in Richard Sylla, Richard Tilly and Gabriel Tortella (eds.), *The State, the Financial System, and Economic Modernization* (Cambridge, 1999), pp. 249–70, and Peter L. Rousseau and Richard Sylla, 'Emerging Financial Markets and Early US Growth', *National Bureau of Economic Research Working Paper 7448* (Dec. 1999).

16. This proliferation of state-chartered banks was a distinct break with the colonial regime, which sharply curtailed bank creation. See Edwin J. Perkins, *American Public Finance and Financial Services 1700–1815* (Columbus, Ohio, 1994), pp. 41, 188, 361.

17. Nettels, *Emergence of a National Economy*, p. 69. The text and commodity lists of the first federal tariff were taken directly from these state revenue measures. E.A.J. Johnson, *The Foundations of American Freedom* (Minneapolis, 1973), pp. 229–33.

18. For more detailed accounts, see Douglass North, *The Economic Growth of the United States, 1790–1860* (Englewood Cliffs, N.J., 1961), pp. 55–8; Stanley Lebergott, *The Americans: an Economic Record* (New York, 1984), pp. 126–30.

19. Frank Taussig, *The Tariff History of the United States* (New York, 1898), pp. 29–36.

20. Robert Zevin, 'The Growth of Cotton Textile Production after 1815' in Robert W. Fogel and Stanley Engerman (eds.), *The Reinterpretation of American Economic History* (New York, 1971), pp. 139–43.

21. C.K. Harley, 'The International Competitiveness of the Antebellum Cotton Textile Industry', *Journal of Economic History*, 52 (1992), 559–84.
22. This analysis is elaborated more fully in Gavin Wright, 'Can a Nation Learn? American Technology as a Network Phenomenon' in Naomi Lamoreaux, Daniel Raff and Peter Temin (eds.), *Learning by Doing in Markets, Firms, and Countries* (Chicago, 1999), pp. 295–326.

CHAPTER 21

Economic policy and Australian state building: from labourist-protectionism to globalisation

Christopher Lloyd

ORIGINS AND COMPARATIVE SIGNIFICANCE OF THE EMERGING AUSTRALIAN STATE

The emergence and development of the Australian state and economy from the initial precarious penal colonisation of New South Wales (NSW) in 1788 must be understood within the context of British imperialism and the world economy of the nineteenth century. The early economic development depended to a large degree upon state direction of investment, labour and land use. Early political/administrative struggles concerned the control and alienation of land, access to foreign currency in order to import luxuries and control of the convict labour supply.[1] The lands of Aboriginal inhabitants were simply expropriated by the crown under the legal fiction of *terra nullius*. A free, proto-capitalist economy soon burgeoned within the imperial framework, especially after a couple of decades of uncertainty. Unlike almost all other parts of what became the industrialised world of the early to mid-twentieth century, and in comparison with other former settler colonies in the Americas, Australia was founded *within* and was an *integral* part of the world economy *from the very beginning*. The Australian colonies and later the independent federated Australian Commonwealth owed their existence, their character and their development to these overlapping forces. There was no other background or significant pole of attraction or alternative developmental trajectory possible. Australia was born as a *modern* component or offshoot of the British state and developed in such a way that no pre-capitalist or anti-modern forces were permitted to influence significantly the infant society. No peasantry or aristocracy impeded the accumulation of rural and urban capital. In the beginning the idea was to subjugate, develop and civilise the alien land and so the concept of a physical alteration process has been a central component of nation building. Subjugation was not just environmental but also of the native people. That the Aborigines have survived to the extent they have, in order to reassert

404

ancestral land and cultural rights and become a potent political and cultural force within a new era of nation building or national reorientation from the late twentieth century, is one testament to the failure of a certain form of exclusiveness that was central to the national project until the 1960s.

When Britain emerged from the Napoleonic Wars as a more politically, militarily and economically powerful nation but even more riven by unrest, Australia became a much more valuable possession, full of political usefulness and potential and actual wealth. Thus from about 1815 the real story of the Australian state and economic development began. The two necessities of exiling politically and socially dangerous convicts from all parts of the empire and of finding raw materials formed the dynamic of Australia's early history. By the 1830s Australia had become of major significance to Britain in both penal and economic senses. The actuality and potential of the pastoral wool industry had seized the imagination of metropole and colony, sparking a major free immigration surge and speculative bubble in the late 1830s and a rapid expansion of settlers into the hinterland, with consequent wholesale violent dispossession and partial eradication of the Aborigines.[2]

Ideas of liberalism, democracy and socialism took root at the very early stage of the second half of the nineteenth century in Australia but racial and cultural exclusion was also central. Nationalism in the sense of the establishment of a genuinely independent political entity was underdeveloped until much later. By the late nineteenth century, well before anywhere else, a special form of 'primitive' social democracy, in combination with liberalism, came to pervade the entire interconnection between capital, labour, culture and the state. Instead of the class exclusion of the Old World, this new world's dominant ideology attempted to deliver class *inclusion* while being racially exclusive. And quite unlike the United States experiment in supposedly class-less democracy, this attempt to create a new kind of democratic society around the turn of the nineteenth century was centred on the essential role of the regulatory state. What has recently been called the Australian 'compromise' or 'settlement',[3] in which the state was so central, emerged from the experience of a century of development up to the late nineteenth century and became a nation-building ideology and project in the early twentieth. From the late 1960s and early 1970s, however, the robustness and adaptiveness of the structure to rapidly altering external and internal environments became a major issue facing the political process and its state actors. Since then there has been a rapid and relatively peaceful move towards racial inclusion, although not yet fully achieved, and economic openness.

The very early and relatively successful economic and political development of Australia, compared with Latin American and African settler
societies, and the tropical colonial regions, and compared also in certain
crucial ways with Europe and the United States,[4] and the comparatively
very successful achievement of a peaceful multicultural society in the late
twentieth century, were the result of the interconnections of local, imperial and world cultural and economic legacies as well as local political and
social struggles of a much more contingent kind.[5] In particular, full significance must be accorded to the importance of mercantile capital, representative democracy, organised labour, the protectionist class compromise,
and the cornucopia of mineral and agricultural exports that underpinned
the continuing relative prosperity. But the legacy of violent Aboriginal dispossession, partial extermination and exclusion, which freed the land for
settlement and exploitation, remains the darkest legacy of this comparative
success.[6]

THE DEBATE ABOUT THE AUSTRALIAN LABOURIST STATE

While the concept of a 'settlement' or 'compromise' between capital and
labour via state intermediation has its limitations, it is a convenient way
into examining Australia's historical political economy and nation building. The essence of the compact was that workers, employers (especially
manufacturers), middle-class professionals and the British culture and way
of life would be protected from competition and erosion in the interest of
retaining and building a prosperous, harmonious society of relative class inclusion that liberals believed was the triumph of the post-convict era. Contributing ideological elements to the compromise were British Chartism
and Philosophic Radicalism, Fabian Socialism, Liberalism and an emerging form of half-hearted Australian nationalism. Nowhere else in the world
was there such an apparent compromise by that time. It can be described
as 'labourist-protectionism' in the sense that both organised labour and
elements of capital reached a high degree of influence and integration with
the state from the earliest decades of the twentieth century such that it
benefited greatly those within the protected compromise, especially (male)
trade union members, manufacturing firms, state enterprises, certain professional groups and the necessary bureaucracies. Later the compromise
was joined by family farmers. To call the arrangement 'state socialist', as
some commentators did at the time, is to overstate the significance of state
ownership and control of the economy. To call it 'social democracy' would
be better but there were significant essential elements of democracy missing

compared with the final expression of the arrangement under the Whitlam government of the early 1970s and essential elements of social inclusion were missing compared with Scandinavian post-war exemplars.

The arrangement was widely supported, especially while it delivered profits and high wages, but did not include all interests or ideological commitments. The dominant ideological commitment of organised labour was a mission to civilise capitalism through redistribution and some state ownership, rather than to undermine it. There was also always a minority oppositional anti-capitalist left. Free trade interests, including pastoralists and mining companies, were also marginalised. But they too found they could live with it, especially after the formation of the Country Party in 1919. The compact survived the great crisis of the 1930s, thanks largely to the Second World War, which rebuilt and reinforced the labourist-protectionist commitments to egalitarianism and state centrism, but could not survive the crisis of the 1970s and began to disintegrate.

This way of seeing Australia is not without its difficulties or critics. Many alternative proposals have been advanced for understanding Australia's historical political economy. Left critics have emphasised both the 'capture' of the state by sectional interests of capital and the imperialist/world-economy context of Australian capital, which stunted the development of a vigorous national form of either capitalism or democratic socialism, so making Australia akin to the Latin American form of dependency.[7] But dependency theory fails to grasp the very real differences between the two zones. Liberal parliamentary democracy took firm root in Australia from the nineteenth century and industrial maturity with high living standards were reached by the late 1950s. More pertinently, the concept of a 'dominion' form of capitalism within the British empire has emphasised the special dependent, semi-peripheral, but relatively advantageous relationship the white settler societies had with the British core.[8] Some have also pointed out how the labourists missed golden opportunities at various moments to make major, even revolutionary, reforms to Australian economy and society and were in fact led by class traitors. Labour was never hegemonic. Industrial and political labour were co-opted by the capitalist state and failed in their mission to civilise capitalism, especially in comparison with the Scandinavians.[9] It is argued that class inclusiveness was a sham that bought off the working class. Others from a centre-left perspective have emphasised the positive social democratic outcomes of egalitarianism, social justice and prosperity with low levels of bureaucratic regulation of social life resulting from the 'compromise' and have drawn positive comparisons with southern South America and the US.[10]

Economic analysts and neo-liberal critics have pointed out what they see as the deleterious long-run economic consequences of the labourist-protectionist consensus. Their view is that Australia's long-run performance was poor; for example, the fifty years of relative economic stagnation between 1890 and 1940 was a consequence of the failure to encourage a vigorous national capitalism through an international free-trade framework,[11] and the protectionism and immigration restriction of the post-war decades were the 'Rip van Winkle' years. According to public choice theory,[12] the state was too central, having been captured by sectional, redistributive interests rather than growth-oriented interests. Similarly, the critical designation of 'colonial socialism'[13] as the close, often monopolistic 'partnership' between private business and government, which had roots back to the foundation in 1788, which was then acquiesced in by organised labour, pointed to the power of monopoly as a brake on growth. Sectional capitalist and labourist interests could use the state for private benefit as long as the costs were shared widely.

Thus there has been a vigorous debate in recent decades about the costs and benefits of the labourist-protectionist state and the theorists and critics are certainly right to try to understand the particular institutional developments and policy choices. While it's unavoidable to reinterpret history to some extent from the standpoint of the present and the long-run outcome, are backward-looking criticisms of the policy choices made at certain contingent moments sometimes too filled with hindsight derived from the new theoretical standpoint? Some such politically motivated criticisms are aimed at shoring up ideological commitments in the present and are not sufficiently historical, failing to see the complexities of the forces at work as well as the contingencies and constraints on decisions and outcomes. For example, the recent neo-liberal critique of the labourist-protectionist settlement tends to deny the historical contingency and balance of forces that produced and sustained that structure of regulation at particular moments.

Taking a more complex historical and realist view, we should stress the interconnections between natural conditions and socio-economic structures that have arisen and evolved slowly over time and which set strong inherited frameworks and limits, on the one hand, and the development and impact of social and political events, movements and decisions, on the other. The deep structures of Australian history include the natural environment as discovered, exploited and more or less humanised by Aboriginal and European occupiers. Included here are the Aboriginal inhabitants who were comparatively poorly organised and easily dispossessed,[14] the temperate climate and poor soils but vast open landscape, lack of native domesticates, the huge distances within and without, which restricted trade and immigration, the limited water supplies (natural and corralled), and abundant mineral discoveries. Such an environment, within a world-economy nineteenth-century context, called forth a rapacious capitalist response. The prison-state foundation and the convict egalitarian legacy, combined with the refracted British inheritance of ideologies, cultures and institutions, particularly liberalism and later socialism, and the context of world capitalism with its insatiable appetite for raw materials and profitable investments, were all relevant. The interconnections between these deep structures and local social classes, politics and ideologies produced the peculiar Australian outcome at the beginning of the twentieth century. The entrenchment of liberal democracy in the 1860s with a high degree of affluence was always going to open government to social and economic interests wanting to influence the state. Underpinning it all was the cornucopia of exports that were extracted efficiently from the land. The capitalist rural subjugation and exploitation process produced the necessary foundation for the success and persistence of the protected coalition in the commercial cities.

Therefore, the idea that an inappropriate settlement or compromise emerged around the turn of the century and that there really were genuine alternative paths downplays too far the central role of the state from the beginning and the structural imperative, in a path-dependent sense, of that role continuing in a socially and culturally homogeneous settler society that was strongly influenced by liberalism and chartism and which could not have industrialised without some form of protection. Neither capital nor labour was hegemonic and consequently a special form of social democratic settler capitalism came into being in Australia that was something of an institutional laboratory as well as becoming increasingly ossified until the 'revolution' of the early 1970s[15] paved the way for the eventual radical reconstruction of the 1980s and 1990s.

FOUNDATIONS OF THE AUSTRALIAN STATE–CAPITAL–LABOUR COMPROMISE

Thus to see the economic and political context for the origins of the labourist-protectionist compromise we need to go back briefly to the 1820s, to the sudden irruption into consciousness and practical consideration of the capitalist possibilities inherent in the new continent. The expansion of pastoralism and the widespread phenomenon of uncontrolled land

squatting, with the resulting emergence of a new economic and political class in south-eastern Australia (the 'squattocracy', although this came
to mean all large pastoral land occupiers whether legally entitled or not),
and the near failure of the Swan River colony (1829) in Western Australia
(WA), gave rise to a struggle over land, capital, social ideology and political power that lasted until the 1870s. The influence in the 1830s of liberal
theories of ordered, state-controlled colonisation, especially Wakefield's,[16]
the ending of the importations of semi-servile convict labour to NSW
in the early 1840s with the subsequent almost complete reliance on free
wage labour, except in Van Diemen's Land (later named Tasmania),[17] the
collapse of the first wool boom and severe depression of the early 1840s,
and the gold rushes of the 1850s, all combined to tip the balance of power
away from atavistic landed oligarchs in favour of urban mercantile capital and urban liberal democratic reformers.[18] Land reform was largely
successful by the 1880s.[19] The agrarian/political question was thus more
or less resolved in the period from 1840 to 1880 against the squattocracy
and in favour of closer settlement of family farmers and urban industrial liberal and working-class interests. The particular outcome varied
from colony to colony, depending largely on the physical environment
and consequent form of agriculture and population distribution. Booming
exports of raw materials such as gold, wool, wheat and later base metals, meat and dairy products, the development of family arable farming,
aided by extensive government railway building, and rapid immigration
with urbanisation and associated manufacturing, transformed the colonial societies by the 1880s into the world's most prosperous and urbanised
region.

The struggle over land was closely related to the struggles for political enfranchisement and for employment of the displaced population of
erstwhile miners once the alluvial gold began to run out by about 1860.
In actuality, the struggles for democratisation of representation and access
to land were remarkably peaceful by the standards of Europe and South
America. In terms of formal universal male suffrage (and later female suffrage in all colonies by the 1890s) and parliamentary representation, no
violent upheaval was required to secure the vote, except for the relatively
minor clash at Eureka, Victoria, in 1854 over the issues of taxation and
control of miners, political representation and republicanism.[20]

The issue of post-gold-rush employment was particularly acute in the
colony of Victoria (separated from NSW in 1851), the largest centre of gold
mining and suffering the largest subsequent fall in production and mining
employment.[21] At the same time Victorians, like the rest of Australians, had

seen their average incomes rise to be among the highest in the world with an associated massive thirst for imported manufactured goods. Domestic manufacturing was thus seen as the solution to unemployment and political pressure. Import duties were the means to achieve that and also provide the government revenue with which to service the growing external borrowings to build railways and provide the urban infrastructure desired by the rising, affluent, voting, middle and working classes, and to pay large numbers of immigrants to bring their labour power to the 'working-man's paradise' of the south. Economic and social policy thus converged on protectionism, especially in Victoria, which soon became the most important manufacturing colony.[22] Other colonies, except NSW, were also protectionist to varying degrees. NSW remained free trade, largely due to the influence of the pastoral interest and because of the large reservoir of saleable arable crown land for government revenue. NSW was thus one of the few parts of the industrialising world in the late nineteenth century not to resort to protection or to increase it.

The desired social outcomes – economic and social diversification, social harmony, population growth and general prosperity – could be achieved while the raw materials were exported, import-replacing industry was fostered, the economy grew, and the capital and migrants flowed in. And economic growth enabled the organised working class in the strategic sites of shearing sheds, mines, wharves and ships to enforce the closed shop and redistribute some of the excess profits generated by the long commodities boom. Significant numbers of real estate speculators also thought they could get significantly rich very quickly on the back of the boom that culminated in the late 1880s from the aforementioned combination.[23] But of course it all turned sour in the early 1890s as the economy crashed into a severe depression upon the spark of the Barings crisis. Unemployment approached 25 per cent and at the bottom of the crisis in 1893 a generalised banking failure wiped out the entire savings of most of the population.[24] The shock of the depression and banking failure in a country grown used to great prosperity and confidence was profound. New institution building was the main long-term outcome.

The trade unions of Australia believed they could hold the line in their hitherto increasingly successful campaign for recognition of collective bargaining against the radically altered labour market conditions of the early 1890s. They learnt many bitter lessons in the years 1890 to 1894 and paid dearly for their adherence to collectivism and radicalism in the face of concerted onslaughts. The colonial governments also adhered to the interests of capital and individual work contracts. Democracy in the formal sense of universal voting (for men at least) for parliamentary representation had long since been achieved. While everywhere the unionists were defeated,[25] since they did have the vote a potent weapon remained in their hands if they could but manage to wield it collectively. They began to do so as early as 1891 when nascent labour parties began to contest elections. The effect was an immediate sea change in the political landscape. The labour parties developed during the course of the decade to greatly influence the colonial parliaments as unified groupings that followed coherent ideologies and enforced party discipline. Modern party politics was thus born in Australia in the 1890s and entered the newly federated Commonwealth of Australia as an institutionalised three-party system – Labour, Protectionists and Free Traders.[26]

Federation itself was another institutional outcome of the 1890s upheaval. Federal talk began in the 1880s under the impetus of economic arguments for customs unification, communications and transport harmonisation, political arguments by capitalists needing to oppose organised labour, cultural arguments regarding ethnicity and immigration, and defence imperatives. Strong and determined political leaders from the colonial parliaments took the lead and persuaded the people within a few years to vote for a federation loosely modelled on the American structure whereby states retained a high degree of sovereignty. A group of hard-working enthusiastic visionaries, such as could be found in any voluntary movement, tirelessly persuaded the populace that this was the right thing at the right time and that they should turn out and vote for it. They did so with narrow majorities in all colonies. Here was an example of a completely modern political process.[27]

The national sentiment that helped give rise to federation was not radical republican nationalism of American or Irish sorts although there was a republican current. Rather it was predominantly a nationalism of racial and cultural feeling about Britishness, egalitarianism and democratic social solidarity among the majority rural and urban working population. There was a widespread distrust of rather than hope for genuine independence. Perhaps never before or since has a set of erstwhile colonies exhibited such reluctance to demand and grasp real independence. Genuine political independence (if there could be such a thing in an integrating world) à la the United States was the dream of only a radical minority. Feeling small and isolated on the wrong side of the world, Australians rationally clung to the military and economic benefits of close association with Britain. (That the benefits of this association failed to materialise when sorely needed in 1941–2 was a great shock.)

The third great institutional outcome of the 1890s depression was the reforged and greatly expanded role of the state as the central regulator of capital and labour and defender of social harmony, equality and welfare. The labour parties of the colonies and early federation had as one of their central policy planks the regulation of industrial relations by the state. They were adamant that the defeats of the 1890s resulted from the combination of governments and capital so in the future governments must be not only captured and controlled through parliamentary politics but used to enact laws that would protect unions and give them an equal role with capital in the industrial struggle. Officially registered unions and dispute-settling industrial tribunals were thus supposed to become quasi-state instruments of social harmony through the redistributive mechanism of high wages on the back of employment and profit protection. The income shares for capital and labour flowing from the productive process were to be maintained at 'fair and reasonable' levels in order to maintain the 'social harmony'. Anti-capitalist or communist ideology played no significant role in the thinking of the organised working class or their parliamentary representatives. Recognition, collective bargaining, redistribution, state ownership of elements of significant industries and social welfare under the umbrella of capitalism (i.e. labourism) were the aims. Similarly, the humanisation of capitalism and the institutionalisation of social harmony through egalitarian social policies were the aims of the middle-class liberal reformers who worked together with the labour parties to bring to full fruition and set in powerful concrete in the first decade of the twentieth century the peculiarly Australian 'compromise'. In a country where the industrial working-class had barely begun to form, an avowedly working-class party formed the national government as early as 1904, after having been severely defeated as a movement only a decade before.

Clearly, labourism has to be understood, then, as far more than the 'compromise' of capital with labour. The Labour Party represented from the beginning the essence of a nation-building idea of a fusion of the interests of working classes (plural) in upward socio-economic mobility, an Anglo-Celtic and egalitarian culture, and racial purity, in coalition with the liberal vision of social stability and democracy. The crisis of the 1890s forged this coalition on the foundations of much older institutional and social developments. That labour recovered so quickly from the 1890s defeats is testament to the capacity of labourism to articulate a national consensus and also to the weakness of industrial capitalism. In America the 1890s crisis of labour had a far different outcome.

NEW PROTECTIONISM IN THE EARLY TWENTIETH CENTURY

The new federal structure permitted nation building in the early twentieth
century, especially in the Lib–Lab era from 1905 to 1917 when a succession
of Liberal and Labour governments consolidated the 'compromise' that had
begun to emerge in the 1890s. The constitution and early federal legislation formalised the six main building blocks of the new national framework. First, the surviving Aborigines were unrecognised and the spoken
assumption was that they had no prior claim on land and they would as-
similate and/or disappear. Second, the immigration restriction policy (i.e.
White Australia) was the first substantive legislation of 1901. This effectively excluded non-white immigrants. 'White' was of course a complex
cultural-racial-political-economic category. Most sections of society, especially organised workers who wished to protect their standard of living,
were in favour of the maintenance of a British-only immigrant stream on
economic, cultural and racial grounds.[28] (Some other Europeans were tolerated in small numbers.) Third, the Conciliation and Arbitration Act of
1904 put in place a federal dispute prevention and settlement court with
the power to intervene and compulsorily arbitrate in disputes across state
borders and to set wages. All the states already had their own compulsory
arbitration systems.[29] Unions were required to register, thus legalising and
legitimising them as quasi-official entities. Union formation and density
burgeoned from 1905 so that between 1901 and 1911 the number of unions
grew from 198 to 573 and density from 6 per cent to 28 per cent and then rose
to 52 per cent by 1921.[30] Fourth, large-scale assisted immigration supplied
the labour force for industrial and agricultural growth. The fifth building
block was protectionism, which became a central aspect of policy in 1906–7
with the passing of the tariff acts of those years. By 1905 Labour had come
down decisively on the side of protection and supported the Deakin Liberal
government of 1905–8, which was the original protectionist regime.[31] The
final main building block was state ownership of key sectors of the national economic infrastructure, notably railways, telegraphs, postal services
and, after legislation in 1911, the new 'people's bank', the Commonwealth
Savings Bank.

The building blocks came together into 'New Protectionism', then, under
Prime Minister Alfred Deakin. New protection explicitly linked job protection, profit protection, wage protection and racial/cultural protection. The
Court of Arbitration was the instrument for converting industrial protection into standard of living protection through its brief to determine what
were 'fair and reasonable' wages. The court decided in 1907 that the needs

of workers rather than any other principle, such as general macro-economic conditions or demand and supply in the labour market or capacity to pay of particular employers, should determine fairness. There should be wage equality right across the nation. Henceforth freedom of individual contract and freedom of the labour market would be severely curtailed for ninety years. 'A new province for law and order' had been created.[32]

Enthusiasm among Liberal (conservative) and Labour governments for participation in the First World War in support of 'the empire' was an essential component of the nation-building process, even if a significant proportion of the articulate left and of the population generally, probably even a majority by 1917, opposed the participation, certainly to the extent of twice rejecting referanda on military conscription.[33] The war should be seen as confirming trends already in existence rather than as a break with them even though it threatened to undermine the social harmony. The path of industrialisation, political economy and national culture continued in the same direction afterward, indeed was even more encompassing of all groups, classes and interests, except for Aborigines. The protectionist 'compromise' continued in reinvigorated form (even though the radical left attempted to undermine it in favour of a more militant, class-conscious, direct political struggle for more thorough socialism) strengthened by the newly created ANZAC spirit of blood sacrifice for egalitarian and racial solidarity.[34] Nationalism could at last be built on this new ideological foundation of heroic myth.

MATURATION AND SUCCESS OF LABOURIST-PROTECTIONISM, 1920–74

Australia emerged from the First World War with a more centralised political economy, an enlarged and heavily protected industrial sector, an almost fully unionised workforce, and a greatly expanded opportunity to supply Britain and the rest of Europe with food and raw materials. The early 1920s were thus confident years. But the confidence didn't last and by about 1926 world market conditions had turned adverse, with the revival of competition by domestic and international producers in Britain and Europe for the Australian primary products. And so, once again, Australian policy-makers, along with the populace, lost any desire to even question the protectionist consensus. Even the farmers' party (the Country Party, formed 1919), representative of the efficient, exporting sector most adversely affected by protection, joined the protectionist consensus. Rationally, they believed the pragmatic course was to seek both domestic and international protection through subsidies, organised marketing, prohibition of imports and export assistance. 'Protection all round' then became the chief slogan of the Australian political economy and was to remain largely inviolate in public opinion until the late 1960s. The 'arrogant' attempt by Prime Minister S.M. Bruce to reform significantly the centralised and compulsory arbitration system saw him swept politically and personally from office in 1929.[35]

The major immediate response to the Great Depression was a dramatic resort to further protection and then fiscal and monetary conservatism, including wage reductions, with avoidance of any even partial deferment of loan servicing, let alone moratorium or default, by the moderate Labour federal government that had come into office on the eve of the depression. The Labour Party split over depression policy and conservatism triumphed in politics and policy. The 1930s was thus a significant crisis for the labourist compromise although protectionism was not seriously questioned. But as it turned out, the long-term significance of the depression for the Australian political economy was as an interruption rather than a turning point. The resort to protection and the war speeded up the transformation to an industrial economy.[36]

So, the Second World War was of greater long-term significance, serving to consolidate a more secure foundation for the ANZAC myth and eroding considerably the remaining neo-colonial mentality. The stimulus to industrial development from the total mobilisation effectively completed the transition to a mature industrial economy. The socio-political effects of the depression and war included, as with all industrial countries, the turn to Keynesian macro-economic policy and increased social welfarism. Full employment, fortuitously achieved, became a fundamental plank of the political and social consensus. The 1941–9 Labour government had a socialist agenda in the sense of continuation and extension of public ownership of the 'commanding heights' of sections of the economy, such as banks, coal mines, railways, suburban transport, airlines, ships, electricity, hospitals, universities, insurance, telephones and postal services. The war emergency enabled federal centralisation of economic power via taxation and banking regulation. The subsequent conservative governments from 1949 to 1972 did nothing to disturb the established regulatory pattern, in spite of another split in Labour over communism. No government could have survived electorally without maintaining the centralised labourist-protectionist consensus, certainly while full employment and prosperity continued.

Australia represented in the 1950s and 1960s the epitome of the protectionist state, presided over, perhaps curiously, by liberal conservatives and not social democrats. Behind the protectionist wall Australia matured in terms of the secondary sector's share of GDP and employment by the late 1950s.[37] Nation building reached a sublime height with the Snowy Mountains hydro and irrigation scheme in the 1950s which combined a great wave of European migration with land subjugation on a grand scale, massive investment in agricultural exports and state-induced demand for protected industrial development. The achievements of industrial maturity, full employment, generalised social welfare, and egalitarian income and wealth distribution were all substantial. There was a high degree of political and social consensus on economic, industrial relations and immigration policies. The centralised and unionised industrial relations system guaranteed the maintenance of a high wage structure whatever the skill level. The relatively high price of labour was a crucial determinant of the maintenance of protectionist policy and an affluent internal market.

CRISIS OF LABOURIST-PROTECTIONISM, 1967–86

The crisis of the late 1960s/early 1970s witnessed the beginning of a significant weakening of the Australian compromise and of the nation-building role of the state. The Vietnam involvement, anti-racist social movements and feminism galvanised opposition to the increasingly conservative government and a cultural awakening occurred which, combined with several other factors, produced a watershed. First, the late 1960s and early 1970s witnessed a version of 'Dutch disease' or supply-side-shock economic syndrome consequent upon the rapid rise of the minerals and energy export sector. This shock had deleterious effects on the traditional exporting sector (agriculture) and the import-replacing sector (manufacturing) through the mechanism of exchange rate appreciation caused by balance of payments surpluses. Combined with the other rigidities in national policy the result was stagflation with the onset of the post-oil shock recession. Having become a major energy exporter by then (coal and uranium), Australia was in a more complex position within the world economy. Here was an industrialised country in which the most dynamic sector was minerals and energy exports and the most stagnant sector the import-replacing and exporting secondary sector.[38]

Second, the protectionist consensus began to crumble in the face of the minerals export boom. The intellectual basis had shifted in the 1960s and the first significant steps to reduce the levels were made by the Gough Whitlam Labour government in 1973, which imposed a unilateral 25 per cent reduction in all tariff levels in response to the supply-side shock and inflation.[39]

Third, in response to stagflation there was an intellectual shift, in common with many countries, away from the Keynesian macro-economic management policy focused on employment to a more monetarist philosophy of fighting inflation first.[40]

Fourth, the White Australia policy was scrapped and a trickle of Asian migrants and, indeed, migrants from every part of the world, began arriving, which soon turned into a flood, especially after the end of the Indochina wars when Australia accepted proportionally the largest number of refugees. Thus there was the beginning of a rapid breakdown of socio-cultural-racial exclusion and isolation and a very significant move towards multiculturalism and openness as official policy. The explanation for this relatively smooth and peaceful transition has to be sought in the earlier widening of immigration to include all of Europe and then the Middle East, and in the class inclusiveness of the social democratic tradition which was able to adjust easily to ethnic inclusion as long as, crucially, the other building blocks of egalitarianism and market regulation remained in place to protect living standards.

Fifth, the Aboriginal land rights issue came to the fore as the issue of the legal legitimacy of land domination by the settler state began to be raised by the surviving Aborigines and their white supporters. In 1967 Aborigines were given legal recognition in the constitution and gradually reconciliation has become a central element of the new phase of multicultural nation building from the mid-1980s.

With the re-election of Labour in 1983 Australia witnessed one of the first examples of a deregulatory social democratic government, increasing the move away from state regulation of some areas of the economy, particularly the finance and transport sectors. On the other hand, there was an attempt to introduce a degree of corporatist national management of a quasi-Scandinavian kind. The Prices and Incomes Accord with the Australian Council of Trade Unions was a 'backroom' deal to trade off 'social wage' increases (national medical insurance, welfare increases and tax cuts) for real wage reductions and hence investment growth to generate employment.[41] The 1980s was a period of rapid economic recovery and employment generation as well as growing inequality.

GLOBALISATION AND FORGING A NEW NATIONAL IDENTITY SINCE 1986

Although the settler era has passed, some of its legacies persist and nation building or rebuilding is an ongoing task. The late 1980s and 1990s, after the transitional period of the previous decade, have seen a virtual 'revolution' in economic and social policy and cultural formation such that the nature of the Australian state and society has changed very significantly.[42] From 1986 the Labour government increased the tempo of deregulation corporatisation, privatisation, and Aboriginal reconciliation. *Terra nullius* was judicially overturned and Aboriginal prior ownership recognised. Australia switched from being a non-participant in the GATT negotiations in the 1960s and 1970s to being a leading proponent of multilateral reductions of protection, particularly in the agricultural sector. The levels of protection of agriculture have unilaterally been reduced to levels below 10 per cent in spite of the lack of reciprocation in other OECD countries. Secondary protection has declined generally to 5 per cent except for special higher levels for the textiles, clothing and footwear, and automobiles sectors. Protection all round, the framework of national policy since the early 1920s and the culmination of policy since 1905, has decisively been killed. Even limited deregulation of the labour market was begun by the Labour government with the weakening of the centralised arbitration system and a concerted move towards workplace bargaining. Since 1996, under a conservative government, micro-economic reform has gone further to include a significant assault on the power of the centralised industrial arbitration system, significant reductions in the welfare, education and public broadcasting systems, and even a degree of deregulation and privatisation of the state universities.

In the space of twenty years, even a decade, the structure of Australia's political economy has changed enormously. From being a protected, mixed economy with a high degree of state ownership and regulation, toleration of monopolies and oligopolies, with an egalitarian income distribution by world standards, the economy and society have been opened to global competition and resulting inequality. Multiculturalism displaced 'White Australia'. Aboriginal land rights and reconciliation moved to centre stage as national issues. Indeed, the beginnings of a new cultural formation, focusing on the special characteristics and influence of the natural environment, fusing Aboriginal, European and Asian cultural elements with environmentalism, can be discerned.[43] And the globalisation strategy has provoked a severe political realignment. As the new century dawned the remaining social democrats grappled with how to redefine their role and that of the state in the face of the strength of the neo-liberalism of the economic elites, the anti-globalisation xenophobia and disaffection of the marginalised and increasingly impoverished small farm and urban working classes, and the anti-capitalist reregulators of the left. The social democrats within the Labour Party, as in Western Europe, are starting to redefine themselves as less enthusiastic supporters of but also ameliorators of globalisation. Neo-liberals have largely prostrated themselves before the Washington economic consensus. Neo-social-democrats are still trying to find their feet. The twenty-year dominance of economic ideology over politics and society is perhaps ending and a new political economy is vaguely taking shape around a more self-confident cultural formation and the new watchword of efficiency.

NOTES

I wish to thank Tim Rowse for helpful advice on an earlier draft.

1. The administrative and economic history of early NSW is discussed in G. J. Abbott and N.B. Nairn (eds.), *Economic Growth in Australia, 1788–1821* (Melbourne, 1969); N.G. Butlin, *Forming a Colonial Economy, 1810–1850,* (Cambridge, 1994); B. Fletcher, *Colonial Australia Before 1850* (Melbourne, 1996); J. Kociumbas, *The Oxford History of Australia, Vol. II: 1770–1860* (Oxford, 1992).

2. On the 1813–40 period, see G.J. Abbott, *The Pastoral Age* (Melbourne, 1971); Butlin, *Forming a Colonial Economy*; M. McMichael, *Settlers and the Agrarian Question: Foundations of Capitalism in Colonial Australia* (Cambridge, 1984).

3. The idea of an Australian 'historic compromise' is discussed in F. Castles, *Australian Public Policy and Economic Vulnerability* (Sydney, 1988). See also P. Kelly, *The End of Certainty: the Story of the 1980s (Sydney, 1992),* where the idea of the 'settlement' is given a central place. There is much contention about this concept (see below) but it is a useful place to start for it highlights what is perhaps different about Australia's political economy even at the risk of neglecting the more global and social (rather than economic and administrative) forces at work. See also the many valuable discussions in P. Smyth and B. Cass (eds.), *Contesting the Australian Way: States, Markets, and Civil Society* (Cambridge 1998), where many contributors defend the idea of a broader 'way' instead of a settlement. See also the challenging and intelligent Gramscian analysis in A. Davidson, *The Invisible State: the Formation of the Australian State 1788–1901* (Cambridge, 1991).

4. See D. Denoon, *Settler Capitalism: the Dynamics of Dependent Development in the Southern Hemisphere* (Oxford, 1983). C. Lloyd, 'Australian and American Settler Capitalism: the Importance of a Comparison and its Curious Neglect', *Australian Economic History Review*, 38 (1998), 280–305. On Australian democratisation, see J.B. Hirst, *The Strange Birth of Colonial Democracy* (Sydney, 1988).

5. Cf. H. Schwartz, *States Versus Markets: The Emergence of a Global Economy*, 2nd edn (New York, 2000), for a good analysis of local/global interconnections over time.

6. On the history of Aboriginal dispossession see C.D. Rowley, *The Destruction of Aboriginal Society* (Canberra, 1970); N.G. Butlin, *Our Original Aggression: Aboriginal Populations of Southeastern Australia, 1788–1850* (Sydney, 1983); Butlin, *Economics and the Dreamtime: a Hypothetical History* (Cambridge, 1993).

7. For left criticisms, including ideas of dependency, see K. Buckley and T. Wheelwright, *No Paradise for Workers: Capitalism and the Common People in Australia, 1788–1914* (Melbourne, 1988); Buckley and Wheelwright, *False Paradise: Australian Capitalism Revisited, 1915–1955* (Melbourne, 1998); B. Catley and B. McFarlane, 'Labor and Economic Crisis': Counter Strategies and Political Realities' in E.L. Wheelwright and K. Buckley, *Essays in the Political Economy of Australian Capitalism, Vol. IV*, (Sydney, 1980), pp. 267–310;. P. Cochrane, *Industrialization and Dependence: Australia's Road to Economic Development* (Brisbane, 1980); J.G. Crough and E. L. Wheelwright, 'Australia: Client State of International Capitalism. A Case Study of the Mineral Industry' in E.L. Wheelwright and K. Buckley, *Essays in the Political Economy of Australian Capitalism, Vol. V* (Sydney, 1983), pp. 15–42.

8. Cf. P. Ehrensaft and W. Armstrong, 'Dominion Capitalism: a First Statement', *Australia and New Zealand Journal of Sociology*, 14 (1978, 252–363); W. Armstrong and J. Bradbury, 'Industrialisation and Class Structure in Australia, Canada, and Argentina: 1870–1980' in Wheelwright and Buckley, *Essays in the Political Economy of Australian Capitalism, Vol. V*, pp. 43–74; McMichael, *Settlers and the Agrarian Question.* See also discussion in C. Lloyd, 'Capitalist Beginnings in Australia,' *Arena*, 81 (1987), 35–54, and C. Lloyd, 'Regime Change in Australian Capitalism: Towards a Historical Political Economy of Regulation', *Australian Economic History Review*, 42, 3 (2002), 238–66.

9. See, for example, McMichael, *Settlers and the Agrarian Question*; Catley and McFarlane, 'Labor and Economic Crisis'; Cochrane, *Industrialization and Dependence*; H. Schwartz, *In the Dominions of Debt: Historical Prespectives on Dependent Development* (Ithaca, 1989).

10. For social democratic/Keynesian views see T. Battin, *Abandoning Keynes* (London, 1997); H. Stretton, *Political Essays* (Melbourne, 1987).

11. One of the first important expressions of this view was by W.K. Hancock, *Australia* (Brisbane, 1961: first published 1930). See the excellent discussion of protectionism from a multi-faceted economic perspective in K. Anderson, 'Tariffs and the Manufacturing Sector' in R. Maddock and L.W. McLean (eds.), *The Australian Economy in the Long Run* (Cambridge, 1987), pp. 165–74.

12. M. Olson, *The Rise and Decline of Nations* (New Haven, 1982); Olson, 'Australia in the Perspective, of the Rise and Decline of Nations', *Australian Economic Review*, 3 (1984), 7–17.

13. The most developed form of the argument is in N.G. Butlin, A. Barnard and J.J. Pincus, *Government and Capitalism: Public and Private Choice in Twentieth Century Australia* (Sydney, 1982).

14. The indigenous people were easily vanquished compared with those of all other settler societies such as New Zealand, USA and Argentina, but nevertheless

there was a long campaign of violence on the frontier. See Rowley, *The Destruction*; H. Reynolds, *The Other Side of the Frontier Aboriginal Resistance to the European Invasion of Australia*, new edn (Ringwood, Victoria, 1990). The latest estimate is that the Aboriginal population fell from about half a million to about 100,000.

15. Cf. R. Manne, 'The Whitlam Revolution' in R. Manne (ed.), *The Australian Century: Political Struggle in the Building of a Nation* (Melbourne, 1999), pp. 179–223.

16. See the excellent discussion of Wakefield and other philosophic radicals in B. Semmel, 'The Philosophic Radicals and Colonialism', *Journal of Economic History*, 21 (1961), 513–25; repr. in A.G.L. Shaw (ed.), *Great Britain and the Colonies, 1815–1865* (London, 1970), pp. 77–92.

17. Transportation of British convicts continued to Tasmania until 1853 and occurred in WA between 1850 and 1868. No sooner had transportation to NSW ceased than influential pastoralists and shippers were scouring the world for suitable sources of servile or semi-servile cheap labour for shepherding. Approximately 3,600 Chinese indentured labourers were imported in the years 1848–53; see M. Darnell, 'The Chinese Labour Trade to NSW, 1783–1853' (Unpublished Ph.D. thesis, University of New England, Armidale, 1997). Later, about 65,000 Pacific Island indentured labourers were brought to Queensland between 1863 and 1904 to work on sugar plantations; see A.A. Graves, 'The Abolition of the Queensland Labour Trade' in Wheelwright and Buckley (eds.), *Essays in the Political Economy of Australian Capitalism, Vol. IV*, pp. 41–57.

18. See McMichael, *Settlers and the Agrarian Question*.

19. On land reform, see S. Roberts, *History of Australian Land Settlement*, 1788–1920 (Melbourne, 1924).

20. Thirty-four miners and four troopers were killed. See the account in J. Molony, *Eureka* (Melbourne, 1984).

21. See W.A. Sinclair, *The Process of Economic Development in Australia* (Melbourne, 1976), ch. 4.

22. Cf. Sinclair, *The Process*, pp. 102–3; B. Fitzpatrick, *The British Empire in Australia, 1834–1939*, 2nd rev. edn (Melbourne, 1949), pp. 128–9.

23. On the 1880s boom, see E.A. Boehm, *Prosperity and Depression in Australia, 1887–1897* (Oxford, 1971). A contrary view about the 1880s as not the 'working man's paradise' is in Buckley and Wheelwright, *No Paradise for Workers*.

24. The 1890s depression is examined in Boehm, *Prosperity and Depression*.

25. On the strikes of the 1890s, see R. Gollan, *Radical and Working Class Politics* (Melbourne, 1960); J. Rickard, *Class and Politics* (Canberra, 1976).

26. The early history of labour parties and the party system are dealt with in Rickard, *Class and Politics*.

27. For recent discussions of federation, see W.G. McMinn, *Nationalism and Federalism in Australia* (Melbourne, 1994); B. De Garis, 'Federation' in Manne (ed.), *The Australian Century*, pp. 11–46.

28. Cf. H.I. London, *Non-White Immigration and the 'White Australia' Policy* (Sydney, 1970).

29. On the origins of compulsory arbitration, see S. Macintyre and R. Mitchell (eds.), *Foundations of Arbitration* (Melbourne, 1989).

30. S. Deery D. Plowman and J. Walsh, *Industrial Relations: a Contemporary Analysis* (Sydney, 1997), ch. 7.

31. Cf. W.K. Hancock, 'The Commonwealth, 1900–1914' in E. Scott (ed.), *The Cambridge History of the British Empire, Vol. VII: Australia Part 1* (Cambridge, 1933; reissued 1988), pp. 491–520; Fitzpatrick, *The British Empire*, pp. 261–5.

32. Justice H.B. Higgins, second president of the Court of Arbitration.

33. J. Hirst, 'Labour and the Great War' in Manne (ed.), *The Australian Century*, pp. 47–79.

34. ANZAC stands for Australia and New Zealand Army Corps, in which the Australasian troops fought at Gallipoli and on the western front. The ANZAC experience was deliberately mythologised after the war as a symbol of courage, tenacity, independence, solidarity and equality and ANZAC Day (25 April), the national day of war memorialising, is more solemnly respected than the official Australia Day of 26 January.

35. See Anderson, 'Tariffs and the Manufacturing Sector'.

36. Cf. Anderson, 'Tariffs and the Manufacturing Sector'; Sinclair, *The Process of Economic Development*.

37. On the post-war growth and development, see S. Dowrick and T. Nguyen, 'Measurement and International Comparison' B. Chapman (ed.), *Australian Economic Growth: Essays in Honor of Fred Gruen* (Melbourne, 1989), pp. 34–59. S. Dowrick, 'Economic Growth' in P. Kriester (ed.), *The Australian Economy*, 3rd edn (Sydney, 1999), pp. 6–25; A. Maddock, 'The Long Boom: 1940–1970', in Maddock and McLean, *The Australian Economy*, pp. 79–105.

38. Supply-side-shock economics is discussed in R.G. Gregory, 'Some Implications of the Growth of the Mineral Sector', *The Australasion Journal of Agricultural Economics*, 20 (1976), 71–91; W.M. Corden and J.P. Neary, 'Booming Sector and De-Industrialisation in a Small Open Economy', *Economic Journal*, 92 (1982), 825–48.

39. On the debate over protectionism in the late 1960s/early 1970s, see Anderson, 'Tariffs and the Manufacturing Sector'.

40. Battin, *Abandoning Keynes*.

41. On the accord and its effects, see K. Wilson J, Bradford and M. Fitzpatrick (eds.), *Australia in Accord: An Evaluation of the Prices and Incomes Accord of the Hawke–Keating Years* (Footscray, 2000).

42. On the 1980s and 1990s micro-economic deregulatory programme see S. Bell, *Ungoverning the Economy* (Melbourne, 1997); D. Bryan and M. Rafferty, *The Global Economy in Australia* (Sydney, 1999); A. Capling, *Australia and the Global Trade System* (Cambridge, 2001); P. Kelly, 'Labor and Globalisation' in Manne (ed.), *The Australian Century*, pp. 224–63.

43. This new formation was graphically expressed in the opening ceremony of the 2000 Sydney Olympics. The fight for Aboriginal rights is discussed in B. Attwood and A. Markus, 'The Fight for Aboriginal Rights' in Manne (ed.), *The Australian Century*, pp. 264–92.

Index

For EU product safety concerns, contact us at Calle de José Abascal, 56–1°,
28003 Madrid, Spain or eugpsr@cambridge.org.

www.ingramcontent.com/pod-product-compliance
Ingram Content Group UK Ltd.
Pitfield, Milton Keynes, MK11 3LW, UK
UKHW042210180425
457623UK00011B/137